THE EMIRATES OF NORTHERN NIGERIA

The Sarkin Musulmi, Sultan of Sokoto.

THE EMIRATES OF NORTHERN NIGERIA

A Preliminary Survey of their Historical Traditions

S. J. HOGBEN

AND

A. H. M. KIRK-GREENE

LONDON

OXFORD UNIVERSITY PRESS

1966

Oxford University Press, Ely House, London, W.1

GLASGOW NEW YORK TORONTO MELBOURNE WELLINGTON
CAPE TOWN SALISBURY IBADAN NAIROBI LUSAKA ADDIS ABABA
BOMBAY CALCUTTA MADRAS KARACHI LAHORE DACCA
KUALA LUMPUR HONG KONG

Printed in Great Britain
by Ebenezer Baylis and Son, Ltd.
The Trinity Press, Worcester, and London

FOREWORD

It gives me great pleasure to introduce the new issue of *The Emirates of Northern Nigeria* in the hope that it will continue to inspire the Emirates as a symbol of unity and that these Emirates may continue to find a place of honour in our traditional society.

I feel honoured that a book written many years ago by my old tutor, Mr Hogben, has been brought up to date and that I should be invited to write this Foreword. I have always resorted to it in drawing material for my speeches and it is my earnest hope that the new issue will be a source of inspiration to those in Nigeria who cherish our tradition and are anxious to continue to pilot our nation along the right lines, having regard to its past achievements.

I take this opportunity to express my sincere thanks and appreciation to my former European teachers and mentors who have done so much for Nigeria in very difficult circumstances. I speak on behalf of myself and many others who owe them a debt of gratitude.

Abubakar T. Balewa
Prime Minister of the
Federation of Nigeria

Cabinet Office,
Lagos,
Nigeria.

November 1964

PREFACE TO PART I

THIS book has been compiled in response to pressure from various quarters to reprint a revised edition of my *Muhammadan Emirates of Nigeria*. This, of course, needed the on-the-spot co-operation of someone in Nigeria to examine the latest local records and select material to bring the histories of the various Emirates up to date. Corrections and additions to the original version would also need to be weighed up with a judicious eye.

Alhaji Aliyu Dogondaji did actually start on the work of local collation when he was in Katsina, but on his appointment to the Embassy in Khartoum he had to give it up. I was then indeed fortunate in finding a scholar at Zaria in the person of A. H. M. Kirk-Greene who was ready to do more than collate and to share the authorship. As a former District Officer and now a lecturer at Ahmadu Bello University he has enjoyed special opportunities for local research and he has already established his reputation as an authority on Nigerian affairs with a number of important publications to his credit.

I have completely rewritten Part I in the light of the latest available material. As in the original book it deals in broad outline with the long chain of successive influences, arising from the Sudan and from across the Sahara, which came to affect the people of the northern regions of what is now Nigeria. We have greatly expanded Part II to include material supplied recently by the Emirates themselves as well as the fruit of our own researches together with extracts from contemporary documents.

From the earliest conception of this book I have always had in mind the aim to make Northern Nigerians aware of their own origins and civilization, which derived from sources outside their present boundaries. In the long unrolling tapestry of Nigeria European influences can hardly be discerned until near the end.

Only last century did Europe discover that the Fulani Emirates and Bornu could be reached at all from the coast: up to then they had faced only north towards the desert. A second aim of the book was to encourage local researches and the preservation of local traditions by committing them to writing. I can still recall the thrill of discovering a list of the ancient kings of Zamfara in Anka in 1924 (had not my Resident Arnett recorded in his Gazetteer 'I cannot anywhere find a list of the ancient kings of Zamfara, but this may yet come to light'?), and of hearing a casual reference by a *tsofo* in Ruma that fixed the date and explained the cause of an event in Katsina history.

Memories are proverbially short, and without the written records of a daily press even a brief passage of years can exaggerate mouth to mouth errors until distortion bedevils truth. Of this I have direct evidence. In 1959, when my wife and I were guests of the Government, I revisited Katsina. No one there at the time (I had left the Emir in Kaduna) seemed to doubt the authenticity of the splendid example of Sudanese architecture shown to visitors as the old Habe mosque: its Gobirau minaret would be pointed out with knowing pride, and historical articles such as the one I have before me now refer to its photograph as 'this 400-year-old building—a legacy of the old Hausa city state, built before the arrival of the Fulani conquerors'. Yet I remember it being built in 1927 when I was there by Frank Daniel the District Officer. 'You are quite right about the so-called Habe mosque,' he wrote the other day. 'When I arrived in Katsina there was just a spike left of the original Hasumiya. The idea was to preserve it enclosed within a "gazebo", which would give a view of the town. I seem to remember a suggestion from you recalling the Sankore mosque at Timbuktu.' I am happy to put the record straight and do justice to one of Katsina's greatest friends. On the same visit to Katsina I heard a house in the town (then occupied by Aliyu Dogondaji) referred to as the Gidan Bieneman and believed to have been the recognized residence of the first Principal of the Training College. But this small and very ordinary house was no more than a sort of town rest-house which Bieneman used while he superintended the building of the College and his own personally designed house up in the station. I know this because I lived next door to him in 1924 in the Gidan Power. In those days there were no Public Works officers up in Katsina to build standard types of houses: each officer built his own house to his own design and took pride in what he built.

Let me then recapture some of the engravings on the milestones of my mind that cover twelve momentous years—years during which I watched some of the outstanding African statesmen of the century blossom from the bud. Many of them were my students, and with most of them I played some kind of a game, either fives or polo, cricket or football: my memories of classroom studies, I am afraid, are less vivid. These recollections may have historical value.

The first years of my service were spent in Sokoto Province, which in 1921 had only four schools and no motor-roads. It took sixteen days to reach Sokoto from Zaria, with another six days on to Birnin Kebbi through Argungu. Trekking like this gave you every incentive to learn the language, live among the people and grow to love them. In those days *kurdin makaranta* ('school money') was commonly paid to insure your son against being rounded up for school—a suspect European innovation—so that it was a task to keep even the few schools up to a strength of barely a hundred apiece. At Birnin Kebbi at the end of 1922 I took a chance with the school repairs vote and put up two Eton Fives courts in the embrasure of the school walls. They were an immediate success. Next year, and this time with official approval, I put up four more courts at the Sokoto school. They were constructed of hard-beaten clay, and the only equipment required was an old tennis ball. From these humble and indeed irregular beginnings has grown almost a national game. One of the first to learn the game in Sokoto was a young boy called Ahmadu Rabah; he is now one of the country's leading players as well as being the Premier, Alhaji Sir Ahmadu Bello, Sardauna of Sokoto. When the Sardauna visited the original Fives court at Eton, between the buttresses of College Chapel, the headmaster, Dr Birley, wrote to tell me how he had got the Sardauna on to one of the other courts where 'although considerably discommoded by his robes, he played in great style, displaying a very remarkable back-hand shot at times'. This visit led to an exchange of teams between Northern Nigeria and Eton in 1961, and again in 1965.

May 1924 found me leading a motley procession of fifty-odd carriers, two baggage camels, three polo ponies with one pulling a trap, and two Airedale dogs into Katsina. We had come a difficult way through the Gundumi bush, Zurmi and Ruma. The

Emir, Muhammadu Dikko, proved to be a great patron of sport, curious to observe foxhounds using their noses alongside the local gaze-hounds and enthusiastic about polo, even though it competed with his first love, racing. He soon got a ground prepared and with the help of his numerous sons the game flourished. By February 1929 with three of these same sons, Nagogo, Yusufu Lamba and Dahiru (who replaced Daniel carried off with concussion), we reached the final of the open Georgian Cup against Kano at Zaria, which we lost 4–1. In those days Katsina was the only team with Nigerian players in these tournaments. It was later that Alhaji Nagogo, the present Emir, and three of his brothers became invincible.

Many of Nigeria's present leaders are the product of a system that set great store on the value of games in character building. But perhaps its outstanding achievement was in the perfection of its teaching of English at the Katsina Training College, for which Gerald Power and Charles Whitting were responsible. Long were the hours that my colleagues spent in phonetics and in their patient demand for the repetition of sounds. Some indeed questioned whether such perfection was necessary. We now know that Power and Whitting were right, and all honour to them. Two others of my colleagues whose names will never die were Malam Nagwamatse, a notable Arabist and a bold if rather wild polo-player (does he still play?), and Malam Bello Kagara.

After Katsina a very different kind of teacher-training took me to Toro in 1929 to work with Eric Mort. Our task was to collect young men from the remoter non-Muslim areas with a view to turning them into teachers for their villages which had never seen a school. It was an exciting experience to have had the personal selection of these men in their villages, to have lived with them and taught them for a year, and to have seen them by this time able to read, write and calculate well enough to keep farm diaries and records of crops. Pre-conceived ideas on age and length of schooling seemed to need revision. All the book-work was done in the late forenoon: the early mornings and afternoons were spent on the farms and on practical crafts such as building and thatching their own houses. We also used to go hunting together in the evenings for small game.

A period at the Bauchi Middle School at a time when the present Prime Minister was a pupil there intervened before I was sent to take charge of schools in the Tiv country and Wukari, as well as some in Keffi, Nassarawa and Lafia. Even in 1933, when I left Nigeria, I had requests from parents *not* to put schools in their villages as they feared the loss of their sons' help on the farm.

This type of attitude at that time needs to be recorded since we are now sometimes criticized in Nigeria for the slow pace of educational advance: 'education is a good thing; why then did you not force the people to have it?' As alien rulers from behind the men we had installed we completely depended on the willing consent of the governed. To me it would have been unthinkable to attempt compulsion. History may declare that I was wrong. On the score of quality, however, I have heard no breath of criticism. *Sannu ba ta hana zuwa*. Indeed, those who ought to know seem to be appreciative. A letter I recently received from Sir Kashim Ibrahim, the Governor of Northern Nigeria, concludes with these words: 'It is our hope that you people will find the opportunity to come out to see Northern Nigeria, which is led by people of your own creation. I am sure you will look back with satisfaction at our achievements for which we have a debt of gratitude to you who taught us. Your names will be ever-green with us.'

There remains now the invidious task of selecting from the long list of books that have been helpful those that have been specially so. Among those that belong to Bacon's third category there are some that have yielded particularly valuable material from being read 'curiously'. From these I have quoted and borrowed gratefully—as historians must and as others, I am happy to say, have done from me. I must underline my debt, then, to E. W. Bovill, Basil Davidson, J. D. Fage, Thomas Hodgkin and Roland Oliver, as well as to the French writers Alphonse Gouilly, Raymond Mauny, Jean Rouch, L. Tauxier and Yves Urvoy, not ignoring the two Sudanese authors whose works have been so well annotated and translated from Arabic by O. Houdas and M. Delafosse. This is not to forget my long-standing debt to the older works on which my original book was based, and I continue to be grateful to those mentioned in its preface, particularly my old friends Tom Baldwin and Charles Whitting, whose advice on Arabic words and their spelling we have tried to follow. Sir Richard Palmer, one of the greatest authorities on Bornu, fed me assiduously with his own notes, but my chief inspiration came from Frank Daniel, whose enthusiasm for knowledge about Nigeria's past stimulated my early interest and researches. Forty years on I am still consulting him and his notes for parts of the chapters on Sokoto, Katsina and Kebbi, where we served together.

Alhaji Sir Abubakar Tafawa Balewa, the Prime Minister of the Federation of Nigeria, has done us especial kindness in writing the Foreword to this book with his characteristic generosity. Our deepest thanks go also to the Premier of Northern Nigeria, Alhaji Sir Ahmadu Bello, Sardauna of Sokoto, for his keen help in getting the various Emirates to check and supplement the original draft; and to Alhaji the Honourable Isa Kaita, Minister of Education, and his staff for arranging for this to be done with official blessing. This includes Alhaji Aliyu Dogondaji, the original collator, who has translated a number of chapters of the original book into Hausa.

Finally, we are under a sense of deep obligation to all those unknown people who have worked on the revision of the Emirate sections in various offices. To borrow the words of Abdullahi dan Fodio, may God reward them all with his approval.

Goldsmiths' College,
University of London.

SIDNEY HOGBEN

PREFACE TO PART II

THE need for a republication of S. J. Hogben's *The Muhammadan Emirates of Nigeria*, written thirty-five years ago, has long been felt, both in Nigeria at the secondary and university level and by the rapidly growing number of scholars from abroad working in the field of Nigerian studies. It has, indeed, become a collector's item in Africana; and whereas many a schoolteacher in Northern Nigeria has wished he had enough copies for each of his students, in London, New York and Paris the book has been fetching £5 and upwards from competitive university librarians. When, therefore, Sidney Hogben and the Oxford University Press invited me at the time of Nigeria's independence to help with the revision of this classic, it was clear that plans were at last in hand to meet this persistent demand for a general, introductory history of the Emirates. We have received considerable personal encouragement for this project from Alhaji Sir Abubakar Tafawa Balewa, the Prime Minister, from Sir Kashim Ibrahim and Alhaji Sir Ahmadu Bello, Sardauna of Sokoto, the Governor and Premier respectively of Northern Nigeria, and from Alhaji Isa Kaita, Wazirin Katsina and Minister of Education. For such sponsorship we are indeed grateful.

This book is virtually a new one, yet one that has grown naturally from out of its predecessor *The Muhammadan Emirates of Nigeria*; hence our choice of title, combining the old with the new. The revision of Part I has been carried out by S. J. Hogben, while we have together rewritten and extensively enlarged the original Part II.

Besides the classic texts of nineteenth-century travellers to what are today the Emirates of Northern Nigeria, I have for Part II drawn on four major sources. One is the series of *Provincial Annual Reports* for the North, published in Kaduna from 1926 to 1939 and again from 1950 onwards. These give the official record. Secondly, the manuscript notes, typescript drafts and scattered extracts of provincial history that I have come across in my travels and researches in Nigeria, distinguished by a number of excellent local studies published as gazetteers in the 1920s. Thirdly, the limited but very valuable volume of Hausa literature published for the Northern Region Literature Agency by Gaskiya Corporation during the peak of the *Yaki da Jahilci* campaign, between 1952 and 1958. These vernacular sources I have cited in the provincial bibliography at the end of Part II. Finally, we have whenever possible sought deliberately to include the better-established local traditions, gleaned from reading and from emirate informants, allowing subsequent scholars to assess their full merits.

This last approach is, as is well known, becoming in the context of African history a highly developed science, known as Euhemerism—the acknowledgement of historical validity to unwritten tradition—or oral history or sometimes ethnohistory. Such a methodology has revolutionized the concept and the tools of African historical studies in the past decade. If our materials here add to the scholar's data for further research, so much the better; but our real incentive has been at a lower, homelier level, one well expressed in the following letter from a Sokoto *malam* published in the *Nigerian Citizen*:

> Memories of events as we know easily lapse with the passing of time, and unless we commit them to writing there will come a time when these will completely be forgotten by later generations.
>
> When man first thought of recording history a step forward in bringing history back to life had been reached. Before then however historical events used only to be memorized in a way we now call 'remembered history'—popular legends handed from father to son. These legends were not of course in themselves related, they might in the course of time have been changed or mixed up with incorrect pieces of information; yet quite a lot of facts both historical and fictitious could be acquired from such stories.
>
> It is high time therefore that Nigerians should immediately start collecting what stories they can avail themselves of from elders and old people and commit them to writing before it is too late. We can gain much knowledge about our ancestors and of incidents of the past if we make a close study of these legendary stories which we often hear people relate to us.
>
> It seems these days that the study of these handed down stories is given comparatively less attention; so much so that they are now on

the verge of being in total eclipse! People consider this kind of study as fruitless and so tend to ignore it and to interest themselves only in affairs of current nature. It is this tendency of course that gives rise to our lack of knowledge in even our local history.

Many people assume that as far as our local history is concerned all work has already been done for us by earlier European historians who have devoted their efforts in trying to give it a basis for study and that nothing more of historical value is considered left unrecorded. All we can do, they think, is simply to enjoy the fruit of those historians' work.

No doubt this work of the earlier historians is a great endeavour and worthy of praise but should at the same time be regarded as a start—not an end, and as unfinished, not finished, work. Lots and lots of useful pieces of information could still be collected if only we are to make an attempt to search for them from old people or other sources as has been the practice of the earlier writers of our history.

Therefore let us not allow these legends to die away, something worthwhile can still be done since our living grandfathers and grandmothers are at our disposal to be asked many useful questions with regard to rebuilding our history as far as possible. To this end it would be wise if a country-wide campaign to collect these legends here and there should be organized either under the auspices of the government or by history research students of this country.

Although we have revised *The Muhammadan Emirates of Nigeria* at the sustained request of many of Nigeria's leaders and educationists, we are nevertheless conscious that the present state of research in African history in no way permits of the definitive story of the Emirates yet being attempted. Hopefully the enterprising 1964 Northern Nigeria Historical Research Scheme will do much to accelerate the pace. Our rationalization has been simple. He who awaits perfection and finality may wait for ever; the creative purist who insists on writing only *the* history may end up by writing nothing at all and so deprive the world of much of value. Our *point de départ* has been that what is locally held to be 'our history' should, in the interests of posterity, be recorded against the day when such primary sources will no longer be available. Thus preserved, their value can later be professionally evaluated and finally assessed within the total perspective of Nigerian history. Until that day, all historical traditions at least deserve attention: *le mieux est trop souvent l'ennemi du bien.*

Apart from discarding the unambiguously irrelevant or impossibly claimant, we have therefore gathered all sorts of oral traditions and ancient lore, sometimes conflicting and sometimes confirmatory, believing that such an assembly allows the professional historian a better chance to apply the strict rules of his discipline and reject those local accounts that his detailed research may later prove to contain more 'story' than 'history'. Not all such traditions are worthy of equal credence; not every chronicler is of unquestioned objectivity or total reliability; yet such tales, such traditions, are not only the very life-blood of history in the raw before it is professionally processed but they also constitute a local acceptance, at least until outside scholars confirm or disprove. An historian cannot command his sources; rather is he at their mercy. Our cautious attitude towards the delicate question of source materials is, we trust, apparent in the sub-title of the book and in our accent on its non-definitive approach.

Now for a word on the heart of this book, the Northern Nigerian Emirates. The emirates as we know them today are the outcome of the conquest of the original Habe or Hausa states by the Fulani under Shehu Usman dan Fodio in the jihad at the beginning of the nineteenth century. In this rise of the Sokoto Empire is located the historical genesis of contemporary Northern Nigeria. The jihad of 1804 is a watershed; more, it is an end and a beginning. Had the Sokoto forces been defeated in those moments of peril at Tabkin Kwatto in 1804 and before Gwandu in 1805, had Bornu not withstood the Fulani armies in 1810, had the Kanuri succeeded in their westward thrust of 1826 or the Habe in their last stand at Gawakuke in 1835, then the history of Northern Nigeria and the political context of present-day Nigeria would not have been as we know them. It is therefore, quite apart from any justifiable sentiment of local pride, helpful to our understanding of modern Nigeria to be aware of the rich and colourful history of the Northern emirates.

One more idea for the historically minded. The jihad of Usman dan Fodio should not be viewed in isolation. It was part of a much wider movement in the Western Sudan. There was the Torobe revolt of 1776 in Futa Toro and Bondu; there was the rise of the Fulani kingdom of Ahmadu Lobo in Massina; there was the religious war of Al Haj Omar in upper Niger and Senegal, probably influenced by the *mujahhidin* of Gobir; news of the Sokoto jihad has even been credited with triggering off the revolt of the Hausa slaves in Brazil. Indeed, there is the attractive parallel of the earlier jihad in what is today the Republic of Guinea, where a group of Fulani leaders were converted by the Mauretanian marabouts and announced their holy war in 1725 under Alfa Ba.

But the Guinea parallel with Northern Nigeria goes further than simply the shared experience of a jihad. Just as the Shehu awarded flags and territorial kingdoms to his followers so did the Guinean chiefs divide the conquered land into *diwal* or provinces. By and large, each emirate and each *diwal* was granted to one of the actual campaign leaders. Similarly, each empire crystallized as a major area of political influence, which have both persisted to the present day. Such comparisons can, of course, be advanced too far, but clear points of resemblance can be discerned by those in search of historical similarities. Parenthetically, it is interesting to notice how, whether by design or accident, this division of the Fulani empire followed the old Habe dichotomy between the Hausa Bakwai and the Banza Bakwai, the former conquered states coming under the tutelage of Sokoto and the latter acknowledging the sovereignty of Gwandu. Again, both empires governed their territories with a marked degree of sophisticated administration, giving evidence of such phenomena as a formalized system of justice, institutionalized taxation and tribute paid to their chiefs, and an administrative hierarchy—the key elements, in fact, of what political scientists have defined as characterizing a 'state' and absent in a 'segmented society'. Both these empires yielded to European aggression at the turn of the century. Lastly, and interestingly enough though the coincidence appears to have been made less of than might have been expected, the men who have led Northern Nigeria and Guinea to political independence are direct descendants of two of the most distinguished Muslim soldier-administrators of the Western Sudan: Ahmadu Bello, Sardauna of Sokoto, great-grandson of Sultan Bello, and Sekou Touré, great-grandson of Almamy Samory.

To present the splendid panorama of emirate history has been both our aim and our inspiration. In so doing, we have a number of hopes. One, that this book will serve to impart to young Northerners, at many levels of their studies, a feeling for their early history. Two, that it may help preserve some of the local lore for future generations and here and there reveal a clue or suggest a research line to historians. Three, that it will give visitors to Northern Nigeria a sufficiently attractive introduction to the

2

history of the emirates to lead them on to some of the excellent specialized monographs now available. Four, that it will encourage and maybe assist Nigerian scholars themselves to gather and record the rich traditions of their areas. And lastly, that someone better equipped than we may complete the Northern Nigerian scene by writing a parallel study of the long and varied history of the non-emirate areas of the North, from the great chieftaincies of Tiv, Jukun, Igala and Igbirra to the colourful story of groups like the Birom, Bachama, Idoma and Gwoza-Mandara peoples.

The compilation of Part II of this book in my *heures perdues* would not have been possible without the help of my *malam* and student friends, too many to be named individually but to all of whom I am personally grateful. This includes Alhaji Aliyu Dogondaji, whose change of duties prevented him from finishing what he had started to do in collating local material. Our special thanks go to those Native Authorities (all save six replied) who took the trouble to read our manuscript and to verify and add information; in many cases these amendments were made by the emir or by an *ad hoc* committee of local historians whose suggestions have been a most valuable incorporation. We were unfortunate that the new Chair of History at Ahmadu Bello University was not filled till after our manuscript was completed, but we are grateful for the guidance offered by Professor H. F. C. Smith on various questions, particularly on the most effective order in which to present the individual emirate histories. We also acknowledge the co-operation of the Premier's Office, Kaduna, where Mr J. H. Smith, Deputy Secretary to the Premier, gave our work every fair wind, especially over the final approval of the emirate genealogies and texts by almost every Native Authority. Finally, I would like to mention the perseverance of Sunday Ajai, who spent many of his would-be leisure hours in wrestling with my handwriting and transforming it into a fair typescript, and my students S. J. Yakubu and Bashiru Tukur who helped in correcting the proofs.

Ahmadu Bello University,
Zaria.

A. H. M. KIRK-GREENE

CONTENTS

ILLUSTRATIONS

ACKNOWLEDGEMENT

The authors are most grateful to Dr J. C. Chartres for permission to reproduce photographs 1, 3, 4 and 5, which were taken by his father the late Lieut.-Col. E. A. Chartres, F.R.C.S.I.; to Bernard Fagg, Esq., Curator of the Pitt-Rivers Museum, Oxford, for photographs 6 and 15; to the Department of Antiquities Jos, for photographs 8, 9 and 14; to the Ministry of Information, Northern Nigeria, for photographs 7, 10, 11, 12 and 13.

MAPS

GLOSSARY

In a work of this nature it is inevitable that for the sake of accuracy, and often of brevity, a small number of Hausa terms should be used. Readers unacquainted with the Northern Nigerian context may find the following list of the Hausa and Arabic words that appear most frequently in the text a useful guide.

Ajele: deputy, official, representative. Cf. *Wakili.*
Alhaji: courtesy title granted to a man who has made the Pilgrimage to Mecca.
Alkali: Muslim court judge.
-awa: ethnic suffix, meaning 'the people': e.g., *Gobirawa,* the people of Gobir.
Daji: bush country.
Dan: son of. Cf. *Ibn* or *Bin* (Arabic).
Dutsi: rock, hill; *Hosere* in Fulani place names.
Gida: house.
Gulbi: river. Also *Kogi*; *Mayo* in Fulani place names.
Habe: in practice the 'Hausa' as distinct from the 'Fulani'. Sing.: *Kado,* but popularly *Habe* when adjectival.
Haj: the enjoined pilgrimage to Mecca, one of the five 'pillars' of Islam. Cf. *Alhaji.*
Hanya: road, path.
Hausa: the conglomerate peoples who speak the Hausa language.
Hijra: exile (Arabic). Used to refer to the flight of the Prophet Muhammad from Mecca to Medina in A.D. 622, from which year the Muslim calendar dates. The term is also used to mean the flight of Shehu Usman dan Fodio from Degel to Gudu on 21 February 1804. Since the Muslim year contains 354 days, to convert from A.D. and vice versa the following formula can be used:

$$\text{A.D.} = \text{A.H.} - \frac{3\ \text{A.H.}}{100} + 621 \text{ (neglect fractions).}$$

Ibn: son of. Cf. *Dan.*

Imam: Muslim religious leader.
Jihad: Muslim holy war.
Kakaki: long state trumpets.
Kirari: a praise couplet, epithet or song.
Kofa: town gate. Also 'official intermediary'.
Lifidi: quilted horse-armour.
Mai-: prefix meaning 'owner of'.
Malam: (also *mallam*) Arabic scholar; learned man; courtesy title, cf. Mr. Plural: *malamai.*
-n: genitival suffix of masculine nouns: e.g. *Sarkin,* the chief of...
Salla: Muslim festival, generally either Id al Fitr or Id al Kabir.
Sarauta: office or title, of king or lesser rank.
Sarki: king, chief. *Lamido* in Fulani; *Mai* or *Moi* in Bornu; *Etsu* in Nupe; *Oba* in Yoruba.
Sarkin Musulmi: leader of the Muslims, 'Commander of the Faithful'. Courtesy title of the Sultan of Sokoto (Arabic: *amir al mu'minin*).
Sudan: here used to denote all the country stretching from the southern part of the Sahara desert to the belt of rain forest along the equator. It derives from the Arabic term *Bilad al Sudan,* the country of the Negroes. The expression Western Sudan is often used to differentiate it from the Nilotic Sudan.
Talakawa: the peasants, common people, plebs. Sing.: *talaka.* The opposite, meaning the upper classes or patricians, is *sarakuna* (sing.: *sarki*).
Wakili: deputy, official representative. Cf. *Ajele.*
Waziri: chief minister, senior councillor to the king, vizier. Other common titles at a Hausa/Fulani court include Galadima, Magaji, Madaki or Madawaki, Ajiya, Ciroma, Yerima, Wambai, etc. The exact ranking of these titles differs from emirate to emirate.
Yaki: war.

SPELLING OF PROPER NAMES

Arabic may be transliterated according to either the orthography of the written or the phonemes of the spoken language, which varies with its dialects. Thus the transliteration Es Sadi or As Sadi reflects the pronunciation of the name, though in Arabic it would be written *alsadi,* since in speech the l of the definite article (*al*) is assimilated to a dental, a sibilant, or the letters r, l and n. Some inconsistency in the spelling of African names is almost inevitable. Coming to us, as they often do, via the unvowelled Arabic of a local scribe or traveller and a French translation, there can be strange variations. Which one is to be 'correct', Melle or Mali, Al Bakri or el-Bekri, Gao or Kawkaw or Alkwakwua or Kagh, Usumanu or Usman or Osman or Othman, Ja or Dya or Za, Saifawa or Sefuwa, Macine or Massina?

Apart from the variations in spelling the name Muhammad has numerous variant forms, e.g. Muhammadu, Mohamman, Mamman, Mamma, Mamudu.

Wherever possible we have used the anglicized form of words, now familiar, rather than more correct transliterations which might appear pedantic.

The following abbreviations have now become common Hausa words:

D.O.: District Officer (Hausa = di'o).
N.A.: Native Authority (Hausa = en'e).

PART I

I. 'A PIECE OF THE CONTINENT, A PART OF THE MAIN': NORTHERN NIGERIA AND THE SUDAN

To UNDERSTAND the people of Northern Nigeria one must understand their setting against the background of history. They belong inseparably to the Sudan,[1] the savannah lands lying to the south of the Sahara, and their distinctive characteristics and culture derive inescapably from contacts with their neighbours, particularly those on the north and west. Right up to the nineteenth century there was no known outlet to the sea through the rain forest belt to the south, and the desert cut off all but the hardiest from communication with the outside world to the north. For almost the whole span of history, therefore, the Sudan including Northern Nigeria remained virtually a large land-locked island, enclosed within a continent of desert and forest. Yet no country 'is an island, entire in itself' in being unaffected by outside influences, however remote, and Nigeria is shown by history to be clearly 'a piece of the Continent, a part of the main'.[2]

Today's Northern Nigerians carry the chromosomes of a variety of ancient peoples, including the Berber, Jewish and Arab immigrants from the north, deriving their civilization and traditions from the Mediterranean régimes of Carthage and Rome, Greece and Byzantium, as well as from the Islamic empires of Spain and the Maghrib, Egypt, Syria and Mesopotamia. Mixed in varying degree with these hereditary strains are those of the ancient indigenous peoples of the Sudan, who later absorbed the lighter skinned immigrants from the north and intermarried with them.

No serious study of Nigerian history, therefore, can afford to ignore either the main course of events in the Maghrib and round the Mediterranean when contacts with the Sudan were beginning to be explored, or the strong Arab-Muslim influences which have permeated the whole of the Sudan for a thousand years. The

[1] For the meaning of the word Sudan in this book reference is invited to the Glossary and to page 28.

[2] John Donne (1592–1631).

heights of civilization achieved under the khalifates in Cordova, Cairo and Baghdad at a time when parts of Europe were still uncouth and unlettered deserve to be more widely recognized.

Man apprehends and experiences life in a way that has been determined by his history. His very being has been shaped and influenced by the remote experiences of his forebears.

'Although' says Jung, 'our inheritance consists of physiological paths, it was nevertheless mental processes in our ancestors that traced the paths. If they come to consciousness again in the individual, they can do so only in the form of other mental processes; and although these processes can become conscious only through individual experience and consequently appear as individual acquisitions, they are nevertheless pre-existent traces which are merely "filled out" by individual experience. Probably every "impressive" experience is just such a break-through into an old previously unconscious river-bed.'[1]

It is difficult not to accept in the main Jung's theory of the collective unconscious, which makes the study of our past more than a mere satisfaction of curiosity. The past must illuminate the present and even help to predict the future. Much depends on the accuracy and skill of the historian in recording the past, and even more on our ability to interpret it objectively.

The chapters in Part I which follow contain material selected to act as markers to the main current of events leading up to the study of Nigerian history. But readers are free, which this book is not, to explore the creeks and sidestreams in larger works such as those quoted for reference. Indeed it is of the essence in the study of history that research should be spread as widely as possible to discover different versions and interpretations.

First of all there is the Maghrib, the Western World of the Arabs in north Africa. This was the jumping-off ground for the trans-Sahara expeditions. The rich kaleidoscope of its history gives us a picture of the variety of its peoples and their different cultures before they started to filter across the desert.

Then there is the eventful story of the rise of Islam, from the empty wastes of the untutored Bedouin[2] herdsmen to the splen-

[1] See 'On Psychic Energy', in *Collected Works of C. G. Jung*, London and New York, 1960, vol. 8, pp. 53–4.

[2] The correct transliteration of this word from written Arabic is the adjective Badawiyyi, from the singular noun Bādiyah, plural Bawādi. We use the now commonly accepted form in English.

dours of material and intellectual achievements in the courts of the Khalifs.

Finally there is the impact of these peoples on the indigenous Sudanese, together with the successive chronicles of one great Sudanese state after another until the invasion by the Moors. All this leads up to the point where Sudanese history merges with Nigerian down to the twentieth century.

II. THE MAGHRIB AND MEDITERRANEAN INFLUENCES

THE Maghrib, meaning simply 'West', is the name given by the Arabs to the western part of their world, that is to say north Africa, west of the Egyptian borders. Maghrib-al-Aksa, or the Far West, was the name for what is today Morocco. An older name for this region is Barbary, the land of what the Romans called 'barbarians', or the people who were pushed southwards to the fringe of the desert by the colonists. From this came the name Berber.

Since the Maghrib is easily accessible by sea from Europe but separated by the desert from the rest of Africa, its history has been chiefly influenced by European or Mediterranean civilization rather than African. The north African coastal strip of fertile country is about 2,600 miles long and, except in the far west, is seldom more than 100 miles wide. Towards the west the country becomes increasingly mountainous and the people of these regions have tended to be as difficult as their terrain. Placidity has belonged to the agriculturalists of the plains, who have always been vulnerable to the restless raids of the nomadic hillmen.

As will be seen, the people who came to inhabit the Maghrib from the period of the early Phoenician settlements of the ninth and eighth centuries B.C. right down to the time of the Arab invasions some 1,500 years later comprised a mixture of races with a predominantly Mediterranean type of civilization. The coastal plains came to be occupied by a succession of peoples from across the sea, with a Greek element coming via Alexandria after the Greek conquest of Egypt. With the latter came almost equal numbers of immigrants from Judaea.

The nomad Berber tribes tended to withdraw to the edges of the desert, and we hear for example from Herodotus of the Garamantes of the Fezzan raiding into the Sudan belt.[1] These appear to have been a powerful collection of tribes living in the interior round the oasis of Garama (modern Germa); they were

[1] E. W. Bovill, *The Golden Trade of the Moors*, Ch. 3.

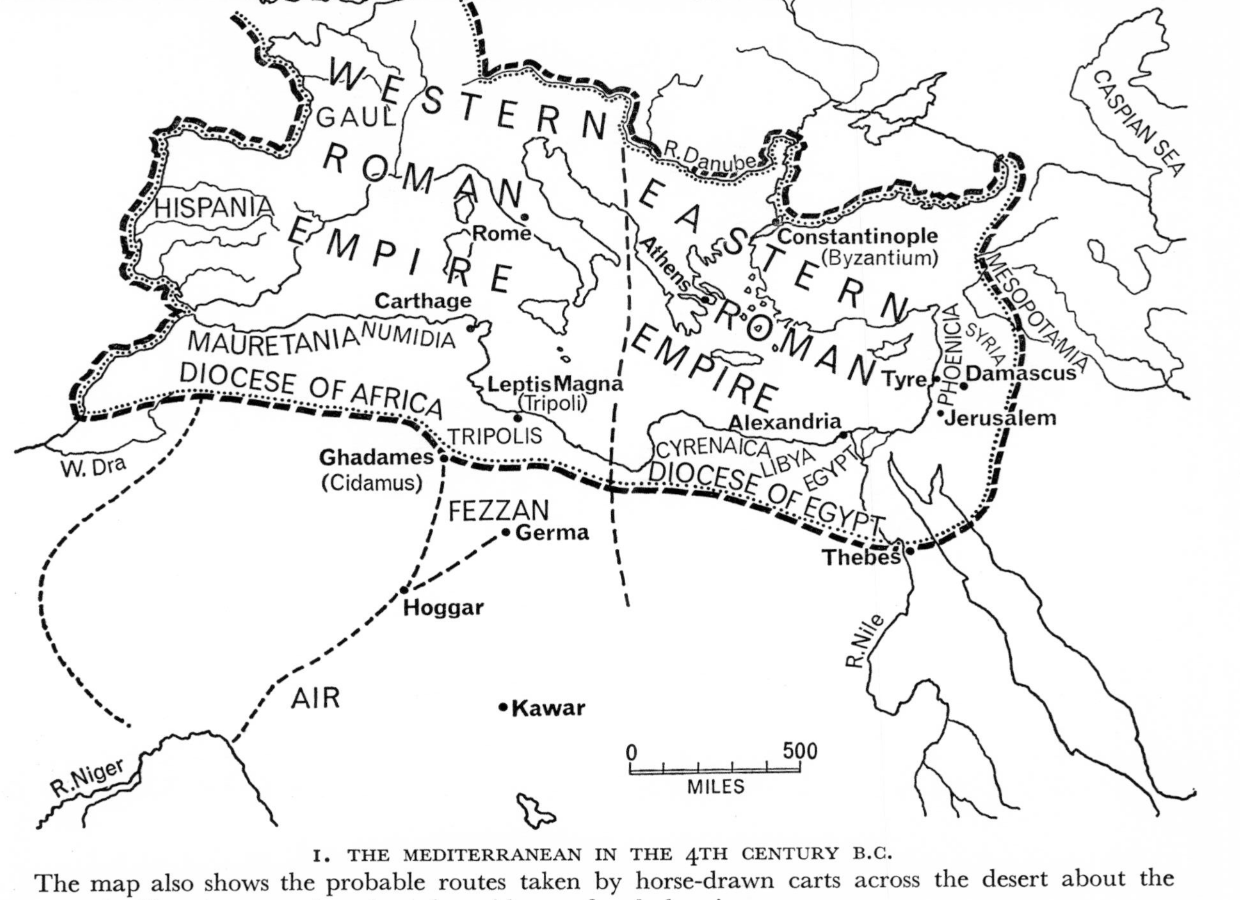

I. THE MEDITERRANEAN IN THE 4TH CENTURY B.C.

The map also shows the probable routes taken by horse-drawn carts across the desert about the second millennium B.C., based on the evidence of rock drawings.

variously described as nomad tent-dwellers and as settled cultivators but their reputation was chiefly for trade and trouble. Over the years more and more Berbers took up work on the plantations of the colonists until there eventually emerged a class of peasant Berber, speaking the Punic language. Many later became Romanized, and in the hills of the interior organized Berber settlements came into being. The fourth and fifth centuries saw the emergence of a powerful tribe of semi-nomad Berbers known as the Zenata, whose depredations on the cultivated areas became a constant source of unrest. But this was over a thousand years after the founding of the Tyrian colony of Carthage in 814 B.C.

THE CARTHAGINIANS

From the ninth to the second century B.C. the western part of this region was occupied by the Carthaginians, originally kinsmen of the Phoenicians from Tyre on the coast of Syria. They were a seafaring people. Carthage itself was near modern Tunis and her trading settlements were dotted east and west along the coast where anchorages could be found. By the fifth century B.C. Carthage sent expeditions into the Sahara to try and capture the important trade across the desert with the Sudan, which consisted largely of animals such as monkeys, lions, leopards and elephants, precious stones like carbuncles, emeralds and chalcedony, and also slaves. By the second century B.C. trade centred on the Tripoli–Fezzan–Bornu (Garamantian) route, which brought much wealth to Carthage.[1] She was powerful enough to exclude foreigners from any lands where her settlements lay, so that the Romans were denied access not only to the African shores but also to Sicily, Sardinia, and southern Spain. The Greeks could come no farther west than Cyrenaica. These frustrating restrictions led to the conquest by Rome in 146 B.C. of Carthage, whose dominions thenceforth became for the most part a Roman province called Africa. The name later spread to the whole continent.

THE ROMANS

The Romans became masters of the art of supplying water to arid regions. The remains of their extensive aqueducts, dams, and

[1] A. Adu Boahen, 'Caravan Trade in the 19th Century', *Journal of African History, III*, No. 2, 1962, and his *Britain, the Sahara and the Western Sudan, 1788–1861;* 1964.

cisterns fed from catchment areas can be seen in most of these parts. Carthage drew its water from nearly ninety miles away. As a result of irrigation corn grew in plenty and vineyards flourished. The provinces of 'Africa' and Numidia became the granary of Rome and the suppliers of olive oil. Much of the labour was provided by the Berbers, who had been gradually weaned from their nomad prejudices by long contact with the farmers, first of Carthage then of Rome.

The Maghrib continued for over five hundred years as part of the Roman Empire until the power of Rome vanished before the invasions of various Germanic tribes. At one time during the first century B.C. the power of Rome extended all the way from Egypt in the east to the Atlantic in the west, including all the lands in Africa north of the Sahara. Two of the better known emperors were Africans: Septimius Severus and his son Caracalla, whose fame rests not only on his baths but on his conferment of the rights of Roman citizenship on every freeborn inhabitant of the empire.

Since 330 the Roman Empire had in effect been two empires: a western empire governed from Rome, and an eastern one governed from the old Byzantium, rechristened Constantinople. The Maghrib naturally came under the western empire, whereas Cyrenaica and the littoral eastwards came under the influence of the eastern empire. It may be significant to note how this division between east and west persisted right into the Sudan. Eastern Mediterranean influences followed the more easterly desert routes through Fezzan and Tibesti from Tripoli and Egypt to the region of Chad; western cultural ideas reached the Niger, and thence the Hausa states, via the routes farther westward through Tuat and Taghaza, or through Adrar of Mauretania and Audoghast. But the two influences, even if they crossed the desert from different sources (and this was not necessarily so), tended on arrival to permeate laterally and intermingle. There was a regular network of trade routes covering the length and breadth of the Sudan north of the forests and these were constantly trodden by traders converging on such regions as Banda and Bono on the upper Volta to collect gold to take back to Kanem, Hausaland, Yorubaland and the Mande areas of the Senegal and Niger rivers.

It was in Roman times that considerable numbers of Jews sought refuge in the Maghrib to join those who had come earlier with Greeks from Alexandria; some are believed to have come even as far back as the time of the exodus under Moses. Some would have come after the revolt against Titus in A.D., 70 and even more after Bar-Cochba's revolt in 135, when Jerusalem was destroyed and the Jews dispersed from Palestine. Another revolt against the Roman power, this time in Cyrenaica about 115, set in motion a migration of Jewish tribes resulting in their widespread dispersal throughout the Maghrib.

Christianity spread under Roman rule, with Alexandria and Carthage as its two great centres in Africa. St. Augustine of Hippo, the devout author of *The City of God*, was a Berber brought up in Numidia and educated in Carthage. As bishop he was constantly engaged in controversy with the various sects such as the Manichaeans, the Donatists and the Pelagians, which developed in the Maghrib in opposition to the mother church of the colonial power. In Egypt, however, it was the Coptic form of Christianity that took firm hold in opposition to the orthodox Melkite church of Byzantium, and in due course it spread to Nubia and Ethiopia.[1]

From the fourth to the seventh centuries there were constant troubles after the weakening of Roman control by the invasion of the Vandals under Genseric in 429. There were rebellions against the civil power and also against the church and its growing persecution. Following Genseric's death anarchy prevailed. In 533 Belisarius landed a Byzantine army and routed the Vandals, but the intransigent Berbers gave their rulers no respite.

ARAB INVASION OF THE MAGHRIB

After the death of Muhammad in 632 the Arabs soon began to penetrate the civilized world. Their bold raiding parties with the rallying cry of Islam easily overran the conscript levies of Byzantium and Sassanid Persia. Under Khalid the Arab armies traversed Palestine and Syria to cross the Tigris and evict the Persian emperor from his throne in Ctesiphon.[2] They even crossed the Oxus to outer Mongolia. Their conquests were generally welcomed rather than resisted by the peasantry, who resented the alien dominance of Greek and Persian imperialism.

Meanwhile another Arab army, quite a small one, came down from Palestine under Amr ibn al As to attack Egypt. The Byzantine rulers received little support from the native Copts, who

[1] R. Oliver and J. D. Fage, *A Short History of Africa*, Chap. 6.
[2] Also known as Mada'in. It lay not far from the site of Baghdad.

quickly came to terms with Amr. Alexandria fell in 642. From Egypt the conflagration spread westwards through Cyrenaica and Tripoli. Periodic waves of Arab invaders followed for many years, which the Byzantine overlords were powerless to check. In 670 the celebrated leader Akbar ibn Nafi built Kairwan some miles south of the site of Carthage as his headquarters, and he extended his conquests as far as the Atlantic. But he was eventually defeated and killed by the Berbers, and in 683 Kairwan fell into their hands.

Over the ensuing years the struggle between the intruding Arabs and the native Berbers waxed and waned; the Byzantines could provide little support for their colonial dependants. At one period the Berbers were inspired by the leadership of a remarkable priestess known as the Kahina by Arab historians. One tradition has it that she was a Jewess of the tribe of Levi. For five years before her death in battle she held the invaders at bay by adopting a policy of 'scorched earth'. There can be little doubt that these constant wars in a country so dependent on man-made water supplies and irrigation must have contributed largely to the desiccation and erosion from which there has been little real recovery.

The Arabs had left their deserts to search for easier living rather than to propagate the new faith; they therefore kept to the comfortably populated areas. But Akbar did penetrate the Sahara as far south as Kawar in 666, and he was persuaded to turn back only a short way from the Bornu grasslands he was seeking.

ARAB INVASION OF SPAIN

Early in the eighth century a certain Musa ibn Nusair, who was then governor of Afrikia,[1] succeeded in his policy of conciliation towards the Berbers to get them to accept his rule. Large numbers of them were converted to Islam and his position in the Maghrib was assured internally. But his coasts were vulnerable to raids. In 711, after capturing the Balearic islands as a measure of protection, he turned his eyes on the mainland of Spain and his general, Tarik, landed near the rock that still bears his name (Jabl al Tarik) and vanquished the Gothic army under King Roderic. This opened the way to the Arab occupation of much of Spain, where they were to remain for some seven hundred years. Spain had prospered under Roman rule from the time of Julius Caesar's

[1] Afrikia or Ifrikia or Ifriqia are Arabic versions of the Roman province of Africa.

governorship, and it had become so assimilated that it had produced some of the shining lights of Latin literature. With the subsequent invasion of the Goths and the Vandals the country had decayed, and many districts had reverted to tribal independence. This weakened Roderic's powers of resistance. The people put up little opposition, and though nominally Christian had no compunction in accepting Islam.

In the eleventh century after the Fatimid centre of power had shifted from Afrikia to Egypt, as is described in the next chapter, there was a long struggle between rival Sanhaja Berber tribes. To meet this situation the Fatimid Khalif eventually hit upon a plan to import into Afrikia a number of Arabs to dilute the strong Berber element. The Arabs selected for this venture consisted of a number of troublesome Bedouin from upper Egypt, including many of the Banu Hilal and the Banu Soleim. The newcomers reduced the Sanhaja kingdoms to the coastal settlements and the Zenata Berber nomads met their match in the ruthlessness and swiftness of the raid. The Banu Soleim got no farther than Cyrenaica, but the Banu Hilal came on westward like a swarm of locusts, killing and destroying as they came. They are held to be more responsible than any others for the denuded forests and ruined cisterns and aqueducts which let in the desert again.

These then were the people who were to provide the first exploratory ventures from the north into the Sudan in the early centuries of the Christian era, and the later more confident journeys in the early Muslim era. The unhappy Maghrib, with its constant subjection to wars and destruction, to invasions and revolts, provided all the necessary stimulus to emigrate in search of a new life. Stories of pleasant green lands far to the south began to be heard from the nomadic tribes, whose mobility had been immensely improved by the introduction of the camel from about the third century. Up till that time the distances between waterholes had made most journeys in the desert almost impossible, though the ox as well as the ass were not quite so inferior as many suppose. The horse by comparison with the camel is almost useless in the real desert, though in the *Sahel* or scrub its speed has certain advantages. For desert travel the camel ousted the horse.

THE CAMEL

The one humped camel (*Camelus dromedarius*) has great natural powers of endurance. It can stand up to abnormal heat, it can store up reserves of energy in its hump, and it can take in over fifty gallons of water at a time. But it is slow: the pack animal covers only about two miles in the hour and even the *mehari* or riding camel does only about four. Neither animal can be goaded to a faster pace for long without breaking down. Though one may hear of special feats, such as covering 150 miles or more within the space of twenty-four hours in pursuit of thieves, one does not often hear of the price—usually death from exhaustion. Though there is evidence of an indigenous long extinct camel in North Africa (*Camelus thomazi*), the later species reached the Maghrib only in Roman times, despite its introduction into Egypt many centuries earlier. If the Hyksos did not bring it from Asia with their invasion of 1680 B.C. the Persians under Cambyses certainly did in 525 B.C. Duveyrier credits Zenata Berbers of Judaic stock with the introduction of the camel when they founded the oases at Gurara and Tuat, during the sixth century perhaps; and it was they who established their chief settlement at Tamentit, where Hebraic inscriptions on burial columns can still be seen. But more modern authorities put the camel's adoption some centuries earlier. After the famous mention of the twenty-two camels captured by the Romans in Numidia at the battle of Thapsus in 47 B.C. we hear of a Roman general demanding 4,000 camels from Lepcis Magna (Tripoli). The Libyan Berbers were using camels well before the Arab invasion of the seventh century, and their spread to Ghana and the Sudan cannot have been much later. In the tenth century Ibn Haukal speaks of an Adrar chief called Tenberoutan sending against his enemies 200 camelmen each with 150 animals in his charge; a century later Al Bakri tells what must be essentially the same story of a chief, now called Tin Yeroutan, of Audoghast, who could put 100,000 camel warriors in the field and still lend 50,000 to his ally Tarin. Such discrepancies offer a salutary caution to the credulous, but even so one can interpret the figures as meaning that camels in those parts were plentiful.[1]

CAUSES OF DESICCATION

Although the evidence of innumerable rock-drawings in various parts of the desert makes it clear that the climate of the desert was formerly far more humid than it is today, it is doubtful whether

[1] Raymond Mauny, *Tableau Géographique de l'Ouest Africain Au Moyen Age*, p. 287.

in Roman times this was so: the drawings of animals that thrive only on abundant pastures such as are now found within the tropics date from an era several thousand years prior to the Romans and point to a wet phase that later came to an end. Had the rainfall two thousand years ago in fact been much heavier than today the bridges whose remains can be seen would not have spanned the rivers and fords could not have been used where they were. The deep, dry watercourses had their origin in a much earlier age, and the occasional scourings of rare storms have perpetuated their scars.

There seems little doubt that the desiccation since Roman times was caused not by a lessening of rainfall but by the destruction and neglect of man.[1] The nomads, Berber and Arab alike, abhor agriculture; down the centuries they have despised farmers and taken no interest in irrigation. The settlements could be protected against the wanton marauder only so long as there was a strong controlling government. But as central control relaxed, so did the farmer's livelihood become more precarious; and like impoverished landlords of decaying property they could no longer keep up with the expense of repairs and maintenance. The aqueducts and the dams collapsed; the wells and water-holes silted up; the farms and vineyards shrank; the desert crept in on the sown. Not only was there the almost seasonal encroachment of the local nomads with their herds, which drought made an absolute necessity for their survival, but in the eleventh century came the devastation of the wild Banu Hilal, who stripped the woods and forests. Up to about that time there was enough natural vegetation to support a wide variety of animals, including elephant, though they tended to run smaller than similar species in the tropics. In Carthaginian times the elephant took the place of the camel as a beast of burden, and Hasdrubal used to capture his elephants in the forests of the Atlas foothills. Bones and teeth of hippopotami have been found in the gravel bed of the Chelif river in Algieria, south of the Atlas. But the wild game had many enemies. The Roman writer, Strabo, in the lifetime of Christ attributed the lack of game to the nomad hunters, the settled cultivators (to protect their crops), and even to the inordinate demand for wild beasts to provide gladiatorial spectacles in the arenas.

[1] E. W. Bovill, op. cit., Ch. I.

THE INTRODUCTION OF ISLAM TO THE SUDAN

Since the seventh century Islam had begun to cross the desert to the south, as witness the Ummayad expedition of 739 mentioned by Al Bakri. It was increasingly the faith or shield of Berber and Arab travelling merchants, since the great Muslim brotherhood of man operated in their favour and assured them of aid and protection from the Muslim trading posts spread out along the routes. This was particularly necessary in a pagan country. With few isolated exceptions the Muslims in the western Sudan were then of the orthodox Sunni persuasion, and had a common bond.

As more and more Berbers and Arabs kept coming to the Sudan there was a natural tendency for those who came in contact with them in the trading quarters to become converts. To the pagan, immense prestige attached to the 'People of the Book' (including of course Christians and Jews), and the commercial wealth and comfort that seemed to accompany the Islamic way of life were obvious attractions. For the Sudani it was a simply understood religion and easy to adopt. He was already used to polygamy, and often to circumcision, and he saw nothing but good in waging a holy war from which he could emerge with slaves and loot. As a Muslim he would be safe from becoming enslaved by another Muslim, and in general he would enjoy better security and status. No wonder that Islam spread rapidly and far.

From about 850 it is believed that the Lemtuna Tuareg (who mainly occupied the west central area north of Audoghast) became gradual converts to Islam, and by 1000 most of the Berbers in this region had also adopted the faith, at least nominally. In the numerous Sudanese towns connected with the desert traffic Muslim communities grew and thrived, and the influence of Islamic civilization on the royal courts became more and more pronounced. Tekrur adopted Islam in 1040, and in 1077 the Almoravids overthrew the pagan king of Ghana—in fact the eleventh century was a period of intense Islamization for the western Sudan. By 1100 Islam was firmly established in all the principal Sudanese states in close contact with the Berbers south of the Sahara and west of Chad.[1] What were the Islamic influences which spread from the Arab world to mingle with the Sudanic cultures and civilization that had grown up south of the Sahara? To understand this requires some knowledge of Arab civilization

[1] Raymond Mauny, op. cit., pp. 521 ff.

as it developed from the days of the Prophet through the succeeding periods of rule under the Ummayads, the Abbasids and the Fatimids, when the great universities of Baghdad, Cairo and Cordova excelled those of Christian Europe and the Muslim empire extended from the Atlantic ocean to the borders of India.

III. ARAB CIVILIZATION AND THE INFLUENCE OF ISLAM IN SPAIN AND NORTH AFRICA

ARABIA

THE new ideas which reached the Maghrib and the western Sudan from the seventh century onwards were imported by the Arabs at the same time as Islam, and one is naturally tempted to identify the one with the other. But Islam at this time was in its infancy, whereas the origins of Arab civilization can be traced back to centuries before Muhammad; some indeed say between thirty and forty centuries. There used to be an advanced civilization in antiquity in the Yemen, which was based on the maritime enterprise of the southern Arabians, who did an extensive carrying trade between the Persian Gulf, India and the West. But this prosperity had dwindled long before the time of Muhammad, possibly because of the establishment by the Romans of a through sea-route from Egypt to the East, which dealt a crippling blow to the caravan trade of the Arabian Peninsula.

Most of Arabia was barren and barely supported tribes of wild Bedouin with their flocks, sheltering in their 'houses of hair' as they called their black tents, and ever shifting their camps in search of pasture. There were only three towns of any importance in central Arabia: Mecca, Medina, and Taif. These had a mixed population of Arabs, Jews, and Persians, and though they carried on a certain amount of trade they were only like so many oases in a desert of rude nomads. There is no evidence that these northern Arabs ever developed a civilization in pre-Muslim times.

MESOPOTAMIA

But north of the inhospitable Arabia lay the fertile crescent of Palestine, Syria and Mesopotamia; and Persia was not so far. In these regions the great empires of Greece and Rome and Persia had held sway for centuries. Learning and the Arts had flourished in the precious shelter of powerful patrons and gracious living.

Into these countries there had been constant migrations of Arabs from the Peninsula; many had found service as mercenaries and had subsequently settled in affluence. In this way rose two important Arab dynasties, the Ghassanids in Syria and the Lakhmites in Hira, west of the Euphrates. The rulers of both dynasties became Christians and surrounded themselves with the pomp of oriental courts. These two Arab kingdoms held a mediating position between the uncouth Bedouin and the great civilizations of Byzantium and Persia. Although Christians, they gave much military assistance to the Muslims during the early wars of Islam. They made it easier for the Muslim conquerors to absorb the civilizations of the countries they overran, and they could point out to their kinsmen the solid advantages of gentle living. They had learned the art of writing long before it was practised in Arabia, and they enjoyed music and poetry.

THE ARABS

The Arabs have never been a nation. Feuds between tribes and between families are characteristic of their impatience of restraint and their unwillingness to take orders from anyone. The sheikh who looks after the tribal interests is by no means blindly obeyed: he must consult with the tribal council composed of the heads of families. The Arab is a born democrat. To quote from Philip Hitti:

> Ability to assimilate other cultures when the opportunity presents itself is well marked among the children of the desert. Faculties which have remained dormant for ages seem to awake suddenly, under the proper stimuli, and develop into dynamic powers. In the Fertile Crescent lies the field of opportunity. A Hammurabi makes his appearance in Babylon, a Moses in Sinai, a Zenobia in Palmyra, a Philip the Arab in Rome or a Harun al-Rashid in Baghdad. Monuments are built, like those of Petra, which still arouse the admiration of the world. The phenomenal and almost unparalleled efflorescence of early Islam was due in no small measure to the latent powers of the Bedouins, who, in the words of Caliph Umar, 'furnished Islam with its raw material.'[1]

And again:

> The two cardinal events of early medieval times are the Teutonic

[1] Philip Hitti, *The Arabs: a Short History*, Princeton, 1943, p. 16.

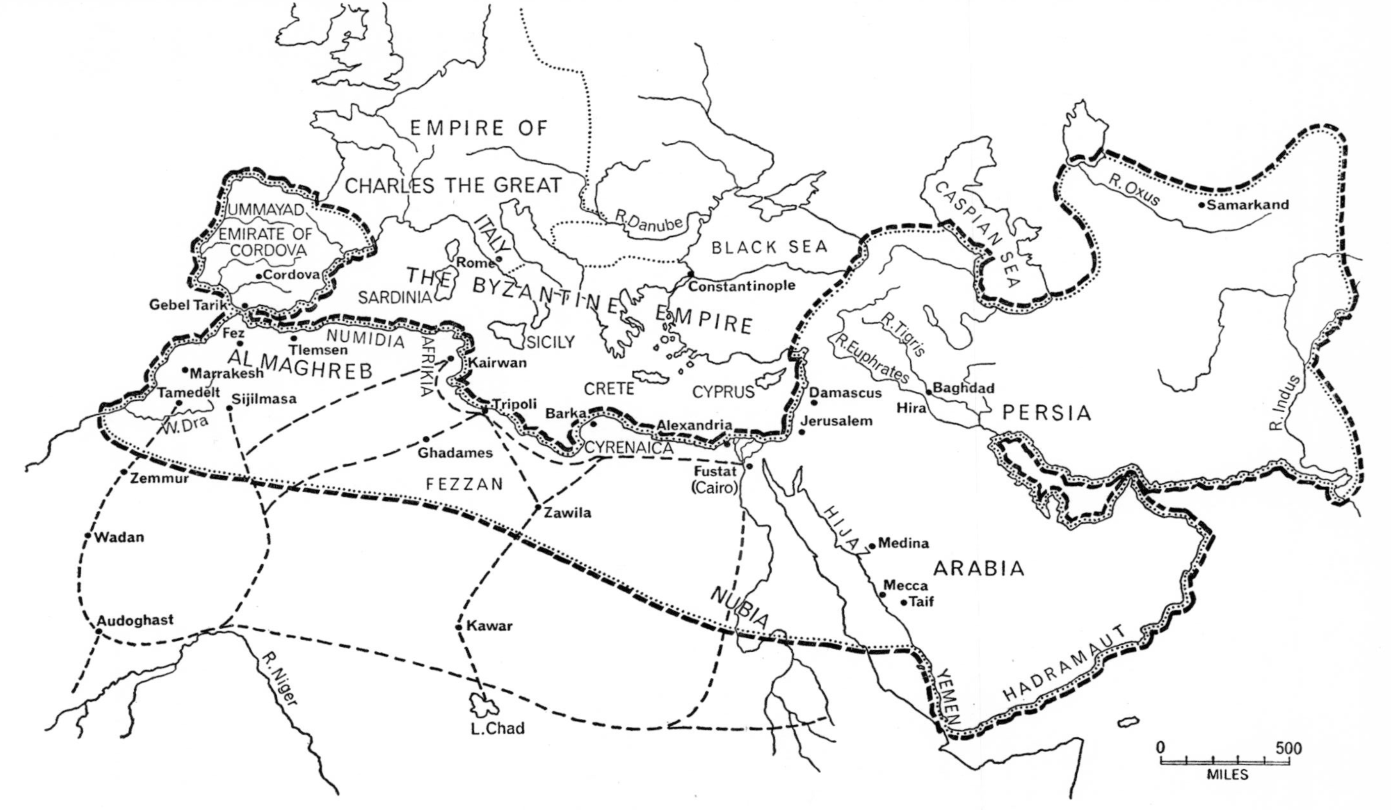

2. THE MAGHRIB AND THE SUDAN EARLY IN THE 9TH CENTURY

migrations resulting in the disruption of the venerable Roman Empire, and the Arab conquests which demolished the Persian empire and shook the Byzantine power to its very foundation. If someone in the first third of the seventh Christian century had had the audacity to prophesy that within a decade or so some unheralded, unforeseen power from the hitherto barbarous and little-known land of Arabia was to make its appearance, hurl itself against the only two world powers of the age, fall heir to one (the Sasanid) and strip the other (the Byzantine) of its fairest provinces, he would undoubtedly have been declared a lunatic. Yet that was exactly what happened. After the death of the Prophet, sterile Arabia seems to have been converted as if by magic into a nursery of heroes the like of whom, both in number and quality, would be hard to find anywhere.[1]

ISLAM

What was there in this new faith of Islam, meaning 'submission' to the will of God, which was to ignite the spirit of these and other peoples and launch them with united purpose into action? It was simply the following of the will of Allah, the only God, as revealed by his Prophet Muhammad in the Book, or Koran. The faith rests on five pillars—its profession in the tremendous formula, 'There is no god but Allah: Muhammad is His messenger'; prayer (through the medium of Arabic); almsgiving; fasting; and the pilgrimage to Mecca. Some have included the collective as distinct from individual duty of jihad against the infidel, but this practice has almost disappeared. The chief strength of Islam rests on its simple enthusiastic monotheism, which engenders resignation and contentment. It offers no unattainable ideal, there are no priests or bishops, there are no complexities of dogma or ritual. But there is the feeling of brotherhood in the faith, expressed in the meeting at Mecca; there is the self-discipline of fasting and public prayer; there is the humanity of almsgiving; and there are no barriers whatever of caste, race or colour.

The educated Muslim is brought up in a knowledge of *al Hadith*, the traditions of the Prophet's utterances, the standard collection of which was made by Al Bukhari, a Persian who taught in Baghdad. Of the 600,000 'traditions' heard by him he admitted only 7,257. His sources were Ayesha, the Prophet's wife; the first four khalifs or 'successors', who had been the Prophet's intimates; and six other recognized companions of Muhammad. Whatever

[5] Philip Hitti, op. cit., p. 46.

1. The Emir of Kano, Aliyu, at Zungeru, in 1903 with George Abadie, the Resident of Kano, on his right, together with the Galadima and H. B. Ryan, D.O.

2. The Governor of the North, Sir Kashim Ibrahim (*left*) with the Premier, Alhaji Sir Ahmadu Bello, the Sardauna of Sokoto.

3. Inside the walls of Kano in 1903, near the Kofar Mata.

4. Outside the walls of Kano in 1903, at the Kofar Gadan Kaya.

in *al Hadith* can be imitated or obeyed is *Sunna* and is compulsory for guidance if connected with religion. Four different schools of the four orthodox Imams followed the death of the first four khalifs, each with its own set of 'traditions' selected to suit the particular school's purpose.

Islam started as a religion, but it later became a state, and finally a culture. It is a fallacy to suppose that the khalif was merely a spiritual leader, a kind of pope with jurisdiction over Muslims throughout the world. Succession ('khilafah') to Muhammad meant succession to the sovereignty of the state. Muhammad as the prophet and messenger of God could have no successor. The khalif was 'the defender of the faith' just as the Christian monarchs often were held out to be. The first Arab conquests were materialistic and secular; the religious conversion of the conquered followed considerably later. The adoption of Islam offered tangible and overt advantages. The culture that came in the train of Islam owed much to the original Hellenistic civilization.

In his lifetime Muhammad was at the same time prophet, lawgiver, chief justice, religious leader, commander-in-chief of the army and civil head of state. His death in 632 raised the great problem of the succession, the bugbear of many constitutions not excepting the Roman Empire. Muhammad's only surviving child was his daughter, Fatimah, the wife of Ali; but succession of Arab sheikhs was not strictly hereditary: it followed rather the elective principle of choosing the most capable leader with due regard to tribal seniority. As a consequence the first three khalifs to be elected were Abu Bakr, the Prophet's father-in-law; Umar, the Prophet's brother-in-law; and Uthman, a former companion and no more. Not till 656 did the Prophet's son-in-law, Ali, succeed as the fourth orthodox Khalif. In his régime the Arab conquests stretched from Persia to Tripoli. With his accession all seemed set fair: he combined the hereditary right with that of election. But his honesty of purpose was to undo him. His forthright dismissal of corrupt governors brought the enmity of the powerful governor of Syria, Mu'awiya, whose forces enabled him to revolt. After the truce talks which ensued Mu'awiya managed by a trick to usurp the khalifate, and he even bought off the legitimate successor, Ali's son Hassan. From this time forward the khalifate was determined on the principle of succession within a dynasty, and there followed the great dynasties of the Ummayads, first in Damascus and later in Spain; the Abbasids in Baghdad; and the Fatimids in the Maghrib and Cairo. Each of these requires some brief description.

THE UMMAYADS IN DAMASCUS

Mu'awiya's dynasty known as the Ummayads ruled Islam from Damascus from 659 until 750. As a man of unusual administrative skill and political sense with his disciplined army he succeeded in developing an orderly Muslim society out of chaos so that most Muslims, and particularly the orthodox Sunnis, accepted him. But the Shi'ites ('adherents', i.e., of the house of Ali), who supported the lineal descent from Muhammad through Ali and Fatimah, were constant in their opposition; and there were also the intransigent Kharijites (the Zealots), a dissident splinter group of former supporters of Ali, to defy authority.[1]

THE ABBASIDS

After ninety-one years the usurping Ummayad dynasty was overthrown by the Abbasids, descendants of the Prophet's uncle, Abbas, and the capital was moved from Damascus to Baghdad. The Abbasids managed to silence the Shi'ite claims by putting out the convincing propaganda that the spiritual headship of Islam had devolved upon their family and not, as might be supposed, upon the surviving son of Hussain, a grandson of the Prophet, after the massacre at Kerbela. The Abbasid Khalifate endured from 750 until 1258, when Jenghiz Khan sacked Baghdad and put the last Khalif to death; but ever since 1055 the temporal mastery of the Muslim world had been surrendered by the Khalif to the Seljuk Turks.

To begin with the whole of the African possessions acknowledged the sovereignty of Baghdad, but in 788 Idris, a descendant of Hassan and the Prophet, escaped from Medina to the Maghrib al Aksa (modern Morocco) and there with the assistance of the Berber tribes established an independent kingdom. It was he who built the capital city of Fez.

THE FATIMIDS

In 800, though it remained within the Abbasid fold, Afrikia (modern Tunisia) became an autonomous principality under the rule of the Aghlabid governor and his successors in Kairwan. No

[1] The *Tarikh al Sudan* refers to Sonni Ali as a Kharijite. See page 72.

longer did the revenues of Egypt have to subsidize its government. Wise rule built up a prosperous economy and fostered learning.

But a century later a Shi'ite was sent from the Yemen to the Maghrib to undermine the Aghlabid government and challenge the long detested Abbasid power. With fervent support from the Berber tribe of Kutama he succeeded in establishing the Mahdi of the time from Yemen as Khalif, thus founding in 910 the Fatimid dynasty of true descendants of the Prophet. As a step towards the mastery of all Islam a long series of attempts began to wrest Egypt from its foreign governors. To secure his base the new Khalif chose an impregnable site for his new fortress capital to replace Kairwan, which he named Mahdiya. To cover his rear he subdued the Idrisids in 922, though the district of Fez was later recovered.

By 969 the conquest of the province of Egypt was eventually made possible when internal troubles caused the notables to invite the Fatimid army to restore order. This resulted in the founding of Al Kahira, The Victorious (modern Cairo), which later became the capital of the Fatimid Khalif Muiz and his successors. Syria and the Hijaz were not long in acknowledging the supremacy of the new khalifate. The Fatimid dynasty continued until 1171, when they were supplanted by the great Salah ad Din, the Muslim hero of the Third Crusade.

THE UMMAYADS IN SPAIN

For the Sudan, however, the chief interest may lie in the glorious achievements of the Ummayad dynasty in Cordova after it had been extinguished in Damascus, since it was destined to be submerged by the Almoravid movement which had its origin in the region of Ghana, as will be seen later.[1]

After the victory of Tarik over the Spanish army and the subsequent occupation of Andalusia by the forces of Musa ibn Nusair, referred to earlier,[2] there was a general migration of Berbers and Arabs across the straits. There they mixed with the descendants of the people whom Rome had nurtured to a high level of learning and culture. This was in the middle of the eighth century. In 758 a new epoch began in Spain with the landing of the fugitive Ummayad survivor, Abdurrahman ad Dakhil (the Enterer), after five years of wandering in North Africa. He had narrowly escaped the vengeful pursuit of the followers of the new Abbasid khalifs in

[1] See page 48. [2] See page 11.

Damascus after the overthrow and killing of the last Ummayad Khalif, Merwan, in 750, by his rival, as-Saffah (the Bloody). All members of the fallen house were pursued with ferocious inhumanity.

Abdurrahman quickly superseded the local governor of occupied Spain and established his independence by sending the governor's head as a present to the Khalif in Baghdad. It arrived beautifully preserved in salt and camphor, wrapped in a black flag and in the royal warrant of appointment. Such were the courtesies of the period. Abdurrahman's thirty years of rule gave the régime a magnificent start and the historians speak well of his successors, who had fluctuating fortunes in contending with internal strife. This perhaps was inevitable. Many moderate Muslims came into conflict with the fanaticism of the newly converted Berbers, and recalled with nostalgia the former days of Roman rule and intellectual nourishment. Christianity found a revival of interest and support. Despite the good intentions of the court, revolts and insurrections kept breaking out.

But under the rule of a later Abdurrahman, the greatest of the Ummayads, prosperity and power returned. His reign lasted for fifty years, from 912 to 961, and during that time Andalusia reached its greatest splendour, which lasted for nearly a hundred years. Hitherto the rulers had the style of Emir; he now proclaimed himself Khalif (929). His lavish spending on building impressed the world by its magnificence but drained the resources of his subjects. The capital, Cordova, became with Constantinople and Baghdad one of the three cultural centres of the world. With over a hundred thousand houses, seventy libraries and numerous bookshops, mosques and palaces, and nine hundred public baths, the city enjoyed international fame. An elaborate system of aqueducts and fountains in parks and gardens kept the city cool and beautiful. One of the lasting gifts of the Arabs to Spain was the introduction of agricultural methods practised in western Asia. They dug canals, cultivated grapes, and introduced many exotic plants and fruits, including apricots, peaches, oranges, rice and sugar-cane. It is scarcely credible that this remarkable standard of living had been achieved in such a short time by people of hardy desert stock: opportunity and environment can work seeming miracles. By contrast across the straits at this very time the marauding Banu Hilal were wrecking the aqueducts and laying waste the countryside; and most of northern Europe was plunged in barbaric ignorance and savage manners.

The real glory of this period, however, lies in the field of learning. We are told that colleges often had the following lines inscribed over their gates: 'The world is supported by four things only: the learning of the wise, the justice of the great, the prayers of the good, and the valour of the brave.' The University of Cordova, founded in the great mosque (which can be seen today), rose to pre-eminence; it preceded Al Azhar of Cairo and attracted students, both Christian and Muslim, from other parts of Europe, Africa and Asia. The general level of culture was so high that some scholars of the period declare that nearly everyone could read and write.

ARAB CONTRIBUTION TO CIVILIZATION

Between the middle of the eighth and the beginning of the thirteenth centuries the Arabs became the worthy custodians of culture and civilization throughout the world, the medium through which ancient science and philosophy were recovered, supplemented and transmitted to make possible the renaissance of western Europe. They are said to have invented the mariner's compass and the telescope; they fostered many of the physical sciences and contributed in no small degree to the development of research in medicine, astronomy (and its mother, astrology), mathematics, and chemistry. There were world-famous historians (Ibn Khaldun was one of the greatest), geographers (Al Bakri of Cordova contributed much to our knowledge of the western Sudan), philosophers and botanists. The introduction of Arabic numerals and the zero opened the door to the science of calculation as we know it today. One great service that Arab writers did was to translate the works of the Greek masters and so preserve the intellectual legacy of Hellenism. But this very service has misled some Arab enthusiasts to claim more than their due for the creativeness of their forefathers. It is, however, true that they did produce the first pharmacopoeia and the idea of chemists' shops, they did make good use of cautery and restrained the excessive use of the surgeon's knife, and by being keen travellers and observers they contributed enormously to our knowledge of the earth and its inhabitants.

Spain in the eleventh century was one of the wealthiest and

most thickly populated countries of Europe. Weaving of wool and silk flourished, silkworms having been introduced from the east; leather work was widely practised; glass was manufactured, as in Syria, and in common use; the various decorative arts such as ceramics, pottery, brasswork, mosaic and inlay with gold and silver work, all prospered. But the local manufacture of writing-paper was one of the most important industries without which the rich accumulation of books would not have been possible. From this Europe was to benefit later.

Until nearly the end of the tenth century women moved freely in society and many of them occupied important public posts. But laxity of sexual morality and the increasing use of concubines gradually forced the respectable citizen to protect his womenfolk from unwelcome attentions, and the practice of strict seclusion and segregation of the sexes became general. The *harem* system, borrowed from the Persians, was exported and adopted in Sudanic countries with the acceptance of Islam. But it had no place in the teachings of the Prophet. The women of his day, like the Bedouin women of the present day, enjoyed considerable freedom, though they lived in a polygamous system where man was the master. Muhammad, contrary to non-Muslim popular belief, by limiting the number of wives of a believer at a time when it was customary to have many, raised the position of women in society.

Many of the sports which are practised today had their place long ago with the Arabs: these included hunting, polo, and racing, as one would expect from a horse-loving people, and also archery, hockey, spear-throwing, fencing and wrestling. Chess, of course, was widely played. Some writers even claim that the games played included a kind of tennis and cricket.

THE END OF THE ARAB OCCUPATION OF SPAIN

At the beginning of the eleventh century the outlook of the Arab world was indeed bright and hopeful, but it was soon to be involved in a desperate struggle for existence with the Crusaders, and no sooner to be delivered from this than to be engulfed by the Tartar wave which swept away all the culture and civilization of the Arab Empire in the East. In Spain, after a period of rule by the Almoravids (1090–1145), a Tuareg movement from Senegal, and a further period under their austere successors, the Almohads (unitarians), persistent attacks from the Christians gradually drove most of the Arabs into north Africa. A small Muslim kingdom of Granada survived until it surrendered to Ferdinand and Isabella in 1492.

Spain's loss was Africa's gain. The great influx into Africa at this time of Andalusians of Arab descent had a far-reaching effect on the civilization of north Africa. This, as we shall see, was reflected in the Sudan. Two famous Arab historians of the thirteenth century, Ibn Ghalib and Ibn Said, testify to the immense debt which Africa owes to the culture and learning of these people whom Spain saw fit to reject. The Hafsid court at Tunis and the Merinite one at Fez continued to reflect a civilization well in advance of that in northern Europe, where classical learning had fallen into neglect with the decline of the Roman Empire. It was not revived till the growing power of the Ottomans drove the learned men out of Constantinople into exile as apostles of Greek culture.

History must record the debt owed to Islam for cherishing during this critical period the treasures of the past. These had reached the Muslim world through Syria, and it was from the Syriac that most of the philosophical and scientific classics had been translated into Arabic. The love of letters and the thirst for knowledge came to the Arabs through their contact with the mother of modern civilization; and this they acknowledge by an ardent devotion to Greece and her achievements. Under Greek influence the Mediterranean world emerged from barbarism and evolved a standard of culture, art and learning that has rarely been surpassed even to this day. At the famous Museum of Alexandria Arab scholars continued the studies that had been begun by such giants as Euclid, the mathematician; Archimedes, the scientist; Aristarchus, the astronomer who demonstrated that the earth and the planets revolve round the sun; Eratosthenes, who rightly calculated the size of the earth; and by successive schools of philosophy down the ages. Aristotle remained to the Arabs as well as to Europe the 'master of them that know'.

IV. THE SUDAN

MEANWHILE, separated from the coastal regions of North Africa by a two or three months' journey across the Sahara desert, lay a belt of savannah and sparse bush stretching all the way from the Atlantic to the Nile and the mountains of Ethiopia. This belt of open country, with its clearly marked dry season of intense heat and its wet season of growth, is bounded along most of its southern edge by thick rain forests; and all along its northern edge laps the desert. The Arabs called this country Bilad al Sudan, the country of the black people; to us it is sometimes known as the Western Sudan, to distinguish it from that other Sudan formerly known as the Anglo-Egyptian Sudan. In this book the words Sudan and Sudanese refer to the countries and peoples south of the Sahara Desert from Wadai westward.

THE SAHARA[1]

The Sahara is by no means the flat expanse of soft sand-dunes that many conceive it to be. The name itself comes from the Arabic *Sah'ra* (with the accent on the first syllable) meaning grey-brown coloured or dun. Most of this huge region consists of stony plains, but about one-seventh of the area comprises what are known as *ergs* or great seas of soft sand. These are almost impossible to traverse except through the *gassi* or lanes of firmer sand that providentially separate the mounds and ridges. Sometimes there are depressions in these dunes as deep as 100 feet below sea-level. Great mountain masses thrust up in parts of the centre like jungles of stone, with chaotic crevasses and gaunt peaks eroded into grotesque shapes. Outcrops of harsh rocks break the surface of the plains. Snow and ice are familiar sights in the Hoggar massif and in the Tassili-n-Ajjer; and one even finds fish in the mountain pools and streams. The highest peak of the Hoggar, Garet al Jenun, stands 8,000 feet high. The interminable stretches of empty desolation, like the Tanezruft and the Tenerere due north of

[1] See Georg Gerster, *Sahara*.

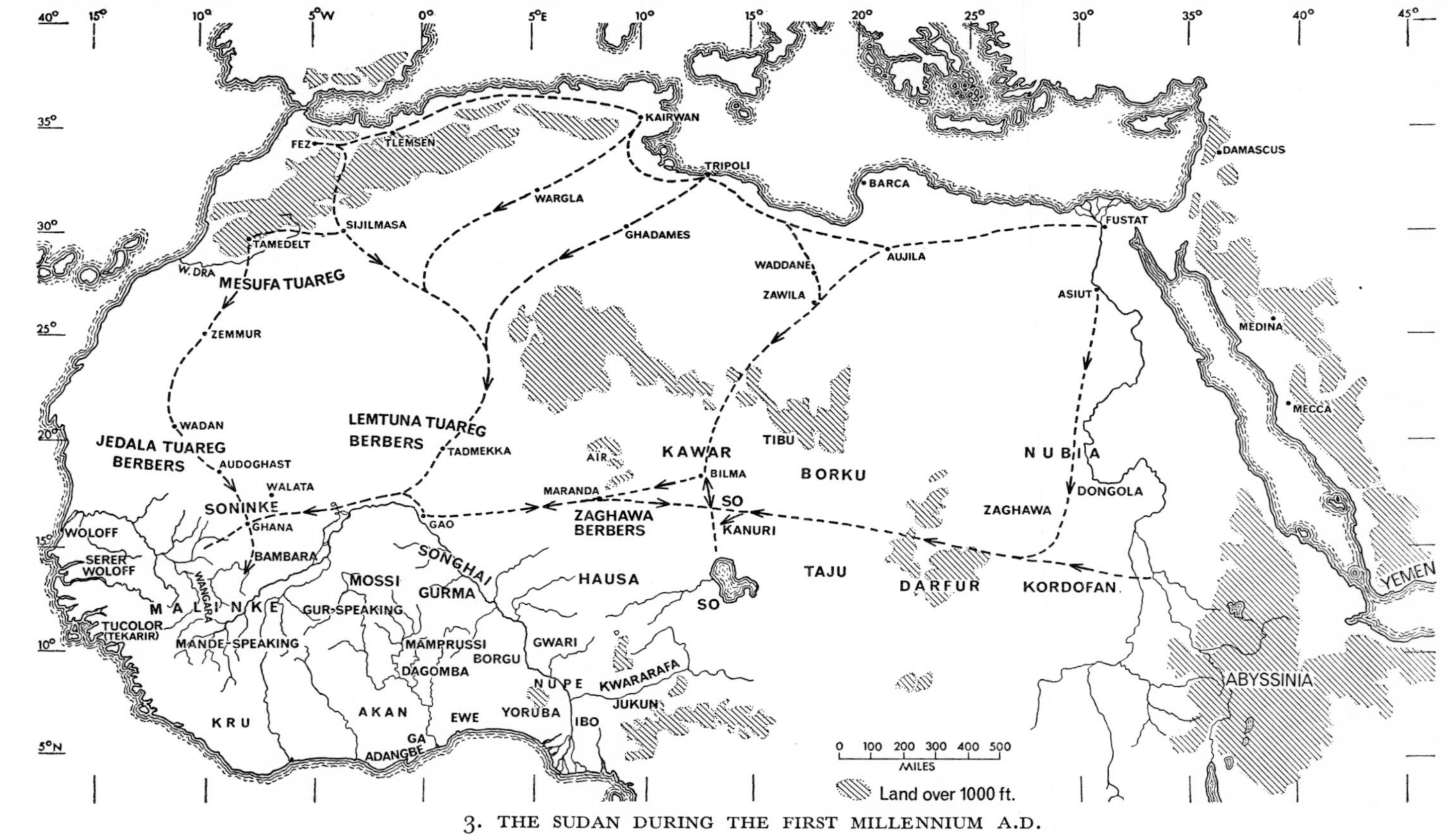

3. THE SUDAN DURING THE FIRST MILLENNIUM A.D.

Bornu, are known as the *reg* and are characterized by a monotonous lack of any sign of life or water in their flinty gravel wastes. Here and there in the sandy areas, where the palm tree can find a bed for its roots, one finds the occasional oasis—particularly towards the north. Without such a refuge the desert nomad could hardly exist.

Modern discoveries of evidence from rock paintings, from ancient rubbish heaps and chance finds now supply what written records have failed to do. It is now clear that the climate in the desert, as already mentioned, has gone through a remarkable change within comparatively few millennia. The earliest drawings discovered by Henri Lhote[1] in the Tassili mountains near Janet show herds of cattle grazing on lush pastures; later drawings of about 4000 B.C. depict only wild animals of the savannah, such as elephants, giraffes, antelopes and ostriches. Later still herdsmen are shown driving cattle across the plains, and there are hunters with bows and arrows. The paintings point to the transition from a land of forests and lakes and rivers to a far drier scrubland with less game; but they also show that negroes must have long occupied parts of the Sahara well over half-way north to the coast. From about 6000 B.C. there seems to have been a highly populous civilization in the Sahara, and by 3500 B.C. or soon after, according to recent radio-carbon datings, the people had entered their Neolithic age of cultivation. Professor Theodore Monod, Director of the Institut Français d'Afrique Noire, at Dakar, calls attention to the great number of settlements of Neolithic man that the finding of fragments of pottery and implements over hundreds of miles reveals. In the foothills of the Tassili these relics lie around in profusion; and the ancient rubbish heaps in the south-west of the Sahara conceal not only axe-heads and arrow-heads of stone but barbed harpoon points and bone fish-hooks.

Quite recent evidence points to a time when horse-drawn carts were in common use in crossing the desert. The drawings date from about 1000 B.C., and large numbers have been found along two of the main caravan routes of historic times, both leading towards the bend of the Niger, one from Fezzan and the other from Morocco. The westerly route ran from Morocco through Zemmur and Adrar of Mauretania to the Senegal and Niger rivers; the other went from Tripoli through Ghadames, Ghat and

[1] Henri Lhote, *The Search for the Tassili Frescoes*, pp. 124–8.

the Hoggar mountains to Gao on the Niger.[1] Some have suggested that the Garamantes used chariots in the desert and that the prosperity of the coastal towns at the head of these two routes in Carthaginian and Roman times can only be accounted for by the volume of trans-Saharan trade with the Sudan. This would have been chiefly gold from Wangara, in the region of the headwaters of the Senegal and Niger. There is no doubt that the coveted prize of gold justified the ardours and hazards of the journeys, and it might explain why these ancient contacts with the western parts of the Sudan so long preceded those with the eastern.

Even when the camel replaced the chariot and other means of transport, the crossing was a severe test of endurance, but there was no other known way. For century after century the only contact between the outside world and the Sudan was the desert. Not until the modern age of railways and steamships had begun did the world learn from Lander and Clapperton that the Sudan could be approached from the Bight of Benin. A map published as late as 1830 (reproduced on page 107) shows a continuous east-west range of non-existent mountains to account for the inaccessibility of the Sudan from the coast.

EARLY INHABITANTS OF THE SUDAN

The origins of the indigenous people in the remote past can only be a matter for conjecture, but it is believed that on the upper Niger one of the earliest systems of agriculture was developed by Mandingo Negroes between 5000 and 4000 B.C. These people are thought to have come many centuries before in a general migration from the east, driving south a Bushmanoid type of people, whose modern descendants are small and lightly-built. Their forebears are said to have been larger and heavier; and they favoured the dry, open hunting country to judge from their rock paintings. The Negro peoples seem to have preferred a more humid region close to forest where they could both fish and farm. There were also in Africa from an even earlier date, perhaps 10,000 years ago, a race of people with Caucasian or Hamitic characteristics, who are thought to have originated in south-west Asia. The Negro is said to have come on the scene later than the Bushman and the Caucasoid, and he is supposed to have moved north during the

[1] Henri Lhote, op. cit.; Raymond Mauny, *Tableau Géographique*, p. 283; R. Oliver and J. D. Fage, *A Short History of Africa*, p. 60. See also Map 1 on p. 7.

wet phase from about 8,000 years ago and taken more kindly to cultivating food when man first learnt the art.[1]

Since few Berbers seem to have ever used bows and arrows, the finding of countless numbers of ancient arrow heads all over the Sahara indicates that at one time, presumably during the wet phase, the occupants of areas as far north as Fezzan may have been of Sudanese origin.

The dating of the wet phase cannot be precise in its limits but radio-carbon tests of material associated with rock paintings and engravings of the Tassili-n-Ajjer give a date about 3000 B.C., so that some 5,000 years ago the Sahara would appear to have provided a vast area of fertile territory, flowing with rivers and streams, covered with trees and vegetation, and abounding in fish and game. In these conditions a New Stone Age civilization undoubtedly flourished, connecting Egypt and the Maghrib with the Sudan and West Africa; and the date from such scientific evidence as is available seems to have been around 3500 B.C. Within perhaps two millennia, however, a disastrous misfortune beset these numerous pastoral communities dotted all over the face of what is now a desert. The land inexorably began to dry up. The rivers dwindled and ceased to flow, the trees died, the vegetation blackened, the game vanished and the people had no choice but to escape. Some went east to the Nile, others to the north, still more to the south. During the period of the second millennium B.C. (before and after 1500 B.C.) the movements of peoples would have been continuous and massive into the grasslands and forests south of the desert.[2]

Coming down to the comparatively modern era of the fourth century A.D. we hear of a great movement of people when the powerful state of Axum in Ethiopia destroyed the thousand-year-old kingdom of Kush and burnt its famous capital of Meroë, on the Nile below the Sixth Cataract. These people migrated gradually west towards Chad, moving through Kordofan, Darfur and Wadai.

In addition to these, there seems to have been a great emigration of Yemeni peasants across the Red Sea into and beyond the Nile valley in about the sixth century, following famine caused by

[1] R. Oliver and J. D. Fage, op. cit., p. 21.

[2] Basil Davidson, 'A New View of the Old Sahara', *West Africa*, 11 January 1964, p. 36.

invasion from the still powerful Axum. The persistent traditions in many of the Sudanese states of their earliest kings having come from Yemen may therefore have a basis of truth and not result from a Muslim wish-thought, as some have suggested. For centuries nomad Berber tribes from the desert kept wandering into the savannah lands of the Sudan. There were thus two main streams of immigration, the one from the Nile valley and the Yemen, the other from the Maghrib. It may be that the Berber influence coming later from the north imposed itself on the already established Negro agricultural society which had preceded it from the east.

By about A.D. 1000 the various peoples inhabiting the Sudan might have been found in the following regions. In the extreme west near the Senegal river were the Tekarir or Tucolor in Futa Toro. These people were in some way associated with the Fulani, or so many think: no one really knows. Here too were the Serer and Wolof. Further east, in the wide tract of country between the Niger and the Senegal rivers, were the Mandingo tribes, the Soninke to the north and the Malinke to the south. In the region of the upper Volta rivers were the Mossi tribes, and east of them astride the southward flowing Niger were the Songhai. East of the Niger in the countries later occupied by the Hausa states and Kanem-Bornu one can safely surmise that there had been considerable mixtures of migrant peoples from the Nile valley and the east to join those from the north in assimilating with earlier elements. The Nilotic influence applied in particular to the people immediately east and west of Chad, though it is said to be detectable as far south as Yorubaland, whose people may have arrived where they are today as early as 1000 B.C.

THE TUAREG

But the desert itself, ever since the drying up phase had put an end to cultivation twenty or thirty centuries earlier, had been occupied exclusively by nomad Berber tribes. By the beginning of the Muslim period in the seventh century the nomad Berbers had become recognizable as Tuareg, akin to but in some ways different from the sedentary Berbers. They have survived as a distinct people until today, with their habitat now largely concentrated within a central Saharan area radiating from the Hoggar mountains to Ghadames in the north, and Aïr and Adrar of the Iforas in the south. Rennell Rodd maintains that the Tuareg of Aïr are not Berbers but a separate race with their own distinct characteristics.[1] Duveyrier asserts, on the other hand, that the Ihaggeren (the red ones) of the Hoggar are descendants of the Aulad Sid ben Sid Malek, Sanhaja Berbers. By the tenth century the Sanhaja Tuareg were in occupation of the desert routes leading north and east from the savannahs and scrub or *sahel* of Ghana and the western Sudan, with the Jedala (Guedala), the most numerous sub-division, in Mauretania towards the ocean; the Lemtuna, the most politically powerful sub-division, in the centre; and the Mesufa, a sub-division based originally round the Wadi Dra, south of Morocco, cornering most of the carrying trade. It was not until the fifteenth century that Berber domination of the western Sahara gave way to Arab.[2]

To this day the Tuareg have remained a mysterious, aloof people, whose very appearance lends an air of romance. By the Arabs they are called Mulaththimin—the people of the *litham* or veil. This is worn by the men, who never reveal their faces below the eyes even when eating. The women, on the other hand, never veil and enjoy remarkable independence and status. The Tuareg have retained the matrilinealism which the settled Berbers abandoned, as well as a form of script known as T'ifinagh, partly derived from the ancient Libyan Berber script, which Arabic has elsewhere supplanted. One can write this language from left to right, or like Arabic from right to left—indeed it can be written downwards as Chinese used to be. It is known as Temajegh or Tamashaq.[3]

To many the Tuareg are the Blue Men because of the sheen which their skins acquire from the long indigo robes (*takatkat*) they constantly wear. Particularly in the Hoggar region, they have kept a class system of nobles, bondsmen and slaves. The nobles or Imajeghan have kept their blood pure down the centuries; their parents must themselves both be nobles, and children by non-noble women are excluded.[4] They wear blue veils, in contrast to the Imghad or bondsmen who wear white ones, and pride

[1] Rennell Rodd, *The People of the Veil.*
[2] Raymond Mauny, op. cit., p. 456.
[3] E. W. Bovill, *The Golden Trade of the Moors*, p. 51.
[4] Oliver and Fage, *A Short History of Africa*, p. 63.

themselves on being warriors with contempt for manual work. They are usually tall, fair-skinned and slender; and by reputation they are not only impatient of restraint but implacable and often ruthless. The tribes are organized in a feudal way under a chief called the Amrar, and the supreme chief of the whole group of tribes (*kel*) is known as the Amenakal (*ama*—possessor, *n*—of, *akal*—country). In spite of now being Muslims, if not very devout ones, they still have certain customs such as monogamy which seem to derive from an ancient Christian tradition. The cross is perhaps their most prominent symbol of ornament, and the position of women in their society contrasts sharply with that of Muslims. The Targuia moves about freely and chooses her husband herself. Though Tuareg society is not a matriarchy it comes very near to being so: a chief is not succeeded by his son but by his sister's son. These then are the people, as old as the desert and as changeless, who in those days connected north with south just as they do today.

LIVING CONDITIONS

Cut off, as we have seen, by the drying up of the desert from almost any contact with the world, life in the Sudan in the early centuries of our era must have been primitive. Few food crops existed and only the smaller livestock were kept. Areas of bush were cleared by burning and when they had produced a few successive harvests they were abandoned and fresh ones cleared. Always there was the necessity to hunt for meat, or fish in the river, and to gather wild fruit and roots. Since iron-smelting was not common in many parts and iron was generally scarce, implements were of the simplest kind. Attack was always round the corner of the path. In these circumstances the population remained low.

But it seems that immigrants from the east brought with them new kinds of food plant, originating (some say) in Indonesia, and the population grew. Conditions in the open savannah areas were far easier than in the thicker bush, where tsetse fly abounded and domestic animals did not thrive. For that reason the more northerly peoples developed a more complex economy and built up greater security against famine and poverty. Grain such as millet grew with little effort by scratching the light soil and the dry season encouraged crafts such as smithing and leather-working. Cotton, too, could be grown and weaving practised.

Among all the people inhabiting the Sudan at this time before the arrival in any numbers of Berbers from the north there was a fairly uniform type of culture. Societies were emerging from kinship or descent groups owing descent to a common ancestor into tribes accepting the authority of priests and chiefs. Tribes again would tend to merge together to form territorial states, especially when threatened from outside. This fusion would sometimes come about from the conquest of one tribe by another and the consequent spread of rule to outlying districts paying tribute to the centre. Speaking of the tribes of the Ashanti hinterland, typical perhaps of most other tribes in the Sudan at that time, R. S. Rattray has this to say:

> These peoples, even where their language differed considerably, had an almost identical social and political organization; the outstanding feature of this was a grouping of totemic clans under Priest-Kings whose influence and authority were considerable, though both depended upon moral and spiritual and not physical punishments; these indigenous peoples inherited through the sister's son.[1]

Each descent-group believed in a supreme God who was the creator of the universe. There was a belief in a life after death and the spirits of the departed were believed to have a strong influence on the present. To label them as pagan, as the Arab writers did, was merely to underline the fact that they were not Muslims. It is true that they also believed in numerous lesser gods, often identified with Nature, such as rivers, rocks or trees, but their animism was not as repugnant to humanity as Europe often quite wrongly assumed from the exaggerated reports of Christian travellers. This is not to say that human sacrifice and other barbarous practices never occurred.

Again, to quote R. S. Rattray:

> Upon these more or less autochthonous peoples, with their very primitive institutions, descended small bands of strangers within comparatively recent historical times. They were better armed, better clothed, familiar with the idea of kingship or chieftainship in our modern sense, in some cases conversant with the rudiments of Mohammedanism and accustomed (even if circumstances had not later com-

[1] R. S. Rattray, *Tribes of the Ashanti Hinterland*, p. xII.

5. Interior of the Emir of Kano's palace in 1903.

6. Interior of the Zaria Mosque; built in 1862 by Babban Gwani, the master builder of Zaria.

7. The Emir of Katsina, Alhaji Sir Usman Nagogo, carrying the famous state sword Gajere outside the Kangiwa.

pelled it) to a patrilineal manner of reckoning descent. These strangers super-imposed upon the primitive tribes, among whom they settled, a new and unheard of political conception, namely the idea of territorial and secular leadership in place of the immemorial institution of a ruler, who was the high priest of a totemic clan and dealt only in spiritual sanctions. These warrior-bands—possibly refugees or off-shoots from one or other of the negro kingdoms of the interior—were composed of males alone. The result was that in a few generations their descendants were speaking the language of the tribes among whom they were compelled to find wives, and whose manners and customs they came largely to adopt.[1]

Unfortunately these people left nothing in writing because they could not write, and they left no lasting monuments in stone because they had no stone to quarry nor the art of fashioning it. In Africa termites and tornadoes leave nothing behind. Though no records of the period exist or are likely to be found it must not be assumed that the 'white people' of Semitic or Hamitic stock, such as the Berbers or the Arabs, brought any superiority in political ideas and systems of government. It is not really known to what extent the indigenous people were organized politically before the newcomers arrived.

But it seems increasingly clear that throughout the whole of the Sudan there evolved a characteristic type of Sudanese state easily recognized by certain common features. These included the seclusion of the king as a remote, mystical being, whose authority was endowed with divine powers. Since his vigour was identified with that of the state, his removal by death became a necessity as soon as his health declined. Power would be in the hands of office-holders chosen by the king to support him rather than in those of hereditary nobles; and chief among the high officials of state would be the king's mother, his sister, and certain of his wives. Trade would be under royal licence and prosperity would be concentrated in and around the court, which would live on the tribute of the outlying provinces with the help of slave labour. Such a state would seem to derive from the conquest of a peasant people by a dominant invader and the imposition of the conquerors' culture on their subjects.[2]

Sir James Frazer's *The Golden Bough* reminds us that similar customs used to exist in ancient Italy, and even until lately in

[1] R. S. Rattray, op. cit., p. xiii.
[2] See Oliver and Fage, op. cit., Ch. 4 for discussion of the Sudanic Civilization.

England there was the ceremony of the king's champion at the coronation, who challenged to mortal combat all who disputed the king's right to the throne. The Shilluk, too, of the Nilotic Sudan had a tradition that any son of a king had a right to fight the king in possession and, if he succeeded in killing him, to reign in his stead.[1]

HANNO'S VOYAGE

The only record that antiquity can produce of life south of the Sahara has no bearing on the Sudan except indirectly. According to an inscription on a temple in Carthage, an expedition set out during the sixth century B.C. under Hanno to sail down the west coast of Africa in order to found new colonies. After landing colonists at a number of places they eventually came to what must have been the Senegal river, followed by the headland of Sierra Leone and, further down the coast, the Cameroon Mountain, which conveniently for identification was in a state of eruption. A few days' sail further on they came to an island inhabited by either gorillas or pygmies, it is not clear which. They captured three specimens, which fought so fiercely that they had to be killed on the voyage home to Carthage, where their hairy skins were displayed.

THE NOK FIGURINE CULTURE

In Nigeria in 1931 there was a sensational find of two pottery heads near the village of Nok, some twenty-four miles from Jema'a. They are believed to date from a period between about 900 B.C. and A.D. 200. Similar pottery work was found in 1944, and since then large numbers of the same kind of figures have turned up in a wide area of central Nigeria, indicating the existence of an advanced culture, which from its iron-using technique would seem to be midway between stone and metal. It would have reached its full development in the last two or three centuries B.C., when iron-working was common in the savannahs but not yet found in the forest regions. Tools dating back as far as the Old Stone Age have been unearthed at Jos.[2]

[1] See *The Golden Bough*, Part I, 'The Magic Art, etc.', vol. II, p. 321, and also Part III, 'The Dying God', p. 22. Compare too the legend of the Karya Giwa in Katsina, *vide* Chapter XVI, pp. 158 and 160.

[2] See Basil Davidson, *Old Africa Rediscovered*, pp. 64–66, and various articles by B. E. B. Fagg.

MIGRANTS FROM THE EAST AND NORTH

There is little enough that is known about the inhabitants of the Sudan before the coming of strangers from the east and north. All over West Africa there are persistent legends of the migration from the Nile Valley, and from the Yemen, towards the setting sun of the descendants of Kush, the son of Ham and the grandson of Noah. These include the Zaghawa, by which name certain people in Wadai and parts of Darfur are still known, the Habesh or Abyssinians, the Copts, and the Berbers. They probably followed the routes that pilgrims have been taking for centuries.

Wahab ibn Munabbeh, who died in 728, wrote as follows:

> Ham, the son of Noah, was a white man. . . . God changed his colour and the colour of his descendants because of his father's prayer. These are the Sudanis. The sons of Ham were Kush, Kana'an and Fut. Fut established himself in the Indies. As for Kush and Kana'an, their descendants are the Sudanis, the Qaran, the Zaghawa, the Habesh, the Copts and the Berbers.[1]

In addition to these Nilotic and Abyssinian-Yemeni immigrants, and probably later, there were the people from the Maghrib, already described in an earlier chapter as belonging to a mixture of ancient Mediterranean and Libyan-Berber peoples, including elements of Jews and others from Palestine, Syria and Egypt, with a later infusion of Arabs from Cyrenaica, Arabia and beyond.

[1] Raymond Mauny, op. cit., p. 446.

V. THE EMPIRE OF GHANA

ONE of the oldest states in the Sudan of which we have any record was Ghana, which occupied the whole region between the upper reaches of the Niger and Senegal rivers and the desert, with its capital some 300 miles west of what would later become Timbuktu. The origin of the people seems to have been the settlement from the second century onwards of groups of Magharibah, chiefly Berbers, in and around Aukar and Hodh, where the local inhabitants at that time are thought to have been Mandingoes. But there may also have been other groups coming by the more easterly routes through Fezzan, including refugees from the Roman provinces of Palestine and Cyrenaica. This would suggest that, as several authors assert, considerable numbers of Jews formed part of these early settlements. The evidence for this, however, is significantly scanty or far fetched, and may be summed up by this opinion of Raymond Mauny—'If there had been any migrations of Jews to West Africa in ancient times—the thing is not impossible—there is nothing that allows us to affirm it and they must be relegated to the realm of legend'. This is not to say that some small groups of Jews did not find their way to the Sudan; they almost certainly did. As we have already seen, the people of the Maghrib included those of many races, and Al Bakri refers to the Jews there; but not a word of them in the Sudan does he utter.[1]

The first mention of Ghana is in the work of an astronomer of the eighth century named Al Fazari, who called it the 'Gold Country'. Al Khwarizmi's chart of the ninth century contains the name of Ghana. In the tenth century Ibn Haukal, who visited Audoghast after a two months' journey across the desert from Morocco, spoke of Ghana's riches: 'The king of Ghana is the richest king on earth, because of the wealth and stocks of gold surrounding him, which have been acquired since olden times by his predecessors and himself.'[2]

[1] Raymond Mauny, *Tableau Géographique, etc.*, p. 439. See also J. J. Williams, *Hebrewisms of West Africa: from Nile to Niger with the Jews*, 1930.

[2] Mauny, op. cit.

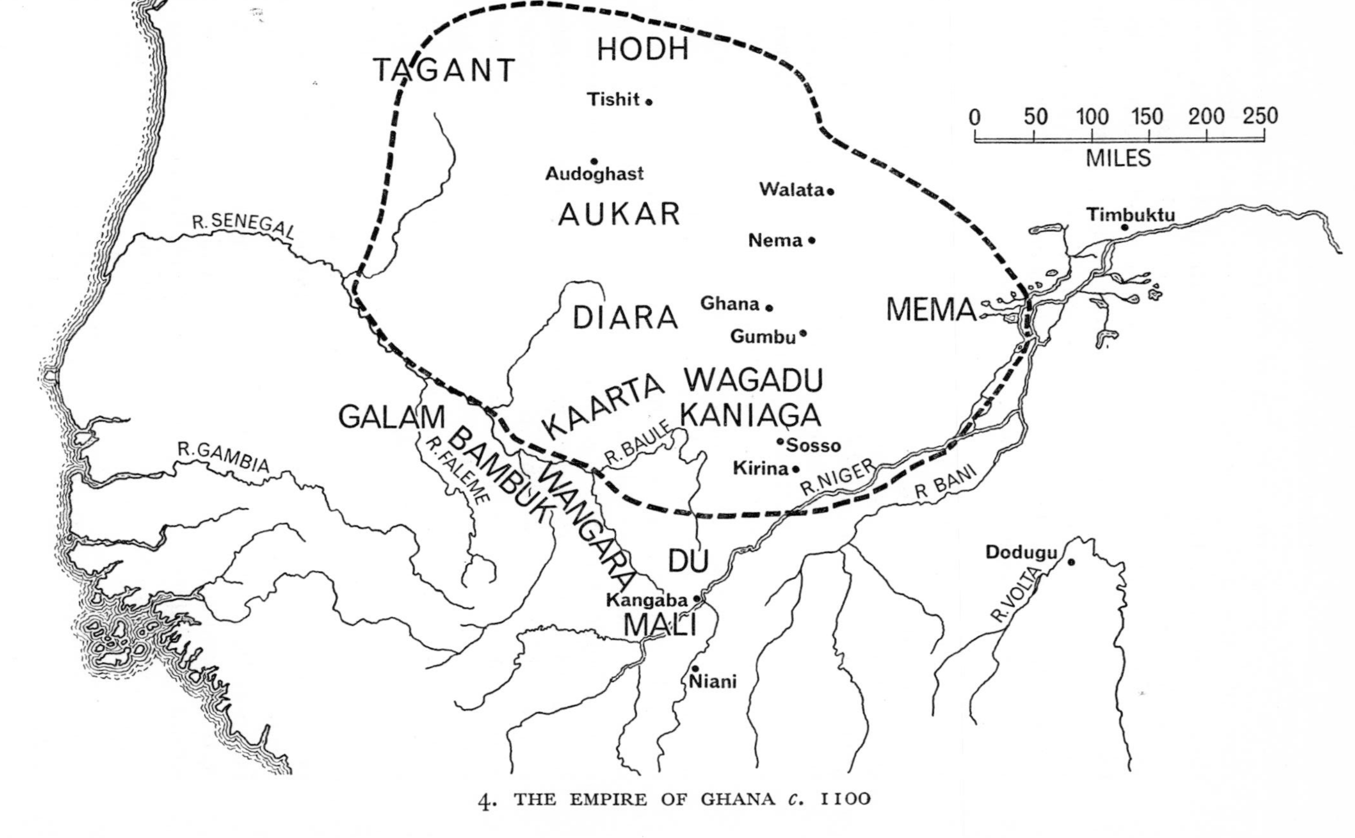

4. THE EMPIRE OF GHANA *c.* 1100

The immigrants to the Sudan at this time would have come from the Maghrib either by the principal route, which ran through Sijilmasa, Tamedelt, and then through Adrar of Mauretania to Audoghast; or by the less usual route farther east through Tuat and Tadmekka. Those from Cyrenaica and Tripoli might have come southwards to Kawar before turning west through Maranda to Gao, or through Ghadames in Fezzan to Tadmekka before hitting the Niger. At that time the occupants of the desert were exclusively nomad Berbers.

SOURCES OF INFORMATION

Apart from the fleeting references to Ghana already noted our chief authority for the events leading to the rise and fall of the great Sudanese empires of Ghana, Mali, and Songhai rests on two remarkable medieval works compiled in Timbuktu. Both cover much the same ground, finishing in the middle of the seventeenth century and starting with the earliest legends.

The first of these works, known as the *Tarikh al Fattash*, has on its title-page: 'Chronicle of the Searcher[1] into the History of the towns, the armies, and the leading men of Tekrur.' In those days the word Tekrur covered much of what is now known as the western Sudan. The work was started by a Soninke scholar named Mahmud Kati in 1519 at the age of 50 and finished by his grandson, Ibn al Mukhtar, in 1665. Mahmud Kati was a personal friend of the Emperor of Songhai, the famous Askia al Haj Muhammad, and accompanied him on his pilgrimage to Mecca. He reached the ripe age of 125 when he died in 1593, a fact attested by the other work, the *Tarikh al Sudan*, and he could bear personal testimony to events as early as the fifteenth century. His chronicle drew on certain earlier works that have now disappeared, and it is the oldest known history produced by a Sudanese author. The manuscript was not discovered until 1911 in Timbuktu and then with the first few pages missing. Two other copies were subsequently found, the second of which though in bad Arabic and difficult to decipher was complete. It is clear that the

[1] Daniel McCall has this comment in his *Africa in Time-Perspective*, p. 4: 'The word ἱστορία meant simply "inquiry". Herodotus worked less with written chronicles than by inquiring of persons who had information of local events in their own times and the times of their predecessors. The oldest written history now extant, that was composed by a West African, the *Tarikh el-Fettech*, uses virtually the same idiom in its title, *The Chronicle of the Searcher*, and Mahmoud Kati went about his task in essentially the same way that Herodotus did.'

authors were using a language other than their own, and the copyists paid more attention to the calligraphy than to the correctness of the Arabic. The work has an appendix by an anonymous writer which contains some useful details of a date around 1660.[1]

The *Tarikh al Sudan* was started by a famous Berber scholar and jurist named Ahmed Baba al Timbukti, who died in Timbuktu in 1627 at the age of 71 after having been transported across the desert and kept captive by the Moors in Marrakesh for nearly fourteen years. He came from the famous family of Aqit, which had provided learned *qadis* for over a century. Some of his writings have survived to this day, including a commentary in manuscript form on Arabic grammar, which is still studied currently in Northern Nigeria.[2] His part of the work is somewhat dry and laconic, with little reference to his authorities for his statements. He would content himself by saying, 'I have heard it said that . . .' The second part of the work, however, comes alive and supplies abundant detail. The man responsible for this was the chief author, Abdurrahman al Sadi, who worked on the book from 1627 until his death in 1655.[3] It was thus both later in starting and earlier in finishing than the other Tarikh. Al Sadi was very close to the events that he wrote about. As *kateb* or Secretary to the Government he took a direct part in the country's political affairs and acted as mediator between various princes. He was born of a highly respected family in Timbuktu in 1590 and his first post was that of notary in Jenne. After some years he became Imam of the mosque in Jenne and then of the Sankore mosque in Timbuktu, a post held formerly by his great-great-grandfather. His mother was a Hausa.

Three manuscript copies of this work were found in Timbuktu towards the end of last century and they were lodged in the

[1] See the Introduction to the *Tarikh al Fattash* by O. Houdas and M. Delafosse, in which they quote the *Tarikh al Sudan* as confirming the date of Mahmud Kati's death as 1593. Mauny supports this and even reminds us of 'l'extraordinaire longévité de l'auteur du *Tarikh el-Fettach*, Mahmoud Kati (1468–1593), mort à 125 ans', *vide* op. cit., p. 534. But M. Hiskett gives 1543 as the date of death of the author, whom he calls 'Muhammad Koti', and an age of 75 is more credible. See *SOAS Bulletin*, xix, 3, 1957, p. 572.

[2] See the article by J. O. Hunwick on Ahmed Baba, *Journal of the Historical Society of Nigeria*, vol. 2, No. 3, December 1962, pp. 311–28.

[3] These are the dates given by Mauny, op. cit., p. 39. But M. Hiskett says that Al Sadi finished the work some twenty years earlier, that is, in 1635 or shortly after. *Vide* op. cit., p. 572.

National Library of France.[1] But several decades before this that great traveller Dr Heinrich Barth had the exciting experience of finding a copy in Gwandu, as the following entry in his journal for 17 May 1853 shows:

> I passed the time during my residence in this place [he had obtained quarters in the house of El Khassa, the chief eunuch of the court in Gwandu] not quite uselessly, especially as I was so fortunate as to obtain here from a learned man of the name of Bokhari, a son of the late Mohammed Wani, a copy of that most valuable historical work of Ahmed Baba, to which my friend Abd el Kader, in Sokoto, had first called my attention, but without my being able to satisfy my curiosity; and I spent three or four days most pleasantly in extracting the more important historical data of this work, which opened to me quite a new insight into the history of the regions on the middle course of the Niger, whither I was bending my steps, exciting in me a far more lively interest than I had previously felt in a kingdom the great power of which, in former times, I here found set forth in very clear and distinct outlines, and I only lamented that I had not time enough to copy the whole.[2]

From these two sources comes most of what we can deduce about the early people of Ghana, who lived beyond the main stream of history. But we have other evidence in the writings of certain Arab authors from about the tenth century. Of these incomparably the most celebrated is Al Bakri (1028–94) of Cordova, but he did not himself visit the Sudan—he merely sifted the evidence of travellers and recorded it. An earlier writer, however, Ibn Haukal, did visit the Sudan at some time in the tenth century from Baghdad. His great contribution, which was unaccountably ignored for centuries, was to confirm the statement of Herodotus that the Niger flowed in an easterly direction. The only other writer whose work has survived and who visited the Sudan prior to the fifteenth century was the renowned Berber from Tangier, Ibn Battuta (1304–68). Though he crossed the Niger and watched it flowing past Timbuktu, he was misled into thinking that it was the Nile. Al Omari (1301–49), who occupied an important position at the court of the Mamluk Sultan of Egypt, has left us some valuable descriptions of life in Mali based on the information supplied by Ibn Said Othman ad Dukkali, who spent thirty-five years in the country of Mali and its then capital, Niani. Ibn

[1] Introduction to the *Tarikh al Sudan* by O. Houdas.

[2] A. H. M. Kirk-Greene, *Barth's Travels in Nigeria*, p. 266; also p. 59.

Khaldun (1332–1406), an Arab settled in Tunis, wrote a history of the Berbers, but it has only slight relevance to the western end of the Sudan.

THE KAYA MAGA DYNASTY OF BERBER KINGS

All we seem to know of the early years is that by about the fourth century some kind of supremacy had been established over the Soninke Mandingoes by an immigrant dynasty of what the *Tarikh al Sudan* calls 'white' rulers. The same authority tells us that there were twenty-two kings of Ghana before the Hijra (622) and twenty-two after, and if the earlier kings reigned for as long as the later ones this would carry us back to the first century for the dynasty's start. The *Tarikh al Fattash* says that 'a reliable informant from Massina gave twenty kings before the Messenger of God. The capital was called Kumbi and it was a great town. An old man has told me that the last of these princes, Kanissa'ai, who reigned at the time of the Messenger of God, lived in a town called Koronga, where his mother lived'.[1]

The first king's name was Kaya (gold) Maga (king)[2] and the dynasty of Berber kings continued until 770, when they were driven out by the Soninke of Wagudu to take refuge in the west in the country of Tekrur. The people of this region bordering on the Atlantic ocean included a variety of Serer, Wolof (or Jolof), Mandingoes and others; it nourished the Tekarir or Tucolor, who continued to make history up to modern times, and the Fulani found themselves there in numbers before they began their gradual migration eastward about the fourteenth century. How they got there in the first place is still a mystery.

The following description of the royal stables of one of the Kaya Magas provided by the *Tarikh al Fattash* hints at a standard of hygiene and cleanliness unequalled anywhere today:

> It is said that he had 1,000 horses stabled in his palace; it was an established custom that if one of these horses died in the morning another would replace it before the evening; it was the same if this happened during the night. Each of these animals always slept on a mat, lightly secured by a silken cord round the neck and foot. Each of them had a copper pot in which it urinated; not a drop fell except into this pot, whether by day or by night. One never saw under any of these horses the least sign of dung. Each of them had three men to look after

[1] *Tarikh al Fattash*, p. 76. [2] Ibid., p. 75.

it, sitting near it; one of them was in charge of the animal's food, the second of its drinking water, and the third took care of the urine and the disposal of the dung.[1]

As will be seen later, Al Bakri's informants speak of a remarkably advanced style of living, particularly in the palace.

THE SONINKE DYNASTY

The Soninke kings who ruled for the three hundred years after 770 proved to be more effective than their Berber predecessors, and by the eleventh century the powerful empire extended some three hundred miles in any direction from the centre. Trade with the Maghrib prospered and multiplied. Great convoys of camels were continually leaving for the north loaded with gold, skins, ivory, kola-nuts, gum, honey, corn and cotton; and the convoys included slaves. On their way they would pass the south-bound convoys bearing salt, copper, dried fruit and cowries, which would later be distributed throughout the Sudan. The life-blood of the country ebbed and flowed vigorously through the desert ports just as it did through the sea-ports of the maritime republics of Venice and Genoa. Great trading companies were established and a regular system of taxation on imports and exports swelled the state treasury.

The gold trade was all important as it had been of old. It was conducted by a curious system known as 'dumb barter', a system exactly described by Herodotus[2] some fifteen centuries earlier when relating how the Carthaginians managed to trade in gold down the coast of Africa. Similar systems have been known in other parts of the world. The sources of gold were always jealously concealed by those who dug for it and the region known as Wangara had always had attached to it an air of deep mystery. The gold merchants would be taken by their local agents in Ghana on a journey of some weeks into this mysterious region until they reached a certain place by a river. Here the merchants, having announced their arrival by loud beating of drums, would lay out piles of goods and merchandise along the bank and then retire out of sight. The local natives would then emerge and place a heap of gold beside each pile and withdraw. The merchants would then examine the heaps of gold and if they were not satisfied they

[1] *Tarikh al Fattash*, pp. 76, 77.
[2] Quoted by E. W. Bovill, *The Golden Trade of the Moors*, p. 25.

would again retire and wait patiently to see if the heap was increased. When the merchants were content they would take the gold and leave, beating their drums as a signal that the market was over. Both sides seem to have played scrupulously fair. In the words of Herodotus, 'neither party deals falsely by the other: for they themselves never touch the gold till it comes up to the worth of their goods, nor do the natives ever carry off the goods till the gold is taken away'.

Not only gold or trade in general accounted for the power and prosperity of Ghana during these centuries of rising affluence under the Soninke kings. The discovery of iron-smelting and its arts brought a new mastery over land and forest, and over the forging of superior weapons of war. The old weapons of wood and bone or stone were no match for these new arms. Besides this, Ghana had immense resources of manpower to draw on. If Al Bakri's informants can be believed, Ghana could put 200,000 warriors in the field, more than 40,000 of them bowmen. Several centuries later Edward commanded only 20,000 men in winning one of the decisive battles of the world at Crecy, and Henry V won his victory at Agincourt with less than 10,000. But Al Bakri has already given us some scarcely credible numbers of camelmen available to an Audoghast chieftain (*vide* page 13) and his figures must be suspect.

Along with the growing prosperity, however, there were always the Berber Tuareg tribes on the borders to be kept at arm's length. Nomadic desert tribes rarely make good neighbours. For their very existence they have to make hot season migrations into areas where pasture is available, and when water-holes dry up they are forced to encroach on more settled lands—if not they and their herds would perish. Caravans are a tempting form of prey for loot or the exaction of 'protection money'. By the time of Ibn Haukal's visit in the tenth century, Audoghast, a Tuareg city lying some 250 miles to the north-west, had become an increasingly threatening disturber of Ghana's peace; yet Ghana's whole survival on a great trade route as an entrepôt demanded complete security for her convoys.

AUDOGHAST

Audoghast was a thriving centre with fine buildings surrounded by groves of date palms, but modern excavations indicate that its population may not have exceeded 6,000—though there may have been encampments outside.[1] The town had been founded about the ninth century by Berbers from the Maghrib and it was a great Lemtuna Tuareg stronghold. The wealthier citizens owned many negro slaves and there was a large trading quarter for the Arab and other foreigners. Contemporary accounts indicate that there was no lack of water. All manner of crops were grown, while cattle and sheep were numerous. As against these reports, modern research suggests that in fact the water supply was limited, and this restricted the growth of the town.[2] Even so, Audoghast earned fame far beyond her borders for luxury and soft living. As far away as Spain Al Bakri had heard of the charm and beauty of her women, with their fair skins and shapely figures, who were reputed to prefer reclining as a posture to sitting so as not to distort the elegant symmetry of their posteriors. The desert too would seem to have had its mariners' tales and dreams of houris in the gardens of Paradise.

In about 990 Ghana's patience gave out. Her trade was being seriously affected and her possessions harried from this hostile Tuareg base. She started to retaliate by dominating the approaches to Audoghast and strangling her rival's sources of strength. Gradually the Soninke prevailed over the Lemtuna, and most of the territory which the latter had occupied was recovered. Audoghast, a Berber city under the influence of an Islamic culture introduced by Arabs from the north and east, became subject to an animist Sudanese Soninke ruler. The event roused the rancour of the Berber and Islamic communities in the Sudan and in the Maghrib. In 1055 they got their revenge.

THE ALMORAVIDS

Some years earlier a certain Yahia ibn Ibrahim, the chief of the powerful Sanhaja Tuareg, had picked up in Kairwan on his way back from the pilgrimage to Mecca a fervent preacher named Abdullah ibn Yasin with a view to receiving instruction from him in the faith and repairing the ignorance of his subjects. At first Ibn Yasin met with resistance and persecution from Yahia's own tribe, the Jedala, and he had to take himself off to a secluded island near the mouth of the Senegal river with only two faithful tribesmen to keep him company. The hermit gradually attracted

[1] R. Mauny, op. cit., p. 482. [2] Ibid., p. 482.

a devout following for his new teaching and in due course the disciples collected themselves together under the name of al-Murabathin or marabouts (monks or hermits) from which they came to be called Almoravids.[1] Setting off on a jihad to the north, in the course of years they had great success against the Christian armies in Spain and Morocco. But before they started to cross the Sahara, Ibn Yasin himself had subdued the surrounding desert tribes with fanatical fervour, and in 1055 his followers sacked the Soninke occupied town of Audoghast. As a stern example to the infidel he allowed his men full licence to loot and rape and kill at will. Three years later he led his men victoriously into Morocco, but in doing so he was killed in battle. So ended the career of an outstanding leader, whose inspiring faith had created the great Almoravid movement; a movement which opened up the channels of intercourse between the Niger lands and Europe.

The movement continued into two quite separate theatres of operation, in the Maghrib and in the Sudan. After Ibn Yasin's death, the chief, Abubakr, relinquished the command in the north to his cousin Yusuf, and concentrated his attention on subduing the unruly desert tribes in the south-west, notably the Jedala, from whom were to come many of the scholars in and around Timbuktu some centuries later. Yusuf achieved remarkable conquests in the Maghrib and in Spain. By 1102 the Almoravid power under the two cousins Yusuf and Abubakr extended from the forest belt in the southern Sudan to the northern borders of Andalusia and the north African littoral.

CAPTURE OF GHANA BY THE ALMORAVIDS AND THE BERBER MUSLIM DYNASTY

In the south, Abubakr continued to harry the pagan strongholds. In 1077 after a prolonged and desperate resistance the city of Ghana fell, and the inhabitants were given the choice of death or conversion to Islam. A Berber Muslim replaced the Soninke king and this dynasty was destined to remain on the throne until Ghana was finally destroyed; it was not disturbed when in 1087 Ghana regained her independence though with her power and possessions reduced. The twelfth century is believed to have contained a period of severe drought and desiccation, resulting in the

[1] The same region bred other fervent religious movements somewhat similar in character in the eighteenth century, *vide* pp. 113–14.

migration of many to the more fertile south. The turn of the century brought disaster to Ghana, when in 1203 the great Sosso chief, Sumanguru, captured the city and incorporated her territories in his empire. But the victory was robbed of much of its sweetness when the Muslim community migrated north to build up a new commercial centre at Walata, taking the city's prosperity with them.

Ghana was near her end. The *coup de grâce* was delivered by a remarkable Mandingo chief named Sundiata Keita. He was the only one of the twelve sons of the king of Kangaba to escape being done to death by Sumanguru; and he was spared because he was too frail a child to be feared. This weakling later managed to revenge his brothers by defeating and killing Sumanguru at Kirina near Kulikoro in 1235. Five years later Sundiata Keita, now king of Mali, completely destroyed Ghana. The year 1240 marks the end of the ancient empire of Ghana.

AL BAKRI'S DESCRIPTION OF LIFE IN GHANA

A vivid picture of life in Ghana during the eleventh century is recorded by Al Bakri. Writing in 1068, on the eve of Ghana's destruction by the Almoravids in 1077, he described the capital in careful detail from reports brought back by adventurous traders and perhaps by participants in the Almoravid movements between the Sudan and the Maghrib. The main route, he says, went via Tamedelt, important for its silver mine, where a number of tracks diverged, and then on to Tinduf and other places before ending at Tegdaoust of the Rkiz (almost certainly Audoghast).[1] The country was called Aukar, and Ghana was the title of the king, who lived in a walled castle built of stone and wood, well decorated inside with pictures and sculpture, and furnished with glass windows. One might note here that window-glass was not used in English dwellings until several centuries later, and that stone was a rare commodity in these parts.

The capital was described as consisting of two distinct towns some six miles apart, the one pagan, where the king lived with his court and followers, and the other Muslim, where the Berber and Arab merchants from the Maghrib lived. The intervening area was also covered with houses. In the Muslim town there were twelve mosques; while the other and native town was surrounded

[1] R. Mauny, op. cit., p. 428.

by secret groves, where priests guarded the sacred idols and kept watch over the tombs of the kings. Here too were the prisons from which none emerged.

The king was a powerful monarch at that time, a Soninke called Tunka Menin (Tunka meant king),[1] but there had been a long line of earlier 'white' or Berber kings. Tunka Menin maintained a court of considerable magnificence by any standards. 'When he gives audience to his people . . . he sits under a huge kind of canopy around which stand ten horses in golden trappings; behind him stand ten pages holding shields and gold-hilted swords, and on his right hand are the sons of his vassal princes, richly attired in silks and brocades with their hair adorned with golden ornaments. On the ground at the king's feet sit the governor of the city and the viziers.' Though unbelievers, the Soninke employed many Muslim officers of state. 'When anyone approached the king he would prostrate himself and throw dust over his head; but as for the Muslims they would content themselves by clapping their hands together as a mark of respect.'

Al Bakri commented on the antagonism in Audoghast between the Zenata Berbers and the Arabs, a reflection of their continual struggles in the Maghrib since the seventh century. He also recorded that 'in the kingdom of Ghana there is a tribe of people called Al Hunahin, descended from the soldiers sent by the Ummayads against Ghana, in the early days of Islam. They follow the religion of the people of Ghana; but they never intermarry with the negroes. They are fair-skinned and handsome. Some of these people are found at Sala, where they are pointed out as Al Faman.' The reference is to an expedition known to have been dispatched to the extreme south across the desert in 739 by the Ummayad governor of the province of Afrikia: it is said to have taken back a number of prisoners.[2]

EXCAVATIONS AT KUMBI SALEH

In support of the written records we now have the confirmation of archaeologists, who have conducted a series of excavations at Kumbi Saleh. This site is almost certainly that of ancient Ghana. It will be remembered that Mahmud Kati's 'reliable informant from Massina' had given the name of the capital of Ghana as

[1] R. Mauny, op. cit., p. 449.
[2] Charles Monteil, *Journal de la Société des Africanistes*, 1950, pp. 158–9.

Kumbi.[1] Raymond Mauny, who took part in one of the more recent expeditions, gives the co-ordinates as 15° 46′ N. by 7° 58′ W., or some 200 miles north of Bamako.[2] So far only the Muslim part of the city has appeared, but there is enough to be seen to permit an estimate of some fifteen to twenty thousand as the possible population, a very large figure for those days. When the buried secrets of the place and tombs of the kings in the Soninke part of the town have been uncovered, we shall know more of the customs of that age. We know that a king would be buried in a large tumulus together with his chief servants and all manner of articles such as he might be expected to need in the next world. The contents of these tombs, reminiscent of those of the Durbawa at Durbi ta Kusheyi in Katsina, will help us to know more of such matters as the nature of the king's divinity, and the system of uterine descent, which as part of a Sudanic civilization operated widely in the Hausa states, in Bornu and neighbouring territories. Here is a description of what has so far come to light:

> . . . Kumbi Saleh had once been great. Among many large dwellings and a mosque, two mansions evacuated by Thomassey suggest something of its scale and comfort. One of these was about 66 feet long and 42 feet wide, and had seven rooms opening out of one another on two storeys connected by an efficient staircase. The other was still larger, and had nine rooms. Built mainly in blocks of slate-like schist cemented with banco, their interior walls had been decorated with a yellow plaster of which a little is still preserved. No objects in silver or gold were found, but a large store of objects in iron: indicating . . . an already advanced civilization, both urban and agricultural. Among these iron objects were lances, knives, arrowheads, nails, a varied collection of farming tools, and one of the finest pairs of scissors of medieval date ever to be found in any country. A large quantity of glass weights, evidently for weighing gold, were recovered; many fragments of pottery of Mediterranean provenance; and seventy-seven pieces of painted stone of which fifty-three bore verses of the Koran in an Arabic script, while twenty-four others had decorated motifs.[3]

CAUSES OF DECLINE

What was the reason for the extinction of the powerful empire of Ghana after all these centuries? The process of decline was

[1] See page 45. [2] R. Mauny, op. cit., p. 74.
[3] Basil Davidson, *Old Africa Rediscovered*, p. 87.

gradual. It was not the conquest of a powerful state by a more powerful one so much as the inevitable fall of a country which had succumbed to the lotus. Her virile neighbour, shortly to develop into the Mali empire, had tasted no such plant. The history of such states is a constant cycle of repetition. We see the hardy peasant, wrestling with nature for his scanty wants—a life entailing activity of body and a lusty arm. Time passes, and girding himself with high principles and stern resolves he ousts his overlord and tastes intoxicating power; a generation or so, and we find him comfortably prosperous, civilized, learned perhaps, self-indulgent more certainly, his arm no longer lusty, the art of war forgotten. His day comes, and it is another's turn to try out his virility with the critical test of power.

VI. THE MANDINGO EMPIRE OF MALI

SUNDIATA KEITA

The empire of Mali, which succeeded that of Ghana, was probably the best known of all the empires of the western Sudan. The name Mali seems to have been more or less interchangeable with Mande. 'The empire of Mali was not really formed until after the destruction of the Kaya Maga dynasty, whose power extended over all this western region without exception. Formerly the king of Mali was only a vassal of the Kaya Maga, one of his officials and of his ministers.'[1] The great Mandingo hero is Sundiata Keita, the conqueror of Ghana, otherwise known as Mari Zata or Jata, meaning Prince Lion. He it was who escaped the assassination of his eleven brothers to build up the small state of Kangaba on the upper Niger into a powerful kingdom. Its kings had received Islam, probably from Abubakr's Almoravids, but its people were still animists. They were ethnically much the same as the Soninke of Ghana. The capital was Jeriba, but Sundiata built a new one down the Niger, some 150 miles farther east, at Niani, more generally known as Mali or Mande. His success was largely due to his building up of a strong bodyguard to maintain order at home and its development into a trained force of disciplined men to fight his battles abroad. After the conquest of the Sosso territories and of Ghana in 1240 his armies extended their conquests to include the gold producing regions of Wangara and Bambuk.

WANGARA

For centuries the exact location of Wangara has been uncertain. It was known to be the region which produced gold but as a measure of protection an air of mystery always surrounded it. Its people were secretive and strangers were never welcome. E. W. Bovill argues convincingly from the accounts of the early travellers that Wangara must have been in the vicinity of Bambuk and Bure, an 'island' of country some 300 miles long and 150 miles broad

[1] *Tarikh al Fattash*, p. 75.

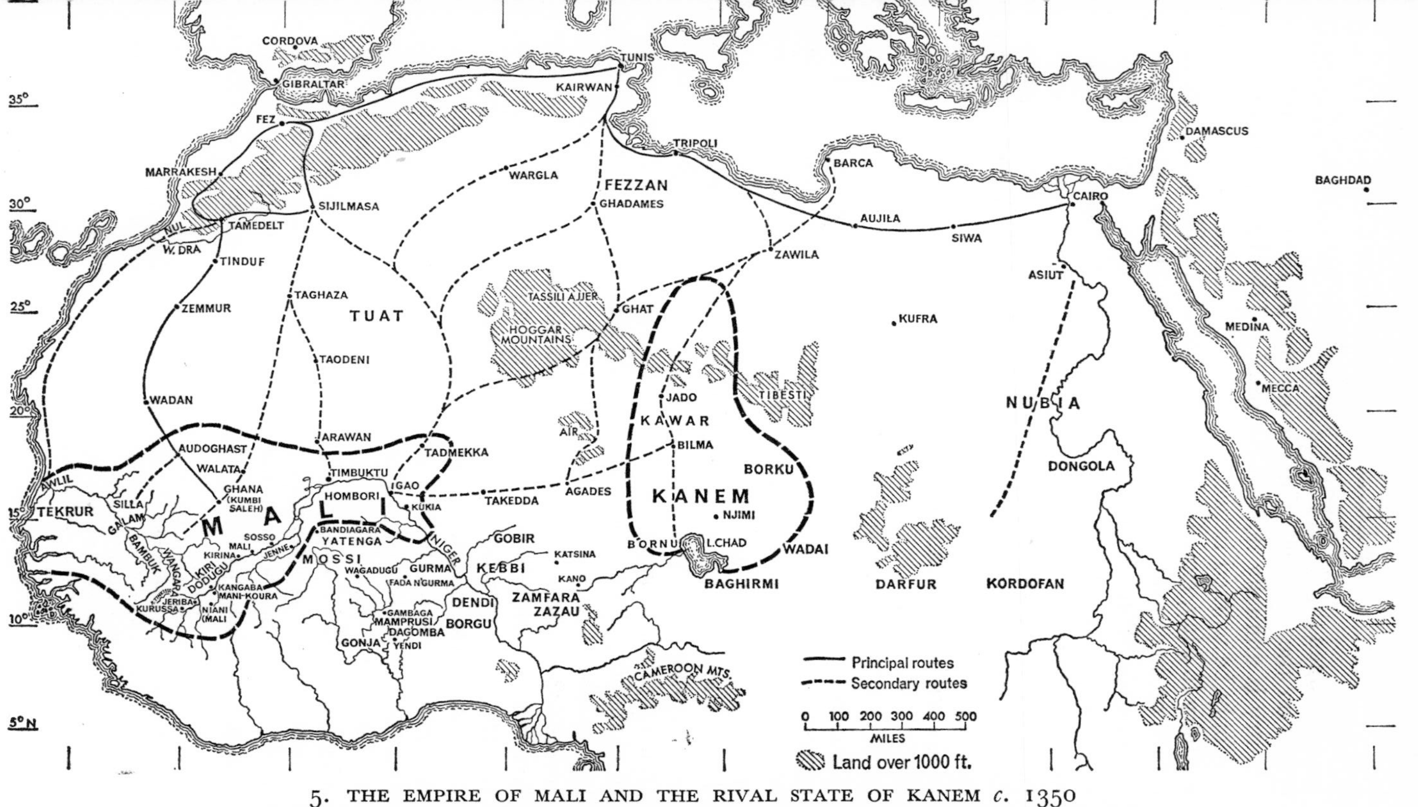

5. THE EMPIRE OF MALI AND THE RIVAL STATE OF KANEM *c.* 1350

The caravan routes shown are those used from the 11th to 13th centuries, the continuous lines representing more commonly used routes.

lying between the rivers Faleme on the west, Senegal on the north, Niger on the east and Tinkisso on the south.[1] In this area the country is annually flooded for much of the year and the gold can only be worked between the rise and fall of the floods, from January to May, exactly as described by Al Idrisi.[2] Gold was also mined or dug for in a few other places, notably Ashanti and Lobi on the upper Black Volta, so that those who merely associated the name of Wangara with a source of gold, as many did, would naturally misinform the inquiring traveller. Then again confusion is caused by the fact that the Hausas identified all Mandingoes or Mali speaking people with the part of their domains they had heard so much about, and various settlements of people of Mandingo origin are locally called Wangarawa by the Hausas.

CONDITIONS IN THE SUDAN

Sundiata's celebrated reign came to an end in 1255 and his successors adopted the title of Mansa. His predecessor, Allakoi Keita, is said to have founded the state in 1213, but records are sparse of all these peoples along the Niger and its tributaries. There was a tendency throughout the length of the Sudan for power to be ever shifting its focal point and for tribes to be ever changing their alliances and their allegiance. In this kaleidoscope of changing patterns it is impossible to be precise about origins nor indeed is it possible to present a neat historical picture of successive empires. The edges are continually blurred, dynastic rivalries and ambitions keep intruding on the political scene, and the travellers to whom we are indebted for such fragments of evidence as we have were severely limited by distances and communications in what they could see and hear. Important towns and trading centres on the main routes became established, such as Timbuktu, Gao, Niani or Mali, Jenne, and others already mentioned. Here were the nerve centres, the rulers and their courts. But for the vast numbers outside these centres life continued as it always had except for the occasional incursion of some marauder. This was always a hazard on the fringe of the desert

[1] See E. W. Bovill, *The Golden Trade of the Moors,* pp. 192 ff.

[2] Al Idrisi (*c.* 1100–66) did not visit the Sudan himself but he is renowned as a geographer for his *Kitab Rujar*, a work commissioned by Roger II, a Norman Christian prince of Sicily with strong Muslim leanings, and based upon original reports submitted by observers who had been sent to various countries to secure data. He was a descendant of the Prophet and of Spanish-Arab parentage.

where the nomad herdsmen in times of drought were forced to move in on the better watered lands. But with it all there continued to be an economic background of peasant cultivation, mainly of subsistence crops, pastoralism, and an occasional barter of one commodity such as millet for an exotic one such as salt. The rise and fall of petty princes in this state or in that made little difference to the rhythms of peasant life but from time to time a great figure would dominate the scene. Such a one was Mansa Musa, the grandson of Sundiata, who came to the throne in 1307, fifty-two years after the latter's death—a subject of sacred legend.

After Sundiata there were eight successive kings before Musa, including Mansa Ule (1255–70) and a usurper, Sakora, who extended the Mali conquests to the east.

MANSA KANKAN MUSA (1307–32)

To quote the *Tarikh al Fattash*:

> This Mali-koi (Emperor of the Mandingoes) was a virtuous, pious and devout king. His power extended from the extreme borders of the Mandingo peoples as far as Sibiridugu, and all the people who inhabited this land recognized his authority, the Songhais included. One of the signs of his virtue was that every day he freed a slave. He made the pilgrimage to the sacred temple of God, in the course of which he built the great mosque of Timbuktu, as well as those of Dukureye, Gundam, Direyi, Wanko and Banko, beyond the river. As for Kankan, she was a local woman, although some say that she was of Arab origin.[1]

The *Tarikh al Sudan* says:

> The Sultan Kankan Musa was the first of the Mali kings to take Songhai. A pious and balanced prince, he was not equalled by any other king of Mali in virtue and uprightness.[2]

But not only in the Sudan was Mansa Kankan Musa famous. His renown spread far beyond Africa. European maps began to appear showing Rex Melly seated on a throne in the middle of the Sahara or with references to the King of Mali. The well-known Catalan Map of 1375 depicting the emperor on his throne, wearing a crown and holding a sceptre in one hand and a lump of gold in the other, bears the inscription: 'This negro lord is called Musa Mali, Lord of the Negroes of Guinea. So abundant is the gold

[1] *Tarikh al Fattash*, p. 55. [2] *Tarikh al Sudan*, p. 13.

which is found in his country that he is the richest and most noble king in all the land.'[1]

MUSA'S PILGRIMAGE

Musa's celebrated pilgrimage to Mecca in 1324, when his spectacular entourage and wealth made a sensational impression throughout the Muslim world, put Mali quite literally on the map. It had for some time been the custom for the Muslim rulers to make the pilgrimage as a religious duty, but this one eclipsed them all for its lavish display. We are told that he was accompanied by 60,000 followers and over 80 camel-loads of gold. His horse was preceded by 500 slaves each carrying a golden bar. He took the route through Walata, whither the Muslim population of Ghana had fled after its destruction by his grandfather eighty-four years previously, thence to Tuat, and probably along the coast of Tripoli where the fame of his arrival would have attracted the attention of European traders. The journey across the desert took its toll of the carriers, many of whom sank to the ground exhausted and were abandoned where they lay. But others in the caravan fared better. The *Tarikh al Fattash* tells us of how Musa's wife, Inari Konte, who accompanied Musa on the journey, complained to him of her discomfort: she was unable to sleep, her body was covered in dirt and she longed to be able to bathe in a river. Now this was between Tuat and Taghaza in the middle of the desert. Musa sat up and called his chief slave, Farba. Never before had his wife asked for anything in vain. Farba promptly summoned the slaves, all 8,700 of them and all from Jenne, and made them dig a ditch 1,000 paces long to the depth of three men. When completed the ditch was carefully lined with stones and logs to give it a smooth surface. Finally, it was filled by emptying into it the contents of innumerable goat-skins so that the surface had the effect of waves. Then 'the princess, accompanied by her women to the number of 500, immediately mounted her mule to take her to the river. When they got there, all the women, radiant with joy, let out cries of happiness and went down into the river to bathe'.[2]

On the way back from Mecca, Musa stopped in Cairo for some time. Local accounts speak of the lasting impression he made not merely because of his riches and display but because of

[1] See E. V. Bovill, op. cit., frontispiece.

[2] *Tarikh al Fattash*, p. 59.

himself. He had a surprisingly pale skin and conducted himself with great dignity and piety. He would not allow himself to show servility in the presence of the Sultan and he established the full rights of equal standing for the Sudanese among the sophisticated orientals of the day. At the same time his lavish generosity was the talk of the bazaars for years. All kinds of adventurers sponged freely on his hospitality and before he left for home he had to borrow largely from a banker named Siraj ad Din, who with his son accompanied Musa back to Mali. There the banker died but the son returned safely with his money.

Legend attaches a traveller's custom to Mansa Musa, as the *Tarikh al Fattash* records:

> Kankan Musa was advised to wait to start his pilgrimage on a Saturday falling on the 12th day of the month to ensure a safe return from his journey. He duly waited in his palace at Mali nine months for such a day, by which time the head of his caravan had already reached Timbuktu. 'Since this time local travellers regard the Saturday falling on the 12th of the month as an auspicious day to start out. There is a local custom to say to any traveller who returns home after a journey in a pitiful condition, "Here is one who did not leave home on the Saturday chosen for departure by the Mali-koi".'[1]

TIMBUKTU AND GAO UNDER MANSA MUSA

The *Tarikh al Sudan* describes Musa's zeal for building:

> On his return from the pilgrimage the people of Songhai submitted to the authority of Kankan Musa. The prince passed through Songhai and had built outside the town of Gao a mosque with a mirhab where he made the Friday prayer. This mosque still exists. Wherever the prince passed through on a Friday he used to do the same. In due course he took the road to Timbuktu; he took this town and was the first sovereign to make himself master of it. He installed his representative and had the royal palace built called Ma'dugu, meaning in their language the king's palace. The site, still well known as that of the palace, now has on it a number of butchers' shops. It was Kankan Musa who built the minaret of the great mosque of Timbuktu.[2]

Timbuktu had its origin in the twelfth century. During the dry season the desert Tuareg used to come down towards the Niger and make their camp near a well there. When they returned north

[1] *Tarikh al Fattash*, p. 57. *Tarikh al Sudan*, pp. 14, 15.

in the wet season the well was left in charge of an old woman called Buktu. Tin Buktu in the Temajegh language of the Tuareg simply means the place of Buktu.[1] This place was ideally situated near the river and on the border of both the desert and the savannah to become an important centre for trade. For this reason it was always coveted by the Tuareg, the Mandingoes and the Songhai; not to mention the Moroccans at the end of the sixteenth century. But Timbuktu also became a centre for culture and learning. When it began to rival Walata in prosperity some of the Jedala Tuareg, who it will be remembered had gone to Walata from Ghana, came east to settle in Timbuktu, bringing their learning with them. The Jedala had always shown a willingness to adapt themselves to new conditions and to foster intellectual pursuits. In Musa's time both trade and learning were flourishing in Timbuktu and his pilgrimage did much to encourage both.

Among a number of cultured men who returned to Mali with Mansa Musa was a poet of Granada named Ishaq al Saheli, who had come to know and admire the Emperor in Mecca. Al Saheli was also an architect and he introduced a new style of building with flat roofs. His fame rests on certain mosques attributed to his design, and in particular to the mosque at Gao which he is said to have built to replace the humble building he found there. It stood for over 300 years and its foundations still remain. He is believed to have influenced the pyramidal form of minaret such as one sees constantly in the Sudan, well adapted to available materials, and he used burnt bricks. He is also reputed to have designed a magnificent audience chamber adjoining Mansa Musa's palace, which was an elaborate affair of stone and plaster, embellished with gold and silver plated on wooden panels.

In Timbuktu he must have been responsible for at least one of the early mosques, though none of them as they stand dates back to the Middle Ages. All three of the ancient ones have been extensively reconstructed several times since the sixteenth century, as is natural in places where stone is scarce. Nevertheless, it seems more than probable that the Jingereber mosque was built or inspired by Al Saheli soon after his arrival. Dr. Barth tells us that he saw an almost illegible inscription over the main gate of this mosque, the only faintly discernible part of which read 1327. Even this no longer exists. Al Saheli died in 1346, so that if, as is sup-

[1] H. Jaunet et J. Barry, *Histoire de l'Afrique Occidentale Française*, p. 50.

posed, the Sankore mosque was not built until the end of the century or later its ascription to him would be false. According to both the *Tarikh al Sudan* and the *Tarikh al Fattash* the Jingereber mosque was entirely demolished and rebuilt in 1570, and the same was done to the Sankore mosque in about 1580. The Sidi Yahya mosque was built later than the others, about 1440, and restored by Alkali al Aqib in 1577–78, this again according to Al Sadi. Its modern transformation dates from 1939. One of these mosques was mentioned by Leo Africanus after his visit in the early sixteenth century as being 'a most stately temple with walls of stone and lime'. Raymond Mauny believes that this can only refer to the Jingereber mosque. There was only one other stone building seen—the palace.[1]

IBN BATTUTA'S DESCRIPTION OF MALI

When Mansa Kankan Musa died in 1332 his empire extended from the borders of Tekrur, far to the west, up to Dandi on the borders of the Hausa states in the east; and from Walata, Arawan and the desert in the north to the forest regions in the south—with the important exception of the kingdoms of Mossi and the trading centre of Jenne, which was so protected by nature as to be well nigh impregnable. This was an enormous empire and its fame understandably spread throughout the civilized world. In 1352 a celebrated Berber traveller named Ibn Battuta (1304–69), who had recently spent twenty-four years travelling in India, China, and in other parts of Africa, was commissioned by the Sultan of Fez to bring back a report on the Bilad al Sudan.

His first experiences in Walata made him rather contemptuous of local habits and some of the customs he witnessed later in Mali evidently shocked him. He was horrified, for instance, when some primitive Wangara visitors to the court were given as a princely token of greeting a female slave for them to kill and eat, which they did with manifest enjoyment. And he professed to being embarrassed when he found that at court even the sultan's daughters were accustomed to moving about with the other women in a state of stark nakedness. But the longer he stayed in the Sudan the more he found to praise.

Mali was an entirely Muslim town and it needed a permit to enter it. When the emperor, Mansa Suleiman, held court, 300

[1] Raymond Mauny, *Tableau Géographique, etc.*, pp. 114, 115; 493, 494.

armed slaves would place themselves on each side of the throne. Two horses would then be brought, saddled and bridled, and two rams to avert the evil eye. The emperor would be robed in a red cloak of European manufacture. 'Before him went singers with hand-bells of gold and silver. He would proceed at a dignified pace, followed by over 300 armed slaves. Over the emperor's head slaves held a silken parasol on the top of which was mounted a great golden bird. If the emperor, in the course of an audience, called one of his subjects by name, the latter would take off his court dress and cover himself with old rags, replace his turban with a dirty cap, pull up his trousers above the knees, kneel down, bump the ground with his elbows, and settle back on his haunches to listen humbly to the emperor's words. Before uttering any word himself he would uncover his back and cast dust over it and over his head. When the emperor addressed the assembled multitude every one present would doff his turban.' Ibn Battuta was particularly impressed by the love of justice and fair dealing above everything. 'In the whole of their country there was complete security. Thieves were either unknown or very severely punished, as was any breach of the laws. When foreigners happened to die, their possessions would be carefully kept until such time as their proper owners came to claim them.' He was pleased to record that in Mali the children were beaten if they did not pray and that they were put in fetters when they showed insufficient zeal in learning the Koran by heart.[1]

The far-flung empire was at that time divided into administrative provinces and districts, zealously ruled by capable governors and well-trained assistants. Regional forces took care of the defence and policing of the country. Soldiers were armed with bows and arrows, and also with spears and shields. The people appeared to be prosperous and happy. The whole picture is of orderly government, security, peace and contentment. Yet before long a rapid decline seems to have set in. Perhaps the very sense of peace and security destroyed the necessary vigilance to resist external aggression. When Mansa Jata succeeded Suleiman in 1362 the rot was well under way.

DECLINE OF THE EMPIRE

Jata allowed his treasury to run dry, no doubt assisted by the

[1] H. Jaunet et J. Barry, op. cit., p. 43.

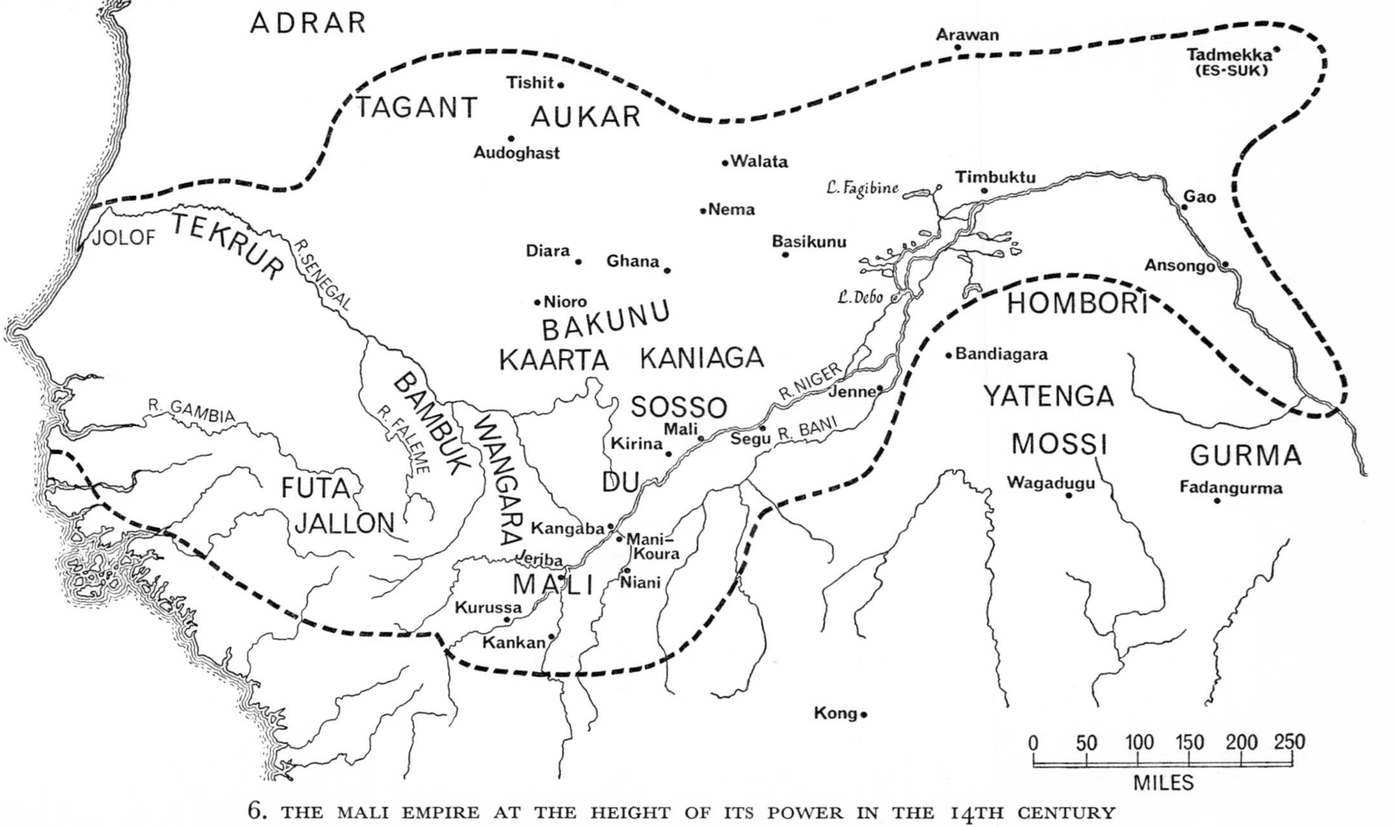

6. THE MALI EMPIRE AT THE HEIGHT OF ITS POWER IN THE 14TH CENTURY

provincial heads or *kois*, who were native and subject kings tributary to Mali. The *koi* was permitted to retain one-third of the taxes, but lax control at the centre would be quickly turned to local profit—another reason to account for the decline of Mali's power. But even before Jata's reign there were inklings of impending weakness. Musa's son Maghan, in a short reign of four years from 1332 to 1336, between his father and his uncle, managed to suffer two major reverses. First, the Mossi, who were never conquered by Mali, raided and burnt Timbuktu; next, he lost the important town of Gao, the Songhai capital.

Timbuktu remained in the hands of Mali for another century, until in 1433 it fell to the Tuareg chief Akil. In course of time Arawan, Walata, and the northern districts all likewise came to be occupied by the Tuareg; the Mossi invaded from the south, and the Wolofs and Tekarir invaded from the west. By 1473 the kingdom of Songhai had completely freed herself to become even more powerful than Mali. Before the final extinction there was a desperate appeal made to the Portuguese, who had recently arrived on the coast, but it produced no help. The seventeenth century saw the last of the Mali rulers reduced to being a mere district head of Kangaba, which is exactly where the first king started four centuries earlier.

VII. THE MOSSI STATES

THROUGHOUT the history of the great empires of the Sudan there is frequent and recurring reference to the Mossi people. These are the inhabitants of the plains and valleys of the upper Black and White Volta rivers enclosed to the north by the great bend of the Niger. They were grouped in three states or kingdoms. The most northerly was Yatenga, in the hills and cliffs between Hombori and Bandiagara. South of Yatenga was the important kingdom of Wagadugu, whose king was known as the Morho-Naba. East of Wagadugu lay Gurma, with its capital Fada-n-Gurma.

South of these three states lay Mamprusi with its capital Gambaga, Dagomba with its capital Yendi, and to the west of these two in the bend of the Black Volta lay Gonja. All of these latter three states have districts in modern Ghana bearing these names, and they probably occupy much the same territory as their ancestors did.

The origin of these people is not known but there is a charming legend about the first king. It seems that in the eleventh century there was a king reigning in Gambaga called Nedega. One of his daughters, Yennenga, was an intrepid warrior who herself used to lead her father's troops in battle. For this reason the king refused to let her be married. Now it happened that one day when Yennenga was returning from an expedition in the region of Tenkodogo, her horse suddenly bolted and carried her far away from her troops. Having pushed its way into a thick forest, the animal was forced to slacken its speed and came to a halt in front of a hunter's hut. This hut belonged to a young man named Riale, the son of a Malinke chief. After quarrelling with his brother over the succession, he had been cruelly banished to live alone in the forest and hunt elephant. When Yennenga appeared at his hut, Riale helped her to master her horse and offered her hospitality. Before long the two young people fell in love and did not want to leave. They had a son whom they named Widiraugo (meaning stallion), in memory of the horse that had brought Yennenga to the place.

Nedega for long sought for his favourite daughter, but without success. He believed that she was dead. When the day came that he heard what had happened, he forgave Yennenga and begged her to come and bring her husband and son. The old king received them with joy and wanted to keep them near him, but Riale feared that he would die if he left the forest. So Nedega let them go back, loading them with presents; and to Widiraugo, now a young man, he gave a troop of soldiers.

Riale and Yennenga lived for a long time in their forest. When Yennenga died her remains were conveyed to Gambaga where she was buried. Widiraugo with his troops took possession of the countries situated in the region of Tenkodogo. To his three sons he entrusted the rule over three provinces of his empire which in course of time became the three Mossi states: Wagadugu, Yatenga and Gurma.[1]

So much for picturesque myth. The facts suggest that there were small tribal groups, most of whom spoke Gur languages but with some who spoke Mande, and these were invaded and dominated by men of Berber origin coming from the region of Chad by way of Zamfara. They had much in common with the Hausa people though they were different and wished to be so. They tended to inter-marry more with the Mande speakers, the more sophisticated of the groups, but in course of time they came to speak Gur and share their religion.

The histories of Mali and Songhai record the major Mossi raids into their territories, including the sack of Timbuktu in 1338 and the daring raid as far north as Walata in 1483, when Sonni Ali routed them near Lake Debo. There is no need therefore to repeat them here. But it should be noted that the Mossi kingdoms had remarkable stability and endurance, beyond that of their greater neighbours. This may be attributable, as some think, to their rulers' success in using ancestor worship and their own quasi-divine position as the descendants of the nations' founders.[2]

[1] H. Jaunet et J. Barry, *Histoire de l'Afrique Occidentale Française*, p. 33.

[2] J. D. Fage, *An Introduction to the History of West Africa*, p. 38. For a detailed study of the Mossi see the writings of Elliott P. Skinner, especially his book, *The Mossi of the Upper Volta*, 1964.

VIII. THE EMPIRE OF SONGHAI

THE ORIGIN OF THE FIRST DYNASTY OF KINGS IN GAO

The Songhai people have always been associated to this day with the middle Niger up and down stream from Gao, which became their capital after an early period in Kukia. Gao has a number of different spellings in Arabic manuscripts, with variants of transliteration into French or English, as for instance Alkwakwua, Kawkaw, Ka'a, Kagh, Gaogo and so on. It is one of the oldest cities in the Sudan, known to Arab geographers from the ninth century. Like Ghana it had two distinct quarters, the ruins of which can still be faintly seen. The discovery of the remains of the royal cemetery at Sane (4½ miles from Gao) has produced evidence to support the belief that Gao was the capital of a powerful empire from the time of its early origins in the ninth century up to the Moorish conquest of 1591. In 1363 Ibn Battuta called it 'a large town . . . one of the most beautiful of the Negro cities, one of the most extensive and well supplied places.' Leo Africanus in 1513 noted that it was a very great town and larger than Timbuktu, but most of the houses were ugly except a few handsome edifices for the king and court. In the *Tarikh al Fattash* it is recorded that about 1585 there was an argument with some inhabitants of Kano, who claimed that their town was more important than Gao. A count was made, which took three days, and without including the grass huts there were found to be 7,626 houses, which could give a population of some 75,000 just before the Moorish disaster. Today one can see the remains of the mosque built by Mansa Musa's architect, with its walls of clay but its *mirhab* of brick.[1]

The river in its wide turning movement to the south flows through arid scrub, but the banks grow a particular kind of succulent grass, which attracts the nomad herdsmen from the parched lands on both sides of the river at this point during the dry season. Along its course are vast expanses of reeds, and innumerable small

[1] Raymond Mauny, *Tableau Géographique, etc.*, pp. 112 and 498–9; *Tarikh al Fattash*, p. 261.

islets are concealed among the devious creeks. Millions of mosquitoes make human habitation barely possible.

According to one tradition, the Songhai migrated westward out of Egypt some time during the seventh century when the country was overrun by Arab conquerors. Their coming to Dandi (Songhai) is thought to fit in with the well-known Hausa legend of the Kisra migration which is held responsible for the founding of Illo, Bussa, and also Kwararafa. The fact that the Dandi region contains many places with names of apparent Bornu-Berber origin supports the theory that the Zaghawa Tuareg, who supplied the early kings of Kanem, migrated westward to the Niger and established their rule there over the indigenous river people. They had an important settlement at Kukia, not far from the confluence of the Niger with the river Kebbi in the south-west corner of Sokoto Province. Some believe that the Lemta Tuareg founded the first dynasty of kings in Gao.[1]

The *Tarikh al Sudan* has an interesting legend concerning the arrival of the first king. Two brothers one day arrived in a state of exhaustion at the Niger near Kukia. The elder was barely able to gasp out something that sounded like Dia Al Ayaman, which was taken to be his name. In reality he was trying to say in Arabic, 'I've come from the Yamen'. He duly recovered and became king in Kukia. At that time there were two rival tribes living on islands in the river south of Ansongo: the Sorko, the fisherfolk; and the Gabibi, the cultivators. The struggle between the two is described as follows:

> At certain seasons of the year the Gabibi used to see an enormous fish appear out of the waters of the river with a ring in its nose. It used to issue commands to the farmers, who were too frightened to disobey. Now it happened that some Berbers on their way from Tripolitania came to settle for a while with the Gabibi. Their chief was called Dia Aliamen. One day when the fish showed itself out of the water, Dia Aliamen killed it with a thrust of his spear, thus delivering the people from their strange bondage. The Gabibi, in gratitude, chose Dia Aliamen to be their king.[2]

The story would seem to depict in the guise of a fish the Sorko fishermen who used to come in their canoes at harvest time to

[1] E. W. Bovill, *The Golden Trade of the Moors*, 1958, p. 100 and M. Delafosse, *Haut–Sénégal–Niger*, vol. II.

[2] *Tarikh al Sudan*, Chapter I.

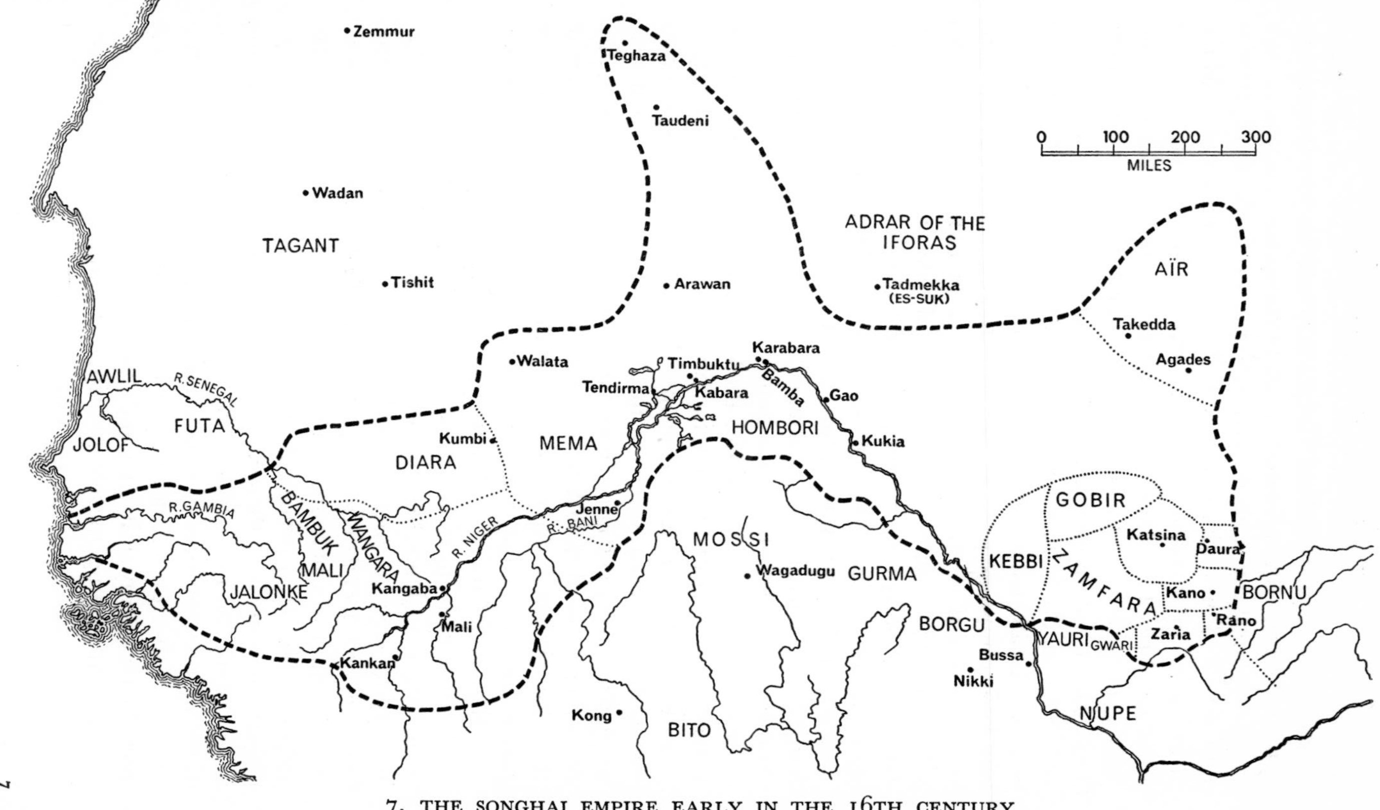

7. THE SONGHAI EMPIRE EARLY IN THE 16TH CENTURY

plunder the granaries of the Gabibi farmers. The docile peasants must have been too terrified of their brutal enemies to put up any resistance until the Berbers arrived to put the Sorko to flight once and for all. The Sorko under their legendary chief Faran Maka Bote[1] went up river to found the town of Gao about 690. But some centuries later they were again driven out by Berbers from Kukia and they finally settled much farther up the river near Lake Debo, where they still get their living from the river as of old. Some of the Sorkawa would have seemed to have found their way to Kebbi, where the people are devoted to fishing and are still known in some parts as Sorkawa. In Argungu the great event of the year is the festival of *Fashin Ruwa*, 'breaking of the waters', when at a given signal vast numbers of fishermen leap into the Gulbin Kebbi with their nets and gourds to celebrate the opening of the fishing season. This is usually about February.

It was in the eleventh century that Gao became the capital of Songhai. At this time Gao rivalled Ghana in its trade between Arabs and Berbers on the one hand and the indigenous Sudanese on the other. Like Ghana and the other entrepôts in the Sudan it had its trading quarter for the foreigners apart from the main town where the king and his people resided. Al Bakri records that 'when the king used to have a meal, a drum would be beaten to stop people from engaging in any business at such a moment, and the women would do a kind of dance with special movements of the head. When the meal was over the remains of it would be thrown into the Niger and criers would announce to the people that they could resume their occupations.'

Gao also came to rival Timbuktu and Jenne in its learning and sophistication. Jenne on the western borders provided another important market. Alone among the cities of this region Jenne remained independent of the power of Mali. The modern appearance of the town helps us to understand how it managed to stay impregnable. It is protected on all sides by waterways that are flooded for much of the year, so that conditions for a besieging army would be next to impossible. Its houses are renowned for their architectural style, which must derive from the sixteenth century under the Askias, with a later Moorish influence, which has affected many of its arts and customs.

Some interesting marble inscriptions found in 1939 at Sane,

[1] Jean Rouch, *Les Songhay*, 1954, p. 9.

about four miles out of Gao, date to the early twelfth century and provide the name of a Muslim king, Abu Abdullah Muhammad, and the date of his death, 1100.

THE DIA DYNASTY AND HOW IT BECAME THE SONNI DYNASTY

The successors of Dia Aliamen are said to have numbered thirty and to have reigned for a period of over six hundred years. It may well have been considerably more. The first king to accept Islam was Dia Kosoi in 1009, the 15th Dia of Kukia. He was converted by traders in Gao. He it was who is said to have taken Gao from the Sorko and transferred his capital there from Kukia.[1] During the latter part of the Dia period the Songhai kingdom came under the rule of Mali, as has already been described. On Mansa Musa's return from his pilgrimage in 1325 he visited the recently acquired town of Gao and received the submission of its king, the 20th Dia; but to ensure the loyalty of his new vassal he took back to Mali with him as hostages two of the king's sons, Ali Kolon and Selman-Nar. Some ten years later the two young princes, who had been allowed to move about freely, managed to escape back to Gao.

SONNI ALI THE FIRST

The second chapter of the *Tarikh al Sudan* tells the story of how the Sonni dynasty was ushered in:

As he is the first Sonni, Ali Kolon's story is as follows. Employed by the king of Mali, he lived near him with his brother Selman-Nar. Both were sons of Dia Yosiboi, and Selman's name was originally Seliman, but altered thus by reason of the barbarous language of these peoples.

The mothers of Ali and Selman were two full sisters. Omma was the name of Ali Kolon's mother, and Fati the name of Selman's. The latter was the favourite wife. In spite of numerous conceptions she had no children, and as she despaired of having any, she said to her husband, 'Marry my sister Omma. Perhaps she will give you an heir, which I have been unable to do'. Dia Yosiboi took his wife's advice. He ignored the law which forbade the marrying of two sisters by one husband. God willed that these two women should conceive on the same night, and on the same night they were each delivered of a son. The two new-born infants were placed on the ground in a dark place. It was only in the morning that they were washed, according to the custom

[1] Loc. cit.

when a child was born in the night. The first washed was Ali Kolon, and because of this fact he was considered the elder. As for Selman-Nar, whose washing followed, he was for this reason declared the younger.

When the two children were considered sufficiently old the Sultan of Mali took them with him. At this time, to be exact, these princes were his vassals, and it was customary for the sons of dependent kings to be attached to their suzerain. It holds to this day in all the kingdoms of the Sudan. Of these young people some used to return after a term of service, others continued to their death living near to their lord and master.

While these two princes were at the court of the King of Mali, at one time or another Ali Kolon used to sally forth on some profitable expedition (to learn the art of war and to fill his pockets). Ali Kolon, who was a very capable and resourceful man, used always to take a different route in order to make himself acquainted with all the roads to and from Songhai. His scheme was to flee one day to his country and make himself independent. To this end he secretly made all preparations, and concealed such arms and stores as he was likely to need on the roads. When these arrangements were completed, Ali Kolon took aside his brother and confided to him his secret plans. Having seen to the feeding of their horses to prepare them to stand the fatigue of a long journey, the two brothers set out for Songhai. Advised of their flight, the King of Mali sent in pursuit to kill them. Every time that they were closely pressed the brothers turned and fought off their pursuers. In these frequent fights the brothers always had the advantage, and without further stoppage they succeeded in gaining their country.

Ali Kolon became king of the Songhai country. He called himself Sonni (or Liberator) and delivered his subjects from the yoke of Mali. On his death Selman-Nar succeeded him. The limits of his kingdom did not go beyond the town precincts until the reign of Sonni Ali, the great Kharijite[1] tyrant. This prince accumulated more forces and showed more energy than all those of his dynasty, who preceded him. He made expeditions, he conquered provinces, and his fame extended to the east as far as to the west, as we shall recount later, if God pleases. One might say that he was the last king of his dynasty, for his son,

[1] R. Mauny op. cit., has the following comment on p. 521: 'One should note that the whole of mediaeval Islam in West Africa was Sunni and orthodox, despite the proximity of the Kharijite and Shi'ite groups of the Maghreb and Tripolitania (Tiaret, Mzab, Jebel, Nefouca, Zawila) and the relations maintained by these towns and countries with the Sudan from the fact that Abu Yezid, the Kharijite agitator, was born in Gao about 885. There were certainly some non-Sunnis in Black Africa, but only isolated individuals or small communities, without influence over the trend of Islam in the vicinity.' Here is yet another reason for the Sunni biographer to be prejudiced against Sonni Ali.

Abubakr Da'u, who ascended the throne after his death, lost no time in falling to the power of Askia El Haj Muhammad.

SONNI ALI THE GREAT (1464–92)[1]

The above extract refers to events immediately after Mansa Musa's death in 1332. The 'tyrant' referred to, Ali the Great, did not start his rule until 1464, but since, as the Tarikh says, Songhai rule during this period did not extend beyond the confines of the city of Gao it is not strange that the records of these 130 years under the Sonni kings are sparse. We gather that Gao's tribute to Mali lasted for little more than fifty years, that is until 1385 or so, and that the town managed to resist raids by another Sudanese people to the south, the Mossi, as well as by various Tuareg tribes from the surrounding desert.

Sonni Ali the Great was the last of the dynasty descended from the original Dia Aliamen eight centuries earlier, and he was reputed to be the eighteenth after Dia Kosoi, who adopted the Muslim faith in 1009. He reigned from 1464 to 1492 and in less than thirty years the power of Gao extended from a town governorship to a wide empire, extending from the rapids at Bussa to Jenne. His chief enemies were said to be the Fulani, the Malinke, the Mossi and all shades of Muslim.[2]

Within four years of his accession Sonni Ali drove the Tuareg out of Timbuktu, where they had been in occupation since their leader Akil had captured it from Mali in 1433. Akil installed a fellow tribesman named Umar as *koi* to govern the city and collect its taxes, but Akil himself insisted on turning up to take the taxes for himself, including Umar's one-third share, and he and his followers would ravish the women as the pleasure took them. In desperation Umar sent secretly to Gao to invite Sonni Ali to deliver them. Ali accepted with alacrity, but when he was near the gates Umar lost his nerve and fled with the assistance he had promised, so that it was a very enraged and vengeful general who finally took the town by assault in 1468.

Written over a century later, the *Tarikh al Sudan* fiercely condemns Sonni Ali's conduct. It follows, as will be seen, the line of an eminent Muslim jurist, Al Maghili,[3] who declared Sonni Ali

[1] The *Tarikh al Fattash* strangely enough does not use the term 'Sonni' and instead uses the title 'Shi' (which the French translators from the Arabic write as 'Chi') for the dynasty of kings prior to Askia the Great.

[2] Jean Rouch, op. cit., p. 9.

[3] See Muhammad Al-Hajj, in *Odu*, July 1964, pp. 53 and 56.

to have been a menace to the true faith. Ahmed Baba, as a pious Berber Muslim, would have had no sympathy in any case with the savageries of this backsliding Soninke adventurer. As a cultured scholar of Timbuktu he must have been horrified by the stories of what happened to his learned ancestors and their literate friends. 'As for this master tyrant, this celebrated scoundrel, Sonni Ali, he was a man endowed with great strength and powerful energy, wicked, vicious, unjust, a bloodthirsty oppressor, he killed God alone knows how many people. He persecuted the learned and pious, aiming at their lives, their honour, and their respect.'[1]

There is a graphic account of how a large number of the learned professors, hearing of Sonni Ali's arrival, had hastily decamped on camels:

> On the day of departure were seen old and bearded men, trembling with fright at having to mount a camel and falling off again when the animal got up. Our good ancestors, you see, used to keep their children tied to their apron-strings, with the result that the children grew up knowing nothing of life, because even when they were young they had never played games. Now this is the time when games mould a man and teach him a great number of things. The parents realized their error, and later when they returned to Timbuktu they let their children have time to play, and relaxed their former restraint.[2]

Another tragic story on an earlier page illustrates Sonni Ali's ruthlessness:

> One day Sonni Ali gave the order for there to be brought to him to become his concubines thirty virgin daughters of the learned men in the town. He was then at the port of Kabara and wished that these young girls should make the journey on foot. So they set forth, going outside their houses for the first time in their lives. A servant of the prince accompanied them and made them walk until they were quite incapable of going any further. When the servant reported what had happened, he was ordered by the prince that they should all be put to death, which in fact was done (may Heaven preserve us!). The place where they finally stopped was somewhere to the west, and very near to Amadagha. It is called Fina qadar el-akbar, which means the threshold of the virgins' fate, or the virgins' uttermost limit.[3]

At Alfa-a-Konko there was a great massacre, 'so that to this day the rainfall is insufficient for crops'. But some of the scholars

[1] *Tarikh al Sudan*, p. 103. [2] Ibid., p. 109. [3] Ibid., p. 107.

Sonni Ali chose to honour, on one occasion sending them a great number of female captives as concubines. 'Those who no longer observed the duties of their religion made them indeed their concubines, but those who faithfully followed its precepts took them in marriage.' Al Sadi's Fulani ancestress was one of these.

TIMBUKTU AT ITS ZENITH

The greatness of Timbuktu coincided with the greatness of Songhai. Its situation, close to a navigable waterway, gave it commercial prosperity. Its port was the fishing village of Kabara, but it is well to remember that there was little timber for boat-building to be found along the length of the middle Niger, which traverses long stretches of desert, and this restricted the volume of trade.[1]

Timbuktu was a city of Muslims from its foundation and it was the proud boast of its people that worship had never been offered to pagan gods within its walls. 'Religion flourished and the Sunna enlivened both religious and worldly affairs. . . . In those days it had no equal in the Sudan, from Mali to the edges of the Maghrib, for soundness of institutions, political liberties, purity of customs, security of life and goods, clemency and compassion towards the poor man and the stranger, and respect for, and assistance to, the students and men of learning.'[2] Learning and scholarship, however, had flourished since the influx of refugees from Ghana and Walata in the thirteenth century.

With the sixteenth century came the beginnings of advance from the study of traditional texts to the creation of original literature, and especially in Timbuktu whose intellectual stimulus had already been making itself felt up and down the Sudan. The teaching was in the hands of famous scholars, who often took their pupils with them as they travelled on the pilgrimage—a lengthy business in those days. Back home again they set up their *makatib* and *madaris*, often in the mosques. These scholars were predominantly Berber by blood and men like Al Sadi were in the minority: such as he, however, were numerous in the other seat of learning up the river at Jenne. His *Tarikh* contains a long list of distinguished scholars at the Sankore University in Timbuktu, with

[1] E. W. Bovill, *The Golden Trade of the Moors*, footnote on p. 101.

[2] J. O. Hunwick, 'Ahmad Baba and the Moroccan Invasion of the Sudan (1591)', in the *Journal of the Historical Society of Nigeria*, vol. 2, No. 3, December 1962, pp. 311–328. The quotation is from the *Tarikh al Fattash*, pp. 312–13.

their attainments. Among them we notice Al Haj Ahmed, who went to Mecca in 1485; he left 700 books in his library. On his return he visited Kano and other Sudanese towns. Makhluf ibn Ali was a geographer who had travelled throughout the Sudan; he went to Kano and Katsina, and died in 1533 of poisoning in Morocco. Aida Ahmed was a learned man who, having come back from Mecca, settled in Katsina, where he was honourably treated and made a judge: he died in 1530. Another was Muhammad ibn Mahmud ibn Abubakr, whose generosity was proverbial; he never refused to lend a book even to strangers, and in this manner lost many valuable works.

JENNE

From Timbuktu Sonni Ali marched against Jenne, which had emancipated itself from Songhai at the time when Mansa Kankan Musa was asserting his domination over Gao and the Songhai rulers. Jenne's position on the Niger, which flooded the surrounding area for several months of the year, made it difficult for an investing army.[1] The town did not capitulate until after a siege said to have lasted for seven years, seven months and seven days.

With the capture of Jenne in about 1473 Sonni Ali had secured one of the pearls of the Sudan. 'This town,' said Al Sadi, 'is great, flourishing and prosperous; it is rich, blessed by Heaven and favoured by God.' He goes on to describe the inhabitants as kind and hospitable, but inclined to be envious of fortune. It was a great market for the Muslim world and an important centre for Sudanese trade. The region was well populated, and Jenne was said to have maintained twelve contingents of troops to the east and twelve to the west to protect herself against Mali, with whom she had eighty-nine battles, all of them victorious.

But above all Jenne had a reputation for culture and learning. Long is the list of notable scholars in Jenne recorded in the *Tarikh* by Al Sadi, who had himself been a notary, and later Imam, in Jenne before going on to Timbuktu. The scholars of Jenne were mostly of Sudanese as distinct from Berber stock.

SONNI ALI'S SUPREMACY

Sonni Ali now had command of the whole of the great waterway of the Sudan, the middle Niger. He repulsed the strong forces

[1] See Raymond Mauny, op. cit., figure 107 on p. 500.

of Mossi to the south, of Hombori in the bend of the river, and of Kebbi to the east, and then established a strong fleet on the river near Timbuktu.

Meanwhile, the Mossi of Yatenga cut across the Niger and the country of Massina, down river from Jenne, and reached Walata to the north, pillaging as they went. After a month's siege they sacked the town and decamped with as many women and children as they could round up and as much plunder as they could find. But Sonni Ali intercepted them at Lake Debo and completely routed them, forcing them to abandon their captives and their booty. This was in 1483 and it settled the supremacy of Songhai over the middle Niger region of the Sudan.

Even so the Mossi still constituted a menace. News of their depredations interrupted Sonni Ali in one of the most fantastic projects ever conceived in the Sudan. He had actually started on the digging of a canal from the western end of Lake Fagibine, a tongue-shaped lake extending some hundred miles or so westward from Timbuktu, to reach Walata, at least 150 miles away on the edge of the desert to the west. According to the *Tarikh al Sudan*,[1] Sonni Ali abandoned his scheme and encountered the king of Mossi at Jiniki-To'oi, 'near Kobi beyond the river', driving him before him into the Mossi country. This was in 1483. Sonni Ali then retraced his steps and marched against Gurma, west of Mossi, which he conquered and sacked. The *Tarikh* says that this was his last expedition but there seems to be a subsequent contradiction. After recording his repair of the ramparts of Kabara in 1485, and the gaoling of the governor of Timbuktu in 1486, which caused many of the inhabitants to seek refuge from his tyranny outside the town, the chronicle says that Sonni Ali died in 1492–93 on his return from an expedition to Gurma, 'where he fought the Zeghrani and the Fulani'. He was apparently carried away and drowned by a flooded river called Koni.

As we have seen, his memory is not preserved by local chroniclers save in terms of condemnation. They cannot forgive the way he treated scholars like themselves in Timbuktu and Jenne, the ruthlessness attendant on his conquests, nor his disregard for religious and social prejudices. Nevertheless, it cannot be denied that he was a brilliant commander and a strong ruler. His allegiance to Islam was perfunctory (he was a Kharijite at that) and his mother

[1] *Tarikh al Sudan*, pp. 115, 116.

is said to have been originally a pagan from the neighbourhood of what is today Sokoto, so that his Muslim biographers were at no pains to suppress current stories that he cut the throats of thousands without any shadow of excuse and that he was a kind of monster. There was a generally accepted belief that he once had a child thrown into a mortar and its mother was forced to pound it with her pestle while it was still living. All are agreed that he had a violent and ungovernable temper, but the outburst was sometimes followed by remorse and he could on occasions be merciful, as when he acknowledged the courage of the young king of Jenne and his supporters by sparing their lives after the town's capitulation.

ASKIA MUHAMMAD (1493–1528)

Perhaps much, if not most, of the credit for Sonni Ali's achievements as a ruler should go to his chief minister, Muhammad Abubakr al Turi, said to have been a pure-blooded negro and a man of remarkable wisdom. For most of the long reign he succeeded in blending Ali's wild brilliance with his own temperate counsels and devout integrity. Shortly after Ali's death he stepped into his shoes. Having wrested the throne from Ali's son, Sonni Bakari, in a sharp fight at the gates of Gao, he proclaimed himself king under the appellation Askia Muhammad.

The origin of the word Askia, which was adopted as a title by all the succeeding rulers of this dynasty, is a matter for conjecture. Some say that it comes from the anguished cries of Sonni Ali's daughters when they saw the usurper instead of Bakari: 'A si kyi a!' (It is not he!) they cried in the Songhai tongue. Others think that it was a disdainful name meaning slave given him by the Tuareg.

The new king brought the long line of the original Dia dynasty to an end. In contrast to his predecessor he encouraged piety and learning, and indeed he seems to have been at pains to justify his usurpation of a throne going back some thirty generations as a jihad against irreligious and barbarous practices. In 1497, with the legitimacy of his rule still worrying him, he left his brother in charge of the kingdom and set out on the pilgrimage to Mecca. As with Mansa Musa, more than a century and a half before, the journey was a kind of royal procession, with an imposing escort of cavalry and infantry. We are told that the Askia took with him

300,000 pieces of gold, of which 100,000 were for the distribution of alms in the holy cities and the purchase of a plot of land at Medina for the use of pilgrims from the Sudan. But Muhammad's chief satisfaction was his confirmation as ruler of Songhai by the religious head of the Muslim world, the Khalif Al-Mutawakkil. In Cairo there were opportunities for conference with some of the leading scholars and statesmen of the day.

During the first years of his reign Askia Muhammad effected a great Muslim religious revival, and on all sides mosques were rebuilt and schools founded. He completely won the confidence and support of the religious leaders. He instituted a standing army, thus doing much to lessen the continual burden of defence and conscription, which in the days of Sonni Ali had fallen so heavily on the peasantry. The civil population could now turn its undivided attention to trade and commerce, and it was not long before the prosperity of the country began to increase. A regular system of market inspectors was introduced, which guaranteed honest measure and fair dealings. Mediterranean goods in large quantities began to find their way into the country, including cloth, brass-ware, armour, weapons, spurs, bridles and the like. These would be bartered or sold in exchange for gold, cotton, corn and other produce.

Politically, the Askia completely reorganized the empire. It was divided up into four provinces, apart from the home districts, which comprised the country lying in the bend of the Niger. The first province, Dandi, lay to the east, spreading from Agades to Bornu, and included the Hausa states. The second, the province of Banku, included the desert to the north-east of Gao. The third, called Bal, took in the desert to the north-west of Timbuktu and reached from the salt mines of Taghaza in the far north right down to Walata. The fourth province, of Kurmina, lay to the west, including the Fulani of Massina, the dismembered remains of Mali, and the pagan Bambara.

This decentralization proved a masterpiece of administration. All the provincial governors as well as the chief office holders were either chosen from the royal family or married to its princesses, with the object of strengthening the bonds of loyalty and mutual concord. But history reminds us that ties of blood and marriage are not always proof against personal greed or ambition: they may indeed afford excuse for a rival supplanter.

Civilization made great strides under the protection of a firm and wise ruler. The study of the Maliki code of laws flourished, systems of banking and credit developed, buildings of more tasteful design began to arise, habits of dress became more elegant; in short, the Sudan began to produce a middle class of cultured people adopting the style of living of their equivalents in the Maghrib and in Egypt. There was only one window on the civilized world, and that looked north across the desert. Askia al Haj and his court were determined to introduce the customs of the Khalif and the nobility of Egypt. These unfortunately included the purdah system of the harem. The absolute seclusion and segregation of women was a late development in the Muslim world brought about by the profligacy of some of the khalifs such as the Ummayad Walid II.[1] This early Persian custom was revived as a measure of protection against the debauched practices of the court, and it was not, as many believe, enjoined as part of the Muslim code of behaviour by the Prophet or by the Koran. The system of the veil and the harem did not become general, even in Baghdad where its protection was first felt to be needed, until the close of the tenth century, under Kadir b'Illah, who is said to have done more to stop the progress of the Muslim world than any other sovereign.

Learning, too, received a great impetus. The university of Sankore at Timbuktu became the centre of Muslim learning in the Sudan, indeed in Africa. It attracted the attention of professors from the Maghrib and Egypt, from the universities of Fez, Tunis and Cairo. Al Sadi records that 'a celebrated lawyer of Hijaz, arriving in Timbuktu with the intention of teaching, found the town full of Sudanese scholars. Seeing that they were superior to him in learning he returned to Fez, where he succeeded in obtaining employment.' Apart from a variety of other studies the art of teaching attracted many scholars. There was no more valued possession in Timbuktu than a book, and infinite care and toil were devoted to collecting libraries which became beyond price. In this manner the Arabic language, script and culture began to spread into neighbouring parts of the country, many of which were still primitive.

It is recorded that the sons of the Songhai kings used to leave the palace in Gao to receive an education in Timbuktu. Here they

[1] Ameer Ali, *A Short History of the Saracens*, p. 199.

rubbed shoulders with rich and poor alike in a common search for knowledge. Among the subjects taught were rhetoric, eloquence, and diction (to enable a student to expound the word of Allah), Maliki law, grammar, astronomy, history, and geography. Mathematics was somewhat neglected, and medicine relied largely on faith-cures.

THE POSITION OF SLAVES IN SOCIETY

Although it is not clear whether slavery was common in the Sudan prior to the coming of Islam, which accepted slavery as an institution subject to certain injunctions, by the time of the Askias in Songhai it had a recognized place in society. Slaves were normally procured by capture in war, and they remained the property of the captor. The slaves performed domestic chores for their masters or worked on their estates: the women would cook, while the men would do weaving, or look after the education of the children, or labour in the fields. The slaves married among themselves, though some became the concubines of their masters, in which case the children became full members of the master's family. All the Askias except the first were the children of concubines. Many slaves rose to hold high position and become truly heads of families themselves. They had a system of gradual assimilation to the artisan class in stages by generations: first the 'horso', next the 'sule', then the 'sule sule', and finally the 'gabibi', the old name, it will be remembered, of the cultivator. Up to the Moorish invasion of 1591 there was little slave trading and it was purely local. Afterwards a real commerce began. Whereas in 1591 only 200 slaves were sent across the desert, in 1593 no fewer than 1,200 were sent to Morocco to join the army being formed there. Later still an extensive trade in human misery grew up and by 1825 we know that Timbuktu got almost all its wealth from the export of slaves and the import of salt.[1]

Askia's first campaign, soon after his return from the *Haj*, was a jihad against the pagan Mossi in the south. He ravaged their country and brought back a number of Yatenga children, whom he had converted to Islam and trained to become soldiers, just like the Janissaries of the Ottoman Turks. He enlarged the empire to the west at the expense of the now feeble Mali as far as Galam on the upper Senegal river. But his most important campaigns

[1] Jean Rouch, *Les Songhay*, p. 40.

came later when in 1512–17, after an inconclusive struggle with the redoubtable Borgu, he overran the Hausa states.[1]

THE HAUSA STATES

These adventures will subsequently be described in some detail in the chapters of Part II covering the individual Emirates. At this stage let it suffice to say that the Hausa states originally consisted of Daura, Kano, Zaria, Gobir, Katsina, Rano, and Biram (identified by some with Garin Gabas, north of Hadejia). These were known as the Hausa Bakwai, the 'legitimate' seven. Another seven, the Banza Bakwai, the 'illegitimate' or upstart seven, developed to the south and west of the original group. These were Zamfara, Kebbi, Nupe, Gwari, Yauri, Yoruba or Ilorin, and (far away to the east) Kwararafa. Bello's *Infaq al Maisuri* gives Gwari as one of the original seven.

Each state had its own traditions and legends of origin, for example those in the Kano Chronicle. There are grounds for believing that some two thousand years ago a number of nomad Berber tribes were finding their way into the grasslands bordering the desert, settling alongside the local Sudanese peasants and eventually gaining ascendancy over them. This happened all the way along the line from Kanem in the east to Gao and Ghana, and beyond, in the west. Maintaining a typically Sudanic form of civilization, the immigrant and local mixture of peoples under the control of the legendary heroes and their descendants began to crystallize into small city states in the area now known as Northern Nigeria and the Niger Republic. These people seem to have been mainly engaged in farming and trade, and to have relied on walled cities for protection. These were of no great political account but they were efficiently ruled under a system of law and administration that owed much to the influence of Islam. It is strictly incorrect to refer to the Hausa people as if they belonged to a separate ethnic race or nation. There are only people who speak the Hausa language and adopt the Hausa mode of dress and life generally. The language is said to belong to the Chadic group,[2] but it has acquired a great many Arabic words, especially to express more abstract ideas, and the Arabic script known as Ajami was used in

[1] Leo Africanus, who visited the country about 1513, lists among the vassals of the 'King of Timbuktu': Walata, Mali, Jenne, Gobir, Zamfara, Katsina, Kano, Zaria, Aïr.

[2] C. K. Meek, in *Man*, October 1959, p. 182, and J. H. Greenberg, *Studies in African Linguistic Classification*, 1955, revised edition 1963.

a slightly modified form for the writing of Hausa before the British introduced the Roman alphabet at the beginning of this century. The Hausa language is a recognized lingua franca of trade spoken by many millions of people all over the Sudan and the Hausa trader has for many years been ubiquitous.

The Askia had a useful ally in Kanta, who later became the celebrated Sarkin Kebbi. As governor of Leka, part of the Songhai province of Kebbi, he had helped in the early campaigns against Zamfara, Zaria, Kano and Gobir. But he was a man of independent spirit. The Askia enlisted his support in a punitive expedition against the Tuareg town of Agades in Aïr as the one way in which to put a stop to the continual raiding by the elusive Tuareg camelry. But Kanta was not to be fobbed off with the jackal's share of the spoils. To quote Al Sadi: ' "Where is our booty?" demanded Kanta's men; "why don't you claim it?" To which Kanta replied: "I am told that if I do I shall be treated as a rebel, and I don't want to be a rebel on my own." "Then we will all be rebels together," said they, to which Kanta replied: "That is all I wanted to hear." ' He set himself up as an independent chief behind the massive walls of Surame in Kebbi, where the ruins can still be seen, and stoutly defied not only the Songhai hosts but the armies of Mai Ali of Bornu. Both enemies were routed before the walls of his impregnable citadel.

The town of Agades has remained predominantly Songhai since the day when Askia occupied it and planted a colony there. The people are mostly negroid and their language is still Songhai.[1] After the defection of Kanta, Askia was content with the extent of the Songhai dominions and the latter part of his thirty-five-year reign seems to have been comparatively free from wars. But his own declining years were a tragic anti-climax for one of the greatest emperors the Sudan was ever to know. He had been staunchly supported for the length of his reign by his able and devoted minister, Ali Fulan (who died later in Kano on his way to Mecca), just as he himself had stood by Sonni Ali. But he got no loyalty from his three sons, who rebelled against him in 1528 and forced him to abdicate in favour of the eldest, Musa, after killing his brother Yahia, who had answered his call for succour. Musa in his turn was assassinated, and succeeded by a nephew of the old Askia, Bankuri, who had been the commander

[1] E. W. Bovill, op. cit., p. 108.

of the defeated force at Surame. He it was who took the shameful step of removing the old monarch, now almost blind and decrepit, from the palace at Gao and incarcerating him on a miserable little mosquito-ridden island among the frogs of the Niger. Fortune, however, smiled just before the end. In 1536 Askia's son Ismail, the governor of Dandi, drove out Bankuri and brought his father back to Gao, where he ended his days in peace two years later. His great square mausoleum can be seen to this day in Gao.

At one time the Askia employed as political adviser a certain Sheikh Muhammad al Maghili, a celebrated Muslim preacher from the Maghrib, who sought refuge from his enemies in Katsina and Kano. He was a contemporary of Machiavelli and he too produced a book of advice on statecraft for princes, this time for the Sarkin Kano, Mohamman Rumfa.[1] Although his preaching resulted in more than one Jewish massacre by Tuareg in the central Sahara, he is still revered as a holy man in parts of the Sudan. He died in 1504.

But Al Maghili's name came to be remembered for more than his piety. It was his famous judgment in regard to the justification of the Askia's action in usurping the throne of Sonni Ali that provided the necessary precedent for the Fulani jihad of 1804 in Gobir. The Askia, recently back from his pilgrimage, was having qualms about the legitimacy of his rule. Al Maghili was specifically asked to decide. His judgment not only vindicated the Askia but declared that a jihad against Sonni Ali and his subjects was more urgent than that against the pure pagans because 'they have covered truth with falsehood in a way that makes a number of the ignorant Muslims go astray'. The Shehu could show an exact parallel between Sonni Ali in Songhai and the Habe kings in Hausaland. In both cases their territories were *bilad al harb*,[2] thus not merely justifying but positively demanding a jihad.

LEO AFRICANUS

But for us a far more illuminating traveller came under the name of Leo Africanus, though he was born Al Hassan and lived in Fez. He seems to have visited the Sudan twice, in 1509 and 1513, as an emissary of the Sharif of Fez to find out about the people whose ruler had created a stir a few years back by crossing

[1] For an extract from T. H. Baldwin's translation of the *Obligations of Princes*, see Thomas Hodgkin, *Nigerian Perspectives*, p. 90 and footnote.

[2] i.e. enemy territory. See p. 385.

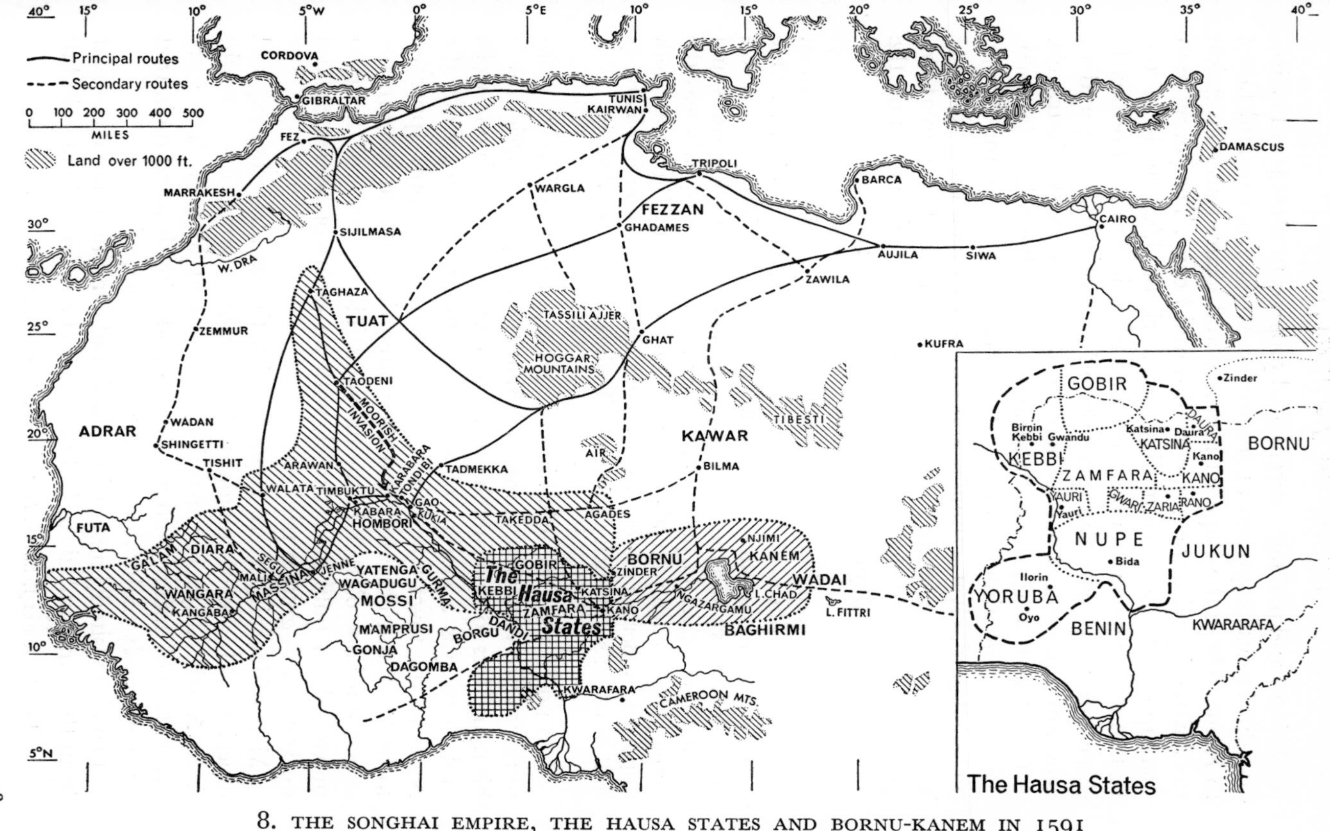

8. THE SONGHAI EMPIRE, THE HAUSA STATES AND BORNU-KANEM IN 1591

the Sahara and making a ceremonial progress to Mecca and Cairo. In 1518 he was captured at sea in the Mediterranean and taken to Rome, where the Pope set him free and secured his conversion to Christianity with the name of Giovanni Leone. The young man thereupon set about compiling his work on his travels in the Italian language based on his original notes in Arabic. For nearly three hundred years European knowledge of the Sudan and its geography depended on the account of these remarkable travels.

It is clear that the trans-Saharan trade was flourishing in north Africa at this time. Important commodities from the Sudan included gold, civet, eunuchs and slaves. Leo took the Sijilmasa–Taghaza–Walata route to Timbuktu, which made no great impression on him as regards buildings, though he remarked on the mosque, as mentioned earlier, and the palace:

> The houses were mud huts roofed with thatch, with the exception of two stone edifices of hewn masonry built by Es Saheli. . . . One could see numerous shops kept by merchants and smiths, and weavers abounded. Slave women were given the job of selling foodstuffs and showed themselves in public with their faces uncovered, whereas the better class women were always veiled. One could buy European cloth imported by Berber merchants, livestock, milk and butter in plenty, as well as corn; salt which came from Teghazza was very dear.[1]

Leo noted that the inhabitants, and especially the foreign community were very rich, 'insomuch that the king has married both his daughters to rich merchants'. There were plenty of good wells and there was a system of aqueducts to bring water from the Niger to the town when the river flooded. The people appeared to be kind and cheerful, and they often danced and sang in the streets until one o'clock in the morning. The governor of the town moved about only on a camel, with an escort of horsemen and decked out in golden trinkets.

Men of learning were received with the greatest respect, and especially Muslim theologians. Any Arabic manuscripts brought from North Africa commanded their weight in gold. 'Here are great store of doctors, judges, divines and other learned men, that are generously maintained at the king's expense.'

Leo also visited Jenne, where he found conditions not dissimilar from those in Timbuktu. In both places he found coin of gold but

[1] H. Jaunet et J. Barry, *Histoire de l'Afrique Occidentale Française*, p. 50.

without any stamp or superscription. In Mali town, where the poor king had been so humbled by the Askia that he was scarce able to maintain his family, he found prosperous conditions in which learning quietly flourished. 'The people of this region excel all other negroes in wit, civility, and industry.' In the great unwalled town of Gao he found the same humble houses as in Timbuktu and the same affluence among the trading community. Imported horses from the north were always eagerly bought by the Askia and the nobility. He noticed the slave market where a young slave of fifteen would fetch six ducats, as would children generally.[1] By comparison horses bought in Europe for ten ducats would fetch forty or fifty in Gao, European cloth would be sold for from three to ten or more ducats a yard depending on its texture. 'The king of this region has a certain private palace in which he keeps a large number of concubines and slaves, which are looked after by eunuchs.'

Leo continued eastward to the recently conquered Hausa states. In Gobir he noted the cottage industries of weaving and leather work; and also the cultivation of rice just as it is grown today in Argungu and parts of Sokoto. In Zamfara, Zaria, Katsina and Kano he found Songhai governors installed to collect the tribute for the Askia. The kings of Katsina, Zaria, and Zamfara had all been slain, but the king of Kano after stout resistance had been allowed to retain his office subject to the annual payment of tribute. He had also taken one of the Askia's daughters in marriage, perhaps as a means to secure his loyalty. One of the Hausa kings 'in my time was slain by Askia . . . and his sons were gelt, and accounted among the king's eunuchs . . . and most of the inhabitants were carried off as slaves by the Askia'.[2]

Finally, before returning north in about 1513 by the eastern route across the desert, Leo visited Bornu, which was beyond the reach of the Songhai armies. The most extraordinary thing about Leo's informative descriptions, to which we were so indebted for our knowledge of conditions of life in the Sudan at the beginning of the sixteenth century, is that he went completely wrong in his description of the direction of flow of the river Niger.[3] 'The Niger flows westward into the ocean . . . we navigated it with the current from Timbuktu to Jenne and Mali.' Yet this was one of the geographical matters about which the world was most

[1] Jaunet et Barry, op. cit., p. 50. [2] E. W. Bovill, op. cit., p. 130. [4] Ibid., p. 130.

concerned. It was nearly three centuries later that Mungo Park in 1796 knew that Leo Africanus had made his great mistake, when with his own eyes at Segu he saw the river flowing to the east. Nothing, perhaps, can illustrate more vividly how remote and isolated from the world was this vast expanse of fertile country nestling in the womb of Africa.

ASKIA MUHAMMAD'S SUCCESSORS

For fifty years after the old Askia's death in 1538 there was no great change within the Songhai empire under the eight Askias who succeeded him. The vassal states, including the Hausa countries mentioned above, continued to pay tribute but from time to time one or other needed the attention of an expedition. One such was sent against Katsina in 1554, when the Songhai force, heavily outnumbered by nearly twenty to one, were captured after a tremendous struggle and chivalrously returned to the Askia with their wounds healed.[1] This was in the reign of Askia Daud, who had succeeded Ishak, the successor of Ismail. Daud (1548–82) proved himself to be no mean member of his dynasty. He took great interest in the mosques and buildings of Timbuktu, causing many of them to be restored. His final exploit was to subdue the Fulani of Massina in the region of the upper Niger.

Within ten years of his death, as we shall now see, the great empire of Songhai was to vanish as the result of a disaster that was as sudden as it was unpredictable.

[1] See pp. 162–3.

IX. KANEM AND THE BORNU EMPIRE[1]

EARLY IMMIGRANTS

Meanwhile, a thousand miles away to the east and confronting the great empires of the western Sudan across the buffer Hausa states, had been growing the rival power of Kanem, the country of the Kanuri and Kanembu people north and east of Lake Chad.

From as early as the seventh or eighth century, possibly even before, there seems to have been a movement of white nomads from the direction of Abyssinia, perhaps initially from the Yemen, into the area known as Borku, which lay to the east of Bilma and Kawar. These immigrants settled here for a time before some moved north to the hills of Tibesti and others moved south to the greener lands of Chad. Tradition has it that the newcomers found in occupation of Bilma and the surrounding country a giant race of people called So, with whom they came to intermingle. The So were supposed to have come originally from Fezzan.

After this first important immigration from the orient there were further migratory movements from the north, originating from the Arab conquests of Egypt, Cyrenaica and Tripolitania towards the end of the seventh century. These later arrivals would have been largely Berbers and their Tuareg kinsmen; and with them may have come the Tubu people including some of the people from Abyssinia who had gone to Tibesti from Borku.

Later still came roving bands of various Arab tribes, from Kordofan to the east, from Tibesti and from Kawar to the north. All of these groups gravitated towards the grasslands of the south. The word Kanem in Tubu meant 'south'[2]—the south or promised land of their dreams. Similar groups were finding their way into the Sudan all along the edge of the desert to the west through the Hausa states to the Niger basin.

[1] This chapter owes much to an admirable translation by Miss Sheila Richards of Yves Urvoy's unfinished *Histoire de l'Empire du Bornou*, carefully compiled in the form of notes based on the researches of the leading authorities on Bornu history. As one of the Nigerian Emirates, Bornu receives detailed treatment in Chapter XXIII.

[2] The name Kanem means South land and was in use (Al Bakri) according to a note by Urvoy, who states that in Tubu the word 'anem' means 'south' and K is a substantival prefix.

One tribe of Berbers, the Zaghawa, made its mark by establishing an ascendancy over the earlier arrivals, mixed to some extent as they were by then with the Sudanese So. Some believe that they may have been the early occupants of Kukia on the Niger, who drove out the Sorko and the Gabibi from Gao to found the Dia dynasty in Songhai. They were powerful in the region of Aïr and in Tibesti, and their influence was both widespread and lasting. To this day people of this name are found in Wadai, and their descendants still work in Nigeria as esoteric groups of metal-workers and leather-workers.

Legend credits the nomad immigrants with a cunning stratagem to gain domination over the local Sudanese by a process of infiltration. They did not dare attack the giant So, but they got the consent of the local chief to live alongside them. After a period of years the So began to admire the way in which the newcomers painted their nails with henna, and they begged to be shown how it was done. The process was then explained by which the hands were stained with henna and then wrapped in leather thongs. Naïvely allowing themselves to become bound hand and fist they fell easy victims to the treacherous nomads. The story turns up again and again as illustrative of the methods of peaceful penetration adopted by the immigrants rather than conquest, and their reliance on their wits.[1]

THE SEFAWA AND THE DUGUWA DYNASTY

The great authorities on Bornu history according to Yves Urvoy, who himself did a painstaking compilation of the work of his predecessors in the form of an uncompleted history published in 1949, were Barth, Nachtigal, Landeroin and Palmer. From the records discovered by these[2] the first king of Kanem is held to be Sef, the son of Dhi Yazan (or D'u Yazan), who was followed by his son, Ibrahim, or Brem as the Kanuri diminutive goes. But the true founder of the first dynasty was probably Dugu of the Beni-

[1] Yves Urvoy, op. cit., p. 23. Cf. the Fika legend on page 360.

[2] Sheikh Masfarma Umr Ibn Othman (*c* 1500) wrote a history of Bornu which is said to exist but which Palmer was unable to trace. Abridgements, however, provided extracts which are found all over Bornu. Two copies of an important one of these called 'The Diwan of the Sultans of Bornu' were obtained by Dr Barth from the Shettima Makaramma about 1853, and a translation is included in H. R. Palmer's *Mai Idris* (1926) together with one of the Kanuri Girgam of the Magumi Mais. This book as well as *Sudanese Memoirs* by the same author contains a wealth of valuable material on Bornu.

Sef (Sefawa or Sefuwa), whom most Arab authorities identify with the Zaghawa. It must have been about 800 that Dugu and his Sefawa carved themselves a slice of So territory and thus originated the Kanembu people. The Dugu family was to rule for over a thousand years over Kanem and Bornu, until 1846, with the title of Mai. Palmer observes that Dugu means 'the son of a daughter of a Mai' and thus 'heir' in a matrilineal society. Dugu, therefore, may not have been the founder's name. Similarly, the name of Dugu's successor, Fune, merely means that he wore a mouth veil. But both words indicate that the Duguwa Mais were of Tuareg affinity, counting their descent through females. Palmer believed that it was not until the adoption of Islam about 1100 that they began to count descent through males, according to the Arab custom, and that they then invented a pedigree stretching back to Sef ibn Dhi Yazan, after first trying out the value of a professed connexion of similar nature with the Ummayad dynasty in Damascus.[1] Sef was a historic Yemeni figure. He descended from the Himyarite kings and after the conquest of Yemen by the Abyssinians in 525, he inspired the Arab resistance, called in the Persians to his aid leading to the Persian conquest of 575, and became viceroy.

The pre-Islam dynasty of Duguwa Mais lasted until the conversion of the 12th Mai, Umme or Hume (1085–97), the first Sultan.[2] Gradually the power of Kanem matured, with Njimi now the capital. The first written records now begin from the pens of Arab writers such as Al Bakri and Yakubi in the eleventh century. They are followed by those of Al Idrisi and Ibn Said in the twelfth and thirteenth. Al Bakri mentions the presence in Kanem in 1068 of people descended from the Ummayad adherents who had fled south to escape persecution at the hands of the Abbasids following their accession to the khalifate in 750.[3]

ISLAM AND THE SECOND DYNASTY OF SEFAWA

The period from 1085 to 1224 was one of growing prosperity and power. Both Hume and his son Dunama I made the

[1] H. R. Palmer's review of Urvoy's work in *Africa*, April 1950, vol. XX, No. 2, pp. 162–3.

[2] See Thomas Hodgkin, *Nigerian Perspectives*, pp. 68–71, for translations of early documents relating to Umme or Hume and his successors.

[3] Raymond Mauny, *Tableau Géographique, etc.*, p. 461.

pilgrimage, the latter three times,[1] and their horizons widened. The Mais had continued the custom of marrying within the noble circle and especially with the Tomagheras,[2] a noble Tubu tribe, but mixed marriages now become permissible and the chronicle tells us of Selma (1193–1210) as the first black king. The word Selma means black and we are told that Hume's father was called Selma,[3] so that perhaps the mixture of blood began much earlier. Dunama's son Biri I was quite ineffective. He was actually put in prison by his mother for executing some thieves instead of following the Muslim law and having their hands cut off—an interesting commentary on the power of the king's mother and the punctilious regard for the *Shari'a* law.

By the beginning of the thirteenth century Kanem was unquestionably the dominant state in the Sudan.[4] A sound political and administrative system of government had been established, with a mixture of Muslim law and pre-Muslim tradition. The Mai, whose legitimacy was by now based on the Arab, non-Sudanic, principle of patrilineal descent, but who retained the matriarchal deference to the mother, sister, and wife of the ruler—the Magira, the Magaram and Gumsu—had supreme though not unfettered power.[5] He was mysterious, withdrawn and semi-divine according to the typical Sudanic pattern. He was advised by a council of twelve, some of whom were sons of slaves. At the same time much of the wealth of the country depended on the export of slaves captured in the south to the markets of Egypt and North Africa.

There were four provincial governors, all of whom were relatives and members of the royal house as a matter of policy. The most important were the Yerima, controlling the lands of Yeri against attacks from the Tuareg, and the Galadima, who controlled the lands to the west. The powerful army was commanded by the Kaigama. The Mai chose his successor from among his sons, or if he had none from among his brothers; until accession

[1] He was drowned on the last pilgrimage in the Red Sea by Egyptians swamping the boat. See 'The Diwan of the Sultans of Bornu' mentioned in footnote 2, p. 90.

[2] Y. Urvoy, op. cit., and Roland Oliver and J. D. Fage, *A Short History of Africa*, p. 63.

[3] Y. Urvoy, op. cit., Book 1, Chapter 3. Hume is said here to be the son of Selma and Taigaram, a Kayi, but the works mentioned in footnote 2, p. 90 refer merely to Umme Jilmi, i.e. son of Jil or Abd al Jalil.

[4] Thomas Hodgkin, op. cit., p. 4.

[5] Ibid., p. 22; Y. Urvoy, op. cit., p. 39.

he was called Ciroma with a seat on the council of twelve. As in the other Sudanese empires, the entrusting of power to close relatives sometimes defeated its object by promoting rivalry rather than loyalty. The intrigues of the Mainas—princes and princesses of the blood royal—gave the Mai constant anxiety. Women occupied an important role in society. The queen mother, or Magira, who was not necessarily the Mai's parent,[1] had enormous power in her right to advise the Mai against any action of which she disapproved, and the Gumsu or first wife held high official status.

During the thirteenth century, just about when Sundiata Keita finally destroyed Ghana, Kanem reached her peak in the reign of the 17th Mai, Dunama Dabalemi (1221–59),[2] with diplomatic contacts in Egypt and North Africa and no rival power in the Sudan.

ARAB WRITERS

Evidence of Kanem's fame and importance comes from the writings of Ibn Battuta (1304–68), the famous Arab traveller, Ibn Khaldun (1332–1406), the greatest of the medieval Arab historians, Al-Maqrizi (1364–1442) from Cairo, and Al-Qalqashandi (died 1418) also from Cairo.

Al-Maqrizi wrote as follows:

> All the Sudanese derive their origin from Fut[3] the son of Ham. Their tribes number nineteen. . . . The inhabitants of Kanem are a great people, and for the most part Muslims. Their city is called Njimi. . . . Their king is a nomad in mode of life. When he sits on his throne his courtiers prostrate themselves before him, and fall on their faces. His army, horse and foot and transport, numbers 100,000. Between Njimi and Yalamlam is an immense number of pagans. The King of Kanem has five feudatory kings subject to him. The war-horses of Kanem are small. . . .
>
> Their king in the year 700 A.H. [A.D. 1300] was al-Hajj Ibrahim of the sons of Saif ibn Dhi Yazan, who occupied the throne of Kanem, which is the seat of power of Bornu. There reigned after him his son al-Hajj Idris. Then Idris's brother, Daud ibn Ibrahim; then Umar ibn Idris; then the brother of the latter, Uthman ibn Idris. A few years

[1] See Palmer's review mentioned in footnote 1 on page 91.

[2] Yves Urvoy gives 1210–24, the period after which he calls the Dark Ages.

[3] Another source says that Fut went to the Indies. See the extract from Wahab ibn Munabbeh on page 39.

before the year 800 A.H. [A.D. 1397] the people of Kanem revolted, and there only remained to the Saifawa the Nubians of their kingdom, who are Muslims and wage holy war on the people of Kanem. . . . The first seat of this empire on the side which is near to Egypt is called Zuwila. Between this town and the town of Kaukau [probably Gao], which is on the opposite [western] frontier, the distance is three months' march.[1]

At that time Zuwila was an important trade centre in the Fezzan, on the Kanem–Kawar–Cyrenaica caravan route. Al Bakri described it in the eleventh century as 'a town without walls situated in the middle of the desert . . . It is from Zuwila that slaves are exported to Ifriqiya and to neighbouring countries. Purchases are made there through the medium of short pieces of red stuff. Beyond the desert of Zuwila, and forty days from that town, is situated the land of Kanem, a race of idolatrous Negroes, whom it is very difficult to visit . . .'[2]

Al Maqrizi goes on to describe some of the habits and customs of Kanem, *vide* a further quotation from his work given on page 310. Some seventy or eighty years later Leo Africanus speaks of the wealth of the King of Bornu, 'his spurs, his bridles, platters, dishes, pots, and other vessels wherein his meat and drink are brought to the table, are all of pure gold: yea, and the chains of his dogs and hounds are of gold also.'[3] The king, he says, used to buy large numbers of horses from the Berber merchants, paying for them at the rate of fifteen and sometimes twenty slaves for each animal. He seemed to grudge paying in gold.

Al-Qalqashandi quotes from a letter sent to the Sultan of Egypt by Uthman Biri ibn Idris, King of Bornu, in 1392, which complains of certain Judhama Arabs who have been capturing 'our free subjects—women and children and old people, and our relatives, and other Muslims . . . they have killed our prince, Umar ibn Idris, a martyr—he is our brother, the son of our father, al-Hajj Idris, son of al-Hajj Ibrahim; and we are the sons of Saif ibn Dhi Yazan, the father of our tribe, the Arab, of the family of Quraysh, as we have been informed by our learned men. . . . These Arabs . . . are selling them to the slave-dealers in Egypt and Syria and elsewhere, and some they keep for themselves.' The writer

[1] Thomas Hodgkin, *Nigerian Perspectives*, pp. 76, 77. The quotation continues on p. 310.
[2] Ibid., pp. 67, 68.
[3] Ibid., p. 105.

implored the Sultan to send messengers to all his lands to have the captives found and put to the test of the Muslim faith, so that they could return to liberty and to Islam.[1]

THE LOSS OF KANEM

Barth's Diwan records that in the time of Dunama Dabalemi 'there occurred civil war through the greed of his children and in his time also the princes went apart into different regions. There was no discord before this time.'[2] Yves Urvoy marks the period 1224 to 1507 as the Dark Ages. For the first 250 years history is confused, turning on civil wars waged between contestants for the throne. It seems that the principle of descent through the male line, adopted from the Arabs with the conversion to Islam of Hume some 150 years previously, was partially abandoned, with the result that there were constant feuds between brothers and cousins. It began with Dunama's two sons, Kade and Kashim Biri, and then, when Kade's line came to an end, it continued with the two sides descended from Idris and Daud, both sons of Haj Ibrahim Nigale. Daud was expelled from his capital, Njimi, about 1386, and his house finally evacuated Kanem about 1400.[3] The chaos caused by incessant war broke off the contacts between Bornu and the outside world from the middle of the fourteenth to the end of the fifteenth century, when the dynasty established itself west of Chad at Ngazargamu under Mai Ali Ghaji Dunamami, and revived its power and prestige.[4] During this time there had been a steady trickle of learned Muslims following on after the fall of Baghdad to the Mongols and there are sufficiently reliable traditions that the court of Kanem still spoke Arabic in the fourteenth century.

The rival house that drove Daud out of Kanem were cousins on the mother's side from the tribe of Kayi or Bulala, who had established themselves in the region of Lake Fittri. The civil war is therefore referred to as the Bulala wars. Concurrent with these wars were the continual rebellions of the So tribes in the south.

The country to the west of Chad, which the Kanuri now came to occupy, was known as Bornu and it had been a province of the

[1] Hodgkin, op. cit., pp. 77, 78.

[2] H. R. Palmer, *History of the First Twelve Years of the Reign of Mai Idris Alooma of Bornu*, para. 17 on p. 87.

[3] Ibid., p. 2.

[4] Ibid., p. 3.

Kanem empire. The origin of the name is said to be Bar-an or place of the Bar-an, i.e. Barbars.[1] Some say that the word comes from Bahr Nuh, the sea of Noah. To begin with, its extent was quite small—hardly larger than the present district of Geidam. To the west and south were the various pagan tribes (known all over the Sudan by a generic name of Lemlem or Demdem or something with a similar sound) until one reached Kano, at that time a modest settlement at the foot of the Dala rock, or the territory of Kwararafa.

After being driven out of Kanem and their capital Njimi, the Kanuri had to make do with a number of temporary resting-places until in about 1470 Ngazargamu was founded on the Komadugu (river) Yobe near Geidam as the capital of Bornu and the Kanuri people. It remained the capital for about 340 years, despite the fact that Njimi was reoccupied at the beginning of the next century. Fortunes began to revive with Mai Ali Ghaji—of the Idris branch. Having killed Othman ibn Kade, the last of the Daud branch to reign, he installed Umr the grandson of Idris and in due course became Mai in about 1475.

REVIVAL OF POWER IN THE SIXTEENTH CENTURY

The sixteenth century was a golden age for Bornu. During five reigns the country was triumphant and prosperous. On the death of Mai Ali in 1503, his son, Idris Katagarmabe, defeated the Bulala and brought Kanem once again under Sefawa rule, after a lapse of 125 years. But the royal house did not resume residence in Njimi. Kanem was run as a protectorate with the Bulala as vassal kings, a situation which continued for about a century though the Bulala made more than one attempt to shake off the mild Sef control.

On the death of Idris in 1526, his son, Muhammad, succeeded to the throne and was reputed to be a 'warrior and fortunate', extending his power to the west. His brother, Ali, who was the next Mai, must have been the famous Bornu king who tried conclusions with the redoubtable Kanta of Kebbi, Askia's rebellious vassal. Mai Ali had been called to the assistance of the Aïr Tuareg to fight off Kanta. He was bold enough to attack Kanta in his fortress of Surame and force him to evacuate it, but fearful of being cut off so far from home he beat a retreat, marching through

[1] Palmer, op. cit., p. 6.

Katsina Laka, south of Katsina. He was hotly pursued by Kanta and got the worst of an engagement near Nguru. On the return journey Kanta was ambushed and killed at Dan Ashita in Katsina.

On Ali's death in 1546 his son, later to become king as Idris Alooma, was either not yet born or was too young to succeed, so that the next king was his nephew, Dunama (1546–63), followed by Dunama's son Abdallah (1564–70).[1] In each reign there was a great famine. Dunama scored a big success against the rebellious Bulala in Kanem, but he had trouble in meeting attacks from the Tubu and Tuareg in the north and from Kwararafa in the south. For a while after Abdallah's death, his sister, the Magira or Queen Mother, Aisa Kili, acted as regent until Idris Alooma was old enough to become king. The latter's mother was the daughter of the Bulala king. During the reign of Dunama and Abdullahi, she feared for the safety of herself and her child, and she is said to have had built for him the Gambaru palace at some distance from the court and capital.[2]

MAI IDRIS ALOOMA (1571–1603)

Of all the Maghumi kings Idris Alooma was the most famous. He was the outstanding figure of the period and during his reign all the neighbouring tribes were subdued, and conquest followed conquest. In contrast was the tragic fall of Bornu's great rival in the west, the Askia of Songhai, before the forces of Morocco in 1591. From that shattering event he learnt the value of fire-arms, and from Tripoli he is said to have secured the services of musketeers to teach his men. After campaigns in the subjugation of the So tribes, he harassed the various settlements of the Kanawa, though he could not actually capture the Kano citadel of Dala. There followed the defeat of the Tuareg of Aïr, and the Tubu in the north, which secured his communications with North Africa, and enabled him to make the pilgrimage to Mecca as befitted a great Muslim potentate. To the end he continued to make successful war against the Mandara and other hostile tribes, with frequent state visits to display his power in Kanem. He met a warrior's

[1] Various sources give various dates. The dates given here follow those supplied by Palmer on the Diwan published with his *Mai Idris* (see above). Urvoy gives Dunama as 1548–66 and Abdallah as 1566–73. Some dates given in Chapter XXIII are inconsistent with these in so far as they draw on different sources. In any case the dates from whatever source can only be approximate.

[2] See page 314.

death in action in about 1603, and was buried near Lake Alo (hence his name), not far from modern Maiduguri.

THE SEVENTEENTH AND EIGHTEENTH CENTURIES

There followed a long period of uneventful history. The three sons of Idris ruled in turn after him and peace reigned. But under Ali ibn Haj Umr, some seventy odd years after Mai Idris, there was trouble from Kwararafa and also from the Tuareg of Aïr. At one time both enemies at once were besieging the capital, but Ali managed to beat them each separately. There was a terrible famine at this time, and again about 1725 there was a famine that lasted for seven years. It is recorded that between 1731 and 1743 Bornu attacked Kano, already weak from wars with Kwararafa, Katsina, Gobir and Zamfara. The last three kings up to 1810 were said to be marabouts.[1]

How eventually Ngazargamu fell to the Fulani invaders and how the fortunes of Bornu were restored by the intervention of Shehu Laminu, Al Kanemi, is told in Chapter XXIII. The Sef dynasty with the firm support of Al Kanemi behind the scenes somehow managed to make a show of kingship in Kukawa until 1846, a span of over a thousand years. Henceforth, after an abortive plot to oust the house of Al Kanemi had failed, the execution of Mai Ibrahim and the death in battle of his son, Ali, obliged Shehu Umar and his descendants to take up the reins and rule as Sultans of Bornu.

[1] See Yves Urvoy, op. cit., Book III, Chapter 3, where they are described as king-priests.

X. THE MOORISH INVASION OF THE SUDAN[1]

MOORISH DESIGNS ON THE SUDAN

Towards the end of the sixteenth century, while the Sudan was basking in the sunshine of peace and order, disturbed only intermittently by minor affrays, and was enjoying the commercial prosperity that comes with firm government, a cataclysmic event shook the Maghrib when in 1578 an army of 26,000 Portuguese was annihilated by the Moors of Morocco at Al Kasr al Kabir, north of Fez. The victor's brother, Mulai Ahmed, on the Sharif's death in the moment of triumph, assumed the title Al Mansur, the Victorious. He found himself in a strong position to extract the maximum of benefit from the ransom of his Christian captives and to establish advantageous relations with the European powers. To the disgust of her Spanish enemies, Queen Elizabeth of England supplied Al Mansur with arms, and timber for his ships, in exchange for saltpetre for the making of gunpowder.

It is clear that the Sharif Al Mansur had his eyes on the gold and riches reputed to lie in the Sudan, and he was determined to fit out an expedition to cross the desert and possess himself of their source. And there was also the possession of the salt-mines at Taghaza to occupy his mind. With no communication routes open to the sea, the Sudanese placed a high value on the supply of salt, one of the few commodities which the people lacked as a normal necessity. Salt was accordingly prized as something for which even gold would be disgorged. The whole process of procuring the salt from inaccessible mines, which required the skilled co-operation of a specialized labour force of slaves under Mesufa Tuareg direction, and transporting it across the desert to exchange with gold, which only certain special agents knew how to get, was as complicated as the diamond trade today.

For no clear reason the salt-mines at Taghaza, though less than a month's march from Morocco, were not under Moorish but

[1] A full and excellent account of the fall of Songhai is given in Chapters 16 and 17 of E. W. Bovill's *The Golden Trade of the Moors*, to which this chapter is indebted.

Songhai control. Efforts to get the Askia to cede them to the Sharif had failed more than once, though the Moors sometimes raided the mines. Eventually, after the Moorish victory at Al Kasr, the Askia tried to appease the threatening Al Mansur by agreeing to lease the mines for a year. This uneasy arrangement continued for a time until Al Mansur sent a force to capture Taghaza; but the plan miscarried when the slaves fled and the Askia forbade anyone to return, so that the mines were abandoned by both sides. This serious loss led to the discovery of other less plentiful supplies at Taodeni, south of Taghaza.

JUDAR PASHA AND HIS ARMY

It was in October 1590 that Al Mansur revealed the outcome of his years of careful preparation when a well-equipped army under the command of Judar Pasha headed south from Marrakesh to invade Songhai. Judar was a young blue-eyed Spanish eunuch, who had been captured as an infant after a raid on the coast of Spain. He had about 4,000 men under his command, all picked troops. Apart from some Moorish lancers and a number of spahis, they largely consisted of Europeans, including Italians, Greeks, French, English, and above all Spaniards. The official language of the force was Spanish. There were Christian musketeers and European artillerymen to serve the six large cannon and other smaller pieces. As with the modern French Foreign Legion there were many adventurers, deserters from other armies and former prisoners, whose aims were more probably plunder than glory. But, like pirates, they were held by iron discipline from the leaders. They had to be. We are told that there were 8,000 camels and 1,000 horses so that the problems of water and forage were formidable.

The route followed was through Lektawa, Taghaza, Taodeni and Arawan, avoiding Walata to the west. This was a tremendous feat of endurance across hundreds of miles of frightful, waterless wilderness. First of all no one in Songhai believed that such a feat was remotely possible; and when rumours of the army's progress trickled in to the Askia, it was felt certain that the attack would come from the direction of Walata to the west. In fact, Judar made the Niger at a place called Karabara (near the present town of Bamba) in the last week of February 1591. All was understandably confusion among the Songhai. Ill fortune also played its part. A stray band of marauding Tuareg happened to waylay the Askia's messengers hurrying to warn the northern chiefs to fill in the wells on the approach trails to the river. Had the wells been denied them, the whole invading army might have perished and the whole course of Sudanese history altered. As it was, according to some estimates, less than half the force survived the crossing and the *Tarikh al Fattash* says that only 1,000 men took part in the first battle with the Songhai forces.[1]

From Karabara, after a few days' rest, Judar marched downstream towards Gao, harried on the way by canoe loads of Songhai patrols. He sent ahead to offer terms for surrender, which were rejected as a sign of weakness. In the middle of April the Songhai army, which greatly outnumbered the invaders, took up a defensive position at Tondibi, near the river and some thirty-five miles from Gao, and here a decisive battle was fought.

The outcome of the battle was, as so often, a triumph for modern weapons and discipline. Twenty to thirty thousand ill-armed warriors crumpled up in the face of the terrors of musketry. Panic supervened: men and animals fled in disorder. It was a complete rout. The *Tarikh al Sudan* says that the Moroccans met the Askia on their way to Gao at a place called Tenkondibo'o, near Tonbodi.[2] The Askia was at the head of 12,500 horsemen and 30,000 foot soldiers. 'When the army was defeated they threw their shields to the ground and squatted on them like seats, awaiting the arrival of Djouder's troops, who massacred them in this attitude without their making any resistance and this was because flight could only end in a rout. The Moroccans stripped them of the gold bracelets they wore on their arms.' Ishak II, 'the last and worst of the Askias', tried to buy off the victors with offers of 12,500 ounces of gold and 1,000 slaves if they would depart at once to Morocco. The offer was sent off to the Sharif with a recommendation for its acceptance, since Judar was anxious to get away from a fever-ridden climate and return home. Meanwhile he was persuaded to move upstream to the healthier region of Timbuktu, a march of about a month, and await the Sharif's answer to the peace proposals.

[1] *Tarikh al Fattash*, p. 264, and R. Mauny, *Tableau Géographique*, p. 286.
[2] *Tarikh al Sudan*, p. 219. Tonbodi is presumably a *lapsus calami* for Tondibi.

GAO AND TIMBUKTU UNDER THE MOORS

Both Gao and Timbuktu proved infinitely disappointing to Judar and his men. They had been led to believe that they would find legendary splendours with gold and riches abounding. Instead they found nothing to compare with what they had left. In a letter to the Sharif of Morocco Judar wrote: 'The house of the head donkeyman in Marrakesh is worth more than the palace of the emperor of Gao.' Judar refrained from molesting the citizens of Timbuktu and the life of the university town continued more or less as before. Timbuktu seems to have enjoyed a position of some independence, having no governor other than the *qadi*, whose authority was widely respected. It was he who managed to keep relations with the Moroccans tolerably sweet.

The Sharif's reaction to Judar's dispatch was anger and disappointment: anger at Judar's clemency and disappointment at the picture of poverty that had been painted. There must be gold there somewhere. Judar had to be replaced. For this the Sharif selected Mahmud ibn Zergun, a Spanish or Portuguese convert to Islam, and, like Judar, a eunuch brought up in the palace. The new pasha crossed the desert with a small escort in seven short weeks and soon showed that this was a measure of his metal. Taking over the supreme command from Judar he set off from Timbuktu in search of Askia Ishak. He defeated the Songhai forces opposing him at Bamba, and Ishak became a fugitive in Gurma, where he lost his life. His successor to his unenviable throne offered submission to the Sharif, but when he arrived with his companions to swear his fealty they were all, on Mahmud's orders, treacherously murdered.

RESISTANCE IN THE SOUTH

A puppet Askia was then installed in Timbuktu, but a real Askia in the south, Nuh, kept up the fight in Dandi. He withdrew in good order to the protection of the dense bush of Borgu and broke the spirit of the invaders by skilful guerrilla tactics. The Borgawa have always been past masters in the arts of ambush and night attack, and they had a reputation for their knowledge of witchcraft and arrow-poisons.

Having to own defeat to the combination of resolute opponents, tropical bush infested with tsetse-fly and mosquitoes, bad water and enervating climate, Mahmud, like others before and since, acknowledged the impenetrability of the belt of forest denying the Sudan an outlet to the sea. He withdrew to Timbuktu and appealed to Morocco for reinforcements.

THE CRUELTIES OF MOORISH RULE

Amidst all the ruthless brutality of the Moors it is pleasant to record the sympathetic and considerate behaviour of the *kaid* Mami, who had been sent by Mahmud from Borgu with a picked force of arquebusiers to settle disturbances in Timbuktu. His benevolent control won over the confidence of the people as never before, and had he remained in unfettered charge the naturally peace-loving population as a whole could have easily come to terms with the Moors, as indeed Jenne started to do. But Mahmud's return from his failure in Borgu changed this happy prospect. With calculated perfidy he tricked the leading citizens of Timbuktu into depositing their valuables in a place of supposed sanctuary before collecting in the Sankore mosque for a ceremony of allegiance to the Sharif. The doors of the mosque were slammed shut on the unfortunate dupes, their valuables were looted from where they had been conveniently deposited, their women were violated and many of the prisoners were slaughtered.

Nor was this the only demonstration of Moorish methods. Envoys were sent to the Sharif in Marrakesh to plead for more humane government on the lines of Mami's. They were received with apparent kindness and escorted on their way home. But a messenger had preceded them to order the arrest of all the scholars and learned men of Timbuktu. A little later they were herded in droves to cross the desert with their families as exiles to Marrakesh. Among them went Ahmed Baba the historian.

Nemesis soon overtook the brutal but fearless Mahmud. The Sharif heard of his iniquities and sent a new *kaid*, Mansur, to take over his post and put him to death. Warned of Mansur's approach, Mahmud cast himself recklessly into a battle with Askia Nuh, who had retired to the hills of Hombori, and died fighting. Nuh himself was killed shortly afterwards by Mansur. This was the last flicker of the Songhai empire.

By the time of his death in 1605 Mulai Ahmed Al Mansur had discovered the emptiness of his conquests in the Sudan that had been so costly in valuable troops and money to achieve. The Eldorado did not exist. The wealth of the country derived from security to move about and trade in peace. This was no longer true of the Sudan, which now seethed with rebels, marauders and brigands across the trade routes. The gold was not safe to move and it remained in the jealously guarded regions of mysterious Wangara. Even to garrison the towns of Timbuktu, Gao and Jenne drained Morocco of ill-spared troops.

After Mahmud's death Judar, the supplanted commander who had gone to take charge of Gao, contrived the death of several *kaids* sent out from home and gradually won the Sharif's confidence as governor-general. He returned in honour to Marrakesh in 1599 bearing as gifts for the king great quantities of gold as well as eunuchs, dwarfs, slaves, and fifteen virgin daughters of the king of Gao to become the Sharif's concubines.

JUDAR PASHA'S SUCCESSORS

Of Judar's successors only Suleiman showed any competence. Conditions became more anarchical and in 1618 Morocco relinquished her rule and support. From this time those Moors who remained elected their own leaders. Chaos prevailed everywhere. Gradually the original Moroccan soldiers were replaced by local recruits and their officers were drawn from the children of Moroccans by local women. These became known as the *Arma* and constituted themselves as a ruling class. Governed by no principle but greed these military ruffians allowed the country to remain in misery. So long as a chief paid his tribute he could do as he liked with his subjects. Thousands perished from famine and disease and no one was safe. The *Arma* chose their own pashas with Timbuktu as the capital; garrisons under *kaids* were kept in Gao, Jenne and in Bamba. But the discipline of the troops became so free that their powers of defence and of internal control melted away.

After the Moorish invasion the centre of power in the Sudan swung eastwards from Timbuktu to Birni Ngazargamu and the Bornu empire, which successfully controlled the desert routes to the north. The Taghaza–Timbuktu route which had hitherto been the most important now became much less so because of its insecurity, and evidence for this can be seen in the decline in size and prosperity of Timbuktu and Gao.

In about 1670 Timbuktu was overrun by the Bambara from Segu, and in succeeding years it suffered from periodic occupation by various raiders.[1] Gao too fell to the Tuareg by the end of the seventeenth century, and Jenne came under Bambara or Fulani control. Between 1660 and 1750 there were no fewer than 128 locally elected pashas, and their authority over the kaids of the other towns increasingly diminished. After 1780 no more pashas were elected and the *Arma* became absorbed into the people, though to this day their ancestry may be detected in their appearance. Moorish influence can be seen in these middle Niger towns, particularly perhaps in the buildings of Jenne. The great mosque which stands today is said to date from about 1300, when the town governor adopted Islam and turned his palace into a temple for the worship of God. The architect is reputed to have been a Moroccan named Malum Idris, who long before the Moorish invasion taught the people of Jenne how to build.

[1] According to the *Tarikh al Sudan*, Timbuktu had been under the following régimes up to the date of writing:
1336–1433 under Mali
1433–1468 under the Tuareg Maghcharen
1468–1493 under Sonni Ali
1493–1591 under the Askias
1591–1654 under the Moors.

XI. THE SUDAN IN THE SEVENTEENTH AND EIGHTEENTH CENTURIES

EVENTS IN THE MUSLIM WORLD LEADING TO THE ISOLATION OF THE SUDAN

We have seen the disastrous effect on the Sudan of the Moorish invasion and its aftermath of chaos in the territories formerly prosperous under the great Askias. As a result trade and traffic with the centres of culture in the north dried up. The desert traffic reached its peak during the period from 1490 to 1590, when Songhai under the Askias and the Bornu empire under the Sefawa dominated the Sahara and the Sudan.[1] Europe began to exploit the sea routes to the new worlds of the Americas and the Indies, and lost interest in trying to cross the Sahara in search of gold. The Sudan became a lost continent like Atlantis. It is true that Bornu, as hitherto, and to a lesser degree the Hausa states, still kept in precarious touch with the eastern countries of the Mediterranean. But these now reflected a civilization as represented by the Ottoman Turks, a crude parody of the old illustrious days of the Arab régime. A new Muslim power had arisen in the East, and this largely contributed to the decline of the Muslim world in the West.

In the thirteenth century the Seljuk Turks overran Egypt, and in 1260 their foreign legionaries, the Mamluks, set up a sultan of their own in Cairo, the Abbasid Khalif merely retaining a nominal and religious supremacy.

At the end of the fourteenth century the Ottoman Turks had pushed their way into the countries on both sides of the Bosphorus surrounding Constantinople. They had an organized military force called the Janissaries, somewhat similar to the Mamluks, which was composed of men conscripted from Christian villages while still boys and trained to form a Muslim *corps d'élite*.

After many years of failure the Ottomans at last succeeded in capturing the Christian stronghold of Constantinople in 1453, and

[1] See A. Adu Boahen, 'Caravan Trade in the 19th Century', *Journal of African History, III*, No. 2, 1962, p. 349.

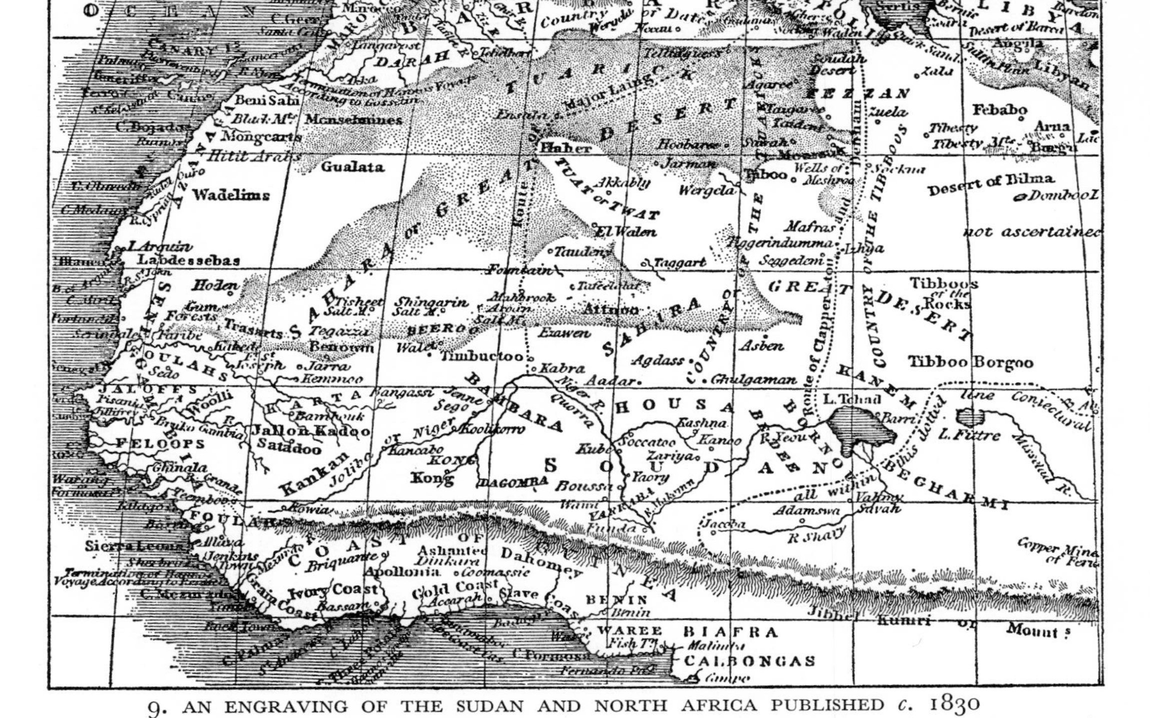

9. AN ENGRAVING OF THE SUDAN AND NORTH AFRICA PUBLISHED *c.* 1830

It will be seen that Major Laing's ill-fated journey of 1825–26 is shown as well as Clapperton's first journey, though it was too early for Lander's discovery of the outlet of the Niger to be included. The cartographer's insertion of a long and non-existent range of mountains, which he calls Jibbel Kumri, must be his way of interpreting the complete inaccessibility of the Sudan from the coast up to comparatively modern times.

thus, paradoxical as it may appear, banished from their midst their one source of culture and commercial prosperity. A wave of alarm immediately went through Europe, which increased to panic when in 1481 the Ottomans pillaged Otranto, a town on the heel of Italy. For nearly a century Turkish fleets continued to command the seas and constantly ravaged the coasts of Spain, Italy, and Africa. It was not until the battle of Lepanto in 1571 that the Ottoman sea-power was broken and trade once more revived.

In 1517 the Ottoman Turks had captured Egypt and Syria from the Mamluks, and gradually the north African states, Tripoli, Tunis, and Algiers, came under their influence.

Meanwhile in Spain, after the sack of Otranto, anti-Muslim revulsion reached a head and in 1492 Ferdinand and Isabella wrested Granada from Islam. In 1502 the Muslims were expelled from Spain.

The expulsion of the Moors from Spain was an emotional reaction to the expulsion of the Christians from Constantinople. Both were acts of senseless folly. Both resulted in far-reaching benefits to the outside world. Scholars of distinction spread into Europe from the East, culture and learning reached out into North Africa. The Eastern Empire of the decadent late Byzantines gave way to a Turkish European state, but the new régime retained all the evils of the old while losing its former markets, its culture and its civilization. The north African seaboard became a hunting-ground for innumerable Turkish corsairs who effectually closed the coast to shipping. Communication between Spain and Africa was cut and so remained. A struggle developed between Turks and Moors for North Africa and large numbers of Spanish Moors elected to remove themselves to the refuge of the desert.

The effect of all this on the Sudan was to stop up the mouth of their only outlet to the living world. The forests sealed off all access to the sea coast at this time, so that news of the exciting discoveries of new continents, of new inventions, of new philosophies, could reach the Sudan, if at all, only from Morocco, itself isolated from Europe, or in a devious way across the desert trails from Egypt. And so it remained for the best part of three hundred years.

THE BAMBARA KINGDOM OF SEGU

From the beginning of the seventeenth century Songhai steadily declined under the military despotism of the Moors. The Askia organization disappeared. The *Arma* (or *Ruma*) controlled only a stretch of the middle Niger. Many petty states had resumed their independence and a small Bambara kingdom came into being around Segu. The Bambara were a Mande-speaking people, who had formerly been part of the Mandingo empire of Mali, and they had spread from further west of the river. The first notable king, who is regarded as the real founder, was Mamari Kulubali. He was commonly known as the *biton* because while still a child he became the leader of a gang of boys. One is not told whether or not he was the king's son, but he is said to have been immensely broad in the shoulders and highly intelligent. The *biton* Kulubali built up a strong army composed of slaves and released criminals, the Ton-Dion. With these he fortified Segu, which was able to repulse the attacks of its enemies from Kong to the south. Some of the Bambara moved away to the north-west to establish a rival kingdom of Kaarta. The two kingdoms were constantly at war with one another but Segu prevailed.

Kulubali and his son, Denkoro, had an evil reputation for cruelty. In order to make Segu impregnable, it is said that sixty young men were buried alive in the foundations of its fort, and sixty young girls were bricked up in the walls. But it was an age of brutality and violence. Denkoro himself was strangled by the unruly Ton-Dion, who put in one of their number to replace him as king. The successor soon suffered a similar fate, and one by one the kings who followed were done to death by the Ton-Dion.[1]

THE FULANI

Meanwhile, paying tribute to Segu as they had been doing to whoever was in power at the time, were a pastoral people known as Fulbe or Fulani who from the sixteenth century onwards, or thereabouts, had infiltrated into the neighbouring territory of Massina. Here was a region of rich pasturelands enclosed between the Niger and the Bani rivers, lying downstream from Segu towards Jenne. The influence of these people on the future history of what is now Nigeria and the Sudan was to be so far-reaching that they deserve more than cursory attention.

The Fulani (sometimes Filani or Hilani) is the Hausa name for the people who call themselves *Fulbe* (singular *Pullo*). They

[1] H. Jaunet et J. Barry, *Histoire de l'Afrique Occidentale Française*, pp. 55, 56.

themselves make a clear distinction between the *Fulbe na'i* (cattle Fulani), sometimes known as *Fulbe ladde* (bush Fulani), and the *Fulbe sire* (town Fulani). The latter include both the aristocratic families such as the Torobe and the small-peasant type of farmers who no longer keep cattle in any number. In Hausa these are called *Fulanin gida* or *zaure*, and most of them now themselves use Hausa rather than Fulfulde except in Adamawa. There is also a further and distinct category of Fulani whom they call Bororo'en —not to be confused with the *Fulbe na'i* or cattle Fulani. The latter think of the Bororo'en as having vast herds of cattle, being less tied to a particular area, and knowing much about cattle medicines. They favour large tracts of bush such as are found to-day only in remote areas mostly outside Nigeria, they speak only Fulfulde, and they are 'unbelievers'.[1]

No one knows with any certainty what the origins of this mysterious people are, though there has been no lack of theories, ranging from the possibly tenable to the fantastic. From a point in the past, admittedly an imprecise point, authorities are agreed in noting that there has been a steady movement of Fulani people from the region now known roughly as Senegal towards the east, through Massina and the Hausa states towards Chad and Adamawa and beyond. But how did they get to the region of Tekrur, Futa Toro and Futa Jallon in the first place?

Muhammadu Bello and certain girgams give the Fulani a Canaanite origin.[2] In his *Infaq al Maisuri*, however, he ascribes the origin of the Fulani to a certain Arab from Arabia named Ukuba, who married a woman of Futa Toro called Bajjomangu and begot four sons, Duti, Nas, Wiya, and Arabu. In course of time Ukuba returned to Arabia leaving his family behind. His children were the first Fulani and they spoke a language that had never been heard before—Fulfulde.[3] Variations of this story are still heard in parts of Nigeria; some give the eldest's son's name as Musa and credit him with being the ancestor of the Torobe clan and therefore Shehu dan Fodio. It is to be noted that all the legends agree in the fact that there were only sons and no daughters of Ukuba, who would seem to have provided the only element foreign to Futa Toro in the Fulani people. The theory

[1] See C. Edward Hopen, *The Pastoral Fulbe Family in Gwandu*, and D. J. Stenning, *Savannah Nomads*.

[2] R. Mauny, *Tableau Géographique, etc.*, p. 40.

[3] C. E. Hopen, op. cit., pp. 6, 7.

that the language sprang parthenogenetically to life is not as wild as might at first appear. M. W. D. Jeffreys believes that since children can and do invent words, they could subject these words to the grammar and syntax of the local Nigritic language.[1]

Sir Richmond Palmer suggested that the Fulani proper were the result of the union of Arabs and Judaizing Berbers who came into the Maghrib between about A.D. 650 and 750 with the Duradae or Taurad, who in Roman times and during the Byzantine era had been inhabitants of the valley of the Draa, which runs from the foothills south of Marrakesh into the Atlantic.[2]

Could this theory link up with the story of the expedition from the Maghrib sent by the Ummayad governor in 739 to the extreme south? We are told that it captured a number of prisoners from the Sudan, and Al Bakri speaks of some descendants of these Magharibah called Al Hunahin in Ghana in the eleventh century. It is suggested that they were driven westwards as refugees to Tekrur, where some maintain that by intermarrying with the local people they evolved as the Fulani.

The origin of Fulfulde is no easier to account for than that of people and even if we could do so it might not help us. The language seems to be closely related to Serer, Wolof and Biafada, which Westermann and Bryan classify as West Atlantic.[3] But a Nigritic language could have been easily adopted by a predominantly male group of immigrants settling down with local wives and falling in with their language and customs.

L. Tauxier in his *Mœurs et Histoire des Peuls*[4] examines at length most of the theories that have been put forward and himself advances one that commands some support. He suggests that the Fulani long ago were a branch of a red Hamitic race who inhabited regions in East Africa close to the Masai people. He thinks that from East Africa they probably went northwards, up the whole length of Egypt, bearing westward along the edges of the desert until they eventually came up against the foothills of southern Morocco. It was from here, in the north, that they came southwards to Tekrur and the Senegal basin to mix, mainly, with the Serer, but also with the Wolof, thus evolving as a mixed

[1] M. W. D. Jeffreys, 'Speculative Origins of the Fulani Language', *Africa*, vol. XVII, 1947, pp. 47–54.

[2] H. R. Palmer, *The Carthaginian Voyage . . . and Sultan Bello's Account of the Origin of the Fulani*, Bathurst, 1931, p. 35.

[3] Cf. the later classification of Greenberg.

[4] See especially his introduction.

pastoral race of Tucolor. The suggestion is that they were under pressure from the Ummayad Muslims to leave the Maghrib at about the same time as the expedition of 739 to the Sudan, and they may have followed in its wake.

There are two main recognized stocks of Fulani (other than those mentioned above), the Dya and the So, which recall the two groups described by Al Bakri as al Faman living in Ghana and Sala. From these two stocks numerous groups have spread over a vast area from the Atlantic to Darfur and from the desert to the coastal forests, which no pastoralist would wish to occupy. Of these the Dya from Futa Jallon (Futa Dyalo) are probably the most numerous and the most characteristic to describe. The Fulani themselves recognize two types: *wodabe* (red) and *balebe* (black). Though not perhaps entirely homogeneous as a type the red Fulani shows fundamental differences from the Negro. His hair is sometimes wavy, but never woolly; his nose is straight or aquiline, but never flat; his limbs are slender, his body usually lean, his features small and sharp. He can be known to blush, and his eyes, according to some accounts, can even be blue.[1]

The above characteristics would seem to indicate clearly that the Fulani are non-negroid, and this is the view taken by most authorities though not by all. C. K. Meek and others believe the Fulani to be physically of Asiatic stock,[2] which accords with Tauxier's theory already mentioned. Kirk-Greene refers to a claim that they are of the same Polynesian stock that colonized Madagascar, and says that some connect them with the Zingari or gipsies of Europe, tracing both races back to a common Indian origin.[3] He too supports a non-negroid descent, and C. E. Hopen categorically states that 'unlike the Hausa the Fulbe are non-negroid'.[4] But Roland Oliver and J. D. Fage observe as follows: 'Although the physical features of the Fulani often seem markedly non-Negroid (a fact that has led some authorities to suggest that they may be descended in part from the early non-Negro element in ancient Ghana), they must today be numbered among the Negro peoples. Their language is certainly a Negro language, and

[1] Charles Monteil, *Journal de la Société des Africanistes*, 1950, 'Les Peuls Rouges', pp. 158, 159.

[2] C. K. Meek, *Man*, October 1959, p. 182.

[3] A. H. M. Kirk-Greene, *Adamawa Past and Present*, p. 22.

[4] See p. 21 of *Africa*, vol. XXXIV, No. 1, January 1964, and an article by C. E. Hopen on a movement to preserve what the Fulani believe to be their superiority over the Hausa and other people in good manners and social conduct.

belongs to the same group of languages as does that of the Tucolor of the lower Senegal, a people with whom the Fulani were closely associated until about the fourteenth century.'[1] Are the criteria for classification by the experts perhaps too technical for some of us to recognize? Of all the many theories there is much that is attractive in Tauxier's hypothesis of a pastoral people of Asiatic origin, starting from the grasslands on the Asiatic side of Africa, where the Masai are now, moving gradually northwards through Egypt and then westwards along the edge of the desert to the Maghrib, possibly acquiring Semitic and Berber elements on the way, and ending up with the Tucolor in Tekrur and Futa after being inhospitably driven out by the Muslims of the Maghrib.

Here they seem to have remained until about the fourteenth century, when they began to work their way eastward into the countryside between the settled areas. By the sixteenth century large numbers of them were grazing their herds in Massina, where they maintained themselves under their own chiefs, the Dyalo, who in turn acknowledged the authority of the emperor or other ruler of the day, with whom they had little contact. The Bororo'en, as most of them then were, remained aloof from the ways of the town or village, pagan and unashamed. But there were exceptions who somehow strayed into the web of urban living; and these tended to float naturally to the top of society for no easily explained reason. Certain clans seemed to inherit a faculty for leadership, such as the Toronkawa and the Sulibawa. The first provided the Sokoto ruling house from Shehu dan Fodio to the present day, while the second supplies the present Emirs of Katsina and Kano, and in the latter case has done so since the days of Dabo, the second Emir. In contrast to the pastoral Fulani the urbanized Fulani quickly took to learning and its close relative in Muslim society, religion. They became experts in Muslim law and the posts of Alkali and Imam gave them a growing influence and authority.

THE FULANI RELIGIOUS MOVEMENTS[2]

From the ranks of the Fulani came the great religious leaders of the eighteenth and nineteenth centuries in the Sudan to launch a movement whose effects would be almost limitless. Starting in

[1] Roland Oliver and J. D. Fage, *A Short History of Africa*, pp. 151 and 152.
[2] Alphonse Gouilly, *L'Islam dans l'Afrique Occidentale Française*, pp. 66 to 60.

Futa Jallon with the Fulani and Tucolor in 1725, carrying on in Futa Toro with Abd el Kader's revolution of 1776, spreading to the east with Shehu dan Fodio's jihad of 1804 from Sokoto, continuing in the bend of the Niger with Shehu Ahmadu's jihad against the pagans of Massina and Bambara Segu in 1810, it reached its climax in the Tucolor empire of Al Haj Omar and his son, Ahmadu Shehu, grandson of Muhammadu Bello.[1]

It was Alfa Ba of Kuranko who took the first decisive step in declaring a jihad in Futa Jallon against the pagan tribes, chief of which were the Dyalonke. His followers were diverse groups of Fulani with little in common but Islam. He assumed the title of Almamy, but died soon after. His successors were a combination of father and son; Ibrahima Sori, a warrior, and Alfa Ibrahima of Timbo (Karamoko Alfa), a scholar. This family alliance of pen and sword acquired great authority over a kind of theocratic confederation, but it never succeeded in islamizing the whole country with its difficult terrain. The dual system of rule continued uneasily for about a century, with 'Alfaya' and 'Soriya' as rivals, until in 1840 a plan suggested by Al Haj Omar was adopted and the power alternated every two years. This reign of the Almamys, as it was called, did not end the rivalry and the system was allowed to lapse under the French.

The next move came in Futa Toro, which had lived for some thousand years or so under foreign dynasties, the earliest of which, that of Manna (*c.* 1250–1300), was itself Muslim. But from the sixteenth to seventeenth centuries power was in the hands of the pagan Fulani Denianke, under whose strict and intolerant rule the Tucolor Muslims suffered. In 1776 Abd al Kader of the Torobe Fulani and his Tucolor supporters threw over the 18th and last of the Denianke dynasty, replacing them by a system of parish priest rule under elected councils presided over by an Almamy. Abd el Kader Torodo was chosen as Almamy and immediately undertook a number of jihads against the Walo, Jolof, Bondu and Galam peoples, who occupied the country between the Senegal and Gambia rivers. Before long, however, Torodo's

[1] Similar reforming movements in other parts of the Muslim world were taking place at the same time but there seems to be no obvious connexion beyond the puritan motive. All were led by *mujaddidun* or revivalists, who exhorted their followers to return to the pure faith of the first four 'rightly guided' khalifs—there were the *Wahhabiyya* in Saudi Arabia, the *Sanusiyya* in Cyrenaica and the *Mahdiyya* in the Nilotic Sudan. See Muhammad al-Hajj in *Odu*, vol. I, no. 1, July 1964, p. 47.

followers wearied of his despotic ways and dissension ensued. After losing and then regaining power he was killed in 1788, leaving behind him the established Islamic state of Futa Toro with its dependencies, Dimar, Damga and Bondu.

XII. THE NINETEENTH CENTURY AND THE FULANI REFORMATION IN THE SUDAN

SHEHU USMAN DAN FODIO AND THE HAUSA STATES

When the nineteenth century opened, the Fulani appeared to be the predominant race in the Sudan. We have seen how for many generations they had been gradually finding their way eastward. There were always a few of the more ambitious of them who found the pastoral life of the herdsman unexciting, and took up occupations in the towns. Here they tended to make their mark and they often came to fill key positions at court. They would then intermarry with the Habe and merge with them in language and customs. The pastoral Bororo'en retained their nomadic instincts and kept themselves aloof with their herds, and the *Fulbe na'i* made a living out of milk and butter which they traded for corn and salt with the settled population.

The outstanding man of the century for the Sudan was a Torodo Fulani, who was born in Gobir territory about 1750. This was Usman dan Fodio, to be generally known as Shehu or Sheikh. He was brought up with his brother Abdullahi as a strict Muslim, and after studying for some years in Agades he felt the call to dedicate his life to teaching the faith. On his return from Agades, Shehu acted as tutor to the Sarkin Gobir's two sons in Alkalawa. One of these was Yunfa, who was later to succeed to the throne; but in the interval before his accession Shehu had felt obliged to withdraw from Alkalawa because of the reversion to pagan practices by the court and the hostility shown towards the Muslim faith. When Yunfa finally became king he sought out his old master in his village of Degel and encouraged him to resume his itinerant preaching. This had widespread and early success, and zealous followers swarmed to Shehu's side. The upshot was that Yunfa and his court grew alarmed. Their authority might be threatened. The austerities of Islam would leave no room for the comforts of the old life. The Shehu and his movement would have

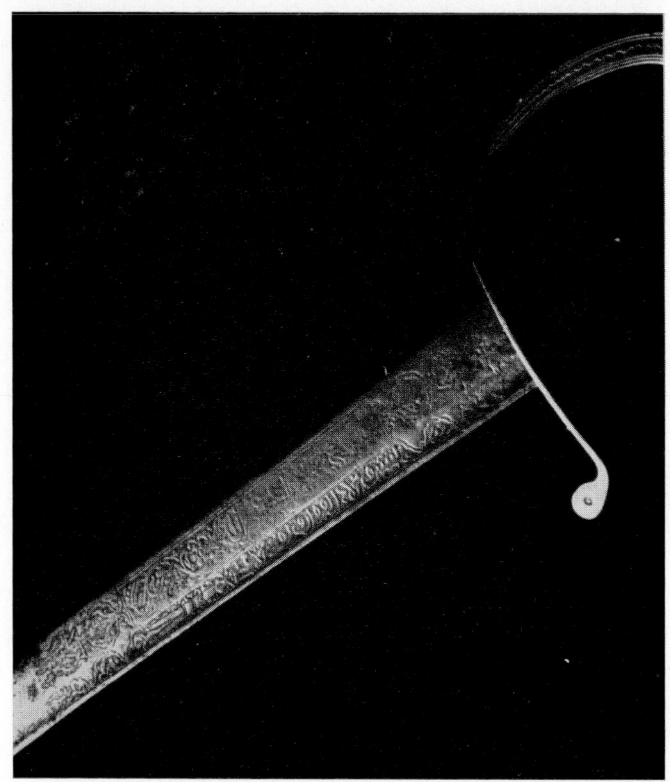

8. Katsina state sword, Gajere, Thirteenth Century, showing Almohad and possible Ayyubid influence.

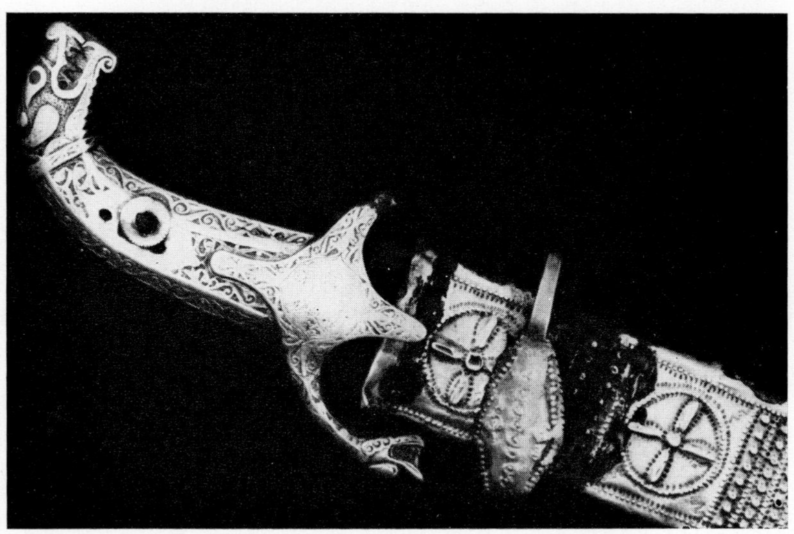

9. Sword of Kanta of Kebbi. Moroccan or Songhai workmanship, fifteenth century.

الحمد لله والصلاة والسلام على رسول الله

١٢٣٨

من عبد الله تعالى محمد الامين بن محمد الكانمي
الى امير قومه ومالك ارضه القائم مقام الولد البار الطائع والنائب
مناب العبد المفيد النافع الامير محمد ابن تنوما صاحب [illegible] السلام
التام ورحمة الله تعالى وبركاته اما بعد فانك ذكرت لنا انك اخرجت
لنا نصيبا من الغنيمة التي غنمتها من بلد كاجكلي [illegible]
مما اخرجته لنا ونسيت [illegible] الان وها هو القادم عليك حامل كتابنا
هذا انسار بابك ابن عم [illegible] الله فادفع اليه نصف ما حصل من
ثمن الرقيق والنصف [illegible]

10. A letter from Muhammad al Amin al Kanemi, Shehu of Bornu, to Muhammad dan Tanoma, Sarkin Gumel (*c.*1830–43): perhaps the earliest surviving Arabic letter of Nigerian origin.

11. The famous well of the Bayajida legend at Daura.

10. THE FULANI EMPIRE AND BORNU IN THE 19TH CENTURY

to be eliminated. From these beginnings arose the eventful years of jihad, from 21 February 1804, the date of the Hijra (flight) of Shehu to Degel, to the slaughter of Yunfa and his Gobirawa at Alkalawa in 1808; and to the subjection of the more distant Hausa States by about 1810.[1]

The histories of the various Hausa States are recorded in greater detail in Part II, but it will be convenient here to provide a summary of the main events in their development. Their legendary origin has already been briefly described in connexion with the conquests of Askia the Great early in the sixteenth century, when their significance on the broad canvas of the Sudan begins to appear. This domination by Songhai lasted effectively only until the end of that century, after which time the power of the new rulers of Songhai, the Moors, was so weakened by internal dissension as to be confined to the riverain cities of the middle Niger.

Though Kano was in many ways the most important of the Hausa States, she had her periods of eclipse. The original legendary warlord of the Hausa Bakwai, Gobir, is said to have been the centre in which the early Zaghawa nobility, or Imajeghan, settled. The leadership of Gobir receives some support from the tradition that the kings of Gobir had a tribal mark under one eye, the *takin kaza* or fowl's footprint, which certain Pharaohs also carried. But Daura was the eldest of the six legendary children of Biram and Diggera, the progenitors of the Hausa States.

The Kano Chronicle records the reigns of forty-two Habe kings of Kano from Bagauda (999–1063) to Alwali (1781–1805), and five subsequent Fulani Emirs up to the last date of recording, in 1892. Kano reached the height of her power under her renowned Mohamman Rumfa (1463–99), in whose reign we find that Sheikh Al Maghili brought a number of Muslim emissaries from Medina. It was for this king that Al Maghili wrote his treatise on kingship, with its memorable injunction, as translated from the Arabic by Thomas Baldwin, 'Ride, then, the horses of resolution upon the saddles of prudence'. Islam had certainly preceded Al Maghili through the medium of earlier Arab and Berber travellers but it had as yet taken no wide hold. Usman dan Fodio quotes the

[1] The main authority is Bello's *Infaq al Maisuri*, from which E. J. Arnett compiled his account of the jihad in his *Gazetteer of Sokoto Province*, pp. 23 to 31. See also pp. 3 to 6 in the Introduction to *The Occupation of Hausaland 1900–04* by H. F. Backwell.

Tarikh al Sudan as having recorded that the lands of Bornu, Kano, Katsina, Songhai, Mali and parts of Zakzak (Zazzau or Zaria) were *Bilad al Islam*, but that near each one of these were territories containing unbelievers.

Early in the seventeenth century the overlordship of Songhai gave way to that of Kwararafa, whose people, the Jukun, had their home far to the south-east on the Benue. For a time they even occupied the town of Kano, the inhabitants fleeing to Daura; but they could make little lasting impression on Katsina, which at this time was much more important than Kano as an entrepôt for the trans-Sahara trade. Kebbi under Kanta also exercised her sway over a wide region. The Hausa States were very far from being united, and the records are full of accounts of internecine strife, with the names of Kano, Katsina, Gobir and Zamfara constantly recurring. And we must not forget Zazzau and her famous Queen Amina, whose younger sister, Zaria, gave her name to the capital. Amina is said to have conquered Kano and Katsina, according to the Kano Chronicle, 'and all the towns as far as Kwararafa and Nupe'. This would have been about 1580. All over Hausa country ancient town walls are called *ganuwar Amina*, although not necessarily built by her, and her fame in war is legendary. She also earned an undying reputation as a consumer of lovers: after each had been enjoyed he would be destroyed.

At the beginning of the nineteenth century, then, when Shehu Usman dan Fodio launched his jihad against what he believed to be the corrupt and irreligious practices of the Hausa rulers, Gobir was all powerful in the north-west, and Bornu was the power in the east, dominating Kano and also to some extent Zaria and Katsina. The Hausa people were living their lives as they had done for centuries, that is as peacefully as recurrent slave raiding would permit. They pursued the crafts of smithing, weaving, dyeing, tanning and leather working. They were industrious farmers and ubiquitous traders. They were law-abiding and well ordered in a culture that owed much to the influence of Islam.

In *Kitab al Farq*, a work on the Habe kingdoms attributed to Usman dan Fodio, the author makes a number of accusations against the Habe rulers. These had to be made to establish the legitimacy under the *Shari'a* law for a jihad, because in Islam rebellion against the ruler is a grievous sin unless his apostasy is proved. The abuses complained of included the imposition of unlawful penalties and oppressive taxation; the use of non-Muslim titles; the practice of *gaisuwa* (courtesy presents) and *gargadi* (conscription); bribery, legal corruption and petty tyranny; and various sins against religion such as the continuance of pagan practices and neglect of the Prophet's teachings.[1]

In reading of the generalship and political acumen of the Fulani leaders it must not be forgotten that Shehu, his brother and his sons, for all their reputation as the founders of an empire, were essentially scholars. All three were prolific writers, in Arabic, and they had a burning sense of mission to educate and to reform. They set a new pace in learning and the language of the Koran took on a new significance.[2] Abdullahi has recorded how he himself was educated. From his father ('he was Muhammad, and his nickname was Fodi. . . . Its meaning in our language is "one learned in the law" ') he learnt the Koran. At the age of 13 he was left in the hands of his elder brother Usman. As he says:

I read with him *al-Ishriniyat*, *al-Witriyat*, and the Six Poets, and I learned from him the science of the Unity from the Sanusi books and their commentaries, and from other works. It was rarely that a book of the science of the Unity reached our country, and I knew of it, and did not copy it down from him. I learnt from him syntax. . . . I learned from him also the knowledge of mysticism which belongs to the forming of good character in oneself and that which belongs to perfecting oneself in science, such as made me independent, if God wills, of other than him. I received from him certain books on law, from which were to be learnt what is obligatory on the individual. . . . I learnt from him Qur'anic exegesis from the beginning of *al-Fatiha* to the end of the Qur'an, more times than I can tell. I learnt from him the science of tradition which comes by knowledge, such as al-'Iraqi, and that which comes by oral tradition, such as al-Bukhari which trained me for [the study of] other works. I learnt from him also the science of arithmetic, the elementary [part] of it, the easy [part], and by the praise of God I came to reflect on religion through the abundance of his light, and through his informative writings, both in Arabic and in languages other than Arabic. . . .

[1] See M. Hiskett in *Bulletin of SOAS*, xxiii, 3, 1960, pp. 558–79.

[2] 'The Arabic of the Shehu is competent, but much of his verse appears to have been written in Fulani. That of Bello is turgid and cumbersome, and his meanings are often obscure. Abdullah, by oriental standards, is a poet of merit. His style is literary and conforms in a high degree to the classical pattern.' M. Hiskett, in 'Material relating to the state of learning among the Fulani before their Jihad', *SOAS Bulletin*, xix, 3, 1957, p. 577.

Many a scholar and many a seeker after knowledge came to us from the East from whom I profited, so many that I cannot count them. Many a scholar and many a seeker after knowledge came to us from the West, so many that I cannot count them. May God reward them all with his approval.[1]

Muhammadu Bello describes his father's intellectual qualities as follows:

He instructed the *'ulama*, and raised the banner of religion. He revived the *sunna*, and put an end to heresy. He spread knowledge and dispelled perplexity. His learning dazzled men's minds. He showed how reality was to be reconciled with the *shari'a*. . . . At the same time he was pre-eminent in knowledge of the *hadith*, and learned in its unfamiliar parts and different branches. . . . He resolved difficulties, acting rightly. His vision was sure. He was trained in the teaching of abstruse matters, pre-eminent in reasoning. Devout and ascetic, he was a leading teacher, spreading knowledge. He filled the western country with learning and with seekers after learning.[2]

In 1804 Shehu had initial success at Lake Kwatto. Here the Fulani herdsmen, brought up from childhood to the use of the bow and toughened by their nomad life, played havoc with the clumsy Gobir horsemen encumbered by their trappings. The Bororo'en, though pagan, supported their racial kin to resist what they thought to be hostility by the Habe rulers to all Fulani; but the ensuing civil war was not entirely of Fulani versus Habe—many of the latter were on both sides, and at first not all Fulani followed the Shehu. The single-minded determination of the Fulani *malamai*, for long established in small but highly influential groups throughout the length of Hausaland, was enough to inspire the ordinary peasants to revolt against the oppression of their rulers. It was the superiority of Fulani leadership that ensured ultimate success for the jihad, which had the twin aims of religious purification and social justice. A later aim, or at least a result, was the improvement in the economy with the replacement of a number of petty warring kingdoms by the Fulani empire. The expansion into the pagan territories of the south brought a plentiful supply of slaves to swell the labour force in the fields.

[1] M. Hiskett, op. cit., pp. 550–78. See also Hiskett's translation of *Tazyin al Waraqat* by Abdullahi, Ibadan, 1964, and its review in *West Africa*, 23 May 1964.

[2] T. Hodgkin, *Nigerian Perspectives*, p. 196. See also pp. 189 and 190.

The victory at Lake Kwatto increased Shehu's following and he offered Gobir peace terms, which Yunfa rejected. This confirmed him in his resolve to extirpate the Habe rulers throughout the Hausa States. As a first move the Shehu selected fourteen of his best lieutenants, and as an emblem of his authority he gave to each a flag which he had blessed. These were to be the true Emirs, or Muslim Governors, to lead the jihad. It is strange how the numbers seven and fourteen recur in Hausa history: the Hausa Bakwai and the Banza Bakwai. The seven important flag-bearers were to take over Kano, Katsina, Zaria, Bauchi, Adamawa, Nupe, and Ilorin. Six others were to possess the less important Gombe, Kazaure, Daura, Hadejia, Misau, and Katagum. The fourteenth was for Bornu, but this mission was never completed. All these were to be independent commands though acknowledging the supremacy of the Sarkin Musulmi in Sokoto. Other smaller chiefs established themselves, sometimes several years later, as subordinate to the true Emirs: and these too came to be called Emirs.

Until 1831 the ever staunch Kebbi remained unconquered and unconquerable, poised on the flank of Shehu's twin capitals of Sokoto and Gwandu: but Birnin Kebbi had to be relinquished to the Fulani and later supplanted the town of Gwandu in importance. Elsewhere Fulani emirs ousted the Habe kings. Gobir and Zamfara disappeared as states, their people being absorbed in the new states of Sokoto and Gwandu, and their neighbours.

The change of ruling dynasty did not alter the system of administration, based on historical tradition and Islamic culture. Nor did it reduce the scourge of slave raiding that depopulated large areas of country, chiefly in a wide belt running east–west along the ninth degree of latitude. The slave trade grew rather than diminished and some Emirs even enslaved their own peasants. Nevertheless we must not let stories about the corruption of some, with their concubines and eunuchs, their embezzlement and extortion, their nepotism and indolence, blind us to the virtues of those other distinguished Fulani rulers who defied corruption.

Shehu lived to see the conclusion of his life's work. He had found Muhammadanism under a ban: he left it supreme. The Filani, from a tribe of nomad herdsmen, had become the ruling race throughout the Hausa states. A man of sincere faith and deep religious convictions, he had implicit confidence in his Divine call, and his personality inspired his followers with a confidence similar to his own. His simple habits and austere life made a profound contrast to the barbaric pomp affected by the pagan rulers. No soldier himself, he attributed his successes solely to the hand of God. After the partition of his empire, he withdrew from the active conduct of affairs and devoted himself to a life of study, first at Sifawa, and later in the city of Sokoto. Here he died in 1817, and was buried within the city walls, where his tomb is still a place of pilgrimage.

Before his death Shehu expressed a wish that Bello should succeed him as Commander of the Faithful.

When Shehu died, Abdulahi was in Gwandu, sixty miles away. As soon as he heard the news he set out for Sokoto, but in the meantime Bello had been formally elected Sarkin Musulmi, and had barred the gates against his uncle.

Abdulahi returned to Gwandu in high dudgeon, and, for the time, relations between the rival courts were highly strained. But soon came an opportunity for reconciliation. The town of Kalambena revolted against Abdulahi, and he and his followers were beleaguered inside the walls of Gwandu. Bello heard of his uncle's plight and immediately came to his assistance. Kalambena was captured, and the revolt stamped out by the combined Filani forces. Abdulahi was generous enough to admit his obligation to Bello for the timely interference. The two met outside the walls of Kalambena. Bello on his war-horse, Abdulahi on the mare which he always rode as befits a Mallam. Bello as the younger man prepared to dismount, as local etiquette demands, but Abdulahi motioned to him to remain in the saddle, and himself bent forward and saluted his nephew as Commander of the Faithful.

The breach was healed, and from that date Sokoto and Gwandu continued to live on the most friendly terms. In accordance with the partition made by Shehu, the Eastern Emirates paid tribute to Sokoto; the Western Emirates to Gwandu.[1]

BORNU

The centre of power in the Sudan that had swung from Timbuktu to Ngazargamu after the fall of the Songhai empire was now to swing west again to Sokoto and Kano. News of the Fulani conquests of Shehu dan Fodio roused the Bornu Fulani to support their kin but their efforts were sporadic. Hostility between Sokoto and Bornu was aroused by Mai Ahmed's treatment of his Fulani subjects, and deepened by the assistance which Mai Ahmed gave to the Hausa kings of Daura, Kano and Katsina. The fires of enmity were fanned by Sokoto charges of blasphemy and religious malpractices levied against the Mai. After a period of fluctuating

[1] F. de F. Daniel, *Journal of the African Society*, xxv, 1925–6, pp. 278–83.

struggles the Fulani under Gwani Mukhtar, a leader from Damaturu who had got a flag from Dan Fodio, drove the Mai out of his capital in 1808.

At this stage the famous Sheikh Haj Muhammad al Amin makes his first appearance on the scene by rallying the Bornu forces to recapture Ngazargamu, reinstate the Mai and kill Gwani Mukhtar. But this success was short lived. Another leader, Ibrahim Zaki, took Ngazargamu for the second time, in 1811–12, and sacked it. It was never restored, though the Fulani did not occupy it for long. Malam Ibrahim Zaki retired to establish the flag in Katagum with the title of Sarkin Bornu. The years that followed were marked by the efforts of the wise Sheikh Haj Muhammad, or Al Kanemi as he came to be called, to maintain the Sef dynasty in power without usurping it. A new capital was built at Kukawa. Efforts to regain the old Bornu ascendancy over the neighbouring Hausa States proved unavailing, and after a defeat of the Bornu forces by Yakubu, Emir of Bauchi, east of Kano in 1826, Bornu gave up further attempts.

THE EMIRATES

Further events during this century in the Emirates are recorded in some detail in Part II. If a general picture is possible it might be one of comparative stagnation during a period when tremendous developments in science, discovery and liberal thought were taking place in the western world as represented by Europe and the Americas. On the other hand the country was free from invasion and the kind of wars that were to beset the western world. In some Emirates the high ideals of the original Fulani founders had shown a tendency to decline, and there was a weakness of internal security; but the mass of the population continued to live as they had always lived under a system that despite its hazards interfered little with their accustomed ways.

Communication with the outside world was still largely trans-Saharan. There were by now four main caravan routes. Starting from the west, the first route ran from Morocco through Taodeni to Timbuktu, with a branch from Mabruk to Tuat; in the centre there were two routes: one through Ghadames to Aïr and Kano, the other from Tripoli through Fezzan to Bornu; to the east there was the route through Cyrenaica and Kufra to Wadai. This latter route assumed increasing importance with the settlement of the

Sanusi in Cyrenaica in the second half of the century. Since the Moorish invasion of 1591 the western routes had been declining in favour because of their insecurity. René Caillié commented in 1828 on the dangers of this road and the poverty of Timbuktu trade; Dr Barth similarly noted the sorry state of Gao in 1854. By comparison the Bornu–Fezzan route was regarded as child's-play by Gordon Laing before setting out in 1825 from Timbuktu on a journey that cost him his life at the hands of Moorish bandits.[1]

SHEHU AHMADU LOBO[2]

While Shehu dan Fodio's jihad was well under way in the Hausa States, the great Fulani religious movement was finding a new outlet to the west of Gwandu, in the bend of the Niger, under the leadership of a certain Ahmadu Lobo of Massina, who had been one of Usman's early supporters in Gobir. In this region the Bambara of Segu had allowed their Fulani vassals to set up a little pagan kingdom of their own in Massina. As already noted, the Fulani had been moving eastward from Futa since the fourteenth century and the fertile lands of Massina had provided such welcome pasturage for the Bororo'en that they had stayed under their own Dyalo Ardo. Prominent in the jihad were both Tucolor and Muslim Fulani, who had developed alongside each other for centuries in Tekrur and Futa. Nevertheless they had always been uneasy partners. Although the Tucolor had come to speak the Fulani language, there were many points of difference between the two peoples. Unlike the Fulani, the Tucolor had been Muslims from a very early date and during the eighteenth century they had been under a strictly puritanical Muslim dynasty of their own. Each group maintained that they, and they alone, were the true Muslims in the Sudan. The preaching of these austere doctrines aroused the fear and hostility of the Ardo of the Massina Fulani, who appealed to his Segu Bambara overlords for help. But already some of the Massina Fulani had joined the ranks of Islam, and in about 1810 (some say later) Shehu Ahmadu Lobo, now proclaiming himself Amir al Muminin, was able to defeat the combined forces of Bambara and the Ardo and create an

[1] A. A. Boahen, *Journal of African History*, III, No. 2, 1962, pp. 349 ff., and E. W. Bovill, *Missions to the Niger*, *I*, 1964.

[2] For a very full account of this period see A. H. Ba et J. Daget, *L'Empire Peul du Macina*, vol. I, 1818–53. See also Alphonse Gouilly, *L'Islam dans l'Afrique Occidentale Française*, pp. 66–70.

independent Muslim kingdom ruling all the inhabitants of Massina. His conquests extended from the Volta to Timbuktu, which he captured from the Tuareg, and the remains of the *Arma*. His fanatical fervour made him the enemy of some who have criticized his altruism and religious sincerity. Others, however, dismiss the criticism as unfounded and due to mere personal prejudice. He was succeeded in 1814 by his son Ahmadu, and in the same year Timbuktu was recaptured by the Tuareg.

AL HAJ OMAR AND THE TUCOLOR EMPIRE

The final act in this great Fulani Muslim enterprise, which had started with Alfa Ba's jihad of 1725 in Futa Jallon, was to start from the same place. A certain Omar, a Torodo Fulani like so many other leaders and connected with the Almamys, went on the pilgrimage to Mecca and after an absence of nearly twenty years returned in 1838 by way of Egypt, Bornu and Sokoto, where he married a relative of Sultan Bello. On his way home to Futa Jallon he passed through Segu, where he attracted a considerable following—so much so that it provoked the king's jealousy. He was put in irons and, after a period in prison, he was told to leave the king's realm and never set foot in it again on pain of death. In Futa Jallon he began the training of an army of religious revolutionaries, and in his stronghold at Dinguiraye he accumulated a supply of weapons and stores, including fire-arms and ammunition.

His first campaign was to invade Kaarta, north-east of Futa across the Senegal river, which he succeeded in conquering though with little sign of the people willingly accepting the new faith. He then recrossed the Senegal to attack Khasso and Galam, where the French had recently arrived. A French outpost at Medina held out against his incessant attacks for three months until it was at last relieved by the French Governor, the celebrated General Faidherbe. When the relief arrived on the scene they found the fort completely surrounded by putrefying corpses, and the garrison were reduced to eating grass and roots.[1] Despite this and other setbacks Al Haj continued his jihad, and in 1859 he undertook new conquests in the direction of Segu. To feed the army, villages were plundered, crops were destroyed, and the countryside left desolate. After occupying Nyamina, and Sansanding on the

[1] See H. Jaunet et J. Barry, *Histoire de l'Afrique Occidentale Française*, pp. 105–7.

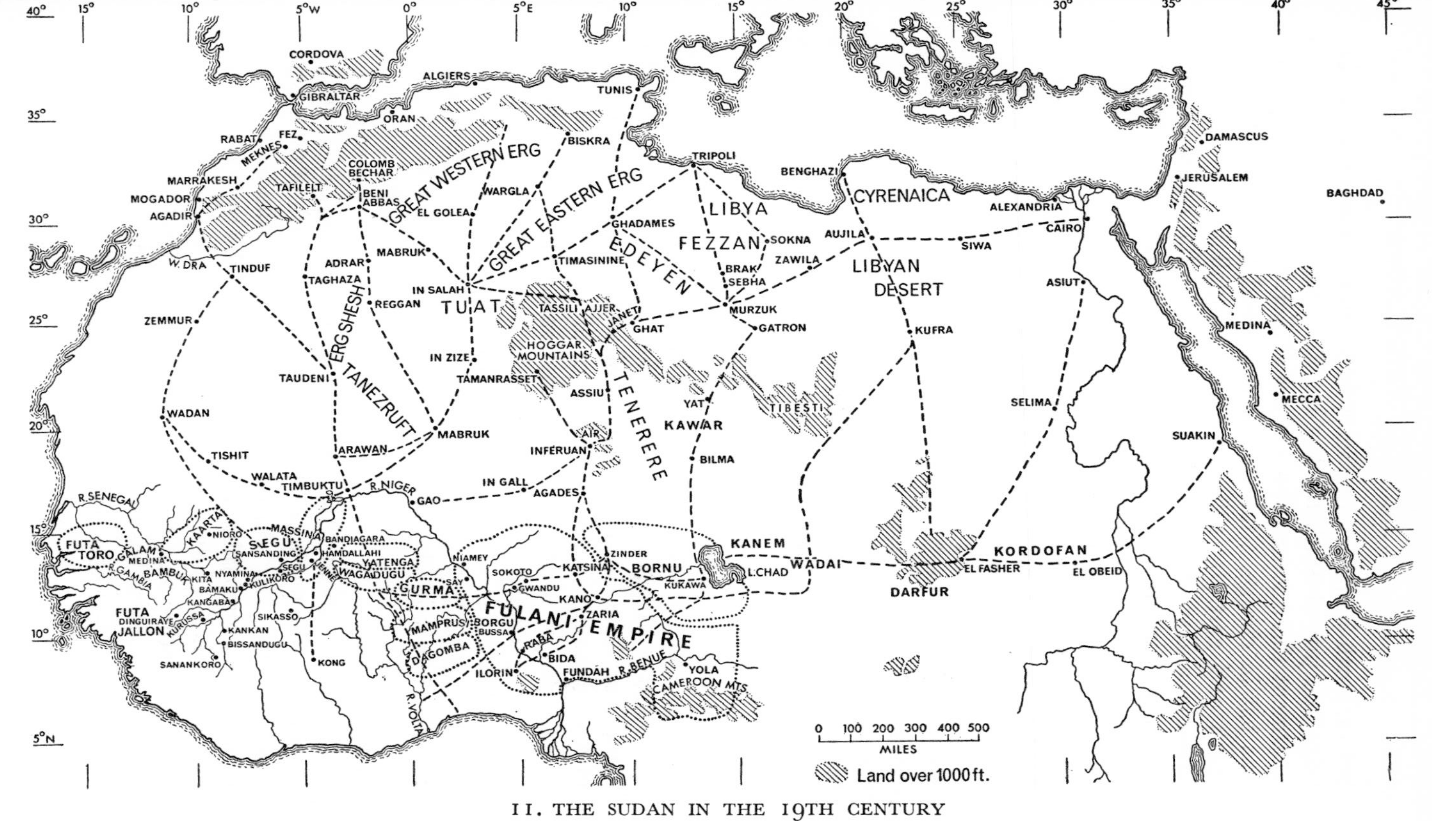

11. THE SUDAN IN THE 19TH CENTURY

left or north bank of the Niger, he crossed the river to capture Segu and put to death the last Bambara king, in revenge for his treatment there some twenty years earlier. Omar's son Ahmadu was left in charge, while Omar continued his conquests to the north and east. In 1862 he took Hamdallahi, the capital of Massina, and went on to plunder Timbuktu. But resistance movements grew in strength behind him. His Tekarir troops were more concerned with loot than with the true faith. A revolt in Massina brought Omar back in haste to Hamdallahi, where he found himself besieged. After some months of siege, the town was reduced to famine, and Omar could escape only by setting the town on fire and slipping out under cover of smoke.

Al Haj Omar took refuge in the rocks of Bandiagara where he died in about 1864. The exact date is not known because his son Ahmadu kept the death secret for about two years for fear of repercussions among the subject peoples. Some say that Omar blew himself up with gunpowder, others that he simply died of hunger. It is even questioned whether Omar ever got away from Hamdallahi.

The Tekrur or Tucolor empire built up by Al Haj Omar extended from the kingdom of Dinguiraye on the upper Niger to the west, to Nioro and the kingdom of Kaarta to the north, to the kingdoms of Massina and Segu on the middle Niger, and even to Timbuktu. The various provinces of this empire were governed by Omar's kinsmen, and the governor of Segu, Ahmadu, who was Omar's son by a daughter of Muhammadu Bello of Sokoto, became accepted as the leader. His rule, however, was increasingly unpopular. After withdrawing to Kaarta, and later to Massina, he was eventually compelled by the French to leave the country. He took refuge in Hausaland, where in 1898 he died.

SAMORY TURE[1]

Somewhere about 1870 a Mandingo named Samory Ture came to power in the territories lying immediately south of those under Tucolor rule. His ambition to recreate a Mandingo empire brought him into collision with the French, who by this time were extending their trading interests from the coast to the interior. Samory's father was a pedlar and the two used to travel from market to market. His mother was captured and held by the chief

[1] Jaunet et Barry, op. cit., pp. 118 ff.

of the Wassulu in the region of the upper Bani, so that Samory went to try and get her released. But he too was held prisoner for seven years, during which time he was trained in the use of arms. On his release he proved himself as a warrior, and proclaimed himself king of his birthplace, Sanankoro. The title went to his head.

He now began to subjugate the small surrounding states, and worked his way north until he was repulsed by the French at Kita, a few days march west of Bamako. Some years later he agreed by a treaty concluded at Bissandugu to confine his dominion to states south of the Niger and Tinkasso. As a mark of his good faith he made over his son Karamoko as a hostage to the French. After spending some years in France and visiting Paris, Karamoko returned with pro-French sympathies, which caused his father to order his death.

Samory continued his dreams of empire towards the east, and his soldiers known as *sofas* (the word means groom in Bambara) terrorized the population. It became habitual for the peasants to take their weapons with them to the fields and to have look-outs posted in the trees to give warning of the approach of the dreaded *sofas*. In 1887–88 he unsuccessfully besieged Sikasso for six long months, forcing the chief of the Kenedugu to seek French protection. He then had a long series of engagements with the French, which eventually forced him to move south to the kingdom of Kong, which he burnt to the ground. In 1898 he made an alliance with a new king in Sikasso against the French, which resulted in the destruction of the town and its fortifications, and in the annexation of the kingdom of Kenedugu by the French. Some time later Samory tried to flee to Liberia, but he was captured and died of pneumonia in Gabon in 1900.

EUROPEAN PENETRATION AND FRENCH COLONIAL POLICY

In 1885 the celebrated Berlin Conference had declared that people of all nations should have freedom of access to the interior of Africa. This was thought to be for the good of Africa inasmuch as what Europeans valued in their own civilization could then spread its benefits to Africans. In practice access was granted in most colonies only with difficulty, or not at all, except to subjects of the colonial power.[1] This was the rule in the French and

[1] See J. D. Fage, *An Introduction to the History of West Africa*, p. 152.

German colonies, where British traders and missionaries were at a disadvantage. French and other foreign companies, on the other hand, competed freely with British firms in British territories. In the latter part of the nineteenth century, when France had had time to recover from the disastrous defeat by Germany in 1870–71, she woke to the conviction that she must acquire as many colonial possessions in West Africa as possible, and she must penetrate to the interior to further her interests. In accordance with this policy of spreading French civilization and the use of the French language, the French attempted the occupation of the Sudan from the Senegal to Lake Chad. Bamako was taken in 1883 and by 1896 they had reached Say, not much more than a hundred miles to the west of the present Nigerian border. By the end of the century the French had reached Zinder and the country to the north and east of Lake Chad. Near here at Kusseri in 1900 they defeated and slew that scourge of Bornu, Rabeh, and later his son, Fad el Allah, which enabled the Kanemi dynasty to be restored under British protection. These events are described in Chapter XXIII under Bornu.

France's policy was to spread what she believed to be her greatest asset—French civilization and culture—as widely as possible in the territories under her control. The benefits of French citizenship were extended to the inhabitants of four communes of Senegal, and they were open to those in other parts of her domains under certain conditions. These were as follows: one had to be prepared to surrender one's rights under native law, to have reached the age of eighteen, to be monogamous, to have been educated in the French language, to have done the military service required of French citizens, and to have been in French employment for at least ten years.[1] This policy of assimilation, as it was called, gave way gradually after 1945, when the French empire became the French Union, to one of loose association, with the formation in 1958 of the French Community. Since then most of the former French colonies have become independent republics in *l'Afrique d'expression française*, though two are independent outside this group and a few are still members of the Community.

[1] J. D. Fage, op. cit., p. 170.

XIII. THE BRITISH OCCUPATION AND INDEPENDENCE

BRITISH COLONIAL POLICY LEADING TO THE OCCUPATION OF NORTHERN NIGERIA

On 1 January 1900, in place of the Royal Niger Company, the Protectorate of Northern Nigeria came into existence, with Sir Frederick Lugard as High Commissioner. Up to that date British interests had been protected by a chartered company and by consuls, not by any Government.

It was only during the latter half of the preceding century that traders, mostly British, had begun to push up country from the southern trading ports; and particularly up the Niger, the lower course of which to the sea had only since 1830 become known to the world. For three centuries at least there had been trade between Europe and the coast, but there had been no inducements to risk the hazards of penetration into the interior. African slave traders had done all that was necessary inland by bringing the slaves to the ports. But with the abolition of the slave-trade, traders found that they needed to go more and more into the interior in search of markets. This in turn led to the demand from traders for British Government protection and the appointment of consuls at places on the coast of Nigeria from 1849. Beecroft was the first.

On the whole, the authority exercised by the consuls proved effective. For some thirty years coastal trade flourished and trade with the interior increased, though it suffered from lack of political protection against lawlessness.

In 1879 Sir George Goldie founded the United African Company, which combined the interests of the competing British firms and managed to defeat the efforts of the French firms to extend French influence from the upper to the lower Niger. A Royal Charter was granted in 1886 with a third change of name to the Royal Niger Company, by which it was to exercise political authority over, as well as trade in, the Niger territories. This Protectorate was later to extend to the country lying on the middle

Niger. 'Since trade cannot prosper in chaos and disorder,' to quote Professor K. Dike, 'Britain had to impose a government of her own making over these discordant elements. The work of state building in Nigeria was, therefore, undertaken by Britain because of the divisions, rivalries and wars between the inhabitants of the Niger territories. Then, as now, men with large capital to invest sought security for their lives and property.'[1]

From 1893 onwards there was continual tension between France and Britain, and the latter decided that the time had come to replace the Company rule. In 1897 Lugard was commissioned to raise local troops to protect the frontiers of the North against French encroachment, and three years later the Protectorate of Northern Nigeria was proclaimed. One reason for the British occupation was that the European powers had agreed after the Berlin Conference that no new annexations or protectorates would be recognized in Africa unless they involved effective occupation and administration.

With his headquarters first at Jebba, then at Zungeru, Lugard found only minor military operations necessary at first. But early in 1903 he had to send a strong force against Kano, which quickly submitted. A spirited action followed at Kwatarkwashi, on the road to Sokoto, before Lugard's troops could approach the Sultan's capital. Details of these actions will be found on pages 204–5 and on page 409. The Sultan having fled resistance was slight, and in due course Lugard installed the successor nominated by the Sokoto Council as Sarkin Musulmi.[2] Apart from the Cameroons campaign against the Germans in 1914–16, the military operations of 1903 were the first and last of major importance during the whole of the sixty years of British occupation.

THE 'DUAL MANDATE'

Lugard's policy of Indirect Rule through the Emirs became a model for adoption in other territories. The authority of the Emir and the Native Court was quietly but firmly supported, so long as the fundamental laws of humanity and justice were observed. There was no tolerance for bribery, extortion or inhuman punishments.

[1] See K. Onwuka Dike, *100 Years of British Rule in Nigeria, 1851–1951*.

[2] See the translation of the 131 letters in Arabic found in the house of the Waziri of Sokoto, Buhari, in 1903, in *Occupation of Hausaland 1900–04*, edited by H. F. Backwell, and Sir Ahmadu Bello, *My Life*, pp. 17, 18.

12. Installation of the 9th Emir of Ilorin, Sulu Gambari, by the Premier, Alhaji Sir Ahmadu Bello, Sardauna of Sokoto, in the presence of the Prime Minister of the Federation of Nigeria, Alhaji Sir Abubakar Tafawa Balewa, in 1959.

13. Crowds gathered to witness the ceremonies in Ilorin.

14. Rock paintings and part of a rock gong at Dutsen Habude, Birnin Kudu; probably representing the humpless 'Hamitic longhorn'.

15. One of the finest Nok figurines collected from the Makabolo River in Abuja Emirate.

The very title 'Resident' emphasized the self-effacement required of the British adviser, who normally left all pomp and ceremony to the Emir and his District Heads. This was true training for self-government and new responsibilities. Lord Lugard, as he afterwards became, coined the classic phrase 'dual mandate' in his reference to the colonial administrator's task.[1] This was to promote at one and the same time the interests of his own country's industrial classes as well as those of the native races in their progress. He maintained that the benefit could and should be made reciprocal.

UNIFICATION OF NORTH AND SOUTH

In 1914 the Northern and Southern Protectorates were united as the Colony and Protectorate of Nigeria, with Lugard as the first Governor-General. The unification of this vast conglomeration of diverse peoples and interests was an achievement the difficulties of which can be too easily underestimated. This remarkable fusion of elements of such differing basic composition could not have occurred but for the provision of flux by an external agent. It is fortunate that the welder was Lugard.

The capital of Northern Nigeria moved from Zungeru to Kaduna in 1916. The First World War of 1914–18 was a setback to progress, and just as development looked promising the depression of the 'thirties put back the hands of the clock. The Second World War of 1939–45 denuded the country of manpower and resources, so that it was not until almost the fifties that Nigeria had an uninterrupted chance to catch up with the modern world.

DEVELOPMENT OF EDUCATION

Though the first Director of Education, Hanns Vischer, was appointed to the North in 1910, he and his little band of assistants could do little until after the war. Katsina Training College opened in 1921 with fifty students, many of whom were to occupy the highest offices of state in the years to come.[2] But the building of an education system is of necessity a very slow process. Teachers take at least a generation to school and train: there is no short cut and time cannot be bought. By 1930, when the Departments of

[1] F. D. Lugard, *The Dual Mandate in British Tropical Africa*, 1922.

[2] See *The Story of Katsina College*, by D. H. Williams from notes by Shuaibu Naibi, Ministry of Education, Northern Nigeria, 1959.

Education in the North and the South were amalgamated, schools were still extremely few. Apart from Middle schools at the Emirate headquarters there would be only a handful of village schools to supplement the popular Koranic schools. There were no secondary schools leading to a university and not till 1928 did the first drive on female education begin with the opening of the Ilorin Girls' School. But within the limits of the foreseen needs of the country the quality was excellent.

Today things are very different. A vast increase in the teacher-training programme makes it possible to predict that primary school enrolment will rise from its present 300,000 to more than 800,000 by 1970, and that the intake of secondary schools will rise from 2,000 in 1962 to at least 8,500 by 1971. Already Ahmadu Bello University is established with its base at Zaria, and a new Polytechnic for post-secondary students is planned.

INDEPENDENCE

In accordance with Britain's declared policy, and after careful preparation, Northern Nigeria became self-governing in 1959, and on 1st October 1960 Nigeria became an independent sovereign state with a federal constitution. Despite its change-over to a Republic in 1963, Nigeria has remained within the British Commonwealth.

The events of the last sixty odd years cannot be satisfactorily generalized in this chapter. They have been recorded in the thirty-seven Emirate accounts which follow in Part II. Though in places they may appear to be parochial, yet for the Nigerian reader they bring the breath of life.

XIV. RÉSUMÉ

In the first part of this book an attempt has been made to provide a backcloth for the histories of the thirty-seven Emirates of Nigeria so that they can the more clearly be understood. But the stage is so vast and the scenes so various that there is a danger that the principal actors in the drama may become lost in the forest of scenery designed to set them off. The following review of the principal events and epochs, therefore, may serve to bring into relief the predominant characters and situations that play the major role and provide the central theme in this complex pageant.

EARLIEST CIVILIZATIONS

Recent evidence from rock paintings in the central Sahara show that as recently as about 4000 to 3000 B.C. the Sahara was enjoying a wet climatic phase that made the whole vast area both fertile and populous. A Neolithic type of civilization seems to have flourished, with numerous groups and tribes dotted all over the area between the Nile and the western Sudan. At this time when Mandingoes are believed to have been developing one of the earliest systems of agriculture on the upper Niger, there is evidence for supposing that the Nile valley and Mesopotamia supported a civilization considerably in advance of any in Europe or Africa, if not in the world. But during the course of the second millennium B.C. the wet phase seems to have come unaccountably to an end, with the result that the dwellers in the Sahara had to seek refuge in the more fertile lands surrounding them, and many groups elected to migrate south towards the Sudanese grasslands. At the same time there was a gradual westerly movement of peoples out of Asia, with the Indo-Europeans going into southern Europe and the Hamitic groups into Africa.

THE EASTERN AND WESTERN ROMAN EMPIRES

With the rise of Greece and the ascendancy of Greek political and cultural influence at the eastern end of the Mediterranean came the beginning of the long rivalry between East and West. History relates how the Persians were repulsed from Greece, and how eventually Alexander of Greece overran Persia and reached India, his successors establishing the Greek empires of the Ptolemies in Egypt, the Seleucids in Syria and the Macedonians in Europe. There followed the rise of the Roman Republic, the destruction of the African stronghold of Carthage, and the growth of the great Roman Empire. This extended to include all western and eastern Europe as far north as the Danube and the Rhine, all Asia Minor and Syria, and all Africa as far south as the Sahara.

This enormous empire, however, broke up into two halves. In the first century B.C. it was divided by the conflict between Caesar in the west and Pompey in the east, and then again by a similar struggle between Augustus in the west and Antony in the east. Finally, in the fourth century A.D., the Emperor Constantine made Byzantium the capital, renaming it Constantinople, and in 395 on the death of Theodosius the two empires of East and West were recognized.

Within two generations the Western Empire had disappeared before the inroads of the Vandals, who also invaded North Africa, and the Goths, Germanic tribes from the north. Following these barbarian invasions there was a flicker of Byzantine life when North Africa was reconquered from the Vandals and Italy regained, but by the end of the sixth century the Eastern Empire had degenerated and become no longer Roman but a heterogeneous compound of Greeks, Slavs and Orientals.

THE RISE OF ISLAM AND THE ARAB CONQUESTS

This was the feeble condition of the Empire when the last and greatest of the Semitic migrations occupied a large part of its eastern dominions. It derived its impulse from the new religion of Islam. On the death of the Prophet Muḥammad in 632 the khalifs who succeeded him organized the wild Arab tribes, and conquered Egypt and Syria. At the same time Arab armies invaded the new Persian Empire.

Thus was founded the Ummayad khalifate of the east with an imposing capital at Damascus. In 750, however, the Ummayads were brutally expelled by the rival descendants of the Prophet's uncle, Abbas, who owed their success to the Persians. The Abbasids transferred their capital to Baghdad, where under the civilizing influence of Persia they built a magnificent oriental city of world renown. One of the Ummayads escaped the massacre of his kinsmen and eventually set up a dominion in Spain, later to become a rival khalifate with another splendid capital at Cordova.

About the tenth century, then, we find at the western end of the Mediterranean the great Arab kingdom of the Ummayads, known to Europe as the Moors, and at the eastern end the even greater empire of the Abbasids, known to Europe as the Saracens. The whole of the Maghrib along the coast of north Africa was under Muslim rule. The remnants of the Roman Empire were a huddled collection of peoples in eastern Europe and Asia Minor, while most of the rest of Europe was occupied by a variety of Germanic tribes.

This was the situation when thoughts of the more adventurous in the Maghrib began to turn to the legendary lands beyond the desert to the south known as the Bilad al Sudan. There were two main caravan routes, one in the east and the other in the west. Just as the rivalry between England and France was continued in the North American colonies, which grew up under different religions, languages and customs, so was the rivalry between East and West continued into the Sudan. The eastern route took the civilization of the eastern Mediterranean to Kanem and Wadai; farther west the Sudan fell under the influence of the civilization in the Maghrib. Islam came to Kanem from Egypt and Mecca, but to Ghana from Morocco and Tunis.

FIRST MIGRATIONS TO THE SUDAN

During the middle centuries of the first millennium A.D., and possibly earlier, there were a few tentative gropings towards the southern grasslands by the more adventurous or desperate of the nomad tribes living close to starvation in the desert wastes. These had migrated earlier from the north and east, and a number had taken refuge in the gaunt, forbidding mountainous regions of Hoggar, or Adrar, or Tassili-n-Ajjer, or Aïr, all of which lay across the trails between the Maghrib and the Sudan.

There are legends of one of these groups from the Zaghawa Tuareg coming down into Kanem, and even making their way across Hausaland to Dandi and the Niger. Certainly many such immigrant tribes were constantly emerging from the desert during the seventh and eighth centuries to settle in the grasslands and subjugate the local inhabitants. In this way, right across the belt of savannah country bordering on the desert, there grew up settlements, then petty kingdoms, then larger states, and finally great empires, all to enjoy their allotted cycle of life and in due course disappear.

GHANA

The first of these was Ghana, which may have had its origin in the settlement in Aukar, as early as the second century A.D., of a group of Berber immigrants among Soninke Mandingoes. In course of time the empire of Ghana, centred on a town of that name, extended over the regions to the north and west of the Niger as far as the desert. The original rulers were supplanted by Soninke in the eighth century and the gold trade flourished. The eleventh century saw a change to Berber rule, under the influence of a strong wave of orthodox Muslim feeling generated by the puritan Almoravids. In 1240 the town of Ghana, whose ruins have been discovered at Kumbi Saleh, was finally sacked by Sundiata Keita of Mali. It never revived.

MALI

The great Mandingo empire of Mali rose on the ashes of Ghana. It grew to world fame under Mansa Kankan Musa, the Rex Melly of the medieval cartographers, whose celebrated pilgrimage to Mecca and triumphal progress through North Africa in 1324 were the talk and wonder of the age. The Mali dominions extended from Senegal as far east as the Hausa States; and from the forests of the south to the desert towns of Arawan and Walata in the north. The towns of the middle Niger, including Timbuktu, and Gao (but not Jenne, which preserved its independence), were at the centre of this empire. Here were the main markets, the mosques and seats of Muslim learning.

KANEM-BORNU AND THE HAUSA STATES

At the eastern end of the Sudan, east of Lake Chad, lay the rival dominions of Kanem, with its Bornu provinces separating it from the conglomeration of petty Hausa kingdoms, as yet in their infancy before the fifteenth century.

But they were soon to assert themselves. Ever since the eleventh century there is evidence of the spread of Islam over the length and breadth of the Sudan, from Ghana to Kanem. With Islam had come the Maliki code of law, together with the customs and administrative systems of the Muslim world. Trans-Saharan trade flowed and prosperity followed. At a time when Kanem-Bornu was passing through a period of relative political weakness, Kano rose to prominence. Mohamman Rumfa, who reigned in Kano from 1463 to 1499, had a wide reputation for his statecraft, his cultivation of learning, and his adoption of modern Islamic systems. Zaria, under Queen Amina, enjoyed the fruits of many conquests; and farther south, Nupe and the Jukun kingdom of Kwararafa were making themselves felt.

SONGHAI

It is the sixteenth century that will be always memorable for the Sudan. It started in triumph and prosperity; it ended in disaster. Mali had declined after Mansa Musa's death. In its place rose the empire of Songhai; first, under Sonni Ali (1464–92), who callously sacked Timbuktu; then under Askia Muhammad I, a born administrator, who outshone even Mansa Musa in his reputation for power and wisdom. He too made the pilgrimage and reminded the world of the riches of the Sudan. The suzerainty of Songhai now extended over the Hausa States, and by the time of Muhammad's death in 1538 the Songhai empire was even more vast than its predecessor. But Kebbi remained unconquered: the valiant Kanta saw to that. Katsina had her period of glory after the successful struggle in 1554 to rid herself of the overlordship of Songhai, and eclipsed Kano as a centre of trade and learning. Away to the east, the century was crowned by the religious and political reforms of the greatest of the Bornu Mais, Idris Alooma, who, like Mohamman Rumfa, adapted the judicial system to Islamic practice elsewhere. He strengthened his expanding empire by the introduction of muskets, which revolutionized the art of warfare.

THE MOORISH INVASION

A tragic demonstration of this novel weapon's power was at this very time being given a thousand miles away to the west. In 1591 a well-equipped army, consisting largely of professional Spanish and Moorish troops, complete with arquebusiers and artillery, descended from the north on the unfortunate Songhai not far from Timbuktu and shattered them. The Sharif of Morocco, Al Mansur, had long nursed the ambition since his annihilation of the Portuguese at Al Kasr to possess himself of the fabulous sources of gold said to lie in the region of Wangara. He had also determined to seize the salt-mines at Taghaza in the desert, which produced the prized commodity most readily acceptable by the Sudanese in exchange for gold. He achieved his objects but they did him little good. The gold was hard to find, the riches of Timbuktu were illusory, and even the salt eluded him since the Songhai slaves who were the only people with the skill and endurance to survive the life fled from the mines.

DECLINE OF THE SUDAN

From the seventeenth century onwards the outlying districts of the Songhai empire fell into neglect, chaos and ruin. The Moorish pashas with their *arma* or *ruma* (as the descendants of the Moorish soldiers were called) could control only the big towns on the Niger, such as Timbuktu, Jenne and Gao. Even the official connexion with Morocco ceased. There was no security for the peasants and trade dried up. Away in Bornu prosperity also declined, but for different reasons: a growing indolence among the rulers and a disinclination to bestir themselves to resist the encroachment of marauding Tuareg or to prevent the secession of the subject tribes. But Bornu still maintained some kind of suzerainty over the nearer Hausa States, though the power of the predominantly pagan Gobir to the north-west was in the ascendant.

THE FULANI RELIGIOUS MOVEMENTS

During the eighteenth century the attitude of most of the rulers in the Sudan was one of *laissez-faire*. But in the far west there were the beginnings of an extensive Fulani religious movement, which was to pursue its course for well over a century throughout the length and breadth of the Sudan. It started in 1725 with the jihad of Alfa Ba in Futa Jallon and the reign there of the Almamys. It continued in 1776 with the revolution in Futa Toro of Abd al Kader Torodo and his Tucolor against the pagan Fulani dynasty of the Denianke, and the establishment of Futa Toro as an Islamic state. Further east, little territorial conquest or change took place, but within the palace courts the Fulani counsellors and intelligentsia were gaining positions of trust that were to prove invaluable in the course of Usman dan Fodio's jihad. At the same time increasing numbers of Fulani herdsmen were migrating slowly into Hausaland from Futa and Massina.

The outstanding event of the next century for the Sudan—perhaps of any of the centuries—was the Fulani revolution in the Hausa States led by Shehu Usman dan Fodio. This started on 21 February 1804 with Shehu's Hijra from Degel to Gudu, as a revivalist preacher in fear of his life. It continued intermittently until 1812, with Shehu's flag-bearers ousting the Habe *sarakuna* from their palaces, establishing themselves and their dynasties in their stead; but maintaining allegiance to one or other of the twin capitals of Sokoto and Gwandu in the Sokoto empire.

The causes of this revolutionary movement are, as ever, susceptible of mixed interpretations. There was undoubtedly the driving motive of the Shehu and his *malamai* to reform the lax standards of Muslim life among the Habe rulers. The movement recalls that of Ibn Yasin and the Almoravids who captured Ghana from the Soninke kings in the eleventh century. The aim was to reform not only the morals but the institutions in accordance with the precepts of Islam. Apart from this, however, the revolution sprang from mis-government. The Shehu had a large measure of support from the peasants and small traders, who were finding injustice and oppression intolerable: few of these burned with religious zeal. And then there was the feeling of racial consciousness among the Fulani as a whole—from the *malamai*, who deplored the crudities of pagan practice and saw in Islam the key to a gentler life of culture and learning, to the herdsmen in the bush, who needed the protection of their kinsmen at court.

The Fulani conquest welded a loose collection of warring city-states into a single administrative unit, with all acknowledging the spiritual and temporal leadership of the Sarkin Musulmi at Sokoto. This over-all control did much to increase security and in consequence the volume of trade. The empire pushed outwards into the forest lands of the south, where pagans could be raided for slaves and sold. While there is no denying the inhumanity of slavery, it must be recognized that many slaves lived perfectly happy lives, secure in their employment and well treated by their masters. Their condition could often compare favourably with that of the working classes in England at that time, when the public conscience was unmoved by the miseries of seven-year-old children at work for sixteen or even eighteen hours a day in sordid squalor.

AL KANEMI AND BORNU

During the century there was a great flowering of learning and scholarship, led by the example of Shehu's successors. It was a remarkable Muslim scholar who stood firm in Bornu to resist the Fulani after their capture of Ngazargamu. Al Kanemi had made the *haj* and had lived for several years in Medina and Mecca before coming to Bornu to bolster up the titular power of the Mai while remaining behind the throne as the Shehu. His statesmanship did much to build up and reform the government. His son, Shehu Umar (1835–80), was forced to oust the Mai in 1846, after an unsuccessful conspiracy with Wadai had been crushed.

REVIVALIST MOVEMENTS IN THE NIGER REGIONS

Outside Bornu and the Hausa states, the first half of the nineteenth century saw the conquests of Shehu Ahmadu Lobo, a Fulani religious leader in the bend of the Niger. In the second half came the domination of Al Haj Omar and his Tucolor (Tekarir) followers in the upper and middle Niger regions; and the depredations farther south of the Mandingo leader Samory between 1870 and 1890. Both came into collision with the ambitions of France, which was bent on a policy of colonial expansion after the Berlin Conference. It was the French who defeated Rabeh and his son in 1900 to save the Al Kanemi dynasty in Bornu.

THE BRITISH OCCUPATION AND INDEPENDENCE

The history of the Emirates from the British occupation in 1900 up to 1 October 1960, the date when Nigeria became independent, is recounted in the chapters which follow in Part II.

PART II

NOTE

The principal problem with Part II has been not only the definition of the term 'emirate' but also the most effective and rational order in which to treat the individual emirate histories. To group them in alphabetical order of Provinces would be to suggest that they are simply administrative units created by the colonial government, a suggestion very far from the truth. To group them in strict chronological order would be to lose an active sense of inter-connecting history. To group them by centuries, with a recurrent examination of emirate history every hundred years or so, would be to confuse the Nigerian reader who is fully aware of the mainstream of his history such as the influence of the Hausa States and the jihad but who is looking for the progressive narrative of his 'own' emirate's history.

In the event, the grouping adopted has, apart from two or three emirates that could justify their inclusion in either of two groups, not only the merit of convenience of reference but also the sanction of the post-jihad vocabulary. Moving from those emirates that spring directly from the Hausa States, both the Hausa Bakwai and the Banza Bakwai, and those of Bornu origin, we find the emirates derived immediately from the jihad already acquiring a regional title. Thus the western emirates were known as the aqalim-al-gharb*; the southern ones as* aqalim-al-yemen, *with the Emir of Adamawa taking the title of Lamido Fombina or Lord of the South; the emirates in the no-man's-land between the Hausa States and Bornu as* Bornu Gudiri *or* Ghaladi*; and the central emirates were, by and large, fiefs of Zaria or Bauchi. The analysis of the emirates' provenance followed here is not to be considered a rigid one.*

In attempting to solve this problem—one that has no complete solution satisfactory to all—we have given preference to the wishes of the Nigerian readers, anxious for a local reference history rather than for the total Northern treatment. At the same time we have been grateful for the advice of other scholars, notably Professor H. F. C. Smith of Ahmadu Bello University, on their ideas about the arrangement of the emirates. We would emphasize that there is no magic in the order finally adopted: those who seek an order of emirate precedence are invited to turn to Appendix B, where the official ranking of the House of Chiefs is recorded; and those who are looking for an integrated history of the North are reminded of the particularism of our title and its qualifying sub-title.

1. EMIRATES DERIVING FROM THE HAUSA STATES

(1) Originating from the Hausa Bakwai

XV. DAURA

OF ALL the Hausa States, Daura claims seniority in its history. A parallel distinction is found today, a thousand or more years later, for of all the emirates in Northern Nigeria, Daura with Abuja, and Argungu *mutatis mutandis*, affords a classic example of a pre-Fulani Habe dynasty and culture.[1] The title to seniority gains support from the very famous legend of Daura's foundation. The *girgam*, or chronicle of kings, of Daura gives this account:

And a certain man named Abuyazidu, son of Abdulahi, king of Baghdad, quarrelled with his father and the people of the city. And they were divided into forty companies. Then Abuyazidu with twenty companies journeyed until they came to Bornu, and they dwelt there. But the King of Bornu saw that Abuyazidu was stronger than he and was of a mightier house, so he took counsel with his people. And they counselled him that he should give Abuyazidu his daughter to wife, and become his father-in-law. And he did so and gave him his daughter Magira to wife, and he married her. Then the Sarkin Bornu said to Abuyazidu that he wished to go to war and prayed him to lend him his horsemen and warriors to aid him against his foe, and he gave him three thousand horses with their warriors, together with princes to the number of seventeen. And he said, 'When we return from this war I will make them princes in my country'. And they went out to war and stayed for six months. Then Sarkin Bornu took counsel to kill Abuyazidu, but his wife Magira heard it and straightway told him. And when he saw all that had been done, that his horsemen had been taken from him and his princes, he saw that it was a plot to overcome him, and he spake unto his people and bade them flee to the north during

[1] The contrast between the Habe and Fulani political organization in a typical emirate situation is excellently analysed in M. G. Smith, *Government in Zazzau*, 1960.

the night. And they obeyed and left him, and he arose with his wife and journeyed to the west. And when they came to a place called Gabas ta Buram,[1] his wife bore a son: and he left her there and passed on with his concubine and his mule, and his concubine also was with child. And they journeyed until they came to Daura at night and they alighted at the house of an old woman whose name was Waira and he asked her for water. But she answered that they could not get water except on Fridays. And he asked her what hindered them, and she told him there was a snake in the well. And he took the bucket which she gave him and went to the well and let the bucket down into the water. When the snake heard the bucket she lifted her head out of the well to kill him, but he drew his sword and cut off her head—and her head was like the head of a horse. And he drew water and took the head of the snake, and it was the night before Friday. And in the morning the people assembled at the well and they questioned one another who had done this thing to the snake, whose name was Sarki, and they marvelled at that part which lay outside the well and that which remained in it. And the news was brought to the Queen of Daura, and she mounted with all her princesses and came to the well, and she asked who had done this thing. And many people spake falsely and said that they had killed the snake, but when she asked to be shewn the head of the snake they were all dumb. Then spake the old woman at whose house Abuyazidu had alighted, and said that a man had come to her house during the night with an animal which was like a horse and yet was not a horse; and he asked me for a bucket and I gave it to him, and he drew water and watered his beast and gave me what remained, perchance it was he who has done this deed. And they summoned him and asked him, and he said he had done it, and shewed them the head of the snake. And the Queen said, 'I have promised that whosoever should do this thing, I will give him half my town.' But Abuyazidu said he wished rather to marry her, and she consented. And he dwelt in her house together with this concubine who was with child. And when the people came to the Queen to bring the news, she would bid them go to the house of Makassarki (the snake-killer).[2]

The ancient well of the Abuyazidu or, more commonly, Bayajida legend, called Kusugu, can still be seen in Daura. It carries a bronze plaque bearing this inscription:

This is the well at which, according to ancient legend, Bayajida, son of the King of Baghdad, slew the fetish snake known as Sarki and afterwards married the reigning Queen of Daura. Their son, Bawo, begat

[1] See chapter on Hadejia, p. 484.

[2] H. R. Palmer, *Sudanese Memoirs*, vol. III, p. 133. See also plate 11.

the first rulers of the Seven Hausa States who were the origins of the Hausa race.

Before this Daura had been ruled by a succession of seventeen queens, as shown on the list at the end of this chapter based on an early girgam. It will be seen that unlike other generally accepted lists which show the legendary Bayajida as marrying the ninth queen, Daura, this one shows the hero coming immediately after the seventeenth queen, Shawata, whom he presumably married. The girgam says that the queens had ruled at Daura since the time of the ninth queen, Daura, which in fact may not have been a name but a corruption of her title, Daurama or Queen of Daura.

It has been suggested[1] that the Daura legend may be considered as celebrating four important new ways of life introduced by the foreign immigrants. First there was the introduction into Hausaland of a new form of worship by the killing of the fetish snake. Then there was the introduction of the donkey, and the art of well-digging through rock to save the dangerous night journeys to the river. Finally, there was the replacement of the traditional Sudanic custom of matrilineal descent by the patrilineal system of the Berbers and Arabs.

In early Hausa history the queen is often known as Magajiya, and the legend indicates that in olden times the Hausa states favoured uterine descent. Daura town is sometimes referred to as Birnin Magajiya Daura. In Kano history, as well as that of Bornu, it is significant how influential a role the king's mother played in political life. The first town founded in this area was probably Tsofon Birni.

An interesting point is the difference in pronunciation of the name of the present town of Daura and the name of the legendary Queen. This may be represented as follows, the grave accent denoting a low tone and the acute accent a raised tone:

Daù-rá—the name of the town.
Daúrà—the name of the Queen.

In the Tuareg language 'Daura' means 'blacksmith'; the Tuareg say that the Daurawa were originally conquered by the Kanuri, who were again overcome by the Gobirawa. The title *Makas-Sarki*, or *Sare-kia*, 'the snake slayer', shortened to *sarki*, became the

[1] We are indebted to Walwyn's 'History of Daura' for both the list at the end of this chapter and for this suggestion. See note 1 on p. 154.

name for king and has so remained in the Hausa language. Similarly, the Galadima of Daura derives his epithet of Babba from this episode, for it is said that it was Babba, who was her Galadima, that the queen sent first to confirm the story of the death of the sacred snake. Next she sent Wan Gwaraje, her Kaura; and since on hearing his corroboration she is said to have conferred on him the rank of War Lord, it has become a tradition in Daura for every Kaura to be Sarkin Yaki, with the praise song of *Kaura gaba, Kaura baya*, 'Kaura to the fore, Kaura to the rear', and that of Wan Gwangu, 'second to none among heroes'.

Some of the first seventeen queens were, according to contemporary Daura historians, the daughters of Abdul Dar, whose ancestors came from Canaan. The first eight ruled at Tsofon Birni, six miles north of Daura. This ancestry is still recalled by the beating of the royal drums, with their call of *Namaruzu dan Kana'an*.

Granted the age of the Daura legend, it is fitting that it should continue by presenting the tale of the origin of the other Hausa States, for Daura is the cradle of the Hausa people. When the concubine brought by Bayajida to Daura gave birth to a son, he was called Karab-Gari, 'the usurper of the town'. A son was then born to Bayajida's wife, the Queen of Daura, and they named him Bawo-Gari, 'bring back the town'. Karab-Gari was now made the ruler of the Maguzawa people and a town was built for him at Yamadawa. The ruins of this place can be seen about five miles west of Daura town on the Katsina road. This Bawo succeeded his father and inherited the royal insignia of sword, dagger and drums, which are still found in Daura today. The present title of Magajiya, conferred upon the senior princess, also stems from this time. Bawo begat six sons, each of whom became a king. They were:

Bagauda, who became king of Kano;
Kazuru (Gazaura), who was of the same mother as Bagauda and became king of Daura;
Gunguma, who became king of Zaria;
Duma, who was of the same mother as Gunguma and became king of Gobir;
Kumaiyau (Kumayan), who became king of Katsina;
Zamagari (Zamna Kogi), who was of the same mother as Kumayau and became king of Rano.

At Garin Gabas (Gabas ta Biram), Magira gave birth to Bayajida's son, called Biram, who became the ruler of the seventh Hausa State.

Another version, while retaining the distribution of the kingdom, has it differently in that Biram is said to have married Diggera, an erstwhile powerful settlement lying to the north of Bornu, and by her begot three pairs of twins: Zaria and Katsina, Kano and Rano, Gobir and Daura. Muhammadu Bello gives yet another account in *Infaq al Maisuri*, where he asserts that all seven were under the tutelage of the king of Bornu who sent his slave Bawo to govern them. It is said in Daura that up to the time of the jihad representatives of the Hausa States used to assemble annually in Daura and thence proceed to Bornu to carry the news of the day to the Mai. Daura tradition has it that Magajin Dankakulema was the representative of the Hausa Bakwai sent by Bawo to Bornu in charge of all the slaves from these states; from there, it is said, the whole caravan of slaves was forwarded to the Bornu representative in Mecca.

Whatever the authorized version, it is generally accepted that these were the eponymous founders of the Hausa Bakwai, the seven original Hausa States. To each was assigned a special duty. Gobir was appointed *Sarkin Yaki*, War Lord, charged with defending the other states from northern invasion, while Zaria was made *Sarkin Bayi*, the Lord of Slaves, and was expected to supply his brethren with abundant labour from the hilly country to the south loosely known as Bauchi. Kano and Rano were, each as *Sarkin Baba*, responsible for industry, especially dyeing and weaving, and Katsina and Daura each became *Sarkin Kasuwa*, responsible for trade and commerce.

Besides these 'legitimate' seven states, there were seven 'illegitimate' sons, known as the Banza Bakwai, where although Hausa is spoken it is not the original language. These were Kebbi, Zamfara, Nupe, Gwari, Yauri, Yoruba and Kwararafa, though in his *Infaq al Maisuri* Sultan Bello places Gwari among the original states and substitutes Borgu in the second list. Some scholars have found support for this in a similarity between the Daura and Gwari facial markings.

There is one further version of the birth of the Hausawa, given here in translation from an old Ajami MS.:

In the name of Allah the Compassionate, the Merciful, and may the peace of Allah be upon him, after whom there is no prophet. This is the history of the Hausa (nation). It has been familiar to every one from the time of their grandfathers and grandmothers, (and) is a thing which has been handed down from the *malamai* and the elders. Any account other than this one is not authentic. If a questioner ask of you (saying) 'Where did the Hausa people have their origin?' say (to him) 'Truly their origin was (from) the Barebari and Northerners'. And this is the account of how this came to pass. The king of Bornu had a horse with a golden horn. This horse did not neigh just at any time, but only on Fridays. If it neighed you would say it was a tornado. It was hidden away in a house. Now the king had a son. He (the son) continually gave him who looked after the horse money and robes in order that (he might persuade him) to bring his horse out, and they should come, and he should mate the horse with his mare. And it was always thus. (And) one day the man who was looking after the (king's) horse took (it) the horse out and brought it. The king's son too took his mare out. They went into the forest and the mare was covered. Now the king has (had) previously said that whoever was seen with a foal from this horse at his house, he would have this throat cut. Things remained at this, (and) one day the mare gave birth, (and nothing happened) till the colt grew up, (when) one day the king's horse neighed, then the young horse answered. And the king said, 'At whose ever house they see it let (that person) be killed (lit. be cut), and do not let him be brought before me'. Then the councillors scattered (to make search) in the town. They were searching for the young horse. And they came to the house of the king's son, and behold as it were the king's horse with its golden horn. Then the councillors said, 'The king has said we must come with you.' Then the king's son lifted his sword. He cut down two men, the remainder were scattered. Then he saddled up the young horse. He mounted. The king ordered he should be seized and brought (before him). The whole town mounted their horses (and) followed him. They did not come up with him. He had gone his way. The king, moreover, has given orders that his own horse is not to be mounted, and if not his horse, then there was not the horse to overtake him. The king's son (rode) went on and (eventually) dismounted in the country of Daura. He stayed with her. And one day she said she wanted him in marriage and he too said he loved her. So they married. The king's daughter became with child. She bore a child, a son. She weaned it. She was again with child (and) bore a girl. And that was the origin of the Hausa nation.[1]

Other Daura sources list fifty-five rulers—the first nine of them

[1] R. S. Rattray, *Hausa Folklore, Customs and Proverbs*, 1913, pp. 1–2.

queens—down to the coming of the Fulani. As some of them, however, are credited with reigns of over 200 years, the genealogy is to be treated with some reservation.

At the time of the Fulani conquest, Malam Ishaku, an Alkalawa *malam* living at Kurneji, studied under Shehu dan Fodio, and was given a flag. According to Daura tradition, the Fulani, unable to take the town by storm, resorted to a siege and finally gained possession by cutting off the corn supplies from the eastern villages. The Habe king of Daura, Sarkin Gwari Abdu, slipped away by the gate called Kidi da Hauka and settled for six months in Kwargwom. In Daura today there is a pond, near where Sarkin Kwargwom lodges when he comes for the *Salla* celebrations, which is still called *Tabkin Kwargwom*, the Kwargwom pool. Abdu retired to Tsirkau (the old town of Kance) and thence to Murya, the daughter of whose chief, Ibil, was his wife, and so to Nguru. When he learned from the Galadiman Nguru that famine had decimated Bornu, Abdu returned to Murya where he stayed for nine years. Then from Yekuwa he waged war on the Fulani. Unable, however, to recapture Daura, he is said in Daura today to have prophesied that one day his grandsons would peacefully reclaim it for his dynasty. On reaching the village of Dukuduku, Abdu learned of the death of Malam Ishaku, but he did not return to Daura. According to tradition, it was at Yekuwa that Sarkin Gwari Abdu died. This story differs from the Fulani one that Abdu was killed in an unsuccessful attempt to retake Daura in 1809. The king's body was, in any event, buried at Yekuwa, where his grave can still be seen.

In Daura, the Fulani rule was continued through Yusufu, Muhamman, Zubeiru, Bello, Altine, Maigardo, Sogiji and finally Murnai.[1] After the Fulani occupation of Daura town, the territory became split into three parts: Daura Fulani, in and around Daura town; Daura Baure, thirty-six miles south-east of Daura; and Daura Zango, focused on Zango, twelve miles east of Daura. From Yekuwa, Yandaje and Toka villages, it was at Daura Zango that the fugitive Habe dynasty eventually established itself after Lukudi, brother of Abdu, had driven out the Fulani from the area. His efforts to unite the two Habe factions, however, failed.

[1] I am indebted to Daura N.A. for this list. I should also like to acknowledge the help derived from my conversations with M. Liman Daura and M. Sani Wali Daura, both students, for their comments on my Daura text. A.K-G.

At his town of Dan Mairam, the king of the opposing Habe group, Danshuhunni, was killed. His son Tsofo fled to Baure and built the town, while his brother Kitari withdrew to Magarya where he was destroyed by Lukudi. The Baure rulers after Sarki Tsofo were Habu, Jibo, Zakari, Abdu and Hallaru. In Hallaru's time, as we shall see, the British brought this Baure splinter-group back into Daura, but Hallaru refused to join and retired to Sitawa where he died.

It was Lukudi's son Nuhu who persuaded the Daura Habe to revolt against their hosts at Damagaram. Later, when Nuhu succeeded his father as king of Daura, the chief of Damagaram, Ibrahim, came to Zango and outlined his plans for a combined Habe attack on the Fulani in Daura town with the help of the exiled Sarkin Kano of Maradi, Sarkin Gobir and Dan Baura Sarkin Katsina. This plot had its mainspring in the fact that Tanimu, Ibrahim's brother, had revolted and fled from Zinder to Daura, where the Fulani emir Bello offered him asylum. Nuhu warned against this scheme. The Daura historians relate the outcome thus:

> And Nuhu's warning was fulfilled, for the attack failed and they were scattered one by one. Ibram Sarkin Damagaram was wounded by a spear and died at Kiru twenty days later. Then Sarkin Gobir counselled Sarkin Maradi to fly. Sarkin Maradi answered that a king does not run away, but Sarkin Gobir replied that if the day is lost even a king runs, and so he fled. But Sarkin Maradi fought on and was killed to the east of the town, and the news was brought to Sarkin Gobir, who said 'was that worth waiting for?'.
>
> So Nuhu returned to Zango and Tanimu became king of Damagaram. But Tanimu hated Nuhu because he had helped Ibram, but peace remained for a time on payment of tribute of a thousand cowries per man.[1]

Daura suffered considerably from the fact that she was situated between Kano and Damagaram, which were constantly raiding each other. Damagaram interfered with Daura, too, and was responsible for the murder of Nuhu and the detention of his son Tafida. Records suggest, indeed, that Daura was virtually a vassal of Damagaram, whose kings at Zinder took the initiative in deposing several of the kings of Daura in the last century, including Muhamman Sha and Dan Aro, sons of Sarkin Gwari Abdu,

[1] From Walwyn, 'History of Daura', quoted in Palmer, op. cit., p. 140.

Suleimanu, son of Dan Aro, and Yusufu, son of Lukudi. Indeed, it was not till the coming of the British in 1903 under *Maitumbi* (Captain H. C. Phillips, who is buried at Hadejia) that Daura Zango became really independent of Damagaram. As a result of the Anglo-French boundary agreement, the Baure group and part of the Zango group were placed under French rule, but the Habe chief Malam Musa and the Fulani ruler in Daura proper came under British influence.

In his desire to unite all the Daurawa under one chief, Lugard, after unsuccessfully approaching Hallaru of the Baure faction, appointed the Habe Malam Musa of Zango as Emir of Daura. Thus Musa brought back the kingship to Daura town, after a break of almost exactly a hundred years since the reign of the previous Habe king there, Sarkin Gwari Abdu. The Habe prophecy of Daura had been fulfilled. Today a plaque outside the main gate of the Emir's Palace commemorates this restoration of Daura to the original Habe dynasty in the following words:

> Praise be to Almighty God and H.M. the King of England who in 1906 on the recommendation of Lord Lugard restored the Habe capital city of Daura to M. Musa, the descendant of the former Habe rulers exiled for 99 years.

On Musa's death in 1911, his son Abdurrahman, then Bunturawa succeeded him as the 58th ruler of Daura.

At first Daura was administered as a Division with Kazaure under Kano Province, but in 1934 it was transferred to the new Katsina Province. In the same year the Emir was commended for his fine leadership and encouragement of mixed farming. The Emir accompanied the Emir of Katsina on an educational tour of Benue and Ilorin Provinces and thence to Ibadan and Lagos in 1935.

Following the dismissal of the Waziri, the post was abolished in 1951. It had never been a traditional Daura office, dating only from 1907, and it was replaced by that of Magajin Gari. The N.A. Council was enlarged in the mid-fifties, and in 1962 the Emir Abdurrahman, aged 82, celebrated his fiftieth year on the throne in a spectacular jubilee ceremony, photographs of which captured a whole page of the London *Times*. It was shortly before this ceremony that the title of Waziri was revived and the unusual step of perpetuating the title Bayajida was taken by its award to the

Premier of Northern Nigeria, Alhaji Sir Ahmadu Bello, Sardauna of Sokoto.

THE HABE QUEENS AND KINGS OF DAURA

Queens

1. Kufuru
2. Gino
3. Yakumo
4. Yakunya
5. Walzamu
6. Yanbamu
7. Gizirgizir
8. Innagari
9. Daura
10. Gamata
11. Shata
12. Batatume
13. Sandamata
14. Jamata
15. Hamata
16. Zama
17. Shawata

Kings

1. Abayajidda
2. Bawo
3. Gazaura
4. Gakuma
5. Jaaku
6. Jaketake
7. Yakama
8. Jaka
9. Ada Hamta
10. Ada Jabu
11. Dagamu
12. Ada Yaki
13. Hamdogu
14. Yabau
15. Naji
16. Gani
17. Wake
18. Kamutu
19. Rigo
20. Gaga
21. Jabu
22. Zamnau
23. Shashimi
24. Ada Inda
25. Doguma
26. Ada Gamu
27. Ada Sunguma
28. Shafau
29. Ada Sabau
30. Ada Doki
31. Nagama
32. Ada Kube
33. Hamama
34. Dagajirau
35. Kamu
36. Ada Guguwa
37. Hamida
38. Abdu Kawo
39. Nagama
40. Hanatari
41. Rifau
42. Hazo
43. Dango
44. Bawan Allah
45. Kalifah
46. Tsofo
47. Jiro

Notes: (1) The above list is taken from Walwyn's *History of Daura*, printed in Palmer, op. cit., p. 142. It derives from an early girgam preserved by the Daura kings but captured in the 1840s from Nuhu with his private papers by Tanimu, Sarkin Damagaram. It came to light again only in Walwyn's time some fifty years ago.

(2) In the absence of the above list other lists were re-written from memory and have gained local credence. According to a Daura MS., *Daura Makas Sarki*, and the testimony of Malam Umaru, Alkalin Abuja, the first queens were Kofano, Gufano, Yakwano, Yakaniya, Waizam, Gadar Gadar and Anagiri. In one list Gamata is the first, in another Yakani, followed by Tabwoi, Waizam and Waiwai. These latter lists unite Bayajida with the ninth queen, named as Daura.

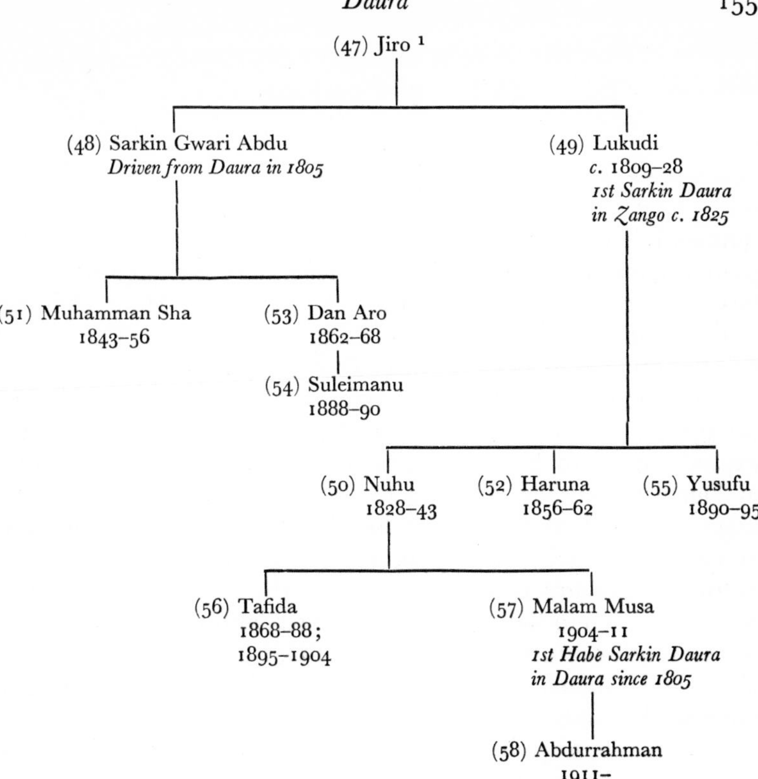

[1] Some Daura historians maintain that Jiro was the elder brother of Sarkin Gwari Abdu.

XVI. KATSINA

THERE is a tradition that the first Katsina dynasty was founded by one Kumayo, a grandson of the legendary Bayajida of Daura fame, and that he ruled at Durbi ta Kusheyi near Mani, eighteen miles to the south-east of the present town of Katsina. The district head continues to bear the title Durbi, and locally the generic name Durbawa is still used to refer to the original inhabitants, though an even earlier group of aboriginals is believed to have existed, similar to the Abagayawa of Kano. The seven large tumuli at Durbi ta Kusheyi are said to contain the bones of the early kings, and indeed are known locally by the names of the first Katsina kings such as Kumayo, Ramba-Ramba and Sanau. Such earth mounds are to be found across the region from Bornu's Komadugu Yo to the buckle of the Niger, and were described by the eleventh-century geographer Al Bakri as tombs of the kings of ancient Ghana. The invaders also settled at Bugaje, twelve miles to the west.

As in Kano, foreigners from the east—in this case Berber—are supposed to have arrived from about the tenth century, but it is likely that Kumayo's dynasty was not founded until the twelfth century or even later. The legend continues that these Berber from Durbi ta Kusheyi and Bugaje used to meet at a place roughly half-way between the two settlements for their annual feast and wrestling display. This meeting-place is said to have been Ambuttai, that is to say the ward of Katsina town where the mosque now is.

It seems likely that these Bornu invaders held sway in Katsina from 1250 to 1468, when Timbuktu fell to Sonni Ali, and Songhai supplanted the dominance of Mali in Hausaland, becoming the chief power in the west. Historically Katsina is, of course, one of the Hausa Bakwai or seven original Hausa States.[1]

The name Katsina, alternatively Kacinna—as sweet-sounding as its female counterpart of Zaria—is said to be derived from a

[1] For the Hausa Bakwai, see section on Daura, pp. 147–9.

princess of Daura who married Janzama, king of the Durbawa, who ruled at Durbi ta Kusheyi. His memory is preserved in the name of a rock close to Mani. Some say that Janzama was conquered by Kumayo. It is also said that the early kings were chosen alternately from the house of Kumayo and the descendants of Janzama. The former by virtue of their descent from Bayajida were known as Larabawa. The latter were called Durbawa from their place of origin. The distinction is still preserved at Maradi, where the Katsinawa Habe were forced to settle after the jihad.

It is said that the last chief of Kumayo's dynasty was called Sanau, and that about the middle of the thirteenth century a certain *malam* of western extraction called Korau came from Yandoto, an ancient capital near modern Chafe, and killed Sanau, thus establishing a new dynasty.

Yandoto, whose ruins are still visible, was not only the name of a town but was also the title of the ruler of the Chafe-Kwotorkwoshi-Kogo region, as it now is of the District Head of Chafe. This area was later known as Katsina Laka or sometimes as Wangara, and some authorities suggest that it was here rather than the town of Katsina—little more than a caravan terminus on the trade route, like Kano—that the *malamai* came from all over the western Sudan and established the great reputation of Katsina scholarship.

The story, which is somewhat reminiscent of Samson and Delilah, is that Korau, whose name possibly derived from *kora*, to drive out, and who was a professional wrestler from Yandoto, was a former playmate of Sanau and that he knew that Sanau was unequalled at wrestling owing to a certain charm which he wore round his waist. It is probable that, though not of royal blood, Korau was a title-holder, perhaps the Kaura or principal chief of Katsina, comparable to the Madawaki in Kano. Korau was invited to a feast by Sanau, and, having persuaded Sanau's wife to steal this charm, he challenged him to a wrestling bout. The contest took place at the traditional place, in the vicinity of the tamarind tree known as Bawada which stood on the site now occupied by Kangiwa ('elephant's head'), as the residence of the reigning king was called. According to custom the king was in honour bound to accept such a challenge. Robbed of his hidden strength, Sanau was quickly thrown and while he was on the ground Korau treacherously stabbed him to death. The fact that among the Emir's *kirari* is *Magajin Korau*, *Mayen Sauri*, *Yanka*

Mashidi Bakon Sanau, 'successor of Korau, wizard of Sauri, guest of Sanau who killed his host', lends credence to the story that Korau obtained the throne by treachery. *The Golden Bough* reminds us of a similar custom whereby to gain the priesthood any aspirant had to kill his predecessor and thereafter remain on constant guard against attack by a would-be successor.[1]

The short sword with which Korau murdered Sanau is still proudly preserved among the magnificent insignia of Katsina, where it is known as Gajere. Its blade, dating from the thirteenth century and showing Almohad and possibly Ayyubid influence, commemorates the famous sword reputedly captured from the Koreish at the battle of Badr near Medina in 624, and given to the Prophet. It bears the Arabic inscription on the obverse: 'Help cometh from God and victory is nigh, so announce glad tidings to the faithful, O Muhammad!'[2] The reverse reads: 'There is no sword save Dhu al Faqar[3] and no hero save Ali'. To this day the Emir carries it in his hand when he addresses the crowd in front of the Kangiwa after returning from his 'Idi prayers, and in 1959 Usman Nagogo made history when for the first time Gajere was allowed to leave Katsina so that he could carry it upright in his hand at the royal durbar. It has been claimed that this sword was Sanau's charm.

The ancient insignia of Katsina, so renowned in the emirate history of the North, include another memento of Korau, the camel-drum or bronze pot of overlapping plates riveted together. A traditional Katsina song refers to *Korau Abu gungurum, Korau mai tukunyar karfe*, 'Korau the invincible, Korau the possessor of the brazen pot'. This was the pot used by the Habe for preparing charms for the king's officers of state on the eve of battle. First a leper had to be found. After he was killed, his body would be cut

[1] See Chapter IV, p. 38 and the footnote. *The Golden Bough* has the following passage: 'When the Muluango or King of Loango, who is deemed the representative of God on earth, has been elected, he has to take his stand at Nkumbi, a large tree near the entrance to his sacred ground. Here, encouraged by one of his ministers, he must fight all rivals who present themselves to dispute his right to the throne. This is one of the many instances in which the rites and legends of ancient Italy are illustrated by the practice of modern Africa.'

[2] We are grateful to A. D. H. Bivar, who provided this description, for telling us that he now puts the date rather later. The obverse inscription is from the Koran 61:13.

[3] Charles Whitting has provided this comment. 'Faqār has been interpreted as (1) cleaving, i.e. "the cleaver", or (2) "the cleaved", i.e. notched after action, or grooved, or with forked tail. Burton, from whom it is unsafe to differ, preferred (1). More modern writers usually prefer (2). It is quite usually done, even today, to engrave superior weapons with a text from the Koran or Hadith.'

up and boiled in the pot, seasoned with other charms. The bronze pot was then ceremoniously carried to the council chamber where each man present drank from it to give him the strength of an elephant and the courage of a lion in battle.

Other items in the Katsina regalia include a second sword, *Bebe* or 'the deaf one'. This was captured from the tent of Sarkin Gobir Yakuba after his defeat by Agwaragi, king of Katsina, in the middle of the eighteenth century. He brought the corpse back and hung up the head on the tree outside his house. Then there is *Gwauron Tambari*, 'the bachelor drum', so named because it is larger and stands alone above all the other royal ceremonial drums. When news was received that war threatened, this drum was continuously beaten from the top of the tower known as Soron Bawada, the double-storied building that once stood on the site of the famous Katsina tamarind tree known as Bawada, at the entrance of Kangiwa. Today its custodian, who holds the office of Tambura and is often a ward-head, is required to beat the drum three times at the turbanning of any of the senior district heads such as Kaura, Durbi, Yandaka, Galadima, and Sarkin Sulibawa, and on the installation of Gazobi, the village head of Karofi, or of Illala, a village head in Mashi. The ancient gate of Katsina, Kofar Gazobi, has been walled up though it is shown in Dr Barth's map. At the installation of an emir, however, the drum is beaten by the Galadima twelve times. It is also beaten at the end of *azumi*, the Ramadan fast. At the festivals of Id al Fitr and Id al Kabir, Tambura rides round the town on a camel accompanied by the rest of his drummers, paying greetings to all the local dignitaries. Tradition forbids him to enter the house of a scion of the ruling Emir.[1]

The change of dynasty seems to have made little difference to the populace. In local Katsina lore, the difference is sometimes expressed by simply noting that Korau was *ja*, 'red', whereas Sanau was *baki*, 'black'. In fact the new Wangarawa and the old Durbawa continued together quite amicably, the latter being particularly respected by the former for their knowledge of magic and the local deities. Possibly for this reason the election of new chiefs rested with the latter, but in course of time the privilege lapsed

[1] Based on three descriptions of the royal regalia of Katsina, given by F. de F. Daniel (1932), R. L. Maiden (1955), and the Katsina Native Authority (1963). See also plate 8.

and chiefs were elected alternately, the right of nomination becoming vested in Kaura Durbi and Galadima.

One of the stories told by Katsina chroniclers refers to the ceremonies attending the election of a new chief. It was the duty of an official called Karyagiwa, 'the elephant-slayer', to strangle the king whenever he appeared likely to die. The title of Karyagiwa has continued in Maradi. The new king was chosen by some rite connected with the sacred snake, or by throwing a spear into the ground. If it remained upright when the name of the candidate was called, the new king was confirmed. The old king's body was then wrapped in the skin of a black ox which had previously been slaughtered over the newly elected king at the Kangiwa town centre so that he became drenched with its blood, and the body was dragged on the ground to the burial place, where it was buried in an upright position. When he had been covered with the hide, the bystanders would slap the corpse and shout 'forget, forget'. It is from this ceremony that the Maradi title of Dan Mari (*mari:* slap) derives. There were various other essential rites in connexion with the election of the new king. The tradition of the Karyagiwa reflects the typical concept of divine kingship common to many Sudanic states, with the king's vigour associated closely with the rainfall and fertility of the land. When the king's physical powers began to fail there was a consequent necessity to have him killed.

Some historians say that Korau lived about 1260 and that he made war on the Kwararafa. His successor Ibrahim Yanka Dari captured Kwiambana and Koton Koro, or so it is believed. After him came Jida Yaki, said to have been the last of the pagan kings. He ruled for forty years and was continually at war with the Gobirawa. Recent research suggests 1492–3 for the accession of Muhammadu Korau, who from his name is assumed to have been a Muslim. He is credited with a reign of fifty years, during which he waged war with Nupe, whose frontier at that time bordered on Katsina.

Muhammadu Korau's successor was Ibrahim Sura—the latter word was a Mali title—who in turn was succeeded by the famous Ali Murabus to whom is credited the commencement of the building of the outer wall, *ganuwar Amina*, of Katsina city. Ali's sobriquet derives from a form of the Arabic *marabout*, an anchorite or religious hermit. There is some dispute about when this was, but we do know that Leo Africanus, who visited Katsina at the beginning of the sixteenth century, speaks merely of grass huts and makes no reference to a walled town. Pory's translation of 1600 reads:

> Casena, bordering eastward upon the kingdom last described,[1] is full of mountains and drie fields, which yield not withstanding great store of barlie and millfeed. The inhabitants are all extremely black, having great noses and blubber lips. They dwell in most forlorne and base cottages; neither shall you find any of their villages containing above three hundred families. And besides their base estate they are mightily oppressed with famine: a King they had in times past whom the foresaid Ischia slew, since whose death they have all been tributaries unto Ischia.[2]

Probably in the lifetime of Muhammadu Korau there was an Islamic revival soon after the visit to Katsina of the celebrated missionary from Tuat, Al Maghili, in 1493. He was once political adviser to the Askia of Songhai. Besides his celebrated *Obligations of Princes*, another of his books is extant, his *Taj-ud-Din*, 'The Crown of the Faith', the manuscript of which was discovered in Kaita district in 1929. It was Ibrahim Maje who ordered his subjects to choose between prayer and prison. It is sometimes said in Katsina that there the *talakawa* eagerly followed the new doctrine while the ruling classes hesitated, the reverse of the Islamic process in Kano where the rulers are said to have led the way. There is a current story in Katsina that after a dispute over the exact orientation of the Gobirau mosque, a certain *wali* or holy man drove his staff into the ground and invited the others to look over it. To their astonishment they could see the Kaaba in Mecca, and the mosque was accordingly oriented in that direction. The *wali*'s tomb is still revered at Guga in southern Katsina. The Gobirau mosque that some say dates from the fifteenth century was not repaired from the time of the jihad (1805) until the 1920s. The longevity of many ancient mud walls and buildings is ascribed to the mixing of the mud not only with a special kind of vegetable matter or *katse* but with blood. A herd of cattle would be driven into the place where communal building was going on,

[1] This was 'Cano'.

[2] Leo Africanus, *The History and Description of Africa done into English by John Pory*, 1896, quoted in T. L. Hodgkin, *Nigerian Perspectives*, 1960, p. 102. Ischia refers to Al Haj Muhammad, Askia the Great, ruler of Gao in the sixteenth century.

and when they were slaughtered to provide meat for the workers their blood would be trampled into the piles of building mud. The *hasumiyar Gobirau*, the tower in Katsina, is not the actual minaret dating back to 1702 but in fact conceals the mud spike which is all that remains of the original mosque.[1] Ibrahim is also remembered for the obscure phrase *yunka yunka*. When he was about to confer an honour on somebody, the Katsina story has it that he would say 'yunka yunka pay a thousand cowries'.

In the *Tarikh al Sudan* we read of at least two eminent malams from the Sankore University of Timbuktu, Makhluf bin Ali and Muhammad bin Ahmed, who also visited Katsina about this time; the latter actually settled in Katsina and was treated with the greatest respect, being made a judge. Islam, therefore, was certainly beginning to take firm root at the end of the fifteenth century, and when in 1512 Haj Muhammad the first Askia of Songhai, a man of singularly devout principles, conquered Katsina, it received a distinct impulse. The bulk of the people, as ever, bore the change with equanimity. It has been observed that the open nature of the Hausa country has afforded ample opportunity for free intercourse between tribes and towns, with the inevitable result that the Hausa-speaking peoples, besides being largely traders, are notably free from ignorant prejudices and highly adaptable to new ideas. These, as in their language,[2] they have a genius for remoulding and remodelling so that they become fully absorbed as Hausa phenomena.

In 1512 came the temporary overlordship of Songhai, when Katsina virtually became a fief of Gao, but she regained her independence at the famous battle of Karfata against Askia Daud in 1554. The chroniclers relate the story:

Askia Daud went to Kukia, whence he sent the Hi-Koi,[3] Ali Dudo, against Katsina at the head of a detachment consisting of 24 horsemen. This detachment encountered, at a place called Karfata, a body of 400 horsemen belonging to the people of Lipti[4] in the country of Katsina. The two forces engaged in a hand-to-hand fight, which was very long and very bloody.

[1] Preface, p. viii, and communication from F. de F. Daniel, formerly D.O. Katsina. The story of the *wali* comes from Mr David Roberts and also the date (fifteenth century).

[2] For a study of linguistic adaptation in Hausa, see A. H. M. Kirk-Greene, 'Hausa Neologisms', *Africa*, January 1963.

[3] The equivalent of the Hausa title *Sarkin Jirgi*, here 'Lord High Admiral'.

[4] Possibly a copyist's error for *lifidi*, meaning that the Katsinawa were protected by horse-armour.

The Katsina people killed 15 of their enemy, among whom was the Hi-Koi, mentioned above. They took the remaining nine, all of whom were wounded, prisoner—including among them 'Alouaz-Lil, the son of Faran Umar-Komzagho and father of Qasem, Bokar-Chili-Idji, Muhammad-Della-Idji, etc. The victors took care of the wounded and gave them the greatest attention. They then set them at liberty and sent them back to Askia Daud, telling them that 'men of such quality, endowed with such great valour and such courage, did not deserve to die'. The vigour and daring of these warriors so amazed the people of Katsina that ever afterwards they spoke of them as models to be followed.[1]

By this time Katsina city had grown to a considerable size with a circuit of seven or eight miles. As an illustration of the diversity of its interests and activities, the number and names of its quarters speak to the great Songhai and Mali influence in the original town. Apart from the smaller wards there were about a hundred principal quarters, such as the official quarter; the old quarter; quarters for people from Bornu, from Gobir, from Mali, from Songhai, from Asben; quarters for the various trades; a students' quarter; a dancing quarter; and a quarter at each of the eight gates. Present-day wards like Ankara and Tudun Mali reveal, as does the title of Dan Sonwe, the vigorous influence of Mali and Songhai in Katsina.

It is hard to trace an exact record of the varying degrees of independence that Katsina enjoyed during this time, but it must have been an anxious period. To the south was the continual thorn of Kano and in later years the menace of Kwararafa; to the east lay the powerful Bornu empire, while from the north or west there was always the liability of an invasion from Songhai or Kebbi, and later from Gobir. Considering all things Katsina was fortunate in steering a safe course amid these perils, which had a damaging effect on trade.

When the Songhai empire was broken up by the Moors at the end of the sixteenth century, it appears that Katsina transferred her allegiance to Bornu. Every king of Katsina on his accession was required to send 100 slaves to the Mai of Ngazargamu and this tribute continued till the reign of Agwaragi in 1784. A similar tribute was exacted from Gobir but was discontinued by Bawa Jan Gwarzo (1777–95). Bornu now protected Katsina, and

[1] Al Sadi, *Tarikh al Sudan*, quoted in Hodgkin, op. cit., p. 107.

in one battle the Mai, Haj Ali, is said to have taken 1,000 prisoners, three of whom were sent back to their chief with their ears cut off and strung round their necks. In about 1680 a famous Katsina *malam*, Dan Marina, whose name is preserved by a cemetery in the town, wrote a song of deliverance for Mai Ali of Bornu to commemorate his success over Kwararafa and their final ejection from Hausaland. Here is part of the poem, in translation from the Arabic:

Ali has triumphed over the heathen, a matchless triumph in the path of God
No Sultan like him; A lath among laths, ever stout of heart.
Has he not brought us succour? Verily but for him
Our hearts had never ceased from dread of the unbelievers.
Narrow had become to us the earth pressed by the foe,
Till Ali saved our children and their children yet unborn.
O people! Say with one accord 'May God grant him recompense for our deliverance'.
He drove back to their furthest borders the army of the Jukon,
And God scattered their host disheartened.

Give thanks again for what our Mai Ali has wrought;
For he has ransomed the whole Sudan from strife.
This is the need of praise of the servant of God,
The Sheikh the Sa'id Hamid,
Upon Ali, King of the two rivers, who stayed war.
I, Dan Marina, fear no one save the savage, whose law is greed.
Praise be to God and thanks for His deliverance from the pride of the rebellious.
And thanksgiving and peace upon the Prophet, the guide to God, our refuge.[1]

It is towards the end of the fifteenth century that history records the first encounters with Kano, a struggle that continued intermittently for over 200 years, though by this time Katsina had ceased to be tributary to Kano. Doubtless some of the rivalry stemmed from a struggle for the proprietorship of the trans-Saharan trade at the western Sudan end. During Mohamman Rumfa's reign in Kano (1463–99), an indecisive eleven years' war was begun between Katsina and Kano. His son and successor, Abdullahi, brought the war to an end by defeating Katsina, but in the 1570s the tables were reversed and Katsina laid waste the

[1] Quoted in H. R. Palmer, *Bornu Sahara and Sudan*, pp. 246–7.

country right up to the gates of Kano. At the end of the century Kano was back in the ascendant under Muhamman Zaki, and on one day at dawn, on the last day of Ramadan, the Kano forces raided Katsina and made away with many prisoners and horses. The Katsina attempt at retaliation failed miserably at Karayi.

A century later, we find Katsina under Uban Yari, otherwise known as Muhammadu Dan Wari, strong enough to defeat and kill the Kano chiefs known as Magani Mai Amfani Baki, Kutumbi and his son Alhaji, and with her confidence established Katsina was in a position to sign a treaty of alliance with Kano in union against their common enemies, the non-Muslim peoples of Hausaland. This was brought about by the increasing gravity of the menace from Kwararafa in the south, beyond the Benue. In 1653, led by their chief Adashu, they had penetrated up to the gates of Kano. Eighteen years later, in 1671, they broke into Kano city itself and slaughtered a large number of the inhabitants including many *malamai*; the Sarkin Kano fled to Daura.

It was about this time that the Kwararafa attacked Katsina. They made a breach in the walls and occupied the western corner of the city. The king of Katsina held out in the inner citadel of the Kangiwa, but many of the inhabitants were seized by the fierce Jukuns and cast alive into a great pit, which is still known as Giwa-Rano. For some reason the Kwararafa did not push home their success. Tradition tells that, thanks to the urgent prayers of the *malam* Dan Masani, the Jukun general was kicked in the groin as he was mounting his horse for the final assault and died on the spot. The Kwararafa fled in dismay.

With the fall of the Songhai empire in 1591, Katsina had gained her independence of Gao. True, to some extent she was now drawn into the orbit of Bornu influence, but at the same time she became in her own right, if not the first, at least one of the leading cities of the western Sudan. By the beginning of the eighteenth century the kingdom of Katsina reached her peak of prosperity and power. The old wealth and tradition of learning of Songhai became diverted her way, so that Katsina found herself a city of wide repute, a conscious apostle of civilization. Scholars now found their way to Katsina instead of to Timbuktu as of old. The leather-working trade for which Agades is famous was introduced to Katsina by the Songhai. Her citizens were renowned for their manners and courtesy, her schools for their learning, her administration and judiciary for their wisdom. Katsina's repute became as fair as her lovely name, and it was to her that Barth awarded the palm of Hausaland:

> Here that state of civilization which had been called forth by contact with the Arabs seemed to have reached its highest degree, and as the Hausa language here attained the greatest richness of form and the most refined pronunciation so also the manners of Katsina were distinguished by superior politeness from those of the other towns of Hausa.[1]

Furthermore, before the Fulani régime Katsina was a very important commercial centre with all caravans converging in her direction. She occupied the position which Kano has since assumed, and in those days Kano was inferior in both prosperity and learning. Her sway extended over Maradi to the north, Zamfara to the west, and all the land to the south as far as Birnin Gwari. But by the 1750s Gobir, freed from her struggles with her hereditary enemies in the north, turned her aggressive attention towards the south. Sarkin Gobir Babari captured Birnin Zamfara but Sarkin Zamfara Maroki made good his escape and took refuge with his vassal Tsaidu in Kiawa. This is an ancient hill fortress on the western edge of the Rubu bush, the natural boundary between Katsina and Sokoto even today. Katsina records say that Babari besieged Kiawa for seven years but Mamman Bello's account gives a siege of fifteen years by Bawa Jan Gwarzo. It is well known that King Agwaragi slew a later Sarkin Gobir Yakuba, when he was called to the assistance of the Katsinawa in Kiawa. This would have been in about 1801, from Maradi records. Kiawa was never taken in the long war between Katsina and Gobir, in which Katsina was more successful than Kano, but in the long run a great deal of Zamfara and territory round Maradi fell to the Gobirawa.

The rise of Katsina was described thus by Barth:

> The town probably did not receive the name of the province till it had become large and predominant; which, even if Leo be correct, we must conclude did not happen much before the middle of the 16th century of our era, while in early times some separate villages probably occupied the site where, at a later period, the immense town spread out. The oldest of these villages is said to have been Ambutey or Mbutey, where we must presume Komayo and his successors to have

[1] Quoted in A. H. M. Kirk-Greene, *Barth's Travels in Nigeria*, p. 95.

resided. After Gogo had been conquered by Mulay Hamed, the emperor of Morocco, and, from a large and industrial capital, had become a provincial town, a great part of the commerce which formerly centred there must have been transferred to Katsena, although this latter place never seems to have had any considerable trade in gold, which formed the staple of the market of Gogo. Thus the town went on increasing to that enormous size, the vestiges of which still exist at the present time, although the quarter actually inhabited comprises but a small part of its extent.

The town, if only half its immense area were ever tolerably well inhabited, must certainly have had a population of at least a hundred thousand souls; for its circuit is between thirteen and fourteen English miles. At present, when the inhabited quarter is reduced to the north-western part, and when this is mostly deserted, there are scarcely seven or eight thousand people living in it. In former times it was the residence of a prince, who, though he seems never to have attained to any remarkable degree of power, and was indeed almost always in some degree dependent on, or a vassal of, the king of Bornu, nevertheless one of the most wealthy and conspicuous rulers of Negroland . . . Katsena, during the seventeenth and eighteenth centuries of our era, seems to have been the chief city of this part of Negroland, as well as in commercial and political importance as in other respects. . . .[1]

At the beginning of the nineteenth century came the jihad and a final change of régime. Fulani herdsmen had for centuries been drifting peaceably into the Hausa states; some had maintained their nomadic habits while others had settled down in these new pastures and a few had become important members of the local community, as *malamai* or teachers. Furthermore, Katsina chroniclers assure us, disaster was augured for Katsina even before the jihad broke out. It seems that the king, Bawa dan Gima, insisted on opening the house which the Habe elders had for hundreds of years kept covered with red leather: any king who opened this 'seat of power' would bring doom to his people by war. Bawa had his way. Thousands of egrets (*balbela*) flew out and filled the whole town. Shortly after the Fulani were astir with rumours of a religious war.

When the news of the Shehu Usman dan Fodio's revolt in Gobir spread like a bush fire through Hausaland, most of these Fulani herdsmen threw in their lot with the new movement. It was their enthusiasm which was responsible for stirring up large numbers

[1] Quoted in Hodgkin, op. cit., p. 118, and Kirk-Greene, op. cit., p. 94.

of the easy-going Hausa peasantry, whose profession of Islam was in many instances only nominal, into a suitably warlike spirit. As usual the excitement of revolt appealed most strongly to the more unsettled members of the community, but among the few rich clans to assist was the quasi-Fulani clan of the Sulibawa, who became prominent supporters of the movement. It must not be forgotten that Usman dan Fodio was in revolt against Gobir, the traditional enemy of Katsina, which meant that support for the jihad was probably warmer in Katsina than in the other Hausa States. The Sulibawa or Sisulbe are said to be of Mandingo origin. At an early date they migrated from the west and settled in the neighbourhood of northern Zamfara to the west of Katsina. The chief of the Sulibawa at this time was Umaru Dumyawa, living near Zandam in Jibiya District. On the outbreak of the jihad Umaru Dumyawa, Na Alhaji, and Malam Umaru of Dallaji near Bindawa all went to assist the Shehu. Na Alhaji is said to have been a teacher, who had married one of the daughters of the Habe Sarkin Katsina. In due course each was given a flag and told to spread the faith in Katsina.

Katsina historians relate the following story about the grant of a flag to Katsina. Usman dan Fodio was unable to decide between Umaru Dallaji, Umaru Dumyawa and Na Alhaji, so he awarded each of them a minor flag and told them to go and say good-bye to his son Muhammadu Bello. It was to Bello that he had previously given the true jihad flag for Katsina, to keep until he could decide which of the three contestants should become the first emir. Impatient at being kept waiting, Na Alhaji and Umaru Dumyawa left Bello's residence and set out for Katsina, saying, 'We have already taken leave of the Shehu, what right has a junior man to trouble us by keeping us waiting thus?' When Bello came forth, only Malam Umaru Dallaji was to be seen. He thereupon gave him the flag and so granted him precedence over the other two claimants, though they were by right the senior ones. Meanwhile Umaru Dumyawa had arrived back in Katsina and, entering through the Kofar Guga, he attacked the Habe and occupied the house of Sarkin Sulibawa. At the same time Na Alhaji entered through the Kofar Yandaka, fought the Habe and occupied the house of Yandaka. This is the origin of the great Katsina families of the Sulibawa of Bugaje and the Yandakawa of Dutsinma, who, by virtue of their being receivers of some kind of flag at the hands of the Shehu, stand in special precedence relationship with the Emir of Katsina.

Another tradition has it that, after their farewells in Sokoto, the three men met at Runka, having travelled via Kaura and Sabri. There they had a quarrel and Malam Umaru is said to have slapped Na Alhaji's face. As a result of this dispute, Umaru Dallaji went off alone to attack the Habe Katsinawa, Na Alhaji retired to Zakka, where on his death he was succeeded by his son Mamman Dikko, and Umaru Dumyawa went back to Zandam in the north. Katsina sources claim that Na Alhaji died of a poisoned *riga* or gown given to him by his father-in-law, the Habe Sarkin Katsina, whose power he had in vain sought to usurp. Umaru Dallaji went from Radda to Bainye and thence to Sabon Birni in Kaura district, where he killed the king of the Habe. Although many of them remained and submitted to the Fulani, the majority now retired to Dankama, some say 30,000 in all, including all the nobility. They rallied to attack Umaru but he again managed to force them back to Dankama. This time, it is said, Sarkin Katsina Halidu threw himself down a well in mortification at his defeat.

The Habe forces, after electing a new chief, made for Damagaram, but, fearful of Bornu under whose tutelage Zinder stood, they went to Maradi and founded the city. Here they more or less settled, despite several periods of revolt, and followed the Sulibawa, paying tribute to Umaru Dumyawa in Zandam who controlled all the country to the north as far as Maradi. Mamman Dikko, who was given the title of Yandaka, controlled the western districts from Sabri. As flag-bearers, both of them followed Sokoto direct and not the Fulani emir in Katsina, Umaru Dallaji, although they each maintained houses in the city. By the Shehu's orders, they had to confer with Umaru Dallaji in Katsina from time to time, and Umaru Dallaji was more or less recognized as the chief by virtue of his activities against the Habe.[1]

It is worthy of note that the Emir of Katsina never attained the extensive position of authority enjoyed by the chiefs of some of the other emirates. Not only Yandaka and Sarkin Sulibawa, but also Maradi of Kurfi, Dangi of Yantumaki, Gatari of Umadau, Dan Yabi of Muniya, and Sarkin Fulani of Yan Rundau all paid allegiance direct to the Sarkin Musulmi and received their turbans at his own hands. Sarkin Katsina, as Emir or governor

[1] According to Yerima Abdu dan Sarkin Katsina Abubakar.

of the Sarkin Musulmi, was no more than *primus inter pares*. In Sokoto, Katsina affairs were entrusted to the Galadima. One such Galadima, who delegated his local authority to one Faruku, has a long story about his son which has given rise to the epigram *kome a ke yi a yi, Dan Maliki ya ratsa Bawada har soro*.[1]

Umaru Dallaji was appointed Emir in 1806, the year in which he finally drove out the Habe. Of the intensity of his war with the Habe, Dr Barth wrote:

> Five princes of Katsina, one after the other, fell in this struggle for religious and national independence; and the Pullo general was not quite secure of his conquest till after the total destruction of the town of Dankama, when Magajin Haladu was slain only four months after his predecessor Mahamudu had succumbed in Sabongari [Sabon Birni].[2]

Katsina was starved by a long siege before Umaru Dallaji could properly establish the Fulani supremacy in Katsina, and he owed a great measure of his success to Namoda, chief of the Alibawa, who brought help from Zamfara, and to Sarkin Ahir of Agades.

Umaru died in 1835. The Galadima of Sokoto, in whose charge lay Katsina, arrived and turbanned Sidiku, Umaru's second son, in preference to the eldest son, Muhamman Bello, on account of the former's learning and piety.

Eight years later a serious attempt was made to reinstate the Habe power in Katsina. Umaru Dumyawa had been succeeded as Sarkin Sulibawa by his son Abubakar, and his demands for money from Maradi fanned the ashes of smouldering resentment into flames. Umaru dan Mari, a direct descendant of the Habe dynasty who had succeeded Rauda as king of the Katsina exiles in Maradi when the latter was killed at Gawakuke after a futile attack on Sokoto, marched south from Maradi through the then well-populated Rubu bush. The Rumawa immediately threw in their lot with him. From Ruma he came to Muniya, thence to

[1] We are grateful to the Katsina N.A. for the following gloss on this: 'This epigram, meaning "Come what may, Dan Maliki has penetrated Bawada and reached the minaret", has important historical significance to this day. Except for slaves, nobody ever rode a horse through the two gates leading to the Emir's palace, Kofar Soro and Kofar Bai. The tradition is still observed, visitors of whatever rank leaving their transport outside the Kofar Soro and proceeding on foot to the Emir's Palace. When a certain Dan Galadima wished to flout the Emir's authority and display his inviolability, he rode through the gate; the next morning he died.'

[2] Quoted in Kirk-Greene, op. cit., p. 95.

Wurma, and finally established himself at Karofi with a strong following. The Emir, Sidiku, hastily sent to Sokoto for help and Kano was told to supply reinforcements. At the battle of Taura near Karofi, Dan Mari was defeated by the joint Fulani forces, but he managed to escape as a fugitive to Maradi. Some say he was later killed at Matazu; certainly this town was destroyed soon afterwards by the Emir Sidiku, who wrought a merciless vengeance on all the places that had harboured the invader. The result of the invasion itself and Sidiku's vengeance is that this once thickly populated Rubu country remained until recently almost uninhabited bush. Most of the villages withdrew bodily to Maradi.

Sidiku had become so self-satisfied and oppressive that in 1844 the Sarkin Musulmi deposed him in favour of his elder brother, Muhamman Bello. Dr Barth made the following notes in his diary of his meetings with the Emir:

> Having assorted such a present as I could afford, I protested once more to Elaiji that, my other luggage having gone on in advance to Kano, I had but very little to offer the governor.
>
> I went about noon with my protector and a great number of Asbenawa to offer the governor my compliments and my present. Sitting down under a tree at a considerable distance from the spot where he himself was seated, we waited a little, till we should be called into his presence, when his brother, who held the office of galadima, came to us—a man of immense corpulency, resembling a eunuch. Indeed nothing but the cut of his face, his aquiline nose, and rather light colour, and the little goatlike beard which ornamented his chin, could expose him to the suspicion of being a Pullo or Ba-Fellanchi.[1]

In 1869 Muhamman Bello was succeeded by Ahmadu Rufai, who reigned only eight months before he died. He was succeeded by Ibrahim, son of Muhamman Bello.

In 1882 Musa, son of Umaru Dallaji, succeeded his nephew Ibrahim, but he was then a very old man. On his death five years later the title reverted to the other branch of the family in the person of Abubakar, grandson of Muhamman Bello, the eldest son of Umaru Dallaji. Musa and his son Yero, who was made Durbi, had spared no pains to despoil Ibrahim's family, especially Abubakar when he was Yerima. On Musa's death Abubakar promptly revenged himself on Musa's family, so that on Yero's accession in

[1] Quoted in Kirk-Greene, op. cit., pp. 89–90; 92–93.

1904 he and his family had been virtually paupers for seventeen years.

Meanwhile, the Habe in Maradi had more than once demonstrated that they were still a power to be reckoned with. They still maintained their own Habe political machinery. The Chief Council consisted of:

> Kadi, the judge;
> Dan Kaka, confidential adviser;
> Galadima, eunuch;
> Durbi, chief lord;
> Kaura, war chief.

Four kings succeeded Dan Mari. Then came Dan Baskori, the greatest of all the Habe generals. He once more devastated the Ruma bush and brought his arms to the gates of Katsina. At Kabakawa, during a night sortie, the Sarkin Katsina only just escaped with his life. After further fighting along the banks of the Jani river Dan Baskori returned to Tassawa. A year later he returned by the *hanyar Hanayi* route, lying to the west of the present Katsina town forest reserve and east of the *hanyar Baturiya*, and penetrated right down to Karayi. These two roads, cut straight through the bush and still traceable, were recognized trading routes, one leading to Chafe and the other towards Kano and Zaria. From Karayi, Dan Baskori marched against Fatika, in Zaria country, where there was heavy fighting. During his reign the Maradi of the Katsina Habe reached the height of her prosperity.

Dan Baskori was followed by his son Bermu or Barafiya. He came down and invaded Kano via Ruma, Rawayo, Kankiya, Kafarda, and Yangworzo near Bici, where he established himself for a while before returning home. Mazawaje, who succeeded him, was a man of peace and refused to war with the Fulani. For this reason, after a period of forty years people began to trickle back to the devastated regions of Ruma, but unfortunately Mazawaje was soon deposed by the Maradi Habe, who could countenance nothing but war with the Fulani. He sought refuge at the court of the Sarkin Musulmi, and was succeeded by Malam.

War now broke out again and once more Ruma was depopulated. From Maradi, Malam invaded as far as Kiru and, after an interval of three kings, Mijinyawa penetrated to Kafur, southwards of Malumfashi. In Mijinyawa's reign Maradi was divided into two camps: one followed Mijinyawa as Sarkin Katsina of Tassawa while the other declared for Mowadaci as Sarkin Katsina of Maradi.

Shortly before the turn of the century, word was sent to Sokoto giving warning of a proposed combined attack by Mijinyawa and the Sarkin Gobir. Abubakar, the Emir of Katsina, was told to provide reinforcements. He dispatched a force under the renowned warrior Muhammadu, Kankiyar Ruma, known as Dan Were; among the other chiefs was the Durbi, Muhammadu Dikko, later Emir. There was a tremendous battle at Chikaji. The late Sarkin Ruma used to relate how he saw his father, Dan Were, spur out of the Fulani ranks and single out the Sarkin Gobir in the very presence of the two armies drawn up in battle array. His father speared the Sarkin Gobir through the chest, whereupon the Habe army turned and fled in confusion. When Dan Were took the horses seized in this battle to the Sarkin Musulmi at Sokoto, he was given the title of Sarkin Yaki and the country of Ruma as his fief. Abubakar thereupon transferred the title of Kankiya to his son. Of this final war between the Katsina Habe and the Fulani we have a graphic account of the personal fight between Kaura Hasau of Maradi and Kaura Wayya of Katsina, when the former invoked the *tsafi* charms of Sarkin Noma Kare and alone beheaded both Kaura Wayya and his brother Yaro whilst they were praying before the battle.[1]

Formerly an annual tribute used to be paid to the Galadima of Sokoto representing the Sarkin Musulmi. This was originally of small value; it was accepted as a present and a portion was remitted to the donors. Latterly the tribute had become a levy extracted from unwilling payers, an imposition that quickly destroyed the close personal relations that had earlier existed between Katsina and Sokoto. We have a hint of this in the following letter sent to Sokoto by the Emir Abubakar:

> After greetings, that is to inform you that my messenger Dan Daura has been sent to enquire after your health and welfare and if you wish to ask about us, we are as well as you could desire. We inform you that the reason that I have been so long in sending to you that which you ordered is the Maradi war. Allah granted me power to go to the

[1] See Mani Kankiya, *Yaki na karshe tsakanin Katsinawa da Maradawa.*

country of Maradi and I myself went with my army to a village called Ungwar Mata, which we sacked and burnt, and in which we found much booty by Allah's will and your blessing. So we have written to you in accordance with what is between us, the love, trust and friendship which we have inherited. Peace. My present to you is five slaves and ten rolls of white turban for your blessing.[1]

Abubakar decided not to offer resistance to the British, despite the exhortations of a strong war party, and he welcomed Lugard as he rode in through the Yandaka gate—an event commemorated by a plaque there. The Emir made elaborate arrangements to receive Lugard, turning out of his palace and offering Lugard accommodation.[2] A charge, which today Katsina historians declare to be false, was shortly brought against Abubakar of polluting the Residency well by throwing a dead dog into it, and in 1904 he was deposed in favour of Yero, son of Musa, and exiled to Ilorin. Yero, however, proved a complete failure, and within a very short time, the Durbi, Muhammadu Dikko, son of Gidado, was appointed in his stead. Lugard described the great ceremony held in Kano to celebrate the installation of the Emir, Yero:

On January 2nd a review parade of all the troops and police was held on the polo ground, which forms part of the great plain surrounding Kano. Thousands of Kano horsemen and of spectators on foot formed a great crescent some half a mile long, facing the hollow-square formation of the troops. The Katsena-Emir-elect, after performing the elaborate ablutions enjoined by the Koran, took an oath of friendship and allegiance on the Sacred Book administered to him by the Alkali of Kano, and I invested him with the insignia of Katsena—a sabre in a silver scabbard inscribed with Arabic—whose origin is lost in antiquity, the drum on which twelve strokes are solemnly beaten, and which is not sounded again till a new accession takes place, the silver

[1] This letter is quoted in H. F. Backwell, *The Occupation of Hausaland*, p. 34. In reply to our question to Katsina, the N.A. supplied the following interesting note: 'The substance of the letter is confirmed. Elderly courtiers add that when Sarkin Katsina Abubakar was ready to take the annual tribute in person to Sokoto, he stopped at Wawarkaza in Kankara district. There his spies told him that the Habe were planning to ambush him and seize the tribute, and that other Habe forces were ready to march on Katsina as soon as he had neared Sokoto. The Emir therefore returned to Katsina, sent the tribute by special messenger and never again visited Sokoto.'

[2] In Katsina today there is nothing to substantiate the earlier assertion that the Emir lodged Lugard in his private mosque . . . a statement that has always struck us as highly coloured and most improbable.

seal, and the new gown and turban. He was received with great acclamations. . . . The troops gave a royal salute and marched past.[1]

Muhammadu Dikko, a Ba-Sulibe, was not a direct descendant of Umaru Dallaji but had risen by his own merits. His grandfather, Dahiru, was a Shinkafi man who was given the post of Collector of Tolls and a house at the Kofar Samri by the Emir Muhamman Bello. When Dahiru's son Gidado grew up as a noted warrior, Muhamman Bello, who had only one son, Ibrahim, took a liking to the young man and treated him as a second son. He first gave him the title of Marusa, then of Kankiya, and finally made him Durbi. When Durbi Gidado died, Musa, who was then Emir, ignored Gidado's family and turbanned his own son Yero as Durbi. On Abubakar's accession, however, Yero was dispossessed in favour of Gidado's younger brother Sada. When Sada died, the Emir appointed Muhammadu Dikko, son of Gidado, to the office of Durbi, and from here he was selected as the ninth Fulani Emir of Katsina. The story goes that Muhammadu Dikko had come to the notice of the Resident, Palmer, when he was urgently trying to build a fort at Katsina after the Satiru rising of 1906. The Emir and his leading men all produced excuses until the turn came of a certain district head. He at once promised to produce over a thousand men and complete the work in so many days. Asked to name his reward, he requested not half the kingdom but the whole of Katsina. This district head was Muhammadu Dikko.

Katsina's eminence among the Hausa Bakwai and her long history of active resistance to Fulani suzerainty did not meet with compensatory recognition under the British administration for another thirty years. To begin with Katsina emirate was included in Kano Province; in 1926 it was transferred to Zaria; and not until August 1934 was the Katsina Province formed, thereby becoming the most recent of all the Northern Provinces till the creation of Sardauna Province in 1961.

Fortunately Katsina's sterling worth established her eminence. A disastrous famine, in which it was estimated that 5,000 people

[1] *Annual Report of Northern Nigeria*, 1904, para. 82. Katsina N.A. has recalled how at the later 1906 ceremony the Emir met the deposed Yero. The latter discourteously addressed the Emir simply as 'Dikko' and was sharply reminded that he, Muhammadu Dikko, was now the rightful Emir of Katsina.

and 10,000 cattle died, rocked the agricultural prosperity of the emirate, but the extension of the railway line from Zaria northwards brought promise of a safer future. Bred from the railway, Funtua developed into an economic centre in the 1920s. Cotton made the emirate famous in this decade, mixed farming in the next. Earlier still, in 1911, an experiment had been made by the Emir with a horse-breeding stock farm in Mashi. A branch of 'Dan Hausa's' Kano Nassarawa school had been opened at Katsina as far back as 1912, followed by a technical school which became the forerunner of the North's craft schools system, but it was in 1921 that Katsina's claim to academic eminence was acknowledged by the foundation of the Katsina Training College, instantly—and prophetically, in the event—dubbed by its pupils as 'the university of the North'. Doubtless mindful of the great Katsina tradition of scholarship and courtesy, the Governor had this to say at the opening ceremony:

> The students should not be careless about the observances of their religious duties nor forgetful of the traditions of their fellow-countrymen, nor lacking in the respect and courtesy which they owe to their parents, to all in positions of authority, and to all old people.
>
> This College is designed to serve all the Muhammadan Emirates in Nigeria, and, as you are aware, the young men who will receive in it their training are drawn from every part of the Muhammadan States. It was necessary, however, to select some place at which to establish this College; and it was for two reasons that I selected Katsina as the most appropriate place for the purpose.
>
> The first of these reasons is that Katsina in ancient days was held in high repute throughout the Muhammadan Emirates as a seat of learning and of piety; and it is good, I think, that this tradition should be perpetuated. My second reason was that Katsina, though it is an important town and the administrative capital of an important Emirate, is not as yet so close to the railway and to the commercial centres of Nigeria as to make it unsuitable for that quiet and tranquillity and that freedom from distractions which are so necessary for young men who are devoting their lives to study.
>
> It is very necessary that the youths who will receive their training in this College, and who will thereafter carry the torch of learning and knowledge to all parts of the Muhammadan Emirates in order thereby to enlighten the ignorance of their countrymen, should concentrate all their energies and all their attention upon the task that is set them during their period of training. That they should cherish no other

desire or ambition than that of fitting themselves by a long course of training for the great work of teaching others the things which they here will learn. And that while living in this College the ordinary lives of young Muhammadan men of birth and standing, they should be subjected to no influences which might tend to make them careless about the observance of their religious duties, forgetful of the customs and traditions of their fellow countrymen or lacking in the respect and courtesy which they owe to their parents, to all who occupy positions of authority and to all old people.

For to these young men will hereafter be entrusted the duty of training and instructing the boys who attend the Provincial Schools in which they will later be employed. And it will fall to them to teach those boys, not only the lessons learned from books which they will here acquire, but the way that good Muhammadans should live, the good manners, good behaviour and the courteous deportment without which mere book learning is of little worth.[1]

The Emir had the gate Kofar Waziri specially built for these students.

In the same year the Emir visited both Mecca and Europe; his diary and photographs of his visit to England are as interesting to study as the record of the Etsu Nupe's visit a generation later. On his return the *bambadawa*, the town's professional beggars, composed a new praise-song:

> You first went to Mecca, you Dikko first went to
> England,
> Brave hero on whom even poison may be tested,
> let others learn from you![2]

A new N.A. Council was formed in 1927 when the old triumvirate of the Inner Council was broken up and the Waziri, Haruna, was removed and made Sarkin Kaita.

In 1929 the N.A. police were formed under a young man Usman Nagogo, one of the royal princes and destined later to succeed to the emirship. It was in that year, too, that the former Waziri, Sarkin Kaita, performed a well-remembered pilgrimage. Rejecting the precedent of seven Katsina pilgrims who, in the previous year, had adventurously travelled to Mecca via Lagos and

[1] From Sir Hugh Clifford's Address.

[2] Cf. the praise-song compiled by the Bida minstrels to commemorate the Etsu's purchase of the first automobile: see p. 276.

Marseilles, he set out from headquarters at Zaria in a ten-ton Ford lorry in the month of March and reached El Obeid after only three weeks' driving. There he sold his lorry, taking the train to Khartoum and thence to Jiddah. Though a similar journey was performed by the Emir of Muri a few years later,[1] Sarkin Kaita is held to have been the first Northern Nigerian to have made the overland journey by car.

Building on the scholarly tradition of Katsina and the success of the Katsina Training College, the town was selected in 1930 as host for the first elementary training college. This was designed for teachers in Muslim primary schools and was balanced by the parallel experiment at Toro for non-Muslim teachers. About this time so much concern was shown over the slaughter of wild life that the killing or capturing of both giraffe and elephant were prohibited for a period of five years.

In 1933 the Emir went to Mecca, and to England when he was received in audience by King George. There is a delightful story of how he met Lugard on this occasion and told him of the plans and counter-plans put forward for ambushing and capturing him when he rode into Katsina in March 1903. At that time he had been the senior councillor and on him had fallen the fearful duty of receiving the High Commissioner. It was Muhammadu Dikko's personal idea that the plaque, now outside the Kofar Yandaka, should be put up to mark Lugard's arrival. During the Emir's absence his son, Muhammadu Gidado, the Durbi, was left to govern the emirate with a Council of Regency. Katsina suffered the death of two prominent leaders during the year, Mallam Alhaji Sayidi, who held the portfolio of education in the N.A. Council—in itself a rare appointment at that time—and the District Head of Kaura, reputed to be over a hundred years old.

Following on the creation of the Province of Katsina in 1934,[2] the Emir of Katsina along with his neighbour the Emir of Daura and a retinue of thirty paid a state visit to the areas of Benue and Ilorin and then on to Ibadan and Lagos. Muhammadu Dikko also made fame by personally paying for the construction of a new mosque, still a proud feature of Katsina town, and by building up

[1] When I arrived in Jalingo in 1950, the highlight of my Hausa lessons was to listen to the account of this pilgrimage across the desert by Ibrahim, the Emir's personal driver.—A.K-G.

[2] I am still baffled by the official map of 1932, now hanging in the Provincial Office, Zaria, which shows Katsina as a separate Province!—A.K-G.

a victorious polo team—in which three of his sons were playing—that won both the Georgian and Nigerian Cups.

On the suggestion of Muhammadu Dikko, committees known as District Economic Boards were set up in 1937. Representing all elements of the community, they were aimed at providing the people with full means to express their needs as well as at facilitating co-operation between the central administration and the districts. In furtherance of the same principles, the Emir increased his Council by three members chosen to represent the ancient hereditary advisers of the Emir, who it was thought would also bring to the Council the broader agricultural basis which it seemed to lack. These were the Kaura, Yandaka and Galadima. The Emir paid his fourth visit to England in 1937, sadly for an operation on his eyes.

After seventeen years of fame in Katsina, the Training College was transferred to Kaduna in 1938. Perhaps in compensation for this educational loss, the Kafinsole farm settlement was opened and the thriving girls' school was moved from its temporary quarters in the Emir's compound to the vacant college buildings. A splendid ceremony to mark the opening of the new N.A. offices was held and was attended by such a throng of royalty as had never been seen before in Katsina, including the Emirs of Kano, Zaria, Bauchi, Hadejia, Daura, Kazaure and Gumel.[1]

On the death of the great Muhammadu Dikko in 1944 at the age of 79,[2] his son Usman Nagogo was appointed Emir. Under his guidance Katsina has fully maintained the illustrious position established under his father. Usman Nagogo had first undertaken the pilgrimage when he was only 16, and was Magajin Gari at the time of his selection as Emir. During the war he became widely known outside his emirate and his country—at that time an uncommon phenomenon—by his visit to the West African brigades in Burma. He was the North's first representative on the Government's Executive Council in Lagos under the 1947 constitution, so that his appointment as a Regional Minister without portfolio in 1956 came as no surprise to his many admirers. His achievements as an outstanding polo player, a sport which was started in Katsina in 1924, and in which Katsina has been unequalled since

[1] In this connexion, para. 40 of the *Annual Report of Katsina Province*, 1938, is interesting.

[2] A moving description, itself a masterpiece of Hausa prose, is given in Muhammadu Bello Kagara, *Sarkin Katsina, Alhaji Muhammadu Dikko*, 1951.

the 'thirties, were yet another way of bringing this remarkable ruler into the public eye.[1] So, too, was his unusual encouragement of his two sons, Hassan and Hamza, to take commissions in the Nigerian Army and the Nigeria Police Force.

On the retirement of the Waziri in 1954 it was decided by the N.A. not to renew the office. The chief Alkali, Alhaji Muhammadu Bello Kagara, however, was promoted to the office of Wali with responsibility for legal affairs and so became a member of the N.A. Inner Council. At the request of the Outer Council, members of the Inner Council now sat as a sort of Government front bench. Further administrative reforms were undertaken in the following year, and as they are to a large extent representative of the reorganizational ideas then in the air in many emirates, it is worth quoting parts of the official report:

> Following on the reorganization of the Central Office last year, an attempt was made to solve the difficulty presented by the absence of a Waziri. Chaos would result on the withdrawal of the District Officer at any time in the foreseeable future. It being apparent that the office of Waziri was neither traditional nor popular, the establishment of a 'Civil Secretary' and a 'Financial Secretary' was considered. This was found impracticable as there was nobody suitably qualified or suitable for the posts, and the suggestion was not popular with the Emir and Council. A suggestion to form an active Council, with members supervising several departments, was readily received and it was agreed to appoint a sub-committee to put up recommendations. The District Officer and three of the more enlightened members of the Council formed the sub-committee and eventually produced a scheme wherein certain members would be responsible for the supervision and financial control of the various Native Authority departments. This was dis-

[1] In Mallam Bello Kagara's *Sarkin Katsina Muhamman Dikko* he writes, 'Tun cikin 1921 aka fara yin *polo*, watau kwallon dawaki, a Katsina. A lokachin nan akwai wani joji a Katsina ana kiransa *Captain Sheridan*. Shi ya yi kokari kwarai wurin koya wa ma'aikatan Katsina kwallon doki.' From my personal recollection I am sure that this statement that polo started in Katsina in 1921 is incorrect. I arrived in Katsina in May 1924 to find Captain Sheridan there but no polo. Having come straight from Sokoto, where the game was in full swing with the Mounted Infantry stables to supply ponies, I was naturally eager to get the game going in Katsina. But apart from Sheridan, who was no expert, and one or two Education Officers such as Norwood, who were keen to learn, we had no European players; nor was there a ground. The Emir soon provided the solution. Ever an enthusiast, he roped in his sons, he lent us ponies, he got prisoners to clear a ground, and he came regularly to watch. His sons included, as I remember, Nagogo (always the best), Yusufu Lamba, Dahiru, Nadada, and Liman. In April 1926 we entered our first tournament at Zaria, and in February 1929 we reached the final of the big event, the Georgian Cup. Our team was the only one at that time to include Nigerians. Shortly after this I left Katsina.—S.J.H.

cussed, amended and agreed to by the full council. The proposals were submitted to the Ministry of Local Government . . . Details as to how much financial responsibility can be delegated by councillors to the Senior Native Administration official in each department and to what extent routine matters such as minor postings can be left to the Native Administration officials, advised by the Government Departmental Officer, have yet to be decided. In the past liaison between Government Officials and the Native Authority has not been all that it might be and nearly everything went through the District Officer. Each Government Official knows his councillor, with whom he should be in almost daily contact. Major matters will of course be referred to the full council but it is hoped many affairs will be settled by the Councillor and Government Official without reference to higher authority.[1]

Mention should be made of the death in 1960 of Alhaji Ulu, who was widely believed to have been one of the first Nigerians to learn to drive a motor-car. He had started life as a poet at the court of Muhammadu Dikko. Later he learned to drive the Emir's horse-trap, and when the Emir bought his first car in 1913 Alhaji Ulu was made driver—a post he held till his retirement in 1957.

To encourage administrative efficiency at the district level, the Emir made a point of attending many of the District Councils and he instituted the annual award of a sword of honour to the most progressive District Head. The title of Waziri was revived in 1962 when the Madawaki, Alhaji Isa Kaita, Chief of Staff to the Native Authority since 1956 and a senior Regional Minister, was turbanned by the Emir. In 1962 the Emir visited Pakistan and the Middle East.

THE HABE KINGS OF KATSINA

Circa 1100	Kumayo. Grandson of Bayajida and son of Bawo.
–1260	Ramba-Ramba.
	Bata tare.
	Jarnanata.
	Sanau. Last of the Durbawa kings, and killed by Korau.
Circa 1260	Korau.
(?)	Ibrahim Yanka Dari.
	Jida Yaki. Ruled for forty years.
1492/3–1541/2	Muhammadu Korau. The first Muslim king.

[1] *Annual Report for Katsina Province*, 1955, para. 3.

d. 1543/4	Ibrahim Sura. Probably from Mali.
d. 1568/9	Ali Murabus, i.e. the marabout or holy man.
d. 1572/3	Muhammadu Toya Rero.
d. 1585	Aliyu Karya Giwa. An eclipse of the sun in his reign.
d. 1589/90	Usman Tsagarana, i.e. Eclipser of the sun.
d. 1595/6	Aliyu Jan Hazo, 'Red like the Harmattan'.
d. 1612/3	Muhammadu Mai-sa-maza-gudu, 'the putter of men to flight.'
d. 1614/5	Aliyu Jan Hazo II.
d. 1631/2	Maje Ibrahim.
d. 1634/5	Abdul Karim.
d. 1634/5	Ashafa.
d. 1644/5	Ibrahim Gamda.
d. 1655/6	Muhammad Wari, son of Abdul Karim.
d. 1667/8	Sulaiman.
d. 1684/5	Usman Na yi Nawa, son of Tsagarana.
d. 1701/2	Muhammadu Toya Rero II.
d. 1704/5	Muhammadu Wari II.
d. 1706/7	Uban Yari. Also known to some as Muhammadu dan Wari.
d. 1715/6	Karya Giwa II.
d. 1728/9	Jan Hazo III, son of Muhammadu Wari.
d. 1740/1	Tsagarana Hassan, son of Toya Rero.
d. 1750/1	Muhammadu Kabiya, son of Usman. Also called Mai-kere, the bearer of the *kere* or throwing club, an ancient emblem of royalty.
d. 1751/2	Tsagarana Yahya.
d. 1758/9	Karya Giwa III, son of Jan Hazo.
d. 1767/8	Muhammad Wari III.
d. 1784/5	Karya Giwa IV.
d. 1801/2	Agwaragi.
d. 1801/2	Tsagarana Gwozo. Buried at Dokau in Gusau district.
d. 1804/5	Bawa dan Gima.
d. 1805/6	Mare Mawa Mahmudu; killed by Umaru Dallaji at Sabon Birni.
d. 1805/6	Magajin Halidu.

THE FULANI EMIRS OF KATSINA

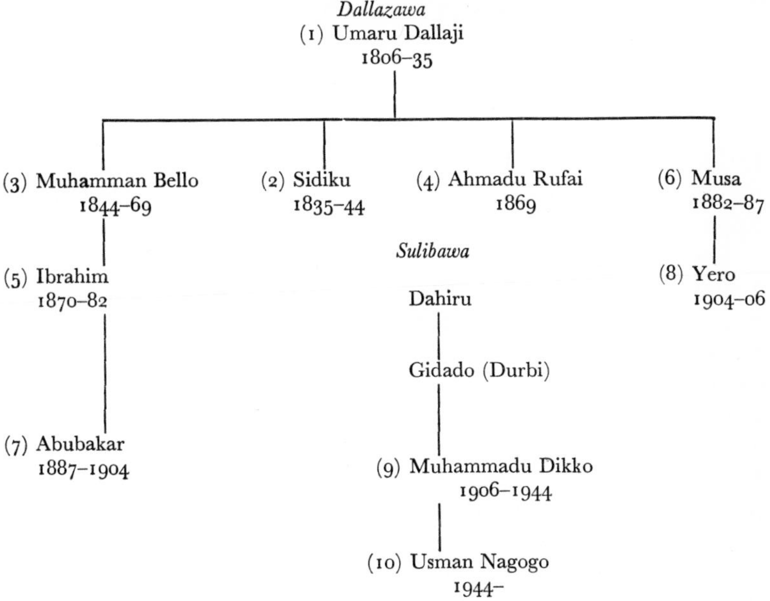

Note: Dates in this chapter and on the above lists have been recently revised in the light of two articles by H. F. C. Smith in the *Bull. of the Hist. Soc. of Nigeria* entitled 'A Fragment of 18th century Katsina' and 'A Further Adventure in the Chronology of Katsina'. Though these still await the acceptance of Katsina, we feel that they are now to be preferred to the earlier inferences of Palmer and Daniel. The revised dates closely follow those collected in 1910 by the French officer, Landeroin, from the oral tradition of Maradi, where the Habe kings retired to after the jihad (see *Documents Scientifiques de la Mission Tilho*, Paris, 1911, vol. 2, pp. 456–61).

The dates of the kings depend mainly on records of lengths of reign but with few firm dates on which to hang them. One such date is the recorded death of Uban Yari in 1018 A.H. but this did not fit in with other records. Daniel appeared to have hit on the answer by suggesting a copyist's error for 1068, but Smith now suggests an error for 1118 (1706/7), which fits neatly with Landeroin. He further suggests that Palmer and Daniel were misled by a faulty transcription of *thalāthīn* for *thalātha* into giving Bawa dan Gima 30 instead of 3 years, and he finds sound evidence for putting Sulaiman's death in 1662/3 instead of 1545, with Karya Giwa on the throne in 1774 and Gwozo in 1802/3, instead of in 1734–52 and 1769–73 as previously accepted. The general effect of the revised dates is to bring all the Habe kings nearer to our era, the later ones by some 35 years and the earlier ones by 100 years or more.

XVII. KANO

IF Daura claims to be the oldest of the Hausa States and the others vied with each other for periodic supremacy, few would dispute the title of Kano as the best-known of the Hausa Bakwai.

The earliest inhabitants of Kano, it is said, were descendants of a Gaya smith named Kano who had come to the Dala hill in search of ironstone. To this day there are people in Kano, generally blacksmiths, who call themselves Abagayawa and are supposed to be the descendants of the original inhabitants. Although there were probably earlier inhabitants, tradition goes no farther; but a Kano manuscript relates the following genealogy. This *Kano Chronicle*, literally written out only in the last decade of the nineteenth century but undoubtedly representing a much earlier record, offers a magnificent source for Kano's pre-Fulani history and lists forty-eight kings from 999 to 1892. 'This is the history', the chronicle tells us,[1]

> of the lords of this country called Kano. Barbushe, once its chief, was of the stock of Dala, a black man of great stature and might, a hunter, who slew elephants with his stick and carried them on his head about nine miles. Dala was of unknown race, but came to this land, and built a house on Dala hill. There he lived—he and his wives. He had seven children—four boys and three girls—of whom the eldest was Garageje. This Garageje was the grandfather of Buzame, who was the father of Barbushe. Barbushe succeeded his forefathers in the knowledge of the lore of Dala, for he was skilled in the various pagan rites. By his wonders and sorceries and the power he gained over his brethren he became chief and lord over them.

Barbushe lived on Dala hill where he officiated as high priest to the god Tsumburbura whose shrine was the tree called Shamus in the area known as Kakua. The tree was surrounded by a wall and none dared penetrate to the shrine save Barbushe: 'whoever else entered, he entered but to die'. Of Barbushe's inner council

[1] This, and most of the following quotations, are taken from the *Kano Chronicle*: H. R. Palmer edition, in *Sudanese Memoirs*, vol. III, pp. 92–132, and translated passages from Alhaji Abubakar, *Kano Ta Ci Gari*. Actually only 47 kings are listed, one twice.

of attendants, legend names them as Tunzagu at Goron Dutse, Damburu from Jigirya, Jandamisa at Magwan, Hambarau from Tanagar, Gumbar Jadu at Fanisau, and many from the hills of Dambokoshi and Dankwai. Barbushe descended from Dala on only two days a year, those of Idi when mystic rites were performed in the grove Matsama at Jakara.

When the days drew near, the people came in from east and west and south and north, men and women alike. Some brought a black dog, some a black fowl, others a black he-goat, when they met together on the day of Jajibere at the foot of Dala hill at eve. When darkness came, Barbushe went forth from his house with his drummers. He cried aloud and said: 'Great Father of us all, we have come nigh to thy dwelling in supplication, Tchunburburai,' and the people said: 'Look on Tchunburburai, ye men of Kano. Look toward Dala.' Then Barbushe descended, and the people went with him to the god. And when they drew near, they sacrificed that which they had brought with them. Barbushe entered the sacred palace—he alone—and said: 'I am the heir of Dala, like it or no, follow me ye must, perforce.' And all the people said: 'Dweller on the rock, our lord Amane, we follow thee perforce.' Thus they spoke and marched round the sacred place till the dawn, when they arose, naked as they were, and ate. Then would Barbushe come forth and tell them of all that would befall through the coming year.

Because of its black water the place was also known as Kurmin Bakin Ruwa. This was later to become the place of execution under the Habe and Fulani kings of Kano.

About the tenth century A.D., a host of strangers from the east came to Kano. Local lore asserts that they came from Baghdad through Bornu and that it was they who introduced the horse to Hausaland. Some say their leader was Bagauda, the son of Bawo of the well-known Bayajida legend of Daura; others that it was Bagauda's grandson, Gajemasu. At first Bagauda settled in Garazawa, the district between Jakara and Damagaram. Then he defeated Jankare and the other pagan leaders and built his town at Sheme. Bagauda is reckoned as the first Habe king of Kano and is said to have reigned at Sheme, between Damagaram and Kazaure, for sixty-six years, dying in 1063. His nickname was Yakano, whence the name of the emirate is said to derive, but it was not till the reign of the third king, Gajemasu (1095–1134) that Kano city was built:

The Sarki consulted the people about building a city. The people agreed. 'Come', they said, 'let us build, for we have the power and the strength.' So they began to build the city. They began the wall from Raria. The Sarki slaughtered a hundred cattle on the first day of the work. They continued the work to the gate of Mazugi, and from there to the water gate and on to the gate of Adama and the gate of Gudan; then past the gates of Waika, Kansakali and Kawungari, as far as the gate of Tuji. There were eight gates.

It was left to the fifth king, Yusa (also known as Sarki), to complete the walls of Kano, in about 1150. In his reign, too, *garkuwa* or hide-shields are said to have first been used by the Kano armies, while tribute, *gandu*, was introduced by his successor Naguji on the basis of one-eighth of every farmer's crops.

The *Kano Chronicle* suggests that the pagan peoples in no way trusted their new rulers, who in turn sought to discover the mysteries of their gods. Typical of this mutual suspicion is the story of Gugwa, the seventh king, who hated the Kano people:

'There can be no plan between them and us, nothing but war; we will conquer them and their god.' When the pagans heard of this they said in secret, 'When the ears hear, then is the body saved.' The chief pagans assembled at dead of night, forty in number, at the foot of the sacred tree. Allah alone knows what took place there. They came forth when the sun rose and went to the Sarki. They said, 'O Sarki, when the night of Idi comes we will tell you the mysteries of our god.' He agreed, for he was glad at heart, and gave them gifts abundantly. That night an apparition appeared to the Sarki in his sleep—a man with a red snake in his hand. He struck the Sarki with the snake and said to him, 'Of two things choose one. Either thou mayest know the mysteries, in which case thou wilt die, or thou mayest not know the mysteries, in which case thou wilt not die.' The Sarki said, 'No! No! No!' Now when the Sarki rose from his sleep he told his men what he had seen in the vision. They said to him, 'What do you see in it?' He said, 'What do you see?' They said, 'We see war!' The Sarki said nothing, he spoke not a word, but suddenly he was struck blind.

Not until the time of Tsamiya, also named Barandamasu, did the royal family learn the secrets of the pagans and thus gain their absolute allegiance:

In his time the cult of Tchibiri was first practised. When he came to the throne he assembled the pagans and said to them, 'Love transmits love, and hate transmits hate; there is nothing between us except bows and spears and swords and shields; there is no deceit and no deceiver except he who is afraid.' . . . When the pagans of Kano heard the words of their Sarki fear seized their hearts. They assembled at the place of their god and prayed to be shown who would gain the mastery, they or the Sarki. It was foretold them that they would be overcome. They knew that their god would not lie. Their chief said, 'I see no means of deliverance from the Sarki except we pay him money.' His men said, 'We agree.' So they were made to pay *jizia*.[1] They collected two hundred slaves within seven days and took them to the Sarki. The Sarki said, 'I do not want your slaves.' So they returned home. Now on a certain Saturday the Sarki sent a messenger called Marukarshi to them saying to him: 'Tell them that on Thursday I am coming to Kagwa, if Allah so wills, that I may enter, and see what is inside. I will destroy the wall and burn the tree.' So the messenger went and told them. When they heard the word of the Sarki, they assembled on the Thursday at the place of their god, pagans of town and country alike—a crowd as had never been seen before. Of drums and cymbals there were a thousand and four hundred and more than four hundred captains of spearmen. They marched round the place of their god from evening until the morning. When the morning broke Sarkin Kano came forth from his house, and went to the place of the god. In front of him were seventy men, each with a shield made of elephant's hide. When the Sarki came near to the place of the god he prevented the pagans entering. As the fight waxed hot, the Sarki cried, 'Where is Bajeri?' Bajeri heard the words of the Sarki, and took a spear and rushed into the battle, cutting his way until he reached the wall of the sacred place. He entered, and seeing a man with his back against the tree holding a red snake, attacked him. The man leapt up and made a great shout; fire breathed from his mouth until smoke filled the whole place round about; he rushed out; and, in his attempt to flee, made for the water-gate, followed by the Sarki, and plunged into the water. The Sarki and his followers stayed hunting for the man in the water, but he escaped and went to Dankwoi where they left him. Hence it is that if any warrior drinks the water of Dankwoi he does not prevail in battle. The Sarki returned to the tree, and destroyed the wall together with all else connected with 'Tchibiri' which was beneath the tree. All the pagans had in the meantime fled, except Makare Dan Samagi and Dunguzu Dan Dorini. The Sarki said to them, 'Why do you not run away?' They said, 'Where were we to run to?' 'Praise be to God,' said the Sarki. 'Tell me the secret of your god.' They told him.

Tsamiya's reign is also marked for the first use of the long horns,

[1] Cattle tax.

kakaki, which played the tune: *Zauna daidai, Kano garinka ne*, 'stand firm, Kano is your city'.

In 1343 Tsamiya was killed by Usman Zamnagawa, who in turn was succeeded by Yaji, 'the hot-tempered one'. About this time Islam seems to have been brought to Hausaland from Mali. Some forty missionaries reached Kano in about 1380, led by Abdurrahman Zaite, Yakubu, Mandawali, Bilkusim and the imams of Jujin Yanlabo and Madatai.

> When they came they commanded the Sarki to observe the times of prayer. He complied, and made Gurdamus his Liman, and Laual his Muezzin. Auta cut the throats of whatever flesh was eaten. Mandawali was Liman of all the Wangarawa and of the chief men of Kano. Zaite was their Alkali. The Sarki commanded every town in Kano country to observe the times of prayer. So they all did so. A mosque was built beneath the sacred tree facing east, and prayers were made at the five appointed times in it.

Opposition was met with from the pagan elements in the city, who continually defiled the mosque until they were suddenly all struck blind and turned away. Yaji is also remembered for his conquest of the town of Santulo, the key to the south, in which one Gwoji so distinguished himself that the king offered him any title. 'I only want to become Madawakin Kano', he replied, and so it is that the Madaki is till today sung of as Gwoji Maikwugi. Yaji's campaigns against the pagans of Panda and Kwararafa earned him the praise-song of

> Yaji, conqueror of the rocky heights,
> Scatterer of hosts, lord of the town.

Under Bugaya, the twelfth king, the Maguzawa[1] pagans of Kano were ordered to leave their rocky fastness of Fongui and disperse themselves throughout the land. His successor Kanajeji (1390–1410), son of Yaji, was the first Hausa king to introduce *lifidi* or quilted-cotton armour, *kwalkwali* or iron helmets, and coats of mail supposed to have been originally obtained as spoils of war from the Crusaders. This was after the lesson learned from the heavy Kano casualties at the battle of Bumbutu against

[1] For the Maguzawa, see section on Zaria, p. 222. The major study of the Maguzawa is J. H. Greenberg, *The Influence of Islam on a Sudanese Religion*, New York, 1946. Further field research was in hand in 1964.

Damagaram. Another of Kanajeji's wars was with Zaria. At first he was repulsed and his army suffered the indignity of abuse from the men of Zaria: 'What is Kano?' they taunted, 'Kano is bush.'[1] Furious at this defeat, Kanajeji renounced Islam, and turned to the Tchibiri *tsafi*:

> The Sarkin Tchibiri said: 'Re-establish the god that your father and grandfather destroyed.' The Sarki said: 'True but tell me what I am to do with it.' The Sarkin Tchibiri said: 'Cut a branch from this tree.' The Sarki cut off a branch. When it was cut, the Sarki found a red snake in the branch. He killed the snake, and made two *huffi* with its skin. He then made four *dundufu* and eight *kuntakuru* from the branch. These objects he took to Dankwoi and threw them into the water and went home. After waiting forty days he came back to the water, and removed the objects to the house of Sarkin Tchibiri. Sarkin Tchibiri sewed the rest of the snake's skin round the drums and said to Kanajeji, 'Whatever you wish for in this world, do as our forefathers did of old.' Kanajeji said: 'Show me, and I will do even as they did.' The Sarkin Tchibiri took off his robe and put on the *huffi* of snake's skin and walked round the tree forty times, singing the song of Barbushe. Kanajeji did as Sarkin Tchibiri did, and walked round the tree forty timer. The next year he set out to war with Zukzuk. He encamped at Gadaz. The Sarkin Zukzuk came out and they fought; the men of Kano killed the Sarkin Zukzuk. The Zukzuk men fled, scattered in ones and twos, and the chiefs of Zukzuk were killed. The Sarkin Kano entered Zukzuk and lived there close to the Shika eight months. The people gave him a vast amount of tribute. [Zukzuk=Zaria.]

In the reign of the fifteenth king, Dauda the Black Leopard, son of Kanajeji (1421–38), a Bornuese prince named Dagaci (Kalnama) came to Bompai at the head of a host of soldiers and malams and trumpets and flags. This was at a time when Bornu affairs were in an unsettled state. Dauda did not know whether it was wise to lodge this huge entourage in his city, so he encamped them at Salanta. When he went away to fight Zaria, Dauda left the affairs of Kano in Dagaci's hands. Dagaci introduced the *banga* drum to Kano, coming with a hundred such drummers.

Abdullahi Burja's reign is chiefly remembered in Kano history for the opening up of trading relations with Bornu (camels first appeared in Kano), especially on the Gwanja route, and for the

[5] Cf. the contrary modern saying *Gari ba Kano ba, dajin Allah*, meaning that anywhere else than Kano is no city but just bush.

exploits of Galadima Daudu in his slave raids to the south. The Galadima is said to have sent back to his king a thousand slaves every month, so that it is small wonder his praise was sung:

Gatherer of the axes of the South; Gatherer of the youth of the South; Drum of Wealth, Galadima; Drum of Land, Galadima.

After seven years, by which time Kano had a surfeit of slaves, the Galadima was ordered back:

When he was returning, he stopped every three miles, and built a town. He left at each a thousand slaves and five hundred females. He thus founded twenty-one towns, before he came to Kano. On arriving there he gave the Sarki three thousand slaves and said to him, 'I have founded twenty-one towns, and in each I have left a thousand slaves, all yours.' The Sarki asked him, 'What are the names of the towns you have built?' The Galadima said, 'Their names are Ibdabu.' The Sarki said, 'I make you ruler of all these towns and their domains.' Because of this the Galadima was called 'Daudu, the strength of the city.'

There are records in Yakubu's time of a considerable Fulani and Wangara influx from Mali, an empire now on the decline. They brought religious books and many of them passed on to Bornu. Many Kanuri came to settle in Kano and the city's trading prosperity increased further.

Yakubu was succeeded by his celebrated son Mohamman Rumfa (1463–99): 'he can have no equal in might, from the time of the founding of Kano until it shall end'. Two tales are told in Kano about the origin of his sobriquet. One is that he was fond of building a grass-mat shelter, *rumfa*, on his travels. Another, less polite, is that after he became king he refused to give up his relaxation of wandering through the city at night. Since there were hundreds of dogs about, the king's food was left for him on top of a *rumfa* out of their hungry reach. Under Rumfa, Kano seems to have emerged as a prosperous and influential kingdom and to have reached the zenith of her power. Shehu Maghili, also known as Sherif Waliyi, brought a number of Muslim emissaries from Medina to Kano. The legend adds that he recognized Kano was his goal by finding its soil the same as that of Medina. He wrote a *risala*, a religious treatise, on Maliki law for the king's guidance, while his classic essay on Muslim kingship, *The Obligation of Princes*, belongs to the class of Islamic literature known as

'Mirrors for Princes': essays written by men experienced in affairs of state and eager to advise their rulers how to comport themselves. Here is an example from Al Maghili's treatise:

> The sojourn of a prince in the city breeds all manner of trouble and harm. The bird of prey abides in open and wild places. Vigorous is the cock as he struts round his domains. The eagle can only win his realm by firm resolve, and the cock's voice is strong as he masters the hens. Ride, then, the horses of resolution upon the saddles of prudence. Cherish the land from the spoiling drought, from the raging wind, the dust-laden storm, the raucous thunder, the gleaming lightning, the shattering fireball and the beating rain. Kingdoms are held by the sword, not by delays. Can fear be thrust back except by causing fear?
>
> Allow only the nearest of your friends to bring you food and drink and bed and clothes. Do not part with your coat of mail and weapons and let no one approach you save men of trust and virtue. Never sleep in a place of peril. Have near to guard you at all times a band of faithful and gallant men, sentries, bowmen, horse and foot. Times of alarm are not like times of safety. Conceal your secrets from other people until you are master of your undertaking.[1]

Maghili also commanded Rumfa to build a Friday mosque whose minaret should stand on the site of the sacred tree Shamus. When it was time for him to move on to Songhai, Maghili left three of his children in Kano, among them Isa (Sidi Fari) to whom he bequeathed his rosary, sword, kettle, Holy Koran, staff and scales. This Sidi Fari dynasty has continued to provide the sharifs of Kano and has kept the family heirlooms.

Rumfa is held to have brought twelve new things to Kano. He extended the walls from Kofar Dagaci towards Kofar Mata and built other sections. At a ceremony where forty oxen were killed, he walled up the gate Kofar Bai built by one Maje-Karofi, enjoining that it should not be opened; not until the coming of the Fulani three hundred years later was it reopened. He established the Kurmi market. He also instituted the practice of *Kame*, appointing Durman to visit the Indabo families and take the first-born virgin for his own palace. He introduced the purdah custom of *kulle* and is acclaimed as the first king to have a thousand concubines. He started the Kano royal regalia of *kakaki* trumpets,

[1] Sheikh Mohammed Al-Maghili of Tlemsen, *The Obligations of Princes*, translated by T. H. Baldwin, Beyrouth, 1932. This edition contains the Arabic text as well. Excerpts are also given in T. L. Hodgkin, *Nigerian Perspectives*, p. 90.

of the *figini* or ostrich fan, and of ostrich-feather sandals, as well as the custom of the spare led horse for the king, known as *dokin zage*,[1] which he started in his war with Katsina. It was in his reign that the *Salla* festival Id al Fitr was first observed, at Shadadoko. He first appointed eunuchs to high office, such as Sarkin Tudu, Sarkin Ruwa, Sarkin Bai, and to the four left without a title he allotted the treasury.

A new palace, the south gate of which exists to this day, was built in place of the old one which used to stand somewhere to the east of Dala. This gate is opened only to allow a new king to enter on his accession. After this event it is walled up until the next accession. The gate is in the inside wall of the palace and opens into the private courtyard through the royal graveyard, called Karofi. The palace is still called the Gidan Rumfa.

In Mohamman Rumfa's reign there began a series of wars with Katsina which, on and off, were to last for about 200 years until a treaty was eventually signed in 1706.[2] Rumfa's successor, Abdullahi, brought the eleven years' war with Katsina to a successful conclusion and also defeated Zaria, but he had to humble himself before Bornu which had advanced into Kano to support the revolt of Dagaci. On Bornu's withdrawal, Abdullahi beguiled Dagaci into submission and turned him out of office.

His warlike son Mohamman Kisoki now avenged this slight, and during his long reign made extensive conquests, driving back the Bornuese and once again establishing the supremacy of Kano in the battle-torn no-man's-land between the two kingdoms. He even captured Nguru. The story goes:

> When he entered the town, Sarkin Kano took his seat beneath the *kuka* tree, at the Kofar Fada, and assembling the inhabitants of the town at the Kofar Bai, reduced them to terrified submission. He gave orders that no men were to be made prisoners, but that only clothes and horses were to be taken. Then he left Nguru and lived for a month in the bush. The Sarkin Bornu sent to him and said: 'What do you mean by making war?' Kisoki replied: 'I do not know, but the cause of war is the ordinance of Allah.' The Sarkin Bornu said nothing more. The men of Kano returned to Kano. In the next year the Sarkin Bornu came to attack Kano but could not take the town and returned home. Then Kisoki said to one of his men, Dunki, 'Mount the wall, and sing

[1] See another meaning given on p. 71 of *The Muhammadan Emirates of Nigeria*.
[2] The less reliable Kano date is 1650. See notes on pp. 183, 194 and 214.

a song in praise of the Sarki and his men of war.' Dunki went. The song that he sung was this: 'Kisoki, physic of Bornu, and the Chiratawa.' He sung it again and again, and after that he praised all those who were present at the fight. . . . Dunki sang their praises for forty days on the top of the wall.

Early in his reign (1512) Kano had been captured by the Askia of Songhai who, having first captured Katsina and Zaria, took Kano after a long siege. He compelled Mohamman to marry one of his daughters and restored him to his kingdom conditionally on his annual payment of a third of all his tribute. This invasion by Songhai is not recorded by the *Kano Chronicle*, although independent evidence is strong. It serves to illustrate either how little this conquest can have affected conditions of life in Kano—an occurrence that was largely repeated after the British conquest of 1903—or, more probably, how biased chroniclers may be by local patriotism.

From 1570 to 1706 there was a renewal of the constant and devastating wars between Kano and Katsina. In the reign of Abubakar Kado (1565–73) the Katsinawa came right up to the gates of Kano and encamped at Salanta. Devastation was carried out with impunity and the country was denuded. The king, who was a deeply religious man, cared for little beyond his religious offices, remaining impotent in prayer, or so it is said. He was deposed in 1573. His successor Mohamman Shashere carried war back into Katsina country, but was repulsed at Kanyika. He, too, was deposed. It was in Shashere's time that the title of Wambai was first bestowed on a eunuch.

For the next fifty years or so the Kano forces prevailed under Mohamman Zaki (1582–1618) and his son Mohamman Nazaki (1618–23). On one occasion the Sarkin Kano, counselled by Abubakar Magarabi, led the Kano army to Katsina during the month of Ramadan and attacked the town at dawn on the day of the *Salla*. They captured many prisoners and spoils of war, including 400 horses and sixty suits of horse-armour. Mohamman Nazaki proposed terms of peace, but the Katsinawa refused them. Instead they attempted an invasion of Kano but were repulsed with great loss at Karayi. Of this town Karayi the following story is told in Kano:

He left the Wombai Giwa behind at Kano because he was sick.

When the Wombai recovered he said, 'What can I do to please the Sarki?' His men said, 'Add to the city.' He said, 'Very well.' So he built a wall from the Kofar Dogo to the Kofar Gadonkaia, and from the Kofar Dakawuyia to the Kofar Kabuga, and to the Kofar Kansakali. He spent an enormous amount of money on this improvement. Every morning he brought a thousand calabashes of food and fifty oxen for the workmen till the work was finished. Every man in Kano went to work. No man surpassed the Wombai in benevolence to Moslems and the poor. The day when the work was to be finished the Wombai Giwa distributed among the workmen a thousand 'tobes'. He slaughtered three hundred cows at the Kofar Kansakali and gave the mallams many presents. When the Sarkin Kano returned from war, the Wombai gave him a hundred riding horses. Each horse had a mail coat. The Sarki was very pleased. He said, 'What shall I do for this man, to make his heart glad?' His men said, 'Give him a town.' So the Sarki gave him Karayi. Hence the song:

> 'Elephant Lord of the town, Abdullah foe of the bull hippopotamus, whose chains for taking captive women are hoes and axes.'

The Wombai left Kano and went to Karayi. Every day he fought the Katsinawa and took much spoil from them in war. He became master of a hundred mailed horsemen and a thousand horses. He was sung as 'The Elephant who reduces his neighbours to servitude.' He became so mighty that it was feared he would revolt. Hence he was turned out of his office in the time of Kutumbi.

By this time the kings of Kano presented a picture of considerable pomp. For instance:

Whenever Kutumbi went to war or to *Salla* he was followed by one hundred spare horses. Forty drums went in front of him, and twenty-five trumpets, and fifty kettle-drums. He was always followed by one hundred eunuchs who were handsomely dressed and had gold and silver ornaments.

But all these worldly emblems of power could not prevent the death in battle of Kutumbi at the hands of the Katsinawa in 1648,[1] when the Kanawa were routed in a night attack outside Katsina. Kutumbi's reign is also remembered for the collection of the Habe cattle-tax of *jizia*, called *jangali* by the Fulani, and for the magnificence of his son Bako: 'no prince could compare with him in anything, in doing good or doing ill, in courage, anger and generosity, he was like a Sarki even while he was only a Prince'.

[1] Revised Katsina dates place all these events over 50 years later. See p. 183.

A year later his son and successor, Alhaji, met the same fate; but this is a Katsina record unsupported by the *Kano Chronicle*.

The Katsina wars did much to weaken the power and domination of Kano. Famine was seldom far away; worse still, in the early half of the sixteenth century Kano had fallen a prey to the Kebbawa under the famous Kanta, a Songhai general who had revolted from the Askia. Kebbi was content, however, to demand tribute without occupying the town.

Besides the attrition of constant warring with Katsina, Kano's domination had been overshadowed from about 1600 by the powerful Jukun people from the south called the Kwararafa, inhabiting the right bank of the Benue. In their own language, the Jukun called their capital Pi, which was about fifteen miles north-east of modern Bantaji in Muri, but the Hausa term is Kwararafa. In the time of Mohamman Kukuna (1652–60) they battered down the Kofar Kawayi; and in 1671 under their king Agwabi, son of Katakpa, they stormed Kano yet again. Of this battle the *Kano Chronicle* records the importance still attached by the nominally Muslim Kanawa to the Maguzawa *tsafi* of Tchibiri:

> The Kwararafa entered Kano by Kofar Gadon Kaia, slaughtered the men of Kano, and reached Bakinrua. The Galadima Kofakani said to the Sarkin Kano, who was in the Pugachin Kishi with his Jarumai: 'Establish "Tchibiri" at Toji and "Bundu" at Rimi Bundu.' The Galadima said to the Sarki, 'Rise up! The Kwararafa have destroyed the best part of your town and have killed many men! They have penetrated to the Kurmi and will attack the palace.' The Sarki mounted his horse and went out, and came to the Kofar Fada with the Galadima and eunuchs and Jarumai. There he met all the Kanawa. He went to Rimi Bundu, took the 'Bundu' and gave it to Dan Durma Mazza Mazza and thence hastened to Kofar Bai. He found the Kwararafa had come near the 'Tchibiri', but every one of them who came close died at once. The Sarkin Kwararafa told his people to take away the 'Tchibiri'. The Kwararafa tried to charge, but they failed to seize it. The Sarkin Kano came to the 'Tchibiri', and took it. On his right hand he had a hundred warriors, in front of him ninety-nine chiefs, all of them mallams, and on his left hand a hundred warriors. They were all slaughtered by the Kwararafa; only a few were left alive. Sarkin Kano fled to Daura. The Kwararafa followed him to Jelli and then returned.

Zaria, Katsina and, later, Bornu were also attacked by these warlike people, and a group of Angas in Plateau Province today claims descent from the Jukun army on their march through Shendam. In the reign of Katakpa, father of the warrior king Agwabi, the Jukun Jumun moved from Pi to Puje, near present-day Wukari, though Pi continued in existence till it was destroyed by Buba of Bakundi (Muri) in about 1860. Wukari was built by Zakanju, also called Tsonkwa, in 1815.

The Sultan of Bornu had become the overlord of Kano by 1734 and tribute was paid to him up to the time of the jihad. Thus Mohamman Kisoki seems to have been the last of the Habe rulers of Kano who enjoyed the honour of paying tribute to no one. It is said that but for the intercession of certain Kano *malamai* the Sultan of Bornu would have burnt the city.

To the west and north-west of Kano two states, Zamfara and Gobir, were now coming into threatening prominence. It is on record that in about 1700 the Kano forces were severely defeated by the Zamfarawa at Argaye. In the reign of Kumbari (1731–43) there was a fierce war between Kano and Gobir, but the result was never decisive, first one and then the other prevailing. The Bornu army under Shehu Mai Ali threatened Kano, camping right inside Fagge, but war was averted. In Kumbari's time shields and guns were first brought from Nupe, while the collection of the tax known as *jizia* was so ruthlessly imposed by the king that the Kurmi market was killed, the Arabs left the city for Katsina, and the *talakawa* fled back to the countryside.

The eighteenth century was marked by continual struggles with Gobir, until in about 1760 Sarkin Gobir Babari, having gradually reduced Zamfara, established his supremacy over Kano. Alhaji Kabe, the king of Kano, rejected Gobir's offer of peace terms by replying: 'I have a cap to fit anyone's head', and was worsted in a bloody battle at Dami. To Babba Zaki (1768–76) is attributed the creation of a royal guard of musketeers, still in existence today. But, as in most of the wars in Hausaland, the losing of this one seems to have had little effect upon the economic conditions of Kano, and the remainder of the century was comparatively prosperous. The internal organization of Kano was unaffected by the reverses abroad and her Habe system of government has largely continued to this day.

It was in the reign of Mohamman Alwali, forty-second king, that the Fulani jihad erupted into Kano. As with the other Hausa states, the Fulani were no strangers. In the fifteenth century there were supposed to have been twelve principal clans of Fulani settled in Kano territory. At the end of the eighteenth century the chief clans round Kano were:

(1) The Modibawa (from Modibo or Malam) chiefly in the city itself. Originally known as Igilawa, they came from Bornu under their leader Malam Atiku, whose wisdom earned him the name of Modibo, 'the learned one'.
(2) The Sulibawa under Malam Jemo in the south-west.
(3) The Daneji under Dan Zabuwa, also in the south-west.
(4) The Yolawa to the west. Their leader was Malam Liman Yafi, who migrated from the village of Yola to the west of Kano during the Kwararafa occupation.
(5) The Dambazawa under Malam Dabo to the north.
(6) The Jobawa to the east.

In 1804–5 Dan Zabuwa of the Daneji clan, who was considered the leader of the Kano Fulani, went to the Shehu, Usman dan Fodio, to obtain his recognition in the form of a flag for the conquest of Kano. The flag was granted, but the Shehu refrained from appointing a generalissimo, possibly fearing dissension and jealousy. The result of this was that a year was spent in spasmodic and disunited contests. Alwali, the Habe ruler of Kano, subdued the Fulani unrest in the eastern parts of his territory, while in the west the Fulani were successful. Finally, the combined Fulani forces met Alwali at Dan Yahaya, twenty-five miles north of Kano, and after a battle lasting three days Alwali was forced to flee for his life and seek shelter in Kano. The Fulani, expert bowmen that they were, did great execution among Alwali's heavy cavalry, despite the protection of their cumbrous *lifidi* armour. The Habe army contained a large element of half-hearted peasants who themselves were vaguely Muslim in an unconvincing way, whereas the Fulani, fighting for a cause, were infused with religious zeal and looked on the Habe as pagans. The bulk of the Habe had no cause to fight for, and were probably only too anxious for a peaceful issue.

The Fulani then took the town of Mariki and went on to capture Kano, forcing Alwali to flee to Zaria. When the men of Zaria asked him why he had left his capital, he is said to have prophetically replied: 'The same cause which drove me out of Kano will probably drive you out of Zaria.' Finding no support he repaired to Burum Burum, where he was discovered by the Fulani, defeated and killed in 1807. It was now necessary for the victors to elect a chief, and the five leaders of the principal Fulani clans went to Gwandu to submit their candidature to the Shehu. It is said that the meeting took place in the country and not in the town of Gwandu. The Shehu asked them to name the most learned man in Kano. 'Sulemanu, a servant of Dan Zabuwa, who is at present at home,' they replied. 'Then he is to be your chief,' said the Shehu. Tradition has it that he sent Sulemanu a knife and a sword as a token of his support when the local Fulani at first refused to allow him to enter Gidan Rumfa, arguing that 'if we enter the Habes' house and we beget children, they will be like these Habes and do like them'.

Sulemanu belonged to the Modibawa clan. His chief counsellor and friend was Malam Jemo, the head of the Sulibawa clan. On Malam Jemo's death, his nephew Dabo gained his uncle's position of confidential adviser.

When Sulemanu died in 1819 after an uneventful reign, the question of succession again became acute. The Sarkin Musulmi, Muhammadu Bello, who had succeeded the Shehu in Sokoto, appointed the pious Ibrahim Dabo on the recommendation of Sulemanu, who, being a *wali* or saint, is said to have been aware of his approaching death.

But there was much dissatisfaction and jealousy amongst the other clans, egged on by the Galadima, Sani, and it took three years of fighting to eliminate this. Dabo's civil campaigns were such that he earned the praise title of 'Bull Elephant', and when he went to war the trumpets played 'The sacker of towns is mounting'. From his war camp on Dala hill he directed his attacks against Karayi, Jirima, Jijita and Rano. Tradition has it that Dabo never shaved his head except when he had sacked a town. Such was the dust raised by his cavalry that it exceeded the harmattan. Dabo became known as 'Cigari'[1] after this struggle, and to this day any man named Dabo (Ibrahim) is liable to receive this nickname. It is of Kano in Dabo's reign that we have this account:

The city is rendered very unhealthy by a large morass, which almost divides it into two parts, besides many pools of stagnant water, made

[1] *Ya ci gari* = he conquered the town.

by digging clay for houses . . . On the north side of the city are two remarkable mounts . . . They are formed of argillaceous iron-stone, mixed with pebbles, and a rather soft kind of marl. The city is of an irregular oval shape, about fifteen miles in circumference, and surrounded by a clay wall thirty feet high, with a dry ditch along the inside, and another on the outside. There are fifteen gates, including one lately built up. The gates are of wood, covered with sheetiron, and are regularly opened and shut at sunrise and sunset. A platform inside, with two guard-houses below it, serves to defend each entrance. Not more than one fourth of the ground within the walls is occupied by houses; the vacant space is laid out in fields and gardens. The large morass, nearly intersecting the city from east to west, and crossed by a small neck of land on which the market is held, is overflowed in the rainy season. The water of the city being considered unwholesome, women are constantly employed hawking water about the streets, from the favourite springs in the neighbourhood. The houses are built of clay, and are mostly of a square form, in the Moorish fashion, with a central room, the roof of which is supported by the trunks of palm trees, where visitors and strangers are received. The apartments of the ground floor open into this hall of audience and are generally used as store-rooms. A staircase leads to an open gallery overlooking the hall and serving as a passage to the chambers of the second story which are lighted with small windows. In a back courtyard there is a well and other conveniences. Within the enclosure in which the house stands, there are also a few round huts of clay, roofed with the stalks of Indian corn, and thatched with long grass. These are usually very neat and clean. . . . The governor's residence covers a large space, and resembles a walled village. It even contains a mosque, and several towers three or four stories high, with windows in the European style, but without glass or framework. It is necessary to pass through two of these towers in order to gain the suite of inner apartments occupied by the governor.[1]

In 1825–6 Al Kanemi, the new leader of Bornu, brought down an expedition and threatened Kano. The Kanawa succeeded in diverting this invasion southwards and a little later Yakubu, Sarkin Bauchi, drove back the Bornuese.

Towards the end of Dabo's reign, a serious attempt was made in 1844 by the Habe, who had collected at Maradi, to oust the Fulani and re-establish themselves in their old position. A similar attempt had been made ten years previously against the Sokoto Fulani, but Bello had inflicted a crushing defeat at Gawakuke

[1] Denham, Clapperton and Oudney, *Narrative of Travels and Discoveries in Northern and Central Africa*, 1826; also quoted in *West African Explorers*, 1951, pp. 247–8.

near Rabah. The Habe forces under Umaru Dan Mari, marching south through the Rubu bush which today roughly separates the Katsina and Sokoto emirates and was then quite populous, established themselves in a strong position at Matazu, where they were joined by many supporters. After a long siege lasting the best part of a year the Fulani captured the town.

In 1845 Dabo died and was succeeded by his son Usman, nicknamed 'Ma-je-Ringim', who reigned ten years and died at Ringim. He was said to be so kind-hearted that highway robbers flourished in his day, confident that the Emir could never bring himself to order their throats to be cut. It was during Usman's reign that Dr Barth visited Kano, and he has left a detailed record of Kano city and government. His description of Kano market is too well known to quote here, but of his audience with the Emir he wrote:

Passing through the market-place, which had only begun to collect its crowds, and crossing the narrow neck of land which divides the characteristic pool 'Jakara', we entered the quarters of the ruling race, the Fulbe or Fellani, where conical huts of thatchwork, and the gonda-tree, are prevalent, and where most beautiful and lively pictures of nature meet the eye on all sides. Thus we proceeded, first to the house of the gado (the Lord of the Treasury), who had already called several times at my house, and acted as the mediator between me and the governor.

His house was a most interesting specimen of the domestic arrangements of the Fulbe, who, however civilized they may have become, do not disown their original character as 'berroroji', or nomadic cattle-breeders. His courtyard, though in the middle of the town, looked like a farm-yard, and could not be conscientiously commended for its cleanliness. Having with difficulty found a small spot to sit down upon without much danger of soiling our clothes, we had to wait patiently till his Excellency had examined and approved of the presents. Having manifested his satisfaction with them by appropriating to himself a very handsome large gilt cup, which with great risk I had carried safely through the desert, he accompanied us on horseback to the 'fada', 'lamorde', or palace, which forms a real labyrinth of courtyards, provided with spacious round huts of audience, built of clay, with a door on each side, and connected together by narrow intricate passages. Hundreds of lazy, arrogant courtiers, freemen and slaves, were lounging and idling here, killing time with trivial and saucy jokes.[1]

[1] Quoted in A. H. M. Kirk-Greene, *Barth's Travels in Nigeria*, pp. 105–6. The famous market description is given at pp. 114–23.

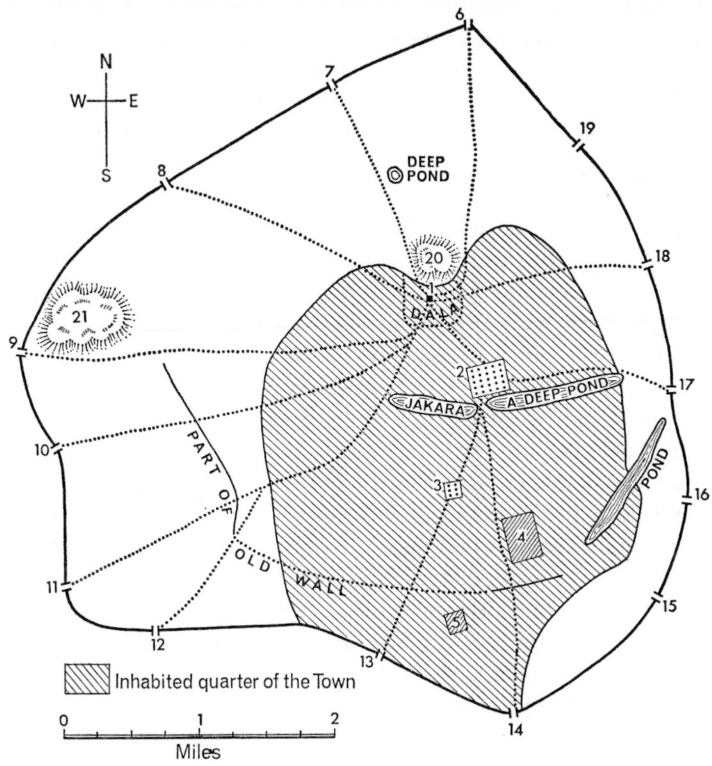

12. A PLAN OF KANO CITY *c.* 1851 AT THE TIME OF DR BARTH'S VISIT

1. Barth's quarters in Dalá. During his second stay in Kanó, he also resided in Dalá, at a short distance from his old quarters.
2. Great market-place.
3. Small market-place.
4. Palace of Governor.
5. Palace of Ghaladíma.
6. Kofa Mazúger.
7. Kofa-n-'Adama.
8. Kofa-n-Gúdan.
9. Kofa-n-Kansákkali.
10. Kofa-n-Limún, or Káboga.
11. Kofa-n-Dakanye, or Dukánie.
12. Kofa-n-Dakaina.
13. Kofa-n-Naïsa.
14. Kofa-n-Kúra.
15. Kofa-n-Nasaráwa.
16. Kofa-n-Máta.
17. Kofa-n-Wambay.
18. Kofa-n-Magardi.
19. Kofa-n-Rúa (shut on Barth's visit).
20. Mount Dalá.
21. Mount Kógo-n-dútsi.

Usman was succeeded by his brother Abdullahi, through whom the succession has since followed, and in his long reign of twenty-seven years he earned the veneration of his people. Unlike his brother Usman, he stood no nonsense from robbers and his nick-name of Abdu Sarkin Yanka[1] reveals that he felt no compunction about cutting off the hands of thieves. Nevertheless he allowed the Ningi pagans, who had for years provided an attractive raiding ground, to become uncomfortably aggressive. In this perhaps he was not altogether to blame. For many years the supreme test of a warrior's courage had been to chase an ill-armed and out-numbered crowd of harried locals from their villages and to capture those who survived as slaves; but in process of time the Ningi pagans had profited by hard experience so that every year found them more confident in their defences—so much so in fact that, turning the tables, they began to become the aggressors and remained a constant thorn in the side of Kano.

Abdullahi built the Emir's 'summer residence' at Nassarawa. He also constructed a new gate, Kofar Fada, and built the great house of Soron Giwa. He rebuilt the mosque and house of the Turaki, and in the present house there stands a store-room said to have formed part of the *turaka* area of the Turaki's house. In the palace, the slaves are said to have become so powerful that the Kanawa thought they must be freedmen. Abdullahi's reign is also remembered for his wars with Dan Baskori, the Habe King of Maradi. He derived one of his *kirari*, 'Son of Ibrahim, a pick-axe to physic hard ground' (*Dan Ibrahim, dagi, maganin kasa mai tauri*), from the great number of people whom he turned out of office, from his own son Yusufu the Galadima and Dogo the Waziri downwards. Another was Ma-je-Karofi, at which town (in Katsina) he died in 1883 on his way to Sokoto. He was succeeded by his brother Muhamman Bello, whose life was uneventful but whose death plunged Kano into a disastrous civil war.

The obvious successor would have been Yusufu, the eldest son of Abdullahi. The Sultan had originally favoured him but his Waziri recommended Dan Lawan, whereupon Nana, the daughter of Shehu Mujaddadi, proposed Bello as the compromise candidate. Yusufu and his brothers had always been looked on with great disfavour by their uncle Bello, who appeared to take a delight in heaping on them indignities, allegedly in order to dis-

[1] *Yanka* = to cut.

credit them in favour of his own son Muhamman Tukur. He made Tukur Galadima and appointed other sons, Zakari and Abubakar, Turaki and Santuraki respectively. Tradition relates that Bello even gave his son detailed instructions about the art of kingship but these fatherly counsels fell on deaf ears, with the result that Bello's designs provoked a needless and bitter civil war. Sarkin Musulmi Abdurrahman disregarded the recommendation of his Waziri Mu'azu, who happened to be in Kano at the time of Bello's death in 1893, and unwisely appointed Tukur in response to some momentary whim. Kano traditions maintain that the Sarkin Musulmi favoured Tukur because of the bravery he had shown in his cause at a battle between Sokoto and Argungu wherein he saved Sokoto from defeat. This is supported by the praise-name given to the Emir of Kano, *Sarkin Yakin Sarkin Musulmi*, 'The Commander of the Faithful's general'. The spear that is carried by Kilishi as part of the Emir's regalia is said to have been given to Tukur by the Sultan of Sokoto.

Many of the Kano leaders supported the Madaki in his protest to the Wazirin Sokoto about this imposed selection of Emir. When the Sultan refused to change his mind, the leaders of Kano society boycotted the mosque and Tukur had to be sworn in by the Waziri in his own house at Sabon Gida. A disastrous civil war now ensued. Yusufu raised the flag of revolt and hundreds of people rallied to him at Takai, beyond Dawakin Kudu. At first he contented himself with putting his army into shape by sorties against Gumel, Misau and Ningi. Then Yusufu felt himself strong enough to march on Kano. Encamping at Fagge after a skirmish, the next morning he fought his way through the Kofar Mata before he was forced to retire. For some months he had to content himself with reducing such of the towns and villages to the south-east as were still hostile, especially Gaya. While thus engaged Yusufu died at Garko in 1894 and his brother Aliyu took his place as Pretender.

Aliyu returned to attack Kano, and succeeded in entering the town by effecting a breach in the walls between the Nassarawa and the Dan Agundi gates. Tukur's stand at the battle is said to have been a silk-cotton tree beside the wall opposite the present Provincial Secondary School where a *kurna* tree now stands at the place one climbs over the wall. Tukur was forced to flee through Kofar Waika. Hearing of this rout of his appointee, the Sultan of

Sokoto ordered Katsina, Zaria and Kazaure to move to Tukur's aid, but they refused involvement with such a bitter family feud. Meanwhile Aliyu pursued Tukur through Dawakin Tofa, Bici and Danzabuwa until he made his war-camp at Macinjim on the Katsina frontier. In a final battle at Tafashiya, Tukur was captured when his horse collapsed under him. On his way back to Kano he died at Gurin, after reigning eleven months.

So ended a most unfortunate civil war which, as always, had a severely crippling effect on the prosperity of the country. The Wazirin Sokoto was in due course sent to invest Aliyu, according to what had formerly been the invariable procedure. On this occasion, however, Kano took the opportunity of showing that it desired no further interference from outside and that it no longer tacitly acknowledged the pre-eminence of Sokoto. Not until the very end of his reign did Emir Aliyu make the customary *mabayia* or fealty-journey to Sokoto, shortly before the British occupied Kano. He also created the office of his own Waziri.

The war with Ningi continued intermittently, though Dan Yaya, the Ningi chief, made overtures for peace. Aliyu included in his armoury a new weapon that the Etsu Nupe is believed to have sent to him. This was *sango*, a sort of elephant-harpoon fired with gunpowder, and its introduction contributed a new name for the Emir, *Maisango*. On one occasion Aliyu was caught by a night attack and barely escaped with his life.

In 1898, at Gezawa, Aliyu defeated the troublesome Sarkin Damagaram from Zinder, who had invaded Kano to within sixteen miles of the city, but in the following two years it is recorded that the Sarkin Damagaram actually penetrated as far as Fanisau, a bare five miles from Kano city.

On the eve of the British occupation Aliyu, who gave asylum to the Magajin Keffi after the murder of Captain Moloney, decided that Kano was a strong enough citadel to hold out against this new threat. 'If a small town like Keffi can do this,' he is said to have exclaimed, 'how much more Kano?' This action on the part of the Sarkin Kano could only be interpreted as a direct challenge and it seemed to Lugard that the future attitude of all the northern Emirs depended on the issue. Hence everything turned on the fate of the expedition which was mounted against Kano. Such was the fame of Kano's walls, 30–50 feet high and 40 feet thick at the base with a double ditch in front and loopholes near the four-foot-thick crest of the wall served by a platform, that the expeditionary force was prepared to encounter a really fierce defence.

In the event, they met with scarcely any resistance. A force of nearly 1,000 men, strongly supported by artillery, left Zaria at the end of January 1903. At the walled town of Bebeji the column was halted. Captain Abadie pluckily rode up to the ramparts to appeal to the people not to fight, but as Aliyu had promised death to anyone who should open the gates the offer of surrender was refused. Bebeji fell and the other newly-walled towns on the Zaria-Kano route decided not to fight. The Emir, Aliyu, had shortly before left for Sokoto, ostensibly to greet the new Sultan Attahiru,[1] but as he had taken 2,000 horsemen with him, Kano city, left merely to the charge of two head slaves, was virtually defenceless. After a fruitless attack on the main gate on the Zaria side, a breach was made in a neighbouring one and the city was captured. The royal palace, which consisted of a network of buildings spread over 33 acres, the whole surrounded by a 30-foot wall, and thus no mean citadel in its own right, was occupied.

Meanwhile Aliyu had been urged to return and defend his emirate, but his heart failed him at Geza when he heard of the occupation of Kano, and after calling on his people to make ready for the morrow's fight he himself quietly decamped in the night. He was eventually caught near Argungu by the Chief of Gobir and deported to Lokoja, where he died in 1926. From the unpublished diary of an officer engaged in the campaign we have this sympathetic portrait of Aliyu at the time of his capture at Chibari:

In the centre was a tall, heavily-built man, intensely black, and enveloped in a dark blue embroidered cloth, baggy trousers and bulky turban, who stood with his hands crossed in front. This was the Emir Aliyu . . . a silent, dejected, tragic figure, no doubt wondering what was going to happen next. He evidently felt his position keenly and when he bent down low in submission I noticed that he was strongly perfumed with musk. He seemed to be almost on the point of tears, but mastering his emotion he addressed me in a deep guttural voice and said simply: 'I am ashamed. If it is the will of Allah that I must die, let it be now.' I replied that . . . he must come with me now, and for

[1] In his autobiography, *My Life*, Sir Ahmadu Bello makes it clear that the Emir Aliyu had not 'fled', as Lugard expressed it in his original dispatch: 'This was due', Sir Ahmadu writes, 'to a confusion with some of the Emir's Councillors who had got away just before the attack.' In her biography of Lugard, Margery Perham draws attention to a discussion of the Emir's conduct in *Gaskiya ta fi Kwabo*, no. 156.

the present let him show the common people how a big chief faces adversity.[1]

There still remains some historic doubt about the accuracy of the published accounts of Aliyu's capture, just as there is dispute about the fate of the flag claimed to be that of Attahiru, Sultan of Sokoto.[2]

The Waziri Ahmadu bravely carried on the advance to Kano, but a small force of Mounted Infantry encountered them at Kwatarkwashi, and in the remarkable fight that ensued the Waziri and seven other title holders were killed and the army scattered. The Wambai, Muhammadu Abbas, a brother of the Emir and the Waziri, had previously held aloof but now he hurried to Kano with his adherents and made his submission to Lugard. In April 1903 he was formally installed as Emir.

Kano was selected as the site for the North's first experiment with Western education, when, after the Government had turned down the offer by the Church Missionary Society in 1906 to open a boarding school in Zaria or Kano to which the emirs might send their sons, Hanns Vischer was seconded from the Administration to become Director of Education and built a number of houses in local style just outside the Nassarawa gate. Gidan Dan Hausa (Vischer's nickname) is still standing. Three kinds of classes were started, one for chiefs' sons, another for malamai, and a third for 'technical and vernacular' classes. The sons of chiefs paid two shillings a month.[3] In 1914 the Kano Native Authority, then comprising the Emir and the Waziri, decided to make an annual contribution of the large sum of £10,000 to the aid-the-war fund.[4]

Muhammadu Abbas was succeeded in 1919 by his brother Usman, who had also been Wambai before his coming to the throne. At that time Katsina Division was part of Kano Province. In 1921 the provincial headquarters were removed from Bompai to Nassarawa. The original Residency in Kano was the present

[1] This is an extract from a private and unpublished diary, to which we were given access by the courtesy of a senior officer of the Nigerian Army.

[2] It will be interesting to see whether the forthcoming account of the Kano-Sokoto campaign by D. J. Muffett, formerly an Administrative Officer in Nigeria, throws any fresh light on this. From what we have seen of the typescript, some new views are likely to be expressed. See also footnote at p. 127 of *Lugard: The Years of Authority*, Margery Perham, 1960.

[3] C. W. J. Orr, *The Making of Northern Nigeria*, pp. 266–74. See also the forthcoming study of Hanns Vischer's work as Director of Education by Sonia Graham.

[4] I am indebted to my student Mahmud Abubakar dan Waziri for his help on a number of matters of local history in this section.—A.K-G.

'summer palace' of the Emir of Kano in Nassarawa, beside the Provincial Office. This was occupied by the first Resident of Kano, Dr Cargill, in 1903 after the capture of Kano. Later, a mud and thatch Residency—afterwards replaced by a building of more permanent material—was erected at Bompai. This was the building used by the Prince of Wales during his visit to Kano in 1925. After this Royal Visit a new Residency, of mud construction and conforming to traditional Hausa architecture, was built in Nassarawa while that at Bompai was handed over to the Royal West African Frontier Force for use as an Officers' Mess; for up to then Kano had been quite a military centre.

Before the 1926 reorganization of the Northern Provinces, no province had more emirates within its jurisdiction than Kano. Besides Kano emirate in Kano Division, there were the emirates of Katsina, Daura and Kazaure in the Katsina Division; those of Katagum, Misau and Jama'are in the Katagum Division; and those of Hadejia and Gumel in the Hadejia Division.

Abdullahi Bayero, who held the title of Ciroma, now traditionally the office of the Emir's eldest son, became the tenth Fulani Emir of Kano in 1926. He broadened the basis of his council by including his younger brother, the Galadima, and followed this step by agreeing to the presence of the Native Treasurer at the weekly council meetings with the Resident as an acknowledgement of the growing importance of the part played by finance in the emirate affairs. In 1930 the N.A. Council was further developed by the appointment of the Ma'aji, so that it now consisted of the Waziri in charge of judicial matters, the Madaki responsible for the administration of the twenty-nine districts, the Galadima holding the portfolio of central departments like police, works, health and Kano city, and the Ma'aji in charge of the treasury. This is the period of which we have the following vignette of a council meeting during the zenith of 'indirect rule':

> Once a week the Emir and his executive councillors meet the District Officer and the Resident (when he is in Kano), generally at the latter's house. A description of such a meeting may give some actuality to the relationship between the Native Authorities and their British advisers.
>
> The Africans, having left their shoes at the door, enter with ceremonious dignity. The Emir takes the Resident's hand in both of his, inclines his body, and seats himself upon a chair. The other three Councillors prostrate themselves and sit behind him crosslegged upon

the floor in front of the Resident and the District Officer. Relations between these people of another race and religion and their British advisers are never one of easy familiarity; they are markedly ceremonious and restrained. It must be accepted as a factor in the administrative situation that full mutual comprehension and, still more, friendly intimacy, can very rarely exist; the relationship rests upon respect and a growing degree of understanding and confidence. Questions of etiquette have always been a serious consideration, as the official files bear witness. Should an Emir be seen alone? Should he interview Departmental Officers or unofficial Europeans except in the presence of an Administrative Officer? Should he be offered a chair, or should a special bed be brought with him on which he can recline? Should he be offered tea? Should he be confronted by an unveiled European woman? (My presence at the Council is a large concession to change if not to progress.) The Emir is dressed voluminously in embroidered robes of white cotton covered by a dove-grey cloak lined with scarlet. His indigo turban, gleaming with hammered indigo, is swathed in thick folds round his head and throat and tied in a rabbit's-ear knot, the prerogative of his blood. His brother, the Galadima, a slighter edition of himself, also indulges in this flourish. He is in charge of the affairs of the city. The Waziri is a little wizened old man with brilliant eyes. His position approximates to that of Prime Minister, as he is general adviser, especially in legal matters. He has the freest manner, and is the only one to smile or laugh, yet he is the pillar of conservatism in Kano. The Madaki is an extremely handsome and benevolent-looking old man, who looks after the affairs of the Districts. The Maaji, or Treasurer, is distinguished from the others by his broad, light face, his father having been a Tripolitan Arab. He has the humblest demeanour, having only recently been put upon the Council, though tradition gave the Treasurer this status. He has been in the Treasury for nearly thirty years, and Treasurer since 1919.

The first question discussed is the local effect of England's abandonment of the gold standard, and the traders' manipulation to their own advantage of the fluctuation of prices. From this discussion turns to the price of ground-nuts and the grain harvest. The Emir, who speaks little and keeps his eyes mostly upon his beringed hands, volunteers a remonstrance against the Government schools being kept open during Ramadan, when the boys cannot eat or drink during the day. The Resident promises to discuss the matter with the Education Officers, but does not hold out much hope of concession. An Agricultural Officer is called upon to explain the economic possibilities of tapping gum in the forests. . . .[1]

[1] Margery Perham, *Native Administration in Nigeria*, 1937 (reprinted 1962), pp. 89–90.

Continuing its tradition of experimental schools in the Western line started by the Nassarawa school for chiefs' sons opened by Hanns Vischer in 1909, Kano opened in 1930 an N.A. polytechnic in Gidan Murphy by Kofar Dan Agundi as well as a girls' centre, and, in 1934, the law school under sheikhs from Gordon College, Khartoum. A court of non-Muslim character was opened in Sabon Gari in 1931 and this Mixed Court, as it came to be called, under the presidentship of a Ghanaian[5] proved a successful innovation. In the following year further devolution of the council's powers was effected by the appointment of four assistants to the Galadima, Wakilin Gabas, Wakilin Kudu, etc., and when the Waziri Gidado went to Mecca the opportunity was taken to delegate some of his powers.

By virtue of its position as the emporium of the Western Sudan, Kano had more to fear from the economic depression of the 1930s than any other city in Nigeria. Fortunately it weathered the slump well and in 1934 the price of ground-nuts jumped 300 per cent from £2 a ton within the first few weeks of the season. With the crisis passed, the Emir of Kano was able to accompany the Emir of Gwandu to England, taking with him the Madaki and his eldest son the Ciroma. He was granted an audience with the king which delighted him. At one of the Kano agricultural shows held about this time, 12,000 tickets at two *anini* each were sold within two hours for the novelty fun fair, described as 'doing for the peasants what visits abroad do for their rulers!' This visit to the United Kingdom led the Emir and his son to arrange for private tuition in English on their return. Whether the unusual trade agreement of 1935, whereby Kano exported 35,000 guinea-fowl eggs at 10d. a hundred, also arose from this visit is not told.

Kano was the delivery point of the first airmail service from Europe in 1936, and almost immediately an emergency flight was necessary to bring in Bank of England currency notes flown out to meet the shortage caused by the purchase of a record tonnage of ground-nuts. Kano had indeed now consummated the re-orientation of her trade outlook away from being the southern focus of camel-borne goods across the Sahara towards her new status of being the northern end of the Nigerian ground-nut trade. The year is also remembered in Kano for the fact that the Governor rode through the streets on horseback in splendid

[1] Mr. C. V. Tay, who later became Ghana's ambassador to Nigeria.

procession with the Emir, a spectacle that could be recalled only as a memory. On the death of Waziri Alhaji Gidado (he was the father of a later Waziri, Alhaji Abubakar) in 1937, the office, which as we have seen was not indigenous to Kano, temporarily lapsed. He was a great old man, who had been appointed Chief Alkali in 1903 and then Waziri in 1909. The new adviser on legal affairs was turbanned as Wali, and the Ciroma was appointed to the Council with responsibility for financial supervision.

In 1951 the Emir Abdullahi Bayero, whose name is still so well-respected in Kano, made his second pilgrimage to Mecca, and on his return he officially opened the beautiful new mosque. The year, however, was saddened by the terrible El Dunia cinema fire, and it is in respect of the dead that the site has since been turned into a memorial garden. Sadness, indeed, seemed the lot of Kano for a while, for the following year brought the death of the venerable Arabic scholar, the Wali, and in December 1953 the Emir died, at the age of seventy. He was succeeded by his eldest son, Alhaji Muhammadu Sanusi, who in a broadcast speech promised a number of administrative reforms such as public sessions of his own court, limitation of the high offices to be held by his own family, retrenchment of his personal household, and land registration and reform in Kano City. The new Emir was also instrumental in forcing through subsidiary legislation to curb the hounding activities of Kano's notorious beggar minstrels. Formerly anyone of rank or wealth had been at the mercy of these minstrels who levied a perennial blackmail: 'there was the choice', noted an official report, 'between paying for their worthless praise or being held up to hatred, ridicule and contempt in an endless calypso in which personal character, domestic difficulties and private affairs were reeled out with pitiless comment for the edification of the vulgar and to the delight of enemies'.

Kano's proverbial preference for commerce over classroom was confirmed in 1952, when the Middle School went on strike, and again in 1954, when not one boy volunteered to continue his education beyond Secondary II. But an improvement was shown in the following year, and since then Kano has made the headlines by its ambitious universal primary education plan. Official recognition of the work of the Emir and his Madaki, Alhaji Shehu Ahmed, later Deputy Speaker of the Regional House of Assembly, in 1955 presaged greater joy for Kano. Sure enough, in 1956 the Queen of England was entertained by the Emir in his palace, the residence of Kano royalty since the time of Mohamman Rumfa. The contingents that took part in the Durbar that year reflected some of the history and traditions of the fighting forces of the Northern emirs of yesteryear. Kano's contingent was led by the *shantu*, trumpeters who used to spur the warriors into action. These were followed by the *kuge*, horn blowers who would warn the people that war was imminent. Then the scarlet-robed *'yan bindiga* with their muskets; the long, silver *kakaki*, blown to announce the arrival of the Emir; the bowmen; the swordsmen; the mounted horsemen in chain mail; more warriors, their bodies and their horses padded as a defence against arrows, and the horses with bells jingling at their necks to frighten the enemy; the *'yan kagura* to acknowledge greetings paid to the Emir; twelve *'yan zage* whose duty is to fan the Emir, steady him on his horse, and remove any dust that may fall on him; and in their midst the Emir himself, mounted and wearing the ostrich feather shoes introduced by Mohammam Rumfa. He was shaded by the *lema* or royal umbrella borne by an attendant selected for his stature and physical strength. Then came the war drums, so heavy that they must be carried on camels, and the spearmen and the lancers preceding the groups of emirate notabilities.

Following this good omen came bountiful 1957, remembered by the Kano farmers as the Year of the Great Harvest on account of its bumper ground-nut and corn crops, a happy memory to contrast with the other still unforgotten farmers' year, the famine of 1914 known as *yunwa mai buhu*. In 1961, Kano City and Waje were separated and each became a district in its own right, the latter under the office of Mai-Unguwar Murdubawa. In 1962 Kano once again made its mark, this time by its ambitious but resolute plan to tackle its problems of rapid urbanization by means of a Greater Kano Town Planning Committee, thinking in terms of a Kano City population of one million souls.

Sir Muhammadu Sanusi resigned in early 1963, after Government had appointed a sole commissioner to inquire into the finances of the Kano N.A., and elected to retire to Azare. The traditional Kano kingmakers—Madawaki, Sarkin Bai, Sarkin Dawaki and Makama—decided to disregard the claims of prominent members of the Bayero and Sanusi families and, in view of the unhappy state of Kano affairs, to look to the cadet branch of

Muhammadu Abbas's family (the eighth Emir). Muhammadu Inuwa, an uncle of the abdicated Emir and then Galadima, was appointed twelfth Emir of Kano and given a caretaker committee until a new Council, including for the first time elected members, could replace the dissolved Kano Native Authority Council.

Muhammadu Inuwa died within a few months and was succeeded by Alhaji Ado Bayero, son of Emir Abdullahi Bayero and at that time Nigeria's ambassador to Senegal. He was installed as Kano's thirteenth Emir in 1963, at the age of 33.[1]

[1] See the portrait-article 'The Youngest Emir', *West Africa*, 11 January 1964.

THE KINGS AND EMIRS OF KANO

The Habe Kings

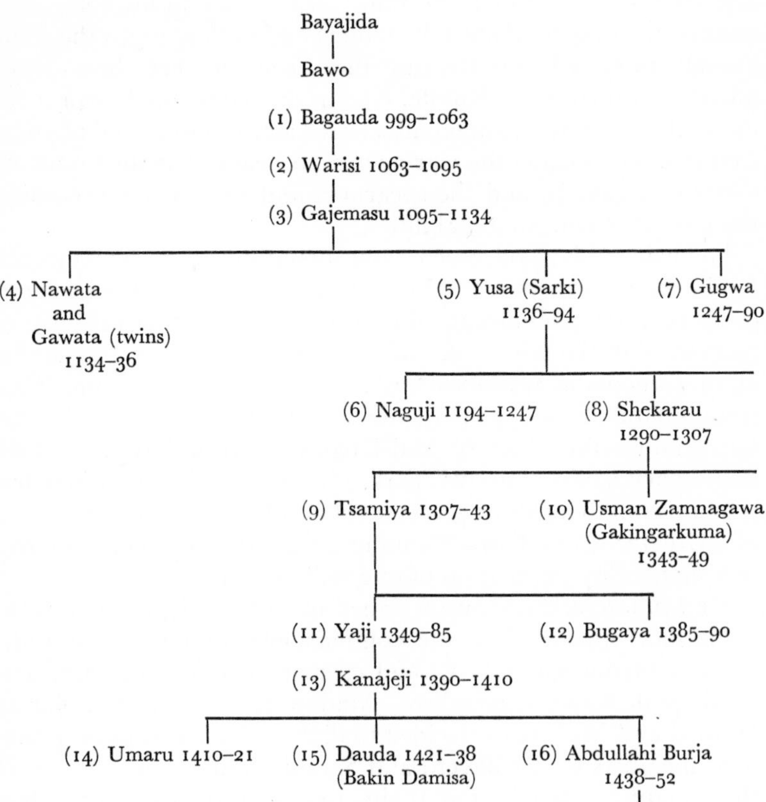

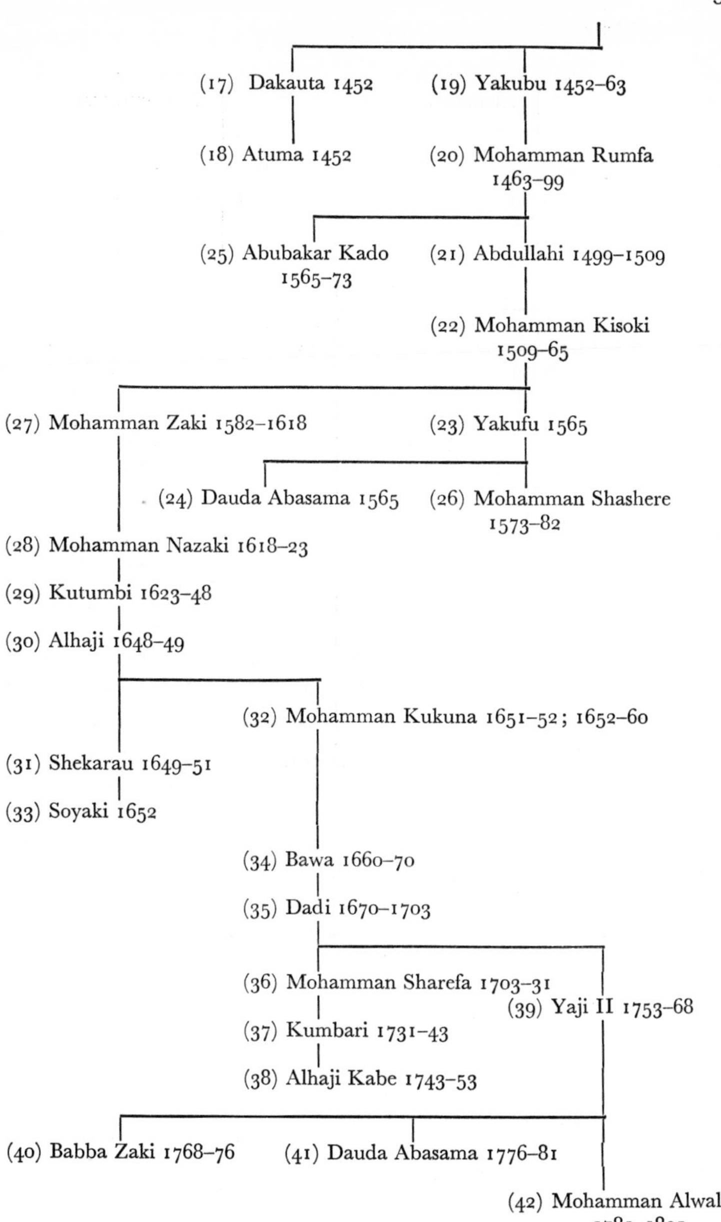

(17) Dakauta 1452
(19) Yakubu 1452–63
(18) Atuma 1452
(20) Mohamman Rumfa 1463–99
(25) Abubakar Kado 1565–73
(21) Abdullahi 1499–1509
(22) Mohamman Kisoki 1509–65
(27) Mohamman Zaki 1582–1618
(23) Yakufu 1565
(24) Dauda Abasama 1565
(26) Mohamman Shashere 1573–82
(28) Mohamman Nazaki 1618–23
(29) Kutumbi 1623–48
(30) Alhaji 1648–49
(32) Mohamman Kukuna 1651–52; 1652–60
(31) Shekarau 1649–51
(33) Soyaki 1652
(34) Bawa 1660–70
(35) Dadi 1670–1703
(36) Mohamman Sharefa 1703–31
(39) Yaji II 1753–68
(37) Kumbari 1731–43
(38) Alhaji Kabe 1743–53
(40) Babba Zaki 1768–76
(41) Dauda Abasama 1776–81
(42) Mohamman Alwali 1781–1805

The Fulani Emirs

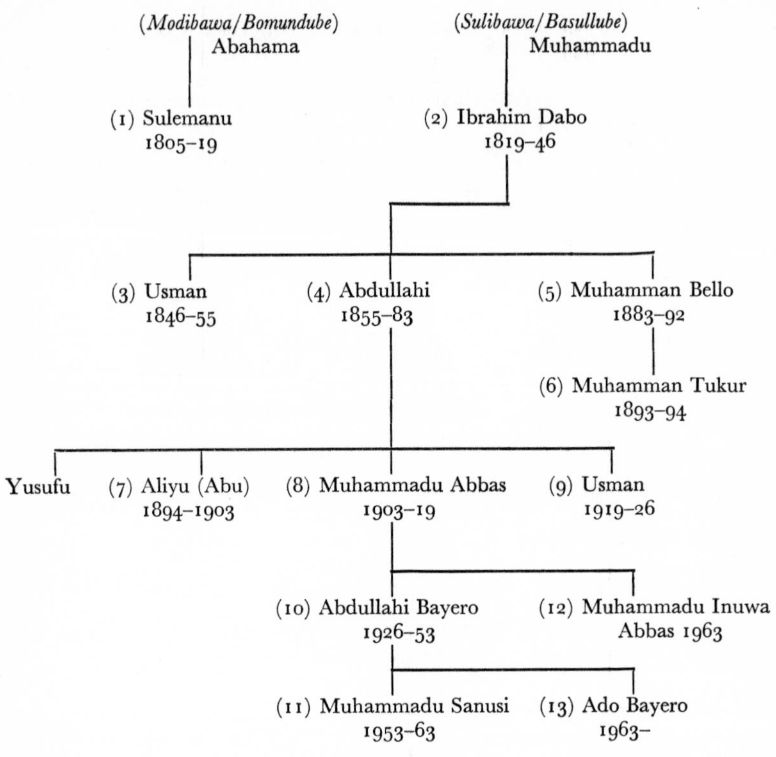

Note: The dates in this chapter and on the above lists owe much to the work of H. R. Palmer on the *Kano Chronicle*, *vide* his *Sudanese Memoirs*, vol. III, pp. 92–132. Recent work by H. F. C. Smith and others on various king-lists indicates that the Kano dates may also need radical revision to bring them into line. See footnote on p. 183 and the last sentence of the footnote at p. 236.

XVIII. ZARIA

ZAZZAU—for such was the ancient name of Zaria—was one of the Hausa Bakwai, the original seven Hausa States. It was also among the largest of the Hausa States, though the British severely reduced its jurisdiction as a punishment for the murder of Captain Moloney at Keffi in 1902.[1] Other names by which present-day Zaria was known are the variants Zakzak and Zegzeg. The people of Zaria are still called in Hausa *Zage-Zagi* or *Zazzagawa* (sing.: *Ba-Zazzagi*).

The Zaria Chronicle,[2] compiled by the Imam of Kona in Zaria, lists sixty rulers of Habe Zazzau before the Fulani conquest of 1804.[2] The first of these, Gunguma, is said to have been the grandson of Bayajida of Daura fame. It was during the time of the eighteenth king of Zaria, Muhamman Abu (*c.* 1505–30) that the rulers were converted to Islam, though another authority suggests 1456.

Writing of Zaria in the early years of the sixteenth century, Leo Africanus noted:

> The south-east part thereof bordereth upon Cano, and is distant from Casena almost an hundred and fifty miles. The inhabitants are rich and have great traffique with other nations. Some part of this kingdom is plaine, and the residue mountainous, but the mountaines are extremely cold, and the plaines intolerably hot. And because they can hardly endure the sharpness of winter, they kindle great fires in the midst of their houses, laying the coles thereof under their high bedsteads, and so betaking themselves to sleepe. Their fields abounding in water are exceedingly fruitfull, and their houses are built like the houses of the kingdom of Casena.[3]

Before the people settled in their present capital town, they resided in Kawar, Rikoci, Wuciciri and Turunku. Tradition maintains that this last-named capital was built by the slaves of

[1] See chapter on Keffi, p. 533. The whole of this Zaria chapter owes a great debt of gratitude to M. G. Smith, *Government in Zazzau*, 1960.

[2] See also Hassan and Shu'aibu, *A Chronicle of Abuja*, 1962, where a local record of the kings of Zaria with their dates is given on p. 37. It differs somewhat from Zaria records.

[3] Quoted in T. L. Hodgkin, *Nigerian Perspectives*, p. 103. (Pory's translation of 1600.)

one Bakwa while she was away warring with the Nupe. The name Bakwa Turunku may mean "the female stranger belonging to the Toronke people" (from Toro in Tekrur). During her reign Turunku was challenged by a rival at Karigi, and tradition has it that the river Galma was the boundary between the two states. The ruins of Turunku are still visible, beyond the hills that lie to the east of the Zaria–Kaduna road some twenty miles from Zaria, and Bakwa's house and tumulus place of burial are an object of pilgrimage.

The story here is a little obscure, but what is locally accepted is the fact that during the reign of the twenty-second ruler, Bakwa Turunku, the people moved from Turunku to Kufena at Zaria, possibly about 1536. Locally, the Emir's palace in Zaria to this day is sometimes spoken of as *gidan Bakwa*, Bakwa's house, while the place where young girls dance in the Emir's palace is known as Kigo after the huge double-storeyed house (*soro*) that Amina built for her own sessions of the *gada* dance. Bakwa perceived that not only would Turunku outgrow its limited water supply but that a stronghold to the north would bring command of the river Galma—so-called from its hoe-like (*garma*) pattern.

The names of Bakwa's two daughters are renowned in the history of Zazzau. One was Amina[-tu], after whom the original wall round the city of Zaria is called. It lies to the north of the town and encircles the prominent landmark of Kufena hill, at the foot of which the capital was first built. From there it joins up with the existing wall at Kofar Doka and again at Kofar Kuyambana. The other daughter was Zaria, who gave her name to the modern emirate and its capital.

The elder daughter, Amina, is said to have built a walled camp wherever she sojourned on her extensive travels. Thus it is that in many parts of Hausaland ancient town walls are called *ganuwar Amina*, 'Amina's walls', even though they were not necessarily built by her. By extension, the phrase now means the site of an ancient town. It has also given rise to the Hausa proverbs for emphasizing respectable venerability: *wane ya cika takama da tsufa kamar ganuwar Amina.*

On the death of Nohir, Amina's grandfather, his younger brother succeeded to the throne in 1535, but he died within the year and Bakwa became chief.[1] In accordance with the Zazzau

[1] There is some doubt in Zaria history whether Bakwa was a man or a woman.

custom, Amina as the eldest daughter assumed the title of Magajiya, at the age of sixteen, and was given the traditional gift of forty female slaves (*kuyanga*). Of suitors she had no lack, even before her mother became queen, but she refused them all. It is said that when the Makama failed to win her hand with a daily offer of ten slaves for every day he made his suit to her, the Emir of Kano sent her fifty male slaves and fifty female slaves as well as fifty bags of white and blue cloth (*kyankyandi*), but all in vain.

Karama became Sarki in 1566. He was a warrior who was never happier than when he was in the saddle, and in these adventures he found an enthusiastic companion in the martial Amina. Her prowess in battle earned her the throne of Zaria on the death of Karama in 1576, and the royal trumpets hailed her: '*Amina, 'yar Bakwa, ta san rana!*'[1] It was of Amina that Sultan Bello of Sokoto wrote:

> Strange things have happened in the history of the seven Hausa States, and the most strange of these is the extent of the possessions which God gave to Aminatu, daughter of the ruler of Zazzau. She waged war in the Hausa lands and took them all, so that the men of Katsina and the men of Kano brought her tribute. She made war in Bauchi and against the other towns of the south and of the west, so that her possessions stretched down to the shores of the sea [i.e. the Niger].

The name Zazzau derives from the famous sword which was honoured by all Zaria people and gave them an ethnic identity long before they recognized any king. When a chief was eventually appointed, they called him Madau Zazzau (from *mai-daukan Zazzau*, 'he who holds the sword') and a retainer would bear this sword whenever the king went forth.

The affairs of state in no way interfered with Amina's love of war. To this the *Kano Chronicle* gives vivid testimony:

> At this time[2] Zaria, under Queen Amina, conquered all the towns as far as Kwararafa and Nupe. Every town paid tribute to her. The Sarkin Nupe sent forty eunuchs and ten thousand kola nuts to her. She first had eunuchs and kola nuts in Hausaland. In her time the whole products of the west were brought to Hausaland. Her conquests extended over thirty-four years.

[1] Literally, 'Amina, daughter of Bakwa, she knows the sun (or day)!', but with a meaning '. . . there are no flies on Amina!' or 'she knows her way about!'

[2] i.e. 1421–38 according to Palmer, and far earlier than the dates here given.

Whether Amina ever married is still disputed in Zaria history, but tradition certainly credits her with taking a lover in every town she conquered; but as camp was broken on the following morning, her brief bridegroom was beheaded so that none should live to tell the tale. Amina died in Atagara, near present-day Idah, for at that time Amina had pushed the frontiers of Zazzau south of the Niger–Benue confluence. Her praise is sung: 'Amina, daughter of Nikatau, a woman as capable as a man' (*kallabi tsakanin rawuna*).

Her younger sister Zaria died at Yauri. As we have seen, she gave her name to the new capital of Zazzau, which either she or Bakwa may have founded. Zaria lore has it that in the village where Zaria was staying there lived a hunter called Bono. One day when he returned from hunting he reported that he had discovered an ideal site for the chief's compound. Bono led his chief to a spot between two rocky outcrops, Madara (today recognized as Madar-kaci, the rock to the east of the palace on which the city's water-tank is so prominently placed) and Kufena. These rocks were two legendary giants, so tall that they are said to have been able to dip their fingers into a bowl of *tuwo* or porridge placed between them, though they were five miles apart. When Kufena came out of his house he would call out *Madara, ka ci?* ('Madara, have you eaten?'), and so the name of Madar-ka-ci arose. Bono's name is not forgotten, for the swampy area to the west of the Emir's palace near Babban Dodo[1] is called after him.

Thus the original site lay at the foot of Kufena Hill, itself an ancient stronghold. At some date before the jihad of 1804 the town moved to its present site on the left bank of the Kubani river. It may be that the silk-cotton trees, so characteristic of the city's landscape, date from this time, for their place in Hausa proverbial lore is an old one: *rimin Zaria sun fi 'yammatan alkawali.* Zaria's walls, stretching for almost ten miles, are pierced by eight gates; a ninth, beyond the Kofar Kuyambana, has been filled in,

[1] This was the nickname of Captain Porch, who built the present house in the city in about 1912. It means 'the big bogeyman'. Abadie's first Residency can still be traced just inside the walls on the main Kaduna road; it was the scene of an abortive dig by the Department of Antiquities a few years ago when they were led to believe that some of the loot from the Kano-Sokoto campaign of 1903 was buried there. K. J. Bryant's guide-book to Zaria City and two articles in *Nigeria Magazine*, one on the city walls (No. 60) and the other on the house decorations (No. 68), make a valuable *vademecum* for the visitor.

for it is through this one that the Habe under their king Makau are said to have been driven southwards to Abuja by the Fulani in 1804. As was the custom in the walled cities of Hausaland, each ward head was responsible for repairing a given section of the wall at the end of the harvest. Not till this communal labour was over could the men leave the city and go off for the dry-season occupations of raiding and trading (*cin rani*). Inside the walls it was usual to leave plenty of open farm land—as, for example, along the north-eastern stretches of the Zaria walls—against the time of siege, when people and their animals might seek asylum within the city.

In Sultan Bello's *Infaq al Maisuri* we find a reference to how 'Zakzak became the most extensive of all the countries of Hausa, for many of the towns of Bauchi were included in it'. Here by Bauchi is meant any pagan area. Kajuru, Kaura, Lapai and Kusheriki were all ruled by Habe chiefs of Zazzau. Zaria's dominance came to an end when Bornu overran the Hausa states in about 1734. One of the royal dynasties, that of Yamusa, is of Bornu ancestry, and the office of Limamin Kona was traditionally reserved to a family of Bornuese extraction. Until the coming of the Fulani, Zaria paid tribute to Bornu; a Bornu emissary, the Kacalla, resided at the court of Sarkin Zazzau; and her kings were installed by a representative of the Mai of Bornu, the Magajin Malam. It is remarkable how many Kanuri links and memories are still to be found in the villages of Zaria emirate.[1]

Though the Habe of Abuja insist that the kings from the beginning of the sixteenth century were Muslims, Zaria traditions speak of periodic lapses into the old *bori* culture.[2] For instance, Jatau (1782–1802), is said to have built a mosque, but his successor Makau demolished it and reverted to animism.

On hearing the news of the Fulani rising in Gobir in 1804 a certain Fulani from Mali, Malam Musa, who had been preaching for many years in Zaria city, went to Gobir. He was present at the defeat of the apostate king of Gobir and then received a flag from the Shehu. It is claimed that there had been Fulani herdsmen

[1] This was borne out by the survey reports produced from 'Operation Zazzau', a village survey project carried out at the Institute of Administration in 1960. The reports were lodged with the Zaria N.A.

[2] The phenomenon of *bori* is dealt with at length in A. J. N. Tremearne, *The Ban of the Bori*, 1914, and S. F. Nadel, *A Black Byzantium*, 1942.

round Zaria right from the time the Habe kings moved from Turunku; certainly the Fulani chiefs of Fatika were recognized vassals of Zazzau, and one of them was rewarded by the grant of a fief within Zaria city (the Fatika ward) for having warned the Habe king of a plot against his life by the Madakin Kankarro.

Musa and a Bornuese Fulani named Yamusa, whose family had settled near Kaduna, returned from Sokoto with a flag and a small army. One legend tells of how Musa took part in the invasion of Kano first and then crossed into Zaria. His party of seventy-four horsemen met opposition at Kudan and again at Hunkuyi, but at Durum he received military assistance from the village-head, who was later rewarded with the gift of vassal status. Either avoiding or defeating the Habe cavalry at Likoro, thanks to the intelligence supplied by the village's Sarkin Pawa, he attacked Zaria from the north-west. The Fulani drove out the pagan Sarkin Zazzau, Makau, who fled with many of his subjects until they settled at Zuba and eventually established the emirate of Abuja.

One story maintains that Yamusa complained to Usman dan Fodio that as a Zaria Fulani he needed no leader from outside and that he sought to be appointed the Shehu's representative for at least the whole of southern Zaria. Zaria history also relates that the Imam Dan Madami, a close friend of Musa's for several years before the conquest, was a prominent horse-breeder whose stables provided valuable mounts for the invading Fulani.

Though Zaria now became a vassal state of the Sokoto empire, she not only was one of the most important but also had several vassals of her own, such as Jema'a, Keffi, Nassarawa, Lapai and Doma; Lafia was transferred to Bauchi in 1812, perhaps in return for Lere. The Waziri of Sokoto was appointed as the official intermediary (*kofa*) between Zaria and Sokoto. Of the tribute due from Zaria we read:

> The Sultan of Sokoto supervised the state of Zaria through his kinsman, the Waziri (Vizier) of Sokoto. This Waziri was the official link between the rulers of Zaria and Sokoto. He was kept informed about local affairs through visits by himself and his agents, and in this way he maintained a continuous contact with the kings of Zaria. The Waziri was responsible for collecting the tribute which Zaria made twice annually to Sokoto, on the occasions of the main Muhammadan festivals of Id-el-Kabir and Id-el-Fitr (known in Hausa as the Greater and the Lesser Sallah). At such times, the kings of Zaria were expected to

visit Sokoto, taking with them tribute in the form of slaves, Zaria cloth, horses, mats, and some cowrie currency. The content of this tribute changed over the century, and its value tended steadily to increase. Apart from the tribute which the rulers of Zaria sent to Sokoto, levies of grain were collected for the Wazirin Sokoto on his annual visits to Zaria. This collection was known as *bani-bani* (give me—give me). By 1860 it had become customary for the king of Zaria to make donations of money and goods to both the Waziri and the Sultan of Sokoto on his appointment to the throne. This *kurdin sarauta* (money of taking office) was introduced in the years between 1835 and 1845, when Sokoto asserted its right to select the rulers of Zaria.[1]

Musa's grasp of the Habe principles of administration was thorough, and onto this structure he grafted Fulani reforms. He eliminated the traditional eunuchs from such offices as Wambai, Dallatu and Galadima; he established the post of Alkali in order to separate the judiciary from the executive; and he created the office of Waziri and, after an unsuccessful palace *coup* by a Fulani, Bagozeki, that of Sarkin Yaki with control over the royal bodyguard. He is also credited with the directive that *hakimai* or district heads should reside in Zaria city, thus reducing their opportunities for either rebellion or oppressive administration by separating them from their fiefs. Musa sought to ally himself by marriage with the leading Fulani families involved in the government of Zaria, and he distributed land round the capital among the four Fulani families that had taken part in the conquest. The Katsinawa received land to the west of the city, the Bornawa and Sulibawa to the south and east, while the Mallawa (his own family) held rights over the northern areas in the Makarfi district. Neither Musa nor his successor was ever turbanned Emir of Zaria, but remained as the deputy of the Sultan. They retained the status of 'malam' and were therefore greeted only with *Allah ya gafarta malam* and never with the royal salutations of *zaki* or *ranka ya dade*. To this day, Musa is always referred to as 'Malam'.

On Musa's death in 1821 he was succeeded by Yamusa. By his immediate dismissal of Musa's office-holders he showed a rupture with Habe patterns of government and declared the political opposition of the Bornawa to the Mallawa dynasty. Yamusa is said to have dropped the office of Waziri and instead to have created that of Wali, in imitation of Sokoto. He placed one of his

[1] M. G. Smith, op. cit., p. 74.

sons, Awaisu, as Sarkin Mai in charge of the Maguzawa[1] in the north of his emirate.

Of Zaria at this time, *c.* 1825, we have the following valuable contemporary account:

> The old city of Zaria . . . only stood siege of two days. . . . The new city built by the Fellatas, the walls of which extend from the south-east side of the old about two miles to the south, enclosing a great space of ground on which are built a number of little villages and detached homes, is surrounded by high clay walls. Near the centre of the wall stands its principal mosque, built of clay, having a minaret about forty or fifty feet high. The principal market is at the south end, inside the walls. . . . The house of the governor is north of the great mosque and is surrounded by a high clay wall. . . . Inside the walls there are a great number of shady trees, which are pruned every year for firewood; they look at a distance like immense poplars: swamps, corn fields and green plats make up the rest of the town. Date trees, palm oil trees, papas, melons, plantains, Indian corn, millet, dourra, rice, yams, sweet potatoes, etc. are in abundance, particularly rice. They say they raise more and better rice than all the rest of Hausa put together. . . . The environs of the city are beautiful, being formed of gentle ridges of land and plains; here and there fine large shady trees, and small streams of water; the rocky mounts to the north and south adding to the beauty of the scene.[2]

When Yamusa died in 1834, the question of succession appeared to be a simple one between the Bornawa and the Mallawa. But, conscious of local political difficulties in choosing either, the council of selectors led by the Galadima Dokaje and the Limamin Juma'a sought a way out by recommending to the Waziri of Sokoto the appointment of Abdulkarim of the Katsinawa *zuriya*, who at that time held the title of Sa'i responsible for the nomadic Fulani affairs. This move not only confirmed Sokoto's ultimate power of decision over Zaria kingship but also necessitated the actual installation ceremony of a king rather than of a deputy as Musa and Yamusa had been.

[1] The *Maguzawa* (sing: *Bamaguje*) are the 'pagan Hausa', today more or less restricted to the southern parts of Kano emirate. They embrace the original Habe groups of the Kutumbawa of the old Kano supremacy and the rural Katsinawa. The leading study on them is J. H. Greenberg, *The Influence of Islam on a Sudanese Religion*, 1946. There are also useful references in J. S. Trimingham, *History of Islam in West Africa*, 1960.

[2] This extract is from Clapperton's journal. He is, in fact, incorrect in his record of the moves of the capital, for he ascribes the move to the present site to the Fulani after their 1804 campaign against the Habe.

In more ways than one was Abdulkarim's accession a turning point in Zaria history, marking the end of Zaria's autonomy. The Wazirin Sokoto, who was the Sultan's *jekada* or emissary to Zaria, now demanded his own tribute in addition to the *gandu* of slaves, mats, cloth and locust-beans annually sent to the Sultan. Furthermore, the tribute was now to include money for the first time. The Sultan instituted the system of *kurdin sarauta*, money for the grant of office, in Zaria at this time, something quite new in Zaria's governmental system. Abdulkarim's authority over his vassals of Keffi and Nassarawa was reduced, while the southern dominions of Zazzau experienced a very loose control. It was, however, in his reign that the Friday mosque was completed, today one of Zaria's oldest buildings.

It is from these three Fulani dynasties, the Mallawa, the Bornawa and the Katsinawa that every successive Emir of Zaria has, with one exception, been chosen. The exception was the appointment in 1854 of Abdulsalami from the Sulibawa dynasty.

Abdulkarim was succeeded by Hamada, son of Yamusa, whom he had dismissed from the title of Madaki, but he reigned for only fifty-two days before he died. His half-brother Mamman Sani was appointed in the same year, 1846. In Zaria it is said that Hamada had foretold his own death shortly after becoming king, but the immediate choice of another of the Bornawa required the active support of Sokoto to overcome the claims of Sidi Abdulkadiri, the son of Malam Musa. The new emir quickly began the redistribution of offices, though he confirmed his rival Sidi as Dan Galadima in order to neutralize him. Mamman Sani was the first Fulani ruler to revive the Habe title of Wan'ya, besides creating a number of new eunuch posts for service in the royal household, such as Kasheka. Major changes were the substitution of a tax on every hoe, valued at 2,000 cowries, instead of the land tax, and the systematic extension of the Habe principle of taxing occupational groups so as now to include caravans, canoes, drummers and butchers as well as the dyers and smiths.

Territorially, Mamman Sani's reign was a busy one, for he undertook military campaigns against the Gwari and other peoples in present-day Kontagora, forced the Kaje in southern Zaria to submit, and attacked Abuja. He gathered to himself a vast booty of slaves with whom he populated many *rumada* or slave-farms, the biggest being Taban Sani which is said to have held over 3,000 of the king's slaves. Zaria traditions rank Mamman Sani as the richest of all its Fulani rulers, crediting him on his death with nearly ten thousand slaves and affirming that the customary third of his corn supplies inherited by his successors to the throne lasted them for eleven years. Mamman Sani sent his troops to support the Kano, Katsina and Bauchi contingents against Hadejia when its Emir Buhari repudiated his allegiance to Sokoto in 1850.

Not until 1853, over thirty years after his father's death, did Sidi mount the throne of Zaria that he so bitterly felt was rightly his. His love for Sokoto was accordingly not great. His rule was brief but dynamic.

Contrary to practice, Sidi appointed none of his own Mallawa dynasty to high office. His brothers withdrew their support. One, Abubakar, hurried off to Sokoto to complain of his disappointment; another, Muhammadu Baki, assembled a force of cavalry with the intention of ousting Sidi by force. The Sultan sent his Waziri to the troubled city of Zaria post-haste.

But Sidi, who had meanwhile suppressed his brother's revolt and imprisoned Muhammadu Baki, was in a fighting mood. He forbade the Waziri to enter Zaria city and ordered him to camp at Gimi, some ten miles away. When the Waziri enquired, in the name of the Sultan of Sokoto, why Sidi had imprisoned or driven out his brothers and had raided his own vassal of Nassarawa, he was bluntly told that these matters were no concern of Sokoto. *Sarauta, na gaje ta*, is the curt reply he is reputed to have sent: 'I have inherited my position of kingship.' The Waziri withdrew to Sokoto; the Sultan commanded the presence of Sidi in Sokoto; Sidi meekly went. He was deposed not a year after his appointment as emir, and was exiled to Wurno, where he remained until his death.

Sidi's deposition—the first Emir of Zaria, though by no means the last, to experience such a disgrace—underlined the power of Sokoto over Zaria. But what of the throne now? Faced with the choice between Sidi's brother Abubakar of the Mallawa, the unsuitability of the Bornawa candidates, and the political weakness of the Katsinawa, Sokoto interpreted the situation in the way most favourable to its own interests: it took upon itself the power to select Sidi's successor. In order to ensure the new king's dependence and increase its own control over Zaria, Sokoto appointed

Abdulsalami of the Sulibawa dynasty of Ibada. Making the best of it, the Zaria Fulani rationalized this autocratic appointment by praising their new emir's advanced years and by pointing out that, since he had seen Usman dan Fodio face to face and known him well, happier days would surely be Zaria's lot. But within three years Abdulsalami was killed in a fight at Munku, shot, according to local tradition, by a client of Sarkin Fada who was greedy for the throne.

Thus by Abdulsalami's death in 1857 the political system in Zaria had crystallized round no less than four competing dynasties, always with a strong element of active supervision by Sokoto. The Mallawa were still discredited by the events of Sidi's reign and the Katsinawa being as weak as before, only the Bornawa could furnish a successor to the late Sulibawa emir. Abdullahi, son of Hamada and now the Madaki, was appointed.

It was shortly after Abdullahi's installation that the remarkable Dr Baikie, trekking from Lokoja through Bida to Kano, passed through Zaria. In his diary he commented how 'the silk-cotton trees, which surround the town, distinguish it in the plain', and estimated that the walls were some ten miles in circumference and between sixteen and eighteen feet high. He noted that the ninth gate had been walled up, and described the mosque as 'a large building, 120 feet long, with two domes and a square tower at the north-east, ascended by steps'.

During Abdullahi's reign the Habe under Abu Kwaka of Abuja made frequent thrusts into southern Zaria, while to the east attacks from Ningi increased. The Emir managed to strengthen his defences in the eastern vassal state of Lere. Then, to restore order among the Gwari, Kaje and Katab of the south, he appointed one Tatumare, an Ikulu convert to Islam who knew the districts intimately, to the military office of Kuyambana, with command of the *lifidi* or heavy cavalry. He also led expeditions against the Kagoma near Kagoro, the Gwari of Dan Bunu and the Katab at Sabon Kaura near Malagum.

Next Abdullahi turned his attention to Keffi, whose vassal chief had been tardy with the tribute. Three times, it is said, Abdullahi was ordered by the Sultan to call off his army from this attack on Keffi, but Abdullahi repeated Sidi's retort that Zaria's dealings with its own vassals were not Sokoto's affair. When in 1871 Abdullahi made the usual dry-season visit to the Sultan, he was told that he had been deposed for his attempted autonomy and *kin umurci*, disobedience.

Following the precedent created on Sidi's deposition, Sokoto itself decided the succession of Zaria without consulting the electoral council. Abubakar, Sidi's brother and a son of Malam Musa, was appointed Emir of Zaria in 1871. The principal innovation accredited to him is the creation of a second Ma'aji title, with responsibility for the Jaba, Ikulu and Kamantan peoples focussed on Kacia. Abubakar undertook only one military campaign, against Gwodo in Jema'a. He died in 1874.

Shortly before Abubakar's death, a new Sultan, Abubakar Atiku na Raba, came to power in Sokoto. He disagreed with the punishment meted out to Abdullahi, who had had no formal indictment or trial, and decided to make amends by reappointing him Emir of Zaria. If the decision was a grave error of judgement, the manner in which it was executed was little short of folly. While the electoral council were actually discussing the question of a successor to Abubakar, they received the startling news that the Sultan had made up their mind for them: Abdullahi was to be restored. 'In its confidence,' historians comment, 'Sokoto had overplayed its hand.'

Trouble at once broke out in Zaria, triggered off by the disputes over the restoration of Abdullahi by the Sultan Abubakar, who made the decision without reference to the electoral council of Zaria, and over the disposition of Abdullahi's concubines, who, in accordance with the custom on the removal of an Emir, had been apportioned between the Emir's suzerain and his successor. The two strong men in Zaria, Madakin Zazzau Ali, and the Galadima, Hamman, who had both received some of Abdullahi's concubines from the hand of Emir Abubakar, gathered their supporters and slaves and withdrew from Zaria to Ifira near Rigachikun. Galadima Hamman was chairman of the Electoral Council of new Emirs of Zaria and had benefited not only from the concubines he had already received but additionally from the distribution of the former Emir Abdullahi's estate. Having crossed the Sayi river, a fairly big stream about four miles from Zaria on the road leading south-west, the two dissidents raised the flag of revolt. When Abdullahi sent one of his slaves, Maigoto, to order the Madaki and the Galadima to return to Zaria, the messenger was put to death by Ali's men.

Abdullahi now sent his army to reduce Ifira and asked Sokoto for support. The Sultan requested the Emir of Kano to negotiate a settlement. Anxious to avoid anything that might lead to a war with Zaria, the Emir of Kano camped at a village near Ifira and sent a message to Madaki Ali offering him the throne after Abdullahi if he called off the revolt. On the triple understanding that he would not be proceeded against by Abdullahi for rebellion, that he would be allowed to retain his portion of Abdullahi's previous estate, and that he would be the next Emir of Zaria, Ali agreed to the terms and consented to accompany the Emir of Kano back to Zaria.

Abdullahi took the unusual step of nominating one of his slaves, Yawa, as Sarkin Yamma and put him in charge of part of the army at Kacia, whose task was to collect tribute from the pagan peoples in the areas. This innovation was to have unexpected consequences in the reign of the next Emir.

Abdullahi's relations with Sokoto worsened. He appointed his son, Yero, as Madaki, but by his inability to recover his former property he succeeded only in exciting Yero's cupidity. Abdullahi showed his annoyance by refusing to make the annual visit of homage to Sokoto, though he sent in Zaria's tribute. His last vestige of hope disappeared with the death in 1877 of Sultan Abubakar, to whom he owed his reinstatement, for his successor Mu'azu had supported the original deposition. On the grounds that his refusal to attend at the Sultan's court was tantamount to disloyalty, Abdullahi was peremptorily summoned to Sokoto and for the second time deposed.

In honour of the promises made on his behalf by Kano, the Sultan appointed Ali tenth Emir of Zaria. When the letter reached Zaria, however, Ali was on his death-bed. In order to avoid Zaria's resentment at the high-handedness of Sokoto's behaviour over earlier appointments to the throne, the Sultan this time instructed the electoral council of the Galadima, Alkali and two imams to send their favoured candidate from each dynasty to Sokoto. From the three recommended candidates—Yero, son of Emir Abdullahi, Sambo, son of Emir Abdulkarim, and Zubairu, an unknown son of Malam Musa but Madaki Ali's choice from the Mallawa dynasty—Sambo was preferred by Sokoto and became Emir in 1879. By ordering Sambo to redistribute the top royal offices of Zaria—Madaki, Wambai and Iyan Kurama—

Sokoto managed to strengthen its own influence over Zaria as well as reduce the chances of attritious dynastic struggles or stubborn kingly rebellion.

In the event, it was one of Sambo's own clients, the Habe Salmanu whom the Emir had promoted from Sarkin Ruwa to Galadima, who plotted to usurp the throne. He sought support from the Habe chief of Ningi, Haruna the son of Hamza who had fled from Tsokuwa in Kano during the reign of Mamman Sani at Zaria (1846–53). Both were hostile to Fulani rule. It was arranged that Haruna would mass the Ningi forces at the old Habe town of Yakasai. From there he would attack Sambo as he set out on the annual journey of homage to Sokoto, while Salmanu, in his position as Galadima and therefore holding the capital in the Emir's absence, would seize the throne.

Sambo duly set out for Sokoto; but by a twist of fate, Haruna's letter to Salmanu listing the final arrangements for the *coup* was delivered, in tragic error, to Sambo himself as he made camp at Tukur Tukur. He immediately ordered a withdrawal back to the city. But even as camp was broken the Ningawa burst upon Sambo before the royal entourage had reached safety. The Wambai, Nuhu, son of Emir Sidi, was killed at the gates of Zaria as he protected his king and some of the tribute intended for Sokoto fell into Haruna's hands. Robbed of his main objective, however, the Ningi chief gave vent to his chagrin by devastating the area round Zaria city and, it is said, taking off 5,000 of Sambo's subjects to slavery. Inside the city, dynastic jealousies and the Habe dislike of Fulani rule made Sambo afraid of taking any action against his treacherous Galadima, Salmanu.

It did not take long for news of Haruna's devastation of Zaria's environs to suggest that Fulani Zazzau was ripe for other raids. Barafiya, the Habe ruler of Maradi, marched through Katsina and captured Kudan, while Ningi thrusts, often as far south as Kacia, became an annual event in the dry season. To repair the losses caused by these invasions, Sambo stepped up his slave raids against the Kagoro, Kadara and Gwari, but his signal lack of success only served to undermine his sinking reputation. Even his vassal states of Keffi and Nassarawa started to fight each other.

In desperation Sambo made one last effort to concentrate enough power in his own hands and give himself real control of his own kingdom. To protect central Zaria against the Ningi incursions and to create a powerful military force removed by 100 miles from the influence of the Galadima in the capital, he built up the command of Sarkin Kuyambana, Tatumare, at Kacia into a sizeable army. As a slave, Tatumare would be fully dependent on the king alone for his position.

But such a redistribution of military resources left the rest of the emirate virtually defenceless. Maradi again captured Kudan; Ningi raided as far as Soba and Makarfi; and Abuja plundered the caravan routes with impunity. Eventually complaints were made to Sokoto by the leading Fulani families as well as the royal dynasties, and in 1888 the Sultan deposed Sambo on the grounds that he was not competent to defend his state. He was succeeded by Yero, son of Emir Abdullahi.

Yero's first step was to recover for the throne all the powers it had lost to the Galadima, Salmanu. To this end he filled all available offices with his own kin. Though he appointed his son Kwassau as Madaki and dismissed most of the Katsinawa title-holders, he stopped short of making any move actually to rid himself of Salmanu.

In contrast to his predecessor, Yero decided to overawe the population with displays of royal strength. He acquired a monopoly of the local trade in firearms available from the Royal Niger Company store at Lokoja, and with these he organized bands of *'yan bindiga*, musketeers, under slave-captains, whom he stationed near the palace both as a reserve against the Galadima and as an offensive arm for local raids. Aiming his vengeance against those families who had gained any of his deposed father's estate, Yero's plundering squads of slave riflemen spread their bullying far and wide. Soon there were bitter complaints against this royal policy of *wasau*, the deliberate spoliation of a citizen's home and property. Ranging further afield, Yero tried to regain control over the southern districts of his emirate, attacking the Pitti and Rukuba peoples on the western scarp of the plateau by Lere, and sending expeditions against Rimau, Kajuru and the Kadara of Girku. This town was completely denuded of its women and children by his brother Ja'afaru. Yero, however, suffered a severe defeat at Abuja in 1893. In another raid, on the Awawa at Riri near Keffi, Yero met his death in 1897, and is still remembered and talked of as Ma-je-Riri.

Yero's death again revealed the power of the Galadima,

Salmanu. As head of the electoral council he persuaded the Sultan this time to send his Waziri to Zaria to crown the next Emir, a move that convinced the Fulani of Zaria that the Habe Salmanu intended to secure the throne himself. Salmanu advised the Wazirin Sokoto to appoint the Mallawa candidate Muhammadu Yero, despite his staggering handicap of being old and blind. Salmanu's motives were as clear as daylight.

The Fulani reacted quickly. They rallied behind Yero's son Kwassau, who was not only Madaki but also commander of the notorious squads of *'yan bindiga*. Thus supported militarily—and some accounts declare that the Emir of Kano rushed down contingents of cavalry to help overawe the Wazirin Sokoto—Kwassau bluntly informed the Waziri that if he was not appointed to the throne peacefully he would seize it by force of arms. Kwassau was crowned.

Kwassau maintained his father's heavy taxation and kept up the terrorizing bands of *'yan bindiga*. The Katab peoples rebelled against their increased tribute of one hundred slaves: Kwassau attacked them, refusing to take prisoners. But the internal security of Zaria was worsening, with forays of armed horsemen, *'yan pila*, from Kontagora joining the constant raids from Maradi. Some Zaria sources declare that the armed incursions by Ibrahim Nagwamatse, Emir of Kontagora, who even attacked and overpowered Birnin Gwari, were intended to punish the local Fulani for having flaunted the Sultan of Sokoto's authority, thus compelling the Waziri to turban Kwassau. On his part, Kwassau could not risk an open breach with Sokoto by waging war against Kontagora: too many Emirs of Zaria had suffered deposition. Nor could he allow Kontagora to lay waste his territory, as such weakness would encourage the Habe elements under the Galadima to seek redress by another coup.

Fate was kind to Kwassau: the British came on the scene as the timely *deus ex machina*. Kwassau begged Lugard to send his troops and put a stop to Nagwamatse's slave raiding. By the end of 1901 there was, on Kwassau's invitation, a British garrison in Zaria. Within a year, however, Kwassau was removed by his guests.

Though Kwassau had wanted British troops in Zaria, they were for his own ends. His heart lay with Sokoto and Kano in their opposition to Lugard's advance. Letters from Zaria to Kano kept the Emir, Aliyu, informed of the movements of the British:

After greetings—to inform you that three Christians and their soldiers have arrived and are camped near the east of their former halting place on the Likoro road. Further the Christians have collected men and made them work. They have given orders that every chief shall set four men to work to clear the road and they have done so. Further we have heard that the Christians from Bauchi are coming to join them. This is to inform you that heavy trouble has come upon us, for by Allah we can neither stand nor sit, and have no power to remain in the same place with them. . . .

After greetings to inform you that the Christians who I told you were coming from Bauchi have arrived. Maijimina has come and those with him and others. Also that you may know that they are assembling and intend to go to Kano. May Allah think of us and protect us. He is the hearer of the prayers of those who pray to him. We beseech Allah to scatter their company and disperse their gathering. May He instil fear and trembling in their hearts and grant you victory over them and also to all Moslems.[1]

Kwassau accordingly instructed his vassal Keffi to withstand the British. As a result, Captain Moloney was killed by the Magajin Keffi, who fled to Zaria and thence to Kano. Lugard reasoned that Zaria was responsible for Moloney's murder and for the Magaji's escape. Kwassau was banished to Wushishi. To emphasize the punishment, the boundary of Zazzau was drawn back to the Gurara river and the vassal chiefdoms of Keffi, Nassarawa, Jema'a and Doma were removed from Zazzau jurisdiction and placed under a different provincial administration when Zaria Province was established in 1902 in charge of Captain Abadie, still remembered by his nickname of *mai-jimina*.[2] A second Divisional headquarters was established at Wushishi, and Zungeru was included in the Province.

For six months Zaria emirate was in charge of the Habe Galadima, Salmanu, who briefly saw his twenty years of opposition to Fulani rule come to fruition. Kwassau was deposed by Lugard and Bornawa rule again gave way to the Mallawa with the accession of Aliyu, son of Emir Sidi. His nomination he owed to Sokoto; his confirmation and appointment to Lugard. Kwassau died in exile at Lokoja in 1907.

Aliyu's first actions were very much his own: a wholesale redistribution of offices, though in the matter of eventually ousting

[1] H. F. Backwell, *The Occupation of Hausaland 1900–1904*, p. 71.

[2] *Mai-jimina* = the owner of an ostrich. Abadie was the first Resident of Zaria.

the Galadima from his stronghold in Zaria city he had to involve the Resident with tales of intrigue against the throne. Thereafter Zaria went the way of all the emirates, with British administrative reforms trying to abolish patronage and nepotism in a reorganized structure and function of a native authority system. In 1905, for instance, the first fief-holder was moved out of Zaria city to live in his fief as a District Head and *alkali*'s courts were set up at Kacia, Birnin Gwari and Paiko. The last-named area was in 1908 transferred to Nupe Province as an independent district along with Kwongoma (Wushishi) Division. Zaria had for some time enjoyed the unusual services of the Salenke's court on circuit, a Habe institution that the Fulani had taken over.

Within two years the emirate had been broken into thirty-two such districts, many titles lapsing in the process of *gunduma* or redistribution of fiefs. An interesting by-product of this was the grant of a small district near Zaria to the Chief Alkali in order to reduce his economic dependence on the Emir. The districts of Jere, Janyalla and Kagarko were transferred from Nassarawa Province to Zaria in 1914. By 1920 the number of territorial districts had been reduced to twenty-seven, five of which—Kajuru, Kagarko, Kauru, Lere and Chawai—were hereditary vassal states.

A *Beit-el-Mal* or Native Treasury was established in 1910 and two years later the old system of taxation was replaced by the taxes of *haraji* and *jangali*. At the same time a prison was built in the city, on the site where Emir Abubakar of the Mallawa dynasty had had his home. This was followed in 1913 by the payment of monthly salaries to district headmen instead of their retaining a share of the tax collected. In 1916 a scribe was allocated to each District Head, being later joined by a messenger and two *dogarai*. A school was opened in Zaria city in 1914, by which time cotton, encouraged by the arrival of the railway, had begun to take a prosperous hold, following the erection of a ginnery at Zaria in 1910. Aliyu also revived the office of Waziri, dormant since the reign of his father exactly fifty years earlier.

No account of the reign of the first Emir of Zaria under British rule would be complete without reference to Dr Walter Miller. He it was who founded the Church Missionary Society station in 1902, holding the unique position of being the only Christian settlement within the walls of a Muslim city by special permission of the Emir.[1] The site is still discernible, among the cactus plants just west of the house popularly known as Babban Dodo, itself the residence of one of the first D.O.s. The mission moved out of the city in 1929 to open its new site at Wusasa.[2]

In 1920 Aliyu had the unenviable distinction of becoming the fifth Emir of Zaria to be deposed within the short space of sixty years—and one of them was deposed twice. In his place the electors nominated Dallatu, a son of Yero and brother to Kwassau. This was the first time in Zaria history that such a promotion had ever been made from the post of Magajin Gari. He died in 1924 and was succeeded by Ibrahim, a son of Kwassau and therefore another Emir from the Bornawa dynasty. This appointment thus marks a significant departure from the traditional system of rotating succession that had guided the council of selectors during the previous century as 'a practical defence against monodynastic absolutism'.[3]

Like his predecessor, Ibrahim made Zaria history by being appointed to the throne from a relatively minor office, that of Dan Madami. It was during his reign that technical departments were developed in the N.A. system. Ibrahim created two new titles of his own, Wakilin Yamma and Wakilin Gabas. His Galadima Hayatu, also his half-brother, was once again entrusted with the administration of Zaria city. Under the 1926 reorganization, Zaria Province consisted of the emirates of Zaria and of Katsina and the independent district of Birnin Gwari which had formerly paid tribute to Katsina though at the actual time the British arrived it had been overrun by Kontagora. Its chief, Abubakar, died in 1935, after thirty-eight years of loyal service, especially to Lugard in the heyday of Zungeru.

A mixed court was set up in 1931 at Kaduna, which despite its status as a Government Headquarters continued to be run by the Magajin Gari as the Emir of Zaria's representative right down to 1956. The Waziri, Yusufu, died in 1933. After the Kaje people from Jema'a emirate joined up with their kinsmen in the Katab district of Zaria in 1934, district boundaries were reorganized and the total reduced to seventeen. The Emir's council was enlarged by the inclusion of Muhammad Tukur, the Galadima, as well as the

[1] See W. R. Miller, *Autobiography*, 1952, and *Reflections of a Pioneer*, 1936.
[2] The full story is to be found in A. H. M. Kirk-Greene, 'Wusasa', *Nigeria Magazine*, No. 76, 1962.
[3] The phrase is M. G. Smith's.

Madaki after Iya had fallen from grace. Ginger became a valuable crop in Kacia and Zonkwa markets about this time.

On Ibrahim's death in 1936 while on tour at Kacia, the British appointed Ja'afaru, a grandson of Emir Abdullahi and at that time district Head of Zongon Katab, as Emir. Zaria historians maintain that since his father had not held the throne he was not eligible and did not therefore appear in the list submitted by the council of selectors. His appointment was also unexpected because it was made from the office of Katuka, another office that had never before supplied the kings of Zaria.

Soon after Ja'afaru's official installation in 1937, a boundary adjustment reunited the Rukuba people of his emirate with their kith and kin in Plateau Province. On the death of Waziri Umaru in 1938, the Emir left the title vacant for a number of years. This was also the time of the well-known Anchau settlement scheme, which provided for 70,000 people to be accepted from tsetse fly-infested areas.

The post of Waziri was revived in 1952 when it was felt that, with the frequent absences of the Emir from Zaria necessitated by modern government, a full-time deputy was needed. The Chief Alkali, Muhammadu Lawal, was appointed to the post, and he then became Adviser on Muslim Law to the House of Chiefs until his death in 1956. Two years later the aged Galadima Hayatudini retired.[1] The position of the southern districts continued to give cause for concern. Factors like long distances from and poor communication with the N.A. executive, 'associated with the inevitable problems existing whenever non-Muslim peoples are administered by a Muslim Native Authority, gave rise to a feeling of isolation, unsettlement and frustration as soon as educational facilities, largely spread by voluntary agencies, grew.'[2] To help counter this, it was decided to build a sub-Divisional headquarters at Zonkwa, thus reviving the unofficial concept of a southern Division that had lapsed in 1912. Recognition of the work of some of the chiefs in this area was made by the award in 1955 of honours to Malam Gwamna, the Chief of Kagoro, and Malam Dogo, the Chief of Jaba for over forty years. The Emir of Zaria

[1] I am grateful to his son, Hayatudin, formerly my student and now Private Secretary to the Premier, for his help on matters of Zaria history. An equal debt in this connexion is due to another student of mine, Macido Dalhat, D.O.—A.K-G.

[2] *Annual Report for Zaria Province*, 1958.

was the only Nigerian to receive an award from the Queen at the time of the Royal Visit in 1956.

For all this, the people of Zaria had been becoming increasingly aware of the need to revitalize the N.A. Various steps were taken to effect this overhaul. In 1953 a number of younger members were injected into the N.A. Council. Next, town councils were established for Zaria City and Tudun Wada. Then it was agreed that in order to sever the tenuous link between the N.A. and the executive machinery, the *magatakarda* post should be abolished and the head of the central office should also be secretary to the Native Authority. Following rather tardily on other N.A.s in the North, Zaria now established an Outer Council to provide for the first time a direct link between the distant districts and the N.A. proper. In 1957 a complete reorganization of the central machinery of the N.A. was undertaken and another infusion of new blood was made to the N.A. Council, which was now increased to seventeen, including three Christian members. The death of Malam Sambo, Sarkin Fada, at this stage was a great loss and necessitated a further reshuffle. A year later yet another improvement was made by the appointment of a full-time administrative councillor, the Wambai.

In August 1959 Ja'afaru died, an old man of great piety and learning who had skilfully managed to control the tempo of his affairs of state despite first governmental and second political pressures. He was succeeded by Alhaji Muhammadu Aminu, District Head of Sabon Gari, whose appointment from the Katsina dynasty broke a run of nearly seventy years rule by the Bornawa and Mallawa. To mark the revival of the Katsina *zuriya* or royal house, the Emir revived the traditional Katsinawa praying ground outside the Kofar Doka for use at Id al Fitr prayers and also resurrected the Zaria ceremony of *hawan daushe* at the Kofar Gaya.

Ja'afaru's reign had brought Zaria through to the time of the North's self-government, with a series of local landmarks starting from the switching-on of electricity in 1938, through the founding of Gaskiya Corporation in 1945 and the opening of the Clerical Training College at 'Kongo' the year after, to the excision of Kaduna in 1956, the closing of *Dan Zaria*, the famous little Bauchi Light Railway, also in 1956, and the building of a cigarette factory in 1958. But it is above all as a centre of higher learning that Zaria has leaped to the front since World War II. The transfer of Kaduna College (the old Katsina Training College) to Zaria as Government College in 1949; the building of the headquarters and the Northern branch of the Nigerian College of Arts, Science and Technology (N.C.A.S.T.) in 1954, the same year as the North's celebrated Institute of Administration was opened; the work of the Agricultural Research centre at Samaru, of the North Region Literacy Agency (N.O.R.L.A.) and Gaskiya Corporation, of many secondary schools and teacher training colleges; and, the glory of them all, the opening of the Ahmadu Bello University in October 1962.

THE RULERS OF ZARIA[1]

Habe There were sixty Habe kings and queens who ruled Zazzau.
The first was Gunguma.
The 18th was Muhamman Abu, possibly the first Muslim ruler.
The 22nd was Bakwa Turunku, the mother of Amina and Zaria.
Muhamman Makau, the 60th Habe Sarkin Zazzau, was driven out of Zaria in 1804 when the Fulani dynasties assumed the kingship.

Mallawa dynasty *The Fulani Emirs*

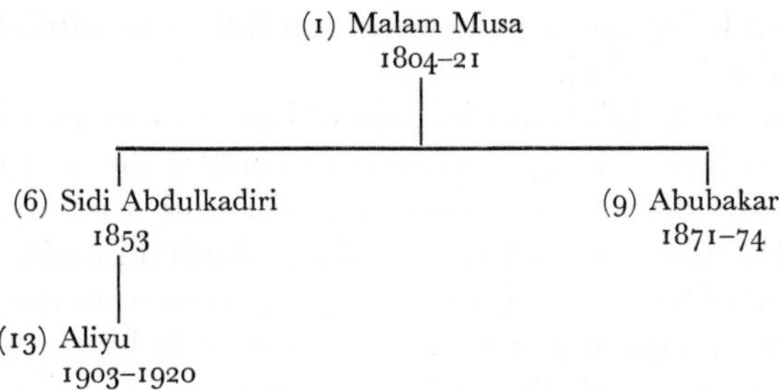

[1] Complete genealogies of the four Fulani dynasties are to be found in the charts contained at the end-cover of M. G. Smith, op. cit. For many years an error in the genealogy of royal Zaria has been continued. Most writers have attributed a reign of 14 years to Mamman Sani (1846–60) whereas modern Zaria chroniclers insist that he reigned 1846–53. The dates we have given in this dynastic tree are those now recognized by Zaria N.A., after checking against a number of hitherto accepted sources. We acknowledge the counsel of M. Hayatu, former Sa'i of Zaria, on this genealogical table. In this connexion, attention is invited to the analysis by H. F. C. Smith, 'The Dynastic Chronology of Fulani Zaria', *Journal of the Historical Society of Nigeria*, December 1961, a scholarly enquiry prompted by doubts on the king-list given by M. G. Smith in his *Government in Zazzau*. At pp. 284–5 H. F. C. Smith gives an interesting comparative table of half-a-dozen sources for the Zaria king-list. Recent discussions by H. F. C. Smith of the Katsina chronology in the *Bulletin* of the Nigerian Historical Society and by Ronald Cohen of the Bornu chronology in *Papers in African History*, reinforced by our own problems in attempting to verify every emirate genealogy, indicate that throughout the North there is still much research to be undertaken before historians can arrive at a final and firm dynastic chronology.

Bornawa dynasty

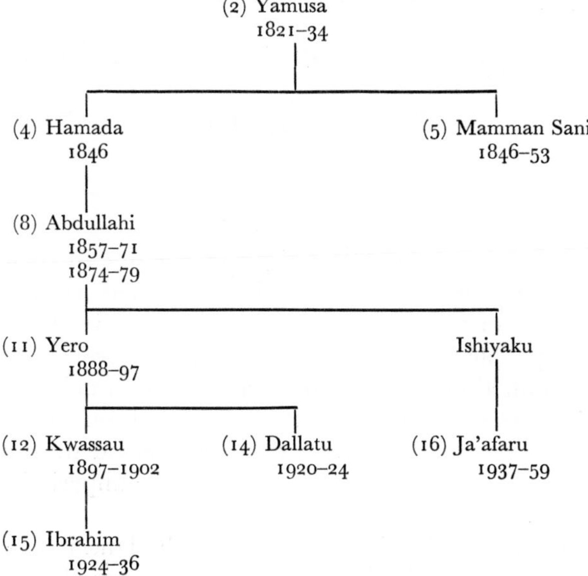

Katsinawa dynasty

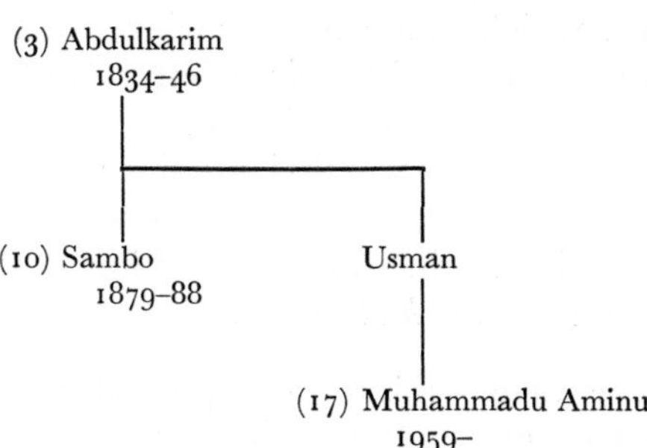

Sulibawa dynasty

(7) Abdulsalami
1854–57

1. EMIRATES DERIVING FROM THE HAUSA STATES

(2) Originating from the Banza Bakwai

XIX. KEBBI

ALTHOUGH the people of Kebbi no longer live in their earlier capital of Birnin Kebbi but have since occupied Argungu, their place in the history of the Western Sudan has remained untouched. A vigorous people, whose very foundation had been in rebellion, and a constant thorn in the side of their Fulani neighbours, the Kebbawa share with the Habe of Abuja and Daura the rare distinction of being the only states to have retained their independence, cultural as well as political, against the imperialism of the Fulani jihad.

In the middle of the sixteenth century the land of Kebbi was on the borders of Dandi, the easternmost province of the Songhai empire, astride the Niger immediately to the west of the Hausa States. These had been conquered in Askia's campaigns of 1512–1517, which made first Katsina, then Zamfara and Zaria, and finally Kano and Gobir tributary to Songhai. Kanta, a *Barde* or one of the great captains in the army of the Askia dynasty and governor of the Songhai province of Leka, had accompanied his king to this war against the Hausa States but, because of some real or fancied slight over the division of the spoils, he revolted. To quote the *Tarikh al Sudan*:

> The cause of this revolt was as follows:
>
> Kanta on returning with the prince from his expedition against Agades hoped to receive, on arrival in his country, his share of the spoils which had been taken. Disappointed in this, he mentioned the matter to the Dendi-Fari (*note:* this is not the name of a person, but the title of an officer) who replied, 'If you make to the prince a claim of such a kind you will get yourself treated as a rebel.' Kanta made no reply. Then when his followers came to find them and said to him, 'Where is our share of the spoils? We have not seen it yet. Why do you not claim it?' he replied, 'I have asked for it and the Dendi-Fari assured

me that if I persisted in claiming it I should be treated as a rebel. Now I do not want to be the only one treated as a rebel, if you will support me I will make a claim.' 'Good,' they cried, 'we will be treated as rebels as well as you.' After this Kanta approached the Dendi-Fari, renewed his request and received a refusal. The rebellion broke out at once. In a great battle, which the rebels fought against the prince's troops they held their own against adversaries and ceased from that time to recognize the authority of Askia-El-Haj-Mohammed. This state of affairs continued till the end of the Songhai dynasty, and Kanta preserved his independence.

Kanta thus set himself up as an independent chief in the large district between the Niger and Zamfara. The Kebbawa were largely a collection of skilled fishermen. It is said in Argungu that the Songhai called them derisively *Turmawa*, suggesting they were as numerous as the *turme* or ant-heaps that are so characteristic of the Kebbi country. Today, outside Argungu emirate, they are known as Sorkawa,[1] whether they fish or not. Though uncomfortably sandwiched between Bornu to the east and Songhai to the west, Kebbi maintained her vigorous independence and remained a stout bulwark for the Hausa states in the three centuries that were to follow. It is thus with the rise of the Kebbi kingdom under Kanta that the history of Argungu—indeed, the recorded history of Sokoto province—begins.

According to one Ba-Kebbi scholar, the title Magajin Leka was that of the Fulani governor of the Songhai province of Kebbi. He was assisted in his authority by Dan Gara, the representative of the Kebbawa: the title obtains in Argungu to this day. The Leka area is now in the Binji district of Sokoto emirate.

The ruling family of Argungu, known as the Lekawa, claims to have emigrated from the East and eventually to have settled in Bawa, today in Sokoto but then under Katsina. Kebbi historians list thirty-nine patriarchs who died in Egypt. Under one Gamba, the Kebbawa moved to Agat and thence to Bawa. His son Makata married Tamatu, the daughter of the king of Katsina, and by her had two sons, Muhammadu (perhaps Mamar Rusu) and Kamce, and a daughter Magajiya. This familial connexion with Katsina is an important one because it explains the *taubashi* or 'tribal cousinship' that still exists between Kebbawa and Katsinawa. An annual exchange of gifts has persisted, the Sarkin

[1] Cf. the Sorko fisherfolk in the early history of Songhai, *vide* pp. 68 and 70.

Katsina sending the *tsintsiya* or 'broom' consisting of turbans, cloaks, gowns and women's clothes, as befits the 'sons of women' on the distaff side, while the Sarkin Kebbi sends the *shara* or 'sweeping' in the form of horses, as befits the 'sons of men' on the male side.

Another prominent group in the Argungu aristocracy, besides the Lekawa who trace pure paternal descent from Kanta, are the Lelabawa. Their name derives from the rock Lelaba lying to the north-west of Argungu, and in pre-Kanta days this was the title of the chief of the peoples inhabiting the Argungu *fadama* or marshland. In the time of the fifteenth Sarkin Kebbi, Sumaila, the title Lelaba was given to his son Badau when he married a woman of this ethnic group. Those who claim descent from this union call themselves Lelabawa.

On Makata's death his son Kotai succeeded him as Magaji or head of the family. Angered at having thus been passed over by his half-brother, though he was much younger, Muhammadu Kanta went off to become a cattle grazer, 'a slave of the Fulani', as Sultan Bello describes him in his *Infaq al Maisuri*. He quickly became adept at boxing, a sport confined to the slaves of the Fulani herdsmen. The Kebbi legend[1] runs as follows:

A certain Fulani came to see the Magaji, and, while seated talking with him and the boy Muhammadu, a young cow was heard to low. The Fulani said, 'Listen to what that cow is saying. Whosoever first drinks my milk and sits on the hide of my calf and eats his meat will be a leader among men and will rule a great kingdom.'

It so happened that one day when the Magaji was not present the cow calved. Muhammadu, who was grazing the cattle, seized her udders and drank her milk. He killed the calf and flayed it and seated himself upon the hide. Having roasted the meat and eaten his fill, he buried the hide and the meat and covered up all traces of the blood. When the Magaji came he asked Muhammadu whether the cow had calved. Muhammadu replied 'No'. The Magaji seeing that there was no doubt that the cow had calved, was very angry and drove the boy forth from his house.

Wandering about the towns of Hausa he became a champion boxer and, in the pride of his manhood, he wore a white ram's skin round his loins, an armlet of the same skin, and his fighting hand was wrapped

[1] Quoted in P. G. Harris, *Sokoto Provincial Gazetteer*, 1938, pp. 26–27, an unpublished source on which we have drawn heavily for these sections.

in the hairs of a white ram's tail: while, after each victory, he shook a calabash rattle and cried out his *kirari*: '*ni a Kanta, ba kidin gwazangwari. Ni a kulkin horon giwa, ko hori sa da ni ya bata.*' 'It is I who am Kanta. It is not the shake of the calabash rattle of the exultant. I am the club with which to beat an elephant. Whoever beats a bull with me [the club] has done the wrong thing.'[1]

At Leka, Muhammadu Kanta is reputed to have floored every boxer who challenged him. Flushed with their success, Muhammadu and his fellow boxers now planned to overthrow the Fulani of Leka. They allotted to one another the titles they would hold: Kanta demanded the title of Sarkin Kebbi, refusing to be called simply a Magaji, and he chose as his councillors such titles as Kokani, Inname, Galadima and Dikko, which have persisted to this day. Some historians see in the ceremonies performed at the installation of the Emir of Argungu traces of the legendary prowess of Kanta as a boxer.

After the revolt of Kanta against Songhai in 1516, Kanta came with his bride Makulo (Ayeshe), daughter of the Sarkin Asben, to the town that is now Birnin Kebbi and captured it. According to some accounts, Kanta then built Birnin Leka, although other historians attribute its founding to Suleimana, the fifth Sarkin Kebbi after Kanta, a century later. Yet another story has it that Birnin Leka was the last of the towns built by Kanta, and it was from here that he set forth on his final campaign at Katsina. At any rate, Leka does not seem ever to have been of much importance so that it may well have been but a *nassarawa* or country seat of the royal family.

Another of Kanta's towns is Gungu, 'the oasis', the ruins of whose massive stone and laterite walls can still be seen at a spot about thirty miles west of Sokoto, half-way between Tozo and Katami. Kebbi legend has it that the stream at Gungu was miraculously brought to the town on the point of the fishing spear of Bawa dan Shiya, led by an intelligent fish. There is also a story about the jealousy of Kanta's wife Makulo, who was angered that she, a royal woman and fair-skinned, should have to take second place to her co-wife, dark and a commoner. One day, incensed beyond measure, she ran off to the west of the town, leaned her head against a lone baobab, and burst into tears. As result of

[1] The earlier legend ended with Kanta's *kirari* of 'I am the black slave of the Fulani', but Argungu N.A.'s committee of historians has rejected this.

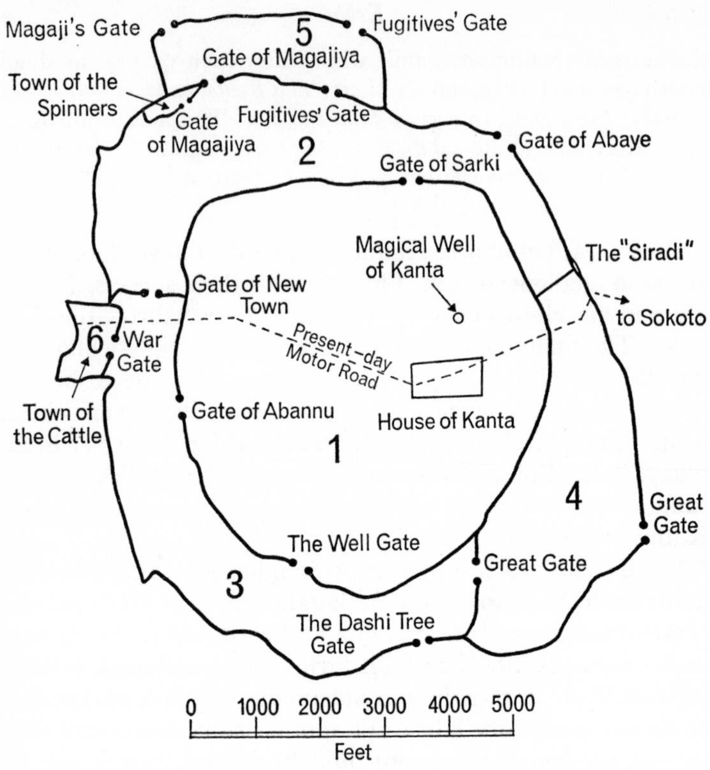

13. A PLAN OF SURAME AS IT EXISTED EARLY IN THE 16TH CENTURY (after P. G. Harris, Sokoto Provincial Gazetteer, unpublished MS.)

this, the local historians declare, the indigo from her head-dress can be seen on that baobab to this day. Kanta, who dearly loved his second wife, followed Makulo and implored her to return. She refused to leave the baobab so Kanta ordered a house to be built for her on the spot. Thus the second town of Gungu came into existence. Later, a third walled town was built to the north, reputedly to appease the smouldering envy of Kanta's first wife. All three towns were linked. Silame, the old walls of which, by the name of Yanta Bornu, can be traced, is said to have been the town of the first Magajiya of Kebbi, called Lame.

It is, however, with the town of Surame that Kanta's name is usually associated. This may well have been the true Kebbi capital, with Leka as a summer retreat and Gungu as a war-base. Its ruins can be seen in the bush some ten miles north-east of Gungu. Tradition has it that when he conceived the idea of Surame, Kanta sent out to all the Hausa states he had conquered and ordered the people to come and build him a town. They came from Bida, Kano, Zaria, Ilorin, Bornu and Gwanja (Zabarma), and the great city of Surame was built in about 1516. It is said that the Nupe delayed their coming, so as a punishment Kanta ordered that the part of the forty-foot walls that they built should have shea butter mixed with the mud to make it especially strong. The Nupe section is today in the best state. Another story recounts how the water used in the construction work had to be carried in leather buckets by a human chain of ten thousand from the River Kebbi five miles away. The city consisted of seven concentrically built towns, each with seven gates. There are also said to have been stables for the cavalry at every one of the forty-nine gates except those of the first town.

The house of Kanta is still an object of some reverence. Local Fulani warn that those who are unwise enough to stay within the deserted walls after dark will have their sleep disturbed by the beating of ghostly drums and the neighing of supernatural horses. The well by the entrance is reputed to have had a miraculous chain that rattled out of its own volition every Friday, the same day that Kanta used to lead his pet black ox and black he-goat in a weekly circuit of the city walls, to the awestruck terror of his people. One of the most interesting features of Surame is the *siradi* to the east of the town. At this point the wall narrowed to a width of eighteen inches for a length of about thirty feet. On either side were dug deep pits in which stakes and up-pointed spears were fixed and fires were lit. Traitors and others who had incurred Kanta's displeasure were made to walk along this thin ledge. Crumbling masonry and fear gave heavy odds against the victim not falling to one side or the other, but if he did cross he was given a free pardon. The name *siradi* derives from the Islamic concept of the narrow way by which all departed spirits pass to life after death, the good crossing over and the evil falling into eternal hell-fire.

One current story of Surame refers to the town's siege by the Bornuese under Mai Ali. After bitter fighting and heavy casualties on both sides, the Kebbawa were driven behind their defences in Surame. Here they gathered their dead, tied each body to a stake, and slit the upper lips of each corpse to make every man look as if he were grinning. These bodies they then placed in likely positions behind the walled defences. When in the morning the Bornu army advanced to what they thought would be an unopposed entry, they found the walls manned by thousands of Kebbawa, each soldier at his post and grinning confidently. Thinking that Surame was still holding out, the Bornu forces withdrew. This is the origin of the phrase heard even today in Binji district whenever accounts of Surame are given: *dariya ba loto*, 'laughter without end'.

An interesting collection of bronze and copper vessels was unearthed in 1920 near Surame at Tumuni and lent to the British Museum. These relics are now in the Nigerian Museum in Lagos.

Of Kanta's numerous wars there is no accurate record. Katsina, Kano, Gobir, Zaria, Aïr all suffered from his invasions. At Bawa there is a baobab still known as *kukar Kanta*, where the king is said always to have camped on his way to his wars in the east. He established a sub-kingdom of Gabi at Mokwa, near Bida. He also made war against Bornu but was defeated before Nguru. On his way back in about 1561 or a year or two earlier Kanta engaged the Katsinawa at Dugul, but at a place known as Rimin dan Ashita, near Ingawa in Katsina emirate, he was mortally wounded by an arrow. There is a persistent story that the leaves of the *rimi*, silk-cotton tree, fell on Kanta and caused his death: certainly the taunt of *rimin dan Ashita* is always used against a Ba-Kebbi in the same way that the gibe of *a mazaya* will provoke a Ba-Gobiri.

Kanta died at Jiriwa and he was carried to his own house at Surame. His faithful warriors made twelve tombs on the way back from Jiriwa so as to conceal the real place of Kanta's body. He was buried at Takwacal Bangi, where a mound is said to mark his grave. Sokoto historians tell how the burial place came to be identified. As Sultan Bello was returning from one of his wars with the Kebbawa, he heard a roar as of a lion coming up from the ground. 'This must surely be the burial place of a great man though an unbeliever,' he remarked. Calling for a stone, he threw it down on the spot.[1] His example was followed by his whole army, so that a huge pile of stones was raised to mark the spot. Kanta's treasure, of which he had amassed a great quantity, is said to have been poured into a certain large flat-topped hill between Gungu and Katami, known to this day as *kabarin Kanta* or Kanta's grave.[2]

The glory of Kanta's reign is recorded in this extract from the *kirarin Kanta*, a praise-declaration in somewhat archaic Hausa enacted by the Maba or royal herald of the Emir of Argungu.[3] Its opening lines are still called out whenever an important visitor enters the royal palace: *sha da azna! ka da azna! zaidi! manzon azna*:

Slaughterer of the enemy
Vanquisher of the enemy
Warrior! Messenger of the enemy.

Kanta! Drummer of rejoicing,
Kanta! Mallet to train an elephant.
Whoso learns from this is hurt.
Kanta! As a field of 'aya' is he
Before him, behind him, the earth is dark.
Kanta! As when a carrier of ashes falls,
Before him, behind him, the white dust is scattered.
Kanta! as a dish of 'Giginya' is he,
Which ensplinters the greedy.
Kanta! the soap for skin sickness
The washers are scratching,
The pourers of water catch the disease,
And rise up afflicted.
Oh! Cruel one, of Birema
Captor of royal drums,
The rainbow is fellow traveller of the sunset.
Oh! Evil dispositioned Camel
Which has no holding rope,
He who wishes death catches (the camel)
Without a rope.
Whoso sees you sees war.
Whoso sees you not
Sees not death.
Father of the town where the medicine of war is brewed,
Even before he set foot in stirrup.
The right ran away,

[1] Present-day historians in Argungu say that Sultan Bello pointed to the grave but did not actually throw any stone. They add, however, and we are grateful for the information, that Kanta's grave is the pile of rocks at Takwacal Bangi.
[2] There is now a fine Kanta museum at Argungu.
[3] Quoted in Harris, op. cit., pp. 236–8.

The left ran away.
Ha! Hear the rattling of shields.
Ha! Hear the rattling of the spears. As they fall.
Ha! Dauntless slayer of the enemy.
Wicked one! Of the blood red spear.
Kanta! Master at Mashaya Kubewa.
Kanta! Master there at Gungu.
Kanta! Master there at Leka.
Of the seed of Gamdazai,
Of the seed of Mardazai,
Between you and God
Nought save thanks.
Fearless one! The dauntless man of Ataku,
The inspirer of fear, of Mohamman.
You are the sun of the kings of the world,
As a strong hide of whip are you,
Son of Ibrahim.
If it falls from above
The angels will use soft words.
If it falls from below
The men of the earth will coax it to cease.
Scatterer of armies, of Arkar.
How those in front he enslaves.
How those behind
(while) the coward clutches at his horse's mane.
An obstacle is the remedy for the guardian
Of a house with one entrance.
A liar is he (i.e. the guardian),
He, the guardian of a house with one entrance.
If not met with in entering
When leaving he is met.
However great the house
It has but one heir.
Kanta! Heir to the house of Makata,
Verily he reigned for thirty-eight years.

At the zenith of its power the Kebbi empire included Yauri and Nupe, and far beyond to the south, where its influence was felt in Oyo and Ibadan. Kanta is said to have given eighty-four towns of Yauri to his daughter when she was Magajiya Kebbi at Silame. Gurma was within the Kebbi boundaries while Arewa and Zabarma followed Kebbi till the beginnings of the present century. Northwards all the country as far as Agades and eastwards the land as far as Zazzau came under the power of Kebbi: after sacking Zaria, Kanta created the slave colony of Zazzagawa, a town near Argungu in charge of Dan Kadu. Songhai made but two serious attempts to reassert its hold over Kebbi. At Wantarmasa, Kanta's army inflicted a crushing defeat on Muhammad Benkan, and in 1552 another battle took place. A peace treaty was signed in the following year.

After Muhammadu Kanta there were ten more kings of Kebbi at Surame. The name of Kanta appears to have become an hereditary title, like that of Askia in Songhai or Pharaoh in Egypt. Notable relics of these times are the ruins of great Surame and the copper-prowed canoe, said to have held fifty oarsmen of Muhammadu Kanta which, brought from Surame by Sarkin Kebbi Tomo and sunk in the pool of Dukku rock at Birnin Kebbi, is said to rise magically from the depths and be visible to all true Kebbawa when danger threatens the state.

In 1591 Timbuktu and the Songhai empire fell to the Moors. The Askia fled to Dandi and thence to Kebbi to implore the protection of Kanta, but the Kebbawa refused asylum to the descendant of their former liege-lord. Dandi—some of whose fair-skinned inhabitants suggest descent from the occupying force of Moorish soldiers—included all that country south-west of Birnin Kebbi to the Niger. It figures in modern history not only by its district name in Argungu and the title of Sarkin Dandi in Gwandu, but also in the Hausa expression of *ya tafi dandi*, which by extension has come to mean 'he went out into the wide world of beyond'. The town of Surame broke up in about 1700 when Tomo, Sarkin Kebbi, perceived the perils inherent in the internal strife and disintegration of his empire and founded the new centre of Birnin Kebbi. Thus was fulfilled the Kebbi adage that 'mark well what we say to you, O men of Kebbi! No war ever waged will take your town but hatred over women will scatter it'. This remained the capital of the Kebbawa until it was sacked by the Fulani under Abdullahi in 1805. Meanwhile the once-glorious empire of Kanta became gradually eroded by the attacks of Zamfara and Gobir, sometimes helped by the King of Asben.

On the death of Abdullahi Toga, the 17th Sarkin Kebbi, in 1775, his son Suleimana, who had been nominated by his father to succeed him, had recourse to witchcraft to consolidate his position. He is said to have poisoned his gown and shoes, which he gave to the Kokani, who called together all the royal sons and said: 'Since you do not want Suleimana, here are the insignia of office. Choose whom you wish and let us return to our homes.' Since each wished to be king but none to die, the council broke up in confusion and Suleimana was left on the throne. When he died in 1803, his son Ukar reigned for only four days before he was murdered by his brother Muhammadu Hodi, who then defeated Moli, the Kokani of Kebbi, and seized the throne.

Hodi had never been on friendly terms with the Fulani before they came to power, and it was ironical that such a man should have come to the throne at the very time when the Fulani became a dominant force in the area. In 1805 the Fulani under Abdullahi made a victorious progress towards Birnin Kebbi, and as town after town capitulated Hodi decided to submit. Abdullahi ordered that no harm should be done to the town, but after Abdullahi's withdrawal his general Aliyu Jedo found Hodi's troops drawn up in battle array outside the town. Abdullahi with the advance guard was already across the marsh, so Aliyu determined to attack at once. Birnin Kebbi was burnt and Hodi fled north-west to Dumana and then to Augi. Before doing so, however, he committed yet another atrocity by murdering Ladi, the mother of his brother Ukar, who had upbraided him for his cowardice with the taunt: 'Is the king of the town also leaving when the rest have gone away?'

The Kebbawa, led by Usman Masa, the son of a former Sarkin Kebbi Muhammadu dan Giwa, formed an alliance with the Tuareg chief Agunbulu and the Gobirawa from Alkalawa, and marched on Usman dan Fodio at Gwandu. Against the advice of Bello and Abdullahi, the Sarkin Yaki Aliyu Jedo moved his men out to meet the Kebbi confederate army. The Fulani attacked them at Alwassa, twenty miles west of Gwandu, and were repulsed with terrible losses, being pursued right up to the walls of Gwandu. After five days the allied forces were driven back and Gwandu could breathe again. Had the Kebbawa been able to follow up their success at Alwassa by capturing the Shehu's camp at Gwandu, the whole course of history in the Western Sudan might have been altered. In one of the assaults on the town, Agunbulu was left wounded. He was stoned to death by the Fulani, and a mound of rocks on the hill to the east of Gwandu now marks the spot where he fell. It is customary to this day for some people in Gwandu to throw stones on the mound and curse the dead unbeliever.

Hodi returned to Augi, but the Fulani captured it in 1808 and the principal Kebbi chiefs of Argungu later submitted to Abdullahi. Hodi retired to the hill of Fakara in the bush between Augi and Bagizza, where he built Birnin Fakara and stayed for seven years before re-entering Argungu. After five years there Bello sent to him, telling him that the Fulani conquest was complete and that he might return to Birnin Kebbi. Hodi went to Birnin Kebbi and made his submission, but after three weeks he realized the shame of this act and was persuaded to move to Kimba. For the next ten years the Kebbawa waged war on the Fulani from Hodi's camps at Kimba, Augi and Argungu. In 1826 Hodi was killed by Buhari, son of Usman dan Fodio; his grave at Madacin Zama is still revered by the Kebbawa of Romo and Keɓɓe.[1]

On the death of Hodi, the Kebbawa split into two. His son Jibrin made submission to the Fulani at Gwandu and was put in charge of Keɓɓe town with the title of Sarkin Kebbi: it is from this branch of the Kebbi ruling family that the district heads of Keɓɓe in Sokoto emirate trace their descent. Samaila, the son of Suleimana, who is better known as Karari, was furious that Jibrin should have accepted the spurious title of Sarkin Kebbi from a Fulani, and at once established a centre of resistance at Argungu. From this date of 1827 Argungu became the capital town of the Kebbawa. At that time the town was better known as Birnin Lelaba dan Badau. It is said to have derived its new name from the Kebbi expression *a yi gungu*, a fishing call meaning 'let us gather in one place' or, less acceptedly, from *arnan Gungu*, 'the pagan people of Gungu town'.

Kebbi's struggle for independence continued throughout the century. In 1831 the Sarkin Musulmi and the Emir of Gwandu combined forces to scotch the Kebbi menace. They took Mera, Kwaido and Bubuci but were unable to capture Argungu though they set fire to it by means of burning arrows. On the second day of the conflagration the women of Argungu came out and begged that the town be spared; in return, they promised that Karari should be driven out. Bello agreed and called off the attack. One day when Karari returned from riding he found the gates of Argungu closed against him. He withdrew to Zazzagawa and gathered a fresh army from among his Zabarma and Arewa subjects, but this force was twice defeated by the Emir of Gwandu. It is said that Karari then decided not to burden the people with more war and advised them to do what everybody else had done and submit to the Fulani. The men of Zazzagawa replied: 'We are the old slaves of Kanta and we shall not drive you out. The Fulani will reach you only over our dead bodies.' Karari refused

[1] Writing in his original book, *The Muhammadan Emirates of Nigeria*, S. J. Hogben notes (p. 104, n.): 'Some dispute the distinction between "Keɓɓe" and "Kebbi" and put it down to affectation, but I had it confirmed by Basheru, the Political Agent in Birnin Kebbi, and amongst others by the District Mallam of Keɓɓe when I stopped there in 1925.' See also footnote on p. 421.

this gallant offer of help and made for Arewa. He was pursued by the Fulani and killed at Galewa. This was in 1831. His son Yakubu Nabame escaped the massacre but was captured and taken to Gwandu.

For the next eighteen years there was an interregnum when Kebbi, kingless, submitted to the Fulani. The country was placed in the charge of the Lords of the Marshes: from Augi to the west was given to the Emir of Gwandu, Baiawa went to the Fulani Sarkin Kebbi of Yabo, and Augi went to the Fulani Sarkin Kebbi of Silame. Yakubu, Karari's son, was sent to Sokoto in 1834, as the Emir of Gwandu regarded him, not without reason, as a source of danger. There he ingratiated himself with the Sarkin Musulmi to such an extent that Aliyu Babba, who grew to love him as a son, gave him a senior command in the Sokoto forces. While on a campaign against Gora in Zamfara, some Gobir princes had taunted Yakubu in battle by accusing him of being a traitor and renegade. Rather than put his loyalty to a further test, the Sarkin Musulmi thoughtfully arranged for the Magajin Gudali to look after Yakubu in the Kebbi marshes, whither he was escorted in honour.

Such is the Fulani story. The Kebbi version speaks of a plot by Lelaba, the pretender Sarkin Kebbi, to murder Yakubu by the hand of Halilu, Emir of Gwandu—a story that is at least consistent with the tendency of the ruling house of Kebbi to fratricide. The tale goes on that the Emir of Gwandu, uneasy at such a criminal plan, sent to Wurno to inform the Sultan. Aliyu Babba, opening his Koran, saw that if Yakubu was killed there would be no rain for forty years. So he despatched Yakubu to Gudali to be out of harm's way!

During his visits to Sokoto in the next two years, Yakubu came under the influence of a certain *malam*, Musa, who prophesied that Yakubu would overcome the Fulani. Yakubu communicated this prophecy to the chief of Zabarma, Dauda dan Muhammadu, who assembled an army of his allies. It is believed in Argungu that the Kebbawa were only too willing to join in this uprising, despite the welcome peace of the past score years, because they had been affronted by the coarse wit of the Emir of Gwandu's wife for whom they had been called upon to build a house. She complained that it smelt of fish (a Kebbi passion) and that the thatch was so poor that she could see the beard of a slave of hers in a town a hundred miles away!

When Yakubu heard that the force was ready, he left Gudali and assumed command. Holding an unbaked pot in his left hand and a raw egg in his right, symbolizing the land he would retake and the enemy he would vanquish, Yakubu was proclaimed Sarkin Kebbi in 1849. The combined force drove back the Fulani, and captured and burned the towns of Silame, Ambursa, Gungu and Gulumbi. At Kibiari, however, Yakubu was killed by an arrow.

Yusufu Mainassara succeeded his brother Yakubu in 1854 and carried on the war against the Fulani till he was slain by Haliru, Emir of Gwandu, in 1859. His nephew Muhammadu Ba-Are avenged his death by killing the Emir in a battle near Tilli in the next year. The new Sarkin Kebbi was another son of Karari, Abdullahi Toga, who reigned from 1860 to 1883. His reign is distinguished by the famous *Lafiyar Toga*, the treaty of peace that he concluded with the Fulani in 1866. The terms were so favourable to Kebbi, including the acknowledgement of its independence of Gwandu and the retention of all the towns then held by the Kebbawa, that the treaty confirms the impression of visitors to the area in this period of 1850–65 that Kebbi was at the very least holding its own in the struggle against the Fulani.[1] This peace was shattered eight years later when war broke out again over the Kebbi town of Giru.[2] In 1875 Abdullahi Toga attacked Ambursa with 5,000 horsemen, supported as usual by Kebbi's faithful allies of Arewa and Zabarma.

Samaila, better known as Sama, was Sarkin Kebbi from 1883 to 1915. A son of Yakubu Nabame, he inherited his father's prowess as a warrior, and Kebbi historians credit him with having burnt ninety walled towns of the Fulani. Three times did the Sarkin Musulmi try to conquer Argungu, but on each occasion the Fulani were repulsed: as the Kebbi chronicles put it, 'so many men were killed that the waters of the Kebbi river could not be drunk'. Incessant hostilities continued to such an extent that Kebbi scholars affirm that when the British appeared in 1902 the area that is now Argungu emirate consisted literally of the three walled towns of Gulma, Zazzagawa and Argungu, all packed with people, and no other inhabited settlement.

The Captain Keyes incident took place in Argungu in 1901.

[1] In particular, H. Barth.

[2] See chapter on Gwandu, pp. 422–4 for a further account of the Kebbi-Gwandu conflict.

Three Frenchmen had arrived with armed carriers and had asked Sarkin Kebbi for permission to trade. Captain C. V. Keyes and a platoon of the West African Frontier Force were sent from Illo to warn the French to quit. When a quarrel arose between the two groups of carriers, Captain Keyes went to disarm the Frenchmen but in so doing was treacherously shot by one of them. The French escaped, disguised, according to local lore, as women, but were captured by the French authorities at Dosso and sent to Jebba for trial. Captain Keyes's body is buried by the mosque at Sowwa.

The site of the fort built the year after can be identified at Bunguji, near Argungu town. In 1905 Argungu Emirate was administered as part of the sub-province of Gwandu, but a year later it was made a separate Division, largely as a result of the disobedience of the headmen of Tilli and Zazzagawa to the Emir which necessitated close administration by an Assistant Resident. The Emir of Argungu, Sama, visited Sokoto in 1907 where a reconciliation between himself and his former adversary, the Sarkin Musulmi, took place. Troops were re-posted to Argungu in 1909 when rumours of disaffection brought about by the Emir's conduct were current, but these were quite baseless. When Sama died in 1915 at the age of 76 he was mourned by all his people, not excluding those Arewa and Zabarma towns of his which had always played such a loyal role in the long struggle against the Fulani but which Kebbi had lost at the time of the demarcation of the Anglo-French boundary in 1907.

The 27th Sarkin Kebbi was Suleimana, another son of Yakubu, who reigned till 1920. He was succeeded by Sama's son Muhammadu, under whom Argungu started to recover and catch up with the other emirates of Sokoto Province. In view of Kebbi's history, it was a noteworthy event that the Emir of Argungu should agree to attend the installation of Hassan as Sarkin Musulmi in 1931, and even more remarkable that the Sultan paid a courtesy call on the Emir in Argungu town in 1934. Muhammadu died later that year from a chill caught when he was out on a *jangali* check.

He was followed by his son Muhammadu Sani (Muza), whose first task was to modernize the administration, which was very much out of date, and to give a lead to a backwater area. He was succeeded in 1942 by Samaila, who was the first Emir to come from the Kamba branch of the Kebbi royal family since the appointment of Muhammadu dan Giwa in 1700.

The dissension and rivalry that marred the good name of Argungu in the 1950s were not out of keeping with Kebbawa history. In 1951 the senior councillor Kunduda was removed for, to quote the official report, 'leading the Native Authority into a web of intrigue and nepotism'.[1] A purge of the administration was followed up by the appointment of a new Emir, Muhammadu Shefe, in 1953. The glory of the 1958 Argungu Fishing Festival, one of the most magnificent yet held, was marred by the open rift that split the Emir and his Council. After a Commission of inquiry had sat, the Emir resigned and 28-year-old Muhammadu Mera Muza, a direct descendant of Kanta the Great, became in 1959 the 32nd Emir to succeed him.

THE KINGS OF KEBBI AND THE EMIRS OF KEBBI AT ARGUNGU

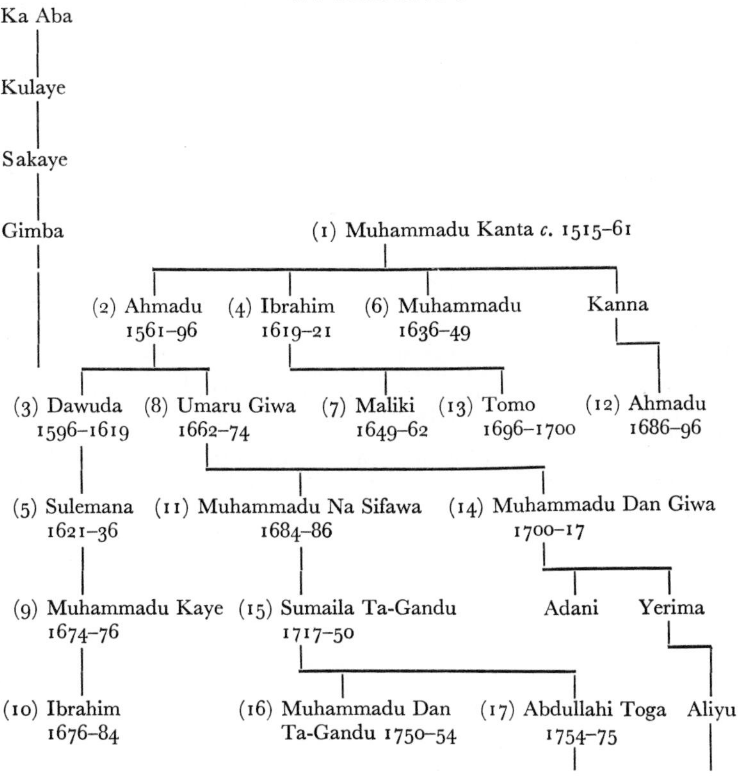

[1] *Annual Report of Sokoto Province*, 1951.

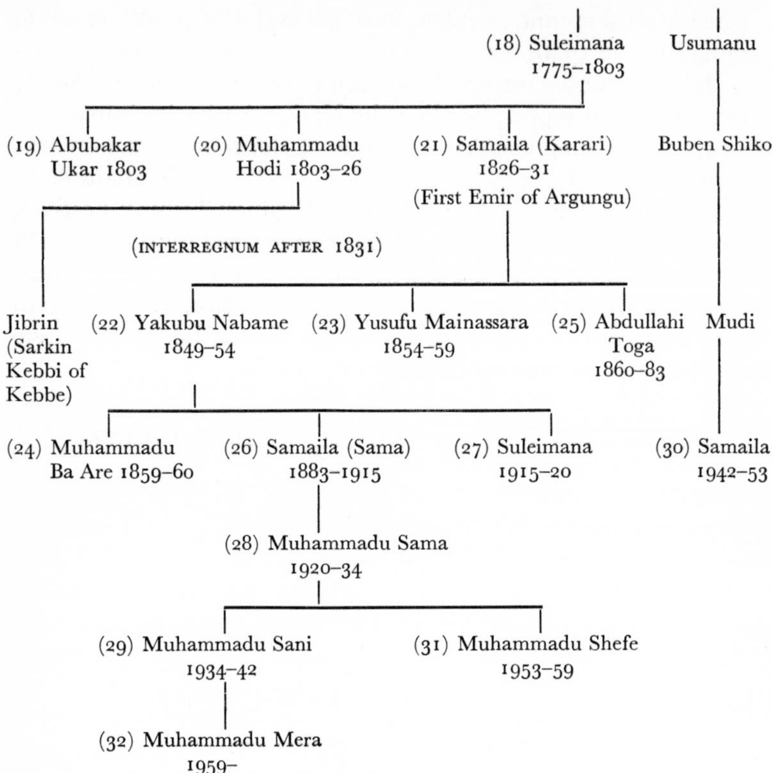

The genealogical tree is as agreed upon by the Argungu Native Authority but there is an unresolved doubt as to whether Dawuda (3rd) was the son of Gimba or Ahmadu (2nd), and whether Ibrahim (10th) was the son of Muhammadu Kaye (9th) or Muhammadu Na Sifawa (11th). It seems unlikely, however, that a father should succeed his son.

The above dates, until those of the nineteenth century, are only approximate, being based on the handed-down recollections of the length of each reign.

XX. YAURI

To a large extent, the early history of Yauri emirate is the history of its principal town, Bin Yauri.[1] The lack of records about Yauri can be attributed to the feuds and jealousies that for years rent asunder its ruling house. Yauri was important among the Hausa states, for it ranked among the Banza Bakwai.

One version of its origin is that it was founded by Katsina hunters who had lost their way. These were followed by the Kebbawa and the Nupe who intermarried and became the Yauri island settlers.[2] Another origin advanced for these Gungawa and Lopawa islanders is that they are the descendants of a Songhai army that was routed by Borgu at Gwangwarake. Whatever the truth—and there are several more legends—it seems clear that the island Gungawa were among the first settlers. The surviving Yauri language of Tsureshe is said to derive from the people who settled in Kambu and Achirra, now ruined towns to the east of Bin Yauri. The chiefs of these two places were treated with respect by Sarkin Yauri and allowed to keep their own royal insignia. The old walled towns of the Kambari and Agwarra, as well as that of Shanga, are of considerable age. Bin Yauri is supposed to be a thousand years old; locally it is known by the islanders as Ireshe or Ireshe Bino. Macipa is a principal Kambari town.

Among the many versions about the founding of the royal house—the only point they all agree on is that no one in Yauri really wanted a king at all—the most credible is that of the itinerant *malam* from the Dabbakar at Magori. He agreed to cure a girl of her madness provided that she became his wife. His charms produced the desired result and the inevitable happened. Their son grew up to be the first wrestler in the land and earned the nickname of Jera Banawa, 'line up the youths'. Later Amina, the celebrated queen of Zaria, came with her thousand horsemen.

[1] Locally called Birnin Yawari.

[2] A large Nupe family in Yelwa today claims descent from this group.

She remonstrated with the people for not having a king. At a loss whom to appoint, they offered the job to Jera Banawa. A dubious gloss upon this legend adds that Amina objected to the name of Rasawa or 'the lost ones', by which the Hausa referred to these people, and instead suggested they be known as Yaurawa, from the strips of dried meat, *yawara* (Sokoto form of *kilishi*), that they had brought to her as gifts.[1] This link is said to be the reason for the close friendship between Zaria and Yauri that exists to this day.[2]

A list of Yauri kings recited in the emirate includes one named Yauri. Both he and the 11th Chief, Jerabana II, have support for the claim to have introduced Islam. Bin Yauri—and the present-day ruins of its huge walls, five miles in circumference, indicate the size and importance of this town—was apparently deserted for a space of thirty years, and not till the reign of Lafiya II, the 22nd king, did the people start to repopulate the town. It was during the time of Albishir (Dan Ayi), the 30th king, that Usman dan Fodio initiated his jihad. Just before this, in the middle of the eighteenth century, Yauri appears to have shaken off its allegiance to the Kebbi empire and established its independence. Mungo Park refers to the 'Sultan of Yauri', and talks of Yauri as 'a populous and important emirate', but with the rise of the western Fulani empire under the Emir of Gwandu the chief of Yauri, Albishir, made formal submission.

Yauri was Mungo Park's last landfall before he and his three surviving companions met their death in the Bussa rapids. He put his guide ashore at Yauri with the customary presents for the chief but they did not reach him. Horsemen were therefore sent post-haste to intercept the boat and to collect the customs dues. They took up their position on an island that commanded the only navigable channel. Tradition has it that Park's men opened fire and those on the bank replied with arrows. In the confusion the boat capsized and all its occupants were swept away and drowned. The Emir's staff of office is made up of Mungo Park's silver-mounted walking stick which was recovered from the river and lengthened. The Chief of Bussa still wears a ring bearing a large

[1] Linguistically, too, the story is suspect, as *yawara* and *kilishi* are different types of prepared meat.

[2] As late as the 1950s, the Yauri *magatakarda* or royal scribe was a Zaria man, M. Aliyu.

silver medal presented by Richard Lander to his forebear, described as a man of great presence.[1]

This overlordship of Gwandu does not appear to have had any material effect on the fortunes of Yauri, which continued to prosper until 1844, when the Emir, Jibrilu, commonly known as Gajere, was expelled by his people who had grown impatient of his cruel maladministration. Gajere fled to Rijau in Kontagora, and Abubakar Jatau was installed in his place. Gajere now succeeded in enlisting the help of a Fulani, Muhammadu Maikarfi, and in 1848 he gave battle to Jatau at Ipanna, near Bin Yauri. Jatau was killed and the Yaurawa fled to the Niger islands opposite Yelwa.

Gajere was killed shortly after this in another fight, this time with Jatau's son, Tankwa.[2] He was succeeded by his son Yakuba, better known as Dan Gajere, who settled at Masambu near Kontagora and proclaimed himself chief of the Kambari. The Yaurawa refused to recognize him and in 1850 they installed Suleimanu dan Addo as their chief, who preferred Ikum island in the Niger river to the exposed Birnin Yauri as his headquarters. The state of Yauri was now split into two factions.

Aided by Umaru Nagwamatse of Kontagora, Dan Gajere carried out a number of attacks on Ikum, but the Yaurawa had impregnable retreats in the numerous islands of the Niger round Yelwa. Though they farmed on the mainland, they could quickly retire to these islands whenever rumour came that Nagwamatse was on the warpath. Dan Gajere was by now so completely in Nagwamatse's power that his death made no difference. At last Almustafa, the Emir of Gwandu, had to warn Kontagora against interfering with his tributary Yauri.

Suleimanu died at Ikum in 1871 and the Emir of Gwandu installed Abdullahi Gallo, the uncle of Dan Gajere, as Emir of Yauri. Two years later Almustafa paid a state visit to Yelwa. Gwandu's protection, however, was more nominal than real, and for the next decade or more the Yaurawa kept to their island refuges for fear of Nagwamatse. Locally it is said that Gwandu in fact cared little for the fate of the mainly non-Muslim Yauri.

Abdu Gallo was succeeded by Abarshi in 1888. He at once got

[1] The claim that the medal was Mungo Park's is no longer valid, as an examination by Messrs. Spink and Son showed that it was of a later minting. The best study of the controversial issues surrounding Park's death is to be found in K. Lupton, 'The Death of Mungo Park', *Nigeria*, No. 72, 1962, pp. 58–70.

[2] Tankwa is commonly used in Yauri for pepper, here meaning a courageous man.

in touch with Ibrahim, Emir of Kontagora and extracted a promise from him that the raids on Yauri would cease if the people returned to the mainland. Abarshi now had to find a new capital. Rejecting the idea of a return to Bin Yauri, perhaps because he was still doubtful whether the Emir of Kontagora would really honour his promise, he selected a new site on the very banks of the Niger. Appropriately he named it Yelwa, 'abundance', for the river front here is lush and lovely.

The Royal Niger Company, who had stationed a detachment of their constabulary in Yelwa since 1896, clashed with the people of Hella island in 1898 and many lives were lost. The then Emir of Yauri, Abarshi, helped in the search for the guilty persons, and it was probably in return for this that Sokoto ordered the Emir of Kontagora to arrest him and seize Yauri. In the event, Yauri was saved by the fall of Kontagora to the British and the flight of Ibrahim Nagwamatse. At a loss what to do about kingless Kontagora, Lugard invited Abarshi, Emir of Yauri, to assume the throne. Within three months he begged to be allowed to abdicate. His son, Muhammadu Gani, found the chieftainship equally impossible and he also quickly returned to Yauri. The rest of the story belongs to Kontagora history.

The British administration now made two mistakes. The first was the amalgamation of the emirates of Yauri and Bussa, never on close terms and since 1885 positively hostile, on the death of the Emir of Bussa in 1914. The combined emirate was given to the Emir of Yauri. Then, as if the initial appointment of Jibrilu had not been crass enough (he was a weak character, who came to the throne only because of a promise made to Abarshi when the British first came to Yelwa, and whose reign was marked by constant intrigue by the kingmakers Ubandawaki, Muta and Ruhubu, who had previously held the power of appointment to the throne), the appointment of the next Emir of Yauri on Jibrilu's deposition was a disaster. One Aliyu of Yabo,[1] a commoner and an alien to boot, was named as chief. He was believed by some to be an adopted son of the Emir, and he had been put in charge of the island district of Gungawa with the title of Tukura.

Aliyu was opposed from the start by the people of both Yauri and Bussa, noted for their vigour. In 1917 Bussa was detached

[1] Not the Yabo of Sokoto but the ward of Yelwa town, originally a Gungawa settlement. The Hella islanders were Gungawa.

from Yauri, which thus regained its sole status as an emirate, enlarged by the retention of Kwanji and Agwarra districts and the Rofia bush to the west of the Niger. But there was little improvement in Yauri affairs. Dukku was taken away from Yauri because of its neglect and handed over to Kontagora, and then in 1923 the Emir Aliyu was, none too soon, deposed.

The recall of Jibrilu was, *mirabile dictu*, seriously considered, but mercifully common-sense prevailed and it was his eldest son, the young Abdullahi, who became the 40th Emir of Yauri, thereby restoring the old Yauri dynasty. The Rofia hinterland was handed back to Bussa in 1927 but Yauri's attempt to recover Dukku district from Kontagora on the death of the Emir in 1930 failed—only just, as Government gave approval and then rescinded it. In 1931 the Emir of Yauri escaped with his life after he had been bitten by a snake, and the temporary curtailment of his personal activities and direction of affairs reacted on the efficiency of the emirate administration. In the following year the District Officer was withdrawn from Yelwa, which was now expected to share the D.O. looking after Dabai N.A., at that time also in the southern Division of Sokoto Province. Official reports throughout the next decade talk of the Emir's remarkable flair for and competence in administration, running his emirate first of all without the supervision of a D.O. and finally, when all his councillors suddenly died or resigned in 1937, without even a council! Emir Abdullahi was, however, gradually being attacked by a debilitating illness, and in 1955 he died. He is still affectionately remembered for his outstanding services. Abdullahi was succeeded by his 34-year-old son Muhammad Tukur who, after a brilliant career as a Hausa teacher at the University of London and Clerk to the Northern House of Chiefs, had just been appointed Commissioner for Northern Nigeria in the United Kingdom. This he gave up in order to return to the service of his emirate. Since then, Yauri has continued in the stable path of administrative progress first brought to it by Emir Abdullahi. Emir Muhammad Tukur has added lustre to the name of Yauri by his appointments as Chairman of the Local Government Reforms Commission in Adamawa and Bornu, of the Northern Nigeria Radio and Television Corporation, and in 1962 of the National Universities Commission.[1]

[1] Acknowledgement is made for the help given in this chapter by my student Mahdi Adamu.—A.K-G.

THE EMIRS OF YAURI

1. Tafarilu
2. Kamuwa
3. Buyanga
4. Sakazu
5. Yauri
6. Kisagare
7. Jerabana I
8. Gimba I *c.* 1578?
9. Gimba II
10. Kasafogi
11. Jerabana II *c.* 1616?
12. Gimba III
13. Kasagurbi
14. Kana
15. Jan Rina
16. Dutsi
17. Lafiya
18. Kada
19. Gamdi
20. Dan Ibrahimu
21. Muhammadu
22. Lafiya II
23. Yanazu
24. Umaru Gamdi
25. Suleimana Jerabana
26. Aliyu Lafiya
27. Ahmadu Jerabana
28. Shu'aibu Madara
29. Mustafa Gazari *c.* 1790

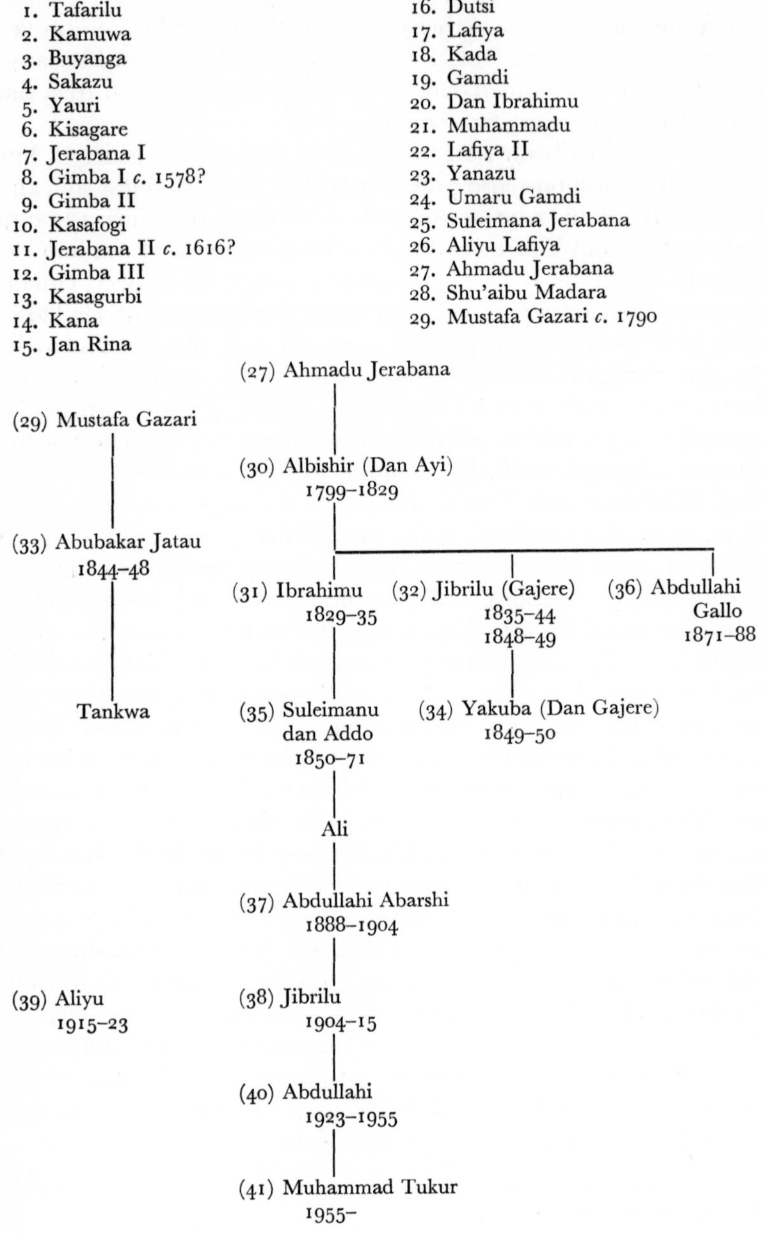

XXI. NUPE

NUPE history focuses on the figure of Tsoede, the culture hero and mythical founder of the Nupe kingdom. His name derives from the Nupe form *Etsu* or *'tsu Ede*, while the Hausa chronicles generally refer to him as Edegi. Inevitably, there are several versions of the Tsoede legend, and the one quoted here is that given by the last living descendant of the Tsoede dynasty, Etsu Umaru of Pategi.[1]

At the time of Tsoede's birth in *c*. 1463, the Beni chieftainships were united in a loose confederacy under the chief of Nku, a village near the confluence of the Niger and the Kaduna. There was no kingdom of Nupe, and the people were tributary to the Atta of Igala at Eda (Idah). The tribute was a harsh one, every family head having to give one male member of his house: Nupe tradition maintains that these were always sisters' sons.

One day the son of the Atta Gara, to give him his correct title, was hunting in Nupe country when he met the young widowed daughter of the chief of Nku who lived at Tafi, near modern Bida. He fell in love with her and they lived together until the prince was recalled to Idah on the death of his father. He left his pregnant mistress a charm and a ring to give to their unborn child. When the child was born, he was given the name Tsoede. When Tsoede was about thirty, he was sent to Idah as a slave. The Atta, recognizing his son in the new slave by the ring he had given him, kept him near his person and treated him almost as if he were his legitimate son. Tsoede spent nearly thirty years at his father's court.

Once the king fell victim to a mysterious illness which nobody could cure. The court diviner prophesied that only a fruit from a very high oil-palm outside the town, plucked by one man, would cure the king. All his legitimate sons tried, in vain, to obtain the precious fruit. Finally Tsoede made the attempt, and succeeded. But in this attempt

[1] This section owes much to S. F. Nadel, *A Black Byzantium*. Currently, research into Nupe history is being carried out in Bida by Miss M. MacReynolds from the University of California.

he cut his lip so badly that he looked almost like a man born with a split lip. From this time—and this still holds true to-day—all hare-lipped boys born in Nupe are named Edegi.[1]

The Atta's love for Tsoede incited the jealousy of his half-brothers, so on his death-bed the Atta advised his son to flee and return to his own country, the rule of which he bequeathed to him. Among the parting presents he gave Tsoede were various royal insignia, including a bronze canoe manned by twelve Nupe slaves, *kakaki* or the long royal trumpets, state drums hung with brass bells, and the heavy iron chains and fetters which became the potent emblems of the Nupe kings' judicial power and are today known as *egba Tsoede*, 'the chain of Tsoede'. These chains were kept in a number of villages along the Niger valley entrusted with the special task of acting as *ledu*, the 'King's Hangmen', for pre-Fulani rulers insisted on their criminals being executed as far away as possible from the king's capital. The nearest *ledu* town to Bida is Giragi. At Tada near Shonga, and Jebba, there are also to be found sacred bronze figures linked with the myth of Tsoede, seven in the first village and two in the latter. These include the beautiful Gara figures, male and female, cast from the ancient *cire-perdu* method.

On his flight up the Niger, hotly pursued by his half-brothers, Tsoede was helped by two men; these he subsequently rewarded by giving one of them, Belenko, the riverain Kyedawa (Kede) to rule with the title of Kuta. Turning into the creek called Ega at the mouth of the Kaduna, he hid there until his pursuers grew weary and returned to Idah. Tsoede sunk his canoe here, and the local Nupe tell how its bright bronze glitters in the water when they perform their annual sacrifice at the spot where their hero holed his sacred canoe. Tsoede now attacked the near-by village of Nupeko, 'Great Nupe', and killed the chief. From here he conquered his uncle's town of Nku in 1531 and made himself ruler of all the country, assuming the title of *Etsu* or king. The twelve men who had paddled his canoe on his flight from Idah he appointed chiefs of the twelve confederate Beni towns of Tafien, Bida, Esa, Doko, Towagi, Egbe, Gaba, Nupeko, Eda, Panjuru, Ewu and Yesa, and today their successors still treasure chains and bangles as insignia of chieftainship.

[1] Nadel, op. cit., p. 73.

Tsoede is believed to have brought back from Idah certain crafts new to the Nupe, such as silver-smithing, glass-making and canoe-building, for which nowadays the Nupe are so celebrated. Their guilds persist to this day, each in its own ward of Bida town, with Muku as the title of the Grand Master of the brass-workers, Masaga for the glass craftsmen, Maji for the bead-workers and Dokodza for the blacksmiths. The *edelucizi* or weavers, however, have no special title for their Nupe head, who is just known as *Ndako* or grandfather, but the heads of the Yagba and Yoruba weavers bear the title of Maji and Leshe respectively.

Under Tsoede's leadership campaigns were undertaken against the Yagba, Bunu, and Kakanda as far as Akobo in the south, and the Kamuku and Kambari in the north. When Nupeko grew too small for his capital, he built the town of Gbara on the Kaduna, which remained the *ezi 'tsu* or the King's Town until the Fulani conquest. The ruins at present-day Jimanli[1] show what a large town Gbara must have been. Nupe traditions claim that Tsoede's royal stables counted 5,555 horses, and in order to quarter them one of his sons, Abdu, founded the town of Dokomba, 'the Place of Horses', on the other bank of the Kaduna.

Tsoede died in about 1591 at the reputed age of 120 years, on a military expedition at Gbagede. His sword and stirrups are looked on almost as a sacred treasure by the people of Gbagede. He was succeeded as Etsu by four of his sons, the eldest being Shaba. Thereafter Nupe history is obscure until the coming of the Fulani, though we know that Jima, Mokwa and Raba joined Nupeko and Gbara as *ezi 'tsu*. The Nupe influence was felt as far south as Kabba and even, some sources would have it, west to Old Oyo. Jima was founded by a descendant of Tsoede, Etsu Abdu Waliyi, who reigned 1679–1700. Etsu Jibrilu, 1746–59, was the fifteenth king of Nupe and its first Muslim ruler; his grave can be seen at Kutigi, where he died in exile. Raba was founded by Etsu Mamma in 1795 after the division of the kingdom of Nupe, on the death of Etsu Ma'azu.

It was during the reign of Etsu Ma'azu, at the turn of the century, that the power of Nupe reached its height; it was also in his time that a certain Fulani from Bangana, near Birnin Kebbi, called Malam Dendo or Manko, 'the Great Malam', who was

[1] Jimanli is about 15 miles south-west of Bida.

destined to alter the whole fate of the Nupe kingdom, is said to have first appeared in Nupe country as an itinerant preacher, diviner and seller of charms.

It was not long before the Nupes' internal quarrels presented the opportunist Fulani with the chance to make themselves master of the country. A feud developed between Etsu Ma'azu's son Jimada, the legitimate heir to the throne according to Nupe rules of royal inheritance, and his father's brother's son Majiya II. The exact origin of this dynastic feud is uncertain, but its outcome is clear: it led to a temporary division of the Nupe kingdom into an eastern half under Jimada at Gbara and a western half under Etsu Majiya at Raba.

For some years previously Fulani cattle-owners had been arriving in Nupe country in search of fresh pastures. In their train had come a sprinkling of *malamai* and missionaries, some at the direct invitation of the local chiefs.

It was Majiya who gained the friendship of Malam Dendo and his Fulani group of followers that had gathered round him. More than this, Majiya installed him in an influential position in his court, trusted his prophecies and rewarded him magnificently, even taking Malam Dendo's youngest son Masaba, said to be born of a Nupe princess named Fatima whom Dendo had cured of sickness, into his house as a foster-son. Thus supported, Majiya took the upper hand, defeated his rival Jimada at Lade and then killed him at Ragada, near Jangi between Raba and Labozhi. Jimada's son, Idrisu, fled to Labozhi and thence to Eggan.[1] Majiya had become the undisputed king of Nupe.

But now Majiya's gratitude gave way to fear of Dendo's power and jealousy of his growing following of Fulani kinsmen. Resolved to rid himself of this potentially dangerous rival, he expelled Dendo and his followers from Raba and drove them across the Niger into Ilorin. Here another Fulani emissary, Malam Alimi, had already established himself as king over the Yoruba of Ilorin, so Dendo and his fugitives received a friendly welcome. In 1806, determined to extirpate Fulani influence from Nupe for ever, Etsu Majiya made a forced march of some 80 miles from Raba to Ilorin in two days and halted his army of 4,000 horsemen and 10,000

[1] Labozhi is about 30 miles east of Raba; Lade is south of the Niger a few miles north-west of Pategi; Eggan is about 40 miles east of Pategi at the confluence of the Niger and Gboko rivers.

foot-soldiers near Sobi hill at the gates of the town. The story of the battle is an epic superbly told in Nupe:

> There were five Fulani emissaries in Ilorin at that time: Mallam Baba, who had fled with Dendo from Raba and later became the first Emir of Agaie; Mallam Dendo himself; Mallam Musa, another fugitive from Raba; Mallam Maliki, who had resided in another Nupe town, Lafiagi, and had been driven from there by Majiya; and Mallam Alimi, the Emir of Ilorin. Dendo was the youngest of the five, but his keen intelligence made him at once their leader. He first sent word to Idirisu, Jimada's exiled son, asking for his support in this fight against Majiya, the murderer of his father. Then Dendo prepared his most powerful *asiri*. Two brave men were sent out at night to steal into the enemy's camp and to bring back some earth. Dendo dug a large pit close to the town wall. He put the earth into this pit, and covered its mouth with grass. On a Friday morning he entered the pit, taking with him fourteen dates. He stayed there till the hour of evening prayer, but what he did in the pit, what secret magic he performed, no one knows. When he reappeared, he called again the two men who had brought the earth the previous night, and ordered them to scatter it by night all round the town walls. Next morning Majiya attacked. A thick mist had fallen over the country. Majiya's troops were unable to move in the mist. Then a sand-storm sprang up, blinding men and horses. The horses bolted, and Majiya's cavalry, placed (in accordance with Nupe military principles) behind the infantry, trampled down their own men. When the small army of Ilorin sallied forth from the gates of the town, it met an enemy already half defeated. Majiya was beaten, he fled across the Niger, back to the protected Raba, with only 1,000 horses and 1,070 men left of his huge army. This was not the end. Idirisu and his followers joined forces with Mallam Dendo. Together they pursued Majiya's troops, marching their men up the Niger as far as Gbajibo, fifty miles north of Raba, where they were able to cross the river unmolested. Here Mallam Dendo is said to have used a clever ruse: for a week he collected horse-dung, and then threw it into the water; drifting down the river it reached Raba; and the Nupe, who had hardly recovered from their defeat at Ilorin, thought that an enormous army of horsemen was approaching Raba and had already crossed the river. Majiya fled into the interior, to Zuguma, leaving Raba unprotected, an easy prey to the Fulani army.[1]

Nupe history now resolves itself into continued play and counter play between the Fulani and the two rival Nupe factions. Later this became still further complicated by a split in the Fulani camp.

[1] Nadel, op. cit., p. 78.

Malam Dendo repaid Idrisu's help badly. He left him as a puppet king at Adama Lelu, near Eggan, while he himself occupied Raba as the real ruler. Idrisu, who had built himself a new capital at Edun, finally rebelled against this treatment in 1830. One story is that he was killed by the soldiers of Dendo, who thereupon turned to woo the fugitive Majiya by offering him friendship and recognition as king of Nupe—always provided he remained in distant Zuguma.[1] Another prefers to suggest Malam Dendo's duplicity. He sent for Majiya at Amgbara and promised him his revenge on Idrisu. Majiya took the bait and, coming down in force, routed Idrisu who fled to Ekagi, near Katcha.[2] It was now Majiya's turn to be favoured. He was recognized as Etsu Nupe by Malam Dendo, and built himself a town called Jangi. Cordial relations were soon cemented between the Fulani in Raba and Majiya in Jangi. Majiya is said to have married his daughter Sofiya to one of Malam Dendo's sons by his Fulani wife, Usman Zaki, and another daughter, Inoga, to Gogo, Malam Dendo's Mayaki. This alliance was in distinct contrast to the Fulani policy in other states, where the Habe rulers were rarely recognized but rigorously ejected. In Nupe the Fulani were sufficiently shrewd to see that they were not strong enough to stand alone.

Malam Dendo died in 1832. Visiting him shortly before his death, a traveller noted in his diary:

> He is an old man, appearing about eighty but said to be a hundred and fifteen; and notwithstanding he appeared in a state of starvation, he gave us some goora nuts and a sealed pot of honey.[3]

Of his diplomacy, a contemporary visitor to his court commented:

> It has been the policy of Mallam Dendo, who by all accounts is an able and crafty chief and a courageous man, to advance foreigners of all nations to certain lucrative and important posts, either about his person, in the army, or as governors of conquered towns; and by this means he conciliates, in a great measure . . . the original population of the country, confirms his reputation, and establishes his sovereignty with little trouble over lands and districts which he may have subjugated and added to his dominions.[4]

[1] Zuguma was about 15 miles north of Raba.

[2] On the Niger opposite Eggan.

[3] M. Laird and R. A. K. Oldfield, *Narrative of an Expedition into the Interior of Africa*, 1837.

[4] From Lander's journal.

Four of his seven sons survived him—Abdu Gboya, Usman Zaki, Mamudu Gwogi, and Mama Saba (better known as Masaba)—and two daughters, Gogo Sabaci and Gogo Wodiko. According to tradition, he is said to have urged his sons to eschew official secular power and to remain what he had been, an emissary of Islam and the uncrowned king of Nupe. Of the capital of Nupe land, Raba, at the time of Malam Dendo's death we have a long contemporary account:

As we rapidly approached the town, it appeared to be situated on the slope of a rising ground; and the houses being built one above the other, to impart to it the appearance of an amphitheatre. With the aid of a glass we could discern an amazing crowd of natives assembled on the banks; but, what was more in accordance with our wishes, we could distinguish horses, cows, bullocks, sheep and goats. As we drew nearer, we found the city to be of immense extent, with villages all round the suburbs. . . .

The King's houses are between thirty and forty in number (each of which is surmounted by an ostrich's egg), and are closed by a very high wall, constructed of mud and red sand.

The outer apartment was the palaver-house, where the chiefs and princes assemble. As we passed through it, there were upwards of one hundred, seated cross-legged, *à la Turque*, together with a great number of Arabs. They appeared to be respectably dressed, and all of them wore a piece of white muslin around their heads, one end of which they brought round over the mouth, and left nothing but the eyes exposed. . . .

. . . It was not until a considerable time elapsed that we could discover which really was his majesty. . . . At length we discovered [him] in the person of Osiman, son of Mallam Dendo. He wore a very common robe, with a piece of muslin over his mouth and nose, which he never attempted to move, but inserted his fingers under his turban, to allow free motion to speak. Close beside him were his sandals, and a silver pot, containing some Goora nuts, which he dealt out with a liberal hand. His manners were dignified and imposing, his conversation free and easy, and his remarks shrewd and sensible. . . . He was rather good-looking about the eyes, which were dark and piercing; and these were nearly all of his countenance that we could discover. . . .

In the afternoon . . . we . . . were conducted to the house of the King's daughter, the Princess of Rabbah, situate near the outskirts of the city. We found everything remarkably neat and clean: calabashes were placed all round the apartment in the same manner that wooden bowls or platters are ranged in a dairy in old England. . . . The lady appeared to be about twenty-eight or thirty years of age, with a remarkably small hand and foot; I never met with one so exceedingly small. She was reclining on a mat in one corner, with a curtain before her, when we arrived. . . .

. . . The city of Rabbah contains a population of nearly forty thousand, natives of Houssa, Yarriba, Ibbodo, and the Nufie countries. Their religion is pagan and Mahomedan. . . . The Felatahs of Rabbah subsist by plundering the weak towns and levying contributions on them. Rabbah is governed by a King or chief, and several elder Mallams. . . . Before undertaking anything important or declaring war, the King is obliged to summon a council of Mallams and the principal people. When his people are successful, which is too frequently the case, the spoils are divided; the King reserving to himself the greatest share. On our first visit it was a matter of some difficulty to ascertain who was really King, owing to the African policy of concealing him from strangers until their views and intentions are known to be peaceful. . . . Osiman, the present King . . . son to Mallam Dendo . . . was reported to be a great and successful warrior, and appeared to be respected by his soldiers.

The King of Rabbah can command five thousand cavalry and twenty thousand infantry. He is daily purchasing horses to add to his troops, who are armed with poisoned arrows and spears, which they hurl with unerring aim a considerable distance. The soldiers also wear knives inside their arms, buckled round the wrist, and also swords slung carelessly over the left shoulder—which latter are brought from Tripoli by the Arabs . . .

The army of Rabbah is composed of liberated slaves, whose freedom is granted on consideration of their taking up arms. In the winter or wet season they follow their ordinary occupations; and in the summer or dry season, when the Quorra is low, they assemble from all parts of the Kingdom of Houssa, Soccatoo, Kano, etc. They travel very quickly, taking the unsuspecting inhabitants by surprise. They seldom fail in capturing hundreds of prisoners, as well as cattle, horses, etc. The slaves are disposed of to the Arabs; and some are sold at towns on the banks of the Niger, and eventually reach the seaside, where they are shipped on board Spanish slavers. The Felatah army of Rabbah is commanded by several Bornouese.[1]

A few years earlier Lander had written of Raba as 'an immensely large, populated and flourishing town built on the slope of a gentle hill, and on a spot almost entirely bare of trees'.

[1] This extract from Laird and Oldfield, op. cit., is reproduced in T. L. Hodgkin, *Nigerian Perspectives*, pp. 239–43. The lower Niger was generally known as Quorra or Kworra.

Malam Dendo's eldest surviving son, Abdu Gboya, took his father's advice in preferring the scholarly profession of *Alkali* to political power. The leadership thus fell to the next son, Usman Zaki, who was still nominally but the spiritual head. He reigned from 1832 to 1859 with a long break of fifteen years. But this was in the teeth of bitter opposition from his youngest brother, the ambitious and popular Masaba. Masaba claimed that, born of a Nupe mother, he was a real Nupe and not the son of a Fulani woman (Adama) like Usman Zaki and Majigi, and that therefore the rank of Shaba or heir-presumptive (held by his other brother, Mamudu Gwogi), if not the very throne itself, should be his. Masaba was driven out of Raba in 1833 and took refuge at Dokun in Lafiagi. He first won the support of the shadow Nupe princes, Tsado in Zuguma and Idrisu at Eggan. Rallying round the pan-Nupe appeal against the Fulani strangers, their combined forces attacked Usman Zaki at Takuma; they were utterly routed. Idrisu's son, Isa, was kept by Usman Zaki as a semi-hostage in Raba. Majiya had accepted the puppet kingship, but soon after his death in 1835 his son Tsado rejected the Fulani overlordship. An indecisive battle took place. Finding the yoking of Fulani spiritual leadership with Nupe secular power to be unworkable, Usman Zaki now adopted the title of Etsu Nupe, declared Raba to be the official capital of the kingdom, and demanded the ancient royal regalia, including the *kakaki* trumpets, from the exiled Nupe king in Zuguma. He also inaugurated the *ajele* or 'deputy' system in Nupeland, whereby the annual tribute payable in slavery was collected by the *ajele* (in Nupe *tuci*) who visited the districts at the head of a small army ready to deal with any recalcitrant taxpayers. From this time the legitimate dynasty of Nupe abandoned all legal claim to its royal heritage and the new Fulani rulers assumed full powers . . . but not without a succession of grave internal intrigues, rebellions and fratricidal wars.

When Tsado instigated yet another rebellion, this time as a protest against the *ajele* system, the opportunist Masaba was tempted to lend a hand from his camp at Lade. This time Usman Zaki was unable to hold off the combined armies: Raba fell and the Etsu fled to Agaie. Hearing of the latest crisis in the turbulent affairs of discordant Nupeland, the Emir of Gwandu, Halilu, came down to Raba in 1841. Here he sent for the following chiefs to meet and discuss the situation: Usman Zaki from Agaie,

Abdullahi Sarkin Agaie, Shitta Sarkin Ilorin, Abdulkadiri Sarkin Lafiagi, Masaba from Lade, Tsado and Isa the two shadow Etsu Nupezhi, Aliyu Sarkin Shonga, and Beji Sarkin Lapai. As a result of his inquiries Halilu decided to remove Usman Zaki to Gwandu and to make Masaba, his brother, Emir of Nupe. Nor was this all. Abdulkadiri, Sarkin Lafiagi, was dispossessed of all his country save the town of Lafiagi itself. Baji, Sarkin Lapai, 'a worthless character', was done away with one night (apparently by Halilu's orders) and his brother Jantabu was turbanned in his place.

Masaba, warrior-king that he was, now proceeded to extend the Nupe kingdom by firmly entrenching himself on the Yoruba side of the Niger and by conquering the Kamuku in the north, the Gwari in the east and the Kakanda in the south. Since Raba was a ruin, he operated from Lade, south of the Niger. Tsado had died in 1836 and his son Etsu Jia was sent to Jangi. For a time Masaba was secure, though only by exercising considerable cunning in the way he played off Etsu Jia against Etsu Isa. It was not long before yet another civil war broke out, in 1843. Once again Halilu came from Gwandu to settle matters. Etsu Jia was defeated at Lemfa, near Eggan, and fled to Yeni, where he died three years later. Maza, his uncle, succeeded him as shadow Etsu Nupe. In 1847 Masaba ordered his general Umar Bahaushe (a one-eyed mercenary adventurer, who had been in Usman Zaki's service) to make war on Etsu Maza and Etsu Isa, but Umar turned traitor and joined Maza. Masaba was forced to flee and was eventually held a virtual prisoner at Ilorin.

Umar soon quarrelled with Maza, over, it is said, a gift of horses from Gwandu. He fought and killed him in Yeni, and proclaimed himself Etsu Nupe. But the Fulani refused to hear of this. Umaru Majigi, son of Mamman Majigi, the eldest son of Malam Dendo, was offered the title but declined. However, he agreed to lead the Fulani against Umar and drove him to Gbobe. Umaru Majigi sent to Gwandu requesting that Usman Zaki might be sent back as Emir of Nupe; he also sent to Ilorin to release Masaba.

Umar collected his forces, and twice defeated Umaru Majigi, driving him back across the Kaduna until he besieged him for three months in the small Beni walled town of Bida. Some say that Umar Bahaushe founded Bida and had long recommended it to his master as preferable to Raba. Usman Zaki and Wazirin

Gwandu arrived from Gwandu, joined later by Masaba from Ilorin. Umar Bahaushe refused to listen to the Waziri, so Umaru Majigi launched a successful night attack, and completely routed Umar Bahaushe. In attempting to cross the Gbako river, Umar was drowned. His body was brought to Majigi, who ordered the corpse to be decapitated and the head sent to be displayed on the walls of Raba. Much credit for the Fulani victory goes to the part played by the twelve Beni towns, whose confederacy was brought into action for the last time in history. It took nine years, from 1847 to 1856, for the Fulani to overthrow the usurper, but in the process the three branches of the royal family emerged united as never before with their family feuds safely buried.

Usman Zaki was reinstated as Emir of Nupe in 1856, but with Bida as the new Nupe capital, Masaba was made Sarkin Fulani and Umaru Majigi became Yarima. Etsu Isa was allowed the empty title of Etsu Nupe but nothing further. Abdulkadiri, Sarkin Lafiagi, and Aliyu, Sarkin Shonga, received back most of their territories that had been confiscated from them in 1841 by Halilu.

Usman Zaki reigned for another three years and died in 1859. During his second reign Glover (later Sir John Glover, Governor of Lagos) and Crowther (later Bishop) visited the new capital from their camp at Wuya and called on the Etsu. In his diary Glover noted:

> Mr Crowther and I were sitting in our hut when news came that the Chief had arrived, and we proceeded to the huts which had been assigned to him and his suite. We found them refreshing themselves from a large bowl of milk and quickly joined them, for it was a treat we had not enjoyed for months. After resting from their long ride, all proceeded on our visit to the King, whom we found seated on a low dais in a large yard. We entered on his left, having to pass through some hundreds of armed retainers, all seated cross-legged on the ground. On his right were, as I suppose, his courtiers and the princes of his family, and before him were spread mats, on which we seated ourselves. He is a very gentlemanly looking man of about 65, drest in the simple robe of the country. He received us most warmly. Then followed our congratulations on his return to his country. He said: 'Yes, God is great. He has brought me back after an absence of eleven years.'[1]

Usman Zaki was succeeded by Masaba, whose second reign

[1] A. C. Hastings, *The Voyage of the Dayspring*, p. 101.

lasted till 1873. Under Masaba, Bida was transformed from an overgrown war-camp into 'a capital worthy of the most powerful kingdom of Central Nigeria'.[1] Many of Bida's notable architectural features date from this time: the three royal palaces within the city walls, the famous night-market, the great mosque. Writing of a visit to Bida in 1871, Dr Simpson recorded in his diary:

August 21. Went to King in the morning, who expressed his pleasure at seeing me. That since he had had communication with white men the Queen had never sent him an Ambassador (as he termed me) before. Proposed his power to be over all the country to Iddah. . . . That he gave all his land to the Queen of England; that once he was weak, now he was strong, through the Queen, meaning the guns, powder, etc., brought by the merchants, and the presents which gave him respect in the eyes of his people and the neighbouring tribes; English people were safe anywhere in his Kingdom; that Lokoja especially was for the Queen; that it was on account of the Queen that he refrained from attacking the people living below Lokoja.

August 25. . . . King informed me the Queen's letter had been read in the mosque this Friday morning. People well pleased and praised him on account of it.

August 29. [The King said] that three caravans with ivory were coming from Adamawa, through Lafia to trade. Had given a camel, an ostrich, and a horse to Abuja, King of Zaria, to permit caravans to pass through his country. Road that way was first open year before last; 2s. was at first charged per head for passing, now 6d. through his intercession (Lafia to Egga, fourteen days; Adamawa to Lafia, forty days).

September 2. Visited King; about 50 tailors at work, making uniforms out of cloth included in Her Majesty's presents; offered me an ostrich, a horse, and a gazelle, all of which I declined, as unable to carry them to England . . . said he was sending to Sokoto, to the Sultan, the Koran and many guns, with other of the best things I had given him, to prove the sort of relations that subsisted between him and the white men; and that his [the King's] traders could supply the interior with all that was wanted; said he cared for nothing himself but guns and powder, and would 'dash' the rest away, but wished his people to trade in everything else they required, or had for sale.[2]

Externally, too, Nupe became a power in the land under Masaba's leadership. He suppressed a revolt in Mokwa and

[1] Nadel, op. cit., p. 82.

[2] W. H. Simpson, *Report on the Niger Expedition*, 1871, quoted in Hodgkin, op. cit., p. 293.

another by the Kede; he waged war against the Kukuruku and the Bassa Nge, he fought the Gwari and even the Fulani of Agaie. Small wonder that the Nupe Kingdom under Masaba is said to have stretched from Mulye and Awawu in Ebe country down to Akpara in Bunu country and in breadth from Yoruba Shari in the west to Payi of the Gwari in the east. Masaba sent Umaru Majigi to enlist the support of Ilorin against a Yoruba chief from Ibadan named Aggeye, who had been troublesome in the Akoko (Kabba-Ilorin) country. The campaign lasted three years. On Umaru Majigi's return he found Masaba involved in the beginnings of another rising, known in Nupe history as the Kwenti rebellion.

At first Masaba had the support of the Kede people. But when their war chief Choida Lumella was drowned in the Niger, owing to an explosion in his canoe, the Kede lost heart. The rebels, consisting of Nupe, Gbedegi, Ebe and others, at first managed to prevail against Masaba, but once Umaru Majigi had taken command of the Fulani army their fortunes began to decline. Within a short time the rebellion was stamped out, over six hundred villages in the Kaduna district being destroyed. A few Nupe still held out, but at Leaba the last remnants were dispersed or captured and sold as slaves. At this period Umaru Majigi stands out from among his fellows in a class by himself. He had already shown all the qualities of a sound administrator, and he now proved himself a master of strategy.

After this rebellion had been put down, a serious quarrel arose between the Fulani at Bida and the Fulani at Agaie and Lapai. A Bida raiding-party had set out against the Kakanda but had been repulsed; they foolishly turned aside and began raiding Agaie and Lapai districts. Masaba attempted to justify such a gross breach of the peace by claiming sovereign rights over Agaie and Lapai. Had it not been for the unfailing good sense of Umaru Majigi and the diplomatic intervention of an Arab, Sharifi-Mai-Bindiga, a disastrous inter-Fulani war would have been precipitated.

The Emir of Gwandu, Abdulkadiri, set out for Nupe to settle this dispute in 1868, but died *en route* at Besse just after the initiation of the famous treaty of Lafiyar Toga.[1] His successor, Almustafa, visited Nupe in 1871, and at a meeting of all the chiefs exhorted them to pull together for the sake of their race and their

[1] See the section on Gwandu, p. 424.

religion. He received many handsome presents and guns from Bida. Not long after his departure Masaba died at Bida in 1873.

It was now the turn of the family of the third son of Malam Dendo to become Etsu in the person of his grandson, Umaru Majigi. For 130 years, right down to the change of 1962, the title of Etsu has alternated with mathematical regularity between the three royal houses of Usman Zaki, Masaba and Umaru Majigi. In Umaru Majigi's reign the Nupe again extended their boundaries, greatly helped by the gunpowder bought from the first Niger Company trading-post, established at Eggan. The Kusopa under a chief from Yeti allied themselves with the exiled Nupe royal family at Zuguma, but they and the constantly rebelling Kede were subdued—the latter with the help of the tributary Kakanda.

With his flag received direct from Sarkin Gwandu, Umaru Majigi spent his first year or two in subduing the Igbirra. He lent assistance to Sarkin Kontagora in quelling a Gwari rising, for several years earlier he had given his daughter in marriage to Isa, the Emir of Kontagora's son, at the same time as Masaba had given his daughter to the Emir himself. He was then summoned to Gwandu with his army to assist Hanufi, who had succeeded Almustafa as Emir of Gwandu, in attacking one of the Kebbi towns. The town fell and the Nupe army returned home after a six months' absence.

There followed a few punitive expeditions and small risings. Etsu Baba, son of Saci, created trouble in the Kontagora country, and was finally drowned in crossing the Niger after being defeated at Leaba. This is known in the Nupe annals as the Fagbagba war.

The next landmark in Nupe history is called the Ganegan war. Masaba had appointed Malam Isatakun to be Kuta of the Kede people on the death of Kuta Bake. But Isatakun had no wish to live at the waterside and eventually transferred the title to his younger brother Usman. Usman was a Kede by descent, and was therefore welcomed at Muregi. After a while Isatakun sent his two sons to be given the offices of Choiwa Kuta and Tsado Somfada, but Usman refused on the grounds that they knew nothing about canoes or fishing, the arts of the Kede watermen. In any case, Usman's own sons held the ranks already. This infuriated Isatakun. 'I gave him meat but he refuses to give me bones,' he is said to have cried. Isatakun did not rest until he had incited Umaru

Majigi to make war on the Kede. Usman was captured and brought to Bida, where he was put to death.

Malam Isatakun now resumed the office of Kuta and lived at Dokomba, giving his two sons rank and power, one in Egba and the other in Muregi. Isatakun remained at Dokomba until the Niger Company campaign in 1897, when he fled to Bida.

Umaru Majigi died just before the end of the Ganegan war. Maliki, who became king in 1884, stands as the wealthiest Etsu in Nupe history, but to acquire this wealth he is said to have increased taxation and tribute until they were almost insupportable. It may be for this reason that he was preoccupied with punitive expeditions against his recalcitrant vassals. He also engaged in several campaigns in the Kabba districts against the Yagba, Kiri and Kukuruku.

It was during the reign of Abubakar that the Royal Niger Company's troops, led by Sir George Goldie in person, moved against Bida. Soon after Abubakar's accession, trouble broke out in the southern areas of the Nupe kingdom, among the Igbirra and the Yagba. The Royal Niger Company, not for the first time, intruded into Nupe politics by promising protection against Bida to these peoples, among whom they had a number of trading-factories. The Etsu, an enemy of the European traders—in marked contrast to his father Masaba who had played such a leading role in the riverain affairs and had befriended and even saved the life of Dr Baikie at Lokoja[1] by sending a protective army of 4,000 men—decided to kill two birds with one stone: to pacify the Kabba peoples and to rid himself of the white man. He ordered his army southwards, under the command of the Makun, Muhammadu.

Abubakar could hardly have made a worse choice. The Makun nursed a grievance against the Etsu for having refused him the title of Shaba or heir-apparent. In exchange for the promise that he would be given the throne, the Makun agreed with Sir William Wallace that he would keep his army out of the way of the Royal Niger Company's march on Bida. The Company found another willing ally in the Kede who, never happier than when rebelling against Bida, manned their canoes, ferried the army and its artillery across the Niger and then guarded the river so that

[1] See H. J. Pedraza, *Borrioboola-Gha*, 1958, for a good account of Baikie's work at Lokoja and a general history of the area.

no reinforcements could reach Bida. Depleted of arms and cut off from help, Bida fell, Abubakar was deposed and Muhammadu was installed as Etsu.[1] The 1897 treaty, written in Arabic and English, is still in the possession of the Etsu Nupe, and the ceremonial staff and spear taken from Abubakar were restored to Bida in 1960. The cannons outside the palace today were a gift from the Royal Niger Company to Etsu Muhammadu after the battle. The Kede were promised semi-independent status and, at the request of their chief Patigi, the land on the southern bank of the Niger opposite his capital of Muregi was excised from Bida's jurisdiction and given to Idrisu, the exiled king of the Jimada branch of the pre-Fulani Nupe dynasty, who had been living in Bida more as a hostage than a guest.

Once the Company withdrew, the imposed Etsu lost his strength, and it was not long before Abubakar was back on the throne. But the Makun was not yet finished. Lugard had at first named Bida as the Riverain District of the Middle Niger Province, placing it under a Resident at Lokoja. But Bida was too powerful to leave it so remotely controlled; closer administration was called for. In 1901 Lugard camped at Wuya and summoned first the Etsu and then his councillors to his presence; only the Makun came. Lugard ordered his army into Bida, Abubakar and his Masaba courtiers fled, and Muhammadu was proclaimed Etsu for the second time. His nickname of 'Etsu with two tongues' is significant, because he was the last of the Fulani rulers who could speak Fulfulde; today the Etsu Nupe joins nearly all the Fulani emirs in Northern Nigeria, other than Adamawa, Muri and Gombe, in their inability to speak their Fulani language fluently. The Nupe Province was created under H. F. Goldsmith, still affectionately remembered by his sobriquet of '*kubelazhin*, 'good-morning'. Abubakar was banished to Lokoja, a haunt of exiled emirs, where he eventually died in 1919, though not without one final attempt to reinstal himself as Etsu.

Muhammadu was succeeded in 1916 by Bello, a grandson of Usman Zaki. Etsu Bello's introduction of the first motor-car into Bida gave birth to a poem that became a favourite of Bida's drummers:

[1] The incident has been recounted in Etsu Ndayako, *In Ji Etsu Nupe,* and A. H. M. Kirk-Greene, 'The Battles of Bida', *West African Review*, July 1955.

The name of Allah is the beginning of all learning.
Let us speak of the day when Etsu Bello bought a motor-car.
On the day when Etsu Bello bought a motor-car,
The whole of Bida went out to build a road.
Younger brothers, they went out to build the road.
All the people on the farms went out to build the road.
The young bride, she went to build the road.
The bridegroom, he went to build the road.
But why did they all go out to build the road?
It was because Etsu Bello had bought a motor-car.
Because of that all the people went out to build a road.
They said: Let us build a road on which the car can travel.
Then the man who wants to go to Baddeggi, in this car he will go.
And Zungeru, the man who wants to go to Zungeru, in this car he will go.
And Wuya, who will travel to Wuya, in this car he will go.
The man who will go to Jima, in this car he will go.
The man who will go to Kacha, in this car he will go.
Thus he will go, they said, and therefore let us make the road.
Etsu Bello has the money to buy the car,
But the car will benefit all the people of Bida, from the farms and from the city,
The great man and the servant.
They thank Etsu Bello because he has bought the car.
Etsu Bello, who has horses, and who now has a car.
Etsu Bello can say: Though the horse may break his legs
We shall go all the same.
On the day when Etsu Bello bought the motor-car,
The bottles of the glass-makers turned into red beads.
And the kernels of the *gombara* grass became necklaces.
In that year when Etsu Bello bought the motor-car,
The men were beating the ground,
And the woman, she was sitting at home.
How did it happen that the woman was sitting at home?
Of old it was the woman who was beating the ground,
And the man he just stood and watched.
But because of this motor-car of Etsu Bello,
All the men were beating the ground, and that is that.
And all the people, the whole of Bida,
They were saying their thanks to *mace da ciki*.
And all Bida was giving thanks to *karan giya*,
Who has sold the car to Etsu Bello.
And all the people were giving thanks to Etsu Bello,

> Because he gave his money to buy a motor-car,
> That motor-car that will become a thing of benefit
> To all the human beings.[1]

Ten years later it was the Masaba candidate Saidu, a grandson of Masaba, who came to the throne. In the same year (1928) the aged Waziri died and was replaced by Muhammadu. The previous years had seen a number of changes in the province. Nupe Province, comprising the three Nupe emirates of Bida, Agaie and Lapai, lost its name when Niger was formed in 1908 by the addition of Kura and Kwongoma Divisions from Zaria; six years later Koton Karfi was transferred to it from Nassarawa Province. The proud title of Nupe Province was regranted in 1918 but it lapsed again on the great 1926 administrative reorganization.

Bida came into unflattering prominence in 1932 when her fair name was spoilt by a sudden tragedy. A hostile crowd in the town set upon three women accused of witchcraft and stoned them to death. As if this were not enough, on the same day the house of one Sokyara, on whom an attempt had been made to assign blame for the murders, was set alight and Sokyara's brother was burned to death. Acting on the assumption that Bida's moral development had lagged behind its material progress and that the N.A. lacked sufficient control, the Government abolished the non-Nupe office of Waziri and a new Council was formed. In the following year, local men of standing were appointed to the Etsu's council, replacing those who had been 'silent spectators rather than advisers'.[2] A parallel reformation was undertaken in the district administration. To mark this new leaf, the Ndeji went on a visit to Sokoto and Zaria emirates, and his *malam* kept a full diary of the tour. The central offices, made from the new Bida industry of brick-burning, had their foundation stone laid and a palace was designed for the Etsu outside the walls of the city on the Wuya road, so as to remove the government of Bida from the bitter factions inherent in its tri-dynastic system.

Etsu Saidu had been in such ill-health for some time that he was persuaded to retire. However, his health gave way completely and he died early in 1935. He was succeeded by the Nagenum and District Head of Jima-Doko, Muhammadu Ndayako, who cele-

[1] Nadel, op. cit., pp. 140–1.
[2] *Annual Report of Niger Province*, 1933.

brated his appointment by a vigorously effective tour of his whole emirate. Following the reduction of the four Trans-Kaduna (as opposed to the Cis-Kaduna or eastern) districts to two, Gbangba and Dakmon Magwe were combined. The same year saw the Emir move into the new palace.[1] Three years later Muhammadu Ndayako made history by being the first Nupe ruler to visit Lagos: he travelled by road. The appointment of the headmaster of the Middle School (Malam Aliyu, later Makama and Regional Minister) to the N.A. Council followed the novel nomination of two women members, the Sagi and the Niniwaye, to the Bida Town Council in 1937, also remembered as the year of the magnificent Coronation regatta at Wushishi. This Sagi—the title originally belonged to the senior Nupe princess, deriving from the martial Habibatu, who founded Badeggi, but today responsible for the problems of the womenfolk of the royal family—was Gogo Safiyatu, who was later succeeded by Gogo Hannatu, an aunt of Etsu Muhammadu Ndayako.

Muhammadu Ndayako visited England in 1952 and, calling on his vivid photographic memory which enabled him in his subsequent years to depict delightful cameos to his guests, he wrote an account of his journey, *In Ji Etsu Nupe*. The reorganization of his Council in 1955 and again in 1959, brought the Emir a wide body of capable counsellors. Despite public worry about his health. Muhammadu Ndayako continued as a remarkably active ruler, and at the Royal Durbar at Kaduna in 1956 he gallantly led his Nupe contingent on horseback. Thus it was amid universal pleasure that Muhammadu Ndayako celebrated his silver jubilee in February 1960 at the age of 76. He died at Kaduna on 29 October 1962 and was succeeded by Alhaji Usman Sarki of the Masaba dynasty, at that time Sardaunan Bida and a Federal Minister. It is of Muhammadu Ndayako's well-remembered reign that we have this vignette of a day of royal routine so typical of the pace and direction of emirate affairs in the late 1930s:

Every morning the Etsu mounts his horse and, accompanied by members of his household and some of his officers of state, rides round the walls of his house. This morning ride is still part of the daily routine of the Etsu Nupe, even up at his modern brick residence which stands by itself on the hill outside the town. He may extend his ride to visit

[1] The famous Kutigi mats found favour in England's markets at this time.

his *esozi*, a short distance away, and inspect his farms, or possibly to inquire after his guests—for visitors of standing who have come from far away are assigned quarters in the *esozi*. Once when I accompanied the Etsu on this ceremonial morning ride he went to see a Nupe Mallam who had returned from the pilgrimage to Mecca and in Bida as the king's guest on his way home. Another time two noblemen from Sokoto, relatives of the Sultan, had come on a visit to Bida and were invited to stay in the *esozi*. Later in the morning, back in his house, the Etsu receives the first official visitors of the day: the Etsu Dogari and the Sarkin Yandoka, the chiefs of the two police forces of the Emirate, who come to bring him the 'news of the town'—arrests made on the market the night before, a case of small-pox in one of the town quarters, and so forth. The Alkali and his Chief Assistant drop in to pay their respects, possibly to report on an important law-case, before they go down to the Court House in the centre of the town. The guild-head of the traders may present himself in order to inform the Etsu of the arrival in Bida of traders or a trading caravan with new attractive goods which the Etsu might care to inspect. Messengers come and go—from the Native Administration Treasury, or the Divisional Office, the Bida Town Council, or from a District Head. In the meantime the highest officers of state, the members of the Emir's Council, have arrived in his house for the daily *nko*, the Council of State. At the *nko* all matters of importance are discussed; or there may be legal cases on the day's agenda. For the *nko* has also judicial functions and tries cases referred to it from a lower court. The session of the Etsu's Council concludes the official duties of the day. In the afternoon the Etsu might see friends or visitors in his house, or drive through the town in his splendid motor-car—one of the modern symbols of royal prestige.

The climax of Bida Court life is the celebration of the Friday. On Thursday night and again on Friday afternoon the Etsu rides in great state to the mosque in the town, and on Friday at his return he holds a reception in his house which is attended by every man of rank and standing. Envisage this Friday procession: king and courtiers on horse-back, in their sumptuous gowns, the king under the great silken state umbrella, the horses with trappings of silver and beautiful cloth; a body-guard carrying swords, and police with their staffs, are running ahead, shouting the Etsu's name or blessing formulae or little proverb-like sentences which illustrate the king's greatness; drummers are beating their drums, three mounted trumpeters blow the huge bronze *kakaki* in an incessant deafening chorus; with it blend the shrill notes of the *algeita*, the Hausa oboe, while another musician is beating an iron double bell with a wooden stick, shouting and singing at the same time. All streets are lined with people, adults and children, who watch, fascinated, this procession, bearing witness to the impressiveness of this display of royal power. And then, back again in the royal palace: the wide place in front of the house and the courtyard are crowded with people; the *talakazi*—the commoners, men without name and rank—sit and stand outside, chatting and watching what there is to watch; the members of the privileged classes, titled nobility, and Mohammedan priests, are sitting in the inner courtyard and in *katamba* (entrance-halls), each *katamba* reserved for a special group. Only royal princes and the highest officers of state are admitted to the presence of the Etsu; they sit in the inner part of the house together with personal friends and favourites of the king. All these people come to pay their respect to their sovereign, to see and to be seen, to exercise prerogatives, or to proclaim their connexion with the privileged and mighty. This external arrangement of the Friday ceremonial is indeed a symbol of the whole structure of Nupe kingdom with its rigid system of etiquette and precedence, its differentiation of status, rank, and prerogatives, and its display of wealth and power.[1]

THE EMIRS (ETSUZHI) OF NUPE

The Nupe Etsuzhi

c. 1531–91	Tsoede (Edegi). He was succeeded by his four sons:
1591–1600	Shaba;
1600–25	Zaulla (Zavunla);
1625–70	Jiga (Jigba, Jia);
1670–79	Mamman Wari.
1679–1700	Abdu Waliyi.
1746–59	Jibrin (Jibrilu), 15th Etsu, and probably first Muslim King of Nupe.
1759–67	Ma'azu; again 1778–95.
1767–77	Majiya I.
1777–78	Iliyasu.
1795–96	Mamma.
1796–1805	Jimada, grandson of Iliyasu, reigning at Jima.
1796–1810	Majiya II, grandson of Iliyasu, reigning at Raba; again 1830–34 at Zuguma.
1810–30	Idrisu, son of Jimada, as Nupe shadow king.
1836	Death of Tsado, son of Majiya.

[1] Nadel, op. cit., p. 91.

The Fulani Etsuzhi Nupe

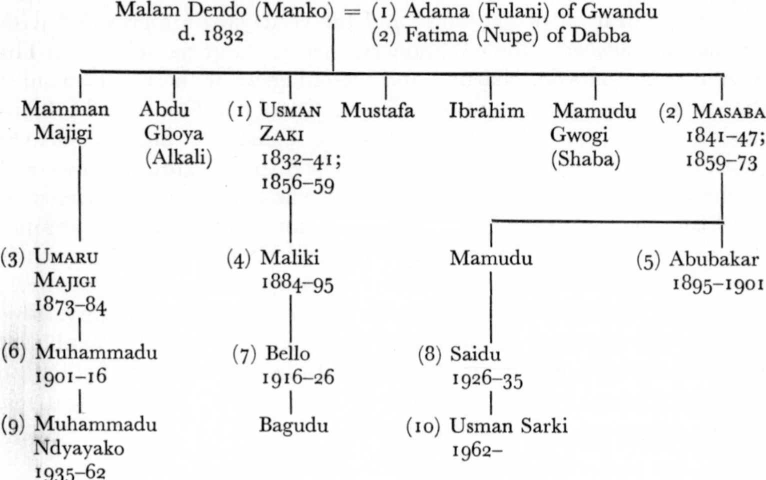

Notes: (1) Between 1847 and 1856 there was civil war between the Fulani rulers and a usurper, Umar Bahaushe, with a consequent interregnum.

XXII. ILORIN

UP TO recently, very little was known for certain of the pre-Fulani history of the Ilorin Yoruba. However, as we write much valuable information is being gathered and examined under the aegis of the Yoruba Research Scheme, so that we may shortly expect something definitive from this historical research. The influential role of the Yoruba on the history of Nigeria has been immense, and though this is today most apparent in the Western Region, it is important to recall that the Ilorin-Kabba axis is predominantly a Yoruba culture-area.

Of the origin of the Yoruba, two explanations are worth quoting.[1] Sultan Bello of Sokoto described them thus:

> The country of Yoruba is extensive and has streams and forests and rocks and hills. There are many curious and beautiful things in it. The ships of Christians come there. The people of Yoruba are descended from the Bani Kan'an and the kindred of Nimrud. Now the reason of their having settled in the west according to what we are told is that Ya'rub ibn Qahtan drove them out of Iraq to westwards and they travelled between Misi and Habash until they reached Yoruba. It happened that they left a portion of their people in every country they passed. It is said that the Sudanese who live up on the hills are all kindred; so also the people of Yauri are their kindred.
>
> The people of Yauri resemble those of Nufe [Nupe] in appearance. In the land of Yoruba are found the birds green in colour which are called 'babgha' in Arabic and which we call 'Aku'. It is a bird which talks and is beautiful.[2]

The Reverend Samuel Johnson, a Yoruba scholar whose work for long remained the standard exposition of the history of the Yoruba, has this to say:

> The origin of the Yoruba nation is involved in obscurity. Like the early history of most nations the commonly received accounts are for

[1] A third, put forward by H. R. Palmer, is that the name derives from Yauri-ba.

[2] Muhammadu Bello, *Infaq al Maisuri*, quoted in T. L. Hodgkin, *Nigerian Perspectives*, p. 58. *Aku* is the Hausa for a parrot.

the most part purely legendary. The people being unlettered, and the language unwritten, all that is known is from traditions carefully handed down.

The National Historians are certain families retained by the King at Oyo whose office is hereditary; they also act as the King's bards, drummers and cymbalists. It is on them we depend as far as possible for any reliable information we now possess; but, as may be expected, their accounts often vary in several important particulars. We can do no more than relate the traditions which have been universally accepted.

The Yorubas are said to have sprung from Lamurudu, one of the kings of Mecca, whose offspring were:—Oduduwa, the ancestor of the Yorubas, the Kings of Gogobiri and of the Kukawa, two tribes in the Hausa country. It is worthy of remark that these two nations, notwithstanding the lapse of time since their separation and in spite of the distance from each other of their respective localities, still have the same distinctive tribal marks on their faces; and Yoruba travellers are free amongst them and vice versa, each recognizing each other as of one blood.[1]

The Ilorin Yoruba claim descent from Oranyan, the great-grandson of Lamurudu. It was his son, Oduduwa, who is supposed to have quarrelled with the authorities at Mecca and in resentment to have migrated westwards with his followers, settling eventually at Ife, the spiritual centre of Yorubaland. The Yoruba are said to have emigrated from Egypt through the Sudan, Bornu and Yauri. Pausing at Bussa in Borgu, they finally settled at Old Oyo. From here their legendary hero Oduduwa moved on to Ife, leaving one of his sons at Oyo. The various places to which Oduduwa's other children scattered from Oyo became the leading Yoruba city-states. Ilorin historians claim that the only families that came from Old Oyo were those of Idiape of the Magaji Are family and of the Baba Isale compound, and Magaji Abdu. Others came to hunt or to trade, or for asylum from the Yoruba wars, and so Ilorin began to grow.[2]

There are two current explanations of the name Ilorin. One is that it means 'the sharpening of iron', *ilo irin*, from the large stone where implements were sharpened; the actual place is identified with the Bandele compound. Another derivation is *ilu erin*, 'town

[1] Samuel Johnson, *History of the Yorubas*, 1921, pp. 3–4.
[2] We are grateful to Ilorin N.A. for this piece of information, among many others.

of the elephant', the founder of the town being said to be a hunter called Ojo Ise Kuse, 'the bad one', who was eventually driven out by a new settler, Eminla by name. In this connexion it is interesting to observe that there is a village just outside Ilorin called Oko Erin, named precisely because an elephant was killed there as recently as the reign of Abdussalami (1831–42).

The emirate of Ilorin is mainly inhabited by Yoruba including the powerful Igbona or Igbomina people who predominate in the area to the south and east of Ilorin town. The Igbona, it appears, were never a very cohesive unit. Of their numerous leaders, one of the most important was the Olupo of Ajasse, who was said to possess an oil with which not only the Oloffa of Offa but even the Alafin himself had to be anointed before the ceremony of installation could be deemed complete. The title derives from *Olu-epo*, 'the lord of the oil'. Small areas in the southern part of the province are inhabited by the Ekiti, and the Igbolo, in the neighbourhood of Offa.

Local tradition has it that one Laderin, who was connected on his mother's side with the Alafin, left Oyo and settled at Ilorin. The famous Afonja, whose praise-name is *'laikya 'loko*, 'the brave warrior in the bush', is said to be his son, or, according to the Oyo account, his great-grandson. Others claim that he was the Are of the Alafin of Oyo. In 1817, after Malam Alimi had left Oyo and settled in Ilorin, the Alafin sent to Afonja to enlist his help in putting a greater distance between Alimi and Oyo. Afonja, who had fled from Oyo because of the Alafin's oppression (this is the Ilorin account), took counsel with Alimi, who reassured him. Afonja decided not to return to Oyo. Instead, his ambitions led him to make common cause with certain Oyo chiefs whose dissatisfaction with the weak and vacillating Alafin Aole (whose father Abiodun is said to have sired 660 children) led to their revolt. Aole's reign is still considered a calamitous one in Yoruba history, for it is sung that

> In Abiodun's reign we weighed money by the bushel,
> In Aole's reign we packed to flee.

The Oyo of those days, commonly known as Katanga, was about half-way between Jebba and Kishi, and as might be expected from its position there was a certain amount of intercourse with the Nupe.

Afonja held the military rank of Are-ona Kakanfo or generalissimo, whereby he was expected once every three years to lead an expedition for the Alafin against any town named by the king and within forty days (some authorities say three months) either to return home victorious or to be carried back a corpse. Having heard of Afonja's intrigues, Aole imposed upon him the apparently impossible campaign of capturing the impregnable town of Iwere, thus hoping to make sure of Afonja's death. Afonja shrewdly explained to the army the impropriety of an attack ordered on a brotherly Yoruba town, and they agreed to ignore the royal command. Aole delivered another message to them: 'Successful or not, let each of you return to his home.' The army took counsel among themselves and sent back an empty covered calabash. The symbolism of this message was known to every Yoruba: it meant 'Send us your head in this'. The Alafin cursed the rebels and their seed for ever, and then committed suicide. The Yoruba historians describe the event thus:

> There being no alternative His Majesty set his house in order; but before he committed suicide, he stepped out into the palace quadrangle with face stern and resolute, carrying in his hands an earthenware dish and three arrows. He shot one to the North, one to the South, and one to the West uttering those ever-memorable imprecations, 'My curse be on ye for your disloyalty and disobedience, so let your children disobey you. If you send them on an errand, let them never return to bring you word again. To all the points I shot my arrows will ye be carried as slaves. My curse will carry you to the sea and beyond the seas, slaves will rule over you, and you their masters will become slaves.'
>
> With this he raised and dashed the earthenware dish on the ground smashing it into pieces, saying *Igba la iso a ki iso awo, beheni ki oro mi o se to! to!!* (a broken calabash can be mended, but not a broken dish; so let my words be—irrevocable!).
>
> He then took poison and died.[1]

To defend himself against the forces sent by the Alafin to bring him back to Oyo, Afonja now invoked the aid of a Fulani *malam* from Sokoto, Alimi by name. He had been sent by Usman dan Fodio to preach in Ilorin, where he had considerable influence with his co-religionists and a great reputation for piety. Afonja also sought the aid of Solagberu, a powerful Yoruba chief who was a Muslim. At Afonja's request Alimi encouraged bands of Hausa

[1] Johnson, op. cit., p. 192.

and Fulani from the north known as *jama'a*,[1] which also included many local Muslim Yoruba, to come to Ilorin, and with their assistance Afonja seems to have declared himself independent. They adopted as their mark of distinction the *kende*, two iron rings worn one on the thumb and the other on the third or fourth finger: they used to greet each other by striking the rings together as a sign of brotherhood. Some historians claim that the Fulani persuaded Afonja to make his new capital of Ilorin on the northern edge of Yoruba land so as to be near to their allies and kinsmen, the Nupe. It is interesting to note that the present Friday Mosque is on the site of Afonja's *tsafi* house.

Afonja, now flushed with success, openly defied the Alafin Maku. The story is a famous one in Ilorin chronicles. The newly enthroned Alafin had sent him a message: 'The new moon has appeared.' To this Afonja insolently replied: 'Let that new moon quickly set.' It was not long, however, before Afonja began to find the presence of the Hausa mercenaries embarrassing. They got out of hand and marched about the countryside pillaging towns and villages. In addition he had the active enmity of the Alafin with which to contend.

Ilorin tradition suggests that Alimi took no active part in these happenings, that he had no personal ambition, and even refused an invitation from Afonja to become a chief. It is said that he exerted himself to restrain the *jama'a*, and that, when they would not listen to him, he went so far as to contemplate returning to Sokoto in disgust. Modern Ilorin historians tell how, when Malam Alimi announced his wish to quit, either to Sokoto or nearer the Nupe for whom he felt a close friendship, Afonja, perceiving that the end of Alimi might in all likelihood spell the end of himself too, dissuaded Alimi and even offered him the throne. Alimi agreed to stay in Ilorin but would not accept the kingship. According to this account, Alimi to the end was only an influential *malam* who exercised no political power and died after living for six years with Afonja and preaching Islam. It should be added that this account does not agree with the Oyo version, according to which Alimi was an ambitious adventurer who conspired to kill Afonja. Needless to say, this interpretation is not accepted in Ilorin.

[1] Cf. Sir Ahmadu Bello, *My Life*, p. 15: 'They say that Alimi, who was in many ways similar to the Shehu, a man of piety and learning, only lent his name and great influence to this force.' *Jama'a* is the Hausa for a group of people.

Afonja unwittingly prepared the way for his own destruction by persuading Alimi to send for his sons. In complying Alimi is said to have made it clear to Afonja that he would find them more ambitious than their father. It may, of course, be that Alimi quietly prepared the ground for his son's accession to power, a phenomenon found in the birth of many of the new Fulani emirates. The two sons, Abdussalami and Shitta, came to Ilorin. Alimi had two other sons: one Abubakar Daudu Saloja, whose ruthlessness later earned him the nickname *Beribepo*, which means 'cut heads, cut posts', and the other Daniyalu, who was born at Ilorin. These two brothers preferred territorial aggrandizement to succession to the throne, and their families have remained the district heads of Malete and Ejidongari. Over 3,000 descendants of Alimi are believed to live today in Ilorin town![1]

In 1831 Shehu Alimi died and the forceable and ambitious Abdussalami, known as *Oba digi aiye*, or 'king, mirror of the world', set about carving out a position for himself. To this end he declared war on the whole of Yorubaland. At that time two men who played an important part in local affairs were Sarkin Gambari and Sarkin Gobir. The former is believed to have established himself at Ilorin some time before the arrival of Alimi, while the latter accompanied the *malam* from the north. They exercised authority over the Hausawa and Gobirawa, large numbers of whom had followed Alimi to Ilorin. The birthplace of Sarkin Gambari[2] is said to have been Zamfara.

When Malam Alimi continued his travels farther south to Ogbomosho and other important Yoruba towns, including Oyo, where he had several audiences of the Alafin, Sarkin Gobir accompanied him, while Sarkin Gambari remained at Ilorin and acquired considerable power. His importance is attested by the fact that he had his own *kakaki* and *tambari*, the state trumpets and drums. On the death of the holder of the title in 1831, Bako the son seems to have gone to Abdussalami to confirm or support him in his office. Abdussalami is said to have deprived him of his *kakaki* and *tambari*, by means of a trick, as a result of which much of his power changed hands. The Sarkin Gambari, however, still ranks next in importance to the Emir, and for long successors traditionally became District Heads of Igponrin.

[1] *Nigerian Citizen*, May 18, 1963, p. 2, 'Focus on Ilorin'.
[2] Gambari is the Yoruba word for the Hausa people.

In the meantime Afonja, resolved to make a supreme effort to get rid of the troublesome *jama'a*, invited the Onikoyi and other powerful chiefs to assist him; but his overweening conduct had alienated the sympathies of many, and he over-estimated his power to achieve his object. A leading Yoruba historian has described Afonja's downfall.

> Afonja perceived his error when it was too late. Haughty and passionate, his very egotism was the cause of his fall. Fortune had carried him to such a high pitch of glory, he thought his fall was impossible; besides, he had unlimited confidence in his Jamas, and was not aware of their growing disaffection and disloyalty towards himself. He thought he could put them down whenever he liked, and was sometimes very severe with any act of insubordination, openly threatening them with suppression and annihilation. This threat only served to increase their disaffection. Too late, he saw what Fagbohun had warned him against. He failed completely to check their ambition, rapine and lawlessness. His threats and warnings were not heeded. Long impunity had increased their boldness.[1]

After some fierce fighting, in which Solagberu, as a Kanuri, stood aside, Afonja was killed. In Ilorin legend has it that so great was the number of arrows piercing him that he died in a sitting posture, the body being supported by the shafts of the innumerable arrows showered on him. His corpse was publicly burnt in the market-place. To this latter fact has been attributed the refusal of the families of Baba-Isale and Magaji Are—the latter of whom is a direct descendant of Afonja—to use ashes in the preparation of food.

Some say that Abdussalami immediately declared himself Emir of Ilorin. Others maintain that at first he adopted a conciliatory attitude towards the Yoruba, siding first with one chief and then with another, sowing discord among them until Hausa and Fulani reinforcements arrived from the north. Only then was Ilorin declared a Fulani emirate. But, as Alimi had died in the meantime, his son Abdussalami became the first Emir of Ilorin, in 1831.

Abdussalami, and Afonja before him, had to withstand several expeditions, sent by the Alafin against Ilorin. In one of the earlier of these, known as the Mugba-Mugba war, Oyo was helped by Raba (Nupe), but the Yoruba had not yet learnt how to cope with the Fulani cavalry. Owing to constant warfare there were no crops, and both armies were obliged to live on the fruit of the

[1] Johnson, op. cit., p. 198.

locust tree, *igba*: hence the name of the war, *mugba-mugba* meaning drink preparations made from the fruit of the locust-bean tree. In another expedition, known as the Kanla war, the Alafin's forces were routed, as a result of treachery on the part of the Edun of Gbogun. Yet another campaign resulted in the battle of Ogelle and the destruction by the Fulani of many towns in Ibolo country. Ilorin also had to withstand an attack by a Nupe army, an indecisive battle being fought near Sobi. The Fulani had championed the cause of Idrisu, a claimant to the title of Etsu Nupe, and it was his rival who led an army to Ilorin.

Solagberu, who lived at Oke Suna just outside the city, had become a thorn in the side of Abdussalami. Matters now came to a head. After much fighting Solagberu was captured and put to death, an event seen locally as nemesis for his defection from Afonja. There is a compound in Ilorin known by his name where Solagberu is believed to have been kept captive for a time. It is said that Abdussalami went out to meet the file of prisoners being brought in, and the place where they were executed, on the present Oyo road, is still called *itaosifila* or 'the street where caps were doffed'.

Abdussalami was now supreme at Ilorin and daily growing more powerful. His name soon became known far and wide in Yorubaland. Among the powerful towns which he conquered were Gboun, Edun, and Ikoyi. An Oyo account speaks of him as having 'subdued all Yoruba proper'. The 36th Alafin of Oyo, Oluewu, was peremptorily summoned to Ilorin, and though treated with the respect due to a powerful king, he keenly felt the humiliation of having to prostrate and, it is said, embrace Islam. A little later he was again bidden to come, but this time he plucked up courage and declined the invitation, with the result that the Fulani went forth and ravaged his country.

Thirsting for revenge, the Alafin now sent round to all the Yoruba chiefs an urgent request to join him in a supreme effort to throw off the Fulani yoke. To this end he also invoked the aid of the Bariba (Borgawa) who had no love for the Fulani. The Bariba leader is variously given as Eleduwe Sarkin Borgu, or Worukura Sarkin Nikki; at Ilorin he is known as *Ikoko*, 'the hyaena'. The Emir of Ilorin, alarmed at the gathering storm, appealed to Gwandu for help, and in 1837 Halilu sent a combined Sokoto-Gwandu force to the succour of Ilorin.

At first the Oyo-Borgu army met with considerable success, but later, in a fierce battle which was waged within the walls of Ilorin city, it was defeated and routed. Eleduwe was slain near a silk-cotton tree not far from Pakata market. The Borgawa attributed the defeat to the cowardice of the Yoruba and alleged that two powerful Yoruba chiefs were in secret alliance with the Fulani. It is only fair to add that the Yoruba were no less scathing in their opinion of the Bariba, whom they depicted as an undisciplined horde intent solely on plunder. Worukura and the Alafin Oluewu were killed, as well as Sarkin Kaiama, Sarkin Wawa, and many minor chiefs. There is a local story that the Ilorin people cunningly pushed forward a naked woman in the forefront of the army, carrying a calabash of charms and shouting, 'Let none look on my person!' The enemy collapsed in confusion.

This Ilorin war proved an unparalleled disaster to Nikki and Kaiama, from which they did not recover for years. The Sarkin Bussa supplied a large force but did not himself accompany it. In the course of the fighting Shitta, the future Emir of Ilorin, was wounded in the thigh, but is said to have been miraculously cured by Abdussalami himself. 'Ikoko' is said to have been buried in the compound of Sarkin Karuma.

Jimba, the Emir's chief slave, pursued the routed army, sacked Oyo, and carried away various insignia of office, including the *egun* dress and one hundred brass pots from the Alafin's palace. These were melted down for ammunition. The capital was deserted and the Fulani pursued the fugitive Oyo forces as far south as Abeokuta. After an interregnum a new Alafin set up his government far away to the south at Ago, which became the new Oyo. One Atiba, the son of the Alafin, was brought to Ilorin as a captive during this war between Ilorin and Old Oyo. The Emir of Ilorin treated him kindly and later allowed him to go and set up a new kingdom of his own. Atiba, who was then living in Otefan Compound in Ilorin town, was accompanied by Magaji Okeogun to his mother's village, called Ago, at the instructions of the Emir. There he was embraced by the people and he set up the place as New Oyo. It was first called Ago-do-yo.

Throughout the long struggle between Oyo-Ibadan and the Fulani of Ilorin the former were always handicapped by internal dissension and petty jealousies. This schism the Fulani were not slow to exploit. Disaffected Yoruba chiefs often betrayed the plan of campaign or else deserted at critical moments. For instance, on one occasion certain Oyo chiefs sent to the Emir a symbolic message of soap, flesh-brush, and the camwood used for preparing a bride for the wedding night. The significance of this message, 'we are bringing the bride [in this case the Alafin] to her husband', was not lost on Ilorin. This astute policy of fostering and taking advantage of dissension in the ranks of opponents was also followed in dealing with the Nupe.

Strange to say, there is considerable uncertainty as to whether Alimi or his son Abdussalami received the flag from Gwandu. Sokoto records say it was Abdul Alimi, but local traditions (and the late Emir Abdulkadiri) maintain that Abdussalami was the recipient after his father's death. Ilorin historians today smooth this out by noting that Malam Alimi was the flag bearer from Shehu Usman dan Fodio as the missionary, while Abdussalami was the flag bearer from Sokoto as the first Emir of Ilorin. Abdussalami created four war lords who bore the title of Balogun. These were Gambari (Hausa), who is said to have come from Katsina; Fulani, whose family had been settled in Yoruba country, at Iresa, for some time; Ajikobi, who had previously lived at Isehin; and Alanamu, who came from Reke and Kuwo. For the three first mentioned the Emir secured flags, while Alanamu was given his later by Shitta.

Shortly after his return from the Pole war against the people of Ijesa—so called in Yoruba history from the cries of the Fulani horsemen in pursuit of the infantry, *pole! pole!*, 'cut him down!'—the Emir Abdussalami fell sick. He died in 1842 and was succeeded by his brother Shitta.

Up to this time the Fulani had been all-victorious, and it looked as if the reputed boast that they would dip the Koran in the sea would be realized on the west rather than in the east where Adama of Yola had already penetrated far south. But in 1843 their army under Balogun Ali suffered a disastrous defeat at Oshogbo, which was being besieged for the third time. Oshogbo sent to Ibadan for help. We have a magnificent account of this great event in Ilorin history:

> When the Ibadan army arrived at the seat of war and saw the situation they had some misgivings as to the probability of success without the aid of Elepo their champion. They could not show their face in the

open field for fear of the Ilorin horse, and for about 20 days after their arrival at Osogbo, they also could not fight outside the town thickets.

Still they were afraid to attack the Ilorins during the morning hours, Osogbo being practically in a plain, the Ilorin horse might have the advantage of them with disastrous results: from prudence therefore they resolved to make the attack in the afternoon, as they might be able to hold on until dusk when the Ilorins would no longer be able to use their horses to advantage, or if defeated, the shades of night would assist them in their retreat.

About 2 p.m. the standard of the Ibadan army left the gate of Osogbo for the battlefield. Again, another council of war was held and it was finally resolved that they should not proceed until dark, as it was necessary that their movements be as private as possible. About sunset they were again on the move and the vanguards were instructed to keep a strict watch and arrest anyone suspected as a spy on their movements.

About a mile from the Ilorin camp they halted and arranged the order of the attack. The Osogbo army and the earlier auxiliaries were to maintain the centre of the battle, Chiefs Abitiko and Lajubu to command the right wing, Balogun Oderinlo with the rest of the Ibadan war-chiefs to form the left wing of the army. About midnight the Ilorin camp was attacked on all sides. The watchword was *Elo ni owo odo?*, 'The fare of the ferry?' (The river Osun had to be crossed in entering Osogbo from the south. Any one who could not tell was known to be an enemy.) The first camp attacked was that of the Elese, and as soon as they rushed in, they set it on fire. The Elese himself was shot dead as soon as he showed his face at the tent door. A panic seized the whole Ilorin army thus startled from their beds; they could not offer the slightest resistance, they simply melted away! Those who fell by the hands of their own friends to make way for their hasty flight were probably more than those who fell by the hands of their enemies. Several who summed up courage enough to saddle their horses had not the presence of mind to loose them and were caught in the stables digging spurs into the poor beasts and wondering why they would not go, forgetting that they were still tethered by the feet.

But Ali the commander-in-chief was calm and resolute; he ordered his horse to be saddled, and gathering around him a goodly portion of his cavalry they dashed through the ranks of the Ibadan army: these quickly making a way for them to gallop through without daring to oppose them, especially as numbers of the men were scattered about on plundering bent.

The principal Ilorin war-chiefs captured in this defeat were:—

1. Jimba the head slave of the Emir of Ilorin;
2. One of the sons of Ali the commander-in-chief;

3. Chief Lateju; and
4. Ajikobi the Yoruba Balogun of Ilorin.

The first two were released and sent home privately by the Ibadan war-chiefs, a form of chivalrous etiquette among the war-chiefs. The latter two being Yorubas by birth were regarded rather as traitors to their country, and were sent home to Ibadan as distinguished captives of war.

Ajikobi being a more distinguished personage was sent to the Alafin of Oyo for capital punishment.

The messengers with the illustrious captive met the King engaged in one of his annual festivals, and he ordered that the *feu de joie* his servants were then firing should be directed on Ajikobi. This was accordingly done, and he was roasted to death with gunpowder.

Besides a large number of captives the Ibadans captured numbers of horses but very few of them were brought home. These hardy people cared very much more for the horses' tails upon which to tie amulets as preventives against bullets in war. These were always a part of their war kits. The only attention bestowed on the hundreds of tailless horses now roaming about the field was for replenishing their larder as occasion required![1]

Following this decisive victory over the Fulani at Oshogbo, Ibadan rose to power and overshadowed Oyo—so much so, indeed, that the Alafin seems to have been uneasy and jealous of this upstart rival. Hence, when some years later the Ibadan army was helping Offa, far from being anxious to promote peace, he was content that Ilorin should keep it busily engaged away from home. He seems to have had secret communication with Ilorin about this time behind the back of the Ibadan chiefs. Once or twice we find Ibadan in alliance with Ilorin. For instance there was a combined expedition against the unfortunate Igbirra and Akoko peoples—always fair game for Yoruba, Nupe, or Fulani—but it was not long before the ill-assorted allies fell out again. It is significant that in these joint expeditions Ibadan, not Ilorin, seems to have taken the lead.

Halilu, Emir of Gwandu, summoned Shitta to a conference at Raba, and afterward visited Ilorin in person. Shitta seems to have interested himself in the never-ending struggles between rival factions of the Nupe, and between Nupe and Fulani on the Niger. He was several times appealed to by one or the other party. The

[1] Johnson, op. cit., pp. 286–8.

stormy petrel of Nupe history, Etsu Masaba, was taken captive by one of Shitta's Baloguns, Usmanu, and detained at Ilorin.

Shitta died in 1860, and was succeeded by Zubeiru, son of Abdussalami, a zealous Muslim who at once burnt the *tsafi* house and swore to put to death all pagans. The people said of him *o gbona bi eleko idaji*, 'he was hot like a dish of steaming gruel'. Constant warfare is said to have been waged against Ilorin during this reign and Awtun became tributary to Ilorin. It had been brought under Ilorin in Shitta's reign and given to Jimba who became its *baba kekere*,[1] but a little later Ibadan ousted the Fulani. Ekiti country was always a bone of contention between Ilorin and Ibadan.

Zubeiru died in 1868, and was succeeded by Aliyu, son of Shitta. During Aliyu's reign the Jalumi war of 1878 occurred, in the course of which Ikirun, aided by Ibadan, routed the Ilorin army under Ajia which had gone to the help of the Ekiti. The Offa contingent is often blamed for the Ilorin disaster at the river Otin, having cut the bridge in the rear of the Ilorin army. Thousands perished in their headlong flight into the river with the Ibadan army at their heels, and local legend has it that the Otin became so choked with bodies at this point that some fugitives were later able to escape by crossing on a raft of corpses. Hence the name, *ogun jalumi*, 'the rush-into-the-river war'.

According to the Offa account, the Oloffa was invited by the Fulani to join in the expedition. This he would not do at first, disapproving of an attack on Ikirun, but eventually he agreed to send a detachment. Ilorin blamed Offa for the defeat, alleging that their support had been half-hearted. So it came about that an expedition against Offa was organized under the leadership of Karara, the Hausa Balogun of Ilorin.

The Emir of Ilorin was lukewarm over the expedition, fearing the anger of the Alafin, who had several illustrious Ilorin prisoners in his hands and at his mercy, but he seems to have been overruled by his chiefs. The war with Offa, often wrongly called a siege, dragged on for ten, some say thirteen, years. In the early stages the Ilorin army was encamped at Ojuko some ten miles distant. Then they moved nearer to Idiagowo and eventually to Iyanago. A huge silk-cotton tree planted by him still marks the site of Karara's camp. In the later stages the Fulani more or less

[1] *Baba kekere* is the Yoruba equivalent of the Hausa *kofa*, 'intermediary'.

effectively cut off the supplies of foodstuffs which Offa had been growing to the south of the town, and the population was reduced to dire straits. Karara, with his legendary monstrous face and hirsute eyebrows, inspired terror in both sides.

Several efforts were made to compose the difference between Ibadan and Ilorin. In 1886 an emissary from Gwandu visited Karara in his camp. Later Sir Gilbert Carter, Governor of Lagos, and Captain Bower visited Karara, and went on to Ilorin to have an interview with the Emir. The latter seems to have been sympathetic; but Karara, who was on bad terms with the Emir and doubtless feared the reception he would get at home if he did not return victorious, was resolved to continue the Offa war. He treated the various envoys sent to him with scant respect, and demanded as a condition of peace that Ibadan should not only retire forthwith from Offa, but also hand over all Ekiti country. The Ibadans tell many stories of Karara's haughty bearing and unconciliatory conduct, and of his final bloody occupation of Offa in 1891:

Next morning when it was known all over the city that the Ibadans had gone and the Olofa with them those hitherto in favour of the Ilorins put leaves on their heads, and went dancing to the Ilorin camp and singing:

'No more are we for the Ibadans,
With the long-bearded our lot we've cast.'

Thus they came and prostrated before Karara. It was said that he asked them, 'Have the Ibadans gone?'—'Yes, they have gone.' He then added, 'Very well, you can go home, I will pay you a visit shortly.'

After breakfast Karara rode up to Offa with his army, and took his seat at the palace gates. His first act was to despatch a body of horsemen to occupy each of the gates of the city so as to allow no exit from any. He next summoned him all the remaining Offa chiefs and the influential men of the city to be brought before him; they came with leaves on their heads as a token of submission. He then said to them, 'You now say you are all on my side, if that be so, why is it you held out so long against me, and did not open your gates secretly for my troops to enter? You know now that the Ibadans have gone then you say you declare yourselves for me.' And when they lay prostrate before him he coolly gave the order, *E maha dumbu won*, 'Slaughter them away'. Thereupon followed the process; a man appeared with a butcher's knife in hand, and another with a basin of water. Seizing these prostrate forms one by one, they were forcibly held down, with head and neck raised and the throat coolly cut, and the blood thoroughly drained and the corpse thrown down. This done, the knife was washed in the basin of water—after the manner of slaughtering animals, and then they proceeded to the second, and third, and so on till they had slaughtered the whole of them! Then he ordered the shade trees of the market place to be cut down as a sign of victory, and the city to be sacked, the inhabitants (such as were left) to be made prisoners. Thus Offa was taken.[1]

With Offa captured and the town deserted, the Oloffa and survivors fled south to Ido Osun, where they built a new town. In 1902 the Emir invited the Oloffa Adigboye to return and Offa was rebuilt. Karara died in camp, but his body was brought back and buried in Ilorin.

For some time the Fulani had no longer been having things all their own way, for their advantage of employing cavalry was now more than counterbalanced by the fact that the Yoruba of the south had learnt to use guns and powder. The Ibadans and the Egbe fell out over alleged traffic in fire-arms with Ilorin, which shows that the Fulani quickly became alive to the necessity of putting themselves on level terms with their more up-to-date opponents.

A visitor to Ilorin in 1890 has left this account in his diary of his interview with the Emir:

Outside our house was an open space, on the far side of which stood the long high wall of the palace, entered by a single and solid-looking gateway. Thither, at 8 A.M., dressed in full military uniform, we repaired. At the gate the chief executioner received us, and, leading the way to a shady spot in the outer courtyard, begged us to wait a little while with patience, as all the important persons of the country had been summoned to meet us, and many were still absent. We were treated with the greatest courtesy by the royal attendants, who formed a cordon round us, to keep back the crowd, and frequently assured us that we should not have long to wait. In an hour or so the head messenger arrived, and told us that all was ready, and that the Emir awaited us; so, following him, we entered the inner courtyard, where, ranged round the wall, stand the dwellings of the royal household, having the appearance of a huge oriental caravanserai. The Emir's private apart-

[1] Johnson, op. cit., pp. 565–6. I am also grateful to my students, Sunday and Akinola Ogundele, for information on Offa history when I stayed with them there in 1962.—A.K-G.

ments face the entrance, and, in front of them, we found that a large opensided mat-shed had been put up, to shelter the assembly of chiefs from sun and rain. As we passed up the centre of the shed, to the verandah of the Emir's house, a murmur ran through the vast gathering of chieftains, who were seated in orderly rows on the ground for some distance around.

The Emir, Alihu, received us sitting in a low doorway, and, shaking us warmly by the hands, motioned us to a seat on some mats opposite him. The customary salutations were of a more lengthy nature than usual, and, though possessed of little variety, took considerable time to get through. The Emir is a stout and pleasant-looking man of about forty-five years of age, his features being of the true negro type, and having none of the refinement of the Fula.[1]

In 1891 Aliyu died and was succeeded by Moma, who at the time was absent with the Ilorin armies in the field. He is said to have returned to Ilorin with an escort of twenty thousand foot and twenty thousand horses.

Moma, being the son of a Yoruba woman from Isehin, adopted a much more conciliatory attitude towards Oyo than did his predecessors. On his accession he exchanged valuable presents with the Alafin. So, too, he welcomed the Governor of Lagos on the occasion of his visit, and terms of peace between the Ilorin and Ibadan Yoruba were arranged. Unfortunately there were many prominent men in Ilorin who did not take such an enlightened view of the situation and trouble was destined soon to break out again.

The Balogun Alanamu was a man of great ability and had acquired unlimited power among the Ilorin people. He joined forces with the Balogun Gambari, the next senior chief, and soon tore away the remaining power from Moma, who became a mere figure-head. These two Baloguns ran riot over the country, seizing and selling slaves and acting in a most outrageous fashion. Their rapacity is still recounted in Ilorin. Rarely a day passed, it is said, but a person was impaled or otherwise tortured outside one or the other's compound, and murder was committed with impunity by their followers.

In 1895 Alanamu intrigued with Alege, a brother of Moma, for Moma's removal. Alege leaped at the idea, and very soon had broached the proposal to the other chiefs, who were only too will-

[1] A. Mockler-Ferryman, *Up the Niger*, 1898, p. 188.

ing to follow any course which Alanamu proposed. The Emir was besieged in his palace, nearly the whole town joining against him. For almost a week he succeeded in defending himself, but eventually, seeing the hopelessness of further resistance, he blew himself up with his chief slave. Alege then put forward his claim to the emirate, but Alanamu expressed his horror and disgust at such an idea, telling the following parable, which has become famous in Ilorin:

> A man desired a woman as his wife; she agreed on the condition that he brought his mother's heart as a gift to her. He did so; and then the woman said, 'You are not fit to live, let alone marry.'

Applying this to Alege, Alanamu asked how, with his hands red with the blood of his brother, he could expect to reign over the people. Alege was dumbfounded, returned to his house, and never again crossed the threshold, dying in 1913.

Alanamu, recognizing the fact that Suleimanu, the son of the fourth Emir Aliyu, was without influence or authority, decided to have him made Emir so that his own power might increase in inverse ratio. Suleimanu was therefore made Emir in 1896. Alanamu became more arrogant than ever, and virtually ruled Ilorin.

Some little time earlier the Governor of Lagos, in order to prevent the Ilorin people continuing their raids to the south, had stationed a post of the Lagos Constabulary at Ode Otin, and in 1894 a boundary was fixed by Captain Bower, representing Lagos, and Captain Lugard, who represented the Niger Company. In 1896 the Ilorin *Ajele* were driven out of Awtun, Ishan, Ikole, and Aiyede.

The result naturally was that these places ceased to pay tribute to or obey Ilorin. The Emir, or rather perhaps Alanamu, decided to send an army under the four Baloguns to retrieve the fortunes of Ilorin. Fighting continued for some time without any apparent result. Early in 1897 Captain Bower sent twelve men and one gun to assist the Ode. The next day the two armies joined battle. The Constabulary set up their gun on a small hill outside Erimopwe near the road, and killed a large number of Ilorins. Adamu, Balogun Gambari, was shot while standing on the spot where the Iloffa Rest-House formerly stood. The Ilorins fled, leaving horses and booty behind, but burying Adamu on a hill near by.

In 1895, in order to protect the neighbouring tribes from Nupe raiders, a post had been placed at Kabba by the Royal Niger Company, who were also not without fear of being attacked at Lokoja. The Nupe at Bida had been for many years growing more and more powerful. Between 1860 and 1870 the Nupe Fulani under the Emir Masaba had overrun nearly all that country now called the Kabba Division. The Aworo, Kakanda, Yagba, Bunu, Igbirra, and Akoko were all attacked in turn. The last named formed one of those unhappy districts alternately raided by Nupe, Ibadan, and Ilorin. In many of these raids the Igbona chiefs joined.

By 1897 the position of the Royal Niger Company at Lokoja was precarious, and to ensure their safety and that of the neighbouring non-Muslim peoples an expedition was decided upon against Bida and Ilorin. Bida was first occupied, then Ilorin, the troops crossing the River Niger at Jebba on their way from Bida to Ilorin. The Ilorin army hurried back from Erimopwe to defend their city. A short fight took place at Ilorin. The palace was bombarded, the Emir and his Baloguns fled, and the Fulani quarter of Ilorin city was fired on 15 February 1897. Messages, however, were sent out recalling the Emir and Baloguns, and a treaty was signed by which the Emir became a vassal of the Company. This treaty is not so well known as some of the other Royal Niger Company ones and is therefore reproduced here:

This Treaty is made on the 18th February 1897 of the Christian Era, and the 15th day of Ramadan, in the year 1314 since the Hegira. The Treaty is between Sir George Goldie, Governor for the Royal Niger Company, and the Emir Suliman, son of the former Emir Alihiu, for his chiefs and people for ever.

1. The Company will recognize Suliman as Emir of Ilorin.
2. The Emir Suliman recognizes that Ilorin is entirely under the protection and power of the Company.
3. He will obey all such directions in respect of his Government as the Company may give him from time to time.
4. The Emir Suliman agrees to make no war without the consent of the Company, and to accept such frontier line between Ilorin and Lagos as the Company may decide.
5. The Emir Suliman agrees to take every step in his power to prevent the further introduction of gin and rum into his country from Lagos, and to destroy all the gin and rum that may be found in his country.
6. All previous Treaties are abrogated, but Ilorin remains under

the protection of Her Majesty, the Queen of Great Britain and Ireland, and Empress of India.

7. I, Suliman, Emir of Ilorin, hereby accept this Treaty, and I, George Taubman Goldie, Governor of the Royal Niger Company, also hereby accept it.

(Signed) SULIMAN (in Arabic)
" GEORGE TAUBMAN GOLDIE.

The town walls were destroyed and a fort built near the Oshogbo gate. In 1898, when Ilorin was held by a detachment of the West African Frontier Force under Captain Somerset, as a result of the broken power of Ilorin all the Ekiti revolted, and at the instigation of the Resident of Ibadan the Ekiti Council was formed with the Ore of Awtun as President.

When the first Resident of Ilorin, the Honourable D. W. Carnegie, soon to be killed by the Tawari in Koton Karfi, was appointed in 1900, a woeful condition of affairs existed. The Emir Suleimanu was a mere puppet in the hands of the Baloguns, especially Alanamu, who was the actual ruler and bitterly hostile to the new Government. He opposed it in every way, warning the people that the stay of the white man would be short, and that on their departure summary vengeance would be meted out to any who dared disobey him. Contemporary reports complain that crime was rampant in the city; gangs of robbers entered houses in daylight, took what they wanted, and did not hesitate to commit murder. No road was safe for man, woman, or child; no caravan was allowed to pass down to Lagos, neither were traders from the Lagos hinterland allowed to enter Ilorin. The larger towns had thrown off their allegiance after Ilorin had been broken by the Company, and the more important chiefs started to raid the smaller ones. Eventually an escort of soldiers from Jebba had to be called in. This changed the aspect of affairs. In a very short time most of the towns except those along the Lagos boundary had returned to their allegiance. The Emir, finding himself backed up by the Resident, broke away from the constraining hand of Alanamu and other chiefs, and began to act up to his position in a way which showed that he realized how the tide had changed. No longer was he depicted as 'a figure-head shaking in his shoes with dread of a sudden death', but as an Emir, supported by the Government, who insisted on the payment of tribute.

Alanamu's time had come. At an enormous meeting outside the

Emir's palace he was judged to be unfit to hold his position, was publicly deposed and stripped of his estates. He left Ilorin for Ogomosho, where he lived till his death in 1910. It is worthy of notice that this man, who had ruled Ilorin for nearly twenty-five years, should have been deposed and disgraced without a single riot or the use of troops.

During the Sokoto-Kano expedition in 1903 a messenger arrived from Sokoto suggesting that Ilorin should create a diversion in order to help them. But the Emir would not listen to the suggestion, and the messenger was driven from the town. Ilorin historians today point out that in so doing the Emir was honouring the peace treaty that had been made with Bida and with Ilorin by the Royal Niger Company. They add that the Emir warned Sokoto to eschew an actual war against the British, as his own experience in 1897 had been a bitter one.

During 1903 the re-enforcement of the tribute was undertaken. Since 1897 practically none had been paid, but little difficulty was found in the collection except on the Lagos boundary. One-fourth of all tribute was paid into general revenue, the balance going to the Native Administration.

The new Native Administration made steady progress until, in 1907, peace was suddenly threatened. Balogun Ajikobi, Magajin Gari, and Ajaji Ogidilolu, the last representatives of the old raiders, held very great power, their followers outnumbering those of the Emir and the other three Baloguns. By passive resistance these three men had always constituted a stumbling-block to progress, viewing with intense dislike the attempts of the Emir to assert his authority. The efforts to win over these malcontents as loyal supporters of the Emir resulted only in the prevention of open acts of hostility. At the end of 1906 and the beginning of 1907 frequent murders were reported at Oluguganga and Bode Sadu, over twenty men and women being shot down in broad daylight by hunters at the instigation of these three men. The Emir's and the Government messengers were openly flouted and threatened. The hunters, some six hundred in number, collected in Ilorin city. The whole town was in an uproar. The three ringleaders urged the hunters to attack the Residency. With the hurried arrival of military reinforcements, order was restored. The ringleaders were sentenced to deportation and many of the hunters were tried for murder.

More rioting occurred in 1913 owing to the levying of a new form of tax. A certain *malam* in the Malle quarter, Liman Omali dan Sarkin Liman Zarumi, who was suspected of being at the bottom of the whole trouble, was arrested by police in his bed and abducted in the middle of the night by means of a ruse. The anti-Fulani element, egged on by Biala, ex-Balogun Ajikobi, seized the opportunity to further their cause, but the arrival of troops soon quelled the disturbances. As a result of an inquiry into this trouble, Government decided that the house of Afonja, represented by Magaji Are and Baba Isale, should always form part of the Emir's Council. But this was not the end of the story.

Baba Isale was leader in 1936 of a revolt in which all the Councillors declared against the Emir, complaining that he had ceased to rule through them and was conducting the affairs of the Emirate with the help of his favourite servants. Baba Isale was brought to heel with the threat of exile and when he died in 1947 the Emir allowed the title to lapse. It was not until 1955 that a new Baba Isale was appointed. The post now carried with it the duties of Ward Head of the Sabon Gari. He was no longer a Councillor.

In carrying through the saga of Baba Isale, we have overshot chronology. Once Ilorin's dynastic troubles had been smoothed over, administration settled down to its normal course. Emir Suleimanu died in 1915 and was succeeded by Shuaibu. On his death in 1919 the succession was broken and the *sarauta*, instead of passing back to Suleimanu's house, went to the Abdul Salami dynasty.

The Lagos railway extension reached Ilorin in 1908, and in 1916 the Niger ferry at Jebba was replaced by the double bridge. So rapidly did Ilorin's economy expand that it soon earned the sobriquet of 'the market garden of Nigeria'. Ilorin Province first comprised Ilorin, Offa and Pategi, to which Lokoja and Kabba Division were added in 1913 and Borgu Division in 1923. An important event, given the history of Ilorin, took place in 1928 when the Oyo-Ilorin *entente* was reconstituted by Ilorin's warm welcome given to the Aremo, the heir-apparent of the Alafin of Oyo.

In the southern districts of Ilorin the replacement of absentee fief-holders by resident District Headmen responsible to the emir did not conform with the local culture, and in the 1930s experiments were made with the revival of the pre-Fulani indigenous system of local administration. The village Council, *ilu*, was a feature of the Igbona and Ekiti areas, where councillors were usually hereditary appointments restricted to certain families. In 1936 the Ekiti of Awtun were allowed, after years of agitation, to rejoin their kin in Ondo Province, on the grounds that by 1900 they had achieved complete independence of Ilorin and that their Ore of Awtun had been recognized by the Governor of Lagos as the head of the Ekiti confederacy.[1]

To consolidate his pride in his Fulani ancestors, the Emir Abdul Kadiri made a tour, in his own car, of the northern emirates in 1935 and was received by the Sultan of Sokoto and the Emir of Gwandu. Shortly after his return he approved a successful reorganization of his Council, with the appointment of two literate members, 'a leaven of progress', as an official report expressed it, 'welcomed by the older councillors as products of modern education who still recognize the deference due to age'.

In the years between 1936 and 1957 the Emir's Council underwent a series of revisions which culminated in there being appointed a large Council, wholly elected from District Councils with the exception of the six leading title holders in Ilorin town who had formed the traditional Emir's Council. This experiment in democracy proved to be too advanced, and it was necessary for Government to dissolve it in 1958. It was replaced by a nominated Council of twenty members which included the six traditional members, senior Native Administration officials, representative Chiefs from the Igbomina, Igbona and Ekiti areas and one or two private persons. This may be looked on as a continuing process that began in 1913 when public opinion successfully demanded the broadening of the Emir's Council by the admission to it of two representatives of the indigenous Yoruba of Old Oyo. In 1937 there died the influential Balogun Gambari Saibu. He traced his descent back to a Malam Dose of Katsina who had been a supporter of Alimi against the Alafin of Oyo, and had been the Balogun of the Hausa quarter of Ilorin since 1900.

Boundary questions with the Western Provinces held up Ilorin's progress in the early 1950s, until the Governor firmly announced in 1952 that there would be no change. A visit to the United Kingdom encouraged the Emir to handle firmly what was

[1] See unpublished manuscript *The People Called Igbomina* (*Igbona*), Paul O. A. Dada, being a paper delivered at Omu-Aran in 1963.

officially described as 'the reactionary opposition of the traditional Baloguns of Ilorin town'. Ilorin now adopted a novel conciliar system with no less than forty-nine members in a full council meeting every six months and a quorum committee of three meeting fortnightly. At the district and village level plans were made in 1954 to reconcile the traditional *ilu* authorities with a majority of elected members in a vigorous conciliar organization which would be fully representative and have statutory powers.[1]

The years 1956–58 saw considerable political tension in Ilorin, by no means divorced from its historical antecedents dealt with so fully in previous pages, and also in Offa. When progress was held up because of local political quarrels, the Government eventually had to issue a stern warning that 'unless the N.A. removes political profiteering from its actions concerning all staff matters and acts in its public duties there will be no alternative but to dissolve the Council'. In July the N.A. Council was replaced by a Caretaker Council which was not cancelled until 1961 when the new N.A. Council was constituted, consisting of thirty-two elected, six traditional, seven nominated and two personal members. Summarizing Ilorin political life, a noted Yoruba scholar has recently written:

> The present-day political structure of Ilorin is a curious blend of Fulani & Yoruba concepts of government. The first Emirs created four Baloguns or war leaders: Fulani, representing the Fulani element in the town; Gambari, representing the Hausa; Alanamu and Ajikobi, representing the Yoruba. Each title is hereditary in the lineage founded by the original holder. Each Balogun is in charge of that quarter of the town peopled predominantly by the tribal groups which he represents. These men are among the most senior chiefs of the town and have in the past exercised tremendous power, often controlling the Emir as their puppet. As in other Yoruba kingdoms, the close relations of the Emirs hold no high political office and cannot effectively support the Emir against his Baloguns. This may, perhaps, account for the great zeal with which Islam is propagated in Ilorin, for the Emir's rule depends not on the physical force which he can command, nor on the myth that his ancestors founded the town, but on his role as the defender of the Islamic faith.[2]

[1] *Annual Report for Ilorin Province*, 1955. Paras 11–13 are very useful for an understanding of the peculiar problems of local administration in Ilorin emirate.

[2] P. C. Lloyd, 'Ilorin', *Nigeria Magazine*, No. 70, 1962. Dr Lloyd is an authority on the Yoruba culture in the Western Region, and his *Yoruba Land Law* is now a standard work.

The Emir Abdul Kadiri died in June 1959, after forty years on the throne. (Another historical death, on a lesser plane, was that of Alhaji Sanusu Alalupupu, the first man in Ilorin Province to ride a motor-cycle.) Following the 1915 precedent in discarding the hitherto usual line of succession, another member of the Abdussalami house was selected as the 9th Emir of Ilorin. The new Emir, Sulu Gambari, was installed at one of the most splendid ceremonies ever witnessed in Ilorin.

THE EMIRS OF ILORIN

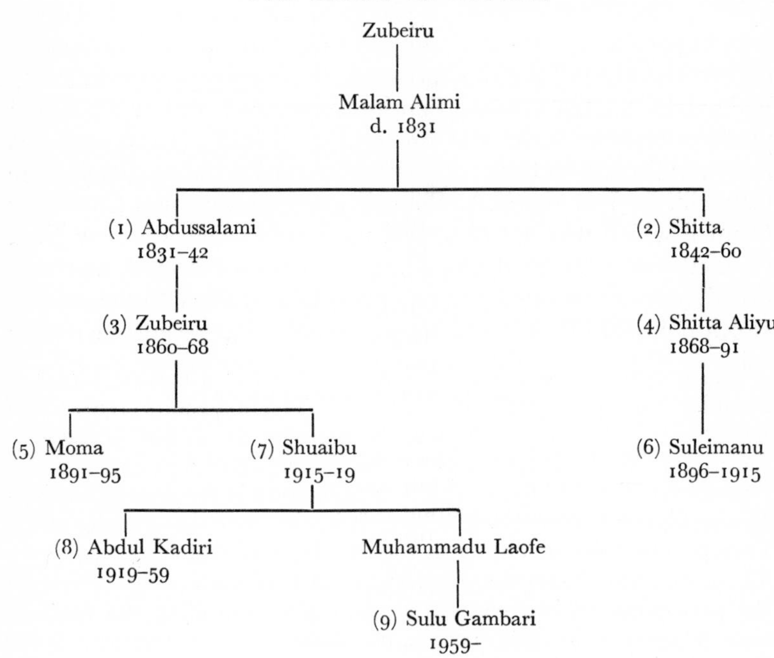

2. EMIRATES DERIVING FROM THE BORNU EMPIRE

XXIII. BORNU

MANY of the emirates of Northern Nigeria have some special claim to fame; but among them few have so many claims to distinction throughout the centuries as does Bornu. For Bornu has one of the oldest histories in the North; Bornu, standing at the caravan junction between east and north, became the host of cultural traits from the civilizations of both the Maghrib and the Orient; Islam left its mark on Bornu before it penetrated the Hausa states; Bornu is rich in written historical records, such as its several *mahrams* or letters patent granted to learned men, its *diwans* or the lists of the Maghumi kings, its *girgams* or lists of ancestors, as well as Arabic despatches in the chanceries of the Maghrib; Bornu repulsed the Fulani attacks consequent on the jihad of the nineteenth century; and today Bornu has a greater share of her sons in eminent positions of leadership, both political and administrative, than has any other emirate, a proud boast confirmed in 1962 by the selection of a Kanuri, Sir Kashim Ibrahim, as the first Nigerian Governor of the North.

The original empire of Kanem was centred on a town called Kawar, some four hundred miles north of Lake Chad. The Kanuri are Kendin and Tubu, 'the people of Kanem'. Even today, at neighbouring Bilma and Fachi in the Sahara, there flourishes a sizeable Kanuri population, engaged in the salt-trade. At Bilma, Tubu tradition relates that:

> The first people of Kawar were Sos (giants) from the Fezzan. Legend declares they were a very big race, while it is still claimed by the natives that the skeletons of these giants, and the great houses where they lived, are even yet to be seen in the Fezzan near Tejerri. These giants were as tall as twenty elbows.

In due course the Sultan of the Beri-Beri[1] came to Bulma and asked the Sultan of the Sos for permission to settle there with his people. Whereupon the giant king, answering nothing, took a wand and, extending it, turned slowly round so that he formed a mighty circle, the edge of which extended to Yeggeba, in northern Kawar and to Dibbela in the south (a diameter of 100 miles or more); and within that area the Beri-Beri were permitted to live.

The Sos were at that time settled in the oasis in the valley of Bulma, the rainfall of which was coming from Jado, and going to Fachi and Termit.

In 800 A.D. there was a great invasion of Beri-Beri, who were Muslims. They came from Yaman in Arabia by way of the Fezzan and Kawar.[2]

The gigantic stature of the So (Sau) is now legendary. Up near Yo, a hill is said to have been the pillow of a So man; the beautiful and characteristic pots found near Ngala (there is one in the Museum at Lagos), the size of a youth, are said to have been easily carried on the shoulder as water-jars, though recent archaeological research suggests they were used for burial purposes; their bracelets would have been too big for the thighs of other men; and an old Bornu manuscript ascribes to the So the power to 'hunt an elephant and carry it away on their head by reason of their strong body and determination'. Monguno, Yo and Damasak are original So settlements and, along with Marte, are among the pre-Ngazargamu towns of Bornu, perhaps a thousand years old. The principal So town was Ndebu, near Dikwa.[3]

From about 800, then, the nomadic Berbers or Beri-Beri began to expel the So from the area north of Lake Chad. They occupied the oases between Bilma and Chad, ejecting the nomadic Koyam inhabitants, many of whom are today found in modern Bornu. The royal clan of these first Beri-Beri kings is known as Sefawa

[1] In reply to our questions, Bornu N.A. gave the following interesting gloss on the term Beri-Beri: 'The word has been used wrongly by historians. Actually the people of Bornu are not Beriberi or Berbers. They are originally Arabs, deriving from one of the Sef Ibn Zuyazan sons. They came from the Yemen in two streams, one through Abyssinia to the Sudan and Darfur and thence to Kanem. This group is also known as the Beni Suleim, whence Silim Bikurmi in Bornu. The second group migrated through Egypt to Kawar via Murzuk, and are known as Beni Hital and then as Kanembu. When the Kanuri came to Kanem from Darfur they found Berbers, Imketa and Kara there, and with these they intermarried. When the second group reached Kawar from Egypt, they mixed with the Tubu of Barku.' This Bornu claim deserves further attention.

[2] H. R. Palmer, *Sudanese Memoirs*, vol. I, pp. 2–3.

[3] An interesting study is Marcel Griaule, *Les Sao Légendaires*, Paris, 1943.

or Maghumi, and their chief took the title of Mai. The founder of the dynasty was Sultan Sef ibn Dhi Yazan, in the sixth century; it was, according to Bornu historians, his grandson who settled in Bornu. A Maghumi tradition has it that whereas the Bulala fought with spears, one of the signs of the new ruling race of Bornu was that they, the Sefawa, always fought with swords. By *c.* 850 the Sefawa seem to have supplanted the former dynasty in Kawar. Of their kingdom Dr Barth defined it as:

an elective monarchy, the privilege of choosing a successor among the sons of a deceased king, without regard to priority of birth, being conferred by the nation on three of the most distinguished men of the country. The three electors proceeded to the apartment of the sovereign-elect, and conducted him in silence to the gloomy place in which the unburied corpse of his deceased father was deposited: for, till this whole ceremony was gone through, the deceased could not be interred. There, over the corpse of his deceased father, the newly-elected king seems to have entered into some sort of compromise sanctioned by an oath.[1]

These Sefawa, who had Berber blood in them, belonged to the nomadic Zaghawa, akin to the modern desert Tuareg. Now they intermarried with and in part ruled over the negro population of the plains of Bornu, in the same way as another race of conquering nomads, the Fulani, were to do a thousand years later. Next they subdued the Tubu (Teda), so that soon the new power of Kanem, based now on the town of Njimi, grew to such maturity that at the beginning of the twelfth century we find Mai Dunama, son of Umme, extending his influence as far as Egypt. According to Dunama's *diwan*, 'his horses numbered 100,000 and his soldiers were 120,000, not counting mercenaries'. The Kanuri claim that Islam came to them direct from the Khalif and that Umme, the twelfth Maghumi Mai, was their first Moslem king (1085–97). The *diwan* of the Mais of Bornu records his successor, Dunama, being drowned in 1151 'in the sea of the prophet Moses'[2]—some say by sabotage—while on his pilgrim's way to Mecca. However, the Arab geographer Al Maqrizi ascribes this distinction to Dunama Dabalemi, who did not come to the throne till 1221.

[1] Quoted in H. R. Palmer, *Bornu Sahara and Sudan*, p. 128.
[2] i.e., the Red Sea.

Under the Maghumi dynasty, the Bornu policy was organized on the basis of one important chief and two of lesser rank to each cardinal point of the compass.

Among the principal officers of state, usually of the blood royal, were the Yerima, the governor (the suffix *ma* meaning 'head of') of the north (*Yeri*); the Galadima, governor of Galadi, the various protectorates to the west (*fune*); the Kaigama, commander-in-chief of the east (*gidin*); and the Zarma, responsible for the south (*anum*). There were also two important eunuchs: Mestrema, escort of the Queen Mother, and Yiroma, escort of the Queen.[1]

A century later Kanem, under the rule of the seventeenth Mai, Dunama Dabalemi (1221–59), reached great heights of prosperity and her influence was felt from the Niger to the Nile and from Fezzan to Dikwa. The celebrated Ibn Battuta could later write of Bornu, a Moslem country of 'excellent slave-girls, eunuchs, and fabrics dyed with saffron', whose king 'never shows himself to his people nor talks to them except from behind a curtain'; while Ibn Khaldun, the doyen of the Arab mediaevalists, noted simply that 'Kanem is the greatest power in the Sudan'. Maqrizi thus describes Kanem-Bornu at the height of its power:

> The inhabitants of Kanem cover the head with a veil. The king does not show himself except at the time of the two religious festivals, in the morning and afternoon; the rest of the year he is not seen and those who talk to him are placed behind a screen. The principal food of this people is rice which grows wild in the country. They have also cheese, guinea corn, figs, limes, melons, pumpkins and fresh dates. As regards money, they use a kind of cloth which they make and which is called 'Wendy'. Each piece is ten cubits long [5 to 6 yards], but for facility of exchange it is cut up into pieces a quarter of a cubit or smaller [about 5 inches]. Other substances such as shells of different kinds and pieces of copper or gold are equally used in commerce and their value is estimated in an equivalent amount of cloth. In this country the pumpkins are so big that they are used as boats to cross the Nile. . . .
>
> They are of the sect of the Imam Malik. They are particular in enforcing justice and extremely severe as regards religion. In the year 640 A.H. [A.D. 1242], they built in the town of Fustat [Cairo], a college for people belonging to the sect of the Imam Malik known as the college

[1] See Yves Urvoy, *Histoire de l'Empire du Bornou*, Book I, chapter 3. Songs praising some of these title-holders are to be found in J. R. Patterson, *Kanuri Songs*, collected from the repertoire of the professional singers attached to the leading dignitaries at the court of the royal Mais.

of Ibn Rashid.[1] It is in this college that members of this nation reside if they come to Cairo.[2]

It was in Dunama Dabalemi's reign that one of the princes of Tunis received a gift of a camelopard or giraffe from 'The King of Kanem and the Master of Bornu':

In the year 635 [A.D. 1257] the Sultan al-Mustansir received a rich present from one of the Kings of the Negroes, the sovereign of Kanem and lord of Bornu, a town situated on the meridian of Tripoli. Among the gifts which this Negro delegation presented to him was a giraffe, an animal whose external characteristics are most diverse. The inhabitants of Tunis ran in a crowd to see it, to such an extent that the plain was choked with people; they felt profound astonishment at the appearance of a quadruped whose strange appearance recalled at the same time the distinctive marks of many animals of diverse species.[3]

It was about this time that the land to the south and west of Lake Chad came to be called Bornu, and in the fourteenth century the kingdom first appears in the works of European cartographers as Regnum Organa.[4]

In common with nearly every one of the empires of the Western Sudan, Kanem's very brilliance had within it the seed of decay; from her splendid zenith she plunged to her sorry nadir. We have seen how the history of these Sudanese dynasties has been a constant cycle of repetition. Ghana gives way to Mali; Mali flourishes and fades and is succeeded by Songhai; Songhai, crumbling before the Moors, leaves a power-vacuum that is only filled three centuries later by the Fulani empire. Contemporaneously with the rise of Mali and Songhai, the Hausa States and the kingdom of Bornu grow to prosperity between the Niger and Lake Chad.

The Berber invaders had joined with their Tubu subjects to give birth to the Kanuri nation, but with the death of their king, Dunama Dabalemi, a series of civil wars played havoc with the empire. No mean contributory force were the setbacks to Islam in

[1] We are grateful to Bornu N.A. for drawing our attention to the fact that today this college is known as Rawak Bornu.

[2] Al-Maqrizi, quoted in T. L. Hodgkin, *Nigerian Perspectives*, pp. 76–77. Hodgkin points out that Leo Africanus had a lesser opinion of Bornu, and quotes *in extenso* at p. 103.

[3] Ibn Khaldun, quoted in Hodgkin, op. cit., p. 74.

[4] The famous Catalan map of 1373 is reproduced in H. R. Palmer, op. cit., p. 208 and in E. W. Bovill, *The Golden Trade of the Moors*, 1958, frontispiece.

the Mediterranean, where the true believers were checked in Spain in 1212 and the barbaric Tartars sacked Baghdad.

In the reign of Umar Ibn Idris, the 30th Mai, the Sef dynasty was driven out of Kanem by their kindred Kayi or Bulala from Lake Fittri, another huge inland sea lying to the east of Chad, after a long struggle with the So, who had broken into rebellion and between 1342 and 1352 had slain four successive Kanuri kings in battles in the Dikwa-Monguno region. Umar's flight is recounted by Bornu chroniclers:

> When his end approached the war with the Bulala waxed fierce; so Umar summoned his Ulema, and said to them: 'What have we to do?' They said: 'Leave this place, our day here is done.' So Sultan Umar ibn Idris sent away his army, and stores, and people to Kaga—and no Sultan has returned to live in Kanem down to this our day, nor will they ever. Umar died in Marghi.[1]

The Kanuri were now forced to migrate to new lands to the west of Chad, where they came up against the expanding rivals of Mali and Songhai. Between the two lay the buffer land of the Hausa States. Thus situated between the two powerful empires of Songhai and Bornu, the Hausa States had already felt the tide of conquest sweep across them more than once in their long existence, but as the waters of war subsided they had always emerged with independence, and by means of stubborn courage and diplomatic payments of tribute they had retained the individuality of their political life. Like a bed of rushes they had ever allowed the storms of encircling forces to beat over their heads. At times they appeared to be laid low, but when the hurricane had passed they raised themselves, no worse for the buffeting of fate.

Hitherto, the Kanuri capital in Kanem had been, as already mentioned, at Njimi, the exact location of which is doubtful. Urvoy puts it some twenty miles east of Mao, itself some hundred miles to the north-east of Lake Chad, but the ruins at this site seem to indicate only a small town. The Kanuri themselves say that the site was in the present Niger Republic not far from N'Guigmi. Michael Crowder, acknowledging the authority of Dr A. D. H. Bivar, discusses the location and mentions the possibility of it having been on the south-west end of Lake Fittri or perhaps on one

[1] Palmer, op. cit., p. 217.

of the three or four ruins of baked brick in fields round Mussoro in Chad.[1]

From Njimi, the Kanuri under their Maghumi kings spent the next hundred years wandering up the banks of the Komadugu Yobe, today the river that marks the northern frontier of Bornu. By its banks they built a series of temporary capitals, such as Wudi, Birni Kimi and Yamia (Muniyo) until, in about 1470, Mai Ali Ghaji Dunamami founded Birni Ngazargamu. Here water was plentiful, contact with Kanem was convenient, and it was a safe distance from the pinpricks of Tuareg raiders operating from their new base of Agades in the Asben Oasis. The story is that the So would sell to Mai Ali Ghaji only as much land as a bullock's hide would enclose. Ali agreed, cut the hide into very thin strips and enclosed the site which became Ngazargamu, 'the ancestral spirit of the Ngazar people'. In contrast to the homogeneous Tuareg community of Njimi, the new Kanuri capital counted very few of the *kokuna* or nobles of Njimi, for the bulk of Ali Dunamami's people were Tuku, Arab and So. A prolific writer on Bornu[2] has pointed out that the Maghumi family was insistent on its claim to a common origin with the Imakitan Tuareg of Asben, the Bulala and the Azgar of Fezzan, whereas the Kanuri of the Birni had no such ethnic connexions with the Tuareg.

For the next three centuries Birni Ngazargamu remained the capital of Bornu. Mai Idris Katagarmabe did, in fact, reoccupy Njimi in 1507, but the Kanuri found their new capital much more conveniently situated. The only change was that the centre of political gravity now moved to the west: Kanem became a province of Bornu instead of Bornu being a province of Kanem, though at first Bornu was little larger than the district of Geidam. At the peak of its glory, Birni Ngazargamu covered six square miles and was estimated to have contained 200,000 souls. An account of the city written in 1658 gives us this description:

> In Ngazargamu there were four Friday mosques. Each of these mosques had an Imam for Friday who led the Friday prayer with the people. At each mosque there were twelve thousand worshippers.
>
> The names of the four Friday mosques were as follows—The first was called Garibaya and the name of its Imam was Sheikh Muhamad Ajirami. The second was called Talusu and the name of its Imam was

[1] M. Crowder, *The Story of Nigeria*, 1962, p. 34. [2] H. R. Palmer.

Sunuramma. The third was called Iyamu and its Imam was called Karagwama. The fourth was called Dayamu and the name of its Imam was Ahmad Bultu Zawamma. The Amir Ali ibn Al Hajj prayed behind the Imam.

At Ngazargamu there were six hundred and sixty roads cleared and widened, called Le. Sixty of these roads were well known to the Amir, for he traversed them, but many of the roads were unknown to the Amir since he did not traverse them and so did not know them. In Ngazargamu were many God-fearing Mu'allims and many blameless nobles and many unworldly people and learned saints.[1]

It was Ali Ghaji, 'he of the tall-walled towns and long spears and mighty horses', also known as Ghazi Din, who finally defeated the Bulala, after a century of their harassing, in a great battle at Lade. Thereafter the Bulala chiefs were reduced to *mainawa* or princes of Kanem and Fittri. Ali Ghaji's reign thus marked the end of a definite period in Bornu history.

The 48th Mai was Idris Katagarmabe (1503–26), a warlike king and grandfather of the most famous of all the Maghumi kings, Mai Idris Alooma. Idris Alooma was the posthumous son of the martial Mai Ali Zeinami Ibn Idris (1545–46),[2] who was killed while fighting against the Bulala: his praise-song is *Ali kange Bulalabe*, 'Ali, the smoke of the Bulala'. The Magira or Queen Mother, Aisa Kili Ngirmaramma, 'Aisa, owner of the great white horse', became Regent on the death of Mai Abdallah in a campaign against the Ngizim in 1562. The title of Magira denotes an official personage and not necessarily the mother of the Mai. According to Bornu traditions, she had great difficulty in preserving the life of the young orphan Idris—his mother had been a Bulala *mairam* or princess—from the machinations of Mai Dunama (1546–55) and his son Mai Abdallah (1555–62).[3] When the Magira became Regent she ordered the building of a special palace and mosque at Gambaru, beautifully situated on the banks of the Komadugu at a safe distance away from the corrupting court manners of the capital Birni Ngazagarmu. This lovely sixteenth-century palace, whose admirably constructed brick walls are yet standing and

[1] Quoted in Palmer, op. cit., pp. 34–35.

[2] Urvoy gives 1544–48.

[3] Palmer gives 1546–63 and 1564–70, whereas Urvoy gives 1548–66 and 1566–73. Urvoy includes Aissa Kili, the Magira, as 58th Mai (1573–80): other authorities give her as ruling from 1562–70, *vide* the list at the end of this chapter. Palmer's Diwan makes no mention of her and she does not appear on his list.

whose shady site by the edge of the colourful river Yo still retains its gentle atmosphere of days of long ago, soon became, in the words of Dr Barth, 'the favourite retreat of the kings of Bornu during the flourishing period of the empire'.

The position of the Magira is of considerable influence in the political structure of Kanuri court society,[1] and even in modern times she, along with the Magaram or the official 'elder sister' of the Mai and the Gumsu or chief wife of the ruler of Bornu, exercises no mean political influence, though no longer do they possess land or towns of their own. Some idea of the status of the Magira—and, incidentally, of the venerability of Bornu—can be gained from this thirteenth-century Kanuri praise-song:

> Magira! Mother of the King. Magira: you the cause of Bagharmi's harrying:
> You the battle-axe, the whip of Wadai: you the leopard (that lies) in the cassia bush:
> You the lion (hungry until) forenoon, with a cub beside it: mother of the King; Magira!
> She is precious, precious as gold: (daughter) of Kadabu Lefamiram.
> Your land Ngalagati, the land of the bush-cow: to the man who likes you, give honey to drink.
> Him who despises you, kill, drag away and leave (unburied).
> You are whiter than milk: (your face) brighter than the moon at its full.
> The river, Magira, is yours; no one will oppress you: yours the games at which are your daughters of four spans; yours the seventy *dandals*:[2]
> At their games one thousand maidens attend. Magira you, too, are a Sultan.
> The fig tree in whose shade the play is held is yours: yours the place of the games which are held every day:
>
> Yours N'gelgusuwa, and Damaya town. The King, the Protector of Islam, was created from you.
> North, Aïr, Damargu is yours; South, Barka Wal;
> There rain is first to fall, and does not cease until all other rains are over: of the slaves Barka Gana and Barka Kura, you are the owner, Magira!

[1] It even extended to the power of imprisonment of the Sultan by his mother, as was the case with Mai Biri I in the twelfth century.

[2] The *dandal* is the characteristic wide avenue in Kanuri towns leading up to the chief's residence.

Yours Mugubi, and Gambaru. In the acacia tree before your house the people pound the honey cakes.
Mother of the King, Magira Aisa, daughter of Dunama Dabalemi, you are as glowing embers in the town of N'jimi.[1]

Idris Alooma—his nickname deriving from the fact that he was buried on the shores of Lake Alo, just outside Maiduguri—who reigned from 1571 to 1603, is today the most famous of all the Maghumi Mais. He was, indeed, the outstanding figure of the century, and his reign marked the recrudescence of Bornu's power comparable to the prosperous days of Dunama Dabalemi. Idris Alooma stands comparison in every way with the glorious reigns of Sonni Ali and his successor, the Askia, in the rival western empire of Songhai. His virtues have been thus eulogized[2]: 'his warlike energy was combined with wildness and intelligence; his courage with circumspection and patience; his severity with pious feelings.' Of his civic principles it is written that:

Among the most surprising of his acts was the stand he took against obscenity and adultery, so that no such thing took place openly in his time. Formerly the people had been indifferent to such offences, committed openly or secretly by day or night. In fact he was a power among his people and from him came their strength.

So he wiped away the disgrace, and the face of the age was blank with astonishment. . . . He kept no secrets from those in whom he reposed confidence. As regards this, if he was upon a journey and heard any news of the enemy by night or day, he did not rest but went forth among his people to the source of the news with the army following him; leading himself for fear any misfortune should befall which he was able to avoid, or by his power to save. He relied on his Lord in everything and God was his support, sure that nothing would happen except by the foreknowledge of God (be He exalted). Hence he was a brave warrior who advanced everywhere, appearing promptly without pausing or beating round, until what he proposed was accomplished. Such was his character and his disposition.

Among the gifts with which God had endowed him, was an impressive appearance. All his followers, small or great, never felt contented except in his presence. Even though he sent large armies in one direction and went in some other direction with a small force himself, his

[1] Palmer, op. cit., p. 233.
[2] By Dr Barth, in his most valuable appendix on the Sefawa of Bornu, given at the end of vol. ii of his *Travels and Discoveries in North and Central Africa*, 1857.

captains were not content to go without him, however large the number of the army.[1]

In the decade of the 1580s he led no less than seven expeditions against the Sultan of the Bulala, Abd al Jalil. Bornuese historians, in particular the Mai's *imam*, Ahmed ibn Fartua, have recounted these Bulala wars in some detail: here is an extract from Idris's final campaign:

> It is told of our Sultan Al Hajj Idris that he attacked Sultan Abd al Jalil at Kiyayaka and that the latter fled to the far desert to escape him. Abd al Jalil and those who followed him and assisted him in his deeds of evil and tyranny, seem in their early days to have been like gazelles pasturing in the desert and browsing on the herbage, who flee in terror to their lairs at the sight of women. Such was the condition of Abd al Jalil and his followers before the battle of Kiyayaka uprooted them; but in their latter days they became like wild cows pasturing in the most inaccessible wilderness who are seen by the eye of no traveller save those whom business or the chase takes to remote deserts.
>
> Our Sultan, seeing this state of affairs, pondered on it, and evolved a plan which would have occurred to no one else but himself on account of its ingenuity. Having thought about the matter he sent for many Bedawin tribes and their leaders, as for example Ali Yarda and his folk and others, and addressing them in complimentary terms, called them to a conference where flattery and blandishment were not absent. In this way Idris attached all of them to Sultan Muhammad Abd al Lahi, and ordered them to assist him against Abd al Jalil to the limit of their power and perfectly openly without slackness or remissness. They fell in with Idris' orders and became Muhammad's right hand, remaining with him until God gave him victory over his uncle Sultan Abd al Jalil.[2]

There were many other campaigns undertaken by Mai Idris, against the Tuareg, the Ngizim and the novel, stockaded towns of eastern Kano.[3] Typical of these is this account:

> They were rebellious and stubborn, and did many evil and wicked

[1] Ahmed Ibn Fartua, *Mai Idris of Bornu*, pp. 12; 53.

[2] Quoted in Palmer, op. cit., p. 239.

[3] 'When the people of the land of Kano sought to bring evil and damage on the land of Bornu, they began a new policy which did not obtain in the days of their forefathers at all. They built a large number of stockades.' Fartua, op. cit., p. 30. Palmer remarks that these stockades lay between Kazaure and Hadejia, and they might include walled towns. 'As the term for this type of town (*birni*) came from the name of the capital of Bornu (Birni Ngazargamu) the Bornu historian was probably unwilling to admit the existence of another Birni and so called other towns stockades though the stockade was built of mud'—op. cit., pp. 73, 74.

actions. They had a false idea of their own strength by reason of two things. Firstly their numerous archers, who used poison arrows, and secondly the strength of their walled towns. These two factors induced them to be rebellious and hostile, as has always been the case with the heathen, and there was no concealment about the fact.

But when our Sultan Haj Idris ibn Ali observed their wicked rebellious acts, he made up his mind to go to the town of Mawa, after celebrating the Id al Fitr in the town of Mugulum.

From Mawa he moved to Gija Gijami, and thence without halt he came to the town of Fika and camped there. On this journey Sultan Haj Idris visited the wonderful water called Jinjina, after crossing Fika country.[1]

It was on yet another expedition, this time against Mandara in 1603, that Mai Idris was ambushed and shot not far from the present site of Maiduguri. He was buried by Lake Alo, where it is said bright lights are often seen on the water at night. A Bornuese *girgam* speaks of:

> Idris of the fair skin and fair town.
> His wars were three hundred and thirty,
> His journeys among the rocks a thousand.

In the next two centuries there followed a series of undistinguished Maghumi Mais, from Muhammad, the 54th, who died in 1618, to Ali Ajimi, the 63rd, who succeeded in 1750. Kanuri historians date the decay and eventual collapse of the Maghumi power to the accession of Ali Ajimi. During his forty years on the throne his war chief, the Kaigama, suffered several crushing defeats not only at the hands of the Mandara but also by the growing numbers of Fulani and Shuwa Arab who had in the last two centuries settled in the Dikwa area.

His successor was his son Ahmed, in whose reign the disaster of the Fulani sack of the Kanuri capital occurred. As the Mai had gone blind, his son Dunama Lefiami was appointed to the throne a few months before the Fulani army under Gwani Mukhtar advanced from Gujba. The attack on Birni Ngazargamu took place in March 1808 and was, according to Fulani sources, provoked by the fact that the Mai had sent the Kaigama and the Galadima to the aid of Daura[2] when the Fulani attacked it. A

[1] Fartua, op. cit., p. 39.

[2] On the advice of Bornu N.A. we have put Daura; earlier sources have the *casus belli* as Kano.

counter-attack by the Fulani drove the Galadima out of Nguru, thereby leaving the road open for the attack on Ngazargamu from the south. The city fell and the Maghumi fled north to Mege in Mobber and thence to Asaga. Thus was fulfilled exactly the Kanuri prophecy that Ngazargamu would last for 333 years; a prophecy that recalls the reputed Fulani one, equally fulfilled, that the empire of Shehu dan Fodio would last for just one hundred years.[1]

A Fulani tradition from Bauchi Province tells how Gwani Mukhtar sent a messenger, one Malam Abare, to Usman dan Fodio to confirm the propriety of attacking fellow-believers. 'Go and tell Gwani Mukhtar that he must fight,' the Shehu replied. He went on:

'Though the people of Bornu pray and follow some of the Islamic laws, they also practise fetishism. Anyone who believes in Allah and His Prophet will never worship anything but the True God.'

The Shehu continued: 'The place where they do their fetishism is their capital. This town has seven gates, each with its own name. They built 490 bowl-shaped earthenware vessels and put 70 of these at each gate. After this, they made another 490 and replaced the old ones. This is a kind of fetishism.

'They choose a beautiful virgin girl, dress her with lovely garments, and throw her in the river when it floods. This too is a kind of fetishism.

'They take a bull with black and red stripes, and drown it as well. This too is a kind of fetishism.

'There is one of their trees, a large gutta-percha, which a newly appointed chief goes to visit. This too is a kind of fetishism.

'There is another tree, called *karimbo* in their language. When a girl is being married and taken to her husband's home, she is walked round and round the tree many times, amid songs and dancing. This too is a kind of fetishism.

'There is a ward in the capital where, when Ramadan is near, they take a big pot and put some water inside. When the new moon is due they go and look in the water. This too is a kind of fetishism.

'Also, when a new wall is to be constructed round their town, they search for a black cow's milk and pour it over the site before the work begins. This too is a kind of fetishism.

'And there is a medicine they have, known as *jiko*, where roots of different types of trees and other such things are mixed together. Some of this is then dropped in water, and the patient takes a bath in it,

[1] See p. 410.

while the rest is thrown on ant-holes. This too is a kind of fetishism.'[1]

Nine months and three days later, Bornu tradition maintains, Mai Dunama, morally supported by the thirty-year-old Sheikh Haj Muhammad al Amin who had recently returned from Mecca and whose help the Mai had invoked in his flight to Mobber, and physically backed[2] up by the redoubtable Kanembu spearmen[3] of the Sugurti and Kuburi, marched against Birni Ngazargamu. One legend asserts that Al Kanemi, as Haj Muhammad came to be known, said he wanted no reward for his services, only four tribes, Kanembu, Sugurti, Zedbo and Tubu. These the Mai gave him, little realizing then that in fact he was giving away his kingship into the bargain. Al Kanemi's father was Sheikh Ninga, a well-known Fezzan *faki* of Kanembu origin. Dunama thus fulfilled Al Kanemi's advice of 'Return to your capital, Allah will restore it to you'. Gwani Mukhtar was killed, the Fulani withdrew, and the Maghumi dynasty was restored. But only for a while. Malam Zaki, the founder of Katagum emirate, hastened to recapture Birni in 1810. Mai Dunama again fled, this time to Kurnawa. Shortly afterwards, on the advice of Al Kanemi, he moved his court to Birni Kabela some nine miles away from Ngornu, where Al Kanemi had settled among the Kanembu. Like all Bornu towns, it had the characteristic *dandal* or wide public avenue leading up to the ruler's house. Though the Fulani evacuated Birni Ngazargamu, Al Kanemi thought it advisable not to allow the Mai to return to his erstwhile capital, and he forbade its reoccupation. Of the Mai in his new town of Birni Kafela in 1823 we have the following description:

> On our arrival at Birnie, which is a walled town, with huts of the same description as those in Kouka, and probably contains ten thousand inhabitants, we were first conducted to the gate of the sultan's mud edifice, where a few of the court were assembled to receive us.
>
> Soon after daylight we were summoned to attend the Sultan of Bornu. He received us in an open space in front of the royal residence:

[1] For permission to publish this passage we are grateful to Mr Victor Low and Salihu Bajoga who in 1959 were the sponsors of a scheme to collect local traditions and stories for the Bauchi Provincial Secondary School Historical Society.

[2] R. Hallett, in his paper on Al Kanemi in *Eminent Nigerians*, quotes the Arab traveller who amused his listeners by telling them of the Bornu army who ran away at the sight of a herd of ostriches, thinking that it was the Fulani who were appearing on the horizon (p. 68).

[3] For a further account, see A. H. M. Kirk-Greene, 'Some Bornu Spears', *Man*, March, 1963.

we were kept at a considerable distance while his people approached to within about 100 yards, passing first on horseback; and after dismounting and prostrating themselves before him, they took their places on the ground in front, but with their backs to the royal person, which is the custom of the country. He was seated in a sort of cage of cane or wood,[1] near the door of his garden, on a seat which at the distance appeared to be covered with silk or satin, and through the railing looked upon the assembly before him, who formed a sort of semicircle extending from his seat to nearly where we were waiting. Nothing could be more absurd and grotesque than some, nay all, of the figures who formed this court. Here was all the outward show of pomp and grandeur, without one particle of the staple commodity, power, to plead its excuse; he reigns and governs by the sufferance of the sheikh, who, to make himself more popular with all parties, amuses the sultan by suffering him to indulge in all the folly and bigotry of the ancient negro sovereigns. Large bellies and large heads are indispensable for those who serve the court of Bornu; and those who unfortunately possess not the former by nature, or on whom lustiness will not be forced by cramming, make up the deficiency of protuberance by a wadding, which, as they sit on the horse, gives the belly the curious appearance of hanging over the pummel of the saddle. The eight, ten, and twelve shirts, of different colours, that they wear one over the other, help a little to increase this greatness of person: the head is enveloped in folds of muslin or linen of various colours, though mostly white, so as to deform it as much as possible; and those whose turbans seemed to be the most studied had the effect of making the head appear completely on one side. Besides this they are hung all over with charms, inclosed in little red leather parcels, strung together; the horse, also, has them round his neck, in front of his head, and about the saddle.

When these courtiers, to the number of about two hundred and sixty or three hundred, had taken their seats in front of the sultan, we were allowed to approach to within about pistol-shot of the spot where he was sitting, and desired to sit down ourselves, when the ugliest black that can be imagined, his chief eunuch, the only person who approached the sultan's seat, asked for the presents. Boo-Khaloom's were produced, inclosed in a large shawl, and were carried unopened to the presence. Our glimpse was but a faint one of the sultan, through the lattice-work of his pavilion, sufficient however to see that his turban was larger than any of his subjects', and that his face, from the nose downwards, was completely covered. A little to our left, and nearly in front of the sultan, was an extempore declaimer shouting forth praises of his master, with his pedigree; and near him one who bore the long wooden

[1] This cage was known as the *fanadir*.

frumfrum, on which he ever and anon blew a blast, loud and unmusical.[1]

Al Kanemi's reputation for piety and learning was widespread. From a visitor to Bornu in Al Kanemi's time, Major Denham, we have a sympathetic portrait of this 'Servant of God', this paragon of a ruler who was so 'greatly loved and respected on account of the extreme correctness of his life and the benevolence of his disposition'. He was good-looking, we are told, with a kind face and eyes that were large and bright. His dress was neat and simple, and his mind was a delight of intellectual curiosity:

Compared to all around him, he is an angel, and has subdued more by his generosity, mildness and benevolent disposition than by force of arms. . . . El Kanemy is a most interesting and aspiring chief, and an extraordinary (if not a solitary) instance, in the eastern world, of a man raising himself to sovereign power from a humble station without shedding blood by the assassin's knife, or removing those who stood in his way by the bow-string or the poisoned cup.[2]

The correspondence between Muhammadu Bello of Sokoto and Al Kanemi of Bornu (as Muhammad al Amin had come to be known) is to be found in a contemporary Arabic work, *Infaq al Maisuri*. For its academic analysis of the disagreement between these two great Muslim leaders as well as the light it throws on the history of the Fulani-Kanuri struggle, it is a work of great importance. From the volume of valuable letters, we have chosen these excerpts:

From Amir ul Muminin Othman, son of Muhammad, son of Othman whom they call Dan Hodio (may God rejoice Islam by prolonging his life, may He grant him peace in his end) to the learned Mu'allim Hajj Amin el Kanemi, greetings to him and all his people. After greetings, the reason of this my letter to you is to inform you of the five matters which were discussed in your letter which you sent to us by Giddado.

Firstly, we would inform you of the reason of our war with the Hausa chiefs: secondly, of our war with the Mai of Bornu and his people: thirdly, that we do not accuse them of heathenism on account of the five acts you mention: fourthly, of the true reason why we accuse them of heathenism: fifthly, that your dwelling in the land of Bornu is unlawful.

[1] D. Denham, H. Clapperton and W. Oudney, *Narrative of Travels and Discoveries in Northern and Central Africa*, 1826, pp. 224–33.
[2] Op. cit., pp. 178–85.

Now, firstly, as to the cause of the war between us and the Hausa chiefs, know that Shehu began to call people to the religion of God and so explain to them all what the true religion was. He taught all of them in language that they understood. He instructed them with great patience and kindness. He endeavoured to remove all cause of doubt. Very many people accepted his teaching and aided him till he became known to the whole country. Then he began to travel with his followers and visited many towns. He spoke to them of religion and many of the ignorant repented.

Still he did not interfere with the customs of the chiefs. Finally his following became very large and they became known throughout all Hausa and were called the followers of Shehu. The people left their towns and came to Shehu. Moreover it was found that some of the Hausa chiefs repented and went to Shehu, leaving their ranks and offices. Now that was what enraged the principal chiefs of Hausa. Shehu's cause was as I have said, and grew until it came to the chiefs' knowledge. Shehu explained it to them and was with them, but they were angry because of the large numbers of his followers and their Islamic religion. The evil spirit of men caused them to make war on us. The chiefs were saying to themselves: 'If we do not scatter this sect, there will be no authority left to us. They are destroying our country.' They began to collect men together, but left us alone until Sarkin Gobir sent to summon us. When we came to him, we saw from his talk and knew that his intention was simply to destroy us and make us return to what we were before.

Then all the chiefs of Hausa rose up and slew the Muslims who were in their towns, and fighting took place between them and the Muslims. But God destroyed them.

After we had routed the Sarkin Gobir we sent to all the Hausa chiefs, we asked them to help the religion of God and to help us so that we might strengthen religion. But they were proud and refused. God destroyed them. That is the cause of our making war with the Hausa chiefs.

Secondly, as to the reason of our making war on the Mai of Bornu. Know you, El Kanemi, that we did not make war on the people of Bornu because of their heathenism. Their heathenism consists in what they do at the places called Kubara and Bukaua, but we do not know the exact truth of it. The reason we have fought with them is that they first began to fight with us and aided the Hausa chiefs against us. And since they aided them, they became like to them. That is the reason why we waged war on the Mai of Bornu.

Thirdly, the reason why we do not accuse people of heathenism on account of their sins is because the Prophet has said: 'Sins are the deeds of the ignorant, but it is not right to accuse those who commit them of heathenism.' That is our reason.

Fourthly, the reason why we do accuse the people of Bornu of being heathen is because they sacrifice to stones and great trees and have great houses for worshipping idols. That is our reason.

Fifthly, let me inform you, El Kanemi, what is commanded in the matter of your dwelling among the people of Bornu; know that your dwelling among them is unlawful, since we have made plain to you their heathenism. We have told you that they aided the Hausa chiefs against us. It is your duty to flee from Bornu and go to a country that is Muslim. So much for that.

But now as to the request in your letter, El Kanemi, that I should command the Fulbe not to fight with the people of Bornu, and desist from waging war on the country of Bornu, that is not possible: it is not lawful. For we know that they are heathen because they aided the Hausa chiefs against us. We will not make peace with them unless they choose one of two things: either let them return to Islam, or else let them ask us to desist from war and make peace and pay tribute.

But do not suppose, El Kanemi, that we accuse you of heathenism or your people because you aid the people of Bornu against us. For how should we accuse of heathenism a Mu'allim learned in law. Further, you say that you do not know the people of Bornu to be heathen. In fact you believe them to be Muslims, while their neighbours, our folk, are Muslims. That is your belief.

Further, you say that our Fulbe began the war with the people of Bornu, and that then you rose up and repelled them. That prevents us from accusing you of heathenism. But had you known they were heathen before you came to them, and had you, nevertheless, come and helped them against us, then, indeed, you would have become like them.

Moreover, as to their character, you know that they sacrifice to stones, and pour blood on the gateways of their towns, that they have great houses for idol-worship, and that they practise rites by their rivers even as the Egyptians did by the River Nile. All this, you know, is heathenism. But you, yourself, El Kanemi, are different from this. You are a Muslim. You are learned in the Law and Tradition. We hear nothing from those who know you but that you are a Mu'allim of great learning.[1]

[1] This, and the following extract, are taken from Muhammad Bello's *Infaq al Maisuri*. Palmer, op. cit., and Hodgkin, op. cit., both quote extensively from this valuable document. The latter has, at pp. 198 ff., some useful notes on the whole correspondence, with a discussion of Professor H. F. C. Smith's translation and commentary from the Arabic edition prepared by C. E. J. Whitting, London, 1951. The Arnett edition, in English, is only partial and is a rendering rather than a translation.

Again, listen to Al Kanemi's reply:

Tell us therefore why you are fighting us and enslaving our free people. If you say that you have done this to us because of our paganism, then I say that we are innocent of paganism, and it is far from our compound. If praying and the giving of alms, knowledge of God, fasting in Ramadan and the building of mosques is paganism, what is Islam? These buildings in which you have been standing of a Friday, are they churches or synagogues or fire temples? If they were other than Muslim places of worship, then you would not pray in them when you capture them. Is this not a contradiction?

Among the biggest of your arguments for the paganism of the believers generally is the practice of the amirs of riding to certain places for the purpose of making alms-giving sacrifices there; the uncovering of the heads of free women; the taking of bribes: embezzlement of the property of orphans; oppression in the courts. But these five charges do not require you to do the things you are doing. As for this practice of the amirs, it is a disgraceful heresy and certainly blameworthy. It must be forbidden and disapproval of its perpetrators must be shown. But those who are guilty of it do not thereby become pagans; since not one of them claims that it is particularly efficacious, or intends by it to associate anything with God. On the contrary, the extent of their pretence is their ignorant idea that alms given in this way are better than otherwise. He who is versed in the books of *fiqh*, and has paid attention to the talk of the imams in their disputation—when deviation from the right road in matters of burial and slaughter are spoken of—will know the test of what we have said. Consider Damietta, a great Islamic city between Egypt and Syria, a place of learning and Islam: in it there is a tree, and the common people do to this tree as did the non-Arabs. But not one of the *ulama* rises to fight them or has spoken of their paganism.

As for uncovering the head in free women, this is also *haram*, and the Qur'an has prohibited it. But she who does it does not thereby become a pagan. It is denial which leads to paganism. Failing to do something while believing in it is rather to be described as disobedience requiring immediate repentance. If a freed woman has prayed with the head uncovered, and the time passes, but she does not repeat the prayer in accordance with what we know they say in the books of *fiqh*, surely you do not believe that her prayer is not proper because she has thereby become a pagan?

The taking of bribes, embezzlement of the property of orphans and injustice in the courts are all major sins which God has forbidden. But sin does not make anyone a pagan when he has confessed his faith. And if you had ordered the right and forbidden the wrong, and retired when the people did not desist, it would have been better than these present doings. If ordering and forbidding are confined within their proper limits, they do not lead to anything more serious. But your forbidding has involved you in sin, and brought evil on you and the Muslims in this world and the next. . . .

Since acts of immorality and disobedience without number have long been committed in all countries, then Egypt is like Bornu, only worse. So also is Syria and all the cities of Islam. There has been corruption, embezzlement of the property of orphans, oppression and heresy in these places from the time of the Bani Umayya [the Umayyad dynasty] right down to our own day. No age and no country is free from its share of heresy and sin. If, thereby, they all become pagan, then surely their books are useless. So how can you construct arguments based on what they say who are infidel according to you? Refuge from violence and discord in religion is with God. . . .[1]

While all this diplomatic exchange of notes was going on, the Fulani were steadily encroaching upon former Bornu territory from Gumel and Hadejia in the north to Gombe and Yola in the south; and Al Kanemi was simultaneously divesting the enfeebled Maghumi dynasty of all power and authority. With his back strategically to Lake Chad, Al Kanemi kept the Mai in Kabela while leaving him the semblance of kingship. Ably assisted by a handful of chosen Arab leaders (his mother was a Tripolitanian Arab) and backed by his own following of Kanembu from the east of Chad, Al Kanemi slowly gained the confidence of the remnants of the Birni Ngazargamu aristocracy. In 1811 he had Dunama Lefiami replaced as puppet-Mai by Muhammad Ngileruma, but finding him less generous than he had hoped, he restored Dunama on condition that he would share the revenues of the kingdom with Al Kanemi.

In the same year of 1814 Al Kanemi decided to move from Ngornu and found his own capital. He chose a site round a group of baobab-trees, *kuka*, by the shore of Lake Chad, and so Kukawa came into being. A Bornu story tells of how Al Kanemi said he would build his capital on the very spot where he reached the last *Sura* of the Koran, which he used to read as he travelled.

Meanwhile the efforts of the Maghumi dynasty to rid themselves of their one-time saviour, Al Kanemi, continued unabatedly. Mai Dunama conspired with the Sultan of Baghirmi, Burgu Manda, to invade Bornu. The Baghirmi army destroyed Al Kanemi's

[1] See footnote on p. 324.

palace at Kukawa, but in an unfortunate disaster at Ngala in 1817 they killed Mai Dunama whom they had come to help. It is said in Bornu that the Mai made no attempt to defend himself when he became unhorsed, as such would have been out of keeping with the royal dignity, but simply sat down under a tree, covered his face with his shawl, and allowed himself to be speared to death. Six of his faithful eunuchs shared his fate.

So emasculated had the Maghumi dynasty become that, according to Bornu historians, Dunama's brother Ibrahim pleaded to Al Kanemi: 'My brother gave you half the power and half the revenues of the kingdom: give me the title of Mai, and you can have them all.' Ibrahim was enthroned. Thus mollified, Al Kanemi now wrote to the Sultan of Sokoto:

> We profess the same religion, and it is not fitting that our subjects should make war on each other. Between our two kingdoms are the pagan Bedde tribes, on whom it is permissible to levy contribution: let us respect this limit: what lies to the east of their country shall be ours: what lies to the west shall be yours. As for Muniyo, Damagram and Daura, they will continue to be vassals of the Sultan of Bornu, who in return will surrender to you all his claims to Gobir and Katsina.[1]

Al Kanemi made one final attempt to wrest from the Fulani the eastern provinces of the Sokoto empire and restore the kingdom of Bornu to its pre-1808 glory. Encouraged by the success of his campaign against Baghirmi in 1824, he pushed his troops westward, drove out the Emir of Katagum and prepared his army for the final march on Kano. Sokoto desperately rallied its forces from all the emirates to meet this threat and placed Waziri Gidado in supreme command. It was, however, the militant Yakubu, Emir of Bauchi, who in 1826 defeated the Bornu army at a place seventy miles east of Kano and so saved the day for the Fulani. Thereafter Kukawa and Sokoto kept to themselves.

Ibrahim found the restraint of Al Kanemi no easier than his predecessors had. His courtiers gradually deserted him. Even Al Kanemi's death in 1835[2] brought no respite, for his son Sheikh Umar made it no less clear that he was the real power behind the Bornu throne. We have this contemporary pen-portrait of him:

[1] Quoted in Palmer, op. cit., p. 269.

[2] The date 1837 is that favoured by Professor H. F. C. Smith of Ahmadu Bello University in his views put forward to the Nigerian Historical Society, *News Bulletin*, iii, 4, 1959. We have retained 1835 as the year insisted on by Bornu *malamai*.

> I found the sheikh (Omar, the eldest son of Mohammed el Amin el Kanemy) a very simple, benevolent, and even cheerful man. He has regular and agreeable features, rather a little too round to be expressive; but he is remarkably black—a real glossy black, such as is rarely seen in Bornu, and which he has inherited undoubtedly from his mother, a Bagirmaye princess. He was very simply dressed in a light tobe, having a bernus negligently wrapped round his shoulder; round his head a dark-red shawl was twisted with great care; and his face was quite uncovered, which surprised me not a little, as his father used to cover it in the Tawarek fashion. He was reclining upon a divan covered with a carpet, at the back of a fine airy hall neatly polished.[1]

Eventually Mai Ibrahim took the only way he knew out of his humiliating, indigent and powerless plight. Seizing the opportunity of the absence of the Shehu on a mission to his province of Zinder, Ibrahim plotted with Muhammad Sharif, the king of Wadai, for a coup against the Al Kanemi family. His treason was betrayed by the husband of one of his daughters to whom he had confided his secret plot. True, the Bornu army was completely routed by the Wadai forces in 1846; but vengeance came swiftly. Sheikh Umar arrested the Mai and his courtiers and had every one of them executed. He bought off the Sultan of Wadai, who was intent on restoring the Maghumi dynasty in the shape of Mai Ibrahim's son, Ali Dalatumi. Sheikh Umar was so relieved at this diplomatic success that he abandoned his plan of fleeing to Fezzan, prompted by the ruthless advance of the Wadaian army and their sack of his capital, Kukawa. Now able to indulge his wrath at Ibrahim's treasonable conspiracy with a foreign power, he sent his brother Abdurrahman in pursuit of Ali Dalatumi, who was killed at Minarge. He had reigned forty days.

With Ali's death in 1846 the thousand-year-old Maghumi dynasty of the Mais of Bornu came to an end. The family of Al Amin al Kanemi, more generally remembered as Shehu Laminu, came to the open as the true rulers of Bornu. They now adopted the royal title of Shehu.

By and large, the change in dynasty and the change in capital made no difference to the general organization of Bornu. The Kanembu did not conquer the country in the sense that the Fulani conquered the western emirates. The transference of influence was gradual and easy, by absorption rather than aggression. The

[1] H. Barth, quoted in A. H. M. Kirk-Greene, *Barth's Travels in Nigeria*, p. 146.

Kanembu dynasty was not, however, able to ensure the continued loyalty of the clans who had supported Laminu, and this may account for the fact that they had little peace after 1880 and eventually suffered such overwhelming defeat at the hands of Rabeh.

It was in the reign of Shehu Laminu's son, Shehu Umar, that Dr Barth sojourned for many months in Bornu, living in 'the English house' at Kukawa. He describes it as 'a small clay house . . . with several small but neatly-made rooms and a yard . . . situated almost in the middle of the town', the courtyard dominated by a magnificent fig-tree.[1] For part of this century it became an official Rest House, but now even its plinth is hard to locate in the barrenness of what was once the glory of Kukawa. Barth's treaty with Bornu, which he signed on behalf of the British Government, is a little-known document even in contemporary Bornu and therefore deserves to be better known. In view of its much wider historical interest, we reproduce it here *in toto*:

The Queen of the United Kingdom of Great Britain and Ireland, being desirous of forming amicable relations with the Chiefs of the Interior of Africa, for the purpose of interchanging reciprocally the merchandise of Africa with that of Europe, has empowered Doctor Henry Barth to make Treaties in her name, and on her behalf, for the purpose above expressed; and the Sovereign of the Kingdom of Bornoo being also desirous of co-operating with Her Majesty the Queen of England, with the view of establishing and effecting what is proposed; Her Majesty has, therefore, named the said Doctor Henry Barth, as her Agent, to conclude the following Treaty, on behalf of Her Majesty, her heirs and successors:

ART. I. English subjects are permitted to enter the Capital of Bornoo and any part of the Kingdom, to travel or establish themselves therein; and English residents shall be treated by the inhabitants of the country as friends; their persons and properties shall be respected; and in case they wish to depart, no impediment shall be offered, either as regards their persons or their property.

II. British subjects may always trade freely, without hindrance by the people of Bornoo, in all kinds of merchandise of lawful commerce, which they may desire to sell or buy in every part of the country. The Sovereign of Bornoo binds himself to grant to English subjects all the commercial privileges which may be enjoyed by the subjects of any other Christian nation.

[1] Barth's original sketch of this house is reproduced in Kirk-Greene, op. cit., p. 168.

III. The communications between the country of Bornoo and other places shall be safe, so that English merchants may, without obstacle, import their merchandise of lawful commerce, of whatever kind, and bring them for sale in Bornoo and elsewhere; and it shall be equally free for them to export from Bornoo such merchandise of lawful commerce, as they wish to sell in other places. Merchants of other countries shall not be prevented from bringing their merchandise of lawful commerce to Bornoo and its Dependencies, or from passing through to Soudan, or elsewhere, when their purpose is to trade with English subjects.

IV. The Queen of England may appoint an Agent to reside in the capital of Bornoo and its Dependencies to protect the interests of British subjects, and to see that the present Treaty is fulfilled. The said Agent shall be respected and protected throughout Bornoo and its Dependencies. The Sovereign will attend to his representations, will treat him with respect, and guarantee his person and goods.

V. The Sovereign of Bornoo, El Emir Omar, son of Mohammed al Kanemy, promises to do all he can to facilitate the passage of couriers carrying despatches to or from the English Nation, within his territories, and to provide for their security.

VI. The Sovereign of the Kingdom of Bornoo will put in execution the present Treaty; will make it public, and cause it to be observed; and it shall not be violated from this day forward for ever.[1]

This, too, was the time of the great Wazirin Bornu, Haj Bashir Ibn Ahmed Tirab, who lost his life in the court revolt by Shehu Umar's brother Abdurrahman in 1853. Barth's account of Kukawa's *kasugu lətəninbe* or Monday market—a Kanuri feature that has continued to this day in Maiduguri—is too well known to repeat here, but here is his description of the city itself:

Having now a horse whereon to mount, I rode every day, either into the eastern town to pay a visit to the sheikh, or to the vizier, or roving around the whole circuit of the capital, and peeping into the varied scenes which the life of the people exhibited. The precincts of the town with its suburbs are just as interesting as its neighbourhood (especially during the months that precede the rainy season) is monotonous and tiresome in the extreme. Certainly, the arrangement of the capital contributes a great deal to the variety of the picture which it forms, laid out as it is in two distinct towns, each surrounded with its wall, the one, occupied chiefly by the rich and wealthy, containing very large establishments, while the other, with the exception of the prin-

[1] See A. H. M. Kirk-Greene, 'The British Consulate at Lake Chad', *African Affairs* October 1959. A photograph of the treaty is in Kirk-Greene, op. cit., p. 149.

cipal thoroughfare which traverses the town from west to east, consist of rather crowded dwellings, with narrow winding lanes. These two distinct towns are separated by a space about half a mile broad, itself thickly inhabited on both sides of a wide open road which forms the connection between them, but laid out less regularly, and presenting to the eye a most interesting medley of large clay buildings and small thatched huts, of massive clay walls surrounding immense yards, and light fences of reeds in a more or less advanced state of decay, and with a variety of colour, according to their age, from the brightest yellow down to the deepest black. All around these two towns there are small villages or clusters of huts, and large detached farms surrounded with clay walls, low enough to allow a glimpse from horseback over the thatched huts which they inclose.

In this labyrinth of dwellings a man, interested in the many forms which human life presents, may rove about at any time of the day with the certainty of finding never-failing amusement, although the life of the Kanuri people passes rather monotonously along, with the exception of some occasional feasting. During the hot hours, indeed, the town and its precincts become torpid, except on market-days, when the market-place itself, at least, and the road leading to it from the western gate, are most animated just at that time. For, singular as it is, in Kukawa, as well as almost all over this part of Negroland, the great markets do not begin to be well attended till the heat of the day grows intense; and it is curious to observe what a difference prevails in this as well as in other respects between these countries and Yoruba, where almost all the markets are held in the cool of the evening.

The daily little markets, or *durriya*, even in Kukawa, are held in the afternoon, and are most frequented between the aser (*lasari*) and the mughreb (*almagribu*) or sunset. The most important of these *durriyas* is that held inside the west gate of the *billa futebe*; and here even camels, horses, and oxen are sold in considerable numbers: but they are much inferior to the large fair, or great market, which is held every Monday on the open ground beyond the two villages which lie at a short distance from the western gate. Formerly it was held on the road to Ngornu, before the southern gate; but it has been removed from thence on account of the large pond of water formed during the rainy season in the hollow close to this gate.

It is interesting to see how the administration of Bornu was organized under the traditional Kanuri system.[1] In pre-Rabeh times the country was administered by the Emir through the Ajia (district head), Lawan (sub-district head), both aliens to the

[1] Based on O. Temple, *Notes on the Tribes, Provinces . . .*, p. 437.

district; the Bulama, their local agent, and the Mbarma (village head). There were in addition two Wakil, special representatives of the Shehu, who resided at Gujba and Geidam.

The largest fief-holders were officials whose tenure was not hereditary. The Magira (the Shehu's official mother) had forty-eight villages scattered over twelve districts, the largest number under any one person.

The officials consisted of:

Twenty-three Kogana (free-born councillors); the largest owner had twelve villages in eight districts.

Thirty-two Maina (princes and princesses); the largest owner had fourteen villages in six districts.

Eight *malamai*.

The Shehu's tailor.

Forty-two Kacalla (slaves of the Shehu, including eunuchs); these were in three classes; the largest owner had twenty-five villages in eight districts.

(a) Twenty-five Kacalla Kazagabe, i.e., captains of spear-men. Their whole estates were escheated on death.
(b) Sixteen Kacalla Turukbe, i.e., captains of gun-men to the Shehu.
(c) One Kacalla Kenyibe, i.e., captain of archers.

In this connexion, too, we have a most valuable contemporary account of the daily meetings of the historic Bornu Council of State, the *Nokena*, which was inaugurated by Mai Dunama Dabalemi in the thirteenth century:

This body is composed of members of the royal family, the brothers and sons of the Shehu, together with the state councillors—the Kokenawa (sing. Kokena)—who themselves fall into two categories: the free-born representatives of different national groups, and the military commanders—Kachellawa (sing. Kachella)—who are of slave origin.

All the state councillors appear in the morning at the royal palace, leaving their shoes, turbans, and burnuses at the entrance. They squat against the walls or on the floor, scattered about the anterooms and the courts, chatting and joking, gossiping and hatching plots, until a musical clamour of drums, pipes, trumpets and horns, electrifies them, and makes them move into the reception and conference hall. This is the sign for the sovereign to leave his private apartments and enter the ante-chamber of the reception hall, . . . attended by some of his brothers and sons and ponderous eunuchs, who together pronounce his praises in short spasmodic bursts—exclaiming, for example—'his wisdom', 'the lion', 'the conqueror'. As the sovereign takes his place on the throne all those present hasten to abase themselves—it is as gross a breach of etiquette in Bornu to remain upright in the presence of a great man as it is to be seated with us, without the great man's permission; and they must sprinkle the dust from the floor on their heads—or at least make a show of this ritual of obeisance, since, with a floor which has been so scrupulously swept and polished, it would be difficult to scrape together the necessary quantity of earth. . . .

Each man has his appointed place, close to or far from the sovereign, according to his degree. Nearest to the throne, against the wall where it is set, right inside the great hall, his sons and brothers take their seats.

Along the sides of the hall, and facing the Shehu, are the ranks of the Kokenawa proper—as those dignitaries are called who, like the princes, have not merely a seat but a vote in the Nokena. These are the freeborn, the Kambe, representatives of the main national groups in Bornu—Kanuri, Kanembu, Tibu, and Arab. . . .

The whole Council of State (Nokena) is only a shadow nowadays, surviving from the aristocratic constitution of an earlier period, and has no longer any effective power. . . . Now it is only the will of the sovereign and the influence of his favourites that count. Of course the free Kokenawa have the advantage of knowing that they are of free descent, as contrasted with the slaves of the Shehu. But, since the Shehu takes no account of noble birth, a free Kokena must bow to a slave who stands higher in the sovereign's favour; though among the free councillors of state there are individuals whom the Shehu esteems—for whom he has affection, either for their own or their fathers' sake. . . .[1]

The tombs of the first four Shehus are still an object of reverence in Kukawa, today but a backwater district town.

By the time of Shehu Umar's death in 1880, the authority and influence of Bornu had declined considerably. Wadai was a constant invader and in 1892 the erstwhile province of Zinder became to all intents and purposes independent. Umar was succeeded by his sons Bukar, Ibrahim and Hashim (Alimi). The fact that none of them enjoyed the strong qualities of their grandfather Al Kanemi is commonly explained in Bornuese circles by the story that the mother of Shehu Umar, a Baghirmi girl, was already pregnant when she arrived to marry Al Kanemi.

In 1893, during the reign of the fifth Shehu, Hashim, the full

[1] G. Nachtigal, *Sahara und Sudan*, 1879, quoted in Hodgkin, op. cit., pp. 291–2.

grip of Rabeh descended on Bornu.[1] The Bornuese army, sent by Hashim to drive Rabeh back across the Shari, was routed at Amja and its general, Muhammad Tar, sewn up in a freshly-flayed bullock hide on the orders of Rabeh. The hide was then exposed to the sun, and Muhammad Tar suffered a horrible death. The Shehu next sent a brash message to Rabeh: 'Do not spoil my country. If you are afraid of me, go away; if not, I will come and fight you.'

Rabeh, who was then at Ngala, realized it would be safer to meet the Kanuri in the open rather than within the town, whose inhabitants might rise against him. He drew up his army on the banks of a small stream just outside Ngala. Rabeh employed skilful tactics similar to those of many generals who have found themselves outnumbered. He allowed the Bornu army to attack over bad ground, and used concealed mobile troops on either flank to take advantage of the confusion that his gunfire caused among the enemy. The Kanuri advanced in a faint-hearted manner and a few volleys put them to flight. In a third battle at Goange, near Kukawa, the Shehu himself was defeated by Rabeh; 'battle' is perhaps too grandiose a word, for it is said that the Kanuri army, doubtless aware of Muhammad Tar's fate, fled without even a shot being fired. Hashim escaped but was soon after assassinated by his nephew, Abba Kiari, who was ashamed of his uncle's cowardice, at Ngalagati near Geidam. The murder was carried out by two of his slaves, Kacalla Ngubdo and Kacalla Abdu, who shot the Shehu while he was saying his morning prayers in his house. Kiari then proclaimed himself Shehu at Gumsa and sent a message to Rabeh that he had raised his royal standard.

Rabeh could deal with Kiari when he pleased. First he wanted to put Kukawa to the sack: to leave it standing would be too great a menace to him. There is extant a Bornu tradition that Rabeh had already spied out the town, disguised as a merchant, and that he secretly dropped certain Koranic verses into one of the wells to turn the Kanuri hearts from fighting. In any event, his rape of Kukawa was as thorough and merciless as any of his deeds in Bornu. Everything that could not be carried away was destroyed. A merchant captured at the time related, on his release two years later, that the loot included 1,000 horses and 4,000 slaves, and from the Shehu's palace alone 70,000 black cloths, 30,000 lb. of

[1] For a fuller account of Rabeh see the following chapter on Dikwa.

red yarn and 700 lb. of gunpowder. The slaughter of the population went on unchecked for two days, and the skulls piled up for counting exceeded 3,000.[1] Kukawa was obliterated.

A rising under a gallant young *malam*, the twenty-year-old Buki, followed in eastern Bornu. Buki defeated the force sent from Dikwa to quell him, but Rabeh then led another army in person. They met at Kuli and Buki was slain.

Rabeh next marched against Shehu Kiari, whose bravery was undoubted and who was said to be at the head of an army on its way to reoccupy Kukawa. Rabeh decided to intercept him, though he had with him a force of only 700 men. He entrenched himself at the village of Dumurwa. Kiari attacked from two flanks simultaneously, with such dash and vigour that Rabeh was obliged to fall back, leaving his camp and women in the hands of the victorious Kiari. This very success was the undoing of the Kanuri. Jettisoning all discipline, the soldiers gave themselves over to wild and licentious looting. At once Rabeh, with his practised eye, saw his chance. At his carefully pre-arranged rallying-point he re-assembled his troops. Then, under cover of darkness, he crept back to the camp. By the light of the burning huts it was easy to spot the Kanuri. Volley after volley was poured into them; Shehu Kiari was wounded and carried away; rumour spread that the Shehu was dead; panic ensued; and the Kanuri retreated in the direction of Gashegar. Of the finale we have the following eye-witness account:

> On coming to his senses Kiari was anxious to again attack. This his people would not hear of, on account, they said, of his wound. As a matter of fact, the unexpected return of Rabeh, whom they thought they had decisively beaten, had greatly weakened their morale. They therefore persuaded Kiari to rest for a day; this he unfortunately consented to. Rabeh, who had his scouts watching them, on hearing that the Bornu army was resting, at once determined to attack. He advanced rapidly and found the Kanuri army, some eating, some sleeping, the women tending the horses. The surprise was complete, and a regular panic ensued. Kiari stood his ground with some fifty of his slaves and relations. These were speedily shot down and Kiari taken prisoner. Rabeh wreaked his vengeance on the Kanuri army, and a wholesale slaughter followed.

The captured Shehu was brought in front of Rabeh, who at once

[1] Verbatim report of M. Abba made to W. P. Hewby and cited in J. Welman, *Gazetteer of Bornu Province*, 1929, pp. 108 ff.

complimented him by saying he was a very brave man, but how foolish it was of him to try and fight against a man who had conquered so many nations. Kiari replied that this was no time to talk, saying: 'Had I caught you, my slaves would have killed you before now.' Rabeh saying he would not hang so brave a man, ordered one of his slaves, Abdullah, who, sitting down, placed Kiari's head between his knees and cut his throat like a sheep's. Two of Kiari's brothers who were taken prisoner had their throats cut in like manner.[1]

A somewhat different and less authenticated story is also heard in Bornu.[2] When Rabeh rode off in person to lead Kiari back on foot in triumph to Dikwa, Kiari cursed his victor and begged to be killed, swearing that the women of Bornu should never see him walk behind any man. Rabeh, a great warrior himself, was always ready to recognize another brave man. Since Kiari would not walk, he had him bound and set on a horse till they reached Dikwa. Here Rabeh had him brought daily into his presence, using all persuasion to gain his submission and even make him one of his generals. But Kiari only renewed his curses, declaring that he was a king and a king he would die. Rabeh, growing weary, accepted the word of his son, Fad-el-Allah, that he knew how to deal with him, and handed Kiari over. Fad-el-Allah then murdered Kiari.

The Al Kanemi dynasty, with the characteristic courage of the Kanuri, made one more effort to scotch this snake. Sanda Limanambe Wuduroma[3] now proclaimed himself Shehu. Within a matter of weeks he had been captured at Konduga, taken before Rabeh at Gashegar, and executed.

For the next seven years, until his death in battle against the French at Kusseri in 1900, Rabeh ruled Bornu with a rod of iron. Signs of his harshness were for some years visible everywhere in Bornu: in political disintegration, in ruined towns, in economic poverty, in maimed old men and women (though today most of these are dead and gone), in the facial 'mark of Rabeh'; and even in the language, for instance the Fulani proverb that 'Rabeh uses a hundred head of cattle for one pot of soup' and the Gujba saying *zakara bai isa ya yi wa yaron Rabeh ba'a ba*, 'even a cockerel may not scoff at one of Rabeh's men'.[4] Yet there is another point of view,

[1] Welman, op. cit., p. 26. The present Shehu was a witness.
[2] Boyd Alexander, *From the Niger to the Nile*, 1907, vol. i, p. 283.
[3] See page 349.
[4] Abdulmalik Mani, *Zuwan Turawa Nijeriya ta Arewa*, p. 161.

expressed by none other than the soldier-administrator, Emile Gentil, who directed the campaign that led to Rabeh's death on the battlefield of Kusseri on 22 April 1900:

In spite of the horror aroused by contemplation of all the crimes which Rabeh committed, one cannot help feeling a certain admiration for him. After conquering Bornu and Bagirmi with a handful of men, he dreamed of the conquest of Wadai, which awaited his arrival in trepidation. Without our intervention, he would have carried out his plan in the course of the very year in which he met his death. . . . Death, fortunately, prevented him from fulfilling his ambitions. Yet they were not without certain greatness, if one may judge by his actual achievements in Bornu. As soon as the country had submitted, the new Sultan set about the task of reorganization. He quickly realized the extreme weakness of the ruler's position—an outcome of the Bornu feudal system, balancing the chiefs' power against the King's, and thus creating a number of states within the state. But he saw also that he, as a newcomer, could not himself undertake the direct administration of a country whose language and customs were unfamiliar to him and his followers. He therefore left the local chiefs in charge of their various districts, so as to provide a liaison between people and ruler; but made them subordinate to his own chief officers, who took his orders, and whose reliability he ensured by keeping them near him. In fact, he replaced the old feudal government by a sort of military dictatorship. He organized taxes, demanding from each district a regular fixed sum, of which he took half himself, leaving half for the military and administrative chiefs to share. His own revenues do not seem to have been spent simply on pleasures and luxuries. He carried out a plan for a public exchequer, to cover the maintenance of his troops, organized in companies of from 150 to 250 musketeers, the erection of healthier and more comfortable buildings, and the storing of provisions with a view to future campaigns. The revenue which he obtained from taxation was further augmented by plunder seized in raids on Bagirmi and the pagan countries; so it may easily be seen that Rabeh, far from impoverishing Bornu, substantially increased its wealth, at the expense of its neighbours. Thus it might have been anticipated—contrary to our original ideas—that after quite a short interval the population of Bornu would have not merely acquiesced in his régime, but even accepted it with satisfaction. . . .[1]

The British did not occupy Bornu till 1902. At that time the French were in control at Dikwa, over what was soon to become

[1] Emile Gentil, *La Chute de l'empire de Rabeh,* Paris, 1902, quoted in Hodgkin, op. cit., p. 320.

known as 'German Bornu', where they had reinstated the Al Kanemi dynasty, first with Sanda Kura and then with Bukar Garbai. When the British heard that the latter had fled to his ancestral Kanem in 1901 because of the heavy tax burden that the French had imposed on him, they offered to make him Shehu of British Bornu if he would return. This he did, and he was installed in 1902.

While Kukawa was being rebuilt, the Shehu resided temporarily at Monguno: 'at present,' commented the Resident, 'Kukawa is one large cornfield,' so the reconstruction of the royal city had to await the harvest. When the Shehu reoccupied Kukawa, a junior Resident remained at Gawange, three miles away, and the principal Residency was built at Magumeri, a healthier spot and administratively more convenient than Kukawa. Mofoni,[1] the site of the present Government station of Maiduguri, at that time consisted of a fort with a company of troops. In 1904 Governor Lugard visited Kukawa to present Shehu Garbai with his staff of office.

Within the next few years it became apparent that, owing to its commercial inaccessibility and climatic disadvantages, Kukawa was unlikely ever to regain its former glory. A new site was wanted for the capital of Bornu. The place now selected lay on a low ridge about a thousand feet above sea-level, on the left bank of the seasonal River Alo, situated between the big market village of Maiduguri and the military fort of Maifoni. It dominated the vital trade route to French Territory and the Nile interland.

On the 9 January 1907 Shehu Garbai moved with his court to the new capital. A telegraph office was opened in July and plans were made for the development of Shehuri, the two royal quarters. Each Ajia was asked to build a mud house as far as possible on the lines of their Kukawa compounds, so as to form the nucleus of the new town springing up round the original hamlet of Kalwa. The capital was christened Yerwa, said to be derived from the Arabic exclamation of grateful pleasure. At the same time as the Shehu moved to his new capital of Yerwa, the Civil Administration took up permanent quarters in Maiduguri, erecting in 1908 the first Residency of sundried bricks, with a wooden ceiling and doors. No review of Maiduguri's history could be considered complete without a reference to Mr W. P. Hewby, the first Civil Resident

[1] Bornu N.A. now prefers this form to the more usual Maifoni or Mafoni.

of Bornu Province. Much of the new capital's healthy infancy must be attributed to his tender care, and the name of 'Mr Ibi', as he was affectionately known throughout Bornu, is still widely remembered today.[1]

Liberty village derives its name from the Freed Slave Settlement established there.[2] Historically, the area where Maiduguri now stands was part of the Uje fief, from which the modern districts of Auno, Dalori and Konduga were carved. Later Yerwa was excised and eventually, in 1957, Yerwa was divided into the urban Yerwa district and the rural Maiduguri district. Strangely enough, Maiduguri has become the usual name for the capital of Bornu outside the town, even though this is a small village well away from the administrative centre. Inside Bornu, the city is better known by the name of Yerwa.

In tracing through the substitution of Maiduguri for Kukawa as the centre of Bornu, we have overstepped chronology. In 1922 Sanda Kura, who had been deposed by the French at Dikwa in 1901, succeeded Bukar Garbai as the tenth Shehu of Bornu. He had already spent fifteen years in Bornu emirate, serving as a district head under his younger brother Shehu Garbai. Once the administration had consolidated itself, its eyes naturally turned to the possibilities of developing the great pasturelands of Bornu for cattle ranching. In 1912 the Shehu despatched the first consignment of cattle by rail from Kano to Lagos, at the handsome return of a ninety per cent. profit. In the following year a ranching scheme was started at Allaguerno, but in the event neither this nor the ostrich farm nor the stallion stud farm proved a success, and all were abandoned. The abundant Chad Game Reserve lasted a little longer, but it too was closed in 1921. The first car reached Maiduguri, from Kano, in 1917, and 1926 saw the arrival of the first aircraft. Photographs of the old fort (on the site of the Provincial Secretary's house) and of Maifoni station at this period vividly illustrate the deforested nudity of the sandy town, while in the station there are still extant the original de Putron double-storeyed houses,[3] whose cool rooms and vaulted ceilings harbour many a tale of the 'holy kingdom of Bornu'.

[1] For the full story of the growth of the capital, see A. H. M. Kirk-Greene, *Maiduguri and the Capitals of Bornu*, 1959.

[2] The story is given in A. H. M. Kirk-Greene, 'The Saga of Liberty Village', *West African Review*, December 1958.

[3] As we write, the sad news of their final condemnation comes down from Bornu.

For historians, 1928 saw an interesting appointment in the turbanning of Abba Musa as Wazirin Bornu in place of Shettima Kolo. He was the grandson of Haj Bashir, the vizier whom Dr Barth had found so outstanding, 'by nature of a superior cast'. The railway extension reached Nguru in 1929. On the death of Ligari Muslim, his place was filled on the Council by the titular head of the Kanuri, Shettima Kanuri. In 1932 the Waziri and Talba visited Kano to study the methods of administration there. Bornu, 'with its large central plain in which vast herds of cattle roam and its broad fertile plains which form the ancient bed of Chad, where in the harvest-season the eye can see nothing but the waving heads of brightly-coloured guinea-corn', was in a better position than most emirates to be cushioned against the trade depression of the early 1930s, though its lacustrine districts suffered terribly from the locust invasions of the period.

Shehu Sanda Kura died in 1937, at the age of 95. An official report had a few years earlier spoken of how:

> his intense loyalty and outspoken criticisms continue to prove of the greatest value, and his liberal attitude towards modern development is remarkable in a man of his age and up-bringing. So far from merely tolerating the products of the age, he has given a valuable lead to his administration.[1]

In his stead Umar ibn Muhammad al Amin al Kanemi, a son of Shehu Kiari and Emir of Dikwa since 1917, was appointed Shehu of Bornu at the age of 65. A year later death robbed Bornu of two more of her leaders, the Waziri and the Talba. The Waziri of Dikwa, Ibrahim, who was already on the Bornu Council by virtue of his title of Shettima Kanuri, now became Wazirin Bornu. The Shehu's visit to Lagos in 1938 was his first journey outside the frontiers of Bornu.

In 1952 the Shehu gave a special party to mark the golden jubilee of a significant event in Bornu history: the restoration of the Al Kanemi dynasty by the British in 1902. Among the guests were all those who had served with Shehu Garbai and 'Mr Ibi'. The following years were critical for Bornu, which by 1955 had plumbed the depths. An N.A. crisis in February 1953 was followed by the removal of three senior councillors. Among the new appointments to the Council were Malam Lawan, who was then

[1] *Annual Report of Bornu Province*, 1934.

Provincial Agricultural Officer and so became the first Government official ever to be a member of an N.A. Council, and Malam Turab, a representative of one of the three leading Arab families traditionally among the closest friends of Shehu Laminu. The purge continued in 1954, under the new Waziri, Muhammadu Ngileruma, who had given up his post as a Minister to accept the office of Waziri. But things were to get worse before they got better. The financial scandals of 1955 brought ugly prominence to Bornu; the Waziri resigned; and to lead the emirate back into its rightful place, two Ministers gave up their office and returned to Bornu. These were Shettima Kashim,[1] who became Waziri, and Zanna Bukar Dipcharima.

Since then Bornu has, apart from an ugly riot in 1958, regained its rank of eminence among the emirates. The Shehu, despite his eighty odd years and almost total blindness, flew to Mecca in 1955, insisted on taking his place on horseback at the head of his contingent in Kaduna during the Royal Visit in 1956, recovered from an emergency operation in 1957, has attended the House of Chiefs, and had a son born to him in 1958. This year was also remarkable in the history of Bornu for the welcome success of two boreholes, sixteen years after the existence of artesian water had been established. The boosting of this water-supply effect on Bornu's economy is likely to be rivalled only by the advent of the railway line from Gombe, opened in 1964.

THE KINGS OF BORNU

The Maghumi (Sefawa) dynasty: they took the title of Mai *or Sultan*

1.	Sef ibn Dhi Yazan	*c.* 570	53.	Idris Alooma	1571–1603
13.	Dunama ibn Umme	1098–1150	63.	Ali ibn Haj Hamdun	1750–1791
17.	Dunama Dabalemi	1221–1259	64.	Ahmed ibn Ali	1791–1808
30.	Umar ibn Idris	1386–1390	65.	Dunama Lefiami	1808–1811
47.	Ali Ghaji Dunamami	1476–1503			1814–1817
48.	Idris Katagarmabe	1503–1526	66.	Muhammad Ngileruma	1811–1814
49.	Muhammad ibn Idris	1526–1545	67.	Ibrahim	1817–1846
52.	Aisa Kili Ngirmaramma (Magira)	1562–1570	68.	Ali Dalatumi	1846

[1] Later Sir Kashim Ibrahim, first Nigerian Governor of the Northern Region. We are deeply indebted to His Excellency for his careful revision of the genealogical tables produced on pp. 342 and 353, and his long note on p. 354.

The Kuburi (Al Kanemi) dynasty: they took the title of Sheikh or Shehu

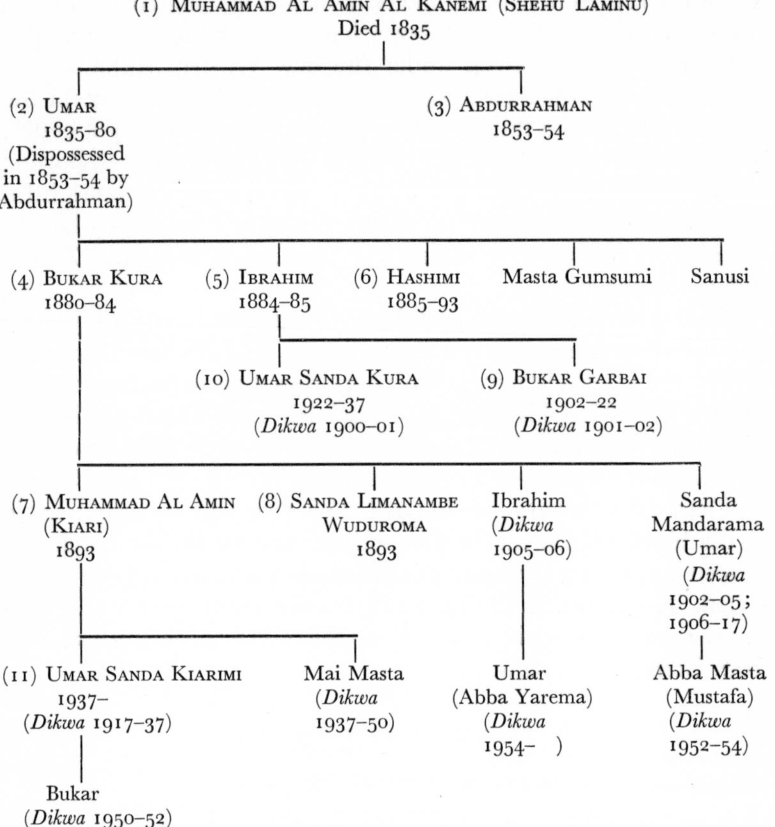

Notes: (1) Up to 1846 the Shehus were merely the power behind the throne of the thousand-year-old Maghumi dynasty of the Mai of Bornu, which ended with the death of Mai Ali Dalatumi.

(2) After the execution of Kiari and Wuduroma by Rabeh in 1893, there was an interregnum until his destruction by the French in 1900, and their re-instatement of the Al Kanemi dynasty in Dikwa—with a consequent installation by the British of a counterpart Shehu, Bukar Garbai, in Bornu.

(3) There is considerable difference between the various authorities on the dates of the Maghumi Mais.

(4) See footnote 2, p. 327.

XXIV. DIKWA

DIKWA history is, up to the end of the nineteenth century, Bornu history. Indeed, this very plea of ethnic sentiment and 'belonging' was, as we shall see, put forward as recently as 1962 to justify the return of Dikwa to Bornu Province. It was only by an historical accident that Dikwa took on the identity of a separate emirate: had it not been for the invasion of Rabeh from the Sudan in 1893 and the machinations of the European colonial powers in the race for Chad in 1900, Dikwa would probably appear in this book under the rubric of Bornu. And that is how we have treated of Dikwa up to the advent of Rabeh, once called 'the African Napoleon'.

Before doing so, however, there is an account of the campaign of Mai Idris Alooma, Sultan of Bornu, against the So towns of modern Dikwa emirate in 1575. Here is the description of the attack on Amsaka:

> Then the Sultan left the country of the Tatala and came towards the region of Amsaka. He pushed on with his army a few days until he reached the town of Kasa. Thence he came to Sangaya which is close to Amsaka.
>
> In the morning the Sultan arose with his army and arrived before Amsaka about 9 o'clock. When the people of the town saw the dust of the Muslims rising to the sky, they mounted onto the tops of their houses and the pinnacles of the walls to observe what the Muslims would do.
>
> The Muslims showed their intention. When the soldiers saw the idolaters and heathen observing them, they wished to charge forthwith upon them.
>
> But the Sultan stopped them from going forward, and ordered them to be patient and restrained. Then he passed by the edge of the stockade opposite the town, and crossed to the South and camped by the East gate about the distance of a short gallop on a 'maidan'. When the camp had settled down the people piled their gear and saddles and slept till the morning.
>
> The people of Amsaka grew even more contumacious and stiff-necked and obdurate, and began shouting in their delight and joy, and cared not at all for the presence of the Sultan and his army threatening them.

They were misled by the result of the former fierce engagement and the strength of their stockade. It is said that in their pride and self-sufficiency they said to the Muslims:

> 'You are as you were before, and we are as we were at first—and neither side will change—and none save the birds will see the inside of our stockade and town.'

Thus they spoke to our people. Then came the Amir ul Muminin to their stockade to attack them in force. The enemy mounted above the stockade, and fired arrows and darts like heavy rain. No Muslim could pause a moment in the vicinity of the stockade without being pelted with arrows and hard stones which broke a man's head if they hit it. The stockade was full of people.

The Sultan ordered the Muslims to fill in the trench which encircled the stockade with the stalks of guinea-corn which the pagans had planted for food. They tried this plan for two or three days, but whenever the Muslims returned to their quarters in the evening, the enemy came out and took out of the trench all the stalks that they had put in it, so that nothing was left. This went on for some time. The Sultan then commanded the whole army to move and encamp close to the stockade to the North. They did so. This fighting took place in the month of God Sha'aban.

The Muslims came to try and fill up the trench of the stockade in the early morning after they had shifted camp close to the town. Horns were blown and flutes sounded. There was all manner of noise and playing in the stockade.

The pagans set themselves to attack the Muslims in every possible way, and to divert them from the ditch by all kinds of wiles and devices; firstly by setting fire to thatched roofs, and throwing them down—a most formidable device; by poisoned arrows; by pots of boiling ordure, or throwing hard clay which would split or break a man's head; then by throwing short spears, or finally by throwing the long spear which is carried by warriors.

All these were among their methods of fighting. They never ceased day or night. One day a section of the stockade, about the length of a spear was broken down. The Muslims thought they would gain entrance through it and follow on. But the pagans built up the place with mud in the open, the Muslims looking on and unable to prevent them building.

The Sultan then ordered the army to cut tall trees to make platforms on three sides of the stockade, so that the gunmen could mount on them and easily shoot at the enemy inside the town in every direction possible.

They did as they were ordered. The people then worked with a will in filling the ditch of the stockade with earth as well as cornstalks, and continued obediently till they had filled the ditch with earth.

The place became flat and even. Then our men began destroying and breaking up the stockade itself with matchet and axes until they had cleared a large amount of the stockade away, and so the enemy were hemmed in.

To the Amir ul Muminin and Khalifa of the Lord of the Worlds, al Haj Idris ibn Ali (may God most exalted ennoble him in both worlds) belongs the credit for an apt device and clever plan by which to fight the enemy—to wit, his order to the army of the Muslims that the gunmen should get in the first discharge so that they should not be forestalled. Thus the enemy's hands would be rendered empty and victory over them would be easy. Thus it fell out. The pagans began to shoot at the Muslims with showers of arrows but our army picked up all their shafts and took them to the Amir in great numbers. It was impossible to count the number of arrows collected. God alone knows. Finally the arrows of the enemy came to an end. Nothing was left.

The heathen therefore assembled all their blacksmiths, and asked their help in making arrows. The Muslims outside the stockade heard the noise of beating of hammers on the big anvils which are placed in the ground [i.e., with a stump fixed in the ground] for the making of new arrows.

The enemy then began shooting with new arrows, covered with mud in place of the former poison just to frighten the Muslims pretending they had poison on them though it was not the case.

The Muslims continued to destroy the stockade with matchets and axes, and filled the ditch, except that they left on the West side a part which they were unable to fill. After a time they destroyed the Eastern part of the stockade, leaving a part in the middle. The enemy then became afraid, and lost their heads, in terror and fright.

The day wore on. It grew hot. Then evening came. It was a Saturday [4th December, 1575] the last day of Sha'aban. After sunset the new moon of Ramadan came out and the people saw it. The Sultan prayed the evening prayer and refused to leave the battle. He ordered his tent to be brought, and slept among his troops. He directed the big drum to be beaten in a changing rhythm, to put fear into the hearts of the pagans.

God cast into their hearts exceeding terror and a great dread. So they remained in fear and trembling, and ran from their stockade under cover of darkness.

The Sultan followed them, killing the men and taking alive the women and children, tracking them down and following far without let or delay, so that none escaped among the heathen save a few.

The Muslims all returned in the belly of the night, safe, with booty, joyful at the enemy's discomfiture, save one man known as Ajima ibn Kalle. He became a martyr in the confusion at night (may God pardon him). That night the Muslims all slept with purpose to keep the fast on the morrow.

On the succeeding Thursday morning, the Sultan ordered his people to cut the trees inside the stockade. They cut them leaving nothing of them. Many of the enemy were slaughtered in the stockade. The stench of the corpses of the slain grew unbearable in our camp. The Sultan ordered his men to gather together the captives into one place. When they were assembled he ordered his Kerde slaves to kill them all. They killed them. No one was left alive.

Then he gave the word to march. The drum was beaten, and he left Amsaka at the head of the army, after there had happened and been brought to light all that has been here related concerning this rebellious and stiff-necked people. It has been published to the four quarters of heaven, so that near and far could hear of the power of our ruler, and commander, and king.

The people of every quarter came to him with many gifts bowing their heads in submission whoever they were or wherever they dwelt.[1]

In 1893 Bornu, which at that time was governed from the city of Kukawa, was invaded from the east by a horde of Sudanese and Arabs under the generalship of the cruel but competent Rabeh. An adventurer of the classical pattern, he was the client (some say foster-son) of the Sudanese slave-raider Zubeir Pasha. His rabble army, estimated at 700 men but backed by formidable fire-power from its modern rifles and cannon, had overrun the countries of the central Sudan and in 1892 penetrated to Baghirmi, growing in numbers as it went.

Apart from accounts published by German and French writers at the beginning of this century, Rabeh's full-scale biography has still to be written in English. Meanwhile, the following eye-witness description may be of value by virtue of its ranking as a contemporary document:

Rabeh decided to move from Bagirmi to a more fertile country in the valley of the Shari; on his arrival at Logone, he decided to make that place his headquarters; he therefore, as was his custom, formed a

[1] Ahmed ibn Fartua, *Mai Idris of Bornu*, pp. 25–28. H. R. Palmer provides the following note on p. 70: —Kaza, one of the old 'So' towns, is about 14 miles east of Dikwa. Amsaka is south-east of Kaza, not very far from Kala Balge. As Amsaka is in the midst of a plain of dead flat black cotton soil, which would be entirely inundated during the rains and well into the dry season, it is possible to fix the date of the fall of Amsaka, from the date given, with some certainty, *i.e.*, 4th December, 1575.

camp, which he fortified with entrenchments and zariba. This was to be his base while he looted the country west of the Shari and formed an advanced camp at Jilbe, from which he conducted his raiding operations, leaving at Logone his women, baggage and other impedimenta. This country west of the Shari, was then under Shehu Hashim of Bornu who was living in Kukawa. On hearing of Rabeh's arrival in his territory he sent Momman Tar with 3,000 men to drive him back across the Shari. Rabeh left his camp and selected a favourable position in the vicinity of the village of Amja; here he waited the attack of the Bornu force; Momman Tar himself was a brave man, his men, however, were not so, and one volley from Rabeh's gunmen put them to flight. Tar was taken prisoner, and hundreds of his men slaughtered. Rabeh was always anxious to save the life of a brave man, with the idea of afterwards making him one of his leaders. After this victory one, Mallam Hiatu from Yola, approached Rabeh asking for his assistance to subdue Mandara and make him king. Rabeh replied, 'When a hunter wounds a beast he follows it until he gets it, so as Shehu Hashim wishes to fight I will not leave him until I have finished him.' Preparations were then commenced for an advance on Kukawa and the subjection of Bornu. Rabeh carefully selected his men; his force when completed numbered 500 horsemen armed chiefly with spears, 1,500 well-trained foot soldiers armed with rifles and the best of his muzzle-loading guns, also two small pieces of artillery.[1]

In this military connexion, we have another piece of original information of interest to the Rabeh researcher in Bornu. A trader taken prisoner by Rabeh at Kukawa, Abba, listed the following dispositions and armaments of Rabeh's army from the observations he made at Dikwa between 1893 and 1895. Rabeh's own regiment consisted of 360 rifles and 44 pieces of artillery of different descriptions, though none of it was mounted on wheels. This regiment used to drill regularly twice a day. Of the score or more numbered *bannières* that made up the rest of his army, numbering between 5,000 and 10,000 men, the biggest were that of Gadim (570 rifles) and those commanded by Babiker (Abubakar) and his second son Fad-el-Allah. The rest, mostly under Jelaba or Arab slaves from Darfur, counted about a hundred cap guns and rifles each. Many of these arms were captured in the rape of Kukawa in 1893.

After he had captured the Bornu capital, Rabeh returned to

[1] Verbatim account given by eye-witnesses to Major A. McClintock, quoted in J. B. Welman, *Gazetteer of Bornu Province*, pp. 22–23.

Dikwa via Alo. For the next seven years this was to be his capital, splendidly isolated in the rains by the impenetrable *firki* swamp. It may be that he was here pausing to recoup his strength before he attempted the most glamorous prize of all, Kano. He kept a regularly drilled army of 20,000 men and every Friday a military parade was held in Dikwa. The importance of the walled town of Dikwa had been commented on by Dr Barth forty years earlier. He had written:

The sight of this town, with its walls over-towered by the regularly-shaped crowns of magnificent fig-trees, was very imposing.

The town of Dikowa, near which we were encamped, seemed well deserving some attention, as having been repeatedly the residence of the rulers of the country, and being still one of the largest towns in the kingdom. I therefore paid a visit to it in the afternoon of the second day of our stay, being accompanied by my friend Billama. We entered the town by the western gate; and I saw that the walls were about thirty feet high, and terraced on the inside like those of the capital, and of considerable breadth at the base: they were in a state of good repair. I was struck by the height and round shape of the huts, which entirely wanted the characteristic tip, or, as the Kanuri people call it, *kogi ngimbe*, and were of the same kind as I had observed in the other towns of this southern province. Every hut had its little courtyard, in some of which vegetation was seen, mostly *karas*.

The further we proceeded, the more I was pleased with the general appearance of the town, the exterior of which had made a favourable impression upon me on our first arrival. Large, beautiful, wide-spreading fig-trees, *ngabore*, *chedia* or elastic gum-trees, and *korna*-trees, spread their shade all around, and two or three isolated pawpaw-trees, or, as the Kanuri call them, *bambus-masarbe*, with their remarkable feathery crowns and their smooth virgin-like stems, formed a lively contrast to the broad-leafed canopy of the other trees, while the hedges and fences of the courtyards were partly enlivened by a luxurious creeper called *dagdagel* by the natives. The real nucleus of the town seemed to consist entirely of clay houses.

After a very pleasant ride, we reached the house of the *mainta*, or governor, who still enjoys a certain degree of independence. The chief ornament of the place in front of his house was the most splendid caoutchouc-tree I have ever seen; indeed I can scarcely imagine that the diameter of its crown, which was so regularly and symmetrically shaped that it appeared as if effected by art, measured less than from seventy to eighty feet. It really formed a beautiful *fage*, or, as the Hausa people call it, *ichenbatu*, or open council-hall, such as are common in these places; but at present no political business of any importance was transacted here, and it formed a favourite lounge for idle people, amongst whom there was a troop of musicians, playing lustily upon their instruments to console the petty chief for the loss of his former power, which had dwindled away to a mere shadow. I would gladly have paid him a visit; but, poor as I was at the time, and without a single article worthy of his acceptance, I was rather glad that I was under no obligation to him.[1]

Now it became Rabeh's town, and there is much to remind the visitor even today of the presence of this remarkable despot. Rabeh's huge fortress-house, reputed in Dikwa lore to have had upstairs the Koran room and downstairs to have contained a thousand rooms each with two concubines, is symbolic and at times almost redolent of the brutal glory that has departed; there stands a monument to Béhagle, the French trader whom in 1899 Rabeh publicly hanged in Dikwa (the executioner was Sururu, later a ward-head in Maifoni where he was in charge of the remnants of Rabeh's Kotoko followers), and within the 1950s it was yet possible to find one or two greybeards who could recount their personal memories of the conqueror of Bornu.[2]

With the murder of Kiari, described in the section on Bornu, Rabeh experienced no more opposition in Bornu. However, Shehu Kiari's brother, Sanda Limanambe, tried to collect the remainder of the Shehu's people at Wuduro, near Konduga, but Rabeh fell upon them and killed Sanda Limanambe. It is because of this that Sanda is still remembered as Sanda Wuduroma. Just for good measure, he handed over the whole country to the doubtful mercies of his army, who looted, pillaged and burned for six months. The Fulani and Koyam of Bornu still use the proverb: 'Rabeh takes a hundred cattle to make one pot of soup.' Rabeh then divided the area into a number of districts and handed them over to his headman who continued to live in Dikwa.

At the close of the century the French made several unsuccessful attempts to break the power of Rabeh, but it was not until they sent a huge military expedition under Colonel Lamy that they defeated him. Rabeh was killed in a battle at Kusseri, by the confluence of the Shari and the Logone, in 1900; Lamy, too, was mortally wounded. According to tradition Commandant Lamy

[1] Quoted in A. H. M. Kirk-Greene, *Barth's Travels in Nigeria*, pp. 215–16.

[2] For the full account, see A. H. M. Kirk-Greene, 'Hanged by Rabeh', *West African Review*, March 1958.

went round all the wounded lying on the battlefield, looking for his great adversary Rabeh, and asking each one 'Are you Rabeh?'. At length he came to Rabeh himself. At the question, Rabeh pulled himself to his feet and buried his dagger into Lamy's heart. His aides immediately struck Rabeh down. The two generals fell apart, dead.[1] Fad-el-Allah, who escaped with several thousand of his father's troops and followers, was driven out of Dikwa and retreated to Kilba. Then he returned to ravage Bornu, until he was killed by the French at Gujba in 1901. Fad-el-Allah made his last stand in a grove of baobab trees which can still be identified, just outside the south-west of the town. When he was shot through the chest, his lieutenant Yerima Lama lifted him back onto his horse and rode off with him. He died within a few hours and was buried in the swamp at Mutwe, but next day the French exhumed the body and took the head back to Dikwa as proof of his end. In 1963 a report from Bornu hinted that Rabeh's daughter was still alive,[2] and in Bornu Province, but this has yet to be substantiated.

Soon after Rabeh's death the French sought to revivify the Al Kanemi dynasty of Bornu. From Zinder, a former state of the Bornu empire, they proclaimed Sanda Kura, one of the sons of Shehu Ibrahim who had died at Kukawa in 1845, as the tenth Shehu of Bornu. He took the name of Shehu Umar and moved to Dikwa. Within a year he had been deposed for intrigues with his brothers in British Bornu. He was replaced by his brother Garbai, from whom the French demanded an indemnity of 80,000 dollars in return for delivering him from his enemies. After only a few months Garbai (Shehu Bukar), who not only had the impossible task of collecting this exorbitant indemnity from his impoverished people but who had also received messages from Colonel Morland, in charge of the British columns marching on Bornu, that if he came across the border he would be recognized as ruler of British Bornu, fled first to Kanem and then to Monguno where he became Shehu. Soon after Shehu Bukar's flight, the French withdrew from Dikwa and set up their base at Kusseri, now

[1] We are grateful to the Emir of Dikwa for confirming this tradition. In his letter he points out that the graves of both Rabeh and Lamy are located near Gamboru and in the colonial days the French held an annual ceremony at the spot. A modern variant on the story is that Rabeh killed Lamy with a small pistol that he had concealed in his tobe.

[2] *Nigerian Citizen*, 10 April 1963, p. 6.

renamed Fort Foureau. The Germans replaced the French in Dikwa, the apparent geographical key to the political control of the Chad basin. The French took with them Abba Sanusi and at Turbon Gida, just east of Maine, they installed him as Shehu in 1904. Shortly afterwards he was deposed and returned to British Bornu, whence he was exiled to Zungeru. During the interim between Shehu Bukar's flight and the German occupation of Dikwa, the people had proclaimed Abba Masta Gumsumi as their Shehu, but the Germans refused to afford him recognition and instead appointed Sanda Mandarama in 1902. Three years later Shehu Sanda Mandarama sought asylum in Mofoni, the British station in Bornu. The Germans installed Ibrahim as Shehu of German Bornu, but a year later Sanda Mandarama returned to Dikwa and was restored to the throne. He continued as Shehu of Dikwa throughout the Cameroons campaign of 1914–16, and on his death in 1917 he was succeeded by Sanda Kiarimi, the son of Shehu Kiari whom Rabeh had murdered.

The French, anxious over the arrival of a large German expedition in the Chad area, had withdrawn from Bornu to Kusseri (Fort Foureau) beyond the banks of the Shari, and the Dikwa area had meanwhile come under German occupation. These territorial adjustments were effected by the Anglo-French boundary commissions (from the Niger to Chad) of 1902 and 1905, the Anglo-German boundary commission (from Yola to Chad) of 1905, and the Franco-German agreement of 1911.

In 1922 Dikwa emirate, which had been taken over by the British in 1916, was recognized as mandated territory under the League of Nations. It now became a separate Division of Bornu Province, and its Emir, Shehu Umar, dropped the title of Shehu of German Bornu in favour of Shehu of Dikwa.

The locust plagues of the 1930s were particularly severe in Dikwa, calling forth a comparison with the ravages of Rabeh. This disaster was followed in 1935 by a series of daylight abductions of young children by a group of mounted horsemen, led by 'the man on the white horse'.

When the Shehu of Bornu, Sanda Kura, died in 1937, Shehu Sanda Kiarimi of Dikwa (1917–37) became Shehu of Bornu and his younger brother, Abba Masta, then district head of Bama was appointed as Emir[1] of Dikwa. During this time, the capital was

[1] See last sentence of Sir Kashim Ibrahim's note on p. 354.

removed from Dikwa to Bama in 1942, owing to the lack of all-season roads during the greater part of the year and to the insalubrious environment caused by the surrounding marshy grounds.

On the death of Mai Masta in 1950, his nephew Bukar ibn Umar El Kanemi was appointed Emir. This was a further linking of the two royal houses, for the new Emir was a son of the then Shehu of Bornu. But tragedy struck Dikwa all too soon. The emirate lost both its new Emir and its respected Waziri, Mamman Tar, by death in 1952. The throne now went to Abba Masta, a son of the Sanda Mandarama who had been Shehu of German Dikwa. Though a graduate of Katsina College, Abba Masta was at this time only village head of Bama. He assumed the title of Mustafa III. Unfortunately serious friction developed between the Emir and his councillors, and after a head-on clash followed gubernatorial warnings Mustafa was deposed in 1954.

Abba Yarema, district head of Gulumba and a son of Ibrahim who had momentarily held office under the Germans, was appointed and took the name of Umar Ibn Ibrahim. A graduate of both Kaduna college and the school of engineering, he gained much from his tour to Europe and quickly infused a new spirit.

A total eclipse of the sun was observed, almost to perfection, in the Dikwa-Gadam-Damasak area in 1959. In the same year, the borehole at Ngala averaged 10,000 gallons per hour—a figure of great significance in the aridity of northern Bornu.

Yet terrestrial events in Dikwa were destined to match the celestial ones. Dikwa was, as we have seen, a mandated territory, renamed Trust Territory in 1946. This meant that the people took part in the 1959 United Nations plebiscite to determine the next stage in their political future. The poll of sixty-two per cent. of the Northern Trust Territory peoples, predominantly from Adamawa and Dikwa emirates, voting against immediate inclusion into Northern Nigeria, was interpreted as a strong protest against the local administration in these areas. As a result of a Commission of Inquiry headed by the Emir of Yauri, sweeping local government reforms were effected in 1960. In response to the separatist sympathies of the Gwoza[1] people, their district was removed from the jurisdiction of Dikwa emirate and created a separate Native

[1] An excellent historical novel of these hill-top peoples is S. White, *Descent from the Hills*, 1963. See also J. Welman's story 'Spears Against Them', in *A Thorny Wilderness*, 1950.

Authority when the Northern Cameroons became the Trust Territory Province in October 1960. At the subsequent U.N. plebiscite held in February 1961 the people, satisfied with the Government's promise that they would retain their new identity as the 13th Province of Northern Nigeria, voted in favour of rejoining their kith and kin. A year later Dikwa requested transfer out of the new Sardauna Province back into its historical home of Greater Bornu. Though Dikwa carries a large Shuwa Arab population, its Kanuri element and its strong ties with Bornu made this plea acceptable and the transfer was effected at the end of 1962.

THE SHEHUS AND MAIS OF DIKWA*

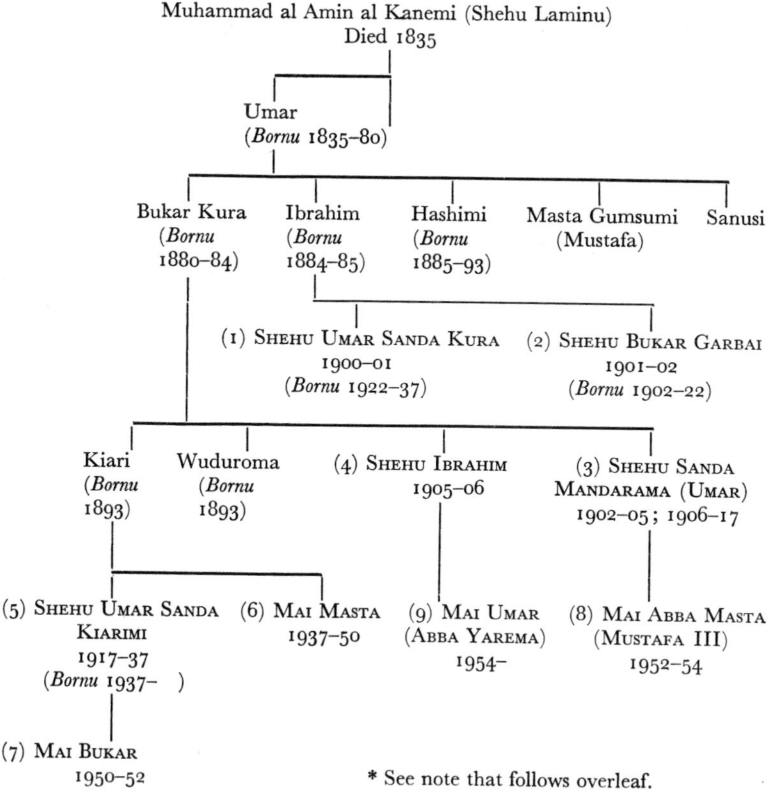

* See note that follows overleaf.

Note: In confirming the order and dates of the Shehus and Mais shown on the genealogical table above, Sir Kashim Ibrahim, Governor of Northern Nigeria, has very kindly supplied the following note.

'When the British and the Germans restored the Kanemi dynasty in Bornu and Dikwa respectively after the confusion and disintegration of Bornu brought about by the advent of Rabeh, a handful of people from Kukawa and Abba Sanusi happened to be at Maine (Turban Gida) in the French sector of Bornu, and they got around Abba Sanusi and proclaimed him Shehu for that part of the territory. Whether that move obtained the backing and approval of the French it was not clear, because when the Shehu and people of Bornu objected to the proclamation and Lugard demanded Abba Sanusi's deposition and extradition by the French, they handed him over and he was taken captive in Lokoja until his death. So Abba Sanusi was never in fact a Shehu although some people still remember him as such.

Masta Gumsumi was merely a stop-gap put in by only one man. When Shehu Garbai fled to Kanem he left Mastirema, a slave, behind to manage affairs, particularly those of his household. But Mastirema wanted to rule, and to make his hands stronger he took it upon himself and appointed Masta Gumsumi as a figure Shehu and relegated him to the background when he carried on what official business there was, if any. Shehu Garbai, although away in Kanem, was still the rightful Shehu until he returned. Masta Gumsumi was never popularly accepted and recognized by the people. . . . *In Dikwa the title of Shehu ended with Shehu Sanda Kiarimi, and all subsequent successors are strictly called Mais.*'

XXV. GUMEL

A CERTAIN Dan Juma, the son of Musa from Kano, came to Dogoma about the middle of the eighteenth century, with a small following of Mangawa, 'the people of the salt'. His nephew Adamu (Karro) was later elected chief owing to Dan Juma's unpopularity. After ruling six years he was killed in a cattle-raid and was succeeded by his brother, Dan Juma, who is said to have founded Gumel in about 1750. The word is said to be a corruption from the Fulani term *gubele* used to describe a short-horned cow, though locally the area is often referred to as Lautaye. After Dan Juma's death Bornu seems to have taken the little kingdom under its wing, and the Shehu of Bornu continued to exact tribute from Gumel during the nineteenth century. Many of the original inhabitants are said to have been from Bornu. Gumel was one of the states in the Hausa-Bornu no-man's land that did not acknowledge the suzerainty of Sokoto.

At the turn of the century, Gumel, under Dan Auwa, engaged in many successful raids, but after his death in 1828 the Gumel fortunes seem to have declined, and on one occasion the town was sacked by Damagaram. Writing of the town in 1851, Dr Barth noted:

March 13. Not waiting for the new horseman whom I was to receive here early in the morning, I went on in advance with my companion, in order to reach Gummel before the heat of the day. . . .

We reached the considerable town of Gummel just when the sun began to shine with great power; and at the gate we separated, the *sherif* taking his way directly towards his quarters in the southern part of the town, while I was obliged to go first to the house of the governor, the famous Dan-Tanoma (the son of Tanoma, his own name being entirely unknown to the people); but on account of his great age, neither on this nor on a later occasion did I get a sight of him. Indeed he was soon to leave this world, and by his death to plunge not only the town wherein he resided, but the whole neighbouring country, into a destructive civil war between his two sons.

However, on my first visit Gummel was still a flourishing place, and well inhabited, and I had to pass through an intricate labyrinth of narrow streets enclosed between fences of mats and reeds surrounding huts and courtyards, before I reached the dwellings of the few Arabs who live here; and after looking about for some time I obtained quarters near the house of Salem Maidukia (the Rothschild of Gummel).

... The next morning I went with Abd el Khafif to pay our compliments to old Dan-Tanoma. His residence, surrounded by high clay walls, and including, besides numbers of huts for his household and numerous wives, some spacious halls of clay, was of considerable extent; and the courtyard, shaded by a wide-spreading, luxuriant tamarind tree, was a very noble area. While we sat there awaiting the governor's pleasure, I had a fair insight into the concerns of this little court, all the well-fed, idle parasites coming in one after the other, and rivalling each other in trivial jokes. The Hausa language is the language of the court; and the offices are similar to those which I mentioned above with regard to Kano. Having waited a long time in vain, the weak old man sending an excuse, as he could not grant us an interview, we returned to our quarters.

To-day being Friday was market-day; and in order to see the market in its greatest activity I mounted at noon on horseback, and went out. In all these parts of Negroland, the customs of which are in every respect so different from those of Yoruba and the neighbouring countries, the market (in Kukawa and Masena, as well as in Kano, Sokoto, and even Timbuktu) is always most frequented and most busy in the hottest hours of the day, notwithstanding the great fatigue which all the people, and particularly the strangers, have to undergo.

The market of Gummel is held outside the town, between the two gates on the west side, but nearer to the *chinna-n-yala* (the northern gate), which is remarkable on account of its well-fortified condition.

Though I had heard a good deal about Gummel, I was nevertheless surprised at the size and the activity of the market, although that held on Saturday is said to be still more important. Gummel is the chief market for the very extensive trade in natron, which, as I have mentioned above, is carried on between Kukawa and Muniyo on one side, and Nupe or Nyffi on the other; for this trade passes from one hand into another, and the Bornu people very rarely carry this merchandise further than Gummel. Large masses of natron, certainly amounting to at least one thousand loads of both qualities mentioned above, were offered here for sale—the full bullock's load of the better quality for five thousand, an ass's load of the inferior sort for five hundred *kurdi*. There were also about three hundred stalls or sheds, but not arranged in regular rows, where a great variety of objects were offered for sale—all sorts of clothing, tools, earthenware pots, all kinds of victuals, cattle, sheep, donkeys, horses—in short, everything of home or foreign produce which is in request among the natives.

Greatly delighted with my visit to the market, though not a little affected by the exposure to the sun during the hot hours, I returned to my quarters; for though a practised traveller will bear very well the most scorching power of the sun, if he sets out in the morning, and by degrees becomes inured to greater and greater heat, he may suffer fatally from exposing himself for a long time to the mid-day sun, after having spent the morning in the shade. Later in the afternoon, the governor sent, as a gift to me and Abd el Khafif, through his principal courtiers (such as the Ghaladima, the Chiroma, and others, who were accompanied by a long train of followers), a young bullock, they being instructed at the same time to receive in return the present, or *salam*, as it is generally called, which we had prepared for him. I gave them a *subeta* and a small flask with rose oil, which is an article in great request with the fashionable world in Hausa and Bornu. In the evening, we received also corn for our horses.[1]

After Dan Auwa's death in 1828 there followed a long record of petty fights with Zinder, Hadejia and Kano until eventually, in 1872, the Gumelawa were decisively defeated by Hadejia at Zaburam. Their Emir, Abdullahi, was killed. This put an end to the protracted Gumel-Hadejia wars.

Towards the end of the century Damagaram seems to have raided with impunity, penetrating right into the town of Gumel on at least two occasions, and the emirate became depopulated. Another pestilential invader was Rabeh: that he threatened to penetrate so far westwards is proved by the following letter sent by Emir Ahmadu to Aliyu, Emir of Kano:

After salutations, the reason for my letter to you is that we have heard news of the accursed evil foe, the enemy of all true believers, Rabeh. He has now come near to us and reached Bedde. He has driven them away, so that their chief has left and gone to Hadejia. And the Sarkin Hadejia took counsel with his people whether to fight or fly. So I have sent to you that you may not hear the news on a sudden that you may know of the matter. Do you arise to prayer. We have collected our *malamai* and they are making prayer for us. May Allah preserve both us and you from this evil affliction. May He grant us victory together over all our foes.[2]

Ahmadu submitted to Lugard in 1903 and after that the people returned in large numbers to enjoy a state of hitherto unaccustomed security.

[1] Quoted in A. H. M. Kirk-Greene, *Barth's Travels in Nigeria*, p. 128.
[2] H. F. Backwell, *The Occupation of Hausaland*, p. 60.

Ahmadu was deposed in 1915 and succeeded by Mamman na Kota. In 1915 the emirate was placed alongside Hadejia to form the new Hadejia Division. Annual reports have so little startling news to tell of this area that the sinking of 200-foot wells and even the opening of the first dispensary in 1931 become significant. Mamman na Kota reigned for nearly thirty years and he was succeeded in 1944 by his son Maina Mamman who became the fourteenth Emir of Gumel at the early age of 32. The Emir's Council was strengthened in 1956 to relieve the overburdened Waziri and again in 1959. The emirate suffered a blow by the death of the Turaki in 1957.

THE EMIRS OF GUMEL

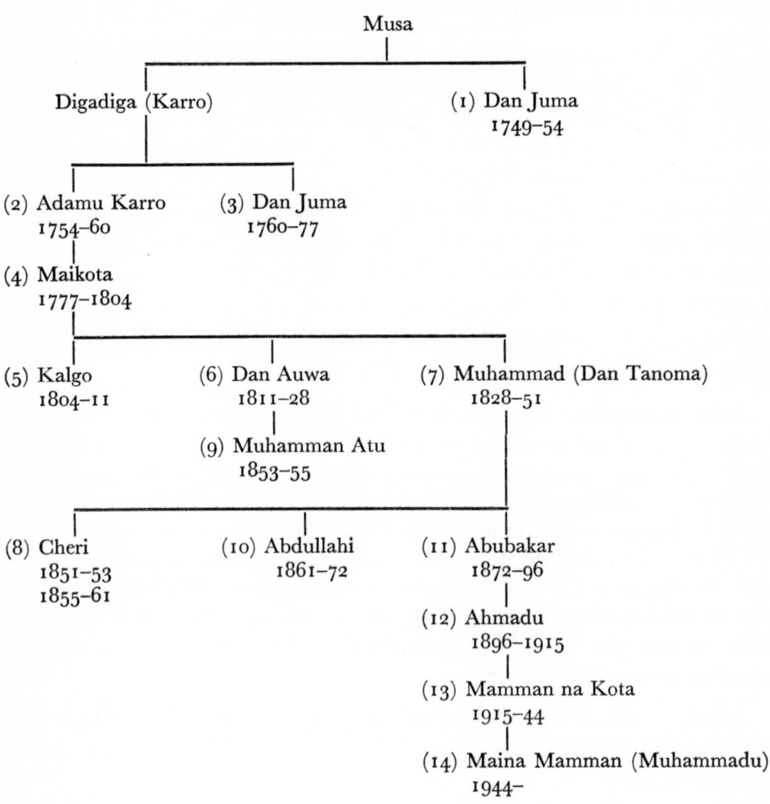

Note: Some of the above dates have yet to be confirmed.

XXVI. FIKA

It would seem that the Bolewa, the ruling people of modern Fika emirate, came from round the shores of Lake Chad. Like so many Nigerian peoples, they claim an ultimate provenance from the Yemen. Their leader was known as Magaji, a title to this day borne by the eldest son of the Emir of Fika. After a number of years in Babur county and in Bornu they settled at Lariski (some say Wuyo), but a few years later, in about 1443, under their *moi* or king Idrisa (Disa) Bunowo, they moved into the hills by Daniski.

According to the local legend, when the chief of the Bolewa reached this place he reined in his horse and shouted to his followers: *daniski*, 'here I halt'. For what it is worth, the story goes on that the Ngamo, who were the aboriginal inhabitants of the area, cried out: 'Why?' and so the newcomers earned their name of 'the why people'. Another ascription, based on the fact that the Hausa used to refer to the Bolewa country as Bolo-bolo, is that in Fika the time for the two daily meals was announced publicly. The people would take up the cry in answer and then eat. Strangers, puzzled by this behaviour, seized on the Bolewa word for two, *bolo*, and called them the Bolo-bolo people.

Of the way the Bolewa overcame the Ngamo the following tale is still told in Potiskum. The Bolewa were not strong enough to seize the land by force; they did, however, possess the secret of a rare red dye. Envious of the beauty of the way in which the Bolewa dyed their bodies a deep red, the Ngamo asked that they too might have the same decoration. The Bolewa now saw their chance. Yes, they replied, it would be possible to allow this for the elders and the best warriors—always provided that the proper ceremonies would be observed. This was agreed by the Ngamo.

Three large bulls were slain and skinned, then their hides still wet, were cut into thongs. Each of the elders and the leading warriors was invited to step forward for the colouring ceremony. Each had to hold his wrists together and insert them into a loop of raw, wet hide. If an initiate succeeded, the thong was tied into a loose, comfortable knot. The initiates were then told to sit down in a circle and after a few hours their skin would turn the desired colour. As the time passed, the hide thongs dried out and tightened round the wrists of the Ngamo men. When the Bolewa saw that the tribal leaders were quite helpless, they fell upon them and slew them all.[1] The Bolewa thus seized the land of the Ngamo.

Tradition has it that the Bolewa lived at Daniski for 361 years and 7 months before their chief Moi Buraimah built for himself a walled town in the plains, called Lafiya Moi; this subsequently became Fika, in about 1805. One of the acquisitions that the Bolewa are reputed to have brought with them from Daniski was the date palm, and today Fika is celebrated for its sweet dates. Chroniclers have listed thirty-five Bolewa kings, with the title of *Moi*, up to the present day. The seven councillors or Magaji are remembered by the continuance of their traditional titles in Fika to this day: they are Tinja, Dalati, Galadima, Ciroma, Tinja Fuya, Tamana and Masaya.[2] There is no record of either the Jukun or the Fulani invasion having had any significant effect on Bolewa history; though they were sorely tried by the ravages of Rabeh, they were never conquered by him. The Bolewa claim to have accepted Islam while they were at Daniski. The Fika Bolewa —there are other groups in the neighbouring provinces—call themselves the Am Fika.

Potiskum, in favour of which Fika was abandoned in 1924 as the emirate headquarters, was founded by a chief of the Ngizim people. The original Karekare town is said to have been captured by a grandfather of Moi Bauya, who came from Birni Ngazargamu. The Ngizim have a number of features in common with the people of Bedde, and it is thought they came into Bornu in the same invasion wave that brought the Bedde to the banks of the Komadugu Yobe west of Geidam. The Ngizim at first centred on Mugni (Kariari) in the Borsari district of modern Bornu. From here they diverged, most of them migrating southwards to Potiskum and the remainder moving up the river to Gaska. Some scholars attribute this exodus to the widespread alarm caused in the area by the fall of Birni Ngazargamu, the capital of Bornu, in 1809.

[1] The same story is told of how the Kanuri overcame the So. See page 90, and also Yves Urvoy, *Histoire de l'Empire du Bornou*, p. 23.

[2] I am grateful to Fika N.A. for this list of title-holders and to M. Gimba Ahmed, Ministry of Information, for points raised when we discussed this text.—A.K-G.

The land round Potiskum at that time was held by the Karekare people, focussed on Pakarau and Langoa. However, Bauya encountered no opposition and was able to build his new town of Potiskum. He then set himself up as Moi, with authority over both his own people and the Karekare. On the coming of the British the Moi, who was then Bundi, was confirmed in his overlordship of these two districts, but in 1909 he was deposed and succeeded by his brother Agudum.

At the same time the Karekare portion of Agudum's kingdom was taken away and given to the Moi Fika, who placed the district in the charge of his son Suleiman with the title of Lawan. Agudum never ceased to intrigue against Lawan Suleiman, with the result that he was deposed and his remaining territory, the district of Ngizim, was transferred to Fika. The headquarters of the reunited districts now became Potiskum. Agudum was not yet finished, however. In 1915 he made a full-scale attack against Potiskum. The Fika officials were driven out and Agudum proclaimed himself Moi again. His triumph was but shortlived: a police patrol restored order and Agudum was hanged for murder. Potiskum has since remained under the Emir of Fika.

In 1955 the two districts that comprised Fika emirate were abolished and replaced by a novel system of village group areas placed under the direct supervision of N.A. Councillors. Further administrative reorganizations took place in 1960 when village group councils were abolished in favour of districts once again: Fika, Potiskum and Nangere.

The present Emir of Fika, Alhaji Muhammadu Ibn Idrissa, is one of the best-loved and best-known emirs in the country. He was appointed Emir in 1922 and has received many honours for his services to the people in his emirate. Within the first few years of his reign he made history by driving his own motor-car. Though now nearly seventy-five years old, he is a bold horseman. His personal leadership of the *jafi* at the time of the Royal visit to Kaduna in 1956 gave rise to a comment from a Fika trader that has since assumed the aura of proverb in Potiskum: 'That will lengthen the beard of the Emir of Fika.'

THE KINGS AND EMIRS OF FIKA

1.	Idrisa (known as Sarki)	7 years
2.	Atman (known as Sarki)	9 years
3.	Moi Albo (the first Moi)	8 years
4.	Mele Manso	17 years
5.	Anbanga	10 years
6.	Bunowo	56 years
7.	Barma dan Moi Bunowo	42 years
8.	Gandowo	15 years
9.	Langawa Daka	10 years
10.	Halbo, son of Moi Langawa	18 years
11.	Mama Kayi	35 years
12.	Bawa Kayi	10 years
13.	Mele Fusan, son of Moi Mama Kayi	25 years
14.	Buraima Wamu, brother of Mele	1 year
15.	Mama Mulu, son of Bawa Kayi	11 years
16.	Adam Bakam, son of Mama Kayi	7 years
17.	Mama Korya, son of Moi Bawa	17 years
18.	Mama Gimsi, son of Mama Kayi	4 years
19.	Sule Ladi, son of Moi Bawa	3 years
20.	Aji Daka, son of Mele	18 years
21.	Langawa, son of Moi Bawa	17 years
22.	Usman Gana, son of Mele	9 years
23.	Mammadi Gizze, son of Mama Kayi	8 years
24.	Mele Filata, son of Mama Gimsi	2 years

The Bolewa left Daniski Hill and moved to Fika.

25.	Moi Buraima	16 years
26.	Adam	22 years
27.	Disa Siri	13 years
28.	Mammadi Gaganga	10 years
29.	Ismaila, 1867–71	
30.	Mammadi Buye, 1871–82	
31.	Aji, 1882	
32.	Mama (Mohammed), 1882–85	
33.	Sule, 1885–1902	
34.	Disa (Idrissa), 1902–22	
35.	Muhammadu Ibn Idrissa, 1922–	

XXVII. BEDDE

ACCORDING to Bornu traditions, the Bade and the related Ngizim of Potiskum—who today comprise the emirate of Bedde—were the first peoples to migrate from Kanem round the north side of Lake Chad and reach the Komadugu Yobe, at the time when the So were still the dominant power in Bornu. They seemed to have paused in their westward migration at Dillawa, east of Geidam; the area is still sometimes referred to as Badar, the name of the site claimed by the Bedde as that of their original home in the east.

When they reached Dadigar in Borsari, they split up under the four sons of their leader. The eldest, Ago, remained where he was and so founded the Bedde dynasty. The second, Muza, turned north and is said to have established a Tuareg dynasty. Amsagiya (Agumsage) or Kwolum continued westwards to found the Ngizim, while Dodo (Buyam) went south to found the Ngazar round Potiskum.

Uncertainty exists about when this took place, but some scholars have estimated that the Bedde arrived well before the foundation of Birni Ngazargamu, perhaps as early as *c.* 1300. During the reign of Dyagana at Tagali, the Kanuri built Birni Ngazargamu. Dyagana travelled thither to salute the *Mai* on behalf of the people of Bedde and obtained the *sarauta* or title of Dugum. The Galadima of Bornu was appointed *chima*, that is to say 'overlord', of Bedde. In the years that followed, the Tagali unit, enjoying the support of the Galadima at Nguru in return for their vassalage, acquired a position of leadership among the other Bedde clans, and the whole group once again moved westwards, this time to the country between the Katagum and Hadejia rivers. It is for this reason that the Tagali Bedde look on themselves as the senior stock.

The present royal family, Gidgid, appear to have moved from Dadigar comparatively late. They were driven out of their first new settlement, at Gazai, by the Fulani, and eventually joined up with their kith and kin at Tagali, in the reign of Mada Zabuwa in about 1790. They were allowed to settle at Gayin, to the north of the town, but when the Tagali people objected for fear that their own chief would have his authority undermined, they moved yet again. This time they settled at Gidgid, some fifteen miles south-east of Gorgoram. But fate was still unkind. No sooner had they established themselves than their chief, Dugum Akuya, was killed in a raid by the Hadejia Fulani under Sambo Digimsa. He was succeeded by his son Lawan Babuje. The Fulani so harried the Bedde that they were compelled to move their headquarters from Gidgid to Agama Kasha, then to Sagmaga, and then to Satako.

Lawan Babuje was a great leader. He obtained his title of Lawan from Shehu Laminu for supporting the Kanuri arms, but soon he began to learn that his connexion with Bornu was not without its drawbacks. When the Kanuri continued to demand large numbers of slaves, Babuje determined to play on the independent spirit of his people and enlist the support of all the Bedde groups in an alliance to defend themselves against the interference of Kanuri and Fulani alike. With the co-operation of Tagali, Katamma, Dumari and the minor chief of Gunghwei, the large fortified town of Gorgoram was built in about 1825. The walled and gated towns of Bedde are a striking feature to this day. So successful was this scheme and so united were the Bedde under Babuje's leadership that neither Hadejia nor Bornu could break the independence of Bedde. Tagali alone succumbed. Unwisely allowing its jealousy of Babuje to win the day, it remained aloof from the pan-Bedde confederation after the initial construction of Gorgoram, and paid the penalty for its isolationism by falling prey to the army of Shehu Umar.

Lawan Babuje, who died seven years after Shehu Laminu, was followed by his son Mai Alhaji, also a mighty warrior. He repulsed Shehu Umar when he attempted to lay siege to Gorgoram, and it was with his own hand that he slew the notorious Buhari of Hadejia[1] when he stormed the walls of Gorgoram. Thus encouraged, Mai Alhaji turned to the attack and Bedde forces began to raid into Bornu territory. In order to put a stop to this, the Shehu sent Abba Bukar against Bedde in 1855, but although he besieged Gorgoram for four months he was unable to take the town and had to withdraw.

[1] See section on Hadejia, p. 485 ff.

Another raid on Bedde followed under Kacalla Ali Fugumami, who was determined to put up a better show than Abba Bukar. But he, too, was defeated by the Beddawa in a bloody battle just west of Gashua. Thereafter there was a period of peace in this no-man's land between Fulani and Kanuri.

Visiting the Bedde country about this time, the great explorer-scholar Dr Barth noted of Gashua, the present capital:

> Three miles further on, turning a little more southward from our westerly direction, we reached the town of Geshiya, once a strong place and surrounded by a clay wall, but at present in a state of great decay, although it is still tolerably peopled, the groups of conical huts being separated by fences of matting into several quarters. Here we encamped on the north side, near a fine tamarind tree, where millet was grown to a great extent. The south and west sides were surrounded by an extensive swamp or swampy watercourse fed by the Komadugu, and, with its dense forest, affording to the inhabitants a safe retreat in case of an attack from their enemies. All the towns of the Bedde are situated in similar positions.[1]

Alhaji was succeeded by his son Duna as Mai. In his reign great disaster struck Bornu, the incursion of Rabeh. Duna was defeated by Shehu Dab, who captured Gorgoram, albeit not without the Bedde forces inflicting heavy casualties on Rabeh's army in a skilful ambush. Shehu Dab summoned Mai Duna's brother Saleh from Allaguerno and appointed him Mai Bedde. Mai Saleh had to defend his position against his brother, who enlisted the help of Hadejia. In this he was successful, and at the time of the British occupation he was recognized as an independent emir. On Saleh's death in 1919, his son Sule became Emir of Bedde. He was deposed in 1941 and was followed by Umara. In 1945 Umar, the eldest son of Mai Saleh, became emir.

Though Gorgoram has given way to Gashua as the capital of Bedde—the old walls of this fortified town are still in fair shape—economically the emirate has perforce looked towards the rail-head of Nguru. There, too, the Divisional headquarters is sited, exceptionally, outside the very emirate from which the Division takes its name. The present Emir, Mai Umar Suleiman, has had a distinguished career and joins the present Emirs of Yauri (Muhammad Tukur), Lapai (Muhammadu Kobo) and Argungu (Muhammad Mera) in proving that big men can come from the

[1] Quoted in A. H. M. Kirk-Greene, *Barth's Travels in Nigeria*, p. 231.

smallest emirates. The Emir of Bedde holds the posts of Deputy President of the Northern House of Chiefs and of Chairman of the Ahmadu Bello University Council.[1]

THE EMIRS OF BEDDE

The Gidgid dynasty

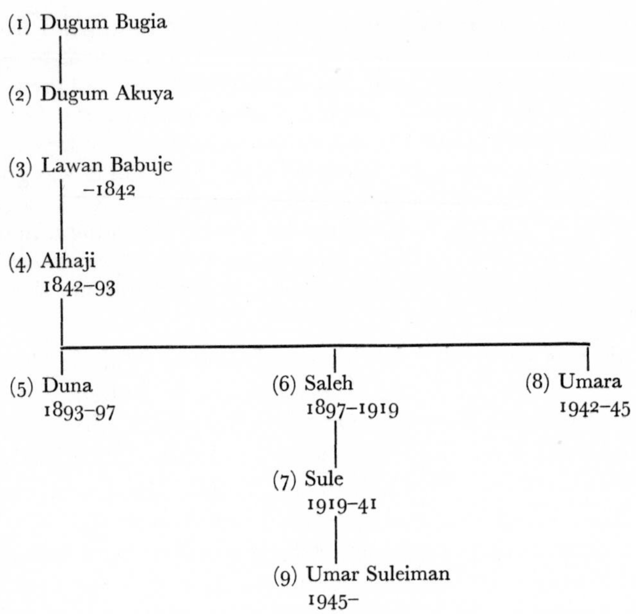

[1] We are indebted to the Emir for his personal revision of our manuscript history of Bedde.

3. EMIRATES DERIVING FROM THE SOKOTO EMPIRE

(1) The North-Western States

XXVIII. SOKOTO

OF THE emirates of Northern Nigeria, Sokoto is the most senior. Its ranking relies less on the age of its ancestry than on Sokoto's dominating position based on its leadership of the jihad under Usman dan Fodio and the consequent establishment of the Fulani empire of Sokoto. From such a history does the Sultan of Sokoto derive both his title of *Sarkin Musulmi*, the Commander of the Faithful, and his status as the most senior of the First Class Chiefs in Northern Nigeria.

If the story of Sokoto proper is the record of the rise of the Fulani power and if Sokoto as a political and geographical unit did not emerge until the beginning of the nineteenth century, the history of the area is nevertheless an ancient one, in touch with the western Sudan empires of Mali and Songhai to the west, Bornu and later Kwararafa to the east, and Aïr or Asben to the north. The Mali tradition is still known in western Sokoto among the Zabarma, an ethnic group whose importance is at its greatest in the neighbouring Republic of Niger. When the two kingdoms of Songhai and Bornu were at their height, in the mid-sixteenth century, the nominal boundary between them was the land of Kebbi, at that time the eastern-most province of Songhai, with a shadowy frontier perhaps following a line running south from Birnin Kwonni east of Gwandu through Keɓɓe[1] to the Niger. In this area, too, were to be found the two Hausa kingdoms of Gobir and Zamfara, whose peoples, along with the Beri-Beri, Burmawa and nomad Fulani, paid yearly tribute to Daura, at that time tributary to Bornu. It is their story that is the early history of modern Sokoto.

[1] See footnote on p. 249.

Today most of the Gobirawa live in the Niger Republic, but a number are to be found in the Sabon Birni district of Sokoto, whose district head retains the title of Sarkin Gobir. The Gobirawa have a genealogy of over 125 kings and claim descent—some say this claim was a recent invention, put forward by Bawa Jan Gwarzo to avoid paying *murgu* or tribute to Bornu—from the nomadic Copts, or Kibdawa, in Arabia. Their history, as preserved in the records of the ruling house, shows a migration from Kabila, north of Mecca, to Gubur (Gobir) in the Yemen and thence through Khartoum and Bornu to Asben, Surukal, Birnin Lalle, Magali, and finally to Goran Rami. It was while the Gobirawa were at Gubur that they created their first king, Bana Turmi. Gobir thus became the most northerly of the Hausa states and her function was, according to the legend, to guard her sister-states from the predatory tribes of the Sahara. Certain it is that the Gobirawa enjoyed a proud martial reputation, perhaps developed by their long history of nomadism.

A manuscript in the possession of the *alkali* of Sabon Birni a generation ago shed more light on the Gobir tradition. It tells of how Muhammad the Prophet called on Bana Turmi, king of Gobir, to support him against his enemy Haibura. Bana Turmi, doubtful of the issue, determined to be on the winning side. He sent half of his retainers to assist Muhammad, half to help Haibura. Haibura was defeated and slain at Badr, and after the battle Muhammad saw a party of Gobirawa in flight. They were captured and brought before him. The Prophet asked them why they fled, for the victory was theirs. They explained that they had been fighting for Haibura, and disclosed the duplicity of Bana Turmi. Muhammad thereupon declared that to the end of time the Gobirawa would suffer from divided counsel and internal dissension.

After the battle of Badr, Bana Turmi left Yemen with his people and, travelling westward, died at the salt wells of Bilma. Bala, grandson of Bana Turmi, led the Gobirawa further west into the land of Asben. Here they found a tribe called Idirfunawa of the Adrar (rocky country), with whom the Gobirawa made common cause against the Tuareg.

It may be mentioned here that the ruling classes of Gobir are entirely distinct from the ordinary people. The latter are of common origin with the rest of the Hausawa, Daurawa, Katsinawa, and so on; but the chiefs of Gobir suggest a Coptic link, for they have under one eye the same mark which is found under the eye of the Pharaohs on the monuments, called in Hausa *takin kaza*, 'the fowl's footprint'.

Since the Asben oasis is so tied up with Sokoto history and since Asben is in a real sense the 'house' of the Gobirawa, it is worth summarizing the four stages of its history. Firstly, it was at one time occupied by Habash, whence its name Ah-bash-an or Absen. These Habash were then conquered by 'Beri-Beri' such as Zamfarawa and Zabarmawa. At a subsequent period a tribe with Egyptian affinities, the aristocracy of Gobir, came along and became masters of Asben. These were the descendants of Bana Turmi who died at Bilma. This was *c.* 1150–1350. Finally, the Gobirawa were driven south by the Tuareg to Birnin Lalle, not far from where Madawa now stands, where they established themselves early in the eighteenth century. This region, 120 miles north-east of Sokoto, is still known as Gobir Tudu.

According to Barth, when the Gobirawa were dispossessed by the Tuareg they made terms with their conquerors that they should not be exterminated and that the Tuareg king should always marry a black woman. Before Tuareg pressure became acute the Gobir capital was moved first to Maigali and later to Goran Rami, close to where Sabon Birni now stands. The people of a small village near Sabon Birni known as Garin Sarkin Asbin call themselves Asbinawa and claim kinship with the ruling family of Agades. They say they are descended from Isun, son of the Sultan of Istanbul by a slave woman. Isun found his mother's people oppressed by the Beri-Beri, and on applying to his father for assistance was given the town of Agades.

Because Gobir history impinges on that of the Zamfarawa in the eighteenth century, we must now turn to this kingdom. The chiefs of both these kingdoms are listed at the end of this chapter.

The contrast between the Zamfarawa and Gobirawa is that the former are in origin regarded as belonging to the Beri-Beri peoples which included the Yoruba, Jukun and Yaurawa, while the Gobirawa are Hausa otherwise Hau-sha or Habash). Zamfara was also one of the Hausa States, but ranked among the Banza Bakwai and not among the true seven. It is worth noting, *en passant*, that no less than four of the old Hausa States still survive in Sokoto Province.

Sultan Bello ascribes Zamfara's origin to a Katsina father

and a Gobir mother. The people of Zamfara generally claim descent from hunters known as Maguzawa,[1] who at one time occupied the bush that was later to become Kano. This would explain the *taubastaka* or cousinship that exists between Zamfarawa and Kanawa. Their first settlement was established at Dutsi in the modern Zurmi district of Sokoto, whose chief today is called Sarkin Zamfara. For seven years they had no ruler, but then they appointed one Dakka as their chief. From this derives one of the titles of every Sarkin Zamfara, *gimshikin gidan Dakka*, 'pillar of the house of Dakka'. Four more chiefs followed Dakka: Jatau, Jimir Dakka, Kokai Kokai and Dudufani; then a woman, Algoje, was chosen. Legend has it that all were giants, Samodawa. At Dutsi it is said Dakka could not only eat a whole ox at one meal but that when he shouted his voice could be heard in Katsina. The six large mounds of earth in Dutsi are claimed to be the tombs of these first Zamfara chiefs, twenty-three in number. Today, the Anka district of Sokoto emirate is the centre of the Zamfarawa,[2] though the title of Sarkin Zamfara has belonged to Dancadi district since it was conferred on Ahmadu Zaruku by the Sultan Aliyu Babba.

From Dutsi the Zamfarawa now moved about thirty miles north to another site, on the Gagare river, near the present town of Isa. Some say that this happened under their seventh king, Bakurukuru, but a much later date is probable. Here they started to build the place which eventually developed into the huge walled town of Birnin Zamfara. The flattened stretch of wall to the east of Isa is all that remains of a city credited with eleven miles of lofty walls and fifty gates. Local historians connect the founding of this city with the origin of the name of Zamfara. Tradition has it that Fara, the daughter of one of the neighbouring kings of Gobir, ran away from her husband and became lost in the bush. She was rescued by some hunters who took her to their village of Unguwar Maza near Dutsi. The hunters looked after Fara, who lived with the youngest of the *samari* and soon became pregnant by him. Anxious to return home, she asked the hunters

[1] For the Maguzawa, see the chapters on Kano, p. 188, and Zaria, p. 222.

[2] The most recent study of this area is K. Krieger, *Geschichte vom Zamfara*, Berlin, 1959. Field research at a doctoral level is currently being undertaken in Sokoto by D. M. Last, whose anonymous suggestions were included in the revision of our draft history returned to us by Sokoto N.A. His theme is the Sokoto caliphate in the nineteenth century.

to escort her back to Gobir country. Soon after her arrival, Fara gave birth to a child. As a reward for succouring his daughter, the Sarkin Gobir gave the hunters all the land between Unguwar Maza and the Niger. They called it Zamfara, being an elided form of *mazan Fara*, 'the men of Fara', and Birnin Zamfara was built on the spot where the hunters first came across her.

During the reign of Babba, *c.* 1715, Zamfara became strong enough not only to throw off the yoke of Kebbi but also to drive their forces back to the Gulbin Ka. This Babba did by forming an alliance with the kings of Gobir and Asben, Muhammadu dan Ciroma and Gabba. Under the leadership of Babba's son Yakubu, the combined army scattered the Kebbawa and captured their king Muhammadu. During the course of this final war with Kebbi, the Zamfara soothsayers prophesied disaster unless a slave was sacrificed. One Acali, a slave of Yakubu Sarkin Zamfara, volunteered his life provided that his family should ever be honoured in remembrance of his deed. Acali was sacrificed; Zamfara overcame the Kebbawa at Tsamiya Maibaura; and Acali's younger brother, Kare, was made the first Sarkin Burmi. At the height of its power the kingdom of Zamfara is said to have extended from Sabon Birni in the north to Kwiambana in the south; from the rocks of Muniya, Rubu, and Duru and the stream Babban Baki in the east to the River Gindi in the west.

Meanwhile, early in the eighteenth century, the peaceful penetration of Zamfara by the Gobirawa had begun. The Tuareg had driven them out of Asben to the country north-east of Sokoto, still known as Gobir Tudu. Casting covetous eyes on the more fertile lands of Zamfara to the south, described by Barth as 'almost the most flourishing country of Negroland', the Gobirawa continued their migration until, in the time of their king Ciroma, they were welcomed as useful warriors and given farms by Maliki, Sarkin Zamfara.

But, while the southern Gobirawa thus established friendly terms with Zamfara and started to farm, those on the northern border had too much nomadic restlessness and pugnacity in their blood to settle for long. Under their 90th king, Soba, they first besieged Zabarma for three years, plundering on a large scale. Then Soba led his forces across the Niger to ravage Gurma. From here they pushed as far south as Ilorin. When Soba turned to go home, a large part of his army preferred the easy luxury of the

Yoruba country to the spartan life of the Gobir land. They stayed and intermarried. From this originates the markedly close relationship between Gobir and Ilorin, persistent to this day. The average Hausa is nothing more than a *Gambari* to the Yoruba, but the term *Bagobiri* has an undertone of affection. The late Waziri of Ilorin's family are typical of this Gobir relationship, and all are proud of their Gobir markings. Another relic of ancient Gobir history is the *kwaraya* or traditional fighting wristlet still to be found in parts of Sokoto emirate. So, too, is the continued title of Sarkin Baura, as the chief of Denge is called, originally conferred by the Gobirawa upon an outstanding warrior.

Elated at their military success, the Gobirawa in the mid-eighteenth century followed up their raids against Ilorin by an attack against Sarkin Katsina, despite his previous role of an ally. A seven-year siege against Maradi failed to capture it. While Soba was away on this expedition, however, the Sarkin Asben descended upon the Gobir capital of Goran Rami. The Zamfarawa came to the aid of their new allies. Secretly by night they surrounded the Asben force with a fence of thorns and then attacked them. On his return from his failure before Maradi, Soba, Sarkin Gobir, at once set out to avenge himself on the Asbenawa. He sacked Manni and Adrar. Then, trying to follow up this advantage, he found his men in mutiny against the incessant campaigning. They deserted their king, who was killed and his body mutilated by the Asbenawa. His son Gofe and his daughter, the Magajiya, both fell fighting beside their father.

Uban Iche or Ibn Ashe, the next Sarkin Gobir, was murdered by his son Babari (1742–70), who then led raids into Katsina, Kano and Shirra in Katagum. After he had been king for nearly fifteen years, Babari began a series of attacks on his Zamfara hosts, regardless of the marriage of his sister Fara to Maroki, Sarkin Zamfara. The Zamfarawa seem to have held their own in these engagements, but their leaders grew impatient of the way their king insulted them. Maroki would taunt them on their return from sorties against the Gobirawa by saying: 'You have not caught the tail of the monkey, what have you been doing?' So the captains of the Zamfara army decided to abandon their capital to Sarkin Gobir Babari, and they escorted him to Maroki shouting: 'See, here is the monkey, even to his tail!' Another version asserts that so vast was Birnin Zamfara that Maroki was happily playing draughts for three days unaware that the Gobirawa had forced an entry. Maroki fled to Kiawa, a town inhabited by Katsinawa some twenty miles east of Kaura Namoda, and took refuge with his vassal Tsaidu. Kiawa is an ancient hill fortress on the western edge of the Rubu bush, the forest which still separates the territories of Katsina and Sokoto. According to an entry in Dr Barth's journal on 29 March 1853, when he was near Zurmi on his way from Katsina to Sokoto, the destruction of the old capital of Zamfara had taken place ninety-seven years previously and this information came from a reliable source: the date therefore might be about 1756.[1] Dr Barth also mentions that the Sarkin Zamfara of Zurmi was no longer the master of the whole of Zamfara as he had been some thirty years earlier.

Babari now laid out another walled town on the banks of the Gulbin Rima as the new capital of Gobir. This he called Alkalawa, because it was built on the *gandu* or official farmlands of the Alkalin Zamfara. These farms had been given by Sarkin Zamfara Malu (or Maliki), father of Babba, to the Gobirawa immigrants. The remains of this city can be seen on the road as one travels east from Dan Tudu to Sabon Birni.

From the time of the fall of Birnin Zamfara to the end of the century it is difficult to place events in their correct chronological sequence because the various accounts differ. Muhammadu Bello, in his *Raulat al Afkari*, says that Sarkin Gobir Bawa Jan Gwarzo besieged Maroki in Kiawa 'for fifteen years until at last he got possession of him'. Katsina records have it that it was Babari, Bawa's father, and the siege lasted only seven years. But it is generally accepted that it was Sarkin Katsina Agwaragi (1784–1801) who defeated Bawa Jan Gwarzo (1777–95) near Kiawa in 1795 and slew his son, Yakuba, not far from there in 1801, so that Muhammadu Bello could be correct.

Whatever discrepancies there may be in the details of the various campaigns the broad truth emerges that there was constant

[1] We do not know whether the 97 years of Barth's informant were in fact 97 Muslim years, which would give a later date than 1756 by about 3 years. It can hardly be a coincidence that 100 Muslim years convert to 97 years of the Christian calendar, and one is tempted to guess that Barth's figure was his own conversion of his informant's round figure of a hundred. In that case the apparent precision implied by 97 years would be false and the date can only be taken as approximate. Arnett on p. 10 of his *Sokoto Gazetteer* notes that 'Barth puts this event in 1764 A.D.', and others have unfortunately accepted this too easily as a fixed date on which to fix others in Gobir history.

war between the Gobirawa, the Zamfarawa, the Katsinawa and the Kanawa. Maradi fell to Gobir and so did Birnin Karfi. The Gobirawa even extended their attacks as far as Nupe, Asben and Yauri. Bawa, Sarkin Gobir, is reported to have received as tribute from Mu'azu, the Etsu Nupe, five thousand female slaves and five thousand domestic slaves, each of whom brought with him twenty thousand cowries. In return Bawa sent 'one hundred horses (of which twelve were Bornu stallions) and two beauteous female slaves, each of whom wore bracelets of silk'.

It would seem that Kiawa, which took the place of Birnin Zamfara as the rallying point for the Zamfarawa, was never taken by the Gobirawa nor was it destroyed. The title of Sarkin Kiawa is still borne by the chief of Kaura Namoda, who is acclaimed as *Gaidagaya Korau Murdagiwa* 'Saluter of the hosts of Korau, strangler of the elephant.' Maroki, according to some accounts, retired to Banga and there, stricken with remorse for the loss of his kingdom, committed suicide. But another version has it that he committed suicide after being surrendered to Bawa outside Kiawa, and that on the orders of Bawa his body was decapitated and his head hung from a fig-tree. This tree is still identified at Kiawa as *durumin Maroki.*

Despite Kiawa's inability to re-establish the suzerainty of Maroki, the town which gave him sanctuary took its revenge on the original instrument of his eclipse by contributing to the defeat and death of his two sons. Just outside Kiawa, at a place called Dutsin Wake, Sarkin Gobir Bawa Jan Gwarzo was decisively defeated by the Katsinawa in a battle whose 'bitterness beggars description' in the words of the Sokoto chroniclers. Bawa was so stricken by grief at this disaster and by the death of his son that he died of a broken heart forty days later. This was in 1795. Within six years Bawa's brother and successor, Yakuba, had also been slain in conflict with Kiawa. He had advanced as far as Shirra, in the Hausa-Bornu no-man's land, after destroying the town of Ruma and attacking Katsina, when he heard of a threat to his rear by the old Zamfara dynasty in concert with the Katsinawa of Kiawa. He hurried back to meet defeat and death. His head was carried on a pole to Sarkin Katsina, Agwaragi, who thus again showed Gobir that there was no fortune to be found at Kiawa. This was the last invasion of Katsina territory by Gobir before it sank into eclipse after the destruction of Alkalawa in 1808.

In one or other of these struggles in the neighbourhood of Kiawa is the origin of the familiar taunt used to annoy a Bagobiri even to this day—*A mazaya a kai iri gida.* These words, meaning 'Let us turn back that our seed may be taken home', are said to have been addressed to the Sarkin Gobir by his men when imploring him to break off the contest and let them go home. Authorities differ as to which Sarkin Gobir it was: Babari, as the Katsina version has it; Bawa Jan Gwarzo, as Bello seems to say; or Yakuba, as others contend.[1]

Yakuba was succeeded by Muhamman, more commonly Bunu Nafata, who reigned for only two years. It was in the reign of his son and successor, Yunfa, that the Fulani jihad began.

As for the Zamfara dynasty, Maroki's son, Abarshi, in due course made his submission to Usman dan Fodio and settled at Sabongari, north of Anka. Many of the Zamfarawa were driven out of Kiawa and went to Banga; under Abarshi's successor, Fari, they went on to Ruwan Gora. It was the next chief, Dan Bako, who helped the Fulani in Bello's reign to drive out the rebel Banaga dan Bature, and was granted Bello's permission to settle in Anka, where his descendants have ruled ever since. The Zamfarawa seem to have been the victims of their geography. Their fertile lands made them content but easy going. They never started a war because they had no need to, but they provided ideal campaigning grounds for the hungry armies of others. Even the Fulani, like the Gobirawa, took advantage of their hospitality. Today the title of Sarkin Zamfara is held not only by the chief of Anka but also by the descendants of Namoda in Zurmi, and of Ahmadu Zaruku in Dancadi. The people of Gummi and Talata Mafara are largely of Zamfara origin but their chiefs are entitled Sarkin Mafara. Kaura Namoda, whose chief is Sarkin Kiawa, and another descendant of the Alibawa Fulani leader who captured Kiawa for the Fulani cause and helped in the downfall of Alkalawa, contains a big population of Zamfarawa.

The fateful first decade of the nineteenth century found the distribution of peoples within the area now known as Sokoto Province broadly as follows. Dominant in the north and north-east, and extending northwards beyond Birnin Kwonni and Marata into the present regions of the Niger Republic, were the

[1] See H. R. Palmer, *Sudanese Memoirs*, vol. III, p. 81. To say '*a mazaya*' amounts to implying 'runaways'.

Gobirawa, with their capital at Alkalawa, near Sabon Birni. But fifty years of insatiable aggression against her neighbours had weakened the spirit of Gobir, whose levies were weary of war. To the south of Gobir lay the fertile lands of Zamfara, across which the Gobir armies had so incessantly tramped, dotted with populous settlements of Zamfarawa wanting only to be left in peace. In the west, Kebbi sturdily maintained her traditional independence despite her shrunken domains. To these three of the original Hausa States should be added the fourth, Yauri, small but powerful to the south-west on the Niger. The picture is completed by including Illo, bulwarked in seclusion by the Niger in the far west, as well as the Dakakari and Kambari people in the remoteness of their hill-top villages to the south.

This then was the setting for an event that marks a watershed in the history of every emirate and of the whole of Northern Nigeria—the Fulani Jihad, which may be said to have dated from the Hijra of the Shehu Usman dan Fodio from Degel to Gudu on 21 February 1804. Whatever truth there may be in the centuries old origin of the Fulani in the east, it has been established at least that in historical times their movement has been from the far western highlands of Futa in present-day Guinea.[1] These immigrant Fulani consisted of two categories: the strictly nomadic class, like the *Bororo'en*, who cared for little but their herds and who generally paid tribute to their host Habe kings, but otherwise held themselves aloof; and the *malam* class, whose scholarship soon earned them high positions of rank at the Habe courts as advisers, judges and the like. Along with the gradual and peaceful migration of these cattle-people into what is today Northern Nigeria was that of the Toronke Fulani clan from Mali, who settled in Sokoto to join their semi-nomadic kinsmen already enjoying the rich pastures of the Hausa states, Adamawa and Bornu. The leader of the Toronkawa, so called because of their provenance in Futa Toro and their early settlement there, was Musa Jakolo.

In 1744 (the date is preferred to the 1754 of many authorities by Usman dan Fodio's direct descendant, Sir Ahmadu Bello, in his autobiography *My Life*) there was born at Marata in Gobir, sometimes called Rugar Fako, to the east of Birnin Kwonni, a son to Fodio, the thirteenth descendant of Musa Jakolo. He was

[1] Evidence based on linguistic research is well presented in J. H. Greenberg, *Studies in African Linguistic Classification*, Yale, 1955. See also pp. 109–14.

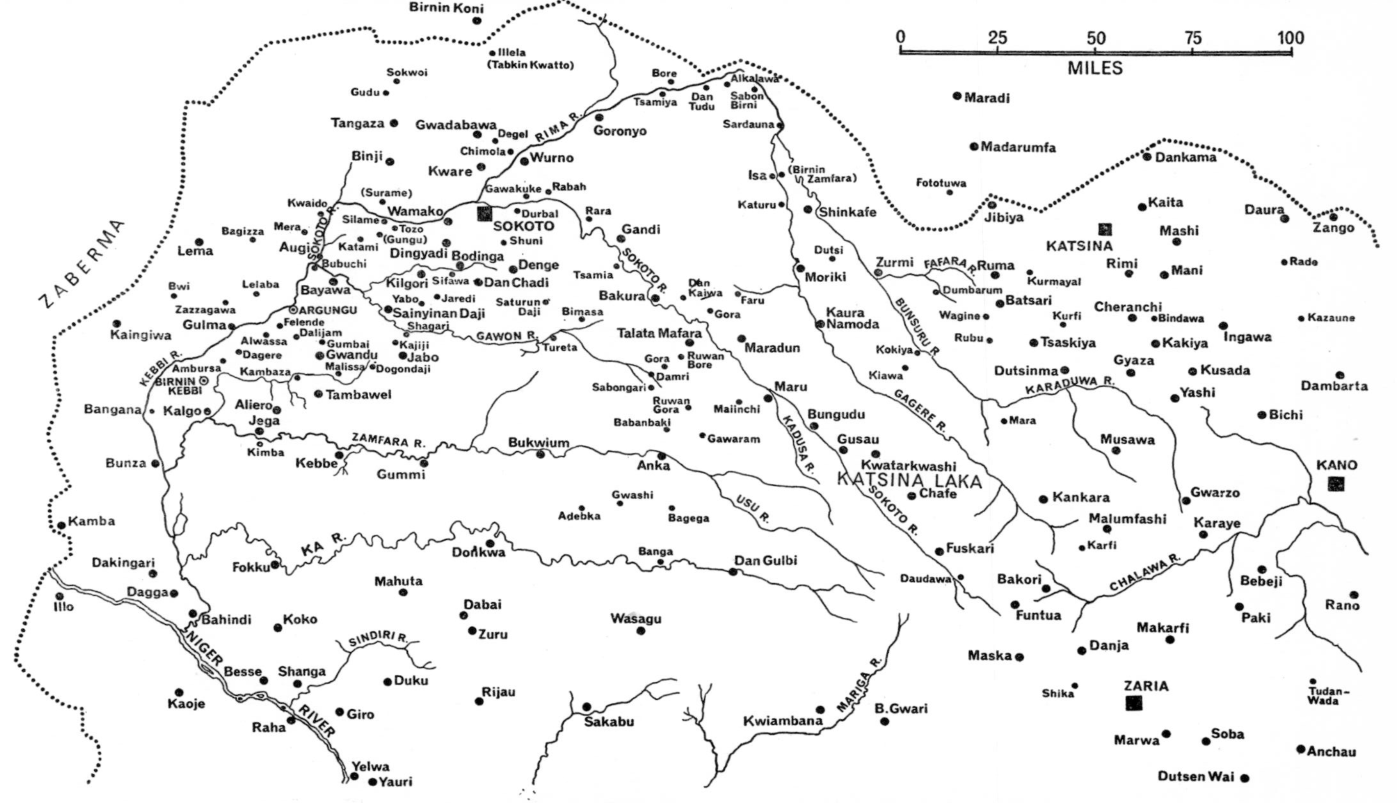

14. SOKOTO AND GWANDU EMIRATES AND THEIR SURROUNDINGS

named Usman. Another son, Abdullahi, followed twelve years later, that is in 1756, or, as some would have it, 1766. Both boys received Koranic and Maliki instruction from the local *malam*, Alhaji Jibrila (Abdullahi's description of his own education is given on page 120). Usman proved an apt pupil, but even more noticeable was the great moral influence and *baraka* that he exercised over all with whom he came in contact. At an early age he spent some years studying in Agades. On his return from Agades[1] he settled at Degel, five miles to the south-east of Gwadabawa, and about twenty miles north of Sokoto from where he undertook frequent journeys to preach Islam in the surrounding Gobir countryside. Bawa Jan Gwarzo, who became Sarkin Gobir in 1777 when Usman was 33, gave the young scholar every encouragement. On one occasion he visited Usman at Degel after a preaching tour in Kebbi and gave him a present of fifty cattle. He finally induced Usman to remove to the Gobir court at Alkalawa and become tutor to the royal princes, including his brother Yakuba and his nephew Yunfa. Another brother, Nafata, seems to have grown up with no love for Islam.

In Alkalawa Usman's piety and magnetic personality soon won him wide respect and influence. Many people now began to adopt Islam and among the converts were some of the Gobir title-holders. According to Muhammadu Bello in his *Infaq al Maisuri*, when eventually Nafata succeeded to the throne in 1801, he was the first to take steps to check the growth of Muslim influence, but without openly breaking with the Shehu. He gave orders that no man should become a Muslim unless a Muslim born, and that all converts should revert to their original faith. He forbade men to wear the turban and women to veil their faces. The latter edicts were prompted by political rather than religious fears for, as has been observed, it was 'these customs which gave to the Shehu's party the cohesion and sense of common identity which the Habe kings feared'.[2] As a mark of his disapproval Usman withdrew from court to his village of Degel.

[1] It is interesting to note that when the Premier of Northern Nigeria, Alhaji Sir Ahmadu Bello, Sardauna of Sokoto, visited the Niger Republic in July 1963, he promised to rebuild the mosque at Agades because it was there that his great-great-grandfather, Usman dan Fodio, received his early education under Malam Jibrilla. He added that one of his uncles, Malam Muhammadu Sambo, was also buried in Agades. The Premier also visited Tafadek, sixty miles north of Agades, where Usman dan Fodio had lived for a while before moving to Degel.

[2] M. Hiskett, quoted in Michael Crowder, *The Story of Nigeria*, 1962, p. 81.

But after two short years Yunfa succeeded his father as Sarkin Gobir and he made a special visit to Degel to salute his old master. Thus encouraged, Usman renewed his attacks on heathen practices and spread the true faith with increasing zeal and energy. So great did the fame of Usman become that it seemed to challenge even the king's position, whose deference to his former tutor was misunderstood. Tradition credits Usman with having persuaded Yunfa to rescind Nafata's edicts. But before long Yunfa's attitude suffered a dramatic change. The growth of the new movement, with its fervour and even fanaticism, especially among the Fulani tribesmen, began to alarm Yunfa and his Habe court, where austerity and asceticism had little appeal. Suspicion quickly turned to distrust and then to hatred.

The final flame of Yunfa's exasperation was lit by an apparent act of defiance to the king's authority when Usman caused some captive Muslims under escort to Alkalawa to be released as they happened to pass by Degel. They belonged to Gimbana in Kebbi, where one of Usman's disciples, Abdussalami of the Arewa (Mantu) people lived. For some reason the latter had declined an invitation to come out of Gimbana and give a holy man's blessing to a detachment of warriors under Waru Sarkin Mafara of Gummi, who was on his way to assist Sarkin Kebbi Fodi suppress a revolt in his Zabarma town of Dosso. A complaint was made to Yunfa, who had ordered that the Muslims of Gimbana be brought to Alkalawa in chains. Abdussalami defied the order and fortified Gimbana, but Waru succeeded in forcing an entry and taking many of the people away as slaves. Usman persisted in refusing Yunfa's repeated orders to surrender the men he had released. By what right, he asked, did they make slaves of Muslims?

Yunfa was furious. He summoned Usman, his brother Abdullahi, and Umaru Mai Alkammu to come to Alkalawa. A story is told[1] of how they lodged in the house of the Dan Galadima. Here they were visited by Yunfa, who fired a gun at them point blank. Miraculous power made the charge blow backwards, burning Yunfa's gown but harming none. Divine guidance had previously warned Usman to decline an invitation to seat himself on a mat which had been cunningly placed on corn-stalks covering the mouth of a well.

[1] The story is one of Abdullahi's own.

Whatever the truth of this story it is clear that Yunfa was determined on a clean break with the Shehu—as he came to be widely known and spoken of with reverence. Yunfa was resolved to destroy Degel itself. But he shrank from openly putting the Shehu to death because of the strength of his following. He accordingly ordered the Shehu to leave Degel before he attacked it. The Shehu refused to desert his followers. Instead, he fled to Gudu, some twenty-five miles away to the north-west and forty miles from Sokoto, quite close to Sokwai in Tangaza. This historic flight is known as the Hijra and is dated 21 February 1804. The Shehu has left us his own explanation of his reasons for the flight from Degel:

I declare, and God the Accomplisher is my witness, that the work of my brother Abdullahi on this subject is sufficient. I said to him on a day: 'Write for us the reasons for our flight from Gobir and our holy war with the Hausa Sultans, to be our apology to whoever reads the book, if he serve God.' He answered that he would write, and wrote:—

. . . Know that our Sheikh, 'Uthman ibn Muhammad Amir al-Mu'minin (may God prolong his life in his service) came forth to call persons, wherever they might be, to the Faith, and to expound to all whom he could reach their duty to God, and noble endeavour, trying to clear away their doubts concerning God, to deliver them from the doom to come and to save them, till his fame spread abroad. There were learned men, his contemporaries, who disputed and denied his mission.

In the beginning he did not address himself to the kings. After a time his people grew and became famous, till they were known in Hausaland as 'The People'. Men kept leaving their countries and coming to him. Of the ruling classes some repented, and came to him with all they possessed, leaving their Sultans. Then the Sultans became angry, till there ensued between them and their chiefs the war we remember. Matters did not rest there.

The Sheikh said: 'I will not interfere between anyone and his chief; I will not be a cause of parting.' He strove to avert a quarrel. But the trouble grew and grew. The Sultans kept sending protests to their people. The rupture became open between the Sheikh and them. They saw the growing numbers of his following and the hold that Islam had gained. Its growing strength made them furious, and devils among Jinns and men urged them on, saying: 'If you do not disperse this concourse of people, your power will be gone; they will destroy your country, by causing all the people to leave you and go to them.'

The Sultan of Gobir sent to us plotting our destruction, as we discovered. This showed us the true meaning of his words and deeds. But God averted from us his evil design. He told us, what we know, namely, that they only wished to kill us. So we returned to our abode. The Sultan of Gobir attacked the Sheikh's people; they fled, for they were afraid. The Gobir army followed them and captured some and slew others, seizing children and women, and selling them in our midst.

This made us greatly afraid. The Sultan of Gobir ordered the Sheikh to leave the country with his children and wives and relatives, but to take no one else with him, and disperse his people. The Sheikh replied: 'I will not disperse my people, but I will go away with any who wish to come with me. Let those who wish to remain, remain.'

So we fled from their land in the year 1218 A.H. on the 10th of Dhu'l-qa'da to a place outside Gobir territory.[1]

The Fulani saw in this threat to the Shehu clear warning of Yunfa's hostility to their race. Not only those who were Muslims but also the non-believing herdsmen 'doffed their caps in salutation to the Shehu'—*sun yi masa caffa.* Since the leaders, however, were *malamai* of the Shehu's school, this insurrection of largely pagan forces against Sarkin Gobir, a Muslim albeit a tepid one, was none the less declared a *jihad* or holy war. A holy man, the Shehu, had been threatened. The actual words used by each man as he acclaimed the Shehu and gave him his hand were *Lamido Julbe*, since the Fulani knew little Hausa. But the news spread far and wide that the Shehu had been proclaimed *Amir al-Muminin*—Commander of the Faithful—or, in the Hausa tongue, *Saṛkin Musulmi*—Chief of the Muslims.

Outstanding among the Fulani leaders were of course Usman's brother, Abdullahi, and his son, Muhammadu Bello; there was also Umaru Mai Alkamma, already mentioned in the story of Yunfa's abortive plot. Abdullahi voiced the thoughts of all: 'Truly this matter has become intolerable; recourse must be had to arms. There can be no doubt that the situation demands a prince to manage our affairs, for Muslims should not be without government.'

And so from Gudu in the early part of 1804 the Jihad began. By the spring of 1810 it was practically ended, with the Hausa states, Nupe, Adamawa, and even parts of Bornu in the hands of the Shehu's emissaries and paying tribute to Sokoto or Gwandu.

[1] Usman dan Fodio, *Tanbikhul-Ikhwan*, 'The Admonition to the Brethren', translated by H. R. Palmer in an article in the *Journal of the African Society*, vol. xiii, 1913, and reproduced in T. L. Hodgkin, *Nigerian Perspectives*, pp. 192–3.

The war, however, was really won in September 1808 with the capture of the Gobir capital of Alkalawa and the extinction of Gobir as a state. Yunfa and all his men were put to the sword, and the Shehu's cause was no longer in doubt.

At first the struggle took the form of raids and skirmishes initiated by both sides with a number of villages the innocent sufferers. But in June 1804, after capturing Birnin Kwonni (north of the present frontier) the Fulani bowmen won a notable victory over the *lifidi*-encumbered Gobirawa horsemen at a place called Tabkin (Lake) Kwatto, some twenty miles north of Gwadabawa.

This early victory put the Fulani in great heart and brought in many supporters. Ambitious plans were made to spread the jihad far and wide. The overall military command was entrusted to Aliyu Jedo with the title of Sarkin Yaki, with particular responsibility for the north; Abdullahi was in charge of the west, and Bello took the east. The forces that these generals commanded were no more than amateur peasant levies with the primitive weapons of the Crusades. Enthusiasm took the place of staff work and looting kept the men fed and clothed.

Specially selected leaders of military missions to the outlying states were appointed by the Shehu to spread the faith and oust the Habe and *Kafiri* rulers. All except one were Fulani. The Shehu's aim was uncomplicated and uncompromising: in his own words, 'a return to the pure and primitive faith of Islam, purged of heresies and accretions'.[1] To each emissary Shehu gave a flag (*tuta*), which he had blessed, as the symbol of his authority, and to each he commended the prayer that he had used before the battle of Tabkin Kwatto: 'If I fight this battle that I may become greater than my fellow, or that my son may become greater than his, or that my slave may lord it over his, may the *Kafiri* wipe us from the land.'[2]

These flags are still preserved by their possessors with great care and reverence, and even when they are brought out on special occasions such as the installation of a new emir, they are never unfurled. It is generally reckoned that the flag-bearers numbered fourteen. Thirteen of them were awarded as shown below in alphabetical order:

[1] Until recently, insufficient attention has been paid to the intellectual aspects of the jihad. Convincing advocacy of this is to be found in Hodgkin, op. cit., p. 10 and Crowder, op. cit., p. 95.

[2] Quoted in J. A. Burdon, *Historical Notes on Certain Emirates and Tribes*, p. 67.

Adamawa: Modibbo Adama
Bauchi: Yakubu
Daura: Isiyaku (Ishaku)
Gombe: Buba Yero
Hadejia: Sambo
Ilorin: Alimi
Kano: Sulemanu
Katagum: Ibrahim Zaki
Katsina: Umaru Dallaji
Kazaure: Dan Tunku
Misau: Mamman Manga dan Gwani Mukhtar
Nupe: Malam Dendo (Danyo in Hausa)
Zaria: Malam Musa

The fourteenth flag was given to Gwani Mukhtar for Bornu, but his mission was never fulfilled. The twin capitals of the Fulani empire, Sokoto and Gwandu, are not of course included in the list; and some of those on this list are omitted from others because of the lateness of the flag's bestowal. Misau and Kazaure come in this category. Shehu Ahmadu Lobo, a supporter of Shehu dan Fodio of former years, also waged a jihad against the Segu Bambara in Massina a few years later, but Sokoto tradition denies that he was one of Usman's flag-bearers, and the same applies to Mamman of Baghirmi. Certain emirates, such as Jama'are (1835) and Kontagora (1864), received flags from the Shehu's successors.

After the battle of Tabkin Kwatto, Shehu conferred flags and titles on some of the local chiefs. For instance, Namoda was made Sarkin Zamfara. The Sarkin Zamfara of Zurmi and the Sarkin Kiawa of Kaura Namoda are descended from him. Moyiju became Sarkin Kebbi of Yabo, a title which his descendant still carries. The titles of Ardon Dingyadi and Ardon Shuni (Dangara) are still held by descendants of the first title holders; and the Sarkin Yaki of Binji is descended from the original Sarkin Yaki, Aliyu Jedo.

No relative of Usman dan Fodio received a flag to found an emirate, though of course his brother and son ruled the Sokoto-Gwandu empire. With the exception of Kano, where Sulemanu died without issue, Katsina, and Daura, where the Habe dynasty was restored by Lord Lugard in 1906, almost every emir has been a direct descendant of one of the original flag-bearers, who were all Fulani except one. It is interesting to compare this list of flag-bearers with today's order of emirate grading and precedence given in Appendix B.

In this context of the jihad's origins it is suitable to cite an

Arabic document that has only recently been made public.[1] This is the *Wathiqat ahl al-Sudan*, a document of undeniable historical significance by virtue of its antiquity as the Shehu's manifesto of the jihad, almost certainly read out to the Fulani congregations in the mosque at the Friday prayers:

This is a dispatch from Ibn Fudi, the Commander of the Faithful, Uthman, to all the folk of the Sudan, and to whomso God wills of the brethren in the (Hausa) States; it is a dispatch advantageous in the present times. Thus speak I, and success comes of God.

Know then, my Brethren:

(i) That the commanding of righteousness is obligatory by assent (literally 'according to the *ijma*' ');
(ii) And that the prohibition of evil is obligatory by assent;
(iii) And that Flight (*al-hijra*) from the land of the heathen is obligatory by assent;
(iv) And that the befriending of the Faithful is obligatory by assent;
(v) And that the appointment of the Commander of the Faithful is obligatory by assent;
(vi) And that obedience to him and to all his deputies is obligatory by assent;
(vii) And that the waging of Holy War (*al-jihad*) is obligatory by assent;
(viii) And that the appointment of Emirs in the States is obligatory by assent;
(ix) And that the appointment of judges is obligatory by assent;
(x) And that their enforcement of the divine laws (*akham al-shar*') is obligatory by assent;
(xi) And that by assent the status of a town is the status of its ruler: if he be Muslim, the town belongs to Islam; but if he be heathen the town is a town of heathendom from which Flight is obligatory.
(xii) And that to make war upon the heathen king who will not say 'There is no God but Allah' is obligatory by assent, and that to take the government from him is obligatory by assent;
(xiii) And that to make war upon the heathen king who does not say 'There is no God but Allah' on account of the custom of his town (*bi-sababi 'urfi'l-baladi*), and who makes no profession of Islam, is (also) obligatory by assent; and that to take the government from him is obligatory by assent;

[1] The following quotation is taken from A. D. H. Bivar's translation in *Journal of African History*, vol. ii, No. 2, 1961, pp. 239–41.

(xiv) And that to make war upon the king who is an apostate (*al-malik al-murtaddu*), and who has abandoned the religion of Islam for the religion of heathendom is obligatory by assent, and that to take the government from him is obligatory by assent;

(xv) And that to make war against the king who is an apostate—who has not abandoned the religion of Islam as far as the profession of it is concerned, but who mingles the observances of Islam with the observances of heathendom, like the kings of Hausaland for the most part—is (also) obligatory by assent, and that to take the government from him is obligatory by assent;

(xvi) And that to make war upon backsliding Muslims (*al-muhammalin min al-muslimin*) who do not own allegiance to any of the Emirs of the Faithful is obligatory by assent, if they be summoned to give allegiance and they refuse, until they enter into allegiance;

(xvii) And that the anathematizing of Muslims on a pretext of heretical observances is unlawful by assent;

(xviii) And that the anathematizing of Muslims for disobedience (*takfir al-muslimin bi'l-mu'asi*) is unlawful by assent;

(xix) And that residence in enemy territory (*fi bilad al-harb*) is unlawful by assent;

(xx) And that refusal to give allegiance to the Commander of the Faithful and to his deputies is unlawful by assent;

(xxi) And that to make war upon the Muslims who are residing in Muslim territory is unlawful by assent, and that wrongfully to devour their property is unlawful by assent;

(xxii) And that to enslave the freeborn amongst the Muslims is unlawful by assent, whether they reside in the territory of Islam, or in enemy territory;

(xxiii) And that to make war upon the heathen to whom peace has been granted (*al-kuffar ahl al-aman*) is unlawful by assent; wrongfully to devour their property is unlawful by assent, and to enslave them is unlawful by assent;

(xxiv) And that to make war upon the congregation of the apostates (*juma at al-murtaddin*) is obligatory by assent, and that their property is booty (*fai'un*), and that in the matter of their enslavement there are two opinions, the widespread one being its prohibition, and the other that the perpetrator of this act does not disobey (the law) if he is following an authority which asserts its lawfulness;

(xxv) And that to make war on the congregation of the warmongers (*juma at al-muharibin*) is obligatory by assent, and that their property is booty, and that their enslavement is unlawful by assent;

(xxvi) And that to make war upon the oppressors (*al-bughat*) is obligatory by assent, for 'Use is made of their armour against them, and afterwards it is returned to them'; and their enslavement is unlawful by assent;

(xxvii) And that in the matter of the property of Muslims who reside in enemy territory there are two opinions, the sound one being that (its seizure) is permitted.

After the rout of the Gobirawa at Tabkin Kwatto and the capture of many of their valuable horses, Yunfa fled back to Alkalawa and sent a message to his brother Habe kings: 'I left a small fire in my country and failed to extinguish it. Now it has burst into flames and burnt me. See that a similar fire does not burn you too.'

The rainy season of 1804 saw a continuance of raids by each side on the other, with the Fulani having to move camp from Gudu to Magabci in search of food. In July the Shehu sent letters to the Hausa kings to explain his cause. Kano and Katsina rejected these overtures but Sarkin Zazzau was more compliant: unfortunately his people were not. Then in October the Shehu moved to Sokoto, at that time a mere camp, where he received the Wazirin Gobir putting out feelers for peace. Terms were offered on condition that Yunfa came in person to conclude an armistice; but Yunfa declined. There was nothing for it but to resume the conflict, and in the dry season of 1804–5 the Shehu's forces suffered a series of reverses round Alkalawa in attempting to assault the town, with a disastrous defeat at Tsuntsua in December. Two thousand Fulani fell including many of the *élite* and learned. With admirable courage the Fulani maintained the offensive until shortage of food in February forced them to retire south to Zamfara, harried all the way by the enemy. With its traditional hatred of Gobir, Zamfara was an ideal base, and was in fact the only one of the Hausa states disposed to be friendly to the Shehu. But as will be seen this friendship was grossly abused by the rough Fulani levies and resentment took its place. A permanent camp was built at Sabongari, twenty miles north of Anka.

The year 1805 opened with the Fulani fortunes at the ebb, with all the Hausa country, except perhaps some of Zamfara, in support of their enemies. In April came a rise in Fulani morale with the capture of Birnin Kebbi and many other Kebbi towns: only for it to fall again with a string of unsuccessful ventures. The incessant pillaging of crops and villages lost them the friendship of their hosts, so that Shehu had to move his camp to Gwandu. Though Shehu's own saintly sincerity of religious purpose was never in doubt, the records show that some of his adherents were no more than callous adventurers. When it came to looting they would despoil believer and unbeliever with ruthless impartiality. Towns were sacked without regard to their religious leanings and even on occasions without distinction between friend and foe. Small wonder that the Zamfarawa came to forsake a leader whose followers had shown such mean ingratitude, and allied themselves with their old enemies, the Gobirawa.

A contemporary account of events some twelve years later graphically illustrates what the people of these villages had to endure in those days:

On receiving intelligence of the death of the Sultan of the Falatahs, the people of Gober, and many of those of the other conquered provinces, impatient of the galling yoke, which they had been compelled, much against their own inclinations, to bear, rose simultaneously into an open and general revolt, and put to death, indiscriminately, every Falatah that had located himself in their country.

Then, forming themselves into a confederation, with a variety of leaders at their head, they for a long time waged an exterminating war with the successor of Danfodio, but their movements being unconnected and irregular, and anarchy having the ascendancy in their councils, Bello had reconquered several of the mutinous districts at the period of our arrival, and made great slaughter of the miserable inhabitants. The towns whose gates were not instantly opened to their summons, the Falatahs surrounded, and intercepting all communication between the people residing in them and those of the neighbouring country, prevented any provisions being obtained by the besieged, and in a manner starved them into capitulation. The insurgents had made, however, for Africans, a gallant defence. And well knowing what they had to expect from their sanguinary adversaries, would not surrender till all their domestic animals had been consumed, and they themselves reduced to the extremity of feeding on decayed vultures, which, next to human flesh, they most cordially abhor.

Having obliged them at length to open the gates, the Falatahs rushed in, and pouncing upon the emaciated and unresisting inhabitants, made dreadful havoc of them, putting the old men and councillors to the edge of the sword. Thrusting a sharp stake into their bodies, and exhibiting them on the tops of the walls and other conspicuous places, as melancholy trophies of their success, and as a spectacle of horror for their shuddering countrymen to profit by. In this situation the ghastly corpses were exposed, till they had fallen to pieces by the action of the air, or been devoured by birds of prey. The old women, and young people of both sexes, who had escaped the general massacre, were driven in triumph to Soccatoo, and retained as slaves by their imperious conquerors.[1]

Meanwhile, in the autumn of 1805 Shehu was encamped at Kambaza, near Gwandu; his forces under Bello in Zamfara captured nine towns, but Abdullahi met with no success in the north, where the enemy strength was gathering. In November a mixed force of Gobirawa, Kebbawa, Tuareg and others who had run foul of the Fulani levies descended on Gwandu. Under the leadership of Aliyu Jedo, the Shehu's forces sallied forth to meet the foe in the open, and, incredible to relate, they are said to have wantonly sacked the friendly town of Kwolda, despite the remonstrances of Bello and Abdullahi. Between Birnin Kebbi and Argungu they met the confederate army in the dry *fadama* at Alwassa, and were routed with the loss of a thousand men. The five days fighting were critical for the Fulani cause, but the enemy failed to push home their advantage and allowed the Fulani time to regroup. Had Gwandu fallen as it almost did, history would have been remarkably different. But it survived, and with the final driving off of the allies the Shehu's cause was never again to be critically threatened.

Meanwhile, in Kano, Katsina, Daura and Zaria, the Fulani were successfully driving out the old Habe dynasties, and the movement was fast spreading through the rest of the Hausa states.

During the early part of 1806, the records speak chiefly of unsuccessful ventures, but Yandoto, near Cafe in Katsina Laka, was captured by Bello. Later a successful expedition was sent north to Alkalawa under Aliyu Jedo, which, although it did not capture the town, laid waste the surrounding crops. Bello meanwhile was victorious in Zamfara and an expedition to Dandi captured many towns. An epidemic seems to have slowed down

[1] Lander, quoted in Krieger, op. cit., pp. 99–100.

operations for some months, but in the following spring Namoda defeated and killed ten of the principal chiefs of Alkalawa at Wanui, and, assisted by Umaru Dallaji, the Katsina flag-bearer, reduced the surrounding country. But it was not until September 1808 that, after great preparations, the Gobir capital of Alkalawa was finally seized. The Kebbawa had already sued for peace and it had now been possible to concentrate all the Fulani forces on Alkalawa. The town was attacked on three sides by the combined forces of young Bello, Aliyu Jedo, Namoda, and Umaru Dallaji. Sarkin Gobir Yunfa and all his men were put to the sword. The power of Gobir was broken; the success of the Shehu's cause was established; those who had been hesitating to declare themselves could no longer be in doubt of where wisdom in their choice lay.

To the east, hard fighting continued throughout 1809 as the flag-bearers carved out the new emirates of Gombe, Katagum, Muri, Adamawa and Bauchi. In Bornu, despite the success in capturing the capital Birni Ngazargamu, the Fulani were checked, though much of the western districts fell into their hands. In the west, the Shehu's brother Abdullahi was equally engaged in extending the new empire, down as far as Kontagora and Nupe, while Bello scored another victory by carrying the faith into the Gwari country. This campaign was celebrated in a poem by his uncle:

> Bello it was who led the horse and foot,
> A raging lion, leading lions to fall
> Upon their courtyards. Thus they were
> Devoured as the straw thrust in the flame.
> And nothing but their silent courts remained.

By 1810, that is within just six years from the Shehu's nomination as Sarkin Musulmi at Gudu, the jihad was practically complete.

Now came the question of administering this vast empire. In 1806 Bello had built the walls of Gwandu for his father's headquarters, and three years later he did the same for Sokoto, from his camp where the Kofar Rimi later stood. It is said that when the Shehu saw the walls of Sokoto for the first time and learned that they had been built by the Zamfarawa, he characteristically remarked that it was a pity they had not been put up by the Fulani. Previously Sokoto had been but a hamlet, but Bello was alive to the natural military advantages of the place. Ali, an elder brother of the Shehu, built the town of Bodinga, close to Sifawa, which Abdullahi for a while made his own headquarters.

At a meeting held in Gwandu in 1809, the Shehu announced his plans for his civil government. He followed the same pattern he had used for his military operations at the beginning of the jihad: Abdullahi was given the administration of the west, Bello the east, and the north was entrusted to Aliyu Jedo, Sarkin Yaki, who nevertheless remained subordinate to Bello. Interestingly enough, though this seems so far to have escaped comment by scholars, this division of suzerainty corresponds to the grouping of the Hausa Bakwai and the Banza Bakwai states. It may well be that at this time there was no intention of permanently dividing the empire but simply of decentralizing its authority.

As his Waziri, Bello chose Muhammadu Gidado dan Lema, a scholarly Toronke *malam* who had married his sister Asma'u (Nana). Sokoto tradition declares that Bello gave Gidado his own flag that he had received from the Shehu.[1] This Asma'u is the authoress of an Arabic ballad commemorating the birth of Islam and the Fulani empire, which was translated into Hausa by one of the Shehu's sons, Isa. Besides the *sarauta* of Waziri, Bello also created the Sokoto titles of Magajin Rafi, Magajin Gari, Ubandoma and Galadima, besides appointing a Koranic *malam* as Alkali.

The Shehu moved from Sifawa to Sokoto in 1814, though there remains some controversy about the exact dates of his movements between Gwandu, Sifawa and Sokoto.

Usman dan Fodio died in April 1817, after a year's illness. He is buried in Sokoto, where his tomb has become an object of veneration for Muslims from all over the Sudan. On his deathbed he warned his son:

> When I am gone, the whole country will go back to paganism. Those who have seen the light, have seen it because of me. You will find yourself in difficulty and there will be no one to help you.

Of his character his son Bello has written:

> Know that he [Uthman dan Fodio] grew up continent and devout, possessed of pleasing qualities. And none was his equal. People trusted him, and flocked to him from east and west.

[1] This may account for the exceptional fact that the Wazirin Sokoto has been accorded the same historical privileges and recognition as an Emir.

He instructed the *'ulama*, and raised the banner of religion. He revived the *sunna*, and put an end to heresy. He spread knowledge and dispelled perplexity. His learning dazzled men's minds. He showed how reality was to be reconciled with the *shari'a*. For years he explained the Qur'an in the presence of learned and righteous men of importance, vying with them, through his reading and the different branches of his learning, in rhetoric, and in knowledge of authorities and of what is written and what is abrogated. At the same time he was pre-eminent in knowledge of the *hadith*, and learned in its unfamiliar parts and different branches. Learned was he also in the religious sources and in the preservation of the *sunna*.

He resolved difficulties, acting rightly. His vision was sure. He was trained in the teaching of abstruse matters, pre-eminent in reasoning. Devout and ascetic, he was a leading teacher, spreading knowledge. He filled the western country with learning and with seekers after learning. The people of his time pause at what he says. He bore the standard of enlightenment, and was a centre of consultation. Revered by both great and small, he was a reformer at the head of this generation, an eloquent orator, a fine classical poet. Excellent in character, good to associate with, and generous in intercourse. Proven, determined in mien, set apart from his kindred, he is immovable in resolution. Filled with humility and compassion towards mankind, he regards himself in his modesty as the least of creatures. He is the defender of the frontiers of the law. Kind and friendly, he was loved and revered by the people even more than they loved themselves. They ask God's mercy on him with shining faces, sincerely and meekly. He was kind and compassionate to the believers, and was accepted, all agreeing on the greatness of his power.

In a word, description falls short of his attainments. He is shaikh of the *'ulama* of his time. Nay, he is a guiding star for the imams of all ages. His qualities do not require comment: for since when has the noon-day sun required to be pointed out? . . . He is meritorious in knowledge of the mystical way, and endowed with strength for effective deeds. He has made a wonderful disclosure of the truth of the Qur'an, and for him the hidden meaning of visions is as an open door.

He is one whom God has made manifest to mankind, and created in his mercy toward men. God granted him complete acceptance among both great and small, entrusted him with the organization of learning and gave him authority to govern. He changed men's customs for him, and made him to speak of the hidden things. God manifested wonders and miracles through his hand. . . .

Know you also that I, Bello, used to see him when he was about to come out to the assembled people; he would stop and stand a little while in the open space of his compound, and he would say a few words which I did not hear. After that he would go out to the people. I asked him about this, and he told me he was reviving his enthusiasm; he was making a promise to God of sincerity in what he was going to do. Further he would pray God to make the people assembled here attend to all he told them. Then, when he came before the people, he would greet them so that everyone could hear. And when he had sat down upon his platform he would salute them three times. He looked pleased and smiled at them. Then he would call for silence. He was never wearied by them and never refused them. He was worried too by some that were badly behaved. When he told them to be silent, when he stopped them asking a multitude of questions, they would not leave off asking.

Then he would begin his sermon to them in a loud voice. He felt no shyness in speaking before this assembly even though there were distinguished *'ulama* assembled. Forthwith he preached his sermon to them all. He cared for none of them except that his words should be useful to them. If perhaps he were asked a question in the middle of his speech, he would stop and answer it. His religion gave him strength and he feared no criticism. He gave his judgments with justice and never departed from the truth.[1]

Abdullahi was at Gwandu when the news of his brother's death reached him. He rode post-haste to Sokoto, only to find the gates shut to him: Bello, then aged 36, had been chosen as Sarkin Musulmi. This was in accordance with the Shehu's dying wish, but Abdullahi felt he had been wronged, as among Fulani a brother rather than a son was the normal successor. Returning to Gwandu, he found that the town of Kalembena had revolted. Bello with his Waziri at once marched to the assistance of his uncle.

It is said in Sokoto that not until Kalembena had been subdued in 1819 did Abdullahi forget his heart-burning and acknowledge Bello as Sarkin Musulmi. Sokoto tradition relates how Bello was mounted on his war-horse and Abdullahi rode his mare which, like the Shehu, he preferred as fitting to a *malam*. Bello, the younger man, was preparing to spur his horse forward and give his elder brother the customary greeting of the *jafi*, but his horse refused to move. Seeing this difficulty, Abdullahi courteously motioned to

[1] Muhammad Bello, *Infaq al Maisuri*, partly taken from H. F. C. Smith's translation of C. E. J. Whitting's version. See Hodgkin, op. cit., pp. 196–8.

him to remain in the saddle and then saluted his nephew as Commander of the Faithful. This pretty incident sealed a close friendship between the two courts that has yet to be broken. Turning to Usman Gidado, Abdullahi took off his gown and turban and handed them to him, saying: 'I was the Waziri of my elder brother the Shehu; now you are the Waziri of our son Bello.' Up to only a few years ago the Emir of Gwandu always used to repeat this ceremony whenever he was greeted by the Waziri on his arrival at the Sultan of Sokoto's palace. For their loyalty to the Sultan, the Katsinawa of Cafe were appointed the regular escort to the Waziri on his official journeys to Kano and Zaria throughout the nineteenth century. The senior status of the Wazirin Sokoto has been retained by his unique appointment to the House of Chiefs with the personal status of a First Class Emir.

As prophesied by the Shehu, his death was indeed the signal for a revolt of most of the Zamfara towns. A powerful chief called Banaga dan Bature, who controlled all the country round Anka and to the south of it, joined with the Sarkin Burmi of Bakura (Habe people originally from Bornu) in leading most of the Zamfarawa in rebellion against Bello, and they even succeeded in capturing his war-drums. But Sarkin Zamfara Dan Bako threw in his lot with Bello in driving Banaga away to the south and moved his people from Ruwan Gora, whither they had come from Kiawa, and later, Banga, to Sabongari north of Anka. He was then given permission by Bello to settle in Anka, which the Zamfarawa have occupied ever since. His successor, Dan Gado, is credited with the building of Anka, where the list of the kings of Zamfara printed at the end of this section is preserved.[1] The regime in Anka seems to have prospered, while Gummi and Bukwium, farther down the Zamfara river, were kept in order. Dan Bako's son, Abubakar, had the satisfaction of invading Banaga territory and recapturing Bello's war-drums for return to Sokoto.

There was also a rebellion to put down in Kware, led by Abdussalami of Gimbana fame. After the destruction of that town he had been entrusted with an important district under Abdullahi, but he had become disgruntled. He argued that the Shehu's movement had lost its reformist character and that all the best posts in the administration had gone to the Shehu's relatives while he, an early adherent, had received no reward. He was summoned

[1] Given in Krieger, op. cit. See also note on page 415.

to Sokoto and ordered by Bello to live at Kware. Here he openly rebelled and was attacked by Bello's forces from Sokoto. Kware was taken and Abdussalami fled to Bakura, where he died shortly afterwards. His son, Buhari, was to lead the Gimbanawa to found the town of Jega, after which he made his peace with Sokoto. Much of Bello's reign was taken up with such punitive expeditions, often accompanied by the eastern emirs such as Kano and Zaria. No fewer than eleven expeditions were directed against the recalcitrant Kebbawa; in the twelfth, in 1831, drastic measures were taken and their king, Karari Sumaila, was killed. The Gobirawa, under their chiefs Gunki and Gunga, inflicted several reverses on the Fulani, and in the reign of their king Ali they managed to penetrate, with help from the Tuareg chief Ibra, as close to Sokoto as Dundaye. To scotch this nuisance, Bello sacked Alkalawa so devastatingly that it has never been rebuilt.[1] He took Katambali, one of the Gobir princesses, as his concubine, and their son Fodio later established the border town of Lajingi. Gunki was killed in a battle at Kadaye in 1820, but it was not until 1835 (some claim 1828), in a great battle fought at Gawakuke near Rabah, that the Fulani really regained their prestige. Sarkin Gobir, Ali, and Sarkin Katsina (na Maradi), Randa or Raud, were slain, and the remnants of the army, except, as usual, those who could recite the *Fatiha*, were made into slaves. There is a legend described by Hajji Sa'id as follows:

> Then they went on and encamped at Gawakuke (Ghuwakuk). Here also the people were violently thirsty, and the Commander of the Faithful took his lance and struck it in the ground, saying to Mash, who was in charge of his water supplies, 'Dig here.' He dug a little, and the water welled up. . . .[2]

Bello's victory was due to a surprise forced march through the

[1] This is perhaps the point to comment on the oft-repeated accusation that the Fulani deliberately destroyed all the Habe records during their jihad. To some extent Crowder and Hodgkin (see note on p. 382) deal with this, but the clearest denial is to be found in E. W. Bovill, *The Golden Trade of the Moors*, 1958, p. 221, n.: 'In his *Caravans of the Old Sahara* the present writer said that the Fulani destroyed most of the local records when they conquered the country. He is grateful to the late E. J. Arnett for having pointed out to him that this was incorrect and unfair to the Fulani. Arnett had been assured by the Sarkin Musulmi that "all records of which memory exists can still be found".' Recent research by the Arabist archivists of the University of Ibadan supports this modern view, and an important collection of documents is steadily growing in the museums and archives.

[2] Hajji Sa'id, *History of Sokoto*, translated by C. E. J. Whitting, p. 6, and his 'Extracts from an Arabic History of Sokoto' in *African Affairs*, July 1948, p. 161.

waterless Gundumi bush, the perils of which wilderness were later painfully experienced by both Clapperton and Barth. Here is an eye-witness account of one of Bello's battles against the Gobirawa:

After the midday prayers, all, except the eunuchs, camel drivers, and such other servants as were of use only to prevent theft, whether mounted or on foot, marched towards the object of attack; and soon arrived before the walls of the city. I also accompanied them, and took up my station close to the Gadado. The march had been the most disorderly that can be imagined; horse and foot intermingling in the greatest confusion, all rushing to get forward; sometimes the followers of one chief tumbling amongst those of another, when swords were half unsheathed, but all ended in making a face, or putting on a threatening aspect. We soon arrived before Coonia, the capital of the rebels of Goobur, which was not above half a mile in diameter, being nearly circular, and built on the bank of one of the branches of the river, or lakes, which I have mentioned. Each chief, as he came up, took his station, which I suppose, had previously been assigned to him. The number of fighting men brought before the town could not, I think, be less than fifty or sixty thousand, horse and foot, of which the foot amounted to more than nine-tenths. For the depth of two hundred yards, all round the walls was a dense circle of men and horses. The horse kept out of bow-shot, while the foot went up as they felt courage or inclination, and kept up a straggling fire with about thirty muskets, and the shooting of arrows. In front of the sultan, the Zegzeg troops had one French fusil: the Kano forces had forty-one muskets. These fellows, whenever they fired their pieces, ran out of bow-shot to load; all of them were slaves; not a single Fellata had a musket. The enemy kept up a slow and sure fight, seldom throwing away their arrows until they saw an opportunity of letting fly with effect. Now and then a single horse would gallop up to the ditch, and brandish his spear, the rider taking care to cover himself with his large leathern shield, and return as fast as he went, generally calling out lustily, when he got among his own party, 'Shields to the wall', 'You people of the Gadado, or Atego', etc., 'Why don't you hasten to the wall?' To which some voices would cry out 'Oh, you have a good large shield to cover you'. The cry of 'Shields to the wall' was constantly heard from the several chiefs to their troops; but they disregarded the call, and neither chiefs nor vassals moved from the spot. At length the men in quilted armour went up 'per order'. They certainly cut not a bad figure at a distance, as their helmets were ornamented with black and white ostrich feathers, and the sides of the helmets with pieces of tin, which glittered in the sun, their long quilted cloaks of gaudy colours reaching over part of the horses' tails, and hanging over the flanks. On the neck, even the horse's armour was notched, or vandyked, to look like a mane; on his forehead and over his nose was a brass or tin plate, as also a semi-circular piece on each side. The rider was armed with a large spear; and he had to be assisted to mount his horse, as his quilted cloak was too heavy; it required two men to lift him on; and there were six of them belonging to each governor, and six to the sultan. I at first thought the foot would take advantage of going under cover of these unwieldy machines; but no, they went alone, as fast as the poor horses could bear them, which was but a slow pace. They had one musket in Coonia, and it did wonderful execution, for it brought down the van of the quilted men, who fell from his horse like a sack of corn thrown from a horse's back at a miller's door; but both horse and man were brought off by two or three footmen. He had got two balls through his breast; one went through his body and both sides of the tobe; the other went through and lodged in the quilted armour opposite the shoulders.

The cry of 'Allahu Akber' or 'God is great', was resounded through the whole army every quarter of an hour at least (this is the war-cry of the Fellatas); but neither this, nor 'Shields to the wall', nor 'Why don't the Gadado's people go up?', had any effect, except to produce a scuffle among themselves, when the chiefs would have to ride up and part their followers, who, instead of fighting against the enemy, were more likely to fight with one another.[1]

Meanwhile the Bornu problem remained unsettled. The eastern frontier had been quiet since the capture of Birni Ngazargamu in 1808 and the seizure of some of the western provinces of Bornu, and Bello and Al Kanemi had preferred an intellectual exchange of polemics[2] to a physical encounter. But in 1824 Al Kanemi, fresh from his victory over Baghirmi, turned his attention to the Fellata threat. Hoping to establish some kind of buffer state in the Shira country against the Fulani empire, he marched westwards and in 1826 ousted Dan Kauwa from Katagum. The way was thus opened to Kano. Bello sent his Waziri to organize the defence, but the situation was saved for the Fulani by the resourceful Yakubu of Bauchi, who late in 1826 defeated the Bornuese army seventy miles east of Kano. With the re-establishment of the emirate of Katagum and the subsequent founding of those of Misau and Jama'are, the political vacuum of the Hausa-Bornu borderland

[1] H. Clapperton, *Journal of the Second Expedition into the Interior of Africa . . .*, 1829, pp. 185–8, quoted in Hodgkin, op. cit., pp. 218–20, and C. Howard and J. H. Plumb, *West African Explorers*, pp. 270 ff.

[2] For some excerpts from this correspondence, see the section on Bornu, pp. 322 ff.

was filled and peace could be permanently observed between Kukawa and Sokoto.

As a statesman, soldier, scholar, poet and administrator Muhammad Bello has been classed as the greatest of the Sultans of Sokoto. His upbringing was a model of filial piety, and in later years it was said that he never strayed from his father's way. His personal bravery was never in doubt—it seems probable that both the Shehu and Abdullahi owed their lives to him in the early days of the jihad—and he is reputed to have led forty-seven military expeditions during his reign. But to give undue prominence to his generalship is to ignore the many other facets of Bello's character. As a scholar, he was constantly quoting classical Arabic authorities in support of his philosophy of kingship, and over eighty of his publications are still well known besides his many poems in praise of the Prophet and the holy war. He was fond of study and encouraged learning, insisting that his sons did not inherit wisdom, as popularly thought, but must acquire it by diligent endeavour.

But he was no mere military tyrant fighting for fighting's sake, for to him war was not justified unless it be for the sake of Islam. He was convinced that it was only by war that paganism could be destroyed in the region of Sokoto, and the security of the Muslim state ensured. Recognizing no distinction between religion and politics he strove for the establishment of the Muslim state where the true law and peace of God might prevail. And he pursued this aim with remarkable determination. By his death the necessary basis of security for the development of Muslim government was in fact assured.

But continual campaigning did not automatically produce Muslim government in the old pagan lands. A new system of administration had to be built up to replace the pagan government which had been destroyed. The teaching of the Shehu had shown that the principles by which this new government was to work were all contained in the Qur'an and the Traditions and the commentaries of the medieval jurists. But to see that these rules were enforced in practice was a different matter. Bello's distinction is that in the midst of all his preoccupation with war he was yet able to lay the foundations of a government based on the requirements of the Malakite *shari'a*. To this task he brought a considerable personal knowledge of the law and much administrative ability. From the beginning we hear of his attempts to restrain the excesses of his soldiery in the conquered territory, and he stood out against corruption in the use of the confiscated wealth of the pagans which formed a considerable part of the revenue of the struggling Muslim government. He concerned himself with the establishment of *shari'a* courts, and gained a reputation for justice and the strict enforcing of the detail of the law. Over the work of his qadis he maintained firm personal control. 'He annulled those of their judgements which showed partiality, and did not let them rest in office.' His heavy hand indeed moved the qadis to warn his successor not to quash their judgements 'as your brother used to do'.[1]

This view of Bello's administrative morality receives strong support from the following extract from one of his directives to his flag-bearers, this one written to Yakubu of Bauchi in 1820:

> Know that on the governor of every region and district . . . seven things are incumbent: first, regard for the organization of the army: and its deployment in the localities, together with the assignment of its pay (provided that the Caliph does not administer and pay it himself); second, regard for the law and the proper following of authority by judges, and other officials; thirdly, the collection of land-tax and the obligatory poor rate, the proper following of authority by the tax-collectors, and the distribution of the legal proportion; fourth, the protection of women from insult and the preservation of religion from corruption and alteration; fifth, the meting out of legal punishment in the enforcement of God's law and the rights of men; sixth, the leading of the Friday and other communal prayers, either in person or by deputy; and seventh, the forwarding of pilgrims, both native and foreigners.

Bello encouraged science and learning, and distinguished visitors were welcome at his court. Among these was Commander Clapperton, who died on his second visit to Sokoto and was buried at the village of Jangebe two miles to the north-east of the city. Of Sultan Bello, whose erudition was a source of amusing embarrassment to Clapperton, he wrote:

> He was seated on a small carpet, between two pillars supporting the roof of a thatched house, not unlike one of our cottages. The walls and pillars were painted blue and white, in the Moorish taste; and on the back wall was sketched a fire-screen, ornamented with a coarse painting of a flower-pot. An arm-chair, with an iron lamp standing on it, was placed on each side of the screen. The sultan bade me many hearty welcomes, and asked me if I was not much tired with my journey from Burderawa. I told him it was the most severe travelling I had

[1] This and the next quotation are taken from the valuable biographical sketch by H. F. C. Smith in *Ibadan*, June 1960.

experienced between Tripoli and Sackatoo, and thanked him for the guard, the conduct of which I did not fail to commend in the strongest terms.

He asked me a great many questions about Europe, and our religious distinctions. He was acquainted with the names of some of the more ancient sects, and asked whether we were Nestorians or Socinians. To extricate myself from the embarrassment occasioned by this question, I bluntly replied we were called Protestants. 'What are Protestants?' says he. I attempted to explain to him, as well as I was able, that having protested, more than two centuries and a half ago, against the superstition, absurdities, and abuses practised in those days, we had ever since professed to follow simply what was written 'in the book of our Lord Jesus', as they call the New Testament, and thence received the name of Protestants. He continued to ask several other theological questions, until I was obliged to confess myself not sufficiently versed in religious subtleties to resolve these knotty points, having always left that task to others more learned than myself. He now ordered some books to be produced which belonged to Major Denham. Before taking leave, however, I had to explain the contents of each, and was set to read them, in order to give him an opportunity of hearing the sound of our language, which he thought very beautiful. The sultan is a noble-looking man, forty-four years of age, although much younger in appearance, five feet ten inches high, portly in person, with a short curling black beard, a small black mouth, a fine forehead, a Grecian nose, and large black eyes. He was dressed in a light blue cotton tobe, with a white muslin turban, the shawl of which he wore over the nose and mouth in Tuarick fashion.[1]

Bello died in 1837. He was buried at Wurno, the town that he had himself founded on the banks of the Gulbin Rima in 1822 as a *ribat* or bastion against the Tuareg as well as an alternative capital. In fact, Bello, like some of his successors, preferred this place to Sokoto and is often referred to as Mai Wurno.

According to Hajji Sa'id:

When the sickness became severe he sent to his son Ali, who was in Sanaki. He came to him and he made recommendations to him, saying to him, 'Do not seek the kingdom after me, but if God gives it to you, then advance those learned in the law—the helpers of the Merciful—and abase those learned in evil—the helpers of Satan. Honour the humble Fulani as you honour their nobles. . . .'[2]

[1] Denham, Clapperton and Oudney, *Narrative of Travels and Discoveries in Northern and Central Africa*, 1826, quoted in Hodgkin, op. cit., pp. 213–14.

[2] Hajji Sa'id, op. cit., p. 12, and Whitting's article in *African Affairs*, July 1948, p. 164.

Hajji Sa'id goes on:

> The Wazir told me that he went in to him on the Wednesday, and he said to him, 'How did you come in without obtaining permission; leave me.' I replied to him, 'I seek God's pardon,' then I said to him, 'will you not authorize me to execute Ali's orders?' He answered, 'No, I do not authorize you in respect of his orders or those of anyone else.' I said to him, 'In whose hands do you leave us?' He replied, 'I leave you in God's hands.'

Another story relating to this period was recently recounted by an old Sokoto *malam* who was discussing the modern interpretation of Islam advanced by some of the city's youth. During Sultan Bello's reign a certain *malam* began to preach that the Prophet had authorized a man to marry ten wives, and that the traditionalists who advocated four were wrong. Summoned before Bello to explain this heresy, the *malam* quoted the Prophet's injunction that a man may marry one, two, three and four wives; which, he pointed out, added up to ten wives. Since he refused to recant, the Sultan ordered him to be put to death for heresy. 'If you do this,' the *malam* challenged, 'the rains will never fall on the farms of Sokoto again.' He was put to death. And even as he died, the thunder rumbled and the first rains of the season broke.

The city of Sokoto in 1823 has been described thus:

> It occupies a long ridge which slopes gently towards the north, and appeared to me the most populous town I had visited in the interior of Africa; for, unlike most other towns in Hausa, where the houses are thinly scattered, it is laid out in regular well-built streets. The houses approach close to the walls, which were built by the present sultan in 1818, after the death of his father; the old walls being too confined for the increasing population. This wall is between twenty and thirty feet high, and has twelve gates, which are regularly closed at sunset. There are two large mosques, including the new one at present building by the Gadado, besides several other places for prayer. There is a spacious market-place in the centre of the city, and another large square in front of the sultan's residence. The dwellings of the principal people are surrounded by high walls, which enclose numerous coozees and flat-roofed houses, built in the Moorish style; whose large water-spouts of baked clay, projecting from the eaves, resemble at first sight a tier of guns. The inhabitants are principally Felatahs, possessing numerous slaves. Such of the latter as are not employed in domestic duties reside in houses by themselves, where they follow various trades; the master, of course, reaping the profit. Their usual employments are weaving,

house-building, shoe-making, and iron work: many bring fire-wood to the market for sale. Those employed in raising grain and tending cattle, of which the Felatahs have immense herds, reside in villages without the city. It is customary for private individuals to free a number of slaves every year, according to their means, during the great feast after the Rhamadan. The enfranchised seldom return to their native country, but continue to reside near their old masters, still acknowledging them as their superiors, and presenting them yearly with a portion of their earnings. The trade of Sackatoo is at present inconsiderable, owing to the disturbed state of the surrounding country. The necessaries of life are very cheap: butchers' meat is in great plenty, and very good. The exports are principally civet and blue check tobes, called sharie, which are manufactured by the slaves from Nyffee, of whom the men are considered the most expert weavers in Soudan, and the women the best spinners. The common imports are Goora nuts, brought from the borders of Ashantee; and coarse calico and woollen cloth, in small quantities, with brass and pewter dishes, and some few spices from Nyffee. The Arabs, from Tripoli and Gadamis, bring unwrought silk, otto of roses, spices, and beads: slaves are both exported and imported. A great quantity of Guinea corn is taken every year by the Tuaricks, in exchange for salt. The market is extremely well supplied, and is held daily from sunrise to sunset. On the north side of Sackatoo there is a low marsh, with some stagnant pools of water, between the city and the river: this, perhaps, may be the cause of the great prevalence of ague, as the city stands in a fine airy situation.[1]

On Muhammadu Bello's death there was much rivalry for the succession. The method of selection is described by Hajji Sa'id. It was the business of the Commander in Chief (Sarkin Yaki) and two other notables, known as the 'flags', to sound opinion in favour of one or other of the late Emir's sons or brothers. The 'flags' had to come to agreement. Approval also seemed to rest with five chiefs named as Ali Jit, the Commander in Chief;[2] Gidado, the Waziri; Almustafa, the Alkali; Bubakr, the Imam of the mosque; and a certain Dusiru. In this case the choice lay between two of Bello's brothers, Abubakar Atiku and Buhari, and one of his sons, Aliyu. Buhari, recently appointed joint commander of a Sokoto-Gwandu expeditionary force to help the Emir of Ilorin against the Borgawa, had a strong following, but in the end opinion swung to 'the house of Inna Gharka', the mother of Bello and Abubakar, Buhari's mother being Zami Gharka.

[1] Clapperton, op. cit., pp. 377–9. [2] i.e. Aliyu Jedo, Sarkin Yaki.

The new Emir, Abubakar Atiku, also known as Mai Katuru, was a sternly devout warrior. 'Dissipation died in his reign to the extent that it was as though it had never been.' We are told that 'the first thing he did in this way was putting to death a kettle-drummer in the middle of his playing so that they abandoned that'. He is described as 'ruddy, short, down-looking—he seldom raised his head, never parting from sword, spear and bow, you would not see him without two of them in his hand, even when he was going in to his house'.[1]

After an expedition in his first year of rule he had to upbraid his people for leaving him unprotected on the march home against possible capture by pagans. Next year in Zamfara before an attack on Gharbad he addressed his men as follows: 'To-morrow, if God will, you will fight perforce, or I will attain martyrdom in front of you, for I will stand before you on the edge of the moat, and do not do as you did last year.' Though his men fought hard and many died, they abandoned the fort and failed to capture it. Some of them said, 'We have fought to the death, and this Emir is not helped (by God).'

In this reign we are told of expeditions against the Gobirawa who were supported by the Habe Sarkin Katsina from Maradi. On one occasion the two wings of Abubakar's army fled, leaving him with only a few in the centre. Among these was a certain Qasar, notorious for his bad language as well as for his bravery. Cursing and swearing, Qasar spurred his horse against the pagans, provoking one of the sons of the chiefs to cry, 'Be careful of your foul language!' Qasar replied, 'Today only one who does not know his father would be careful!' And the speaker, observes the chronicler, was suspected of that.

We also hear of the capture of Bello's son Ali Fodio in Tan-shawar by the Sarkin Gobir. Ali Fodio had an evil reputation for oppression and extortion. 'One of his worst acts to the folk of Gobir was his taking those of their daughters whom he fancied, and putting them into his house. He used to act in a way in which none of the sultans of Gobir had acted, pagans though they were. To this he added much opposition to the Commander of the Faithful Atiqu.'

Abubakar Atiku died in 1842 at the age of sixty at Katuru in Isa district on his way back from raiding in the Gobir and Katsina.

[1] The quotations on this and the next page are from Hajji Sa'id, op. cit., pp. 16–22.

The succession once again presented difficulties and dissension. The army supported Atiku's brother Ahmadu Rufai, as did the Imam of the mosque and the Sarkin Yaki; the Waziri was under pressure from Atiku's son, Ahmadu Atiku, though he secretly preferred Aliyu, son of Bello. The Sarkin Yaki then conferred with his sons, who advanced objections to his choice, Ahmadu Rufai, so that further consultations became necessary. Said the Imam, 'Anyone who is disinclined for Ahmadu Rufai is a plaything of Satan's.' Sarkin Yaki rose and said, 'The Imam has said quite enough for us.' Halilu Sarkin Gwandu then arrived to give his advice. In the absence of general agreement it was left to Ali Jit, the Sarkin Yaki, who had presided at the selection of the Shehu, of Bello, and of Atiku, to make the final decision. The Sarkin Yaki remembered the advice of his sons and chose Aliyu, to be known as Aliyu Babba Mai Cinaka. He reigned from 1842 until 1859.

A son of Muhammadu Bello, Aliyu inherited some of his father's talents, though lacking his energy and firmness of administration, and his reign is still highly esteemed in the Sokoto annals. His Koran reader, Hajji Sa'id, described him thus:

> As for his description—before his succession he was corpulent; then, after his succession, he became fine drawn. He was black, of medium height, with a gap between his front teeth, fond of laughter, with good features and a fine long beard, beloved by the people, beneficent to them. . . . No one could talk him into action against a poor wretch. . . . He did not dispute in theology with anyone without vanquishing him. He was wide awake in ordinary affairs, knowledgeable about current events and the reasons for disasters. Often have I heard him say—'Such-and-such a disaster befell us because we did such-and-such, and through our doing such-and-such we have suffered such-and-such an event.' He fulfilled family obligations, was kind to the sons of his paternal uncle, and in the matter of the marriages of all of them took the responsibility of helping them and advising them. . . . He did not leave off learning by night or day; excessively hated shedding blood, and was on his guard against that. He only put to death him whom the Law condemned, and he attained the highest degree of justice.[1]

Much of Aliyu's time was preoccupied with expeditions against dissident subjects, especially within the borders of the present-day Sokoto and Katsina provinces. The heyday of the Sokoto empire had passed with the loss of Usman dan Fodio's moral impetus and

[1] Hajji Sa'id, op. cit., and quoted in Hodgkin, op. cit., pp. 220–2.

Bello's brilliant administration; from now on the empire, like all of its kind, was faced with the threat of internal decay and disintegration. Aliyu's last campaign was against Buhari, the rebel Emir of Hadejia, who had inflicted a severe defeat on the Sokoto forces in 1852.

Aliyu during his eighteen years' reign appointed the quite remarkable number of sixteen emirs to the Hausa emirates; five of these were to Zaria, where dynastic troubles at this period vexed the emirate. In addition to this confirmation of original flag-bearers' families, the emirate of Kontagora was founded in 1864, by Umaru, son of Abubakar Atiku and the *mauvais sujet* of the Sokoto royal house. Sokoto's own historians accuse Umaru Nagwamatse of conferring upon himself the grandiose title of Sarkin Sudan in imitation of the same title that Muhammadu Bello had once bestowed upon his son Aliyu Babba.

Dr Barth was hospitably entertained by Sultan Aliyu, who 'received me with the utmost kindness and good humour' when he visited Sokoto in 1853 and again in 1854. He signed a treaty with the Sultan, and as this document is not widely known, it is reproduced here in the original text:[1]

The Queen of England, Victoria, wishing to conclude a Treaty of Commerce with the Emperor of the Believers, has sent Abd el Kereem, Henry Barth, and the Emir of Sokoto, Aliu Emir el Mumeneen, after having heard and fully understood the discourse of Abd el Kereem, the messenger of the Queen of England, has given his consent, and has given to the English security of commerce under the following conditions:

The merchants of the English Empire shall travel in security with their people, their merchandize, and their beasts, in the whole extent of the empire of Aliu Emir el Mumeneen, and not even a rope shall be lost, while they may come and go at their pleasure.

They (the merchants of the English Empire) shall not hear an offensive word, nor shall anybody wrong or injure them, nor shall a Governor in the Empire of the Sultan Aliu be allowed to lay hold of them, or do them any injustice.

They shall return home in safety with their property; and if any body denies them payment of a debt, the Sultan Aliu will pay them, or take care of their being paid.

If any body among them should die, the tenth part of his property

[1] Quoted in A. H. M. Kirk-Greene, 'The British Consulate at Lake Chad', *African Affairs*, October 1959.

will be claimed by the Sultan, and the rest shall remain in his hand, till he has sent news to the nearest among her British Majesty's Agents, who will take care of it.

They may buy and sell every thing except slaves; but the Emir el Mumeneen will not allow them to buy slaves.

These are the Articles of the Treaty.

Written and signed, at Wurno, the 2nd May, 1853, corresponding with the 23rd Rejeb, 1269.

Barth described, however, the uneasy state of the empire at that time, rent by Kebbi and Gobir raids executed with bold impunity, to 'the weakness and unwarlike spirit of Aliyu and the complete nullity of Khalilu [Emir of Gwandu]', coupled with what he sensed as a patent feeling of jealousy between Sokoto and Gwandu. Among his valuable journals Dr Barth has left this account, along with a sketch-map of the royal city of Wurno:

The market is held on a natural platform spreading out in front of the north-western gate, and surrounded and fortified by a ditch, as, in the present weak state of the Fulbe, the market people are liable to be suddenly attacked by the enemy. This place, as well as the whole of the town, I visited the following day, in company with my friend Alhattu, who, in acknowledgement of the present I had given him in Gawasu, and in expectation of more, took me under his special protection; but in crossing the town, in a westerly direction from our quarters, I was surprised at its neglected and dirty appearance,—a small ravine which intersects the town forming a most disgusting spectacle, even worse than the most filthy places of any of the deserted capitals of Italy. Emerging then by the western gate (the Kofa-n-sabuwa), through which leads the road to Sokoto, and which was just being repaired by the people of the ghaladima, in order to make it capable of withstanding the effects of the rainy season, we turned northwards round the town. In front of each gate, on the slope of the rocky eminence on which the town is built, there is a group of wells, each with a little round clay house, where the proprietor of the well has his usual residence, levying on each jar a small contribution of five shells; but there are also a great number of wells facing the north-western gate, close to the market.

After the luxuriant vegetation of other parts of Negroland, I was astonished at the naked appearance of the country around the capital, only a few kuka or monkey-bread trees being seen; but the country presented a very different aspect on my return journey the next year, at the end of the rainy season.[1]

[1] Quoted in A. H. M. Kirk-Greene, *Barth's Travels in Nigeria*, pp. 253–4.

On Aliyu's death at Wurno in 1859, Ahmadu, the eldest son of Abubakar Atiku was appointed Sultan. He is also known as Zaruku. His reign is remembered for his encouragement of markets and caravans, and for the fact that he ordered the making of metal gates for all the large towns in his emirate. The town of Acida was founded by him as a bulwark against the Gobirawa. Ahmadu, too, is credited with the courage of having summoned the leaders of the proud Sulibawa clan of the Fulani, centred on Wamako and Shuni, and insisting on their obedience on the five issues that he laid down:

(i) No buying or selling of farms;
(ii) No reward to be demanded for the restoration of fugitive slaves;
(iii) Prompt response to any summons by the Alkali;
(iv) Obedience to the call of the Sarkin Musulmi to the jihad;
(v) To honour and obey their chiefs.

Ahmadu founded two towns, Sabon Birni and Cimola. He preferred the latter to Wurno, hence his nickname of Mai Cimola.

When Ahmadu died in 1866, another son of Bello, Aliyu Karami (i.e. the Small to distinguish him from Aliyu Babba, i.e. the Big), was selected in the mosque at Cimola. He took the court back to Wurno, but he died within the year. The next Sultan was Ahmadu Rufai, a son of the Shehu, then aged about fifty-seven. He is the only one of the Sultans of Sokoto, before or since, to come from outside the 'house of Inna Gharka'—the mother of Bello and Atiku. He was elected at Wurno but moved to Sokoto. He drove out the Kebbawa from Silame, which they had taken from the Fulani, and then made a peace with them which lasted for eight years. In Sokoto he is remembered as a peaceful king who was as generous and merciful to the poor as he was merciless to the wrongdoer: it is said that in his time the amputation of the hands of thieves was introduced instead of death.

Abubakar Atiku, the son of Bello, reigned from 1873 to 1877, and was preoccupied with a perilous invasion by the combined forces of the Gobirawa and Katsinawa. He destroyed the towns of Gidan Garere, Fototua and Madarumfa, but was unable to capture Maradi because Damagaram sent reinforcements from Zinder. Abubakar Atiku was succeeded by his brother Mu'azu, but his short reign is remarkable only for the revolt of the Gobir chief of Sabon Birni, Dan Halima, whose town he twice attacked but failed to take.

Umaru, the son of Aliyu Babba and a grandson of Sultan Bello, was appointed Sarkin Musulmi in 1881. For many years he made expeditions, supported by the eastern emirates, against the Gobirawa and the Kebbawa, but success eluded him. It was he who signed the original treaty with Joseph Thomson on behalf of the Royal Niger Company in 1885. Sokoto historians do not look well on Umaru's reign, reproaching him for having imposed an illegal capitation tax of 1,250 cowries (then worth under 1*s*.) and accusing him of preferring the advice of dubious *malamai* and servile underlings to that of his proper councillors. So critical did the situation become that the Waziri, Buhari, the Galadima and the Magajin Gari decided to take the grave step of either calling for the Sultan's abdication or asking him to accept their resignation. However, Umaru was taken ill and died at Kaura Namoda.

His successor was Abdurrahman, a son of Abubakar Atiku, who is widely known as Mai Kano or Danyen Kasko. The latter epithet in Hausa refers to the fact that in the same way as an unbaked pot will not hold water, so can the person thus nicknamed neither keep a confidence, nor finish properly whatever he undertakes. It reveals the low estimation in which his people held him. Of all the Sultans, his reign was the least popular, and his incompetence brought Sokoto into disrepute and ridicule. At home, he angered his councillors by his blatant nepotism; abroad, not only did he make the disastrous mistake of refusing Waziri Buhari's warning and appointing Tukur as Emir of Kano, resulting in a terrible civil war, but he also led three expeditions against Argungu, each of which was humiliated by the Kebbawa. Also in his reign came the angry alliance of Hayatu, son of Sa'idu of Gandi and a grandson of Sultan Bello, with Rabeh, whose daughter he married. For his own purposes, Rabeh acknowledged Hayatu as the rightful heir to the sultanate of Sokoto, but after a stormy career in the north-east Hayatu quarrelled with Rabeh's son Fad-el-Allah and was killed by him in 1900. Hayatu was the father of Malam Sa'id, the centre of the Mahdi incident of 1923; his deportation order was rescinded as one of the first acts of an independent Government of Northern Nigeria. In Abdurrahman's time a section of the Fulani called Mallawa or Tijani established themselves in Sokoto.

We have the following analysis of the empire's administration at the end of the nineteenth century by a French observer:

The Hausa Empire is divided into provinces, each of which has its governor, bearing the title of 'Sarki'. Within his province the Sarki has the right to administer justice, both in major and minor matters; he raises troops, and receives taxes. The office is hereditary in the same family, except that the appointment must be ratified by the Emperor, who performs the investiture.

Next in rank to the Sarki comes the Galadima, a kind of lieutenant, nominated by the Emperor, but always chosen among those who stand high in the order of succession, when he is not the heir presumptive himself.

The Sarkis of the various provinces owe the Emperor entire obedience. They furnish him with a military force, armed and maintained at their own expense, for his expeditions. They also pay him an annual tribute deducted from the receipts of taxation. Apart from these ties of vassalage, they administer their provinces in an almost independent manner. None the less, the Emperor reserves a right of control over their administration: hence those who hold high office at the imperial court have allocated to them a certain number of provinces, which it is their responsibility to inspect, over whose affairs they exercise a central oversight, and on which they report to the Emperor.

Thus the Galadima, the heir presumptive of the Empire,[1] has in his charge the provinces of Katsina, Kazauri, Magazingara (the neighbourhood of Magami n'Didi), and Kebbi. Sokoto and Wurno came under the special administration of the Sarki n'Kebbi. The Sarki n'Saffara, son of the Commander of the Faithful, supervises Zamfara and Daura. The Waziri has responsibility for the provinces of Kano, Zazzau, and Adamawa. But, in view of the multiplicity of his functions, the Waziri delegates some of his powers to Bandawaki, King of Gandi, . . . whose principal duty it is to visit Kano, Mauri, and Adamawa, and speed up the collection of their taxes. Every year

[1] We are grateful to Sokoto N.A. for pointing out that this observation of Monteil's is not correct. They have given this useful extra information on the supervision of the Fulani empire by Sokoto title-holders: 'The Galadima was the councillor in charge of Katsina, Daura and Kazaure, and was one of the king-makers but never the heir presumptive. Sokoto and Wurno were under no councillor. The Sarkin Zamfara, one of the princes, at first supervised Sokoto but when he was moved to Dan Cadi the town came under the charge of the Galadiman Gari: this was at the time of the British occupation. When the Galadiman Gari was moved to Durbawa, the town of Sokoto came under the Waziri. The Waziri had originally been responsible for Kano, Zaria, Yola, Katagum, Misau and Jama'are, but he used to delegate the supervision of Yola to his *wakili* at Gandi. Bauchi came under the Magajin Rafi and Muri under Sarkin Rabah.' Monteil's observations are notoriously unreliable.

Bandawaki sets out to make this tour of the provinces, which lasts seven or eight months.[1]

The Council of Selectors or king-makers (*sarakunan karaga*) comprised the following, in order of precedence: the Waziri, the Sarkin Yaki of Binji, the Galadiman Gari, the Magajin Rafi, the Magajin Gari, the Sarkin Kebbi of Yabo, the Ardon Shuni, the Ardon Dingyadi, and the Barden Wamako. Of these the choice of the two first named outweighed that of all the others. It is noteworthy that the ancestors of four of the above were granted flags by the Shehu, and four others were holders of offices created by his son, Muhammadu Bello.

Abdurrahman, who generally resided at Wurno and retained Sokoto as an alternative capital, died at Wurno in 1902, shortly before the British turned their attention to the conquest of the powerful northern emirates. He it was who sent the now famous retort to Lugard when the High Commissioner sought his assistance in appointing new emirs to Kontagora and Nupe:

> From us to you. I do not consent that any one from you should ever dwell with us. I will never agree with you. I will have nothing ever to do with you. Between us and you there are no dealings except as between Mussulmans and Unbelievers (*Kafiri*) War, as God Almighty has enjoined on us. There is no power or strength save in God on high. This with salutations.

Muhammadu Attahiru I, the grandson of Abubakar Atiku, was appointed Sarkin Musulmi in late 1902, and it was unfortunate that almost at once he had to deal with the advance of the British who had taken up the challenge contained in Abdurrahman's letter just quoted. After the fall of Kano on 16 February 1903, the column set out for Sokoto. A fierce engagement occurred at Kwatarkwashi before the British troops joined up at Shagari with their reinforcements from Illo. A battle took place on the *hurumi*, or communal open land just outside Sokoto town, to the south-west, on 15 March 1903 in which, despite the heroism of some of the Fulani cavalry, the Sokoto forces were defeated. Submission was made at the foot of the famous lone *giginya* palm on this Sokoto maidan, still standing; the great mud fort was demolished in 1930.

[1] P.-L. Monteil, *De St. Louis à Tripoli par le Lac Tchad*, Paris, 1895, quoted in Hodgkin, op. cit., p. 316. See, however, footnote at p. 408.

Sultan Attahiru fled first to Gusau and thence, with a large following, to Burmi. Here he was killed in the battle fought in July, 1903, the first Sokoto notable ever to meet his end on the field of battle. The flag captured from Attahiru, believed to be the standard of Shehu Usman dan Fodio, was carefully preserved in the West African Frontier Force museum and was returned to the Sultan at a special ceremony in 1961. It is interesting to note, too, that the deliberate date selected by the Premier for Northern Nigeria's self-government in 1959 was 15 March, the anniversary of the battle of Sokoto.[1]

One often comes across the alleged prophecy that the Fulani empire of Sokoto would last for exactly one hundred years; and that is the time span from the acknowledgement of Usman dan Fodio as Sarkin Musulmi at Gudu and the victory at Lake Kwotto in June 1804 to the death of the fugitive Sultan Attahiru in July 1903. Lugard credits this prophecy to the Shehu in person. Of Lugard's two senior Residents, Major Burdon of Sokoto emphasizes that he had never heard of such a prophecy[2] (his choice of terminal dates is, however, suspect), but Sir William Gowers narrated how he had been told of it by the Fulani headman of Goila in Adamawa, who declared he had read it in a manuscript of Sultan Bello.[3] For what it is worth, the legend is mentioned here while it awaits substantiation.

The Sokoto Council of Selectors, headed by the blind and noble figure of Waziri Buhari, now named Muhammadu Attahiru II as the Sultan. Tradition has it that it was in fact he who had been nominated to succeed Abdurrahman but that in order to avoid civil war he had withdrawn. It is also on record that in 1903 the selectors first chose Umaru, the son of Aliyu Karami, but as he was old and had lost an eye the choice eventually went to his cousin. The fine old gentleman Waziri Buhari, who, as we have seen, was descended on the distaff side from Usman dan Fodio through his daughter Asma'u, who had married the first Waziri, Muhammadu Gidado, died in 1910 and was followed in office by Ambo and then Macido. Lugard's historic speech at the installation of the 12th Sultan of Sokoto is too well known to quote here.[4]

[1] See A. H. M. Kirk-Greene, 'The Choice of March 15th', *West African Annual*, 1960, and D. J. Muffett's forthcoming *Concerning Brave Captains*.

[2] *Annual Report of Northern Nigeria*, 1902, para. 25.

[3] Quoted in J. A. Burdon, *Historical Notes on Certain Emirates and Tribes*, 1909, p. 67.

[4] It is to be found in *Annual Report of Northern Nigeria*, 1902, Appendix III.

The only set-back to the early administration of Sokoto emirate came with the Satiru disaster of 1906. One Dan Makafo persuaded the village head Isa to rebel. Two Administrative Officers and nearly half a company of troops were killed, while the Maxim gun was captured. But at this critical moment the Sultan did not hesitate. He at once sent the Marafa with 3,000 men to subdue the rebels in Satiru. After order had been restored, the Sultan determined to make an example of the village by ordering that it should be razed to the ground and the soil never tilled again. Satiru has remained a wilderness.[1]

Muhammadu Attahiru II died in 1915. The year was indeed a sorrowful one for the Province, for it lost all three of its First-Class chiefs by death and the Emir of Yauri by deportation. Attahiru II was followed by Muhammadu, better known as Mai Turare,[2] who had up to then been Marafa of Gwadabawa. As his mother was a daughter of the ruling house of Gobir, he had an added advantage in his popularity. Sokoto tradition maintains that he had been a strong candidate for the throne in 1903 but that he had refused to accept while an heir of the senior branch of the Dan Fodio family survived. Towards the end of his reign Mai Turare, who died in 1924, became unpopular with his lesser chiefs and appealed to the Governor that he was the victim of a plot. His son Muhammadu succeeded him. He was known as Tambari because his maternal grandfather, an Asben from Aïr, had held this title. He never really enjoyed the confidence of his people, whose trust and affection he had alienated, and in 1931 he abdicated. Then, hoping that his mother's connexion would entitle him to the Asben office of Sarkin Musulmi granted by Usman dan Fodio to Muhammadu Kamma in 1810, he made a precipitate flight to Niamey. Later he returned to Nigeria and was banished to Wukari, where he died in 1935.

Hassan, a grandson of Sultan Bello, was in 1931 appointed the 15th Sarkin Musulmi after Shehu. He immediately reorganized his Council. In 1933 he and the Emir of Gwandu visited Lagos, and in the following year, accompanied by the Emirs of Gwandu and Kano, he went to England and was received in audience by

[1] A photograph of the famous machine-gun used in this engagement (*bindigar ruwa*) and a note on the story attached to it are now in the Museum of the Nigerian Army, Zaria.

[2] *Turare*=civet-cat scent. Clapperton noted the passion of the Sultan for cats; he had more than two hundred of them in his palace.

the King. Hassan did much to improve the administration of his emirate which had so deteriorated under his predecessor, including his brave advocacy of female education throughout the Province and his no less enlightened support of an Ibo State Union school in Gusau, so that his sudden death in 1938 genuinely deprived the people of a ruler whose probity and interest for their welfare had endeared him to all. Once again history repeated itself, for the Province quickly suffered another blow through the death of the Emir of Gwandu. A moving tribute was made in the official annual report of the Province, a document not normally known for its warmth of human feeling:

> Hassan, the late Sultan, had experienced to the full the hazards of outrageous fortune. Recalled from obscurity in 1931 to assume the role of Sultan—at a most difficult time, when years of misconduct and maladministration had culminated in the abdication of his predecessor—he at once took a grip of affairs, and by personal example rather than by forceful leadership quickly restored a standard of integrity in administration and strengthened the morale of a then distressed and disheartened Emirate. Hassan very soon endeared himself to his people to whose welfare he was devoted. A man whose tastes and standard of living were of marked simplicity and whose genuine smile and courteous and charming manner will long be remembered, he exerted a tremendous influence for good. By the people he was revered as is a saint; by all Emirs and Chiefs he was held in the highest esteem. His sudden death, of which we were given not a day's warning, came as a calamity and disaster: high Native Officials and the lowliest peasant felt that there had passed not only a wise and just ruler but also a personal friend. In all my years out here I can truthfully say that never have I seen such depth of feeling as was made manifest by all; and most moving were the tributes paid to the memory of their lost Chief by each member of the electoral Council—even by those not normally given to many words. During his lifetime Hassan had begged, as his dearest wish, the privilege of a grave situated to the east of and under the shadow of the tomb of the revered Shehu dan Fodio: this was willingly granted, whereupon he strictly enjoined the Waziri and other councillors that no monument or tomb should be erected over his grave: this request was typical of the late Sultan, a man whom I am proud to have known as a friend.[1]

Hassan's successor was his thirty-seven year-old nephew, Abubakar, who held the new (1933) office of Sardauna and was at that

[1] *Annual Report of Sokoto Province*, 1938, paras. 52–53.

time district head of Talata Mafara, and who had already been to the United Kingdom with his uncle. One of his first acts was to recognize the growing importance of Gusau, a railhead boom town, by posting a senior Council member there with an executively free hand, and persuading the Administration to complement this with the permanent stationing of a senior D.O. and the establishment of a sub-treasury. District administration has always been a feature of Sokoto, and in 1951 a joint Committee from all the emirates within the Province published its guide to district heads, known locally as *mai rigar fata* from the leather binding of the original.

A major reorganization of the Council and the district administration took place in 1952 as a result of the departure to Kaduna of the Sardauna, Malam Ahmadu, to take up his appointment as the first elected Minister of Northern Nigeria—a position from which he soon rose to become Premier. It is of interest in our emirate context to note that on receiving a knighthood for his distinguished services, the Sardauna adopted the name of his royal great-grandfather and expressed a wish to be known as Sir Ahmadu Bello. The Sarkin Musulmi's personal charm and popularity as both a Minister without portfolio and Sultan of Sokoto have been evident to every visitor to his palace.

The year 1961 thrice revived memories of Usman dan Fodio. First, by the ceremony at which the Sultan received back the Shehu's personal standard said to have been captured in 1903. Secondly, by the death of Inna Wuro at the age of ninety-seven, the last grand-daughter of the Shehu and for many years the custodian of the relics of Usman dan Fodio. Thirdly, by the pious appeal of his great-great-grandson, Alhaji Sir Ahmadu Bello,[1] Sardauna of Sokoto and Premier of Northern Nigeria, for funds towards the rebuilding of the two historic mosques in Sokoto town, the *Masallacin Shehu* and the *Masallacin Bello*.

[1] See his autobiography, *My Life*, 1962, and its Hausa version, *Rayuwata*, 1965.

THE SULTANS OF SOKOTO*

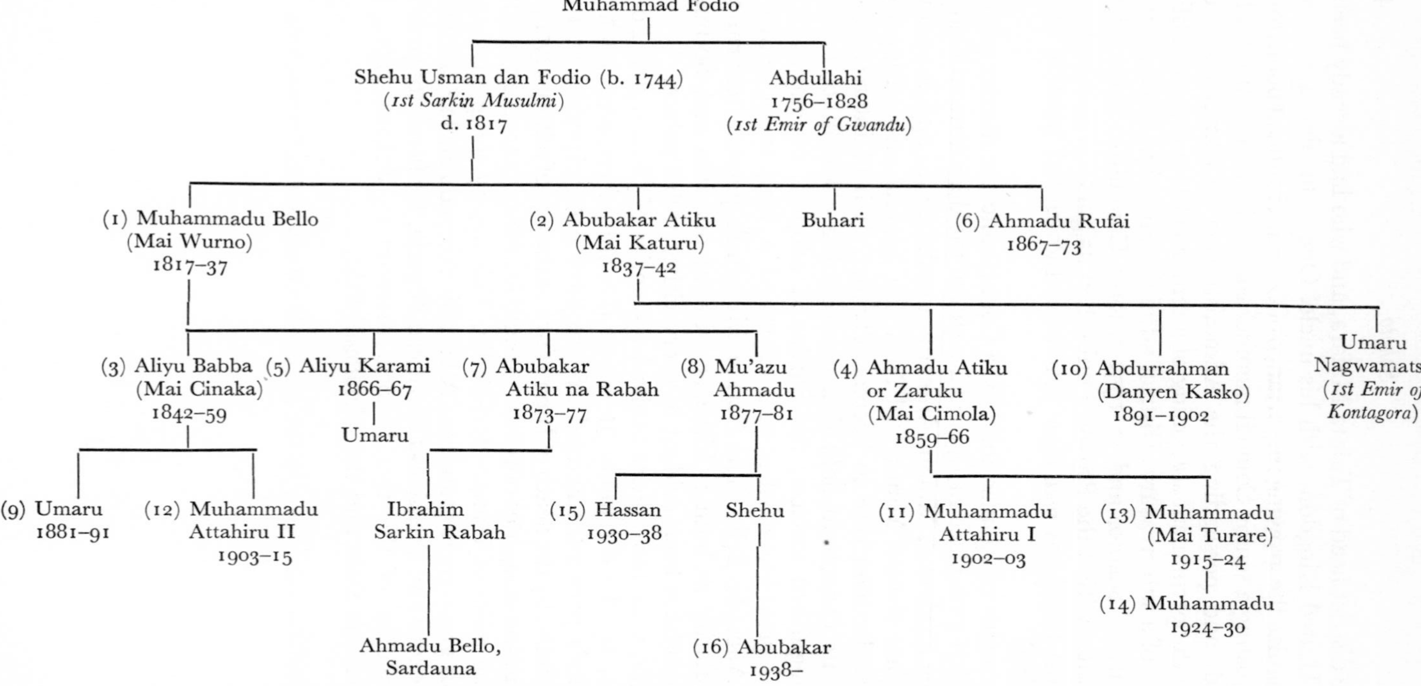

*Based on the dynastic House of Fodio reproduced in Sir Ahmadu Bello's autobiography, *My Life*, p. x.

THE KINGS OF ZAMFARA[1]

(According to a list in the possession of the Sarkin Zamfara of Anka, Muhammadu Fari)

1. Dakka I (rulers at Dutsi)
2. Jatau (rulers at Dutsi)
3. Jimir Dakka (rulers at Dutsi)
4. Kokai Kokai (rulers at Dutsi)
5. Dudufani I (rulers at Dutsi)
6. Algoje (female)
7. Bakurukuru, *c.* 1300
8. Bakawa
9. Gimshikki
10. Karafau
11. Gatamma
12. Kudandam
13. Bardau
14. Gubarau
15. Tasgarin Burum
16. Durkusa
17. Mowashi
18. Kigaya
19. Tabarau
20. Dudufani II
21. Burum I (twins *c.* 1550)
22. Burum II (twins *c.* 1550)
23. Taritu
24. Fati I (twins)
25. Fati II (twins)
26. Zartai (Zaudai), *c.* 1625
27. Dakka II
28. Tasau
29. Zaude
30. Aliyu (perhaps the first Moslem king)
31. Hamidu Karima
32. Abdu na Makaki
33. Suleimana
34. Muhammadu na Makaki
35. Abdu na Tamane
36. Maliki (Malu)
37. Babba I, *c.* 1715
38. Yakubu I
39. Jimirra or Jirau
40. Falkari or Fashane
41. Babba II, *c.* 1734
42. Yakubu II (from Birnin Lalle to Zamfara)
43. Maroki, *c.* 1756 (driven out by the Gobirawa)
44. Abarshi, *c.* 1805 (to Sabon Gari)
45. Fari (from Banga to Ruwan Gora)
46. Dan Bako (to Sabon Gari)
47. Dan Gado (to Anka)
48. Tukudu, *c.* 1825
49. Abdu Fari
50. Abubakar, 1829–53
51. Muhammadu Dan Gigala, 1853–77
52. Hassan, 1877–1896
53. Muhammadu Farin Gani ('the Handsome') 1896–99
54. Abdullahi Gado, 1899–1904
55. Abdu Caccabi, 1904–16
56. Muhammadu Katar, 1916–28
57. Muhammadu Fari, 1928–46
58. Ahmadu Barmo, 1946–

THE KINGS OF GOBIR

At Gubur in Arabia and later at Suakin

1. Bana Turmi
2. Gubur
3. Sanakafo
4. Majigi
5. Sarki
6. Bartuwatuwa
7. Bartadawa
8. Bartakiskia
9. Kartaki
10. Sagimma
11. Baran Kwammi
12. Masawana Jimri Gaba

[1] There are some discrepancies between the lists given in Krieger, op. cit., and P. G. Harris, *Sokoto Provincial Gazetteer*, 1938. In his *Sokoto Gazetteer*, 1920, E. J. Arnett reports that he was unable to trace any list of the kings of Zamfara. S. J. Hogben found this list at Anka in April 1924.

At Khartoum

13. Ciroma
14. Dan Goma
15. Sakidamma
16. Matsaura
17. Duguma
18. Zaberma
19. Umi
20. Gozo
21. Banizam
22. Beyamusi
23. Gosi
24. Jimri Gaba
25. Ciroma II
26. Majejeri
27. Kasimu
28. Cida

In Bornu

29. Gojo
30. Dara
31. Jelani
32. Bataji
33. Babba
34. Munzakka
35. Munzakka II
36. Munzakka III
37. Alazi
38. Kana Ju'un
39. Baciri
40. Hunda
41. Dalla Gungumi
42. Dalla Kure
43. Hammadmi
44. Humadi
45. Arkal
46. Babba
47. Humdu
48. Ubandoma
49. Baciri II
50. Ubandoma (possibly Ubandoro)
51. Ubandoma II
52. Baciri III

In Asben

53. Ubandoro II
54. Abdulla
55. Keji
56. Dunsumi
57. Akwai Allah
58. Zamai
59. Falali
60. Gintsarana
61. Dalla
62. Baciri IV
63. Muhammadu
64. Dara
65. Ciroma III
66. Mundagas
67. Baran Kwammi
68. Ashafa
69. Baciri V
70. Bustadana Gingama
71. Ashafa Dara
72. Kawami
73. Mundagas II
74. Ciroma IV
75. Muhamman
76. Kazgaba
77. Muhammadu
78. Maji
79. Ciroma V
80. Arkal II
81. Usmanu
82. Ushuwa
83. Makuwa
84. Muhammadu Dan Ciroma, *c.* 1715
85. Baciri VI
86. Muhamman Mai Gici
87. Akali
88. Arkal III
89. Muhammadu
90. Soba
91. Uban Iche (Ibn Ashe)

At Alkalawa

92. Babari dan Ibn Ashe (1742–70)
93. Dan Gudi dan Babari (1770–77)
94. Gambai (1777)
95. Bawa Jan Gwarzo dan Babari (1777–95)
96. Yakuba dan Babari (1795–1801)
97. Nafata dan Babari (1801–03)
98. Yunfa dan Nafata (1803–08)

At Tsibiri

99. Salihu
100. Gwamki
101. Ali
102. Mayaki
103. Baciri VII
104. Bawa Dan Gwamki
105. Ibrahimu
106. Mainassara Maji
107. Almu
108. Ibrahima Na Mai Fura
109. Bakon Dare
110. Umaru Dacili
111. Bature
112. Dan Bude
113. Dan Magaji
114. Tumbulki
115. Gulbi
116. Salau

At Sabon Birni

117. Dan Halima
118. Gaude
119. Kasso
120. Ishaka
121.
122. Belarabe
123. Jari
124. Jadi
125. Umaru Shawe

The above list with that of the Kings of Zamfara is based on that in the *Sokoto Provincial Gazetteer* compiled by Mr P. G. Harris (duplicated typescript, August 1938). Two other lists are known to exist. One, given in Arnett's *Gazetteer of Sokoto Province*, was based on a list found at Yankaba, in Kaura district, by Mr H. F. Backwell when he was Assistant District Officer; it gives Yunfa as the 58th king. Another list in the possession of the Alkalin Sabon Birni gives Yunfa as the 45th king; it agrees with the Yankaba list in the eight names from Ibn Ashe to Yunfa, but there are discrepancies in the earlier names and omissions on the Sabon Birni list. All lists agree on Bana Turmi as the first king.

The relationships of the kings of Gobir in the years before the jihad were as shown below:

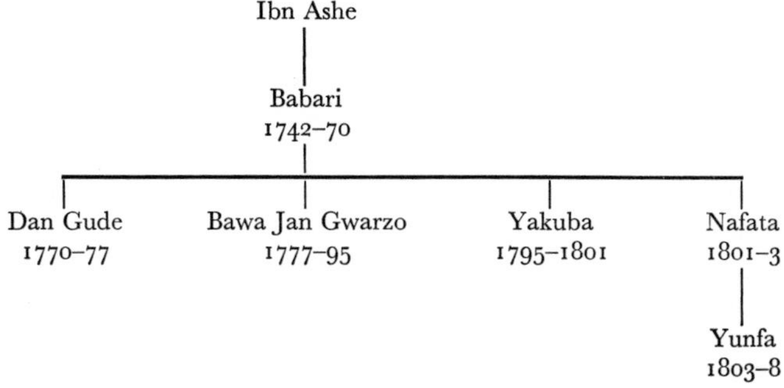

XXIX. GWANDU

To a very considerable degree the history of Gwandu is part and parcel of the history of the Fulani jihad in Sokoto. The detailed story of Usman dan Fodio's holy war and the part played in it by the founder of Gwandu, Abdullahi, we have already treated under the Sokoto section, so that what remains is the history of Gwandu emirate from its creation in 1808 as the guardian of the administration of the western part of the Sokoto empire. We thus reject the claim advanced in some quarters that the history of Gwandu emirate dates from only 1817 because Abdullahi, with his expectations of succeeding the Shehu, never cared to govern Gwandu but preferred to reside in Bodinga and leave the administration to his son Muhamman. We prefer to accept the theory that to begin with no clear-cut division between Sokoto and Gwandu was considered, but that when the Shehu delegated the military command of the western areas to his brother Abdullahi, Gwandu became the focus of this new power.

The Fulani had withdrawn to Gwandu after their initial setback against the allied forces of the Gobirawa, Kebbawa and Tuareg at Alwassa at the end of 1805. They had already established a base there a few months earlier when the resistance of the Zamfarawa and a food shortage combined to cause them to retire from Sabongari. Gwandu at this time was within the Kebbi sphere of influence. A year later the Gobirawa were routed by the Fulani and in 1806 Bello started to build the walls of Gwandu.

The name Gwandu derives from the term *gandu*, or 'royal farmlands', belonging originally to Kanta, the great Sarkin Kebbi. His head farmer enjoyed the title of *sarkin gandu* and his village gradually grew into the sizeable settlement of Gwandu. At a later date Fulani nomads, finding the area a fertile one in pastureland, settled there.[1] When Usman dan Fodio used Gwandu as a base for his early campaigns against the Gobirawa, these Fulani rendered him valuable assistance. Later he returned to Gwandu and built a house there. Gwandu district today contains many relics of

[1] See C. E. Hopen, *The Pastoral Fulbe Family in Gwandu*, 1958, for a fuller study.

greatness of the old Kebbi empire, specially the deserted towns such as Birnin Barama, Birnin Magum, Birnin Ginga and Birnin Langarma, located in the bush known as Dajin Barama between Gwandu and Argungu.

Gwandu's *raison d'être* was the Shehu's realization that as long as Kebbi maintained her strength and independence, the Fulani empire was threatened: a bastion in the west against the Kebbawa was imperative. Accordingly he sent Abdullahi to drive the Kebbawa out of their capital, Birnin Kebbi.

Two campaigns of Abdullahi have special relevance to the formation of Gwandu emirate. One was his expedition to Gurma; the other, that against Dendi and Zabarma. At the latter's capital of Dosso, Abdullahi left his representative as Sarkin Zabarma, whose descendants have continued to hold the office of Zerinakoi. In a third expedition, Abdullahi's son Muhamman is said to have installed Sarkin Illo as a vassal of Gwandu, though this is hotly denied by Illo people who claim descent from Kisra and insist that Illo was never dependent on any state, being at the most an ally of Kebbi.

After the Zabarma campaign Abdullahi took up his residence at Bodinga. The Shehu now divided the administration of his empire, giving Abdullahi the western provinces and Bello the east. Abdullahi's last major expedition was in support of Malam Dendo's struggle for the Nupe throne. We have discussed Abdullahi's failure to succeed his brother as Sarkin Musulmi. In his later years Abdullahi withdrew more and more from Gwandu's affairs of state, which he was content to leave to his son Muhamman and to his nephew Buhari, a son of the Shehu, and instead devoted himself to books and writing. Abdullahi died in 1828, at the age of seventy-two.[1]

It was in Abdullahi's reign that one of Gwandu's most prosperous towns was founded, that of Jega. Its founder was Buhari, the son of Abdussalami, the Ba-Are disciple of Usman dan Fodio whose discontent at what he considered to be his shabby treatment by the Shehu led to his rebellion against Bello and his eventual capitulation at Kware. On Abdussalami's death, Buhari made his submission to Abdullahi, now Emir of Gwandu, and with the approval of Bello he was permitted to take his large Arewa following and settle on the banks of the River Zamfara.

[1] For the discrepancy in dates, see the section on Sokoto, p. 376.

The importance of Jega as a cross-roads market was pronounced throughout the nineteenth century: what gave rise to its importance is still a matter of controversy, though it is significant that most of the dominant markets of the Western Sudan, like Kano, Wagadugu, Kukawa and Jega, lay along the twelfth parallel of latitude, a line which it has been suggested represented the southern limit of animal transport. These markets thus became the great exchange marts and clearing houses for the produce of the open savannah of the north and that of the southern forest regions.[1]

Abdullahi was succeeded by his son Muhamman, who was confirmed in his appointment by Bello on a special visit to Gwandu. His reign is largely remembered for the hard fighting against Karari, Sarkin Kebbi, which has been described in the chapter on Kebbi. To prevent the Arewa towns again revolting in support of Argungu, Muhamman sacked Beibei, Damana and Birnin Debi, and forbade them ever to rebuild their walls. Other campaigns which Gwandu led during this reign were those against the Yoruba, in which Kwajobi was captured, and Wawa in Borgu, which was not successful.

Muhamman died in 1833. He had left a testament that he wished his brother Halilu to succeed to the Gwandu throne. Bello came from Sokoto and confirmed this appointment. Halilu's reign of a quarter of a century was to be a momentous one for Gwandu; much of it resolved itself into a series of military expeditions.

Halilu's first preoccupation was the threat from Borgu, whose forces had attacked Kaoje and encamped in the bush to the south-west. The fame and prosperity of Kaoje were in earlier times its horses, bred on the rich Niger *fadama* or marshland and nearly always sold for a handsome profit in the Bida market. From his base at Kassara in Zagga, Halilu sent Muhamman Sambo against the Borgawa. The Fulani of Zagga are known to this day as *Toronkawa Sabulde* or 'the Toronkawa of the Soap', because such was the gift of their chief Abdulkadiri when all the Fulani came to make obeisance to Usman dan Fodio at Gwandu in 1805, each clan bringing the customary present of a typical local product. The battle was a disaster to the Fulani, for Sambo was pursued in headlong flight as far as Butuli and Isiaku, the youngest son of

[1] For a discussion of Jega's importance and of this thesis of the 12th parallel, see the remarks of E. W. Bovill in *The Geographical Journal*, vol. CXXIV, 1958.

Abdullahi, was killed. Regrouping his forces, however, Muhamman Sambo fared better in a second campaign and succeeded in reoccupying Kaoje and driving out the Borgawa.

Halilu met with no better luck in his first attempt to subdue Gurma. He halted at Say and sent Muhamman Sambo, supported by Sokoto troops, to attack Botu. They were repulsed and many of the Gwandu-Sokoto army died of thirst before they reached their camps at Zongori and Say. Halilu hurried back to Gwandu and implored Sokoto for reinforcements. Bello gave him all the Sulibawa Fulani, under the command of the Barden Wamako. This time the campaign was successful, Botu falling and its chief Bunewal being killed. The Barden Sokoto also lost his life in this battle.

The years 1836 and 1837 saw Halilu operating in the Nupe and Ilorin country. The Emir of Ilorin, Abdussalami, had appealed to his liege-lord Gwandu for help against the Borgawa who had invaded Ilorin at the request of the dissident Yoruba elements opposed to the Fulani régime. The combined Fulani army, made up of contingents from Sokoto and Gwandu, was commanded by Buhari dan Shehu and Muhamman Sambo. The Borgu forces drove the Fulani back to Ilorin town, but when their chief was killed in an assault their morale collapsed and the Fulani were able to repulse them. Halilu left some of his men in Ilorin as an added defence against the Borgu inroads.

Muhamman Sambo, the Gwandu general, was killed in 1838 when Halilu organized a campaign by his own army along with contingents from Nupe and Ilorin to subdue the Dakarawa who had been plundering traders' caravans. No sooner was this dealt with than the towns of Gummi and Keɓɓe[1] revolted. Halilu called on the Etsu Nupe, Usman Zaki, to assist. Two years later Halilu had to go to the assistance of Usman Zaki, but the Nupe forces were too strong and drove the Fulani out of Raba. Halilu returned to install Usman Zaki in Raba.

[1] The town of Keɓɓe on the Zamfara River is not to be confused with Kebbi. The chief of Keɓɓe bears the title Sarkin Kebbi in common with the chiefs of Jega, Silame, and Yabo, apart of course from the Emir of Argungu. The Fulani chiefs of Silame and Yabo were governors of parts of Kebbi during the period of Kebbi submission from 1831 to 1849. Keɓɓe, which revolted against Halilu at the end of this period, was eventually brought to heel but petitioned to be subject to Gwandu direct instead of through an intermediary, Tambawal. Halilu refused, but Sokoto arranged a compromise that Keɓɓe should follow Sokoto direct. Thus it has remained. See pp. 249 ff. and footnote on p. 249. See also E. J. Arnett, *Gazetteer of Sokoto Province*, pp. 39 ff.

There was more trouble on the home front in 1845 when Halilu had to deal with revolts in Kebbi. Ever since the defeat and death of Karari in 1831 the Kebbawa had been kingless and subject to Fulani governors. At first defeated in front of Argungu, Halilu was later successful with aid from Sokoto and reduced to submission the town of Keɓɓe. More trouble then came from revolts in Zabarma and Arewa, which resulted in the setting up of Karari's son, Yakubu, in 1849 as Emir of Argungu. Since 1834 he had been under loose surveillance in Sokoto.

After his Zabarma campaign of 1849, Halilu undertook no more expeditions in person. This military retirement seems to have developed into a general withdrawal from the administrative cares of his emirate, for Dr Barth, visiting Gwandu in 1853, found Halilu 'a man without energy', who 'lived in a state of the greatest seclusion, well fitted for a monk but by no means suited to the ruler of a vast empire'. His whole impression of Gwandu at this period is a sorry one, that of a kingdom faced with serious internal threats from the vigorous Kebbawa and external troubles in its provinces of Nupe and Ilorin, without a strong character at the helm. Of the town Dr Barth wrote:

As we approached the town of Gando, I could not help wondering how the people had been led to choose this locality as the seat of a large empire, commanded as it was by hilly chains all around, while the rising ground would have offered a far more suitable locality. But the situation of the town is on a par with the character of its dominion—without commanding strength, and quite incapable of keeping together that large agglomeration of provinces which have gathered around it. However, for a provincial town, the interior is very pleasant and animated, being adorned with a variety of trees, among which the banana is prominent. . . .

The interior of the place was not quite without its charms, the whole of the town being intersected, from north to south, by the broad and shallow bed of a torrent, which exhibited fine pasture-grounds of fresh succulent herbage, while it was skirted on both sides by a dense border of exuberant vegetation, which altogether is much richer in this place than either in Sokoto or Wurno, being surpassed only by the fine vegetable ornament of Kano. The rains are extremely plentiful in Gando, causing here quite an exceptional state in the productive power of the soil; and to this circumstance we have partly to ascribe the fact that very fine bananas are grown here in considerable quantity: and the fruit being just ripe at the time, formed a very pleasant variation to my usual food. The onion of Gando is remarkable for its size and quality, compared with that of all the neighbouring districts; and it is well for the traveller, in whatever direction he may intend to go, to lay in a supply of this wholesome article. But the place is extremely dull, and the market very insignificant—a fact easily to be explained by the desperate state of the provinces around, although the situation of the capital, as a central place for commerce, is rather favourable.[1]

It was, of course, in Gwandu that Barth made one of the most important academic finds; this was the Arabic manuscript *Tarikh al Sudan*, a document of monumental importance to the study of the history of the Western Sudan. He was allowed to copy it, 'which opened to me quite a new insight into the history of the regions on the middle course of the Niger'. The pass over the Dutsin Duku, where Dr Barth's camels stuck as he was leaving Birnin Kebbi, is still known as *hanyar Barth*, 'Barth's route'.

Halilu was succeeded by his younger brother Haliru in 1858. His first campaign against the Kebbawa brought a great victory; the second, in 1860, cost him his life at the battle of Tilli. Yet another son of Abdullahi, Aliyu, now became Sarkin Gwandu. A few months after his enthronement, Aliyu moved the emirate headquarters from Gwandu to Ambursa, the site of the old town broken by the Kebbawa in their 1849 uprising. This town was an original Fulani settlement, populated by the Wagawa, under their chief, Ardo Wago, as the ruling clan, and the Kasarawa and Ujaria groups. At the time of the jihad Ardo Wago made submission to the Shehu. The reason for Aliyu's move was to afford protection to the towns situated on the south bank of the River Kebbi[2] which were in danger of being overwhelmed by the Kebbawa.

From this base Aliyu spent the four years of his reign fighting off the Kebbi threat. On his death in 1864 he was succeeded by his brother Abdulkadiri who, in 1866, managed to conclude a peace treaty with the Kebbawa through the intermediary of the Sarkin Musulmi. The terms, which were highly favourable to Argungu, were that:

(*a*) Argungu should be independent, a vassal to neither Gwandu nor Sokoto;

[1]Quoted in A. H. M. Kirk-Greene, *Barth's Travels in Nigeria*, pp. 264–7.
[2] Or River Sokoto.

(*b*) all the towns then held by the Kebbawa should remain under Argungu;
(*c*) there should be no exchange of slaves captured in the previous fighting.

This treaty is known as *Lafiyar Toga*, 'the peace of Toga', after the name of Sarkin Kebbi, Abdullahi Toga.

On Abdulkadiri's death at Besse in 1868 while on his way to Nupe, he was succeeded by Almustafa, a grandson of Abdullahi. In 1871 he paid a state visit to Kontagora and Bida, receiving a present of many guns from the Nupe, who were on very friendly terms with the river merchants at Lokoja. Three years later an incident occurred at the Kebbi town of Fanna, which ended the eight-year *Lafiyar Toga*. The inhabitants of Fanna sent a deputation to Almustafa to say that they wished to follow Gwandu. When the Emir agreed to this, Sarkin Kebbi naturally interpreted it as a treacherous breach of the peace treaty and ordered Sarkin Shiko, the chief of Fanna, to seize all the Fulani cattle he could lay his hands on: it is said that he rounded up ten thousand head in the Fanna and Giru districts. Almustafa marched on Giru but was unable to capture the town. He now summoned Etsu Nupe to come to his aid, but he died before the Nupe army arrived. His successor Hanufi, another grandson of Abdullahi, waited for the arrival of the Nupe reinforcements and then attacked Giru. In retaliation, Sarkin Kebbi sent raiding parties against Ambursa and finally launched a full-scale attack on the Gwandu capital with a combined force of Kebbawa, Arewa and Zabarma. Abdulkadiri, Sarkin Kalgo, stoutly defended Ambursa in the absence of the Emir, driving off this attack and another one by a Kebbawa raiding party on Randali whose inhabitants, hearing the firing at Ambursa, had hurried in for the kill, only to find Sarkin Kebbi had withdrawn and that they were trapped. Meanwhile, Hanufi captured Giru after a four-month siege. He also killed Sarkin Shiko of Fanna.

Another grandson of Abdullahi, Maliki, came to the throne in 1876, and the Sultan sent his Waziri Buhari to confirm the appointment. Within a year disaster struck Gwandu. The Kebbawa made a vigorous attack on Ambursa and captured all the Emir's thirty guns. They also seized Ruga Shehu. Mortified at this defeat, Maliki abandoned Ambursa as his capital and returned to

Gwandu. During his reign Joseph Thomson visited Gwandu to make treaties on behalf of the Royal Niger Company. He gave Maliki a present of cloth valued at forty million cowries; that to Sokoto was worth sixty million.

The 10th Emir of Gwandu was Umaru Bakatara, another grandson of Abdullahi. Two of his chiefs, Haliru of Kalgo and Haliru of Raka, led a number of expeditions against the Kebbawa, with varying degrees of success. His reign saw the catastrophic rinderpest epidemic of 1887–91, still mournfully remembered as the *sannu*, from the Hausa expression of condolence and sympathy:

> The older men tell one terrible stories of those days. Attempts were made, by some, to fly from the disease and preserve their cattle. Fulani, having lost all—or nearly all—their cattle, became demented: many are said to have done away with themselves. Some roamed the bush calling imaginary cattle: assaults on persons for imagined provocation or suspected derisive remarks as to loss of cattle were common. When the outbreak had spent itself and passed on, Fulani of the eastern area of what is now Nigeria renewed their cattle from parts of Adamawa that had escaped, while those to the West obtained the almost humpless 'Keteji' type kept by the Borgu Fulani from time immemorial, hardy cattle of the bush and hills of Borgu, Kaiama and Jikki, which had apparently escaped the ravages of rinderpest to a considerable extent. So great was the demand for cattle that, locally, it was common in many places to offer large prices for the unborn calf.[1]

The loss of their herds forced many *Fulbe na'i* or nomadic Fulani to turn to farming and so join their kinsmen the *Fulbe sire* or agricultural Fulani. Gwandu, and to a lesser extent Sokoto, are characterized by the high percentage of non-pastoral Fulani, partly because of the drastic change in the economy brought about by this rinderpest epidemic and partly because here are the traditional strongholds of the Toronkawa, 'the land of the faithful' as the local historians call it.[2]

Umaru Bakatara was succeeded by Abdullahi Bayero, who reigned for but a year before he died and was followed by yet another grandson of Abdullahi, Bayero Aliyu. Gwandu offered no resistance to the British occupation in 1902 when troops were around Kebbi. Bayero Aliyu died in 1903 and his successor

[1] F. St. Croix, *The Fulani of Northern Nigeria*, p. 13.
[2] See Hopen, op. cit., pp. 1–5.

Muhammadu was deposed in 1906 after the Satiru incident.[1] Haliru reigned from 1906 to 1915 and then his son Muhammadu Bashiru till 1918. Haliru was the first of the Emirs of Gwandu to be installed at Birnin Kebbi, the new headquarters of the emirate.

Usman became the 16th Emir of Gwandu in 1918; his reign of twenty years was the first substantial one since that of Halilu, the third Emir, who had died sixty years earlier. If his period of rule was an uneventful one, apart from the Mahdi unrest in Besse in 1923, it reflected the quietness of a country contentedly ruled. His official obituary was later to speak of him as

> forceful, ambitious, and endowed with boundless energy. He could never forget the glories of the past nor how, after the British occupation, the area over which his ancestors ruled had been reduced. To keep Gwandu in the forefront of the picture despite its handicaps he never spared himself.[2]

Yauri emirate and Dabai were transferred from Gwandu Division in 1932, the latter ending up in Niger Province. The Emir of Gwandu undertook a number of notable journeys, such as that to Lagos in 1933 and to England a year later, with six followers paid for at his personal expense, along with the Sultan of Sokoto and the Emir of Kano.

Towards the end of his reign Usman was handicapped by ill-health. On his death in 1938—the same sad year in which Sokoto Province also suffered the loss of the Sultan—he was succeeded by his younger brother Yahaya, who had up to then been the Sarkin Gobir of Kalgo and had accompanied the Emir to England a few years earlier. His reign, unlike so many in royal history throughout the world, fulfilled all the early hopes and promise, and when Sir Yahaya (as he deservedly became,) died suddenly in 1954 he had acquired a reputation for wisdom, selfless devotion and unlimited integrity that was acclaimed far beyond the boundaries of Northern Nigeria.

The new Emir was Sir Yahaya's forty-one year-old nephew, Haruna, up to then Sarkin Gobir of Kalgo. In his time, the name of the emirate became known in connexion with such development projects as the UNICEF malarial control scheme and the Gwandu rice scheme. The Emir was honoured by his elevation to the

[1] See section on Sokoto, p. 411.
[2] *Annual Report of Sokoto Province*, 1938.

Presidency of the House of Chiefs in 1958, but bleak days marred the emirate in 1962 when a commission of inquiry into the administration reduced the Native Authority to a state of virtual dependence on the District Officer.

THE EMIRS OF GWANDU

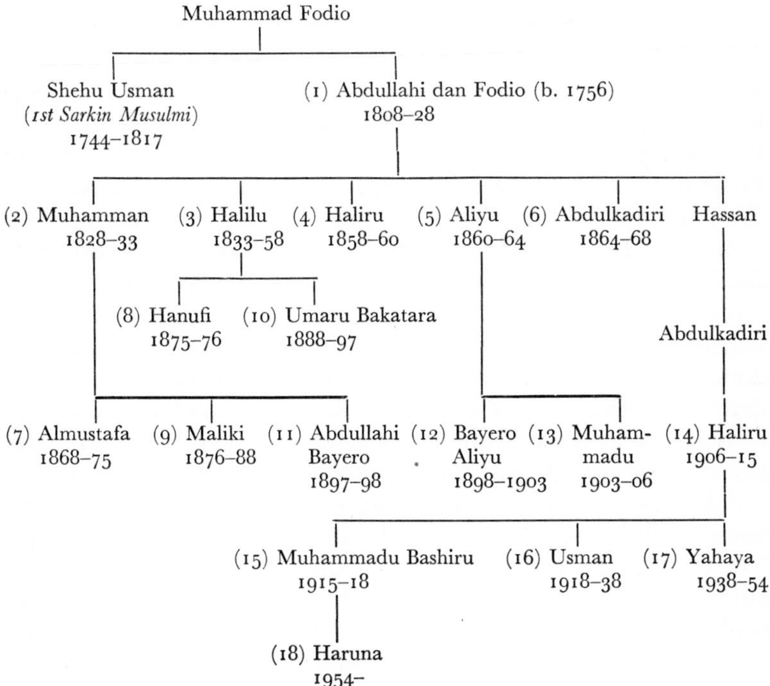

3. EMIRATES DERIVING FROM THE SOKOTO EMPIRE

(2) The South-Eastern States

XXX. ADAMAWA

THE nineteenth century name of Adamawa was, in emirate history, dropped in favour of Yola during the early years of the British administration, but in 1926 it was revived to describe both the emirate and the new Province of Adamawa. It derives from the name of the first Emir, Adama. The Emir of Adamawa is known by his Fulfulde title of *Lamido*. Adama's full title was *Lamido Fombina* or *Aminu Yemen*, 'the Lord of the South', which properly denoted those great areas of the southern (i.e., from Sokoto) districts conquered by the Fulani. At one time this kingdom stretched from Marua and Madagali in the north to Ngaundere and Tibati in the south and from Lere and Rei Buba to Mayo Lope in the west, but the Fulani emirate of Adamawa was carved up by the Cameroons mandate agreement of 1922.[1]

Adamawa, along with Muri and Gombe, are the sole emirates where Fulfulde continues to be the language of daily intercourse. Yet there is more than this in Adamawa's claim to be unique among the emirates. It would appear that the large middle class of traders and artisans that existed in the Hausa States had no counterpart in this region of the Sokoto empire. Again, whereas in the Hausa States the conquered by and large absorbed the conquerors—so that today, for instance, very few if any of the Fulani Emirs outside Adamawa and Gombe speak Fulfulde, and the Emirs of Bida are culturally more Nupe than they are Fulani—in Adamawa the distinguishing ethnic characteristics of the Fulani have not been nearly so absorbed by miscegenation and concubinage, nor has the social amalgamation been anywhere as pervading and

[1] The chapters on Adamawa and Muri lean heavily on A. H. M. Kirk-Greene, *Adamawa Past and Present*, and *Stories of Old Adamawa*, ed. R. M. East. Grateful acknowledgement is also made to the suggestions of M. Muhammadu Song of Adamawa N.A. and M. Bashiru Tukur.

persistent as it has been in the Hausa States. Furthermore, in contrast to the Hausa emirates, Adamawa is marked by the absence of walled towns. Again, to quote an official report:

[Here] the administrative organization differs from those in Hausaland in the traditional status of the office of district headman: in the latter, before the British occupation, he was generally an absentee landlord, in the former invariably a resident fief-holder with local ties. The position of their successors still rests, in local eyes, on the original conception and constitution of the office whereby the holder was spokesman for the people in his charge and authorized agent of the emir in the latter's dealings with them. In that traditional duality lies its strength, for Fulani and pagan have been associated in this area for close on two centuries.[1]

The first record of the Fulani presence in the eastern side of Northern Nigeria dates from *c.* 1300, when a party of them came from Futa Toro to Bornu. The early migrations of the Fulani were caused rather by their need for new pasturage than by any idea of conquest. They used to pay grazing dues to the pagans in whose country they herded their cattle, to whom they often acted as herdsmen, and were generally so subservient that they are said to have acceded to the *jus primae noctis* claimed by these chiefs. The general conversion of the Fulani to Islam was slow, owing to the innate conservatism of a pastoral people, and only a minority had become Muslims by the time Adama launched his jihad at the beginning of the nineteenth century. Numerous clans, though supporting their kinsmen in the holy war, retained their totemic cults, and today the Bororo'en and Kesu'en remain predominantly un-Islamized while the Kiti'en, who settled among the Gongola valley tribes, are scarcely Islamized at all.

The Yola royal family, which is of the Ba'en clan, preserves the tradition that its ancestors were driven out of the Damaturu neighbourhood by the Kanuri in the fourteenth century and entered Adamawa by the Yedseram valley. It seems that the main penetration, however, did not occur till the eighteenth century, though there were advance parties in Bornu and Bauchi during the fifteenth century and some Fulani had reached Baghirmi by about 1550.

Two main branches are distinguished in this stream of migration. The first consisted of the Wolarbe, the Ba'en, and several

[1] *Annual Report of Adamawa Province*, 1936.

smaller clans, while the Ilaga'en constituted the bulk of the second. The fission appears to have taken place after the foundation of settlements in the Upper Yedseram valley by both sections. The Wolarbe and the Ba'en, with some of the Ilaga'en, with the Mbewe'en and Gara'en, turned eastwards through the mountains and penetrated the basin of the River Kebi before settling around Marua.

The Mandara empire—later the most powerful and highly organized enemy that the Emirs of Adamawa had to face—was hostile to the Fulani long before the jihad and blocked their approach round the northern tip of the Mandara hills. Thus the eastern movement of the Ilaga'en could not be achieved until they had reached a point well south of the Mandara territories—probably from Mubi, itself a settlement of this clan, through the narrow Ba'a valley which is the only practicable opening in the seventy-mile mountain barrier that separates the basin of the Kebi from those of the Yedseram and Kilengi rivers.

The western branch of the migration continued south-westwards, crossing the Yedseram and Kilengi watershed and so entering the basin of the Benue. For some time its southern front paused in the highly organized kingdom of Kilba on terms dictated by the tribal chief, and a great deal of intermarriage seems to have taken place, the effects of which are still discernible in the physical characteristics of a people otherwise indistinguishable from the southern Marghi. Thence the expansion pushed on into the Benue valley proper, where its immediate range was limited by the Verre hills to the south and to the west by the intractable hostility of the tribes occupying the Gongola valley and the Mumuye plateau. Eastwards from this barrier the Benue lowlands were occupied by centralized Bata principalities, with whom the Fulani came to terms.

By the end of the eighteenth century the immigrants were established in numbers throughout the Bata territory. The whole of this region, watered by the Benue and its tributaries and rich in large marshes, fertile cotton soil, and good grazing pastures, was dotted with growing Fulani settlements, each under an *Ardo*, a title originally given to chiefs owing allegiance direct to the Lamido; nowadays it has lost its meaning of family leader, though it still retains among the settled Fulani an archaic suggestion of respectability and blue blood. These settlements remained in a state of subservience to the pagan chiefs until the time of the Fulani jihad. Furthermore, the eastern and western branches were once more in contact: the former had reached the Benue by way of the Kebi and Tiel valleys and settled in some strength in the Bata state of Demsa, near Garua, while the latter, passing eastwards along the south bank of the Benue, had crossed the River Faro into Bundang, another Bata state.

As the Fulani influence with the indigenous chiefs increased, often by way of intermarriage, subservience became distasteful to the immigrants, particularly when emphasized by the insistence of the Bata kings on their *droit de seigneur*. Such a demand in about 1803 by the chief of Bundang was, according to legend, the occasion of the first direct step towards the establishment of the Fulani supremacy in Adamawa. Ardo Jobdi, head of the Wolarbe around Song, slew his daughter rather than yield her up, then turned and killed the chieftain lest he demand again what had been refused beyond recall. His deed was the signal for war and the Wolarbe withdrew to the Verre hills where, under Ardo Hamman, they entrenched themselves at Guriga Hosere. A pagan force from Song attacked them but was repelled. The Verre, however, afraid that they might be drawn into the quarrel, refused to allow the Fulani to remain, and in 1804 the latter moved down to the plains and camped on the west bank of the Faro on the site of what was later to become Gurin town.

In this first battle perished Ardo Hassana, a Ba'ajo noble. His son Adama, fancifully said to be a great-grandson of Jobo Rum, a Persian, returned to his people at Weltunde near Guriga in the following year after a period of travel and study in Bornu, under Malam Kiari of Kukawa, and in Sokoto, during which he had perfected the learning and piety that won for him the title of *Modibbo*, 'the learned one'. Adama brought the news that Usman dan Fodio had declared a jihad against the heathen. Many of the local Fulani had already embraced Islam, and Adama persuaded the various clans to combine and follow the crusading example of Sokoto. A mission was sent to Usman dan Fodio, the Commander of the Faithful, to request his sanction and support for the jihad in the east. The party included Adama and Kokomi, the Bata chief who, having seen that the Fulani must become the dominant power, had thrown in his lot with theirs. By his foresight Kokomi secured the confirmation of his office for himself and his descendants, and also the title of Magaji, with authority over all the riverain Bata later subjugated by the Fulani, and a monopoly of ferry rights, while his whole clan was granted immunity from enslavement and taxation.

The Shehu received the mission favourably and gave a flag to Ardo Boronga of the Wolarbe, the senior clan-chief, whom the delegates had nominated as their leader in the Holy War when Adama declared that he preferred to abstain from secular command. The grant of the flag and the commission which it signified were conditional upon the sending of a yearly deputation to Sokoto with a regular quota of slaves: the latter presented no difficulty, but the idea of a recurrent pilgrimage involving over a month's journey was disagreeable to the Adamawa delegates, who determined, in Adama's absence, that the conditions attached to the commission should be disregarded. This dishonesty came to the ears of Adama, the leading spiritual force of the party, and indignant at such perfidy he reported it to the Sultan at a public audience.

Usman dan Fodio recalled the mission and publicly took back the flag. He then presented a new flag to Adama:

> When you return tell them this is what Shehu gave you. Say also that I accept their greetings. Bid them place their hands in yours; whoever gives his hand to you, join hands with me. Tell them I greet them. Make flags for them like this that I have given you, and give them the flags, with the orders I have laid upon you. You are the envoy; whatsoever they desire let them tell it to you, then do you come and tell me.[1]

As a special mark of favour and honour, the Shehu is said to have unwound Adama's turban and crowned him with a fez from his own head. In his letter of appointment he conferred on Adama the title of *Lamido Fombina*, with a firman to propagate the faith from the Nile to the Bight of Biafra, and allowed him to recruit Fulani volunteers (Toronkawa) in Sokoto. Their ranks were swelled by Hausa mercenaries, fired by the prospect of slaving, and Adama thus acquired a nucleus for the Adamawa army which he was to raise on his return. In fact, Adama never adopted the title of Lamido, for he was always—and still is—known as Modibbo, the learned one.

[1] This and the next quotation are from R. M. East, op. cit.

Adama arrived back in Gurin in 1806. He initiated his campaign by sacking the neighbouring Bata towns of Pema, Turuwa, and Tepe. Another tradition maintains that he obeyed the commands of Usman dan Fodio and waited three years before undertaking any conquest; this was in contrast to the zeal of Buba Yero of Gombe, whose conquests of the Yungur, Lala, and Hona areas were taken away from him by the Shehu, as a punishment for his precipitancy, and handed to Adama. For the next forty-two years Adama was occupied with extending his conquests and subduing rebellious vassal-governors of his provinces as he gradually carved out the kingdom of Adamawa.

First to fall was the Bata capital of Demsa on the Benue, which was conquered by Ardo Hamman. The sultanate of Mandara, under Bukama, was a tougher nut to crack, but by the end of the 1820s Adama had added Mubi, Moda, Micika and Uba to his kingdom. It is from Modibbo Adama's campaign against Mandara that the Fulani legend of *Balewu Yola*, 'the black horse of Yola', derives. Fulani chroniclers relate it thus:

> Whilst they were attacking them in this fashion, one of the people of Modibbo called Bakera, who had a black horse, was about his own business, and did not hear what was happening to his countrymen. What engrossed his attention was this: There was a house standing by itself which he discovered close to the side of the moat. In this house he found one of the best-looking women in the city, and went in to her. With this woman he was so preoccupied that he was quite unaware that the Mandara had returned and driven out his countrymen. When the woman heard that her people had come back she tried the more to detain him, and Bakera stayed on until the husband came and arrived at the entrance, all without his knowing. Then the Mandara woman said to him, 'Get up, my husband has returned!' He got up, and made ready. The woman saddled his horse, put his girdle on, and held the stirrup for him. He mounted. Then the Mandara man came to enter his house, and espied someone on a horse inside. (The house had a wall round it.) Then he said to Bakera, 'You there! Get ready, and look where you can escape!' Bakera leant over, took his spears from the hand of the woman, and said to the man of Mandara, 'In the name of God! Prepare yourself, I am going out!' At this he made his horse plunge forward towards the entrance, and the man made quite ready and awaited him. Bakera went up to him as though they would meet right in the entrance, and then turned his horse back into the courtyard at full gallop. The man followed and they went through the courtyard

together. They reached the wall, Bakera pressed his horse forward to the jump, and it took both the wall and the moat at one bound. Then came the man of Mandara, he urged his horse forward, but jumped the wall only; it could not clear the wall and the moat. Then Bakera turned, and struck his horse's quarters. 'My black horse is not like your roan,' he said. 'It is on such a day as this that horses prove their worth; to-day he has paid for his fodder!' Thus he escaped from them and departed. The fame of this horse has lasted in the East even till now.

Further conquests were made in the Kilba, Holma, Song and Malabu areas, and with the move of his capital to Yola in 1841 Adama was able to press home his campaigns against the Verre and Bata peoples. The name Yola derives from the Fulfulde *yolde*, meaning a settlement on slightly rising ground. Then, while he turned his attention to the Marghi and Mandara territories in the north, his lieutenants Ardo Hamman Joda, Sammatu and his son Hamman Gabdo Dandi extended the frontiers of Fombina to the east by seizing Laro, Koncha and Banyo, and others such as Ardo Jobdi and Hamman Sambo occupied Tibati and Ngaundere.

Rei Buba was more difficult.[1] In the early days of the jihad one Ardo Yajo, son of Ardo Bondi from Mali and cousin of the Sultan of Sokoto, passed through the Mandara country from Bornu and, reaching the upper waters of the Benue, settled on the edge of the Dama and Laka territories, where he was appointed lieutenant by Adama and given a flag. Yajo died soon afterwards and was succeeded by his son Jidda, who made his headquarters on the banks of the River Rei and entered into a treaty with the Dama chief, cementing this by the marriage of the latter's daughter to his son, Buba Jirum. Despite this treaty, the Dama were soon reduced to serfdom. Jidda then extended his conquests into the Laka and Baya country and consolidated his position by allying himself with the governors of Tibati and Ngaundere. A climax came when he called on the governors of the minor provinces of Balda, Njarendi, and Wuro Mayo to throw off their allegiance to Adama and acknowledge him as suzerain; at the same time he sent an embassy to Sokoto with a large present of slaves and a request for the recognition of his independence of Yola. This appeal was refused; at the Sultan's orders, Jidda returned his allegiance to Adama.

[1] In the *National Geographic Magazine*, August 1959, Maurice Fiévet has some fine paintings of Rei Buba and the northern parts of the Adamawa province.

In the following spring, according to custom, Adama ordered Jidda to send a force to take part in the annual slave-raid on the Namji pagans. No contingent from Rei appeared, the raid failed, and Adama retired defeated. Immediately Jidda demonstrated that he could succeed where Adama had failed; he attacked the Namji with his own forces and captured a number of slaves, some of whom he tauntingly dispatched to Yola. He was soon summoned thither himself to explain his conduct to the Emir, who made a show of accepting the proffered apologies but in fact planned to procure Jidda's death by drowning on his way back from Yola. Hearing of this plot, Jidda, on his departure, dressed his brother Umaru in the blue gown which he himself habitually wore and sent him to take his own place in the canoe; as Jidda had expected, an upset was staged and his brother was drowned. The same night Jidda fled overland to his capital; the revolt of Rei was on.

Jidda's first rising was easily put down by Adama, who punished his rebellious henchman by taking all his territory north of the River Shina and giving it to Ardo Bibeme. The second uprising was disastrous, for Adama actually entered Rei, deposed Jidda, and appointed his son Shehu governor in his stead. Yet no sooner had Adama left Rei than Jidda rallied his remaining forces and retook his capital, Shehu being killed in the assault. Adama hurried back but was unable to recapture the town. Thereafter he was obliged to tolerate the virtual independence of Rei, the successive chiefs of which nevertheless continued to recognize the spiritual leadership of the emirs of Yola and to furnish in normal years nearly the whole of the annual tribute of slaves payable by Yola to Sokoto.

It is from Rei Buba that the legend of the Fulani drum *tumbal sardi* comes. During all the wanderings of the Fulani until they reached Adamawa, this war drum, an heirloom of great ancestry, remained in the possession of the Jillaga clan right up until the time when the Ardo Jajo was pasturing his herds in the Mandara mountains to the east of Mubi. While the old man was still alive dissension arose among his six sons for the inheritance of the drum named by the Fulani *tumbal sardi*. To end this and ensure to his eldest son Bondi the precious heritage, and with it the succession to the rule over the tribe, Jajo hid the drum by night in a ravine in the mountains. He marked the site with a stone, and shortly before his death entrusted Bondi with the secret. But when the latter went to recover the drum, he could not find the spot: a gazelle in flight had knocked the stone down into the ravine. It fell upon the drum, the head of which gave out a hollow tone. It was never seen again; only the traveller journeying at night through the mountains is alarmed by its hollow notes. To replace it, Bondi had another drum made out of a mighty stem, which was exactly like the sacred one; it also was named *tumbal sardi*. Its hollow tones, accompanied by the throbbing of a second one, made by Buba Jidda, still herald the approach of the mighty Ardo of Rei, accompany the songs of the men and the women at the dance, and inspire the warriors in desperate encounter.[1]

By this time the Fulani migrations and campaigns in Adamawa had resulted in three clearly defined divisions:

(*a*) To the east, the Fulani kingdom of Fombina.
(*b*) To the west, the Fulani kingdom of Muri and the area governed from Wase.
(*c*) In the centre, a block of unconquered pagan tribes, such as the Mumuye and the diverse tribes of modern Numan Division, with groups of people, such as the Kilba, Higi, Fali, and Koma, who maintained varying degrees of independence according to the inaccessibility of their hill-top villages to the Fulani cavalry.

Following on Rei, a similar bid for independence was made in 1842 by Ardo Hama-Sambo, Governor of Chamba, who sent a magnificent present of slaves and merchandise direct to Sultan Atiku of Sokoto. Contrary to precedent, Atiku granted him a separate flag of office, whereupon Adama, despite his advanced years, decided to retire to Mecca for the pilgrimage. He set out from Yola with a very large following, but before he had reached the limits of his territory he was overtaken by messengers bearing the news of Atiku's death and a petition from all his vassal chiefs, except the governor of Chamba, begging him not to desert them. Adama at once summoned his recalcitrant vassal to a meeting at Beka, ten miles south of Gurin. It is said that this meeting took place before the greatest host of horse and foot ever assembled in

[1] Based on a translation from the history of Adamawa compiled by the German Resident F. Strumpell, 1912. I came across this document in the Residency, Maiduguri.—A.K-G.

Adamawa. Hama-Sambo did public obeisance and was ordered to return his flag and commission in person to Sokoto.

In 1848 Modibbo Adama died in his bed at the age of seventy-seven. His piety is still revered in Yola, and is enhanced by contrast with the ostentatious behaviour of Sanda and later Lamidos. It is said that at his death Adama left only his Koran, his simple clothes, and one female slave. He had the reputation of being a man of great learning and much energy, and as a leader was bold and able. In disposition he is said to have been mild to a fault, though inflexible once his mind was made up. He was by preference a scholar and saint rather than a warrior, universally respected and even beloved by his people. He made no less than eleven pilgrimages to Sokoto.

Of Adama's wives, Yasebo bore him two sons, who were said to have been excluded from the succession because one night their mother kept Adama waiting outside her hut in the rain; Astajam was the mother of Lawal, Sanda, and Mansur. Jara, said to be a Marghi concubine given him by his wife Mamare, bore Zubeiru and Bobbo Ahmadu. It is remarkable that Adama was succeeded by his four sons in turn, three of them in accordance with his dying testament, as will be seen. Adama had altogether eleven sons and four daughters. The great pride that the Fulani of Adamawa take in Modibbo Adama is amply illustrated in the following tale told by Yola historians:

> One day the Lamido had come out and was sitting at the entrance to his house in the evening, when he caught sight of his brother Hamma [Hamidu?] swaggering on his way to the mosque. So he sent a man to tell Hamma when he came out of the mosque to come and see him. When Hamma came he asked him, 'Why are you swaggering like that?' Hamma said, 'Three things cause me to walk with a swagger.' 'What are they?' he asked again. Said he, 'If you pick up your slate and come here I will teach you knowledge. Again,' he went on, 'if I meet a hundred horsemen of the enemy, when they see me they will not stop and wait for me, for they feel that they are standing on my old home.' Thirdly he said, 'It was Modibbo Adama who begat me.' Then Lamido Lauwal said, 'You are right. Go and be proud of yourself.' Hamma got up and walked away, swaggering as he went.

Adama was succeeded by Hamman, better known in Yola history as Lawal. It was Lawal's destiny to consolidate the empire which his father had carved out. His reign was largely occupied

30

with wars against the Fali of Mubi, the tribes of Lere and the Logone valley, and the Bata of Bagale hill, while much of his energy was expended in dealing with the turbulence of his governors, especially those of the southern provinces. He founded the fiefs of Girei and Namtari which, like his father's Gurin, have remained as traditional appointments of the Lamido, conferred as a personal reward.

Apart from campaigns against the Fali round Mubi and Tibati, one of Lawal's most spectacular victories—and one celebrated by Yola historians—was his conquest of the Bata stronghold of Bagale in the hills behind the Benue opposite Yola. Under their chief, Geloya, the town had resisted assault for many years, but in 1853 it was betrayed by one of its women, a concubine of Lawal's.[1] She secured admittance by pretending that she had escaped from her master's harem and wished to take refuge with her relatives. A few days later the Fulani forces made a night march to the point nearest to the town affording them concealment. In the morning this woman set fire to some houses at the opposite side; the Bata garrison rushed to that quarter to repel a supposed raiding party and the Fulani captured the stronghold almost without opposition. Thus was Lawal able to fulfil the promise he made when he marched out of Yola that he would not return from his war-camp until Bagale had been stormed. To quote from a Fulani chronicler:

> Lamido Lauwal had reigned for three years when he decided to make war on Bagale. He collected his forces, and went and encamped round the foot of the hill. He said, 'Listen, my people, to what I say. I am Lauwal, Death or Glory!' He remained two years, and the women-folk kept on sending out dried meat from the town. For this reason they gave his camp the name *Takkande*. Every morning they would go out to fight until the sun had passed its zenith at the time of afternoon prayer, then they would return to the camp for the night. They beat the drums at the crack of dawn; the foot-soldiers took up their shields and weapons; the horsemen put on their chain armour and coats of mail, their girdles and their helmets, they slung their swords round their shoulders, took their spears in their hands, and went out to fight.

It was at this time that the village of Girei was founded, after the Bata menace had been scotched.

[1] So say the Fulani chroniclers. However, modern Yola Fulani lay the blame on Arnado, Bagale's wife; we are grateful to Adamawa N.A. for this amendment.

Lawal died in 1872, at the age of seventy-five. Barth described him thus:

The governor was very simply dressed and had nothing remarkable in his appearance, while his face, which was half-covered by a somewhat dirty shawl, had an indifferent expression.

Today in Yola, Lawal is often regarded as the *beau idéal* of the Fulani administrator: warrior, scholar, and religious ascetic. He enforced a strict censorship of moral conduct and even of dress, for makers and wearers of short garments were severely punished, and whistling, guitar-playing, and smoking or snuff-taking were absolutely forbidden. He founded many schools with the help of Adama Gana (held by many to have been a fellow-student and friend of Adama and known as Modibbo Adama the lesser; but claimed by others to have been Adama Aganna, chief of Bundang, whom Lawal had captured), who is buried in his house near the present Yola town rest-house.

The succession was claimed by two of Modibbo Adama's sons, Sanda and Hamidu, each of whom sent a deputation to Sokoto; the Sultan decided in favour of Hamidu, but as he died before the emissaries returned to Yola, Sanda Umaru obtained the Sultan's commission.

Fulani chroniclers have recorded the dispute:

Mallam Hamidu said that he did not agree—he should be Lamido himself. But the chiefs objected, for Modibbo Adama had already enumerated his sons who should rule after him as follows: 'La-U-Zu,' that is to day La: Lauwal, U: Umaru, Zu: Zubairu. The fact that Modibbo had enumerated his sons in this manner was the reason that the chiefs refused to give the Emirate to Mallam Hamidu. But in spite of this Mallam Hamidu would not consent, till he had written a letter and sent it to the Sultan, stating the reasons why he should get the Emirate rather than Sanda. He said he surpassed Sanda in valour and in learning, and, moreover, he was before him in seeing the light of day. Then the Sultan sent a letter to the chief men of Yola telling them to appoint Mallam Hamidu, for all his reasons were strong ones. And the chiefs sent back a reply to the Sultan and told him what Modibbo had said before he died. But after they had sent back the answer to Sokoto, Malam Hamidu collected the people of Vere, and came and encamped in a circle right round Yola, saying he would seize the power by force. Then finding it could not be done, he turned round and went back to Nyibango. In less than a week after his return he died. Thus the Emirate was assured to Sanda.[1]

The new Emir was weak, and the provincial governors were quick to take advantage. Buba Jirum, who had succeeded Jidda at Rei, demanded the return of the territory of which his father had been deprived by Adama as a punishment for rebellion, and the case was referred to Sokoto. The Sultan ordered the disputed lands to be restored on payment of 1,000 slaves each to himself and to the Emir and of 100 to the Yerima, or heir-apparent, of Yola. The dispute was settled on these terms, and the fact that all three payments were promptly made suggests that Rei's claim to independence had never been substantiated. Ngaundere and Banyo remained in revolt throughout Sanda's reign, while in the north Buba Ciuto, whom Lawal had exiled from Madagali, defied the Emir until his defeat and capture in the Gulak campaign.

Sanda died in 1890. Indolent by nature, preferring ease and the delights of his harem to the active affairs of state—from which he at one time tried to abdicate in favour of his son Iya (later the 6th Lamido)—his reign was unfortunate for Adamawa. It was while Sanda was ruling at Yola that the Royal Niger Company first appeared on the scene.

A Fulani manuscript relates:

> When Sanda was dying, he commanded all his slaves to come and encircle his house after his death and tell the people to bury him there and not take him anywhere else. So the slaves encircled his house, and when he was dead they said he was to be buried there, and even started to dig his grave. Then one came and filled it in, saying: 'Cease this folly of yours; take him up and carry him to the tomb of his father, so that he too may receive his father's blessing.' Then they took him up and carried him to Modibbo's house and buried him there.[2]

Zubeiru became the 4th Lamido. He was a man of very different character. He at once set about reforming abuses which had flourished in his brother's reign. A strict moral and social code was enforced; former sumptuary laws were repealed; professional dancers were banished; and corruption amongst the officers of state was severely punished. These measures naturally excited much hostility among his subordinates, who are said to have made several attempts to poison the Emir.

[1] East, op. cit., p. 85.
[2] East, op. cit., p. 91.

Having set his capital in order, Zubeiru next turned his attention to the provinces. Of his zest for campaigning, a Fulani relates:

> Lauwal Zubeiru was a very keen crusader and was always making preparations with a view to war. On account of his love of crusading men used to cry out against him, 'Alas! Month after month the people have been in a state of war. When are they going to stop?' Whenever they came back from an expedition, and before the people had dispersed, he had a proclamation made that they were to get ready and make every effort, for he was not sitting down.

But his military skill was offset by his impetuosity which on many occasions brought him near to disaster. His first campaign, against the Fali, was successful. His second, against the Mundang pagans, was less so, for in the course of the fighting he lost his son Sa'adu who was captured and tortured to death.

One of the most serious rebellions that Zubeiru had to face was that of Hayatu, an exiled scion of the royal house of Sokoto. He settled in Yola for some years. During his stay he is said to have bought only bridles in exchange for everything he possessed—for such was his ruling passion; even Lamido Sanda's farewell present he sold for more bridles. Hayatu left Yola to settle at Marua, where Sali was the chief. There he built up a large following, founded the town of Balda, and began to attack Marua. Sanda had been too weak to intervene, but now Zubeiru led an army against him and the two forces met near Marua. It is said that two days before the battle a leader carrying the local title of Sarkin Katsina, who was senior captain of the Hausa troops from Yola, made the last of many appeals to Zubeiru to avoid this conflict, for he deemed it shameful and irreligious that a son of Modibbo Adama should join battle with so near a kinsman of the Sultan. Zubeiru refused, whereupon Sarkin Katsina withdrew and, assembling the other Hausa commanders, made public intercession that he might not himself be permitted to see the day of such internecine strife. His prayer was granted; that same night he fell sick and died next day on the eve of the engagement. The battle was counted the most disastrous since the beginning of the jihad. Hayatu's army totally defeated that of Zubeiru, which had to retire in disorder; but meanwhile the Fulani of Marua had fallen on Hayatu's camp and destroyed it, carrying off women, slaves, and beasts of burden. Deprived of transport and supplies, Hayatu was unable to follow up his victory, and retreated northwards. Fulani chroniclers hold that neither party gained any advantage, Zubeiru's losses in the field—including his brother Aliyu and much of the flower of Yola's youth—and in prestige being offset by the destruction of Hayatu's camp and by his retreat. Hayatu was later killed when fighting Rabeh near Dikwa.

It was of Zubeiru that one of the Royal Niger Company's agents wrote in his diary:

> He was not only mallam by name but a highly educated scholar of the Mohammedan school. . . . He was continually at war with the surrounding pagan tribes and, while sometimes successful when he caught a number of slaves who mostly went as tribute to Sokoto, frequently he came off second best. . . . During the whole of this period I can say that one man saved the situation time and again: that was the Emir's Majindadi, Arkal. He nursed the Emir and acted the go-between for years until he was killed by pagans on one of the Emir's mad raids. The Emir, with all his faults, was a real ruler, but I think during the last years of his career he was more or less mad. I was told that overstudy during his youth had affected him before he became Emir.

Zubeiru was a man of great bravery, personal strength, and energy, gifted with much astuteness and a sense of almost harsh discipline, and at times a fanatical Muslim. He would, it is said, enslave dark men, angrily denying that they could be Fulani; his reign was marked by many slave-raids, at Dakka, Mubi, Uba, Hildi, Marua, Ga'anda, Demsa, and the greatest of all, Gulak; and it was Yola's intolerance and hatred towards the infidel Europeans that brought about his eventual overthrow. He executed as an example one of his own nephews who had indulged in robbery on the Yola-Banyo road, and he caused to be amputated in Yola market-place the foot of a grandson of Modibbo Adama for a similar offence. It was to this constant severity that his critics ascribed the several calamities of his reign, such as the great cattle sickness of 1891, the locust plague, the menace of Rabeh, and the invasion of the British. Mizon was told that Zubeiru had a chronic illness and that once a fortnight he used to spend a whole day shut up alone. Local belief was that he suffered from fits[1]—one is reminded of Macdonald's comment that fits of temper seem to be hereditary in some Yola families—which the Fulani considered a sign of possession by the devil. It is even told that the Sultan of Sokoto had been so displeased by the accession of the epileptic

[1] Though this is the report of all visitors to Yola at that time, it is today denied by Yola historians.

Zubeiru that he had sent, for his coronation, a black gown and turban instead of the white ones traditional for a royal investiture.

On the capture of Yola in September 1901, Zubeiru and most of his courtiers fled and headed for Gurin. After a fugitive life for a year, during which he harassed both the British and German administration, Zubeiru and the faithful Lamdo Marua determined to make a final stand. The battle that followed at Marua is renowned in the annals of Fulani history. Four hundred and twenty-four of his picked corps of *Sikirri*, 'those vowed to die', made an heroic stand round the green flag and were shot down to a man by machine-gun fire. Zubeiru was rushed from the field by his immediate attendants and took refuge in the Mandara hills, still accompanied by Lamdo Marua. He was killed in early 1903, reputedly by the Lala pagans. There are, however, still Fulani in Yola who are convinced that the decapitated body belonged to Bakari, Zubeiru's close friend, and that Zubeiru himself was mysteriously lifted to the skies in a thick protective mist sent by the guarding hand of Allah.

After the defeat and flight of Zubeiru, the succession passed to Bobbo Ahmadu. Soured by the loss of territory and prestige consequent upon the 1907 International Boundary Convention, he became intractable and in 1909 was deposed for misrule and exiled to Lokoja, but on account of his old age he was allowed to return to Yola, where he died in 1916. He was succeeded by Iya, who was so weak and extravagant that he abdicated in 1910 in favour of his cousin Abba.

By now the Administration had so far extended its control over the remote tribes of Yola Province that it was possible for the Lamido to tour among them. Various devices for better government had been tried, just as the original Fulani administration had taken different forms in different areas. In 1909 the province was reorganized in five Divisions, designed to suit supervisory touring rather than with regard to political or tribal boundaries—the fifth Division, for instance, contained the heterogeneous population of four districts of Adamawa Emirate and five independent pagan tribes. This unnatural arrangement soon ended, and in 1912 all the pagan tribes within the borders of the emirate were placed in charge of *kalifaen*, or Fulani guardians, who were supposed to act through tribal authorities. This system, too, proved a failure and was abandoned in 1913.

Abba's able handling of Yola's frontier affairs during the difficult Cameroons campaign of 1914–16, when a German patrol even penetrated into Yola town and shot up the hospital, earned him a reward. He was succeeded in 1924 by Muhammadu Bello, better known to the Yola Fulani as Maigari.

On Maigari's death in 1928, a great-grandson of Modibbo Adama, Muhammadu Mustafa, became the 9th Lamido at the youthful age of 28. His reign and generous character are still recalled. During his reign his capital of Yola was amalgamated with the cosmopolitan waterside settlement of Jimeta under the direct administration of the Galadima.[1] The Chamba districts became a subordinate federation, and in 1937 the people of Koma paid their tax, at 1*s.* 3*d.* per adult male, in full for the first time.

Ahmadu, who succeeded as Lamido in 1946, started off well and the following account of a visit to Yola by the United Nations illustrates his early charm:

> The colourful receptions which the Lamido gave in honour of the Mission will always remain outstanding in the memory of the members of the visiting Mission. . . . Riding on colourfully-adorned horses, surrounded by some twenty or thirty footmen carrying ceremonial weapons or playing drums, flutes and horns, the chiefs, one after another, would extend their greetings by first raising their right fists, then dismounting from their horses, and finally kneeling in front of the Lamido. . . . Every chief was a knight in shining armour, every woman an adornment with her colourful attire, and every child a gala participant in the whole joyous affair. Over that tumultuous parade presided the Lamido, a tall, young and handsome man, whose white robes added to his impressive dignity as he watched his people and received their homage with imperturbable eyes. His princely bearing was matched by his perfect courtesy. His eminent position did not detract from his kindness to his guests.[2]

In 1951 Ahmadu accompanied the Emir of Gombe on a six weeks' tour of Europe, during which he visited Oxford, Ascot, and Paris. But the glory of his 1949 performance had begun to tarnish; all that glisters is not necessarily gold, and those in closer and more constant touch with the Emirate administration than an ephemeral mission were disturbed by the evident backsliding. Measures taken in 1952 to try to improve Ahmadu's administra-

[1] The story of the vicissitudes of Adamawa's capital is given in detail in Kirk-Greene, op. cit., Appendix A.

[2] *Report of the United Nations Visiting Mission to the Cameroons*, 1949.

tion and his personal conduct, by placing him under the surveillance of the traditional Council of Selectors, were unsuccessful. Official reports speak of his character as inflexible to change; his inability to work with his councillors; of his failure to regain the confidence of responsible people in the Emirate. Matters came to a head in June 1953, with a rowdy, organized demonstration against the Council. Ahmadu abdicated. Aliyu Mustafa was recognized as the 11th Lamido of Adamawa.

Continuing the process of broadening the N.A. Council, which in 1952 had welcomed its first representatives from outside Yola and had included three non-Fulani members in the persons of the traditional chiefs of Kilba, Yungur and Sugu, the Lamido increased the non-Fulani membership to a third of the Council. This was followed up by the appointment of Santuraki, Til Kilba, as a portfolio holder and the promotion of the first two non-Fulani as heads of N.A. departments. In 1956 the council was again reorganized so that it now consisted of three traditional members each from Fulani and non-Fulani title-holders, six elected and two nominated members.

The Waziri, Alhaji Muhammadu, retired in 1957, after forty-four years service to the N.A., thirty-five of them in the office of Waziri. The ex-Lamido Ahmadu, who had been living in exile in Biu, was nominated as a candidate for one of the southern Adamawa constituencies at the 1959 national election, but nothing came of it.

No mention of Adamawa emirate history would be complete without reference to the Northern Cameroons. Under the League of Nations mandate of 1922, certain areas of the former German Kamerun, such as the Madagali, Micika, Mubi, Maiha, Belel, Sorau, etc., districts, were administered as an integral part of the main Yola Province, and a separate Cameroons Division was created. In 1923, however, it was decided no longer to exclude the mandated territory from the jurisdiction of the Lamido. After the inception of the Trusteeship Council in 1947, the would-be separate identity of these districts was brought into emphasis by periodic visits from the United Nations. With the approach of Nigeria's independence, it was agreed in the United Nations to hold a plebiscite in the Northern Cameroons. This was held in November 1959 when the electorate were asked to say whether the Northern Cameroons should be part of the Northern Region of Nigeria or whether the future of the Northern Cameroons should be decided at a later date. Out of the eighty-seven per cent who voted, sixty-two per cent preferred the second alternative, the figure for Adamawa emirate being sixty-nine per cent. This result was largely a verdict on local issues coupled with a natural tendency to procrastination. Reforms in local government were swiftly effected by the dazed Adamawa N.A. When the final plebiscite was held early in 1961 to answer the question whether the area preferred to join an independent Nigeria or an independent Cameroun Republic, the majority voted for reunion with their kith and kin in Nigeria. But Nigeria's gain was Adamawa's loss, for a condition of voting in Nigeria's favour had been the promise of a separate administration. Sardauna Province was formed from all the previous Trust Territory. The ancient kingdom of Fombina was drastically cut down and murmured echoes of a previous Lamido's broken heart were heard: 'They have left me merely the latrines of my kingdom . . . they have left us the head but they have cut off the body.'

THE EMIRS (LAMIDOS) OF ADAMAWA

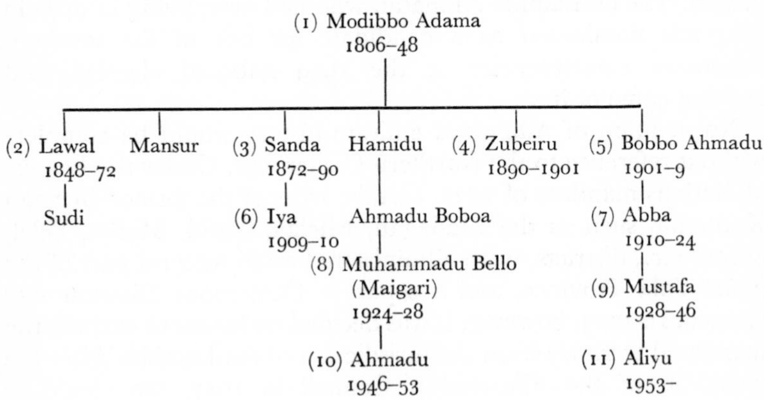

XXXI. MURI

THE first aggressive contact of the Fulani with the pagan tribes of Muri occurred at the end of the eighteenth century, when Buba Yero of Gombe, anticipating the declaration of the jihad by Usman dan Fodio, conquered the tribes of the Gongola valley. He ravaged Yungur, Song, and Holma, and defeated the Fali pagans at Bulmi. Here he received orders from the Sultan of Sokoto, who, incensed at his general's precipitate campaign, commanded him to return at once to Gombe; and it was on his way back that he marched through the country of the Wurkum.

Buba Yero's younger brother,[1] Hamman Ruwa, remained behind on the western edge of the Wurkum territory, and when the jihad was declared in 1804 he waged war in this area as a general in the army of his brother who had been appointed Emir of Gombe. By 1817 Hamman Ruwa had overrun the greater part of the present emirate of Muri, except Wase and Bakundi, and was appointed governor of his conquests. For many years he followed his elder brother and went in his train to do homage at Sokoto.

In 1833 Buba Yero, who was then about seventy, was anxious to secure the succession of his son Kwairanga to the Gombe throne. Fearing that the people would choose Hamman Ruwa, the natural heir, he summoned him and his eldest son, Bose, to a conference at Gombe. As soon as they arrived he had them executed on the pretext that they were scheming for the secession of Muri from Gombe. The people of Muri thereupon appealed to the Sultan for their independence, and he gave the deputation a flag to take to Hamman, the eldest surviving son of Hamman Ruwa. Finding popular opinion against him, Hamman retired in favour of his brother Ibrahim.

Little is recorded of Ibrahim's reign. About 1836 he became insane for a brief period, during which Hamman acted as regent. In 1848 he was finally deposed in favour of Hamman.

Hamman's reign was troubled by internal dissensions. Shortly

[1] This relationship is now questioned in Gombe.

after his election he had to deal with trouble between his son Burba and his nephew Hamadu, the son of the murdered Bose and founder of Gassol town on the banks of the River Taraba. Burba, who had settled near Wurio, accused Hamadu of misappropriating tribute in transit from Donga and Wukari to his father at Muri. The Emir, fearing open warfare, placed the two leaders under arrest in the capital and put garrisons at Wurio and Sandirde under trusted slaves to prevent an outbreak of trouble. He also put his sister Maryamu, nicknamed Gogojam, at Sandirde which he had recently founded, and ordered that all tributes from Donga and Wukari should be directed to her. The nickname, Gogojam, and the name of the new town, Sandirde, are Fulani words meaning 'peaceful aunt' and 'arbitration'. Hamadu begged for his release and permission, which was granted, to return to Gassol where his slaves and properties were.[1]

Hamadu escaped and returned to Gassol. Two years later the Emir, during a visit to Sandirde, was attacked and wounded by Hamadu and his followers while riding on the Taraba sands. Burba, who was in the Emir's retinue, asked to be allowed to exact vengeance, but the Emir refused and returned meekly to Muri. Hamadu immediately captured Sandirde, and Burba left his father in dudgeon and re-established himself near Wurio. This weakness over Gassol brought the Emir into disrepute with the Muri Fulani, who accused him of insanity and degeneracy, and of caring only for the pleasures of female company. He was deposed in 1861 and died at Mayo Ranewa.

It was during the first year of Hamman's reign that his slave Kuso attacked and overcame the Jibu stronghold at the junction of the Donga with the Benue. The Jibu fled south to the Wurbo country, where they founded the town of Beli, on the Taraba. About the same time two other slaves, Bula and Aliyu, founded settlements at Ibi and Bantaji, which were thus added to the emirate; Ibi, dating from 1855, became an advanced post for the *bayin Fulani* or Muri slave bands.

Baikie, who visited Muri during Hamman's reign, has left the following description:

Hammaruwa is a powerful Pulo province, tributary to the Sultan at Sokoto, and considered but little inferior to Adamawa. It comprises a

[1] We thank Muri N.A. for this new piece of information.

considerable extent of country, on both sides of the river, extending from Kororofa and Bautshi or Baushi to Adamawa. Prior to its occupation by the Fulatas, this country was occupied by various independent races, the Muri being on the north, and several races speaking dialects of Djuku on the south. Different tribes still remain in a state of semi-independence on the confines of Adamawa, and to the eastward along the river, they are all heathens, and are considered very barbarous. Several countries pay annual tribute to Hammaruwa, among which are Wukari, as having been conquered by the brother or uncle of the present Sultan, and Zhibu, as a Pulo dependency. The tribute consists chiefly of slaves, and the amount varies according to the success met with in their annual predatory excursions. In what they look on as a productive year, Wukari sends from thirty-five to forty slaves, carried off mostly from the Mitshis, or from the barbarous natives living beyond Kororofa.

Muri he describes as a large town, measuring two miles by one and a quarter, but carrying a population of only 8,000.

After the deposition of Hamman in 1861, the people chose his rival, Hamadu of Gassol, and as the representative of the Sultan of Sokoto was opportunely in Muri at the time, the appointment was ratified without delay. Hamadu lived part of the time in Muri, where his son Umaru Sanda took charge during his absence, and part of the time in Gassol, Sandirde, and Wurio, in each of which he placed a son in command. His cousin and old enemy, Burba, retired southwards and founded Bakundi. The Wurbo pagans were then living in a village built on piles in a lake close to the site of Bakundi, but when this tribe, together with the fugitive Jibu people at Beli, agreed to follow Burba, he broke up this village. It is said to have been built about 1800 to protect the Wurbo against raids from the Chamba.

On the death of Hamadu in 1869, the Sultan of Sokoto directed that Abubakar, a son of Hamman Ruwa, should be appointed Emir, but the people refused to accept him and chose the rebel Burba instead. Burba's first act was the arrest of the three eldest sons of the late Emir, who had come to Muri as claimants to the throne. They escaped and raised the standard of revolt at Gassol and Wurio. Burba himself attacked Gassol, while another force was dispatched under the Kaigama to subdue Wurio. Both enterprises were successful at the time, but four years later Gassol again revolted and before Burba could organize a punitive expedition he became insane and was deposed. He later recovered his sanity and returned to his old home at Bakundi, where he remained as an independent ruler, paying tribute direct to Sokoto, till his death in 1892.

Burba was succeeded by Abubakar, the original nominee of Sokoto. He died within seven months of his appointment and was succeeded by his son, Muhammadu Nya, in 1874.

Muhammadu Nya, an able and energetic Emir, first established friendly relations with Burba at Bakundi; both parties agreed to live in amity and to combine, if necessary, against the house of Hamadu. Thus secure against Gassol, the Emir set about extending his dominions. He undertook no less than four campaigns against the Tiv, penetrating as far as Katsina Ala, which he sacked and burned. He found himself unable to hold his Tiv conquests and withdrew his garrisons.

The next campaign was against the Jukun stronghold of Kona.[1] The original Jukun settlement of Kuro, some five miles north of modern Kona, had been sacked by Hamman Ruwa, and when smallpox followed on this catastrophe the Jukun left and built Kona under their chief Aganwa. They paid tribute to Muri in the shape of slaves, food, and labour. During Nya's reign the Jukun slaves managed to escape. They assembled at Sonko, a town about sixteen miles south of Jalingo, today in ruins. Nya collected his army, crossed the Benue, and camped at Hosere Bolere, to the south-west of what is now Jalingo. Meanwhile Aganwa gathered a force of Bacama and Mumuye pagans and placed this reinforced Kona contingent under a Demsa Bacama named Panabuguri. This general, before setting out for the attack on Sonko, swore a vinic oath that he would bring in the Emir of Muri dead or alive.

The pagan force fell on the Fulani camp, but much of their ferocious energy was dissipated in shooting at each other from the opposite directions of attack, so that the Muri troops were able to escape with only a few casualties. The Emir rallied his men and cornered the jubilant pagans in a marsh, where many were slain, among them Panabuguri. A younger brother of Aganwa, named Dau, declared that he would seize the Emir dead or alive and thereby prove the superiority of a Jukun over a Bachama oath. He charged the Emir's party, threw two spears at Nya, but missed him. The Emir, on learning that this was the brother of the Kona

[1] This is the Hausa name, from *kona*, to burn.

chief, drew his sword, cut his steed's tethering rope, set his horse at Dau, drove him back into the bog, and dispatched him with a spear.

This war with the Kona pagans continued for the next four years, until Aganwa sent his messenger, Fokuru, to the Sultan of Sokoto with a promise to follow the Emir of Muri and to pay an annual tribute of 100 slaves. In 1892 Aganwa's successor, Yinu, led another uprising, which the Emir put down with the assistance of the adventurer Mizon,[1] breaking the town with the French cannon. It was Mizon who, defying the authority of the Royal Niger Company, took his ships up the Benue as far as Yola with the aim of securing Adamawa, Bornu and Baghirmi for France. He succeeded in establishing a proper protectorate of Muri in 1892, but was then firmly escorted out of the Company's territories.[2] From this war-camp at Jalingo the Emir later undertook a number of raids against the Mumuye plains settlements, but he made little impression on their hill villages.

Of Jalingo—the name derives from the Fulani word *jala*, meaning 'to conquer'—at this time one of the Niger company's agents wrote:

> The camp itself is a settlement of, I should think, 1,000 people, built in a circle with four gates at the N.S.E.W. aspects respectively. A high mud wall surrounds the whole place with loopholes for guns about every two feet. . . . Contrary to the usual custom, the houses are not packed together, each house having a small farm attached, this being in the event of a siege.

On the death of Muhammadu Nya in 1897, his son Hassan returned to Jalingo from Mutum Biu, where he had settled in 1895 after his defeat at Yola Mbodewa when Nya had sought to make him Yerima of Gassol. Though his father had supplied him with rifles and about fifty cartridges, the Gassol army had waited till all the cartridges had been exuberantly fired off and then they advanced on the town and forced Hassan back to Mutum Biu. It is said that his younger brother, Muhammadu (Hamman) Mafindi, had refused to be nominated, probably because of his

[1] I am grateful to Julius Aje, a student of mine and later D.O. Muri Division, for this interesting note on Mizon: 'The elders here often refer to Mizon as Aguda. They have no explanation for this. I am apt to think that it is a nickname originating from the South, as I know it to be common in Lagos and the West. For instance, the Roman Catholic Church there is often referred to as the Aguda Church. Is this perhaps a Portuguese term for European?'—A.K-G.

[2] See Kirk-Greene, *Adamawa Past and Present*, pp. 37–39.

exiguous following. However, emboldened by a delay in the Sultan's recognition of his brother, Muhammadu Mafindi joined forces with Abubakar of Wurio in an attempt to seize the power and divide the kingdom. The Emir scattered their armies at Wuzu, the port of Muri. Hassan died at Jalingo in 1903, shortly before the High Commissioner approved his deposition for slave dealing.

After his defeat at Wuzu in 1897, Muhammadu Mafindi took refuge with Abubakar in Wurio until 1899, when the Royal Niger Company put him to flight after a company of troops entered Wurio in order to arrest the two leaders, who were suspected of aggravating the tension between the Emir and the Taraba chiefs. Travelling through Bakundi and the Dakka country, Muhammadu Mafindi arrived at Zubeiru's court at Yola and offered his services. He was given Mayo Belwa as his residence, to control the Mumuye with whom he had considerable influence. It may be added here, in parenthesis, that when Muhammadu Mafindi died in 1953, the Mumuye spoke of the passing of their *babban dodo.*[1] After the fall of Zubeiru in 1901, Muhammadu Mafindi was the first to tender his submission and, continuing to play his cards well, he later escorted Dr Cargill and Captain Ruxton through the Mumuye country to Jalingo, where a truce was patched up between him and his brother the Emir. It was agreed that Muhammadu Mafindi should henceforth live at Bamga, in Yola Province.

Immediately on hearing of his brother's death, Muhammadu Mafindi hurried to Jalingo. Tradition has it that for three days he sat in silent prayer in the middle of the mosque, conspicuous to all but conversing with none, until the council of selectors became so anxious about the meaning of this unusual behaviour that they elected him Emir. Muhammadu Mafindi informed the Resident that he had become the chief, and a fortnight later he was installed at Lau.

At first Muri was a Province in its own right, including many of the riverain areas on both banks of the Benue that later became part of the Province of the name. Under the great 1926 administrative reorganization, however, Muri lost its provincial status: the Ibi and Tiv units were transferred to the new Benue Province, Shendam became part of Plateau Province, and Muri emirate joined Yola Province, now renamed Adamawa. From

[1] 'Great god'.

1910 to 1917 the Emir had his headquarters at Lau instead of Mutum Biu, his predecessor having given up the old capital of Muri town for the war-camp of Jalingo.

In 1930, thanks to the high standing of the Emir among the Mumuye, their traditional rain-maker was persuaded to accept a district headship. This apparent advance was halted two years later by the assassination of the Mumuye leader Zamvoro, the District Head of Zinna. Muhammadu Mafindi made the pilgrimage to Mecca across the desert by car in 1934.[1] His personality dominated this semi-backwater, for he was a remarkable man, and it was with widespread rejoicing that in October 1952 the Emir, at the age of 84, celebrated his golden jubilee on the throne. He died a few months later, the last of the emirs to have been installed by Lugard.

Muhammadu Mafindi was succeeded by his seventy-year-old younger brother Muhammadu Tukur. Unhappily his accession was quickly followed by an ugly riot in Wurkum, his former district. Later the Emir was able to set about reorganizing the N.A. Council and enlarging its basis. Under his sage guidance Muri has now emerged into the modern world after half a century of Muhammadu Mafindi's benevolent but inevitably conservative personal rule.

THE EMIRS OF MURI

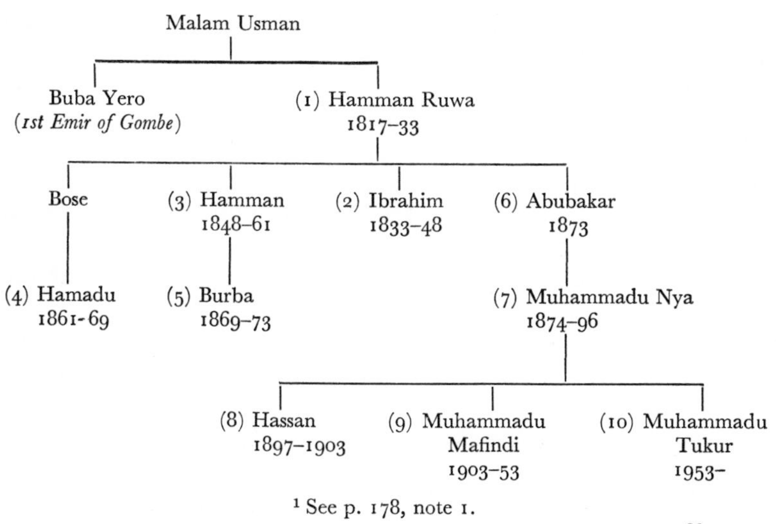

[1] See p. 178, note 1.

XXXII. BAUCHI

UNLIKE the Hausa Bakwai, Bauchi has no history of successive Habe kings. There is one tradition that one of the kings of Kano, Alwali (1781–1805), fought a battle with the Jarawa at Gwangsam, south of Bauchi, which he renamed Bununu (Dass) because of the great multitude of its inhabitants (*bunu:* grass), and another one that Lari was first settled by a Zaria migration. Instead, along with many other emirates in the eastern half of the north, Bauchi history takes as its focal point the advent of Usman dan Fodio's emissaries, the *masu-tuta* or flag-bearers. Among these, it was the destiny of Yakubu to found the Fulani emirate of Bauchi.[1]

Exceptionally, Yakubu was not a Fulani himself, and was thus the only non-Fulani to whom Dan Fodio gave a flag. Nevertheless, he came of Muslim cattle-rearing stock and was 'of pale complexion'. His great-great-grandfather was a local man, born at Gilliri, the main town of the Gerawa. Some sources maintain that this stock was originally from Mandara. His grandfather, Abdullahi, son of Yangiri, was a respected *malam* there. His father was Dadi. It is said that when Dadi moved from Gilliri to Yuli to pasture his cattle, the chief of Yuli refused him permission to settle there. When he was asked why by the chief of Miri, he replied: 'That man has something inside which, if it should ever escape, will bring this whole country under his rule.' The chief of Miri scoffed at this story and approved Dadi's request to move to Tirwun. 'As you wish, then,' replied the chief of Yuli. 'Yet know that my prophecy concerning Dadi will be fulfilled after my death and that you will be the first to fall beneath it. . . . It is known in Tirwun that some day a great man will appear and upset the whole world.'

Yakubu himself was born about 1753 (some authorities give 1765) at Tirwun, near the present town of Bauchi. At the age of

[1] We wish to acknowledge the contribution made to the chapters on Bauchi and Gombe by Victor Low and Salihu Bajoga of Bauchi Provincial Secondary School, who generously allowed us access to their collection of material on local traditions in the Province's history assembled by the school's Historical Society. Mr Low is now undertaking field work for a doctoral study on Bauchi history.

eighteen he was sent to Gobir where he studied under Usman dan Fodio until 1792. Usman dan Fodio is said to have married Yakubu as a reward for his diligence to Yaya, the daughter of a friend of his named Bazam Pare. This girl was a sister to Ahmadu, father of Gorkwa of Bauchi. The story of how Yakubu came to be sent to Gobir has been handed down in Bauchi from Malam Mustafa, later the tutor to Yakubu's sons:

> A great and wise man, Malam Ishiyaku, came from Bornu to reside at Jetar, close to our town of Tiruwin, where a certain man called Dadi was his friend and well-beloved. One day Dadi said to his friend Malam Ishiyaku:—
>
> 'This my son is the coolness of my eyelids, my love for him is fixed in the circle of my heart, I have many children besides him. I desire that Allah may bless him, wheresoever he may be. I give him to thee, thou shalt be his father and *malam*, he will be to thee both son and pupil, and he shall render to thee such service as he has been accustomed to give his father. Guard thou him as a father is a protection to his son, so that he may obtain a blessing from thee. Whatsoever work that thou desirest to be done thee, appoint him the task.'
>
> On whatever journey Malam Ishiyaku went, Yakubu was with him and carried the Malam's book. They heard of Othman dan Fodio and Ishiyaku went to him at Degel where for seven years he remained as his pupil. After this time Ishiyaku returned to his home but left Yakubu to the great Malam.

Other sources say that Ishiyaku was the younger brother of Adama, who had married the sister of Dadi, and that it was Adama rather than Ishiyaku who was Dadi's great friend. Ishiyaku died on the way back, at Yakwante Zayal, near Kano.

The chief imam of Bauchi, Alhaji Mahmud, used to relate the Bauchi tradition how Yakubu was wont to say that Usman dan Fodio prayed to Allah for four things for Yakubu's new kingdom:

(i) To bless its people with sufficient wealth with which to keep them from evil and false pride;
(ii) To bless its people with continued faith in Islam;
(iii) To avert misfortune;
(iv) To have a dwelling-place ever prepared for any stranger that might appear.

There is another story current in Bauchi about Yakubu. Yakubu was the youngest and smallest of the pupils who gathered to learn at the feet of Usman dan Fodio. One day the Shehu rode out with his boys to take the air. As they passed a huge stone, Usman dan Fodio remarked how nice it would be to have such a stone in his compound to sit on. The pupils thought he was joking; all but Yakubu. When they had returned home and he had stabled the Shehu's mare, Yakubu hurried to where the stone was lying. He managed to struggle back with it to the Shehu's compound. The next morning Usman dan Fodio asked in surprise: 'Who brought this heavy stone?' 'I did,' said Yakubu. The Shehu blessed him and thanked him for his thoughtfulness. Again, one day when lessons were over, Usman dan Fodio told his pupils that he wished them to go the next morning and collect some corn from a village six miles away. After every one had gone to bed, Yakubu walked to the village and by dawn had brought home all the corn, so that none of his fellow-pupils had to go the next day. It is also claimed in Bauchi that Usman dan Fodio once said Yakubu was like his own son, created from his own heart.

Yakubu's father, Dadi, died while he was still with Usman dan Fodio. The Shehu advised him not to claim anything from the inheritance except a single bow and seven arrows which Dadi had used for hunting. These were the famous *zagbai* and *kardangi* of Bauchi legend which, along with Yakubu's sword ring and flag, have remained among the revered insignia of each successive Emir of Bauchi. The Galadima presents the flag, the Muezzin the ring, Sarkin Yaki the knife, Baraya the sword, and Ubandoma the bow and arrows. At this time there probably existed five independent centres of authority, each having a number of peoples owing sovereignty. There were the Jerumawa at Ganjuwa, to whom the Gerawa and Denawa were subject; the Zaria settlement of Lere; the Hausa town of Mar, towards Ningi; and the chiefs of Miri and Tukunya, the latter being a Gobir settlement.

On the outbreak of the jihad Yakubu, who had lain low in Warunje for two years despite his possession of a flag, was ordered to see which peoples would follow his standard in Bauchi. A considerable following attached itself to him, though not his own people, the Gerawa. Bauchi traditions maintain that Yakubu read a message from Usman dan Fodio to the Gerawa, his own people, though none of them heeded it, enjoining Yakubu to mind seven things:

(i) Unity in all affairs;
(ii) Building the mosques;

(iii) Saying five prayers constantly in these mosques;
(iv) Learning the Holy Koran and teaching it;
(v) Seeking knowledge of Islam and spreading it;
(vi) Improving the markets and forbidding in them what is disapproved;
(vii) Waging holy wars because they are compulsory for true believers whenever they occur.

His first victories were at Kan Yallo, Miri and Gubi. The stone at Taghaul on which Yakubu sat in his battle with the pagans is still pointed out. Within a few years he had subdued the whole country within a wide radius, penetrating as far as the Rivers Benue and Gongola, the Wurkum hills, Lafia Beri-Beri, and Lere. Lere offered stubborn resistance and Yakubu, faced at Pyem by a huge host of mounted spearmen from Sura and Bokkos, decided to exercise the better part of valour and withdrew.

He made Hassan, Faruku, Muhammadu Kusu and Abdu his generals, the first three being his pupils and Abdu his slave. Hassan was given the title of Madaki and head of the Ganjua Fulani; Faruku that of Galadima and head of the Bayak Fulani; Muhammadu that of Sarkin Yaki and head of the Zaranda Fulani; and Abdu became Wambai and head of the Yuli Fulani. Hammadi, the son of Malam Adamu, was turbanned Ajiya and head of the Ganjua Fulani. Yakubu, who had repulsed Buba Yero of Gombe when he sought to extend his kingdom west of the Gongola, next assisted the Emir of Kano against Bornu. Bauchi traditions accuse the Kano army of turning tail, though Yakubu engaged the Bornu forces at Fake. Hassan, his Madaki, was killed in this battle. In Bauchi the battle is described thus:

The King of the Kanembu now got ready for war. He advanced into the Kano country and the country could scarcely supply his host with enough food. Many people were alarmed.

Shehu Osman sent to Yakubu. He said, 'Mount your horse and go and meet the Kanembu, whenever you meet them fight them'; and the Sarkin Bauchi said, 'I obey. It shall be done.' The message found him still at Dass. He summoned all his people and told them of the message that he had received. He said, 'My supreme Chief has ordered me to fight the Kanembu. . . .'

Yakubu said to his malams: 'What is your advice? Ye behold the multitude of his horses. Ye behold also the number of my horses, 2,500. What say ye?' They replied, 'The king's word is ours.'

Yakubu said, 'I know not how to defeat him, neither do I know how he may be killed, but one thing I do know. I know that he has no power to raise the dead; that he has no power, if rain be lacking, to cause it to fall; that he has no power, if the grass does not spring up, to cause it to do so.' The followers of Yakubu said, 'As for these things, Allah alone is able to do them.' Yakubu replied, 'Since ye know this, that no one is able to do anything save Allah, let us take courage and fight with him, for we shall defeat him and kill him, because no one is powerful save Allah. . . .'

He went and he fought and all the Kanembu were afraid of him, and smote them by the power of Allah, in Kano country. Then, without resting, and with all his people, he followed them to Ganzul and they came close to one another.

Hassan led the Bauchi troops. The battle continued four days, and on the fifth Hassan called in Hammadi and sent him to Yakubu to say the Emir should move closer to the fighting, as it was growing fierce. Yakubu replied that if he, the commander, was afraid, he might come himself and jump into the Emir's pocket. When Hassan heard this, he told Hammadi, 'Go and ask Emir Yakubu if his pocket is better than paradise. Tell him that if I am killed, and he finds my face turned in his direction, not to pray for me. Also inform him that I hope we shall meet in heaven.'

Hammadi carried this message to Yakubu, who said, 'Thank you for bringing this reply. I shall give you a kola nut in gratitude when I get home, if Allah so decides.' He then prepared for action, but another messenger arrived first with news that Hassan was dead. Immediately the Emir and his men pushed forward. As they were approaching the enemy camp, the Bornuese were disputing whether it was Yakubu they had killed or a servant of his. The severed head was brought to El Kanemi, who gathered his men together and said, 'Here is the head of Yakubu, Emir of Bauchi.' The majority agreed, but one stranger, said to have been an Arab, examined the head and told everyone it was not the Emir's. This man, who served in the Bornu army, explained that he had lived at Bauchi a long time, and knew that Yakubu was pale in complexion, with a large head and a few tribal marks on his face, and had a short grey beard. El Kanemi listened carefully, and, seeing that the head lacked these features, decided it must be that of a Fulani. The Arab then said it was from Madaki Hassan's body. 'Since Hassan is now dead,' he announced, 'you will soon meet Yakubu.'

A moment after he spoke, the Bornuese heard the beating of drums and other signs of a new struggle approaching. The Arab departed with his camel, leaving El Kanemi and the rest wondering at the fact that they had been fighting only Yakubu's Madaki. Soon the Sheikh learned that Yakubu was near Kwaikwai, their encampment. It was the Emir who ordered the drums beaten. He had collected some archers, and rode out himself. A poet wrote, 'With them was a gathering like a hedgehog's back. It was a group of bows mingled with arrows. . . .'

They beat their drums; when Yakubu's army and the Kanembu met, no man could be seen, so thick was the dust and the smoke. They fought, and day became night; no one spoke, only their form spoke, it spoke as it met iron and as it cut flesh. The bows spoke and the arrows spoke, all the place was dark, and the man by your side was invisible. Yakubu alone could be heard, and he said, 'Shoot whether you see them or not.' They shot; even Yakubu shot. Then the darkness lifted, all the dust lay down, and the Kanembu ran so fast that Yakubu could not catch them.

When Yakubu entered the Sheikh's encampment, El Kanemi escaped out the back way, leaving behind his bed, silver gourd (*sintali*), carpets and drums. Some of the Emir's men urged that El Kanemi be pursued and taken prisoner, but others disagreed. Yakubu ordered his servant, Maigonso, to beat the royal Bornuese drum which he found there. When the enemy heard it, he said, they would turn round. This was done, and they began pouring back towards the camp in great numbers, saying to each other, 'It must be the Sheikh.' The Bauchi soldiers killed them from evening until the next day. Yakubu did not wish to have any Bornuese slaves.[1]

Later Yakubu besieged Misau, which he starved out and then handed over to his ally Mai-Munga. Bauchi historians sing Yakubu's praise that *ya yi jihadi har arba' in da daya*, 'he undertook no less than forty-one campaigns', as *Bajimin Bauchi*, 'the bull of Bauchi'. Bauchi tradition relates how the royal Bauchi drum, acclaimed as the sweetest-toned in the whole of Hausaland, is in origin a Bornu one, left behind when the Kanuri musicians were driven out of the town at the time of the Bornu war.

For seven years Yakubu made his headquarters at Inkil. Then in 1809 he moved a little westward and laid the foundations of the town of Bauchi. He built the first wall, from Unguwar Bakaro to Jakan, near the market, to Kobi on the west side and to Unguwar Jakun on the south.

Of the founding of Bauchi it is said that Yakubu went to Sokoto to seek Usman dan Fodio's advice. The Shehu replied that it was not for him to decide, as Yakubu was the king. Yakubu then put

[1] This, and the first quotation on p. 455, are taken from a MS. history of the emirs of Bauchi belonging to M. Mustafa, tutor to the sons of Yakubu. It is quoted in A. Schultze, *Das Sultanat von Bornu*, and again in the manuscript notes on Bauchi Emirate compiled by the Hon. Oliver Howard, Resident, *c.* 1908.

forward four ideas for his capital. The first was Inkil, then his residence. The Shehu agreed that the place was healthy, yet he warned that if Yakubu were to settle there permanently even the most zealous of his Islamic followers would backslide and become dancers and singers. Yakubu then suggested Zaranda. A fine place, the Shehu agreed, where people could raise many sheep and grow rich, but they would surely forsake their God. So Yakubu proposed Wase, then better known as Gauron Dutse. Again the Shehu warned that if he settled there, the people would prosper but would lapse into unbelievers. 'What, then, of Baba,' asked Yakubu, 'the place where Malam Idrisu's grave lies?' Said the Shehu, 'If you settle there, your people will surely harvest corn in abundance, yet their religion will not last till the coming of the Mahdi!'

It is said their while Yakubu was making other suggestions, an old slave of the Shehu, Modegel, whose job was to fill water pots at the Friday mosque for the ease of worshippers in their ablutions, begged his master to make the decision for Yakubu. The Shehu then urged Yakubu to found his capital a few miles to the west of Inkil, where Islam would thrive for ever. The area might be poor and so, in order to prevent the spread of poverty, Yakubu should take special care over the distribution of amenities. Yakubu thanked the Shehu but pointed out that the hilly area west of Inkil was full of snakes. 'By God's power,' replied the Shehu, 'snakes will not harm your followers. The number may be large indeed, yet they shall be in no danger. If anyone is bitten, he shall not die unless the snake is charmed.' He then declared that if any stranger visited Yakubu's new town and stayed for but seven nights, he would remember it for a whole year after his departure. 'There is one more thing,' the Shehu went on, 'that you must know. Your people will never be rich, or never as rich as most others. But if amongst them you find some who value money overmuch, your subjects must neither spend time nor eat with them.' Finally, the Shehu appealed to Yakubu to include Warunje hill within the town walls. 'If you follow my wishes,' he concluded, 'I promise you that your capital will become celebrated everywhere, always a haven of peace and never conquered in war.'

Yakubu then went home to search for a suitable site west of Inkil. One day he met an old man returning to his home on the top of the hill called Dutsen Idi. Yakubu asked him who he was, and he answered that he was a hunter whose real name was Baushe.[1] The children of the village had altered this to Baushi, by which name he was generally known. So Yakubu promised that his new capital should be called after Baushi. This Baushi is said to have been the subsequent founder of Shendam.

Here, at Bauchi, after a memorably wise reign, Yakubu lived in comparative peace until his death in 1845. For many years afterwards the town was known as Yakoba rather than Bauchi. In Bauchi today Yakubu is remembered as one who was loved by those who surrounded him and who accepted their shortcomings graciously. He especially looked after the orphans and those unjustly treated, so much so that he is credited with having built wooden reservoirs in which *miya* or soup was prepared daily and supplied to the poor and the strangers.

Yakubu was succeeded by one of his twenty-five sons, Ibrahim, during whose reign many of the subjugated peoples, such as Ningi and Dass, revolted and re-established their independence. He partially conquered the Angas and Montol, but one Hamza from Kano stirred up a revolt among the Ningawa, whose chief he was; though he was killed, Hamza's successors at Dua, Kisalla and Ahmadu, continued to rebel against Bauchi and even killed the Dan Iya of Kano in battle. In Dr Barth's estimation, Ibrahim, who was also a man of learning who loved to invite scholars to his court, ranked high among the Emirs of the North:

> The second, as regards real power, after the Governor of Kano, is . . . Ibrahim ibn Yakubu, the Governor of Bautshi, for although he has a force of only 2,000 horse, his troop of archers, the best known in the Sudan, are numberless.

It was during Ibrahim's reign, too, that his Madaki, Abdulkadiri, was sent to build a walled town as a *zaman ribatsi*, a defence against the Ningi inroads. This is the town of Kafin Madaki, some twenty-eight miles north of Bauchi. Here the Madaki's magnificent house, named Babban Gwani after the skill of its builder, stands today as an hundred years old monument to local architectural ability. When Abdulkadiri died in 1897, he was succeeded as Madaki by his son Muhammadu Fate, who was killed in the Gworam affair of 1900.

[1] Possibly Ba-haushe, meaning a Hausa man.

The gentle Ibrahim eventually abdicated in favour of his son Usman in the year 1877. He removed his court to Rauta, where the remains of his palace can still be seen thirty-five miles north-west of Bauchi. Among his praise-titles in Bauchi is this one:

> You have tried to make yourself into a river.
> Flowing till all the land is covered
> And nobody is left in thirst.

Usman's reign opened forebodingly, for the first thing he had to do was to appeal to Misau for assistance in driving out his uncle Halilu, who also claimed the throne. Halilu had a strong following both outside and inside the city walls. It is said in Bauchi that the rival followers of the Emir and of Halilu walked about armed in the streets, and that when they met at the mosque on Fridays the whole town considered a fight to be imminent. When the Misau force arrived, a terrible battle broke out, with brother killing brother and father son. Even today the results of the desperate conflict that ensued can be seen in Bauchi town, where whole quarters were ruined and the population decimated. The pretender Halilu was captured and executed, but not long afterwards Usman was himself deposed by the Sarkin Musulmi.

Umaru, who succeeded him in 1883, had an equally disastrous reign. More of the subject peoples threw off the Bauchi yoke; from Gombe, the religious rebel Malam Jibrilla raised the standard of defiance, successfully repulsed the combined forces of Bauchi, Katagum, Misau and Hadejia at Bajoga, and laid waste the neighbouring countryside. Embittered by this series of misfortunes, Umaru resorted to a tyrannical oppression. In 1900 this culminated in a wholesale massacre in the town of Gworam, which had refused to allow slaves to be levied from the Muslim population. Umaru sent to Misau for help. The Emir of Jama'are, whose daughter was married to Lawal, the chief of Gworam, also came, ostensibly to make peace between the contending parties. On the arrival of the Misau-Jama'are forces outside Gworam, Lawal was invited to parley with his father-in-law. As he left the town to meet the Emir, the Misau cavalry rode into the town from the other side, pillaged and plundered it, and massacred its inhabitants. Lawal was murdered; duplicity and barbarism had won the day.

Before Umaru had time to try the patience of his people much further, the British forces under William Wallace reached Bauchi with a military force in February 1902. They were allowed to occupy the town without any resistance. Umaru was promptly deposed and subsequently deported to Lokoja and then Ilorin. His grave is in the market-place there. Lugard had meanwhile written to the Sultan of Sokoto about the Bauchi problem:

> I have heard that you sent a letter to the Emir of Bauchi warning him to desist from oppressing his people, but he does not obey your instructions nor listen to your words of wisdom. I have, therefore, been compelled to send my troops to compel him to act properly. I do not know whether he will oppose them and fight. If he does so, he will probably lose his place. But I do not wish to drive out the Fulani and the Mohammedans, I only wish that they shall rule wisely and with humanity. If, therefore, the Emir is driven out because he himself attacks my troops I shall endeavour to find his proper successor and shall install him as King if he is a man who will rule well.[1]

Umaru's successor Muhammadu died shortly afterwards, and Hassan succeeded him until 1907 when Yakubu II, great-grandson of the original Yakubu, acceded.

In 1911 the provincial headquarters were transferred from Bauchi to Naraguta, because of the need for close administrative supervision over the rapidly expanding tin mining industry. They returned to Bauchi in 1917, but were again moved to Jos, because of its urgent growth, in 1924, where they remained until the creation of the new Plateau Province in 1926. In that year the Jos and Pankshin Divisions were transferred out of Bauchi into this new province. Bauchi made history by opening the first teacher training centre, at Toro, for non-Muslim teachers in 1929, but thereafter it suffered hardly from the depression of the early 'thirties.[2] The hill Angas of Lere district chose this time of strain to attempt to reassert their independence but they were unsuccessful.

It was a sad blow to Bauchi emirate when Alkali Muhammadu died in 1938, a man who during his twenty-nine years of office had acquired a reputation for integrity and learning that had spread far beyond the borders of Bauchi. Even sorrier was the news of the

[1] H. F. Backwell, *The Occupation of Hausaland*, p. 13.

[2] The *Annual Report for Bauchi Province* contained a reference to the example set by the Emir and the Alkali in this crisis, when they offered to eat cassava (the emergency food crop) even though it was never part of the diet of the upper classes. However, Bauchi N.A. has asked that this quotation should not be given prominence in the text itself and we have acceded to their request.

death of the Emir in 1941, after a reign of nearly thirty-five years. He was succeeded by Yakubu III, who thirteen years later abdicated because of his age and his 'inability to adapt himself to the change from Sole Native Authority to Chief-in-Council'. He retired to Wase.

The new Emir, Adamu Jumba, had been Wakilin Gona and then Waziri, a new office created in 1952 for the senior N.A. Councillor. This post of Waziri seemed an unfortunate one in 1955, for its holder Ahmadu Jika died and so did his successor, within a matter of days. A new one, Ibrahim Jalo,[1] was appointed in 1956. The opening of the railway station in Bauchi town has been the most significant event in Bauchi's recent history, topped only by the emirate's pride in producing Nigeria's first Prime Minister, Alhaji Sir Abubakar Tafawa Balewa.

THE EMIRS OF BAUCHI

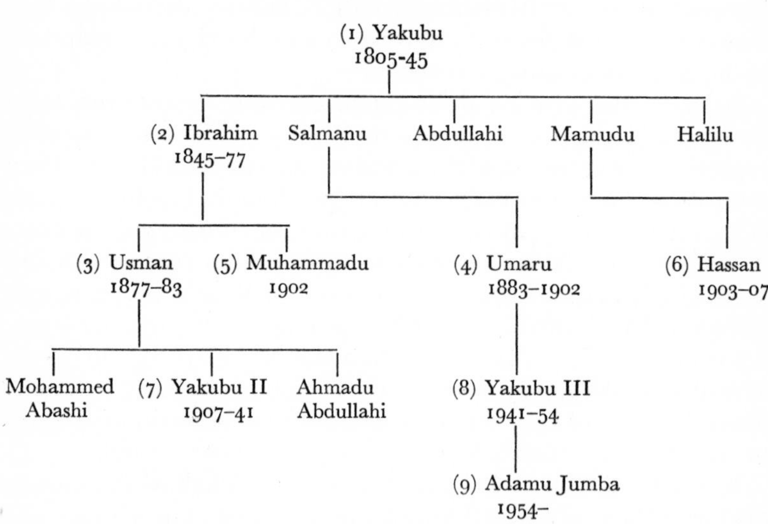

[1] Later Speaker of the House of Representatives in Lagos.

XXXIII. GOMBE

BUBA YERO, the first Emir of Gombe, was of Fulani extraction. He was born about 1762 near Mada (old Shellen) now in Numan Division, his father being a Kitije Fulani and his mother a Kanakuru. The offspring of such mixed marriages was known locally as Kambarijo.

Buba Yero's grandfather, Aliyu Ukuba, was a Koranic *malam* who married the daughter of a wealthy man in Tihati. Their son Usman settled at Lakumna, in Shellen, and took to preaching Islam. Gongon, the *amna* or chief of Shellen, was a friend of his and gave him his daughter Janaba in marriage. A son, Abubakar, was born in the year of Usman's death at Gombe, whither his religious wanderings had taken him. Abubakar was taken back to Shellen by his mother, where his grandfather nicknamed him 'Buba Yero' because of his large eyes—*yero* being the Kanakuru (Janafulu) word for 'eyes'.

He was left an orphan while still a child when his mother died of smallpox. When he was a youth he set out for Bornu to study, but on the way there he was captured by the Ngizim and kept as a slave at Potiskum for three years. On obtaining his liberty he went to Gobir to study under Usman dan Fodio. Gombe tradition claims that he did in fact reach Bornu, after escaping from his captors, and there he became a Muslim and ultimately a *malam*.

After some years he returned to Shellen, but Gongon now became worried about the effect of his missionary fervour among the pagan Kanakuru and drove him out of town. So Buba Yero withdrew to Bobini (Numan) and built a mosque there. Later still he moved to a new settlement, called Furakayo after the Kanakuru word for 'welcome', and thence to Gombi (now Little Gombi in Adamawa) and Song. He was working on the conversion of the population of Petembere (Numan) when word reached him of Usman dan Fodio. So Buba Yero went back to Gobir.

On the way he stopped at Daura, whose chief gave him his daughter Hawa to wed. Other sources suggest that Hawa was in fact a Kano girl. He is also said to have stopped at Katsina, where he was given the chief's daughter Zulai in marriage. Here he met Yakubu of Bauchi and became friendly with him. Yakubu, who was an old friend of the Shehu, strongly recommended Buba Yero to him, and so the Shehu gave Buba Yero a flag. He is said to have been the first person to receive a flag from Usman dan Fodio. Buba Yero started for Old Gombe via Kano, where some say he married Hawa. Pushing past Gombe, he went to the Bolewa town of Ako, where he became the lifelong friend of the grandfather of the late Galadiman Ako.

Buba Yero now persuaded the Ako Fulani to follow him, and began to subdue the country. It is believed in Gombe that this was contrary to the instruction of the Shehu, who had directed them to wait in Gombe until the order was given. His first campaign, in which he was helped by his loyal friend and fellow-student with the Shehu, Ahmadu Gora, son of Ado Sule of Pandaya, was against the former Jukun settlement of Pindiga, which at that time shared with Kalam the authority over most of what was to become Gombe emirate, including the Tangale and Waja peoples and the land lying to the east of the Gongola. One of the praise-titles of the chief of Pindiga has derived from the days of its power: *Dodon Tangale*, 'the Lord of the Tangale people'. The Fulani gradually seeped into the Jukun settlement and established their own centre of Sumbe, just outside the town. As was their practice everywhere in their peaceful pre-jihad penetration, they intermarried and looked after the locals' herds.

Buba Yero first settled in Shani (Biu), where his wife Zulai gave birth to a son, Suleimanu. From Shani he moved to Gulani, and here his wife Hawa delivered a son, Muhammadu Kwairanga. This is the reason why the Gombe royal dynasty is known as Shanima Gulanima Fulbe Janafulu.

He next established himself in the Bolewa country at a Fulani settlement around Old Gombe. There is a story that he built the walls of Gombe in seven days and seven nights. He overran the country systematically, even crossing the Benue to the south. Being of Bole blood himself, he refused to let his followers exterminate the Bolewa, and even offended his men by appointing the Sarkin Dukku, a Ba-Bole, one of his chief advisers.

A story is told of how a Bole clan was induced to move from its impregnable position on the top of a high hill near Gombe. A message was sent by Buba Yero to say that he had built the walls of Gombe in seven days and to remove their hill would require no longer a period. One morning the Fulani gathered round the hill and at a concerted cry of *hoku, hoku,* 'lay hold', they began to remove the big stones as fast as they could. Legend goes on to say that the panicked Bolewa at once vacated their hill top. To the east of the Gongola, Buba Yero subdued the country as far as Adamawa and then turned his attention to the north. It is said that he joined Misau in capturing Birni Ngazargamu, the capital of Bornu; certainly Misau was always on very friendly terms with Gombe.

Yakubu, Sarkin Bauchi, refused to allow any expansion west of the Gongola, and repulsed Buba Yero at Beri-Beri. Although Buba Yero objected when Yakubu took Darazo and Lago, which he claimed as his, he was unable to do anything about it.

To the south the Muri Fulani at first were subject to Buba Yero. But when dissensions rose, culminating in the killing by Buba Yero of the Muri chief Haruna, the Muri Fulani broke away and followed Sokoto direct. Buba Yero had hoped to be rewarded by Usman dan Fodio with the grant of suzerainty over all the country he had conquered, but the Shehu clipped his wings and gave him only the governorship of Gombe. Some maintain that this was because Gombe was nearer to supervision from Sokoto than distant Adamawa; others that it was a punishment for Buba Yero's impetuosity in declaring a jihad in the east—maybe inspired by his years of sitting at the Shehu's feet in Gobir—and ravaging the peoples of the Gongola valley before he had been given the signal by Usman dan Fodio. For his presumption, which possibly occurred as early as 1798, the Yungur, Lala and Hona areas were transferred to Modibbo Adama of Yola. Buba Yero's younger brother,[1] Hamman Ruwa, became the first Emir of Muri.

Buba Yero led an expedition across the Benue to Kwararafa and scattered the Jukun. On his return he settled at Gulani and then moved to Gurbol, today known as Ribadu, Kubto and Dukku. There was a civil war between the Fulani of Gombe and Dukku, which is said to have lasted two years and to have been brought to a conclusion on the orders of the Sarkin Musulmi through the direct intervention of Yakubu, Sarkin Bauchi.

After three years in Dukku, Buba Yero decided that he wanted to settle in a town of his own. So he sent his nephew Umaru, the son of Hamman Ruwa the Emir of Muri, to reconnoitre in the

[1] See note on p. 447.

bush. Umaru—who later married Buba Yero's daughter Ayisha and whose son Haruna became the first Magajin Gari of Gombe—recommended a site among the hills some twelve miles west of Dukku, where Buba Yero built a fort near a mahogany tree known to the local Bolewa as Gambe Memosiri. Some of the Bolewa came down from the hills to live with the Fulani, and they called the stockaded settlement Guru Gambe Memosiri, *guru* being the Bolewa word for 'fortress'. They intermarried with the Fulani and their children began to refer to their village simply as Gambe.

Buba Yero died at Gombe in 1841. Like so many of Usman dan Fodio's flag-bearers, he never publicly assumed the title of Emir of the kingdom he founded; instead, Buba Yero preferred the title of Modibbo Gombe. On his death the town was named Gombe Aba in his memory, and by this name the town of Old Gombe is still known. He was succeeded by his son Sule, who captured the town of Gadam in the Wawa bush and publicly sat on top of its chief's corpse as a warning never to rebel again. Sule's followers grew tired of his continual campaigning and when they complained to Sokoto the Sultan summoned the Emir of Gombe to warn him to pay more attention to his capital of Gombe Aba. On his way home Sule died in Kano in 1844.

The next Emir was Muhammadu Kwairanga, another of Buba Yero's sons. He subdued Tangale, Waja, Dadinya and Cham. He was succeeded by each of his four sons in turn. The first was Zailani, also known as Abdulkadiri, who came to the throne in 1882. It was in his reign that Malam Jibrilla began to cause trouble. Jibrilla, also known in Gombe history as Malam Zai and Modibbo Burmi, came from Jebdo in Katagum. After a quarrel with the Emir there he migrated to Zai in Fika, then to Zange and finally to Nafada. This was originally a Bolewa town which is said to derive its name from the following story. The Fulani herdsmen used to visit a local Hausa hunter who lived on the banks of the Gongola. They used to annoy him by upsetting his hut, whereupon he would shoot at them: *na fada maku kada ku zo nan*, 'I told you not to come here'. So the Fulani grew accustomed to telling each other they were off to Nafada.

Jibrilla asked the new Emir, Zailani, for a place to farm and he was given some land at the village of Kafi Wol Burmi on the Gombe-Fika border. Jibrilla built a settlement there and called it Burmi. Gombe tradition accuses Jibrilla of approaching the Emir disguised as a beggar and thus receiving the royal hospitality under false pretences. At any rate, it seems that once he had ensconced himself at Burmi he began to win a reputation as a magician. Gombe historians relate tales of how Jibrilla claimed to be able to tie his tongue round his head like a turban and of defying the laws of gravity when seated on a goatskin. This *léger-de-main* gained him a large following, among them many fugitives from enslavement or from justice. Soon Jibrilla proclaimed a revolt against Gombe and began to ravage the Nafada area.

When in 1888 Jibrilla refused to desist, the Emir Zailani marched on Burmi with a large force. Encamped at Sangaru, the Emir one night said to one of his followers, Layiwa, that when Burmi was taken he would dismiss the powerful Ajiya and give the title to Layiwa. One of the Ajiya's servants overheard this promise and ran to tell his master. Ajiya, a powerful office-holder, at once summoned all the district heads and persuaded them not to fight on the morrow. On the next day the Emir led his forces into battle, but when he called on his district heads to charge not one of them moved. In fury, the Emir rode forward alone and attacked the wall with his sword and spear. He was badly wounded in the head by an arrow and carried back to Birnin Bolewa where he died.

Zailani's younger brother Hassan succeeded him. His prodigality dissipated the wealth of Gombe Aba. It is said that out of the 700 horses in the royal stables, there remained only seven at his death. Even with the assistance of the armies of Bauchi, Katagum, Hadejia and Misau, Hassan was unable to subdue Jibrilla. One story has it that Jibrilla shrewdly bought off the Emir by presents and promises of allegiance . . . until the armies withdrew. Hassan died in 1895, and as none of his sons was old enough to govern Gombe in time of danger, his brother Tukur was appointed Emir. Tukur had been the favourite son of Kwairanga, who had urged the council of selectors to prefer him to his elder son Umaru. He reigned for only three years.

On Tukur's death in 1898, Umaru came out from his refuge with the Galadima Bubawa at Ako, where he had been hiding from his brother's envious hatred. There ensued a bitter struggle for the throne. The people of Gombe Aba chose, without consulting the district heads, Tukur's younger brother Jalo. This abuse of tradition so incensed the leaders of the emirate that they joined the Galadima, who marched on the capital, bringing his nominee

Umaru with him. He camped outside the town and announced to the people of Gombe that he had brought them their new Emir. After lengthy discussion Jalo was driven out of the palace.

Umaru's reign could hardly have opened less auspiciously. The support he had had from the Galadima meant it was almost impossible to resist the claims of Ako district for independence of Gombe, especially when Galadima Bubawa enlisted the support of Manga, Emir of Misau. Worse still, Jibrilla at Burmi continued an active menace to the peace of Gombe, at one time even allying himself with Rabeh, the usurper of Bornu. It was not until the arrival of a British force at Gombe Aba early in 1902 that the Jibrilla affair was clinched. A battle took place at Tongo, and soon afterwards Jibrilla was captured and exiled to Lokoja.

Burmi, however, was destined to reappear once more in the history of Gombe emirate. In July 1903 an extremely fierce battle took place between a column of troops led by Major Marsh and the remnants of Jibrilla's followers under the inspired leadership of the fugitive Sarkin Musulmi Attahiru, the ex-Emirs of Bida and Misau, the Magajin Keffi and a number of other important men from Sokoto, Kano, Gombe and Misau who had been deposed or dismissed from office. This movement of religious dynamism of the ex-Sultan's was known as *Perol*, a cause dedicated to avoiding British interference in the affairs of the Sokoto empire and to a great pilgrimage to Mecca. But when Attahiru learned that his way to Mecca was barred by the French round Lake Chad and by Fad-el-Allah in southern Bornu, he determined to defend Burmi against the aggressors. In the flight that followed the battle of Burmi, where the casualties were heavy, it is said that much property was hidden in a well to the west of the town; but this well has not yet been located. The graves of both the ex-Sultan Attahiru and Major Marsh are to be found near the ruins of Burmi, a town which now remains but in history. Many believe that the flag handed back to Sokoto at a special ceremony in 1961 was the personal green standard of the Sultan taken in this battle.[1]

In 1913 the Divisional headquarters of Gombe was moved from the isolation of Old Gombe to Nafada, being more accessible both from Kano and from the river. However, a new site was selected

[1] A somewhat colourful version of the incident is to be found in F. Crozier, *Five Years Hard*, 1935. See also the section on Sokoto, p. 410. A study of the Burmi episode will be found in D. J. Muffett, *Concerning Brave Captains*.

at Doma in Ako district and here the Emir took up residence in 1919, renaming the town Gombe. Umaru died shortly afterwards and was succeeded by his son Haruna. A clash of interests between the Emir and the Alkali led to the dismissal of the latter in 1930. On Haruna's death in 1935 his younger brother Abubakar, district head of Nafada, became Emir at the age of 33. He visited England in 1951. His reign will be remembered by the honour done by the upgrading of Gombe emirate to a first-class chiefdom in 1955. Gombe suffered the loss of its Waziri in 1951 and again in 1955, on both occasions by their death while away on the holy pilgrimage.

With the Bornu railway extension coming to Gombe town in 1962, the emirate's growth to great prosperity over the past decade has crystallized. The railway station at Gombe was officially opened to passenger traffic in April 1963. It is interesting to compare the thriving communications junction of Gombe today, a vast centre of trade in the east-central area of Northern Nigeria, with the gloomy statement of thirty years earlier that the emirate 'is not one of the principal focal points of the North and where the possibilities of expansion are confined by the paucity of local resources'.

THE EMIRS OF GOMBE

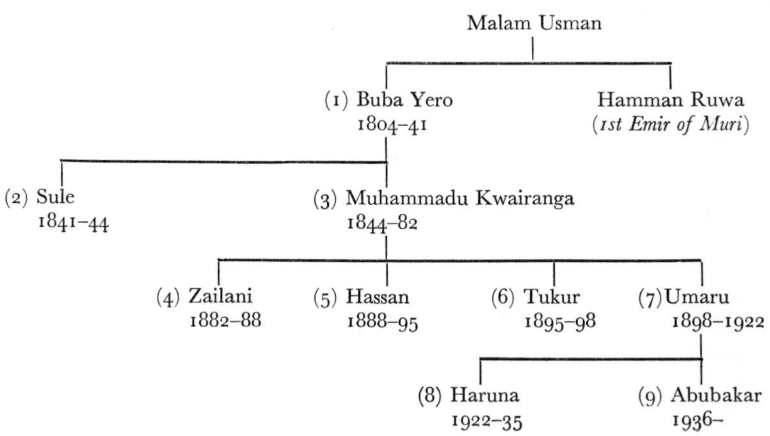

Note: Buba Yero never assumed the title of Emir.

3. EMIRATES DERIVING FROM THE SOKOTO EMPIRE

(3) The North-Eastern States

XXXIV. KAZAURE

DURING the reign of Sulemanu, Emir of Kano, the Sarkin Musulmi carved the emirate of Kazaure out of the adjoining states of Kano, Katsina, and Daura to make a kingdom for a favourite chief, Dan Tunku, a Fulani of repute who had settled at Dambatta[1] and helped to drive out the Habe kings of Kano, Katsina and Daura.[2] Kazaure historians claim Dan Tunku (his real name was Ibrahim) as a Fulani from Egypt. He was one of three brothers, but while Gege (Geibi) and Daniya settled in Bornu, Dan Tunku settled at Dambatta. Because his brothers lived with the Yerima of Bornu, they came to be known as the Yerimawa people.

Kazaure was placed under the suzerainty of the Emir of Kano, but on the Emir's death in 1819 Dan Tunku refused to follow his successor. A force was sent to subdue him but he repulsed it, and is said to have raided up to the walls of Kano.

On another occasion Dan Tunku was driven back from his raids on Kano territory and withdrew to Kazaure, then no more than a stockaded village. The Kano forces won the day and occupied Kazaure. Dambo, the son of Dan Tunku to whom part of the Kazaure forces had been entrusted, secretly moved his men round behind the hills lying to the north of the town and made a surprise attack from the west. The Kano army was driven back in confusion across the stream Korammna or Burdungu, about six miles south of the town, which was Bello's choice of boundary with Kano when Kazaure became independent in 1824.

The reason why Dan Tunku left Dambatta was that his brother

[1] Seventeen miles south of Kazaure.
[2] See Arnett's *Gazetteer of Sokoto Province*, p. 25.

Geibi went to greet the Emir of Kano, Dabo, and elicited from him the promise of Dan Tunku's *sarauta*. When Dan Tunku's son Dambo heard this, he called Geibi back to Kurfi, a village a few miles north of present-day Kazaure. Dambo pursued him right up to Kazaure but the Kano army was pushed back to the present Kazaure-Kano boundary. Six months after this engagement Dan Tunku died, from gun wounds received when his rifle exploded accidentally while he was loading it. He was succeeded by his son Dambo, who was the first Emir to occupy the royal compound in Kazaure town. This had been intended for Dan Tunku but he did not live to see its completion. The palace is the one used today by the Emirs of Kazaure.[1] Because it was impossible to sink wells by local methods inside the town, Kazaure differed from most of the northern fortified towns by being quite unsuited to withstand a siege.

The Emirs of Kazaure claim that, because of their history of establishing some kind of independence against the Habe kings of Kano, their appointment was never officially approved by Sokoto. Nevertheless, by the end of the nineteenth century we find Kazaure listed, with Katsina and Kebbi, as being in charge of the Galadima of Sokoto, at that time the heir-presumptive.

On the death of Emir Muhammadu in 1922, Kazaure and Daura were formed into a separate Division of Kano Province, later named the Northern Division. The creation of Katsina Province in 1934 necessitated another change and Kazaure now came into Kano Division. The official reports that 'Kazaure is unimportant and has nothing to record' may reflect on the author rather than the emirate, though life in a northern area like that of Kazaure and Gumel does indeed continue in a tranquil way.

On the death of Umaru in 1941, his nephew Adamu, who was then District Head of Roni, and the son of the Magajin Gari, became the 7th Emir of Kazaure. In contrast to some emirates, the Emirs of Kazaure have enjoyed long reigns and long life.

[1] I am grateful to the Kazaure N.A. and to my student Zubeiru Mahmud for some of the facts given in these paragraphs on a recent sojourn in this lovely town. —A.K-G.

THE EMIRS OF KAZAURE

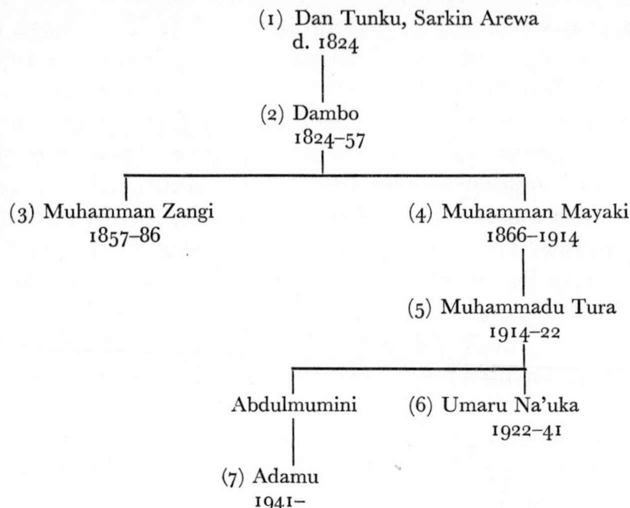

XXXV. KATAGUM

THE two outstanding figures in Katagum in the religious wars which owed their inspiration to Usman dan Fodio were Malam Zaki and his nephew Dan Kauwa. The former's full name was Ibrahim Zakiyul Kalbi and he was a native of Yayu in Cinade district east of the Misau river, his mother being a daughter of the chief of Yayu, a Bauchi title. His father was Lawan, an Arab from Baghirmi who had settled at Nafada and then moved to Yayu. There is a local legend that the first person to settle in the modern capital of Katagum, Azare, was a hunter called Zirai; whence the name derives. Others claim that the original site was thickly populated by hyaenas, for which an early Habe word was *zarai*.

At the beginning of the wars Malam Zaki was driven out of Yayu by the Bauchi people. He settled at Laimari and from there, collecting a following of Tashena men from his wife's (Kankama) district, he made an unsuccessful attack on Udubo, and finally joined Dan Audure Umaru, who had received a flag about 1807 and was then besieging Auyo. Malam Zaki went to Sokoto in 1807 to obtain his flag. After the fall of Auyo its people helped him to capture Tashena. He stayed at Tashena for a time until he heard that Shira and Gadau had been captured by Malam Bakatsine and Barden Kano Bagel. He hurried off south and, persuading them to hand the towns over to him, he installed his nephew Dan Kauwa as chief of Shira. Malam Zaki then returned to Tashena via Misau, conquering Udobo and Gamawa on the way. Tashena, however, did not satisfy him and he started work on the present town of Katagum, using labour from Tashena for the purpose. This was in about 1814.[1]

Usman dan Fodio now ordered a second attack to be made on Bornu, presumably to re-establish the prestige lost when his general Gwani Mukhtar was killed in 1808. This attack was primarily made by Katagum and Hadejia forces under the command of Malam Zaki. The expedition defeated Mai Ahmadu of

[1] This is the date now preferred by Katagum N.A., whose counsel we acknowledge. Other commentators have given 1810.

Bornu and captured Ngazargamu. Then it at once retired westward under orders, it is stated, from Usman dan Fodio. Malam Zaki returned to Katagum, where he stayed until his death in 1814. He now ruled this former Kano territory and his title became Sarkin Bornu. By that time he was in control of most of the old kingdom of Shira, except the westerly section, which was still under Kano, and the southerly portion of Misau which retained its independence. In addition he held the much smaller kingdom of Tashena, akin to Bedde. The main subordinate offices, such as Azare, Shellen Chinade, and Udubo, were in charge of his sons.

Malam Zaki was succeeded by Liman Adandaya, his brother, who ruled for only two years. During this disastrous period his title was twice usurped. The first occasion was due to interference from Hadejia, which took advantage of an obvious state of weakness. This was corrected by the Sarkin Musulmi. The second was a more serious matter, and was in effect a successful Habe revolt which only came to an end with the assassination of Tushum, the Habe leader, who actually occupied Katagum for some months.

Owing to his proven unsuitability Adandaya was deposed in 1816 and was succeeded by Dan Kauwa, one of the two original leaders. His is the great name of Katagum emirate. His reign was disturbed by considerable trouble with the conquered Habe, who were encouraged by the active offensive policy at this time being pursued by Bornu under the vigorous guidance of Al Kanemi. This culminated in the expedition of Shehu Laminu about 1826, which was received with open arms as a band of deliverers by the Shirawa, and for a short time Azangu, the son of the last Habe king, was restored in Shira. The Fulani withdrew precipitately before the Bornu advance and Katagum itself was evacuated. Dan Kauwa retired to Hadufia, a very strong position near the junction of the Kiawa and Katagum rivers. The defeat of Shehu Laminu at Fake by Yakubu of Bauchi, however, led to a complete reversal of affairs. Dan Kauwa now joined Yakubu in recapturing Shira where Abdurrahman, to mark the end of the Habe rule, abandoned the town east of Shira hill and built the present town in the centre of the hills, which he called Dar es Salaam. From Shira Dan Kauwa went on westwards, and on the wave of Fulani ascendancy captured Jalam.

Later, in about 1828, he and Yakubu again combined and captured Misau, the last Habe stronghold in this borderland area. A subsequent dispute between them as to who should hold Misau was settled by the Sarkin Musulmi giving it to Mamman Manga as a reward for the services of his family in Bornu. Dan Kauwa died in 1846.

It was in Dan Kauwa's reign that Captain Clapperton visited Katagum in 1824. He described it like this:

> It extends nearly one day's journey to the northward, and five days' journey to the southward, where it is bounded by an independent territory, called after the inhabitants Kury-kurry. On the east it is bounded by the kingdom of Bornu, and on the west by the neighbouring province of Kano. From the best information I could obtain, the whole province can send into the field about 4,000 horse and 20,000 foot, armed with bows, swords, and spears. The principal productions are grain and bullocks, which, with slaves brought from the adjoining territories of the Kafirs, are the staple articles of trade. Here we found, for the first time, kowrie shells in circulation as money; for hitherto native cloth, or some other commodity of standard price, had been the common medium of exchange. This city was the strongest we had seen since we left Tripoli. It is in the form of a square, the sides facing the cardinal points of the compass, with four corresponding gates, which are regularly opened and shut at sunrise and sunset. It is defended by two parallel walls of red clay, and three dry ditches, one without, one within, and the third between the two walls, which are about twenty feet high and ten feet broad at the base, gradually decreasing upwards to a breadth just sufficient for a narrow footpath. This is protected by a low parapet, and is ascended by flights of steps at convenient distances. Both walls are of the same height, without loopholes or towers and, instead of being crenelated, terminate in a waving line. The gates are defended by a platform inside over the entrance, where a body of townsmen take their station to repel assailants. The three ditches are of equal dimensions, each about fifteen feet deep and twenty feet wide. There is only one mosque, and this almost in ruins. The governor's residence is in the centre of the city, and occupies a space of about 500 yards square. The governor and principal inhabitants have houses made entirely of clay, besides the coozees already described. They are flat-roofed, in the Turkish style, and sometimes of two stories, with square or semicircular openings for windows. The city may contain from 7,000 to 8,000 inhabitants; including all merchants and tradesmen, together with the servants or slaves of the governor.[1]

Of the Emir, Clapperton noted that he was 'a stout, tall fellow,

[1] This extract from Clapperton's diary is reproduced in C. Howard and J. H. Plumb, *West African Explorers*, pp. 235–6.

blunt and good-natured', whose personal band sang his praises thus:

> Give flesh to the hyaenas at day-break:
>   Oh! the broad spears.
> The spear of the sultan is the broadest:
>   Oh! the broad spears (*repeat*).
> I behold thee now—I desire to see none other.
> My horse is as tall as a high wall:
> He will fight against ten, he fears nothing:
> He has slain ten—the guns are yet behind:
> The elephant of the forest brings me what I want:
> Like unto thee—so is the sultan:
> Be brave! be brave! my friends and kinsmen:
> God is great!—I wax fierce as a beast of prey:
> God is great!—To-day those I wished for are come:
>   Oh! the broad spears (*repeat*).[1]

Clapperton's companion Dr Oudney died here and was buried at Murmur, 'about five yards to the north of an old mimosa tree a little beyond the southern gate of the town'.

The fourth Emir, Abdurrahman, second son of Malam Zaki, was previously Sarkin Shira, this being recognized as the most important subordinate office in the emirate—indeed, in some respects it seems almost to have formed a separate unit.

Abdurrahman opened his reign by attacks on towns along the western border of Bornu. These expeditions, however, were overshadowed by events in Hadejia which directly affected Katagum. Ahmadu Emir of Hadejia, had been driven out by his brother Buhari.[2] The Sarkin Musulmi, Aliyu Babba, ordered Katagum to help to restore him. This was done without much serious fighting. Shortly afterwards Abdurrahman died, having ruled for only five years.

Abdurrahman was succeeded by Abdulkadiri, the eldest son of Dan Kauwa. Thus the title returned to the house of Dan Kauwa, where it has remained ever since. His first war was with Buhari, who had had Ahmadu assassinated and had proclaimed himself Sarkin Hadejia. Abdulkadiri was a member of the expedition under the Waziri of Sokoto which was sent to deal with Buhari,

[1] Ibid., p. 231.
[2] See pp. 488 ff.

and which was totally defeated in the campaign known as the Yakin Kuffur. In the months of Buhari's raiding and destruction, in revenge for the Sarkin Musulmi's refusal to recognize him as emir, Katagum suffered severely.

In 1868 Abdulkadiri was succeeded by his brother Haji, Sarkin Shira. He carried out the usual attacks on towns on the Bornu boundary and also on the Keri Keri. While on his way to Sokoto in about 1883 he heard that the Ningawa were approaching. He met them with an inadequate force at Tumfafi, east of Shira. He was defeated but he managed to escape to Zadawa. The following year he took part in a combined attack on Ningi with Haruna, Emir of Hadejia, and Muhamman Sambo, Emir of Jama'are. This was moderately successful, although the allied forces retired rapidly with some loss.

This was followed by a Mahdist outbreak at Dutsi in Kano under one Liman Ya Musa. He collected a large following and set out eastward on the pilgrimage in defiance of Sokoto. He was, however, stopped at Gwadayi by the presence of a large combined force from Katagum under Sarkin Shira Abdulkadiri (Haji himself had gone to Sokoto) and the Emirs of Hadejia, Misau, and Jama'are. Liman Ya Musa surrendered himself without fighting and his large following at once dispersed. He was taken to Sokoto and was treated well, though his property was divided up by his captors.

The second appearance of Mahdism occurred about 1888. In the previous year Katagum, Misau, and Jama'are had made an attack on the Keri Keri with Malam Jibrilla, also known as Gaini.[1] He was a native of Katagum but he seems to have begun to set up on his own in the Keri Keri country, where his presence was not regarded favourably by Misau. After this war Malam Jibrilla moved to Nafada, being forced to do so by pressure from the local emirs, who thought he was becoming too powerful. He shortly extended his power over most of Gombe, and successfully defied an attack by Misau and Gombe on the town of Burmi, where he had established himself. He was sufficiently important at the time of Rabeh to be accepted by the latter as his ally, and he also had diplomatic relations with the rebel Malam Hayatu.[2] Jibrilla was finally defeated and captured by Colonel Morland in 1902.

[1] See p. 468.
[2] See pp. 407 and 441.

The Emir Haji also took part in several expeditions organized by the Sarkin Musulmi, including the Madarumfa war and attacks on Gobir and Maradi. Haji died in 1896 and was succeeded by his son Abdulkadiri II. Of his appointment we have the following letter written to Sokoto by the Sultan's envoy to Katagum:

From Magaji Muhammadu Buhari son of Muhammadu Sambo to the Sarkin Musulmi Abdurrahman, greetings, etc.

I enquire after your health and welfare and after inform you that Allah the Almighty has granted me to reach Birnin Katagum in safety and good health. We have carried out your orders and have invested Abdulkadiri Sarkin Shira with the title of Sarkin Bornu[1] and seated him on the seat of his fathers and forefathers in health and prosperity. Further the Sarkin Azare has been put on the throne of Shira and the Sarkin Sokwa in the land of Azare in health and prosperity. Therefore we have written to you to tell you by letter. Our messenger will go to you by the grace of Allah. May Allah prolong your life and give you victory. My present to you is three gowns. Peace.[2]

Abdulkadiri's early years, however, were full of disturbances, arising from the advance of Rabeh. The latter was to a considerable extent dependent on Kano and the west for his supplies of powder, and the Sarkin Musulmi accordingly ordered that such trade with Bornu must be stopped. Katagum, being in an extremely exposed position and also seeing possibilities of considerable profit, did not obey fully. The Emir Haji had moved the main market from Katagum to Gamawa so as partly to shift his responsibility, a move that resulted in large tolls being collected at Gamawa. In the end, Sambo Sarkin Gamawa, who was being handsomely enriched by this, refused to obey an order from Abdulkadiri the Emir to arrest the Kano traders. Meanwhile, Muhammadu Sarkin Sokwa, eldest son of Abdulkadiri, had caused general bad feeling owing to his oppressive methods, which came to a head when he looted Zubuki (Gadau) on his way back from an attack on Ningi.

The four senior subordinate chiefs—the Yerima, Sarkin Shira, Sarkin Azare, and Sarkin Udubo—complained to the Sarkin Musulmi, who ordered Abdulkadiri to come to Sokoto. The latter merely sent his representatives, refusing to go in person. As a result

[1] Courtesy title of the Emir of Katagum since the days of the first Emir and flag-bearer, Malam Zaki.

[2] H. F. Backwell, *The Occupation of Hausaland*, p. 18.

the Sultan ordered the Katagum chiefs to follow the Yerima and ignore Abdulkadiri, a reprisal in which the Emir of Hadejia was to support them.

Sarkin Gamawa now sided with Yerima, but before active operations could be taken Sarkin Sokwa attacked and defeated him while the Yerima was still on his way north. Sarkin Gamawa withdrew, but the Katagum forces had to return home at once because it was rumoured that the Emir of Hadejia was advancing to help Gamawa. It is said that this is indeed what he intended to do, but he was dissuaded and instead tried unsuccessfully to reconcile Katagum and Gamawa, without success. He sent help later to Gamawa, as did the other Katagum chiefs of the Yerima's party. This did not prevent Sarkin Gamawa's forces suffering a severe defeat in which he himself was killed, and Gamawa again was brought under Katagum in 1900.

Prior to this, the Emir of Hadejia had threatened to put in by force Sambo's son as Sarkin Gamawa. This son had gone to Bagam, then held by Hadejia, and had been very well received. Before this was attempted, however, the Sarkin Musulmi pardoned Abdulkadiri, a reprieve encouraged, it is alleged locally, by gifts from the loot taken at Gamawa. The other Katagum chiefs were reconciled, but the distrust between the ruling family and the Yerima lasted until the latter's death in 1925. There was also considerable ill feeling against Hadejia for a time.

The first sign of the British occupation was the arrival in 1902 of a column from Bornu which, however, only came as far as Yayu and returned. The next year Captain Sword's column in pursuit of Attahiru, Sarkin Musulmi, passed through to Misau. The only chief of importance who actually joined the Sarkin Musulmi was Usman Sarkin Shira. Others, however, including Muhammadu, then Sarkin Azare, the conqueror of Gamawa, were preparing to do so.

The flight of the Sarkin Musulmi and his defeat not long after at Burmi stopped any further ideas of opposition. Following the capture of Kano, Katagum acknowledged the new rule and in December 1903 the Katagum Province was formed.

Abdulkadiri died in May 1905, and was succeeded by his son Muhammadu, who had made his reputation at the capture of Gamawa.

Muhammadu's death in 1909 caused considerable difficulties as regards the succession, one party supporting his son Abdulkadiri, and another his brother Mustafa. The former was appointed, and this led to the 'Katagum flag incident'. Mustafa, looking round for some method of getting Abdulkadiri into disfavour, arranged for the theft of the flag from the house of Major Fremantle, then Resident in charge of the Division. A search was started as soon as the loss was discovered but the flag could not be found. It was subsequently discovered beside the Katagum river, having been smuggled out of the town. The persons concerned were eventually traced and arrested and Mustafa was deposed from his *sarauta* of Azare.

Certain minor territorial adjustments have been made for administrative reasons, such as the move of the Divisional headquarters from Kano to Azare in 1916 when Hadejia was removed from Katagum Division, and the transfer of Katagum from Kano to Bauchi Province in 1926, but except for the transfer of Hardawa to Misau in 1913, the present Emirate of Katagum is very nearly the same as in the time of Malam Zaki.

During the 1930s Katagum's leadership left it behind the other emirates in this Fulani-Kanuri no-man's land, an area known locally as *Bornu Gudiri* or Little Bornu. Emir Abdulkadiri died after reigning nearly forty years, spanning the national governorships from Lugard to Macpherson. With the appointment of Umaru Faruku as Emir in 1947 and a vigorous modernization reshuffle of the Council in 1951, followed by a further redistribution of portfolios in 1958, Katagum underwent a positive transformation, so that in recent years its competent N.A. staff have earned it an enviable reputation among the emirates, and official reports gladly hold up 'the high standard of Native Authority administration now characteristic of Katagum'.[1]

[1] *Annual Report of Bauchi Province*, 1961.

THE EMIRS OF KATAGUM

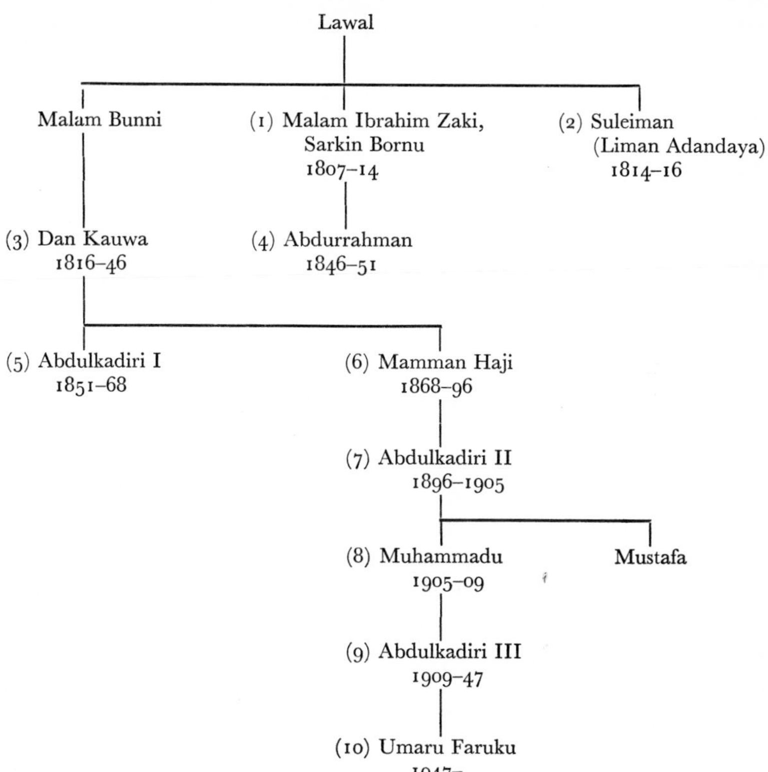

XXXVI. HADEJIA

BEFORE the Fulani conquest at the beginning of the nineteenth century, the country now known as the Hadejia emirate was composed of seven separate kingdoms, whose chiefs received their titles from, and owed allegiance to, the Habe Galadima of Bornu. These were Auyo, Hadejia, Garin Gabas (Mabudi), Gatarwa (Sarkin Dawaki), Kazure (Sarkin Arewa), Fagi (Sarkin Arewa), and Dawa (Ciroma).

One authority claims that the most ancient and important was Auyo, said to have been founded in 1400 by a Baghirmi of that name, whose brothers Tashe and Shira are reputed to have founded Tashena and Shira (in Katagum) at the same time. Another authority gives pride of place to Garin Gabas which, it is said, was originally called Biram. The well-known legend is that Biram was the father of the Hausa States and one of the Hausa Bakwai.[1] A story goes that the town was founded by Arabs from Baghdad. One, Muhtari, also known as Bayajida, came from the East. In Bornu the reigning chief gave Muhtari his daughter Magira in marriage. Muhtari subsequently went to Daura, where he slew the sacred spirit and married the queen, but on the way his Kanuri wife gave birth to a son called Biram—or some say Burkimu, meaning 'welcome'—who founded the town. Yet another version says that it was Muhtari's younger brother who was called Biram; and another that the town where Magira gave birth to her son was known as Gabas ta Biram. The chiefs of Garin Gabas claim descent from this Arab family.

There is yet another tradition that Hadejia was founded by a Kanuri hunter named Hadejia, who came from Macina, and was the first of a long line of thirty-two kings. This version draws some authority from the manuscript of the Ḳano Chronicle, where it is stated that during the reign of Yakubu the nineteenth Habe king of Kano (1452–63), Agalfati, chief of Gaya and son of the chief of Macina, came to Kano with his three brothers. One

[1] See pp. 145–9 for the story of Bayajida and the Hausa Bakwai.

of them became king of Hadejia with the title of *Sarkin Gabas*, 'Lord of the East'.

Towards the end of the eighteenth century a certain Fulani cattle owner named Umaru settled close to Hadejia and succeeded in obtaining the title of Sarkin Fulanin Hadejia. His father had originally come from Macina, and settled at Jarmari, a few miles north of the town.

On hearing the news of the jihad in about 1805, Umaru at once sent his brother Sambo to the Shehu for a flag and the Habe king Abubakar submitted without delay. Within a few months Auyo, Gatarwa, Garin Gabas, and Kazure had submitted to Umaru, while the two remaining kingdoms of Fagi and Dawa were given by the Shehu to Larmina, a cousin of Umaru, who styled himself Sarkin Marma.

In 1808 Umaru was allowed to transfer his title to his son Mamman Kankiya, but within the year both father and son died. Umaru's brother Sambo succeeded and from him have sprung all subsequent Emirs of Hadejia. The emirate may thus be said to have been founded in 1808. Sambo now moved from Umaru's residence at Rinde, just outside the northern gate of the town, and took up his abode in Hadejia town itself, which he considerably enlarged. On his entry the Habe inhabitants left the town and settled outside the eastern gate.

After a comparatively peaceful reign of thirty-seven years Sambo abdicated in favour of his eldest son, Garko, who died two years later, in 1847. His brother Abdulkadiri, who succeeded him, himself died within a few months, to be followed almost at once by his aged father.

Sambo's third son, the Ciroma Buhari, now succeeded to the throne against the dying wish of his father, who had nominated his fourth son, Ahmadu. An Hadejia tradition accuses Buhari of impersonating Ahmadu at his father's death-bed and thus deceitfully obtaining his father's blessing. The story goes thus:

Sambo gave him [Buhari] the name Hite-hari. But his brothers and sisters changed it round and amended it to Buhari. Formerly he had been called by a girl's name, because his father did not know that he was a boy, and it was only when he realized this that they altered it in this manner. [*See extract below on page 487.*]

When he reached years of discretion he was taken to Miga to receive his schooling. There he attended school until he reached puberty, when he left off and came back home. He was unable, however, to return to his father's house, for he was not in favour there. Thus he wandered from place to place, until his father fell sick of the illness of which he died. He was very ill, and at last knew that he would not recover. Then one morning his eldest son went to pay him his respects. He came in, and when he was about to rise his father said, 'As for me, my span is ended; yours still remains. Go now, and come back at mid-day that I may tell you.' Now their step-mother, who preferred Buhari, heard when he said this. Buhari was in the town, but had never come to greet his father, for he was afraid. So his step-mother sent to look for him, and he came and found her in the house. She said to him, 'To-day when the sun is overhead come in good time, go and find your father, and tell him you have come. He has told your elder brother to come at mid-day, but I think he means to give him his royal power. If you get there before him, it is you who will get it.' 'Good,' he said. He went and waited for the sun, and when it was nearly overhead he went to their house, entered in and found his father and said, 'I have come.' His father said, 'Have you come, Hamman?' 'Yes,' he replied, 'I have come.' His father said, 'Come close to me.' He drew near to his father. His father took the insignia of office and gave them to him, he gave him all his secrets of kingship and of war. Buhari expressed his pleasure and gratitude. Then his father said to him, 'But I warn you about Hite-hari. That man is an infidel, and if you do not beware of him he will snatch the power out of your hands. Go then, as for me now my time is passed.' Then they prayed each other's forgiveness, and Buhari went out and departed, having obtained the royal power.

When the sun had reached its noon the eldest brother went and announced his presence to his father. When his father answered, he said, 'I have come.' His father asked him, 'Who are you?' He said, 'I am Hamman whom you told to come at noon.' Then his father asked again, 'Who came and went away just now? Was it not you who came?' He answered his father, 'It was not I who came; I have only just this moment arrived here.' His father said, 'Woe and alas! Then it must have been Hite-hari who came. Now there is nothing that can be done, save that you seek a way to escape from his wickedness.'[1]

Buhari proved to be a bold and cruel ruler, whose name became a bloody byword in the stormy marches of eastern Hausaland. It is said in Hadejia that on his accession, he called all his people to assemble under a baobab tree laden with fruit; he shouted, and not one pod was left on the tree. Then were the people of Hadejia

[1] R. M. East, *Stories of Old Adamawa*, pp. 75–77.

seized with fear, for they knew he would gain the mastery in whatever he decided to do.

One of his first acts was to have his cousin Nalara, the Sarkin Auyo, assassinated. He thus early fulfilled the dark prophecy said to have been made by Usman dan Fodio before Buhari's birth. The chroniclers relate:

Before Buhari was born his father used to go to Sokoto to visit the Shaihu. Every time he went to greet the Shaihu, if he found him with his children and grandchildren, when they saw him they would run into the house. Then Buhari's father asked the Shaihu, 'Shaihu, what makes these children run away from me?' The Shaihu answered, 'There is an infidel they see in your loins whom you will one day beget, a killer of men, that is what makes them run from you.' He asked the Shaihu again, 'Shaihu, shall I beget an infidel and a murderer?' 'Yes,' replied the Shaihu. 'Thus it is.' He pondered and resolved in his heart to give up all intercourse with his wives, lest he should beget the infidel about whom the Shaihu had told him. He went back to live in his town Hadejia, and left off all intercourse with his wives for a long time. Then they said to him, 'It is not right that for the sake of one child you should be denied the rest of your heritage. How can you act thus, when you might be the father of many children?' Then he answered, 'True. That which God has ordained shall come to pass.' He started to have intercourse with his wives again; nevertheless, whenever his wife bore a male child he killed it, but if it was a female he let it be. Whenever a male child was born to him he thought it would grow into the infidel of whom the Shaihu had spoken, and he killed it.

After a time Buhari was born, but his womenfolk hid him, saying it was a girl, and when the time came for the naming ceremony he gave him a girl's name. The child grew and came to boyhood, and they began to tie a cloth round him and put a necklace round his neck like a girl. They continued to treat him in this way until one day, when his father was sitting at the entrance to his house, he was sent on an errand. As he came and was about to pass close to his father, his cloth came unfastened and dropped off. Thereupon his father saw he was a boy and started up after him. He ran into the house. His father went and found him and took a spear to kill him. All the people in his household made a ring round the child, weeping and praying him not to kill him, but to spare just him alone. For if every child that was born were killed, when would one be born that would be left alive? 'So let him be', adding, 'but at least he shall not grow up in my house. Let his mother take him, and let them get out of my house, and go and live wherever they like.' His mother departed with him, and brought him up to boyhood in another place. But his father had formed the opinion that this was certainly the child who would become the infidel of whom the Shaihu had spoken. So he gave him the name Hite-hari.[1]

Because of his raiding of brother emirates the Sarkin Musulmi, Aliyu Babba, sent word to have him deposed, but Buhari refused to do more than meet the Wazirin Sokoto at Katagum. On the approach of the Katagum forces under the Waziri of Sokoto, Buhari retired with his followers, and Ahmadu was installed as Emir in 1850. Having defeated the Sarkin Macina, Buhari returned to Hadejia reinforced by the Shehu of Bornu who was quite ready to put a spoke in the Sokoto wheel. He routed the Katagum forces, and put Ahmadu to death. This was in 1851. Local Hadejia traditions ascribe Ahmadu's death blow to the hand of the celebrated warrior Tatagana, Sarkin Arewan Hadejia, who was one of Buhari's right-hand men in his wars. Buhari later gave him the house of one of Sambo's leading courtiers, Musa Maisarki, and finally turbanned him 'Chief of Northern Hadejia'. In return, it was destined to be Tatagana's firmness that obliged the men of Hadejia to bring back Buhari's body from the battlefield at Gorgoram and bury him in the town of Hadejia.

Having now openly defied the Sultan and repudiated Hadejia's allegiance to Sokoto, Buhari proceeded to enrich himself by a series of raids and expeditions on all sides. Marma was captured after tunnelling under the walls and became part of Hadejia, thus bringing the emirate to its present size. Buhari died in 1863 in an unsuccessful expedition against Bedde at Gorgoram. His reign furnishes a remarkable record of combined courage and ruthlessness, and drew the following observations from Barth:

> Bohari, or, as the Bornu people call him, Bowari, . . . had been governor of Khadeja, but being a clever and restless man he, or rather his jealous brother, had excited the suspicion of his liege lord Aliyu, the ruler of Sokoto, who had deposed him. . . . [He] had just now set out to try his fortune against his brother. . . . Predatory incursions are nothing in these quarters, where several provinces and entirely distinct empires have a common frontier; but this, as the event proved, was rather a memorable campaign for the whole of this part of Negroland, and was to become 'the beginning of sorrows' for all the country around. For Bokhari, having taken the strong town of Khadeja and killed his

[1] East, op. cit., pp. 73-75.

brother, . . . spread terror and devastation to the very gates of Kano. . . . Districts, which on my former visit I had found flourishing, and populous, had been reduced by this warlike chieftain who, instead of founding a strong kingdom and showing himself a great prince, chose rather, like most of his countrymen, to base his power on the destruction and devastation of the country around him, and to make himself a slave-dealer on a grand scale. Tens of thousands of unfortunate people, pagans as well as Mohammedans, . . . have been carried away from their native home into distant regions.[1]

Buhari was succeeded by his son Umaru, despite the strong protests of Buhari's brothers, one of whom, Haru, in 1865 eventually succeeded in obtaining a sufficiently strong backing to force Umaru to abdicate. Haru then reigned for nearly twenty years. He defeated and killed the Sarkin Gumel at Zaburam in 1872 and thus brought to an end the Hadejia-Gumel wars, but he did not fare so well against Ningi nor against the Badawa, who severely defeated him at Gorgoram in 1869.

Haru was succeeded by his son Muhammadu in 1885. Most of his reign, like that of his predecessors, was spent in fighting. After the Kano civil war of 1893, he pretended that he had been promised Miga and Kwanda, although he had rendered no support, and promptly annexed them by force. Muhammadu, however, had bigger trouble on his hands when Rabeh was believed to be marching on Kano by way of either Hadejia or Katagum. Muhammadu's warning letter to the Emir of Kano, Aliyu, has been preserved:

After salutations the reason of my letter is to tell you the latest news here. Rabeh has sent twelve standards of his people to Bedde. They came there and fought with the people of Bedde and were not able to conquer them. When the Bedde people saw no way out, Sarkin Bedde Maiduma got up, he himself with all his people, great and small, free and slaves, male and female and came to us and remained with us. They are here now and have left Birnin Bedde. The people of Rabeh entered Bedde and the inhabitants of the villages and farms of the Bedde country were all scattered and of them some came to us, and some went into the bush. Therefore I tell you that between us and Rabeh there is no one who has power over him save Allah. It has also been heard that Rabeh has moved and intends going to the west. Some say he is going to Kano by our road, others that he is going to you by Katagum and others that he will go to Kano by Damagaram. May Allah preserve us

[1] Quoted in A. H. M. Kirk-Greene, *Barth's Travels in Nigeria*, p. 131.

both from his mischief. Do not be surprised that Galadima has not come to you sooner. He has been delayed by this affair. Peace.[1]

He was killed in April 1906 while defending Hadejia against the British, and the annexed districts were returned to Kano. After Lugard's messenger had had his face slapped and one of his soldiers had been killed in cold blood, a force was sent to Hadejia to compel the Emir's submission. Muhammadu perished with three of his sons in a gallant but vain stand. Neither this incident nor the celebrated Moloney affair in Keffi has ever been fully or satisfactorily explained.[2]

Haruna, his son the Ciroma, was appointed to succeed him, and on his death in 1909 his son, Abdulkadiri, who was then only a youth, was appointed Emir. Hadejia was combined with Gumel in 1915 to form the Hadejia Division. In 1925 Abdulkadiri died, and was succeeded by his brother Usman. It was Usman who showed considerable courage in his personal handling of a riot among the stranger elements in Malam Maduri on Christmas Day, 1934. The following year saw a milestone in Hadejia's history, the huge opening ceremony of the hospital. Apart from a broadening of the Emir's Council by the inclusion of the Ma'aji and a legal scholar in M. Haruna, the rest of the decade is notable chiefly for a remarkable storm bringing five inches of rain one April morning. The Emir, who had never been further afield than Kaduna, visited Lagos in 1937.

On the death of Usman in his twenty-fifth year on the throne, the council of selectors chose Haruna, son of Emir Abdulkadiri and then District Head of Guri, to be the 14th Emir of Hadejia. The aged Turaki, the senior councillor, died in 1957, and Hadejia suffered another loss by the death of the Ciroma in the following year.

[1] Quoted in H. F. Backwell, *The Occupation of Hausaland*, p. 61.

[2] A new version of the Moloney incident by an eye-witness, Hassan Keffi, is quoted in the forthcoming account of the Kano-Sokoto campaign by D. J. Muffett, entitled *Concerning Brave Captains*. See also the Keffi chapter, page 533.

THE EMIRS OF HADEJIA

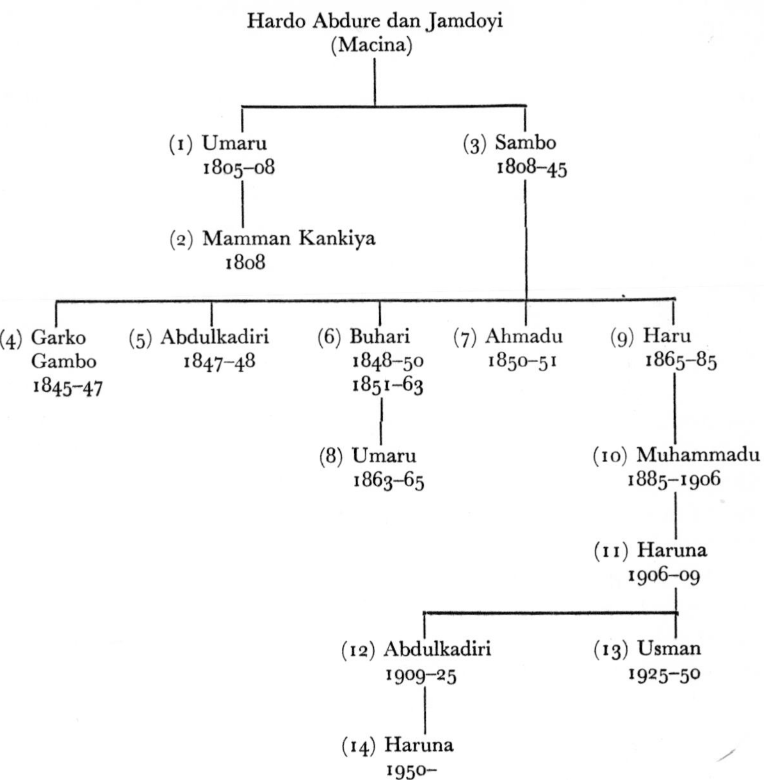

XXXVII. JAMA'ARE

LIKE Misau at the outbreak of the jihad, the people of Jama'are were in Bornu, their chief town being Dilara, near Lake Chad. Among the titles of the Emir of Jama'are to this day remains that of Sarkin Dilara. Some say that the name of the emirate derives from an amalgamation of *jema'a*, meaning 'people', and Mari, an alternative name for the Dilara plain. More likely is an extension of the Fulani form *jama'are*, 'people'.

When Usman dan Fodio started his campaigns, Muhammadu (Hammar) Wabi, the son of Ardo Sale the then chief, joined the side of the Fulani and probably took part with Gwani Mukhtar in the capture of Ngazargamu (Birni Bornu) in 1808. It is believed that Gwani Mukhtar, the founder of the Misau emirate, offered Muhammadu Wabi the *sarauta* of Madakin Bornu. There is some doubt whether Muhammadu Wabi actually accepted this title or not, but at any rate he refused to join Gwani Mukhtar permanently; in consequence he was not directly involved in his subsequent defeat. Muhammadu Wabi—he is also referred to locally as Watsi—is said to have received a flag from Usman dan Fodio about 1811 while the latter was still at Sifawa, though some sources maintain that a flag was not given until Sambolei received it from the Sarkin Musulmi in the 1830s. The re-establishment of the Bornu power under Al Kanemi drove the Fulani steadily westwards. In the course of this movement Muhammadu Wabi, who was then at Dawasa, attacked the Keri Keri of Gwajin near Potiskum about 1824. He died soon after.

He was succeeded by his brother Sambolei, who urged his people to go yet farther west until they should find fertile lands on which to pasture their herds. They finally came to a spot a little north of the present town of Jama'are, on the banks of a river. But no sooner were they settled than they received the full force of Shehu Laminu's attack in 1826. Many were captured and taken to Shira, but subsequently released on its recapture by Sarkin Bauchi, Yakubu, and Sarkin Katagum, Dan Kauwa. After this the site of the town was moved west of the present area, but was still without a wall. Sambolei took part in several raids into Bornu, the largest being about 1834, when with his allies the Emirs of Hadejia and Misau an attack was made on the border *Kacellawa* or slave-chiefs, established by Bornu for frontier defence, in which the latter were defeated with considerable loss.

Sambolei's outstanding exploit, however, was at the battle known as Yakin Gawakuke in 1835, in support of the call to arms by the Sarkin Musulmi, when he killed Rauda, the Habe King of Katsina. For this the Sultan offered him all the land he wished. But Sambolei is said to have replied that since his followers were so few, he would be content with the area encompassed by half a day's ride out from his town in each direction. This the Sultan of Sokoto granted him in recognition of his feat in having saved the Fulani empire from a Habe revolt and attempt to overthrow it. Thus the emirate was founded in the area of Gijip, the old Habe capital of Shira. Jama'are, however, had again to be evacuated about 1851 as a result of the Buhari wars with Hadejia. Gijip was sacked by Buhari's forces, and the people went to Tumfafi in Shira for six years. Sambolei was wounded at Juga, near Azare, in 1854 while on a raid to Bornu with Katagum and Misau, and died shortly afterwards at Jama'are. Jama'are was much too small to carry on wars on its own and was always the ally of some stronger emirate. It is, however, claimed that its smallness was made up for by military skill, particularly when led by Sambolei.

Sambolei was succeeded by his son Muhammadu Maude, who returned to Jama'are and started to build a walled town on the present site. Its walls were twenty feet high and pierced by four gates. Before this, however, he had taken part in the successful attack by Misau and Bauchi on Wase and the Tiv. Buhari's capture of Tashena about 1861 and subsequent raids again caused Jama'are to be evacuated. The population this time retired to Bana Kadai in Shira, and it was seriously considered whether they should go to Adamawa and rejoin the portion of their group who had gone there from Bornu in the days of the religious wars. Muhammad Maude died at Bana Kadai in 1862.

The new Emir was Muhammadu Sambo, a son of Muhammadu Wabi. During his reign the Ningawa were in the ascendant under Sarkin Ningi Haruna. Several raids were made by them, and in revenge Muhammadu Sambo joined Katagum and Hadejia in the rather profitless attack on Ningi about 1884. He gained a few local successes, but soon retired hastily, with Haruna in pursuit. Muhammadu Sambo also took part in the expedition to Biu with Sarkin Misau Sale in 1882, and was present at the capture of Liman Ya Musa at Gwadayi.

Muhammadu Sambo died in 1886 and was succeeded by his son Muhammadu Wabi II, who occupied the throne until his death in 1918. About 1887 he accompanied the Emir of Gombe to the Keri Keri country in the expedition in which Mallam Gaini (or Jibrilla) took part. This was shortly before Jibrilla's Mahdist operations in Gombe. Jama'are joined Sarkin Kano Aliyu in the attacks on the Ningawa. To this campaign Muhammadu Wabi sent his son Muhammadu (later the 6th Emir), who also represented him in the unsuccessful attacks on Malam Gaini after he had established himself at Bima. Jama'are took a more prominent part in the attack on Gwaram[1] in 1900 by Misau and Bauchi, being personally interested because Muhammadu Wabi's daughter was married to Sarkin Gwaram.

Jama'are was not much affected by Rabeh's presence. Trading relations existed, and the Jama'are representative only just escaped with his life when Fad-el-Allah was defeated by the French. Indeed, in a way, like other border emirates, Jama'are benefited by Rabeh's presence, as a considerable number of persons escaped from Bornu with property of which the Fulani emirs took due toll. Soon after the turn of the century there occurred the incident remembered in this part of north-eastern Nigeria as the *Perol.*[2] When the first Europeans were sighted in Jama'are, led by one nicknamed Mai Tuke, the people thought that the world was coming to an end. They packed their bags and fled eastwards, heading for Mecca. It is claimed that some got that far, but most returned to Jama'are soon after. Muhammadu Wabi submitted to the British after the capture of Kano in 1903. There is extant a letter from the Emir of Jama'are to the Emir of Kano giving information about the movements of the Europeans just before the conquest. It reads:

From Sarkin Dilara Muhammadu Wabi, son of Muhammadu Sambo. May Allah have mercy on him. Fullest greetings and blessing and good-will and honour and rest to the bull among Kings, lion of battles, refuge of small and great, who is above all his contemporaries

[1] See p. 462. [2] See p. 470.

in generosity and courage, the succour of mankind, Sarkin Kano Aliyu Baba, son of Sarkin Kano Abdullahi. May Allah be merciful to him and cause his reward to be in paradise. Amen.

After asking after your health I inform you that Sarkin Azare has said to us that Allah has been kind to us in the matter of the Christians, for they have returned to the east by way of Yaiyu. The Sarkin Yaiyu fled, and they settled down in Yaiyu and have made his relation chief of the country. They have declared Yaiyu to be part of Bornu and the river to be the boundary. Further to give you information about Ahmadu Sarkin Bornu,[1] he and all his people have fled to the west and we have not heard news of their return home. The Waziri of Azare returned home on Friday. This is the news we have to tell you. May Allah favour us with you. My present to you is two robes.[2]

Jama'are, like the other emirates in the Division, was for a few years made subordinate[3] to Katagum, but it was restored to its former independent position in 1907. Muhammadu Wabi died in 1918. Part of his marked influence may be ascribed to his relationship by marriage to Kano, Katagum, and Misau. This gave him considerable weight, although not enough to save Sarkin Gwaram from being executed.

He was succeeded by his son Muhammadu Goje, then Waziri, who ruled for ten years. By sending three of his sons to the royal school at Kano, opened in 1912, he gave a lead in western education. Emir Muhammadu divided his emirate into five districts, each under a councillor such as the Galadima and Dan Buram, while he himself was advised by a council consisting of the Waziri, Sarkin Yaki, Sarkin Fada and Majidadi.

On Muhammadu Gaji's death in 1928, his eldest son Muhammadu Wabi III, district head of the town, became Emir, at the age of twenty-eight. Shortly before his accession Jama'are was transferred from Kano to Bauchi Province. In 1932 the emirate administration was reorganized by eliminating districts and allowing the four village-area heads to deal direct with the Emir. An annual revenue of only £2,000, however, did not allow the N.A. much scope, so that Jama'are played a quiet role for many years.

[1] This refers to the Emir of Misau, who since the days of Gwani Mukhtar had borne the courtesy title of Sarkin Bornu ta Gabas in recognition by Sokoto of the part played in the wars with Bornu.

[2] H. F. Backwell, *The Occupation of Hausaland*, p. 68.

[3] Although this appears in official documents of the time, it is now denied by Jama'are N.A.

In the 1950s the Emir made history by personally leading a team composed of nearly every able-bodied man in the emirate on a community development project of constructing the Jama'are-Desina road, camping with them and encouraging them daily till the work was finished. A similar piece of exemplary self-help was recorded in 1959, again under the Emir's leadership. The joint veterinary service shared between Jama'are, Katagum and Misau has been a successful model for other emirates of similar limited resources faced by the demand for expensive services.

THE EMIRS OF JAMA'ARE

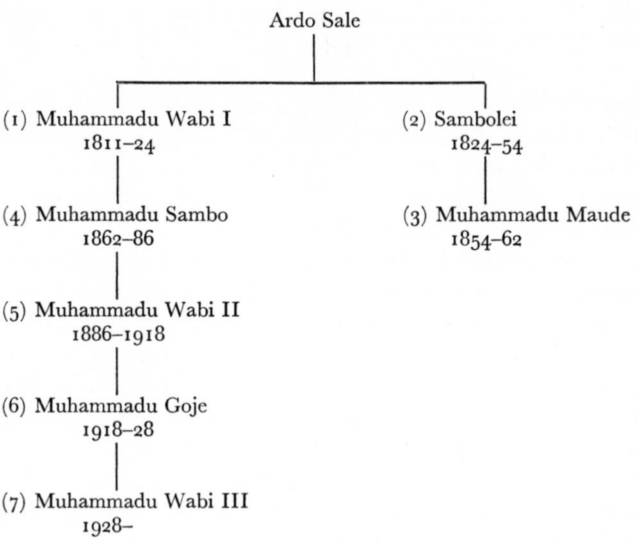

XXXVIII. MISAU

MISAU emirate is the creation of Gwani Mukhtar, the Fulani general who destroyed the capital of Bornu, Birni Ngazargamu, in 1808 and drove the Sef dynasty to seek refuge over by Lake Chad.

The earliest known leader of the Bornu Fulani was Akibu (sometimes Ukuba). He was followed in direct line of succession by Akibu II, Ardo Sulaiman and Yaro Fate. The last-named had a son, Sambo, a herdsman at Wuro Bokki in Bornu, who in due course became the *Ardo* of the Fulani. His son, Abubakar, married after he had attended a Koranic School, and his first child was named Gwani Mukhtar. When Gwani Mukhtar grew up, he was taught Arabic by a *malam* at Wuro Bokki, by name Gwani Lawal, whose daughter he eventually married. On Lawal's death, Gwani Mukhtar became the village head and *imam* of Wuro Bokki.

Gwani Mukhtar's early campaigns belong to the history of Bornu rather than Misau.[1] In outline, however, this is what happened. When Gwani Mukhtar heard of Shehu dan Fodio at Sifawa he paid homage to him, refusing allegiance to Mai Dunama, the king of Bornu, on the ground that the people of Bornu were not true Muslims. Then he proceeded to attack the non-Muslim towns in his country. On hearing of this, Mai Dunama sent his Madaki, Gangarama, to Gujba against Gwani Mukhtar, but the Madaki was defeated. Gwani Mukhtar now became a powerful chief, conquering all the neighbouring pagan districts, and finally proceeding eastwards without strong opposition until he reached Birni Ngazargamu, the capital of Bornu, which he took after a siege of seven days.

Gwani Mukhtar sent many of the spoils to Shehu dan Fodio, and stayed at Ngazargamu for seven months until he was ordered by Dan Fodio to return. It was during his journey back that Mai Dunama followed him and killed him. Gwani Mukhtar's son, Mamman, sent to Shehu dan Fodio and informed him of what had taken place. The Shehu sent Mamman a flag as head of the Bornu

[1] See pp. 318 ff.

Fulani. Thus, though the people of Misau were originally from Bornu, from now onwards they looked to Sokoto.

Mamman lived at Gujuba for five years and then founded his own town, Damaturu, a little to the north. During this time Aliyu, Manga's younger brother, complained to Sokoto that the people preferred him to Manga. Manga was deposed by the Waziri of Sokoto, Gidado, but all the Fulani followed him to his exile at Lafiyaji in Bornu, leaving only the Kanuri with Aliyu in Damaturu. When the Sultan heard this, he ordered the reappointment of Manga. From Damaturu, Manga moved to Guber, but was driven out by Shehu Laminu to Bauchi country.

Yakubu of Bauchi gave the fugitives land at Buri-Buri and, as he was then starting on a visit to Sokoto, Mamman Manga accompanied him. The Habe town of Misau was claimed by both Yakubu of Bauchi and Dan Kauwa of Katagum, who had captured it in 1827. But Mamman laid his case before the Sultan, who ordered Yakubu to give Misau to Mamman Manga. This is generally believed to have been in 1831. Manga and his people would really have preferred to return to Bornu, but the Sokoto Fulani were not strong enough to support such an inroad into Kanuri country. In Sokoto, Misau's title was, somewhat hopefully, *Sarkin Bornu ta Gabas*, 'the lord of Eastern Bornu'. He was empowered to levy *jangali* and *haraji* on all the Fulani of Bornu wherever they happened to be living at the time, a privilege that he exercised till about 1880.

Mamman Manga lived at Misau for two years until his death in 1833. He was succeeded by his brother, Ahmadu, in whose reign the town wall was built. He fought several campaigns against Bornu and captured many towns.

On Ahmadu's death, the Sultan of Sokoto appointed Usman, son of the first Emir of Misau, who was in turn succeeded by his brother Sale when the Sultan of Sokoto deposed him in 1861. Misau historians declare that Sale usurped the throne while his brother was away fighting for Sokoto. Usman died in exile at Yelwa near Bauchi. Sale was renowned in his long reign for his successful generalship in no less than seventy-two campaigns—the name of one of his horses is still remembered, Wauaro—and his pious observance of Islam. He died in 1886, aged seventy-two. Sale's son Mamman Manga became Emir but he died at Dafo on his way back from a visit to Kano in 1900. His brother Ahmadu joined the forces of the ex-Sultan of Sokoto at Burmi, from where he fled to Mecca. He and his followers settled on both banks of the White Nile in the Sudan. On Ahmadu's deposition the throne went to his brother Alhaji Tafida. Misau was placed under the Emir of Katagum in 1904, but its independence was restored in 1907 as a separate emirate in Kano Province.

In 1915 the minute and historically nebulous 'emirates' of Dambam and Jellum were brought under Misau as districts. On Alhaji's death in 1926, his son Ahmadu, then Waziri, became Emir. Youthful (he was only twenty-six) and educated, he made a significant impact on his emirate, closely supervising the work of Misau's six districts and personally giving the Native Treasury staff tuition in reading, writing and keeping the books of account. The Emir gained the reputation of being so knowledgeable about his Treasury office that he could tell within a matter of shillings the exact balance under each head of the estimates!

THE EMIRS OF MISAU

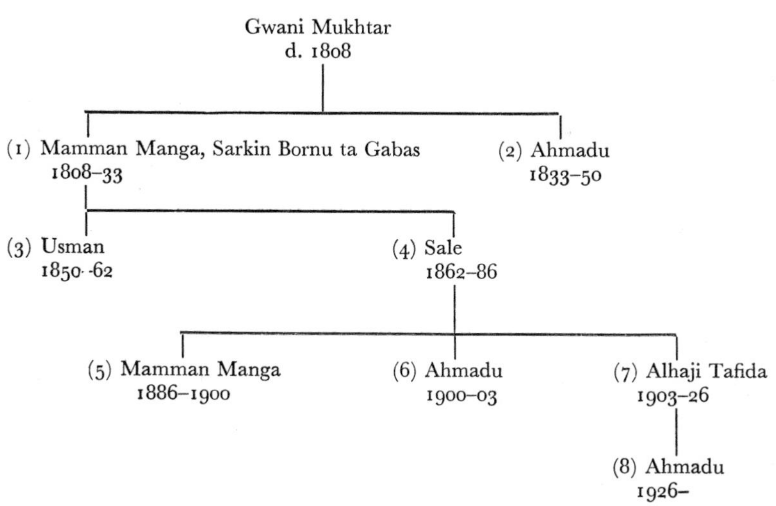

3. EMIRATES DERIVING FROM THE SOKOTO EMPIRE

(4) The South-Western States

XXXIX. KONTAGORA

THE founder of the present Kontagora dynasty was a famous Sokoto warrior called Umaru Nagwamatse. The origin of the name has yet to be clarified. One version is that Ahmadu dan Atiku built for Umaru the town of Gwamatse (five miles south-west of Wamako), but that the town would not fill owing to Umaru's tyrannical disposition, and on his return to Sokoto he became known as *Na Gwamatse*, 'the man from Gwamatse'. Another is that when Umaru was sent to Agwaragi to help in a campaign, the latter exclaimed *Asha! An gwamatse ni!*, 'alas! I have been put upon!' Yet a third interpretation is ascribed to Umaru's satisfied boast after his slave-raids: *na gwamatse* [*su*], 'I have harried them.' The rendering of Nagwamatse as 'the destroyer' would appear to be a *post hoc* derivation.

Umaru was born in 1806, the tenth son of Abubakar Atiku (2nd Sultan of Sokoto) and a grandson of Usman dan Fodio. This historically close relationship between Kontagora and Sokoto was poignantly illustrated on the death of the 4th Emir of Kontagora in 1961, when the Sardauna of Sokoto made an immediate air journey to Kontagora to offer his sympathies.

A typical adventurer, full of character and impatient of authority, Umaru proved a somewhat difficult person in Sokoto. It is said that he even snatched the hat from his father's head as he lay dying so that he might inherit his power. At the age of forty odd we find him entrusted with the command of a post on the Sabon Birni-Isa-Kaura road at Katuru, north of Kaura Namoda, to prevent the Gobirawa from raiding Zamfara by this route. His personality, his influence and his private fortune amassed from capturing slaves and levying exorbitant taxes on such a busy caravan route, were too much for his elder brother Ahmadu Zaruku (subsequently 4th Sultan of Sokoto). He grew jealous of him and caused Umaru to be recalled. Back in Sokoto he was humbled and stripped of his wealth.

But Umaru was too fine a fighting man to be kept in permanent idleness, so when a revolt broke out in Zamfara he was sent to Gummi to assist Agwaragi, Sarkin Mafara. This was the title given to the chiefs of Gummi who had submitted to the Sokoto Fulani. Nagwamatse spent two years raiding the surrounding country and again accumulating much spoil, but Agwaragi eventually complained to the Sarkin Musulmi that Nagwamatse was exceeding his instructions in an offensively high-handed manner. So powerful had he grown, however, that it was feared at the Sultan's Court that any letter recalling him would be bluntly ignored. By a stroke of good luck, a military expedition was about to be despatched to Hadejia under the Waziri, who was ordered to arrest Umaru on the way. He was brought back to Sokoto under escort. Tradition has it that the devout Muslims were so shocked at the sumptuous and gaudy robes in which Umaru was dressed that they persuaded the Sultan to have such finery destroyed as a humiliating punishment to the proud warrior.

Not long after this Umaru visited Gwandu, and hearing of the civil war raging in Nupe, he decided to go south and try his fortune. Welcoming the opportunity to reduce the claims of the many royal scions in Sokoto and particularly pleased to be rid of the troublesome Umaru, the Sultan sped his younger brother on the way with a string of horses to trade in Bida. When he arrived there, Umar Bahaushe had just revolted against Masaba, the representative of Gwandu in Nupe (the Etsu Nupe and 2nd Emir of Bida). Nagwamatse's assistance was refused, so he passed on to Abuja, Nassarawa, where he stayed two years, and Bauchi. He founded Ugu and Kagara, near Tegina, and then settled at Lalle. On the subsequent defeat of Umar by the combined forces of Umaru Majigi, Usman Zaki and Masaba, he made friends with his kinsman, and having attached Umar's defeated followers to himself he assisted Usman Zaki (now Emir of Nupe) to subjugate the surrounding country.

On Masaba's re-accession in 1859 Nagwamatse received permission to establish himself at Bogi, near Wushishi, where he

34

stayed for many years living on the spoils of his forays. There is today a large group of Nupe living in Kontagora emirate at the town of Zuguma, chiefly made up of those who fled and settled there during the Nupe wars of succession and perhaps increased by Umaru's troop of forty horsemen whom he was now allowed to recruit from Bida. Umaru was thus at last able to fulfil what must have been his life-long dream: to carve out a territory for himself of which he should be the undisputed king. He had an effective fighting force under his command, he had a secure base, and above all he was expanding into an area where there was little likelihood of his coming into conflict with any other Fulani ruler, for the people round Bogi were isolated groups of pagans such as the Gwari in the north and east and the Kamuku and Kambari to the west. Umaru's tactics were brutally successful and have been described in strong terms:

> He would descend on an area, send out raiding parties to harry the outlying hamlets, thus forcing the people to take refuge in the town. The town would then be besieged and systematically starved out—Umaru had no scruples about setting fire to the crops at harvest time and so adding the misery of famine to the other horrors of war in order to achieve his ends. From towns that agreed to surrender Umaru would demand immediate tribute in the form of slaves. He would then appoint an agent to take charge of the town and superintend the levying of taxes; taxation was at the exorbitant rate of ten thousand cowries a year from every household, no less than four times the rate being levied in Kano at the same time. In addition any member of Umaru's household or any official messenger was entitled to demand a dash of ten thousand cowries from any place in which he spent the night. If a town refused to surrender, it was taken by assault and all its inhabitants butchered or sent into slavery. It was the crudest, and cruellest form of imperialism; to satisfy one man's ambition families were torn asunder and flourishing communities wiped out.[1]

The extent of his conquests became more and more considerable, and in 1859, when his elder brother Zaruku became the Sarkin Musulmi, one of Zaruku's first acts was to confer the title of *Sarkin Sudan*, 'King of the Blacks', on his younger brother, doubtless in the hope of keeping him at a distance. Nagwamatse responded by large presents of slaves and horses to Sokoto. Communication with Sokoto, however, was threatened by the hostility

[1] R. Hallett, in his contribution on the kings of Kontagora in *Eminent Nigerians*.

of the Kamuku at Koton Koro, situated across the caravan route, and this led to a long and desultory war with their chief, Sarkin Bamu.

Nagwamatse now turned his eyes to the Kambari and Yauri country. At this time there were two rival chiefs of Yauri, Dan Gajere at Masamagu, some fifteen miles west of Kontagora, and Dan Addo on an island in the Niger called Ikum. Nagwamatse assisted Dan Gajere, but in doing so he established himself strongly in the Kambari country, building himself the town of Kontagora in about 1864. According to tradition, Umaru at the end of a long day's march through the bush came across a site that appealed to him and said to his followers *kwanta gora*, 'lay down the water-bottle'. Another story is that in those days every traveller carried his gourd with him. When Umaru's men had finished building their new town, he wanted to tell his people that they could now put aside their water-bottles; but instead of saying *ajiye gora*, 'put down your gourds', he said *kwanta gora*, 'lay down your gourds'. Whatever the origin of the name, it was from this new headquarters that Umaru waged war afresh with the Kamuku, and eventually succeeded in capturing Koton Koro and Womba, driving away a Maradi chief named Dan Zambari who had come down to assist the Kamuku.

Nagwamatse at one time or another raided the Bassa, Kambari, Tauri, Gwari, Kamuku, Dakarawa, and Dukawa towns round Kontagora; but in 1871 Almustafa, Sarkin Gwandu, came to Kontagora and warned him to keep his hands off Yauri, which was under the suzerainty of Gwandu.

Nagwamatse died at Anaba in 1876 at the age of seventy, being succeeded by his son, Modibbo, who had settled in Wushishi. Modibbo died in Kontagora four years later and was succeeded by his brother Ibrahim, a young man of twenty-three, who was officially installed as Sarkin Sudan from Sokoto.

Ibrahim soon made himself felt by assisting Umaru Majigi, Etsu Nupe, to exterminate the last remnants of the Habe Nupe under Etsu Baba in Zuguma and Leaba. After this he made several raids on the Gwari, at one time coming to his father's old headquarters near Wushishi, after Umaru Majigi had been repulsed from Minna by the Gwari. His raids extended to the River Gurara, and his kingdom now stretched from the Gurara near Abuja right across to Leaba on the Niger, a belt one hundred and fifty miles long and perhaps fifty miles broad. Kontagora itself was now a vast war-camp, with a population of over twenty thousand.

Returning to Kontagora, Ibrahim was summoned by the Sarkin Musulmi to aid Tukur, Sarkin Kano, against Aliyu, but he wisely excused himself.

Again he attacked the Gwari and besieged Birnin Gwari. The Gwari were assisted by the Gobirawa and Habe from Maradi, but Ibrahim severely routed them and captured the town.

He continued to raid the Zuru-Dabai and Yauri country to the north, usually with success, but suffered severe reverses at the hands of the Dakarawa at Penin Amana, barely escaping with his life, and again in Abuja emirate. We have an excellent account of this second battle:

> When Ibrahim Nagwamatse, Emir of Kontagora, the Sarkin Sudan, . . . came down to raid the town of Kurmin Gurmana, they sent to the Emir of Abuja to help them. . . . The Kuyambana advised that he should go himself against the Fulani whilst the Madawaki stayed to help the Emir with the defence of the town and countryside in case of surprise. He asked for footmen and horsemen of the best, so the Emir gave him four hundred foot and two hundred horse; but some of the foot went back for they could not keep up with the horses, and the Kuyambana sent back some of the horsemen to help the Emir, keeping only one hundred and fifty with him.
>
> Now the Kuyambana told the men of Gusoro and the men of Kurmin Gurmana to take twine from the *kalgo* tree and bind elephant grass on their heads so that he should know them from the enemy and not kill them by mistake in the heat of the battle. So the men of these two towns did as they were told; Gusoro bound their heads with twine from the *kalgo* tree, and Kurmin Gurmana wore elephant grass. When the battle began, the Fulani saw the men of Abuja give ground, and they pressed forward to rout them, for they did not know that this retreat was a trick. But when he had drawn the Fulani away from Nagwamatse's camp, the Kuyambana ordered the Gwari of Gusoro and of Kurmin Gurmana to make their way round to the rear and set fire to it, for when they should see their camp on fire, the Fulani would surely rush back to it. So, whilst the fight went on, the Gwari set fire to the Fulani camp.
>
> When the Kuyambana saw the smoke rising up, he called out, taunting the Fulani, 'I see clouds of smoke behind you. Is yours a dye-pit or a war camp that such fires burn in it?' And when the Fulani saw the fires, they wheeled round and galloped back to their camp, but they could not get in, for the Gwari of Gusoro and of Kurmin Gurmana

covered it with their arrows. Now the Kuyambana and his people drove the enemy before them with great slaughter, until the Emir of Kontagora saw that there was nothing for it but to abandon his camp with his store of kolanuts to the flames.

At dawn the next day, the Gwari went back to the Fulani camp and came across countless piles of kolanuts, all scorched. They had never seen kolanuts before, so they began to pick out those which were not too badly charred and to cook them like yams, for they supposed that it was some kind of food. When the nuts were cooked, they pulled them out to cool, and when they were cool, each man took one and put it in his mouth. But the taste was bitter, and when they tasted the bitterness they spat it out.

So the Fulani of Kontagora had neither pleasure nor profit from their meeting with the Kuyambana, for the numbers who were slain were beyond reckoning. They went back about seven hundred and fifty horses fewer than they came, without counting those who were picked off in the bush, for it was the arrogant custom of the Fulani to go out to battle dressed in their finest Feast Day robes, voluminous garments which prevented them from moving fast. But when the men of Abuja went to war, they put on short trousers to the knee, and coats reaching only to the trousers top; and in the bush, amongst the trees, they could move freely, for they carried no great banners of flags but could gallop their horses through copse or gorge or thicket.[1]

Armed horsemen, *'yan pila*, from Kontagora ravaged rural Zaria at the turn of the century and extended Ibrahim's marches right up to the south-west boundary of Zaria emirate. In 1899 Ibrahim led his Kontagora forces right into Zaria territory and overpowered the Habe chiefdom of Birnin Gwari, situated in the no-man's land between Zaria and Katsina. Zaria chroniclers ascribe this incursion into a brotherly emirate as being undertaken at the instigation of the Sultan of Sokoto who wished to inflict a sharp lesson on the Zaria Fulani for their snub to his authority by their compelling through force of arms his Waziri to recommend the accession of Kwassau instead of the Mallawa candidate to the throne on the death of the Emir of Zaria, Yero.[2]

When it was heard that Abarshi, Sarkin Yauri, had assisted the British troops at Yelwa, Ibrahim received orders from Sokoto to arrest Abarshi and take over Yauri. He summoned Abarshi to meet him at Shonga, but took no further action and returned to Kontagora, where another Nupe revolt was in progress. He

[1] Hassan and Shu'aibu, *A Chronicle of Abuja*, 1962, pp. 17–18. [2] See p. 230.

quelled this drastically. A few months afterwards the British forces, alarmed by the defiant menace of Sarkin Sudan, advanced into Kontagora. Early in 1901 Lieut.-Colonel Kemball attacked Kontagora town from the west or Niger side, Yauri having already submitted. The resistance was slight, and the Emir and his army were hotly pursued eastwards. Lugard then sent a letter to the Sultan of Sokoto in which he said:

In the name of the Most Merciful God. Peace be to the Generous Prophet.

Salutations, peace, and numberless honours. To the Emir of Mussulmans in Sokoto, whose name is Abdul-Lahai, the son of the late Emir of the Mussulmans, whose name is Atiku.

I desire to inform you who are head of the Mohammedans and to whom the Fulani rulers in this country look for advice and guidance that the Emirs of Bida and Kontagora have during many years acted as oppressors of the people and shewn themselves unfit to rule. More especially in these latter days they have raided the towns and villages in the districts close to their own cities, and have depopulated vast areas so that the fields are lying uncultivated and the people are destroyed or fled. Moreover they have gratuitously attacked my men when proceeding with mails or canoes, and have seized the mails, and stolen and destroyed goods in the canoes. I have therefore found it necessary to depose both these Emirs, and to place troops near their respective cities to keep the peace and protect the people. . . .

In the case of Kontagora, many evil people tried to burn the town. It may have been the slaves who had been ill-treated by their masters or it may have been the carriers with my troops. But through all the night the Commander of the Force made the soldiers and carriers extinguish the flames, so that the town has not suffered.

I desire that the people shall return and live in peace under a just ruler, and I write to you to appoint a man who will rule justly, and if he does so I will support him and uphold his power; send him to me with a letter, and I will install him as Emir of Kontagora with pomp and honour. But warn him that if he acts treacherously and with deceit he will share the fate of Kontagora the Gwamachi.

With peace from your friend Governor Lugard.[1]

As all the Nagwamatse family had fled, Abarshi Sarkin Yauri was installed. But neither he nor his son Gani could tolerate the position, so that a trial was made with one Mayaki Ibrahim, a

[1] This appears as an appendix to the *Annual Report for Northern Nigeria*, 1902.

Nupe who had taken service with Sarkin Yauri and had accompanied the British troops entering Kontagora.

Early in 1902 Ibrahim, who had collected another large following running into several thousands, made a camp for himself at Kaya in Zaria emirate and started to terrorize the country round about by his raids. The end came suddenly. Early one morning two British officers and a handful of troopers galloped into the camp and arrested Ibrahim before he could resist. One of these officers was Captain Abadie, the first Resident of Zaria and still remembered as *mai-jimina* because of his pet ostrich. We have an interesting eye-witness[1] account of this bold event:

> The Emir of Kontagora had sworn that when he took Zaria, which seemed to be very imminent, for the people were running away in numbers in sheer terror, ours would be the first heads to fall! . . . Bargery and I were sitting about 11 a.m. in the little room which had been given to us and which we used as bedroom and sitting room, a mud-grass hut when, to our surprise, a man appeared with a 'chit' in a cleft corn-stalk. I opened it and read:
>
> 'Dear Miller, will you come out to the "Kofar Gayam" this afternoon at 5 p.m. and have tea with me? I arrived an hour ago with Nagwamachi in chains.
>
> Yours sincerely
>
> George Abadie.'
>
> I went to the Emir to tell him what had happened—he had already heard. In the afternoon I found Abadie, as he had said, and Nagwamachi with chains on wrists and ankles. We sat down to a delightful little tea which might have been in a West End drawing-room instead of a dusty plain in Central Africa, and Abadie, an old friend, then told me his story, which was one of the most romantic I have ever listened to or read. I give it as far as I remember almost in his own words so vivid was the impression on my mind.
>
> Lugard, having heard at Zungeru of the peril to Zaria, had given Captain Abadie, a senior administrative officer and a great friend of Lugard's, fifty Mounted Infantry, Hausas, with three or four English non-commissioned officers, the whole under Major Porter, with instructions to ride 'Hell for leather' and take Nagwamachi prisoner. They had ridden their horses almost beyond endurance and done a thirteen days journey in under five days. Nearly all the men and their horses were tired out and when Abadie and Porter with the N.C.O.s and about four or five native Mounted Infantry arrived at the top of

[1] The writer is Walter Miller.

a hill and saw Nagwamachi's huge camp spread out below a quick decision had to be made; to wait for the rest of the detachment would ensure detection . . . So Abadie rapped out to Porter, 'Can we do it?' and the typical English soldier's 'of course we can' was as quickly given. The seven or eight of them putting spurs to their tired horses, galloped down the side of the hill, made for the biggest hut which would be the Emir's, found him, and, through sheer bluff before any of that enormous crowd could show any resistance, they clapped hand-cuffs on the Emir's wrists, and then, through one of the Hausa soldiers, proclaimed that the White man had no quarrel with any but the Emir and his chiefs and that they might all go home—which they did. And so Abadie brought his prisoner with the grandiloquent title 'King of the Sudan' into Zaria. In all my experience of Nigerian events this was, I think, the epic.

Ibrahim was first imprisoned in Lokoja and then exiled to Yola. His chiefs had almost all escaped capture and had fled to Sokoto, but a great number of his followers submitted and were allowed to return home. In 1903 it was decided to allow Ibrahim to return, but his powers as Emir were greatly curtailed. Shortly afterwards he was charged with slave-dealing, but was pardoned by the High Commissioner. Not for nothing does the legend still live that on being urged to give up slave-raiding, Ibrahim replied to his British captors: 'Can you stop a cat from mousing? When I die, I shall be found with a slave in my mouth.' But the terrible effect of this slaving can be seen even today in Kontagora emirate:

If you make the journey, just over a hundred miles, between Jebba and Kontagora, you will find yourself travelling for miles and miles without catching sight of a village. The map—especially the map which shows the density of population—makes the same point. Kontagora has a lower density of population than any other district in the Northern Region, Borgu in Ilorin Province alone excepted. But much of Borgu is waterless and so uninhabitable; there are no obvious geographical reasons to explain why Kontagora should be so thinly populated, to account for the fact that when the first effective census of Northern Nigeria was taken in 1921, it was found that there were less than seven people to the square mile in Kontagora, while the average for the north was well over twenty. The reason why Kontagora is still so bereft of population is a simple and terrible one—for fifty years first Umaru, then Ibrahim made the area their hunting-ground for slaves. If you travel through the bush in Kontagora District you still can see the ruined walls of wasted and desolate towns, unoccupied since they were destroyed sixty and more years ago. Often, as with the battlefields of France after the First World War, or the shattered towns of Germany after the Second, the destruction caused by war is effaced in remarkably few years. In Kontagora this has not happened; despite the progress of the last fifty years, the land is still disfigured by the scars of the wounds caused by the slave-raiders.[1]

Back in favour, Ibrahim was recognized as a first-class chief in 1906 and all his districts, except for the Dakarawa and Gwari areas, were restored to him. An artificial emirate had been created in Sakaba in 1903 but its incumbent, a Nupe of humble birth called Ibrahim who as a favourite of Sarkin Yauri had been appointed Mayaki, became so involved with his Waziri in highway robbery and extortion that he was obliged to retire in 1913. The Dakarawa now became a 'Pagan Division', whose chiefs were directly responsible to Government, but in 1919 their Sarkin Dabai was recognized as a paramount chief of a loose federation which eventually developed into the Zuru N.A. Another change in the emirate structure occurred in 1907 when part of Borgu Province was amalgamated with Kontagora. This lasted till 1925 when the whole of Kontagora Province was broken up and Kontagora emirate became a separate Division in the new Niger Province.

Ibrahim, 3rd Emir of Kontagora, had shown a remarkable ability to move with the times, for after his chequered career at the turn of the century he was in 1929 honoured by an award bestowed at Zungeru in the presence of all the Niger chiefs in July. Sadly enough, he was not destined to enjoy this new honour for long, for he died suddenly on 26 October of the same year, aged seventy-two. So passed away the last of the Emirs who had made personal submission to Lugard. He was succeeded by his eldest son, Umaru Maidubu, who was installed in 1931. The new Emir's progressive views, it was reported, did not find favour with the ultra-conservative councillors or with the district heads.

The chiefdom of Wushishi, Nagwamatse's erstwhile war-camp, was in 1933 transferred from Zungeru to Kontagora Division, along with the Kamuku and Allawa Gwari chiefs. The Sarkin Wushishi, though *de jure* independent, was so closely related to the

[1] Hallett, op. cit. There is some ground for believing that Nagwamatse's career has been over-blackened, and an Arabic MS. discovered in Kontagora by E. Lannert of the U.S. Peace Corps in 1963 may shed fresh light on this. It has been sent to the Secretary of the Nigerian Historical Society.

Emir of Kontagora that he was often described as the Emir's lieutenant. Wushishi had been a great help to Lugard.

The following year saw a big change in the emirate administration. There appeared to be no good reason for the maintenance of no less than eight district-headships, so when the aged district head of Kontagora District retired, no successor was appointed by the Emir. Instead, village-heads had direct dealings with the Emir. The same process was repeated on the dismissal of the district head of Rijau, and the tribal groups of the Dukawa, Kambari and Hausa-Fulani were also brought under the direct control of the Emir. This was not a popular move, as the village heads soon expressed a desire for the intermediate authority of a district head, but it suited a forward-looking Administration that, a score of years ahead of policy, envisaged district councils functioning without an official chairman.

Umaru Maidubu was one of the first people in Kontagora emirate to buy a plough and a yoke of oxen, thus giving the area a good start in mixed farming. Figures show, however, that his enthusiasm received no support from the people of Kontagora. Happily, cotton caught on well and restored Kontagora, so long in the development doldrums, to the economic map. Within a year the purchase of cotton-seed jumped from 29 to 120 tons; only in neighbouring Kamuku had the Resident to report that 'a few clodhoppers used their supply of cotton-seed for making soup'! In 1935 the Emir made his first visit to Lagos. In the next two decades Umaru Maidubu succeeded in welding his council together into what was officially acclaimed as 'an admirable example of teamwork between age and youth, both working together and combining sage experience and drive for the benefit of the community'. The Emir's council was enlarged in 1955, including the first representative of the Kambari. Three years later a joint committee was set up with tiny Wushishi to look after financial and police affairs. The Kontagora Land Settlement Scheme, one of several experiments in resettlement made after the war with uneven results, was liquidated in 1956.

The Resident reported that the destruction of the Native Treasury records in a mysterious fire in 1959—alleged to have been caused by lightning, despite the absence of any thunderstorm conditions reported by the meteorological authorities—revealed that the administration of the emirate had fallen away. The Emir was too old to take matters in hand, and as some of his councillors were involved Kontagora had perforce to undergo a long period of stagnation. Umaru Maidubu died early in 1961 and was succeeded by his sixty-year-old brother Mu'azu Sarkin Bauchi, previously the district head of Rijau for thirteen years.[1]

THE EMIRS OF KONTAGORA

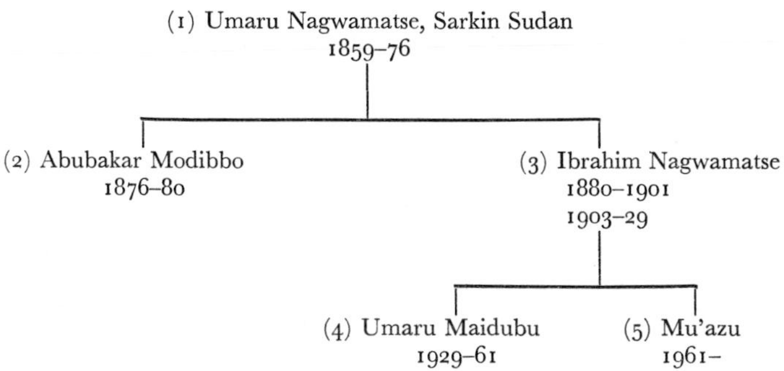

[1] As a matter of historical curiosity, Kontagora and Bida shared the dubious distinction of being the only courts of first-class Emirs without full grade A powers, namely those of trying capital offences. In Lord Lugard's time the Resident recommended Grade A court powers for the court, but the proposal was not acceded to by the Lieutenant-Governor of the day, and the powers were not exercised by the court. In a despatch to the Secretary of State dated 13 October 1915, Lord Lugard pointed out that the number of courts with full powers had increased since he left Northern Nigeria in 1906; and it may have been that Kontagora was one of these. In 1935, however, a reduction in the powers of six courts with full powers took place, and Kontagora was one of these.

XL. AGAIE

BEFORE the advent of the Fulani the country was in the hands of the Ganagana. This is the Hausa term for the people known today among the Nupe as Dibo or Zitako. Before them again there are vague traditions of a people called the Mama, whom the Ganagana are said to have ousted. Etsu Majiya I (*c.* 1770) was the overlord of the Agaie Ganagana.

Among the companions of Malam Dendo, the Fulani founder of the Fulani dynasty in Bida, was a Fulani friend of his, Malam Baba, son of a certain Katsina *malam*, Attahiru. Baba had fled to Ilorin with Malam Dendo when Etsu Majiya II drove the Fulani *malamai* out of Raba at about the turn of the century. Now he set out to conquer a kingdom for himself. Following the counsel of Malam Dendo, he and his party of twelve men headed northwards, raiding the countryside as they went but always travelling by night for fear of interception by Nupe soldiers. His troop grew into a small army as he marched into the heart of Nupe country. Finally he camped at Nko-Shepa, some three miles west of present-day Agaie, in a spọt still marked by the *rimi* or silk-cotton tree, and established yet another Fulani emirate in Nupeland.

Crushing local Nupe revolts and repulsing the attacks of Etsu Majiya who claimed sovereignty over Agaie, Malam Baba next turned to the offensive and enlarged his kingdom by new conquests. He subdued part of the Bataci people on the river and made himself master of a wide tract of land stretching southwards to the Niger and westwards to the Kaduna river. Though he also seized Katca and conquered the Gwari of Payi, the first subsequently fell to Bida and the second became the emirate of Lapai under Daudu Maza. The latter had been Baba's chief general or Mayaki but he had preferred to cut loose from Agaie and establish his own independent kingdom.[1]

[1] I have to express my thanks to a large number of Agaie *malamai* who helped me put together an outline of the emirate history when I was A.D.O. Bida in 1954. The original MS. is in the Agaie District Notebook. Since then, an Agaie *malam* has compiled a local history.—A.K-G.

In 1832, after a rule of ten years, Malam Baba obtained permission from Gwandu for his son Abdullahi to be installed as Emir, he himself merely acting as Regent. He lived until 1848.

Muhammadu, known as Mamman Dikko, succeeded Abdullahi in 1857. In alliance with Jantabu, Emir of Lapai, he had joined Masaba, Etsu Nupe, in the struggle against his foreign mercenary rebel, Umar Bahaushe. Masaba one day unwisely started to raid the Agaie farms, and only desisted when the Emir of Agaie appealed to the Sarkin Sudan of Kontagora for help. On a later occasion, the boot was on the other foot, for the Emir of Agaie raided the territory of the Etsu Nupe and was only stopped by a full-scale campaign led by the Emir of Gwandu in person, acting as the highest feudal overlord of all the Fulani emirs in the western half of Usman dan Fodio's empire. Thereafter Agaie seems to have co-operated with Bida in her slave-raiding expeditions.

Against the advice of their Emir, Nuhu, the Agaie chiefs assisted Bida against the Niger Company, and suffered as a consequence. Agaie was occupied and Lapai was burnt. Abubakar succeeded Nuhu in 1900, but this time Agaie took no part in the subsequent battle of Bida. After a wise and successful rule of nineteen years he died at an advanced age in Agaie in July 1919. He was succeeded by Abubakar, Kpotun of Kuturiko, who reigned until 1926, when Abdullahi, the grandson of Muhammadu, the 3rd Emir, came to the throne.

In 1921 the headquarters of the Agaie-Lapai Division were returned to Agaie from Baro, whither they had been transferred at the time of the building of the Baro-Minna railway line some twelve years earlier. A further administrative reorganization occurred in 1933 when the Division was broken up and Agaie was joined with its Nupe brothers in Bida Division. In the following year the emirate was reorganized into a single unit by eliminating the office of district heads and allowing the village-heads to come under the direct control of the emir.

On the death of Emir Abdullahi, suddenly from a chill, in April 1935, the council of selectors chose Aliyu. At the time of his appointment he was in the curious position of being the only surviving member of the Agaie N.A. Council. After a shaky start the new council settled down. It required strengthening on several occasions, notably in 1938 and in 1952 by the appointment of a wise old ward head from Agaie town.

On succeeding to the throne in 1953, the new Emir, Muhammadu Bello, found the council facing yet another crisis and a complete reorganization was undertaken. This was continued by the introduction of an elected majority on the N.A. Council in 1958.

THE EMIRS OF AGAIE

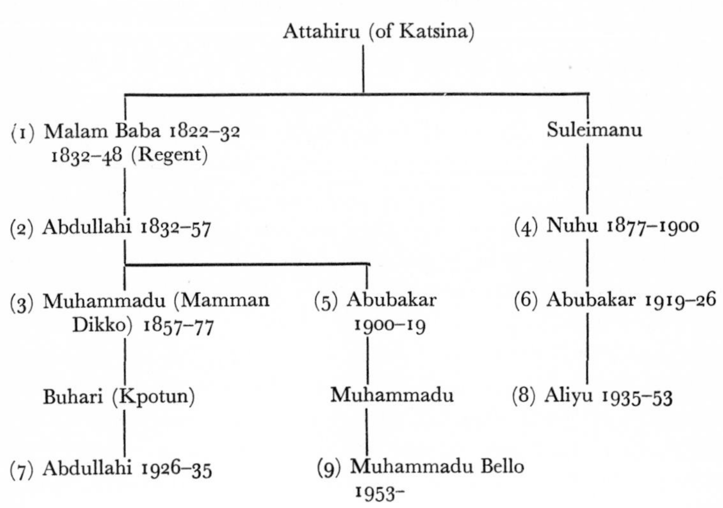

XLI. LAPAI

The first records of the Fulani settlement at Lapai date from the arrival of one Dampami, a Cow-Fulani from Damatumaki. He owed allegiance to Isiaku, the Habe king of Zaria at the end of the eighteenth century, and bore the title of Sarkin Fulani. At that time the dominant Gwari of Lapai, then known as Payi, were ruled by Habe vassal chiefs of Zazzau.

Of the establishment of Fulani rule in Lapai there are two tales. One is that Dampami's grandson, Daudu Maza, was head of the local group of Bororo'en, nomadic Fulani, around Lapai when the jihad broke out in Gobir. He travelled to Sokoto, received a flag from Abdullahi, Emir of Gwandu, and was entrusted with the conquest of the country round Lapai. The more probable version is that Daudu Maza was the war general or *Mayaki* of Malam Baba, founder of Agaie, and on one of his forays for his king in which he overran Lapai he decided to break away and set himself up as an independent chief. Makau, the ousted Habe king of Zaria whom the Fulani had driven south to Abuja, tried to overpower Daudu Maza but was killed near the gates of the present town in 1825.

Once firmly established in Lapai, Daudu Maza asked the Etsu (Emir) Nupe to be his overlord in preference to the Emir of Zaria, whose vassal Lapai had remained despite the change of dynasty from Habe to Fulani in Zaria in 1804. The Emir of Bida reported this request to his liege, the Emir of Gwandu, who was suzerain of the western states of the Sokoto empire, and Daudu Maza was recognized as Emir of Lapai.

Daudu Maza died in 1832 and was succeeded by his brother Yamusa, who reigned for four years. Popular opinion was against the next brother, Jantabu, so that a younger brother, Baji, was elected Emir in his stead. In a fit of disgusted fury, Jantabu withdrew from Lapai town and started to build the settlement known as Birnin Jantabu, fifteen miles south-east of Lapai near the Gurara river. In the event, no more than the walls of the town were built, for he was soon able to depose Baji, weak and licentious, without difficulty. Jantabu had him arrested and sent to the Emir of Gwandu. Lapai historians agree that Baji died shortly afterwards in mysterious circumstances. In Sokoto there is a tradition that he was executed by the Emir of Gwandu on a charge of highway robbery and the murder of some pilgrims on their way back from Mecca.

Jantabu is the great figure in Lapai Fulani history. Under his strong and able leadership for thirty-six years the emirate prospered. During his reign imported cloth first made its appearance in Lapai. Jantabu extended the borders of Lapai down to the Niger. On his death he is said to have left a vast personal fortune, including 2,000 cows, 600 horses and over a thousand slaves. In about 1872 the Emir of Gwandu found it necessary to journey to Bida in person and iron out the rival claims of Lapai, Agaie and Bida over Nupeland.

Lapai now lapsed into a sorry state. Atiku, Jantabu's son, who succeeded him, died a year later; a second son, Bawa, something of a profligate, died in 1893. His brother, the 7th emir, Abdulkadiri, was little better, and was extremely unpopular owing to his drunken habits. The Yerima, Ibrahim, his brother, was approached with a view to deposing him, but Ibrahim refused. So bitter was the feeling against the Emir that, according to Lapai historians, yet another claimant was brought forward and the traditional insignia of royal office, turban, *alkyabba*, gown and trousers, were prepared for him. The resolute attitude of the Emir was not without its effect. On his defying the revolutionary party and declaring that he would never leave his palace alive, it was agreed that the real power—though not the outward signs of power—should devolve upon the Yerima, Ibrahim, who should act as a sort of regent. This compromise satisfied the Emir's followers, obviated the necessity of outside intervention by Government, and pleased the people of Lapai.

In 1907 Abdulkadiri abdicated, dying three years later, and Ibrahim became the 8th Sarkin Lapai. He died in 1923 and was succeeded by Aliyu Gana, a grandson of Daudu Maza. Ten years later Lapai was transferred to Abuja Division on the break-up of the Agaie-Lapai Division; memories of the old wars between Lapai and Abuja were only momentarily recalled. Another change took place in 1936 when it was decided to move the emirate headquarters to a healthier site at Badeggi-Lapai, nine miles to the west of the old capital. This took place two year later.

Emir Aliyu died in April 1937. 'He was of the older generation,' the provincial annual reports comment, 'was impatient with progress and reform, and his administration . . . occasioned adverse criticism.' Furthermore, petty dynastic quarrels had marked the last years of Aliyu Gana's reign. He was succeeded by Umaru, son of the 8th Emir Ibrahim. On his installation he was plainly reminded of the need to survey and improve the 'administration left by his high-handed predecessor'. One of the first steps was to reform the N.A. Council, which merely comprised the Emir's son and his cousin. Then, admirably assisted by his new councillors, the Wakili (ex-Alkali) and the Ndeji, the Emir set about the task of bringing back the flesh and blood of a healthy district administration.

During the final years of his reign, Umaru was so bed-ridden that the day-to-day affairs of the emirate were left in the hands of his council. On his death in November 1954, at the age of seventy-two, the selectors chose Muhammadu Kobo, then Tswaida and a councillor in Bida N.A., to be Emir. Because of the Emir's resentment at the decision on ethnic grounds to remove the Gawun enclave from his jurisdiction—still officially described as an 'obsession' as late as 1961[1]—it was some time before the new Emir was officially installed. In 1956 the emirate was brought into Bida Division, not without some reluctance on Lapai's part. Two years later the Emir of Lapai played a distinguished part in leading the Northern Nigerian Government's judicial survey delegations to Pakistan and Libya, and in 1961 he was appointed chairman of the Government's commission of inquiry into the maladministration of a major sister emirate.

[1] *Annual Report for Niger Province*, 1961.

THE EMIRS OF LAPAI

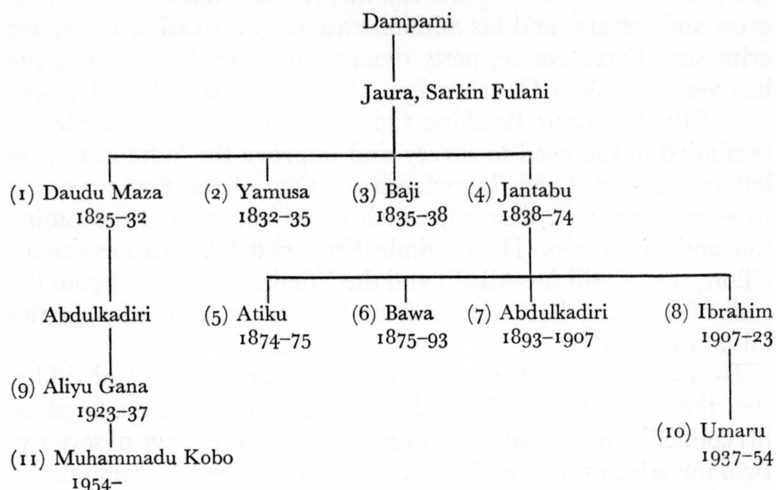

XLII. PATEGI

THE history of the emirate of Pategi—the name derives from a Nupe word meaning 'a small hill'—is of unusual interest because it is based on the reinstallation of a pre-Fulani local dynasty. In this respect, Pategi merits classification along with Daura; and it is because of this unique emirate feature that the Nupe of Pategi strongly reject Bida's claim to the title of *Etsu Nupe* or 'king of the Nupe people', insisting that they alone are the original Nupe royal family. They point to a descent unadulterated by marriage such as had occurred in the Bida, Agaie, Lapai and Lafiagi royal houses and claim direct descent from Tsoede, 'he of the scratched face'. The royal family today proudly bears the traditional stomach marking of the royal house of Tsoede.[1]

We show, in the chapter dealing with the history of Nupe, how the Fulani dynasty of Bida maintained the aboriginal Nupe royal house in that town, nominally as honoured guests but in practice as little more than hostages. Many Nupe had, for fear of Masaba's Fulani in Bida, emigrated to the Yoruba country, from where they paid tribute to Ma'azu Isa, the son of Idrisu, whom alone they recognized as their Etsu. On Ma'azu's death in 1872, it is claimed by Nupe historians that the Sultan of Sokoto agreed that Idrisu Gana, Ma'azu's son, should be acknowledged as Etsu Nupe. In the event, power remained in the hands of Masaba though Nupe on both sides of the Niger continued to pay tribute to Idris Gana.

When the Royal Niger Company occupied Bida in 1897, the Etsu of the non-Fulani Nupe at Jimada, Idrisu Gana, refused to help the Fulani Nupe in their defence of the town. Indeed, he played a material role in contributing to the downfall of Bida, for he concentrated all the canoes belonging to the riverain Nupe at Pategi and thus prevented the Bida armies, then operating south of the Niger in Kabba country, from joining up with the main force in Bida. History suggests that while the Bida Nupe were content to live under the Dendo dynasty, the Jimada Nupe had

[5] See the photograph in *Nigeria Magazine*, No. 50, 1956, p. 268, and the Nupe chapter, pp. 261 ff.

never really accepted the alien imposition and were throughout the nineteenth century seldom slow to seize an opportunity for disaffection. Now, on the withdrawal of the Company troops from Bida, the Agent-General, William Wallace, took Idrisu Gana with him to Pategi, opposite the confluence of the Kaduna and the Niger. The town had been founded at the end of the sixteenth century by the Etsu Nupe, but it shrank to nonentity when a later Etsu moved his headquarters elsewhere. Not until 1845 did Pategi come into prominence again, when Masaba of Bida built the fortified town of Lade, nine miles west of Pategi, as his war-camp against the Yagba; and power returned to the Pategi area. Here, as a reward for his services, Wallace installed Idrisu Gana as an independent Etsu Nupe in 1898. With him came a group of traditional Nupe blacksmiths, under their own *Dokodza*, from Gbara, the ancient residence of the Jimada branch of the aboriginal Nupe dynasty.

Idrisu, the 1st Emir of Pategi and the 23rd Etsu Nupe as some would have it,[1] died in 1900. He was succeeded by his son Ma'azu, who reigned for twenty-three years. The next Emir was Idrisu's brother, Usmanu. A clash of interests between the Yagba and Nupe elements in the local administration led to an inquiry into the affairs of the emirate. Usmanu abdicated in 1931 and in his stead Umaru, grandson of Pategi's first Emir, was appointed to the throne. Soon after his accession, the Yagba district of Pategi was transferred to Kabba Province.

The Emir's superior education in a Government school, at that time an unusual qualification for a chief, at once endeared him to his people, whom he has now led for over thirty years. In 1956 Pategi tried to amalgamate with Lafiagi as a federated Native Authority, but this move came to naught apart from a joint police force with the Federated N.A. of Lafiagi, Shonga and Sharagi. From about the same time dates the fame of Pategi for its river regatta, a colourful spectacle that attracts thousands of visitors at the beginning of each year,[2] and has to some extent superseded the popularity of the traditional Nupe masquerades of the Gugu and Ndekogboza cults.

[1] Historians may find a parallel confusion in the title of Queen Elizabeth II of England . . . or of Scotland. Cf. James I of England and VI of Scotland.

[2] See H. O. H. Vernon-Jackson, 'The Pategi Regatta', *Nigeria Magazine*, No. 54, 1957.

THE EMIRS (ETSUZHI) OF PATEGI

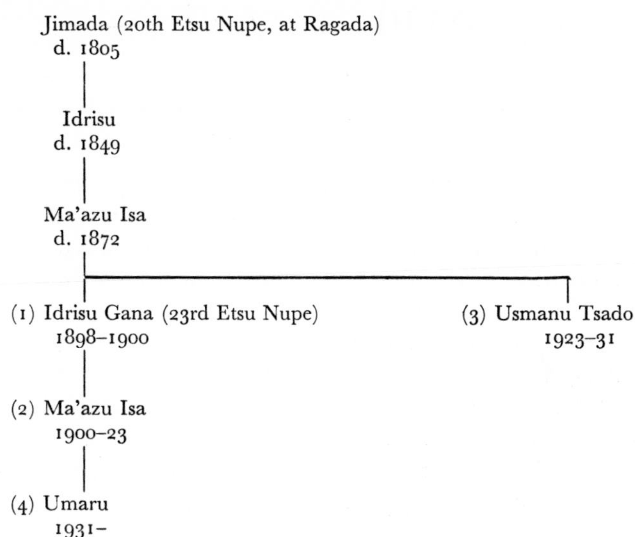

XLIII. LAFIAGI

THE history of the Nupe emirates of Bida, Lafiagi, Pategi (and the former Shonga)—and to a lesser degree of Agaie and Lapai—are so closely interwoven that reference to the general Nupe history recorded on page 261 under Nupe emirate will be a useful introduction.

Among the Fulani emissaries from Gwandu to the south-west was Malam Maliki. He and his brother Manzuma took part in Malam Dendo's skilful repulse of Etsu Majiya's attack on Ilorin in 1806. Pursuing the broken Nupe forces northwards, Malam Maliki decided to settle near the River Niger and in 1810 founded the fortified town of Lafiagi, the remains of whose strong mud walls can still be traced.

On Malam Maliki's death in 1824, his son Aliyu was too young to succeed. In his stead, Maliki's brother Manzuma was appointed and it was to him that the Emir of Gwandu presented the insignia of kingship. Manzuma thus ranks as the first Emir of Lafiagi. Aliyu, unhappy at this preference, retired to Shonga, where he built the town and founded the royal house of Etsu Shonga.

Etsu Idrisu, the dynastic Nupe king, chafed under the rule of the Fulani and gathered the Nupe people against them. First, Lafiagi was attacked on four sides. The town was burnt, and the Emir Manzuma fled to Ilorin. Raba was next threatened by strong forces. Malam Dendo, the Fulani leader of the Nupe, appealed to the rival Nupe Etsu, Majiya, to come to his help. At the sound of Majiya's trumpets, legend has it, Idrisu fled, escaping to Ekagi, near Katcha. Manzuma's authority was restored at Lafiagi but only with the stationing of a Fulani *ajele* in every important Nupe centre.

After the death of Malam Dendo in 1832, his son Usman Zaki came to an agreement with Manzuma, whereby the latter retained the land south of the Niger, which is approximately the area of the Pategi-Lafiagi Division of today, while Usman retained control of the Nupe country north of the Niger along with the Share districts, today in Ilorin.[1]

When Manzuma died in about 1833, Maliki's son Aliyu, Etsu of Shonga, was appointed Emir of Lafiagi. This was the outcome of a pact that Manzuma had made with him, whereby Aliyu should succeed to the Lafiagi throne provided that he gave Manzuma's son Abdulkadiri the title of Yerima or heir-apparent. Usman Zaki, the Muslim leader in Nupe, was at this time ruling north of the Niger at Raba. His youngest brother Masaba, an important figure in Nupe history, rebelled against him as he thought he should have rightly been made Yerima. After a fight at Raba in 1833, Masaba was driven out and fled to Lafiagi. Emir Aliyu refused to receive him, though he eventually gave him permission to settle at Lade, now in Pategi country. Masaba was not one to let grass grow under his feet. He sent a messenger to the Emir of Gwandu, protesting that Aliyu was not a fit ruler of Lafiagi, and that Abdulkadiri, son of the late Emir Manzuma, would make a better chief. Halilu, Emir of Gwandu, did not question this report from Masaba. Aliyu was promptly deposed and in about 1834 he returned once more to Shonga. Abdulkadiri, the Yerima, now became Emir of Lafiagi.

Usman Zaki's ambition to assume the title of Etsu Nupe on the death of Majiya led to a second revolt of the Nupe. Masaba, whose mother was a Nupe, fostered this rebellion against his brother, and in 1840 he tried to persuade the Emir of Lafiagi to support the forces that he sent to help the Nupe who were besieging Raba, but Abdulkadiri refused on the grounds of horror of a fratricidal war among Fulani.

The siege of Raba lasted for a whole year, and slowly the people began to die of starvation. Appalled, the Emir of Lafiagi went to Ilorin to ask the Emir to assist to raise the siege. The column arrived too late to save the town. Usman Zaki fled to Agaie, and the Emirs of Ilorin and Lafiagi returned to Ilorin.

Incensed at this civil war among his own people, Emir Halilu, having the previous year found the enemy too strong for him, again

[1] This action is attributed by some historians to an older son, Mamman Majigi. But the latter did not survive his father (cf. Nadel's *A Black Byzantium*, p. 79) and in any case had no ambition for temporal power. For the events in Nupe following the death of Malam Dendo, with the conflict between the Fulani and the Nupe contenders for power, and the rivalry of the brothers, Usman Zaki and Masaba, see pp. 269 ff. in the Nupe chapter.

marched southwards with an army from Gwandu and summoned all the local Fulani chiefs. He deposed Usman Zaki and appointed Masaba in his place. The Emir of Lafiagi was retained at Lafiagi, but lost most of his territorial power, including the country now known as Pategi. Masaba did not go to his brother's capital of Raba but returned to Lade, opposite Muregi, which, as his capital, was eventually to become the centre of the powerful state of Pategi.

Masaba still nurtured a grudge against Lafiagi for Abdulkadiri's lack of support over the Raba siege and for other occasions of lukewarm reaction. He therefore secretly arranged with Usman, the Yerima of Lafiagi and a brother to the Emir, to conspire with the principal men of the town against Abdulkadiri. At the critical moment Masaba would arrive with an army and drive the Emir out, installing the Yerima in his place. The intrigue was entirely successful. The wily Masaba, however, having ousted Abdulkadiri, had no scruples about his promise to the Yerima. Treacherously, he recalled Aliyu from Shonga, and made him Emir of Lafiagi for the second time about 1845.

A little later, in 1847, Masaba's foreign general, Umar, determined to revolt against his master. To this end he made common cause with the Etsu Maza and with Usman, the Yerima of Lafiagi who had been so bitterly deceived by Masaba over the Lafiagi succession. The combined forces marched on Lade. Masaba fled southwards, whither he was pursued by Yerima Usman, while Umar stayed in Lade. It is said that Usman caught up with Masaba, who had become separated from his followers, but magnanimously spared his life, stating that he was satisfied to see his enemy thus humbled. He then saw Masaba's wife standing nearby, and told her she must come with him so that he might restore her to her father, the Emir of Ilorin, as her husband's days were numbered. She refused. In the struggle that ensued when Usman tried to drag her on to his horse, the girths broke. The opportunist Masaba sprang at Usman and cut off his head. He then made his escape on Usman's horse.

The Lafiagi forces, now commanded by Ibrahim Halilu, brother of the Yerima Usman, seized Lafiagi and put the adherents of Aliyu to the sword. Aliyu was sent to Umar and ultimately returned to Shonga, and Abdulkadiri was brought back from Ilorin and restored as Emir in about 1853.

Umar was eventually defeated and slain by the united Fulani forces, under the leadership of Umaru Majigi, reinforced at his request by Gwandu. In 1856 Usman Zaki was installed as Emir of Bida by the Waziri of Gwandu, with Masaba as his Sarkin Fulani, while Abdulkadiri was confirmed as Emir of Lafiagi with his territory much as it is today.

The fifteen years of Abdulkadiri's second reign were untroubled by war. His brother, Ibrahim Halilu, followed as Emir of Lafiagi in 1868 and reigned for fourteen uneventful years.

Masaba had by this time become very powerful and had come into conflict with the Emirs of Agaie and Lapai in his continual slave-raids. In about 1873 Almustafa, the Emir of Gwandu, came south in person to check his activities, and it was only by dint of a host of expensive gifts that Masaba prevented the Lade country, today recognized as Pategi, from being taken from him and given to the Emir of Lafiagi.

Halilu, Emir of Lafiagi, died in 1882 and was succeeded by his younger brother Aliyu. There are two stories told locally of his succession. One is that, because the Nupe were in insurrection in Bida country, the Emir of Gwandu was unable to give Aliyu his turban. Instead he deputed the Emir of Ilorin, Shitta, to act for him. This story is disputed by Lafiagi historians, who say that it was Abdurrahimi, son of the Sarkin Lifidi of Gwandu, who brought the turban. They maintain that the Emir Shitta was already dead and that the troubles in Nupe did not break out till three months later.

In any event, a discontented faction of the Nupe under Etsu Baba, son of Saci at Leaba, now rose against the Bida Fulani. They were defeated by Umaru Majigi and their leader Etsu Baba was drowned during the retreat. The Nupe, however, reassembled their forces south of the Niger under Nda Legbo, son of Majiya, and Kolo Shuaibu, son of Etsu Baba. They proceeded to conquer Shonga and threatened to sack Lafiagi if the Emir Aliyu did not throw in his lot with them. Discretion being the better part of valour, Aliyu agreed. Furthermore, he sent his brother Abdurrahim and his nephews Ahmadu and Umaru to join the Nupe army.

After sacking Egga, Umaru was sent with half the army to attack Budon. Umaru Majigi's army now came on the scene, supported by arms and vessels from the Royal Niger Company, under the command of the Yerima Maliki. The Bida forces relieved Egga and marched on Lafiagi, but the town was deserted, the Emir and all his followers having fled to Oke Ode.

While at Lafiagi, Maliki heard of the death of Umaru Majigi at Bida, and he was installed as Emir of Bida in Lafiagi town. Maliki wished to put Lafiagi under Bida, but the Emir of Gwandu insisted on the return of the Emir Aliyu. He came back from Oke Ode and made his peace with Maliki but he never regained his lost power. He died in 1891 and was succeeded by Abdurrahim, the last of Manzuma's sons. He in turn died after only eighteen months and was followed by Ahmadu, son of Abdulkadiri, the 3rd Emir.

After the fall of Bida and Ilorin to the Niger Company's forces in 1897 Nupeland was in a state of unrest, as people thought that the Fulani power had been broken. In Lafiagi they rose against the Emir of Lafiagi and burnt the Fulani quarter of the town. Ahmadu fled to Shonga, but was escorted back and reinstated by Niger Company troops. Yet as soon as they left he was again driven out, until once more the Company's troops had to intervene. On this occasion two of the leaders of the rising, Ndeji and Nefenni, were sent to prison at Lokoja.

On the advent of the British administration the Nupe empire, which had stretched from the Benue in the south to Gbagede in the north, was shorn of some of its power and jurisdiction, for Lugard felt that the Bida-Kontagora complex was too strong to leave intact. Yagba, Bunu, Bassa and Kakanda became independent districts, while the Nupe territory lying to the south and west of the River Niger was transferred to Ilorin Province. Here they were, between 1900 and 1905, shared out among the Emirs of Ilorin, Lafiagi and Shonga. This last-named emirate had, as we have seen, been founded by the deposed Emir of Lafiagi, Aliyu. At that time it was a village subject to the Nupe-Yoruba settlement of Share, famous then as now for the cultivation of onions. After an internal quarrel among the Yoruba ruling families, the chief of Share, the Olupako (he had cast off the Nupe title of Ndakpoto), was removed in 1905. Since 1946 Shonga has been a district in Lafiagi Emirate. It houses at Tada nine magnificent examples of the famous Nupe bronzes.[1]

Ahmadu died in 1915 and his son Bello was appointed.

[1] Some good photographs are to be found in *Nigeria Magazine* No. 73, 1962.

Shu'aibu, the Kpotun, who claimed superior rights to the throne,[1] had been rejected on account of his previous bad record, having been twice in prison for extortion. Disgruntled at the perverse decision of the council of selectors, Shu'aibu collected a force of hunters from Lafiagi District and forcibly deposed Bello. He then proclaimed himself Emir. The Resident and a force of police escorted Bello back to Lafiagi from Oke Ode, whither he had fled, and restored him to the throne. Shu'aibu was banished to Katsina for six years.

In 1920 Lafiagi—and Pategi—recovered their independent status by being granted their own Native Treasuries. Eleven years later another landmark was reached when Lafiagi celebrated the first-ever visit of the Lieutenant-Governor of the Northern Provinces. The long reign of Mohamman Bello came to an end when the 8th Emir of Lafiagi died in 1945. He was followed by Abubakar Kawu. Immediately after this, the district of Oke Ode, which had featured so often in Lafiagi history, was transferred from the emirate to Ilorin on the ethnic grounds that the majority of its inhabitants were Igbomina Yoruba. In return, and on the same ethnic plea, Lafiagi acquired from Ilorin the predominantly Nupe districts of Shonga and Sharagi.

On the deposition of Abubakar Kawu in 1949 (he died in Lafiagi in 1961, whither he was allowed to return in his private capacity in 1955), the title of Emir of Lafiagi was replaced by that of Chief of Lafiagi, and its first holder was Maliki. He died in 1951 and was succeeded by Abubakar, who up to then had been the *alkali* of Bode Sadu in Ilorin emirate. Three years later the Federated Council of Lafiagi, Sharagi and Shonga was established, but its N.A. Council of over fifty members proved too cumbersome. It was replaced in 1958 by a more streamlined Federated N.A. Official reports in 1961 pointed out how, for Ilorin, 'it has been the Northern People's Congress which has dominated the active political life and set the pace' in the Lafiagi, Sharagi and Shonga Federal Native Authority.[2] The local party branch organized a powerful albeit peaceful demonstration against the alleged corruption and inefficiency of the chief, Abubakar Ceceko. He resigned and withdrew to Bida, and in his place Umaru Oke-Ode was appointed.

[1] He was the fifth son of the Emir Ibrahim Halilu.

[2] *Annual Report of Ilorin Province*, 1961.

High hopes are held in Lafiagi emirate of the Bacita sugar plantation. A delightful link between modern Lafiagi and the emirate's founders, Maliki and Manzuma, is the historical night-market, an attractive phenomenon peculiar to many of the Nupe-Yoruba towns such as Bida, Offa, Ilorin, Shonga and Share.

THE EMIRS AND CHIEFS OF LAFIAGI

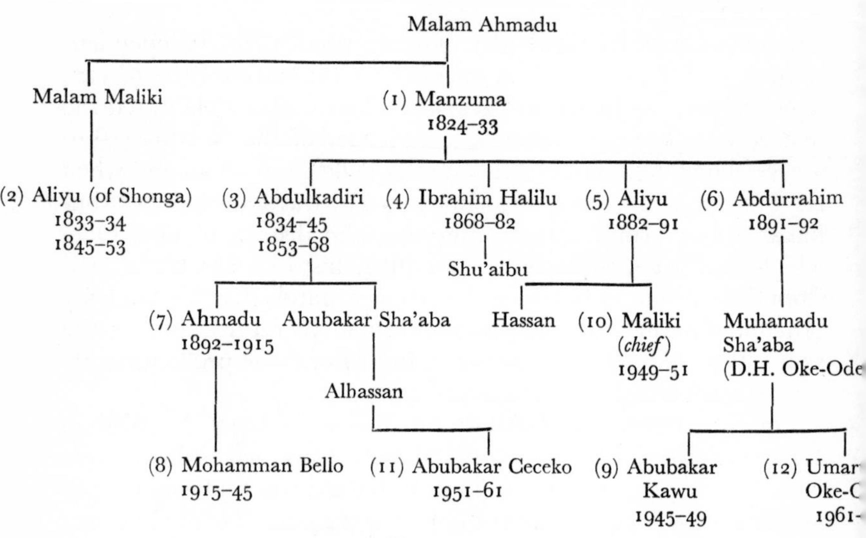

Note: Some Lafiagi records prefer not to count Aliyu of Shonga among the Emirs, though admitting that he twice reigned in Lafiagi, and therefore re-number the Emirs from Abdulkadiri as the second.

3. EMIRATES DERIVING FROM THE SOKOTO EMPIRE

(5) The Central States

XLIV. KEFFI

THE original inhabitants, that is, those occupying the country at the time of the earliest local accounts, were the Gade, the Yeskwa, and the Bassa. Tradition has little to relate about the origin of these peoples. The first invaders of whom we have any sure record were the pagan Hausa from the north—the Gwandara, the Toni, and the Koro.[1]

Of these, the Gwandara were the most important immigrants. It is said that a certain Kareshi, son of Sarkin Kano, was expelled by his father for refusing either to accept Islam or to give up his pagan religious dances. Hence, it is claimed, the name of Gwandara was attached to his followers, the original and full appellation being *gwanda rawa da salla*, 'rather dance than pray'. The Gwandara under Kareshi went south and founded Kareshi town and kingdom, their king being recognized by Sarkin Zazzau. They established an ascendancy over the surrounding Gade, Bassa, and Yeskwa peoples.

The Kareshi kingdom seems to have reached considerable proportions and is even reputed to have extended at one time as far as the Benue in the south and the Niger in the west. If this is so, the Igbirra, coming from the west, must have driven them north and east again out of the territory in which they then founded their powerful kingdoms of Koton Karfi and Koton-Panda, which were still flourishing in the time of the first Emir of Keffi, Abdu Zanga. But it is probable that the authority of the Gwandara in the distant parts of their empire was but shadowy and that they offered little serious resistance to the invasions of the Igbirra.

[1] I am grateful to my student Abdu Abubakar, now a District Officer, for the long discussions we had on Keffi history.—A.K-G.

The first blow at Gwandara ascendancy was the arrival of a band of Arab horsemen from the region of Lake Chad, who expelled the Gwandara and their Yeskwa and Gwari subjects from the surrounding country and founded the town of Bagaji in about 1750. The Gwandara took refuge with the Yeskwa in the Gitata Hills to the north, while the Gwari fled west to their own country round Karu and Kurafi.

There is in Keffi emirate a place called Kokwana, which has a legend dating back to the eighteenth century. It was recounted by Emir Abdullahi (1902–21). A devout *malam* named Ahmadu settled in Kokwana, which at that time was continually being attacked by the people of Ninkoro. Ahmadu possessed a long stick, and whenever he led the men of Kokwana in defence against the men of Ninkoro, the assailants fled. On Ahmadu's death he was buried just outside Kokwana, with the stick placed lengthways on his grave. Then the people of Ninkoro came stealthily by night to steal the stick, but as they seized it the stick turned into a pillar of stone. It was now too weighty to remove, so they hacked a piece off, about two feet long, and carried it back to Ninkoro where they planted it and where, they used to declare, it grew. Ahmadu's shrine and its stone pillar with a piece chipped off are still visited by travellers anxious to ensure good luck on their journey, while the small pillar at Ninkoro corresponds exactly to the one at Kokwana with a piece missing.

Shortly before the Fulani rising in Gobir at the beginning of the nineteenth century, a certain Fulani cattle-owner from Zanga, named Muhamman Gani, had been in the habit of bringing his herds from Katsina to graze every dry season on the grasslands in the area that is today Keffi. His son Abdullahi continued this annual pasturing and was known by the name of Zanga. Abdullahi eventually decided to settle in this district altogether, and built a stockaded village which he named *Keffi*, 'a stockade'.

The probable reason for the lack of resistance encountered by Abdu Zanga on his settlement at Keffi was that the Gwandara were fully occupied by far more pressing dangers from the newly established kingdom of Abuja. Though the Habe kings of Zaria had been expelled by the Fulani, they continued, despite the fallen fortunes of their house, to exact tribute from their former vassals. Thus the unfortunate kingdom of Kareshi had to pay tribute both to Abuja and to Zaria, and was also raided by Abuja for slaves.

It was no surprise that on the arrival of the British a century later the Kareshi Gwandara stoutly refused to follow Abuja at any price, and were instead placed under the Fulani Emirate of Keffi.

Tradition relates that when Usman dan Fodio sent out his call to all the Fulani, the ambitious Zanga decided to hurry to Sokoto in the hope that he would be given a flag for himself. But he was turned back by the first Fulani Emir of Zaria, Malam Musa, who made it quite clear that the country round Keffi and beyond as far as the Benue had been granted to him as his fief. Keffi thus joined Nassarawan Kwotto and Jema'an Dororo among the larger vassal states of Zaria and paid *gandu*, tribute, and not *kurdin kasa* or tax. Zaria expected not less than a hundred slaves annually from Keffi and allowed her vassals to make war independently on the neighbouring pagans or on Abuja but not on one another.

Zanga now turned back and started to consolidate his settlement at Keffi. Yet this does not seem to have prevented the Zaria horsemen from making a demonstration of force and raiding the village with fire and sword. Keffi was rebuilt, with mud walls replacing the original stockade. Zanga now received a flag, but from the Emir of Zaria and not direct from Sokoto. It thus became customary for the Emir of Keffi to be crowned in Zaria after his nomination by the local council of selectors, but after 1840 Zaria lost this power though it retained its suzerainty. At times this too became somewhat notional, for Keffi lay so far to the south that close control from Zaria was out of the question. This vassal relationship was effected by the appointment of a *kofa* or intermediary. These were generally Zaria titleholders, who communicated with the vassal states through their own *jekadu* or agents. Keffi was at first allotted to an untitled pilgrim, Alhaji Musa, whose religious scruples prevented him from assuming territorial office. Later Keffi came under the supervision of the Madaki of Zazzau, together with Jema'a.

Abdu Zanga died in 1820 and was succeeded by his brother Maizabo. On his death in 1835 he was succeeded by Jibrilu, son of Abdu Zanga. During this time Keffi was famous for the exploits of a great warrior known as Makama Dogo, later to become famous as the 1st Emir of Nassarawa.[1]

Makama Dogo—his real name was Umaru—had attached himself to Emir Abdullahi. When the Emir noticed his courage as a

[1] The chapters on Nassarawa and Keffi should be read together at this stage.

fighter he presented him with a horse, and on the submission of the Afao people Makama Dogo was appointed as their *kofa* or intermediary in Keffi. About this time a Katsina man arrived in Keffi and claimed Makama Dogo as a runaway slave belonging to his wife. The Emir Abdullahi offered to redeem him with two slaves. One was accepted, the other was to be sent later to Katsina. Some months later the man returned, this time with his wife, to demand the balance of the second slave. The Emir is said to have handed over a young female slave belonging to the household of one of his courtiers, Ahmadu. Thus the redemption of Makama Dogo was completed.

While the new Emir, Jibrilu, had gone to Zaria to attend before Sarkin Zazzau, and Makama Dogo was visiting his fiefdom of the Afao country, this Ahmadu identified his former slave, who is reputed to have grown into a very beautiful girl, in the compound of Makama Dogo. Ahmadu complained to one Tabo, whom the Emir had left in charge of Keffi, and was advised by him to resume possession of the slave. This he did. On his return from Afao, Makama Dogo complained to the Emir but Jibrilu refused to do anything. Makama Dogo, cursing the new leaders of Keffi for treating him in a way that his old master Emir Abdu would never have done, vowed that he would take his complaint to Sarkin Zazzau. Nassarawa historians relate that Abdulkarim, Emir of Zaria, dismissed the complaint, but the chroniclers of Zaria claim that on the contrary it was heard sympathetically by the Emir who then ordered the deposition of Jibrilu as Emir of Keffi and nominated Makama Dogo in his stead. The Fulani of Keffi rejected Makama Dogo and shut the town gates against him on his return from Zaria. Abdulkarim was forced to accept this rebuff when he learned that the Keffi Fulani had the moral support of Sokoto in their refusal to accept a Habe ruler.

The outcome of this belongs to the history of Nassarawa emirate. When, however, Makama Dogo was an old man and near the end of his days, he wrote a letter to Emir Jibrilu from Agaza, in his own kingdom of Nassarawa, expressing a wish to die at peace with his former master and now brother emir. On his death-bed, and in the presence of Jibrilu, Makama Dogo charged his son Ahmadu that he should follow the Emir of Keffi. He told him that if he failed to carry out this dying request, the people of Zaria would one day make him captive. In the event, Ahmadu ignored his father's wishes and lived to rue the day that this prophecy was fulfilled. Makama Dogo died in 1858 but his wish that his body should be carried to Keffi and buried close to the grave of his foster-father, the late Emir Abdu Zanga, was rejected by Jibrilu.

Jibrilu died in 1859 and was successively followed by four of his brothers, Muhamman (1859–62), Ahmadu (1862–77), Sidi Umaru (1877–94), and Ibrahim (1894–1902).

During this time there was continual slave-raiding, and by the end of the century the whole country had become seriously depopulated. Every year large caravans of slaves burdened with crops and livestock were sent northwards to the suzerain Emir of Zaria. It is on record that during the reign of Abdullahi at Zaria he in person raided Keffi in the early 1870s when the annual tribute had fallen into arrears. This forced collection, however, angered Zaria's liege-lord, the Sultan of Sokoto. Three times did he order Abdullahi to withdraw from Keffi, but Abdullahi continued his forays, retorting that Zaria's dealings with its vassal were no concern of Sokoto. This recalcitrance led to Abdullahi's deposition. In Umaru's reign Keffi went to war with Nassarawa. With the backing of Sokoto, Sambo, Emir of Zaria, levied a large fine on both of his vassals, payable in slaves.

Naturally the arrival of the British was not welcomed by the men who made a profitable livelihood out of plunder and slaving. The last thing they wanted to see was peace and justice. Such a man was the Emir of Zaria's representative in Keffi, the Magaji. In July 1902 Provincial headquarters were established at Keffi, Abuja was occupied after sharp measures had been taken against the brigands there, and troops were stationed within the emirate of Keffi.

The Resident, Captain Moloney, who had accompanied the expedition to Abuja, attempted to come to an amicable understanding with the Magajin Keffi, hoping that the lesson of Abuja had been sufficient and that he would use his influence to secure a bloodless submission. But the Magaji evidently feared for his life. On 3 October Captain Moloney and the Assistant Resident, Mr G. W. Webster, proceeded to the square fronting the Emir's and Magaji's residences, and summoned the Magaji to attend. He declined to do so. The Assistant Resident was then sent to fetch him, but was attacked by the Magaji's retainers and eventually thrown out, narrowly escaping with his life. Captain Moloney at once sent Mr Webster to call up the troops. The Magaji, seeing that his arrest was imminent, rushed out of his house, killed Captain Moloney, who was without protection and was a one-armed man, and fled northwards. He was sheltered in turn by the Emir of Zaria, the Emir of Kano, and the Sultan of Sokoto, but ill fortune rewarded them for their hospitality. It cost Zaria her lower Benue provinces of Keffi, Nassarawa and Jema'a, and the Emir Kwassau lost his throne; it precipitated the British occupation of Kano, when the Emir Aliyu was captured and deported; it hastened the fall of Sokoto, when the Emir Attahiru fled, to be killed eventually at Burmi in 1903. The Magajin Keffi was also killed in the same battle. The true reasons for what happened at Keffi on that sad day in 1901 are unlikely ever to be established, but the generally accepted story told in Keffi is that Moloney's political agent, Audu (who was also killed by the Magaji), mistranslated the Resident's message. Another version blames Audu for deliberately leading Moloney into the private apartments of the palace where he was easily attacked. Captain Moloney's grave now lies on the top of the hill overlooking Keffi. The original plaque, inscribed 'murdered in the fearless execution of his duty', did not find local favour and was replaced by the present one which simply says 'killed in action'.[1]

The aged Ibrahim was removed and Abdullahi, sixth son of Jibrilu, was made Emir in 1902. Because of Government's displeasure with Keffi, it became only a Division and the junior emirate of Nassarawa was selected both as the headquarters and as the name of the new Province. Abubakar succeeded to the throne in 1921 and Abdullahi two years later. He was obliged to resign after an undistinguished reign that left Keffi in the last position among the emirates of the Province, but under the leadership of the new Emir, Muhammadu Mayaki Isa, the emirate's administration showed an initial welcome improvement. In 1928 the Divisional headquarters moved from Keffi to Nassarawa; a decline in Keffi affairs marked the last years of Emir Muhammadu Mayaki. Ex-Emir Abdullahi died in Kaduna in 1929.

[1] The initial resentment cooled down enough to allow Keffi N.A. to recommend the name of Moloney to be given to a house in the Teacher Training Centre and to one of its primary schools. The latter was renamed Ahmadu Maikwoto Primary School in 1963. See also p. 490, n., and the Keffi chapter in Muffett's forthcoming account of the Kano–Sokoto campaign.

New life came to the emirate with the appointment of a Waziri in 1930. Muhammadu Mayaki was succeeded as Emir by his cousin Abubakar in 1933, who in the following year attended the experimental conference of Northern Chiefs held at Kaduna. This afforded Abubakar and his brother-Emirs of Nassarawa and Lafia an opportunity to meet the other emirs of the country from whom they had always felt somewhat isolated. The mid-thirties saw a growing demand for land for tin-mining. In 1937 a reorganization took place in the three emirates that made up the North Benue Division, resulting in the emergence of a Yeskwa tribal area within the Keffi emirate.

Later, the Division was reconstituted and Keffi-Nassarawa became a Division in its own right. On Abubakar's death in 1949, his son-in-law Ahmadu Maikwato, then Galadima, became the 13th Emir of Keffi. The opening of the North's second Government College, in 1955, at Keffi has brought great fame to the town. Keffi emirate reorganized its district administration in 1956 by converting its four districts into five and one town.

THE EMIRS OF KEFFI

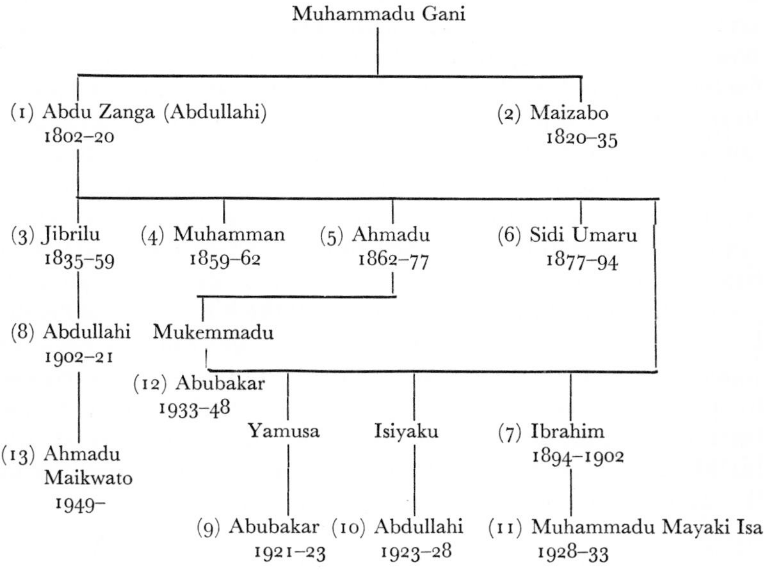

XLV. NASSARAWA

BEFORE the founding of Nassarawa emirate, the area was one of the vassal states of Fulani Zaria, together with Keffi and Jema'a, and was long known as Nassarawan Kwotto or simply Kwotto. These three states shared with Fatika and Bagaji the *kofa* or intermediary of Madakin Zazzau, who represented the Emir of Zaria and through whom tribute was despatched (less one-fifth for the *kofa*) to Zaria. The town and emirate of Nassarawa were founded by Umaru Makama Dogo in about 1835, though local historians claim that recognition was personally given by Shehu Usman dan Fodio to the first Emir of Nassarawa earlier when he attached him to the Emir of Zaria.

Umaru was a slave, who as a boy had run away from his Fulani master at Ruma in Katsina and had attached himself to Abdullahi Zanga, the founder of Keffi.[1] Other sources claim that he attached himself to Usman dan Fodio. His father was Usman Rabawawa and his mother was called Amina. Nassarawa chroniclers relate how Umaru—soon to become known as Makama Dogo—stayed for two years in Zaria before the Emir, Musa, sent him southwards to spread the Faith. Arriving at Zanga, he met Abdullahi Zanga and Gunki rearing their cattle. Urging a superior claim to Keffi, Nassarawa elders declare that it was Umaru who suggested to Abdullahi and Gunki to present themselves to the Emir of Zaria and seek recognition. This they did, but when the Emir asked them where they would like to settle, they answered that they preferred to remain where they were, by the hill known as Piyanku. Umaru, it is said, was detailed off by the Emir of Zaria to supervise this, and on his return to report to the Emir his request to stay with Abdullahi and Gunki was granted. Abdullahi now became the Emir of Keffi, with Gunki his Madawaki and Umaru his Makama. Later, misunderstandings arose, which resulted in the Madawaki breaking away from the Emir and withdrawing

[1] The chapters on Keffi and Nassarawa should at this stage be read together. We are grateful to Nassarawa N.A. for the detailed memorandum they compiled on the emirate's history.

from Keffi to Agwadu. Abdullahi is said to have assembled all his sons and told them that he had promoted Umaru Makama Dogo to the office of Madawakin Keffi and that they were all to obey him.

On Abdullahi's death, his sons approached Umaru and warned him to prepare himself to accept the title of Emir. He was actually installed by the Emir of Zaria, Nassarawa historians maintain, but on their way back to Keffi the people all deserted him. On complaining to Zaria, he was advised to attack the treacherous Keffi people. Umaru replied that it was not wise to kill the goose that laid the golden eggs; instead, he begged the Emir of Zaria to accord him recognition as Emir of Kwotto, with jurisdiction over the pagan peoples to the west. Another explanation to account for the conferment of the chieftaincy over Kwotto on Makama Dogo is provided by the following version of a story related in the Keffi chapter.[1]

Not long after Jibrilu became Emir of Keffi in 1835 a quarrel sprang up between him and Makama Dogo. While Makama Dogo was away fighting, a man named Ahmadu heard that a handsome female slave of his was living in Makama Dogo's house, and resumed possession of her. This girl had been originally given by Abdullahi, Sarkin Keffi, to Makama Dogo's former master from Ruma in part redemption of the freedom of Makama Dogo. On Makama Dogo's return he could get no satisfaction from Jibrilu, so in a fit of wrath he took his complaint to Zaria. Abdulkadiri, Emir of Zaria, at first counselled him to let the matter rest, but when Makama Dogo became adamant Abdulkadiri saw a fine opportunity to halt the growing power of Keffi of which he was becoming jealous. He decided to weaken Keffi by offering Makama Dogo the *sarauta* of the Igbirra or Kwotto kingdom of Panda. This he reckoned would reduce Keffi's strength by drawing off the powerful Makama Dogo faction.

On Makama Dogo's return to Keffi he found the gates shut against him. One story is that the Emir of Zaria had nominated Makama Dogo as Emir of Keffi but that the Fulani of Keffi revolted against this Kado and drove him out. At any rate, he departed and went with his following to a place called Yankardi. Nassarawa chroniclers add that Yamusa, the son of the Emir of Keffi, and the father of the Magajin Keffi who was subsequently

[1] See p. 532.

involved in the *affaire Moloney*, offered to follow Umaru Makama Dogo. Umaru refused this support but told Yamusa that if he occupied and remained in his *gidan Makama* he would surely become an important person in Keffi.

One of Makama Dogo's daughters, Halimatu, was married to Jibrilu, Emir of Keffi. When she heard of her father's treatment, she left her husband and made her way to his camp at Yankardi. But Makama Dogo ordered her to return, explaining that 'this is a matter between men, it is not the concern of womenfolk'. He now considered where he should settle. There came into his mind a certain pleasant place by a river where he and his old chief, Abdullahi, Emir of Keffi, used to pitch their war camp. He recalled how whenever Abdullahi had camped there victory had always been won against his enemies, and even how the Emir had prophesied that one day a town should spring up on that spot. So Makama Dogo proceeded thither and he called his new town *Nassarawa*, 'the victorious ones'.

From Nassarawa, Makama Dogo conquered both the Igbirra and their subjects the Bassa, broke up their kingdom and destroyed the town of Panda. Many Igbirra refugees from Panda fled west to the rival Igbirra kingdom of Koton Karfi or Kwotton Karfi, 'the strong or unconquered Kwotto'. On his return from Panda, Makama Dogo assumed the title of Sarkin Kwotto, which is held to this day by the Emir of Nassarawa. It may be that 'Kwotto' was the Hausa corruption of Okpoto.

Makama Dogo also made war on the people of Toto. They sent to Abuja for help and in the battle that followed three of the sons of Abu Ja, the Emir, were taken prisoner. We are told that Umaru Nagwamatse, Emir of Kontagora, was with Makama Dogo and urged him to send back to Abu Ja his three sons. But the Emir of Nassarawa refused to listen to this advice and put the three young men to death; whereupon the Emir of Kontagora withdrew to his own country in disgust.

In his old age Makama Dogo restored his friendship with Jibrilu, and sent his daughter Halimatu a present of a tall lamp, captured from the chief of Panda. Halimatu had been entrusted with the lighting of the lamps in the mosque. She placed this lamp in the mosque at Keffi where it can been seen to this day.

When Makama Dogo felt that his time had come, he wrote to Jibrilu, Emir of Keffi, and said that he wished to die at peace with him. So Jibrilu gathered his people and went to visit Makama Dogo at Agaza. On his death-bed Makama Dogo charged his son Ahmadu, Madakin Kwotto, to follow the Emir of Keffi, else 'you shall surely behold that which will not please you, and Zazzau shall make you captive'. Ahmadu promised his father that he would respect his wishes. Makama Dogo died in 1858, but his request that he should be buried next to his old master, Abdullahi, at Keffi was refused by Jibrilu on the grounds that as the founder of Nassarawa his body should lie there so that the people of Nassarawa might enjoy his blessing for ever.

Makama Dogo was succeeded by his son Ahmadu, who together with Jibrilu, Emir of Keffi, made war on Akewa. On his return to Nassarawa he was acclaimed as Sarkin Kwotto and at once disobeyed his father by proclaiming Nassarawa's independence of Keffi. Within a year Nassarawa experienced the cruelty of Abdullahi, Emir of Zaria, who sent his Makama Abdusallami to raid Kwotto and collect its overdue tribute. His severity was illustrated by ordering the execution of two men for theft, even though one of them was his client. A little later Ahmadu again crossed swords with Zazzau and, again as prophesied by Makama Dogo, he was taken as a prisoner to Zaria. He was later pardoned and sent back to Nassarawa. During his twenty years' reign he conquered a number of small towns.

At Panda, Makama Dogo had captured an Igbirra concubine named Waji, said to have been the favourite slave of Ohegu, King of Panda. He lay with her but she then ran away or was sold. Hearing that she was with child, Makama Dogo had a great search made for her. She was found and according to Nassarawa tradition Makama Dogo predicted that her son would be a mighty man. This son was called Muhammadu, and he it was who succeeded to the throne of Nassarawa on his brother's death in 1878. His name is that of a great warrior in the history of Nassarawa. He conquered Akum, Iguehi and Kuradu, and extended the borders of his emirate so greatly that, according to local traditions, only the coming of the British prevented him from establishing a really powerful kingdom of Nassarawa. Nassarawa also engaged in a war with Keffi, which resulted in the Emir of Zaria imposing a heavy fine on the two vassals with the support of Sokoto. The fines were payable in slaves.

Of Nassarawa's second war with the people of Toto, when

Abuja tried to support the town's Habe population against its Kwotto elements, we have a detailed account by both the Nassarawa and the Abuja historians. The Emir of Nassarawa, in his role as Sarkin Kwotto, at first sent his slave Magayakijaki with his troops from Afako to help the Kwotto, but he soon realized that they were up against the whole might of Abuja:

Then the Emir of Nassarawa sent out a summons to a certain town called Katakwa to come and help him, and they sent twenty men armed with harpoon-guns such as they used for hunting elephant, and six hundred bowmen. When he saw how strong these reinforcements were, that day he divided his forces into two parts, intending to trick the Madawaki by sending some to fight on the usual battle-ground, whilst he himself with his horsemen and the harpooners and two hundred bowmen moved round the back of the Abuja camp to burn it. You see his cunning!

When the men of Abuja saw the enemy come out to battle as usual, they left the camp to come to grips with them, but Kauran Chachi, the Jarmai, said, 'There is something strange in the fighting today. I shall not go to the usual place, but I shall patrol the camp.' So he got on his horse, and whilst he was patrolling round with a few other mounted warriors, he came suddenly upon the Emir of Nassarawa and the harpooners. He did not know that they were harpooners and he charged towards them, but they did not stir. He made another charge towards them, but still they did not move, so he stopped short and did not come right up to them. Then he called to another great warrior, the Sarkin Fada, saying, 'Today these men come in strength; you see that when I feint at them they do not stir.' So the Sarkin Fada answered, 'Then we must attack them without delay.' So they fell upon them and drove the Emir of Nassarawa from the field; they killed the harpooners every one, and the men with muskets; they drove all the archers in flight, and the Emir of Nassarawa led the flight. Our men pursued him up to the gate of the town, and for all his hurry he hardly reached it in time; they captured many harpoons and muskets and arrows, but they lost six horses by the harpoons.

So the fighting continued without respite, and the men of Abuja came together in council. They said, 'Let us dig a deep ditch round our camp, for who knows when this war will end?' So they began to dig a ditch round the camp, but the warriors spoke together and said, 'Let us end this digging like slaves, and finish the war by our valour in battle.' So they ceased digging.

Then our men heard that a certain robe was being brought to the Emir of Nassarawa. Now had they done nothing to prevent it reaching him, they would have been lost, for this was a magic robe, and if he had put it on and gone out to fight wearing it, he must have destroyed them. So the Madawaki chose some of the boldest of his warriors, the Jagaban Dawaki, the Barden Galadima, the Madawakin Barde, and other horse and foot, telling them to block the road from Nassarawa and to seize the charm before it could reach the Emir. So they went and hid on the road between Barno and Buga. Then the Nassarawans came, at their head was the Dallatu, but the warriors fell upon them, killing the Dallatu and seizing all the loads together with the magic robe which they brought to the Madawaki.

Now when the Emir of Nassarawa heard this and learned that his charm had been captured, he was mad with fury. He collected all his men and rushed out to battle, and on that day the Barden Zuba, one of the Abuja warriors, was killed. After this the Emir conceived a stratagem. He found some white gunpowder and sent certain evil men of his company by night to the Abuja camp. At dawn the camp was fired, and the fire spread over the whole camp so that it was utterly destroyed and not a hut remained standing. Then when the Nassarawans saw that the fire had taken hold, they fell upon the men of Abuja to slaughter them. But when our men saw this, they left the fire to burn itself out, and rushed to battle, driving the enemy right back to the gate of Toto. And this day we beheld a wonder, for we had taken a pagan of the Gade tribe prisoner and had tied him fast. We took him out to an open space and threw him to the ground to slit his throat like a sheep, but he disappeared from the sight of all men and was never seen again.

Then at last the Nassarawans took counsel of each other; they said, 'We must end this war.' The Emir sent his son, the Chief of Chiji, to the Madawakin Abuja to say that he wished to end the dispute there and then. So the Madawaki called the men of Abuja together to tell them the words of the Emir of Nassarawa, and they said, 'Let us end it.' They said to the messenger, 'Go then back to the Emir and say that we are agreed; we will meet him at Sharu to settle the quarrel.' So they met, and agreed upon the day when they should come together in Toto. There the quarrel ended, and they said, 'Never again will we fight one another till the end of the world, but live in peace and confidence.'[1]

The Nassarawa version goes thus:

A quarrel broke out between the Habe population of the town of Toto and the Kwottawa (Igbirra) of the town. The former invoked the help of the Emir of Abuja while the latter appealed to the Emir of Nassarawa. Abuja sent 600 horsemen but the Nassarawa force numbered only 33 horsemen under the command of one Dan Ahoda. Seeing

[1] Ḥassan and Shuʼaibu, *A Chronicle of Abuja*, pp. 26–28. The writers are Abujans.

the superior strength of the foe, Dan Ahoda asked for reinforcements, and the Emir of Nassarawa sent 70 horsemen under the Madaki, Usmanu. The war lasted for twenty-one months. The Emir of Nassarawa moved to his war-camp at Toto and summoned the help of the armed hunters from Bakono, celebrated for their skill with harpoon guns. So heavy were the Abuja casualties that some of their office-holders, such as the Dan Galadima, the Sarkin Gaya, Kaura Caci and Alawa dan Koko, decided to seek for terms of peace. They were taken to the Emir of Nassarawa by the Alkali, Adamu, and it was agreed that representatives from both sides would meet in the village of Sharu and swear on the Koran that never again would Nassarawa and Abuja war with each other. When they met at Sharu, the terms proposed were that there should be no more fighting along the highways known as Hanyar Giwa, Hanyar Bakono, Hanyar Loko and Hanyar Ramin Gishiri (Awe). On Abuja's request, the last-named was excluded from the terms so that they could continue to use the Awe route for their salt supplies. Peace was agreed by Abuja and Nassarawa and there would be no more war until the end of the world.[1]

Muhammadu was one of the first Emirs to make submission to Lugard, in 1900, and was rewarded by seeing the name of his kingdom given to a whole Province and his capital made its headquarters at the expense of the senior emirate of Keffi.

After the great provincial reorganization, in which Nassarawa Province disappeared, the North Benue Divisional headquarters of the Keffi-Nassarawa Division were in 1928 moved to Nassarawa. The 'thirties saw the development of gold and tin mining in the emirate. In 1937 the Afu and Gade peoples were formed into a tribal area within Nassarawa, and in the following year the North Benue Division was broken up to allow Keffi-Nassarawa and Lafia to become two separate Divisions.

In 1951 Nassarawa lost one of its princes, Sambo Assabango, who had been the caretaker president of the Gade Federation Council until they could find a leader acceptable to them all. An event of some historical significance took place a year later when the Emir of Nassarawa consolidated his gradual reconciliation with the Chief of Umashia by recognizing his traditional Igbirra title of Ohimegi Panda. The Emir, along with the District Officer and the District Head of Afo, received a special commendation for bravery for his outstanding conduct in handling the ugly mines labour disturbances at Udegin Bekin in 1956. Recently a novel and adroit

[1] This new account is given by courtesy of Nassarawa N.A.

administrative experiment was made by the N.A.'s use of the district councils as a sounding-board in confirming the appointments of district heads.

THE EMIRS OF NASSARAWA

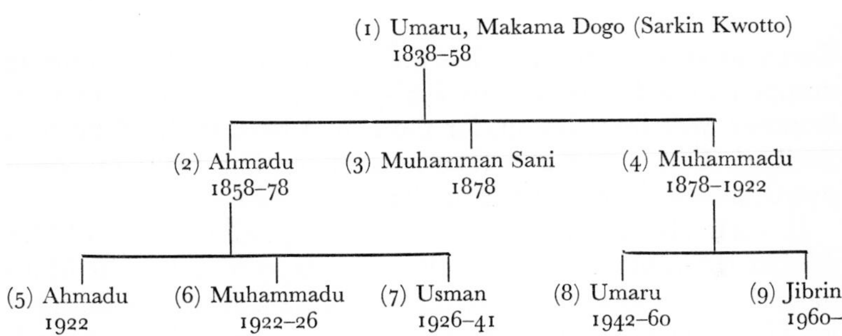

XLVI. LAFIA

ONLY in very recent years has the capital town of Lafia emirate dropped its suffix of Lafian Beri-Beri: the indication that its founders were from Bornu, for the Hausa refer to the Kanuri as Baribari. One might also take note of the fine make of Bornu sword known throughout Hausaland as *ba-barbara.*[1]

It was in about 1790 that one Dunama—possibly the son of Mai Ali bin Hajj Dunama, whose disastrous expedition against Mandara did much to weaken the empire of the Sef dynasty of Bornu—left Birni Ngazargamu, the seat of the Kanuri *mai* or king. According to Lafia lore, they are said to have had an intimate connexion with the Yemen of Arabia Felix, Medina and Mecca. With his followers, they moved southwards into the pagan country north of the Benue. The tradition that these Kanuri were despatched as a garrison in the upper Benue valley is less acceptable than the other one that, since Dunama's followers were predominantly traders, it was the constant wars in the no-man's land between the Hausa states and Bornu that prompted them to seek asylum elsewhere.

Travelling via Kano, Zaria, and Bagaji (near Keffi), they eventually reached Shabo, at that time inhabited by a section of the Gwandara tribe. Still restless, they continued their journey to Shendam, then in Wukari country. From Shendam they crossed to Kambari near Lau, where to this day the baobab trees are pointed out as having been planted by Dunama; they have given rise to the town's nickname of Kukan Kambari. After a brief stay, they again turned their steps towards Shabo, where they settled and started farming. Unfortunately, disputes over the farm-lands led to a fracas in which many were killed. Embittered by this, Dunama's band once more collected their household goods and started on their homeward journey to Bornu. At Kwandare they were met by the chief of that town, Akwoki, a man of much learn-

[1] We are grateful to Lafia N.A. for the lengthy memorandum they produced on the emirate's history.

ing and skill, who invited them to stop in his country. This they consented to do.

Chafing at their lack of a fixed abode, they turned longing eyes towards Anane, at that time a small Arago town under Doma which paid tribute to Wukari. The Doma had broken away from Atagara, near Idah, about the first half of the thirteenth century, under their leader Andoma and his lieutenant Keana.[1] Keana later built his own town at a rich salt-pit some four days march from Doma. When his people refused to fight their kith and kin to recapture the salt-pit at Keana, Andoma cursed them with the abuse 'Aragogo', by which sobriquet they are still known. After the Fulani pushed the Jukun back across the Benue, the Arago became a vassal state of Zaria until 1812 when Sarkin Zazzau transferred the Lafia districts, lying north-east of Doma and centred on Bagaji, to his neighbour the Emir of Bauchi. He allowed them to settle in the plains between the Mada and Tiv peoples, today the heart of Lafia emirate. Thereafter the Arago split up into many small towns that today are in Lafia Division.

With the assistance of Sarkin Kwandare the Beri-Beri managed to capture the town of Anane. This was in about 1780, though some sources post-date it by forty years. Here they decided to settle at last, much to the delight of Sarkin Kwandare, who thereupon expressed the wish that they would settle down *lafia*, 'comfortably'. Hence the name of the present town. The Doka ward of modern Lafia town is built on the site of Anane, and Arago aboriginals still live here.

Under the guidance of Dunama, there began an era of great prosperity for the new settlers, who were reinforced by an influx of Beri-Beri from Bornu. Dyeing was one of their mainstays. Many of the older Lafia immigrant families still bear the Kanuri facial markings, although very few can speak the language. Among Dunama's close Kanuri associates who are remembered to this day were, besides the later Emirs, Madaki Dibi, Zanuwa Bisami, Dalatu Marami, Gayam Laminu, Moyi Barguma, Ahoda, Wambai Magaji and Galadima Umaru, all of whom founded influential houses in Lafia.

It is said that Dunama's help to the Jukun in capturing the town

[1] The chiefs of Doma and Keana are listed in S. J. Hogben, *The Muhammadan Emirates of Nigeria*, p. 150. They have not been included in this revised version of that book because the areas are no longer recognized as 'emirates'.

of Wuryo was rewarded by the grant of a flag and the title of Sarkin Lafia by the Aku Uka of Wukari. The Jukun connexion can be traced in several titles, such as that of Makwongiji or 'the one who sleeps in the house [of the king]'.

On Dunama's death while on an expedition to Awe, where he was buried, he was succeeded by Musa dan Jaji, since his two sons Ari and Dalla were too young. Musa was a man renowned for his warlike capabilities. Under his leadership the new Lafia people increased their dominions, conquering the tribes of Koro, Gwandara, Mama, and Aike, advancing even as far as Monkwor at the foot of the Bauchi plateau. It was during the reign of this powerful chief that the walled town of Jankwe, near present-day Gidan Rai, was broken and the population completely scattered. This was no mean feat, as legend has it that the town was larger than Kano and had withstood even the attacks of the Nupe armies.

But the Lafia people were not to be permitted to harry the borders of Bauchi with impunity, for during the rule of Umar the first, who succeeded Musa and was an even greater warrior, the famous Yakubu of Bauchi determined to wage war on Lafia. With a considerable army behind him he marched on Lafia town. On his arrival he divided the army into two, sending the Madakin Bauchi with one half to besiege the west and part of the north sides while he himself attacked from the east and the remaining part of the north; the south was guarded by a broad and deep stream. Though undefended by any wall, it is said that the people of Lafia gallantly withstood the siege for sixteen days of incessant fighting. At length their valour was rewarded, for on the sixteenth day Umar, by dint of a brilliant sortie, captured Yakubu's principal war-drum. This drum is today numbered among the prized trophies of the Emir of Lafia.

Discouraged by this loss, Yakubu decided to return to Bauchi. But on reaching Adabu he was overtaken by the Madakin Lafia, Dibi, who, as representative of the Emir of Lafia, offered to submit if suitable terms could be arranged. No tribute was to be exacted, but Lafia would send one *riga* or gown each year to Bauchi as a token of allegiance. Peace was arranged on these terms. This was a considerable triumph for the people of Lafia, for in the time of Dunama they had been forced to pay a tribute of eighty tobes at harvest time and another twelve gowns after the rains, besides certain other presents to Bauchi. Yakubu of Bauchi now presented Umar with a flag; this also is still in the possession of the Emir of Lafia.

As a result of this siege, a wall was built round Lafia by Laminu, the successor of Umar. It was not till the time of Abdullahi Dalla (1849–66) that the now famous war wall was built, a second one outside the first to enable the people to farm all the year round without fear of slave-raiding expeditions. But of Dunama's wall, only the names of the four original town gates have survived: Kwandare, Ramin Gishiri (Awe), Dan Banja and Keffi. It was in Laminu's reign that the post of Alkali was created, the first holder being Maina, a scholar from Bornu, whose family has continued a distinguished record of judicial service in Lafia. Islam had become so tainted by Arago customs that one Salihu Buzu, a Katsina *malam*, was sent to prevail upon the people of Lafia to revert to the faith of their forebears. He organized the building of a mosque on the site of the pagan shrine. This was made of *zana* mats but in Emir Abdullahi's time the present mosque was put up on the same site.

When Musa Gana died, the council of selectors found so many able candidates for the throne that they decided that lots should be drawn. It is said in Lafia that Abdullahi Dalla, one of Dunama's sons, drew from the calabash a paper bearing the Arabic inscription, 'It is not for man to decide, but Allah.' He was thereupon installed as Emir. He is chiefly remembered for the building of the war wall round the town.

The reign of Umar (1868–73) is sorrowfully remembered for the capture of Lafia by the roving marauder Bayero, a wayward son of the Sultan of Sokoto. On an earlier visit to Lafia he had felt himself slighted by what he considered Umar's shortfall of presents and attention. Perceiving the military nakedness of the town, Bayero determined to avenge this affront. He rallied the Arago, Koro and Gwandara to his standard, though he could not subvert the Gwandara of Kwandare or the Arago of Obi who had close and affectionate links with Lafia. Marshalling his forces at Kadarko, Bayero marched on Lafia. From his camp on the hill at Kawari, just to the south of the town, he laid siege to Umar. Treacherously seizing the Magajin Lafia, Abdullahi Dalla Bahagu, who had been sent to seek terms for peace, Bayero attacked the town and captured it. The Emir Umar fled through the Keffi gate and reached Bauchi, where he subsequently died. Bayero showed no mercy. The Lafia chroniclers aver that he publicly slaughtered in cold blood many persons at the Keffi gate as a sign of his fury at the Emir's escape, while hundreds were enslaved. The town was burnt. For his services in the attack, the chief of Keana was presented with the engraved wooden door of the Emir's palace, a relic that has been preserved at Keana. As the new Emir, Bayero installed Abdullahi Dalla Bahagu, who it now transpired had all the time been in league with the invader. Shortly after the ceremony, Bayero was recalled to Sokoto just as he was about to attack his former ally Doma.

To restore the damaged emirate, Abdullahi resorted to slave-raiding, his most profitable area being the Ankwe of Shendam. In this he was aided by the Emir of Nassarawa.

During the reign of Mohamman Agwe, slave-rading expeditions were increased, still with the assistance of the Emir of Nassarawa, but now into Tiv territory. But Mohamman Agwe was unpopular with his people, his alleged faults being his intense nepotism and his miserly distribution of the spoils of war, in particular the slaves. Assured of public support, the influential Gayam, Mammadi Chillum, son of Emir Laminu, marched on the palace and demanded the Emir's resignation. The Emir abdicated and fled to Bauchi. Eighteen months later Mammadi and the elders of Lafia were summoned to Bauchi, where the Emir Umaru is said to have taken it upon himself to imprison them and order the reinstatement of Mohamman Agwe.

It was the Emirs of Lafia and Nassarawa who opened the trade-route from Lafia to Loko and established the Lafia market as one of the chief centres for the Benue trade. Loko came into prominence in the first decade of this century when it was the terminus for the head-loaded caravans of porters bringing the tin straws down from Naraguta on the plateau to the Benue for onward shipment by canoe to the ocean-ports of the Niger delta. But after the opening of the Bauchi Light Railway in 1911, Loko declined in importance.[1] Curiously enough it was the railway that brought Lafia back on the economic map, first of all when the Port Harcourt—Kaduna line was built through the emirate, and secondly in 1928 when there were good prospects of a new line being built through Shendam to Bornu from the take-off point of Lafia.

[1] The full story of the Bauchi Light Railway is to be found in A. H. M. Kirk-Greene, 'The Last Journey of Dan Zaria', *Nigeria Magazine*, No. 65, 1960. The spot where the tin-headloaded carriers assembled at Jos for the march down to Loko is on the present site of the Nigerian Airways office. The engine is in the Museum.

Lafia Division was created in 1933 by the addition of the independent district of Awe to the emirate of Lafia. In the same year Muhammadu Angulu died and was succeeded by his cousin Mohamman Agwe II. Though he took the title of 14th chief of Lafia, he was in fact only the 4th Emir of Lafia, as the rank was not current until Lugard recognized it in 1903. A year after this move, Lafia was involved in another administrative reorganization when it was placed with the Keffi-Nassarawa Division to form the new North Benue Division of the three emirates officially described as 'outwardly small replicas of the Northern emirates'. This amalgamation was rescinded in 1938 when Lafia became a Division in its own right.

On the death of the Emir in 1949, a dynastic deadlock ensued and, to the detriment of Lafia affairs, no successor was agreed on for three years. For some time now the principle of selection had become accepted that the Ari and Dalla moieties of Dunama's family should provide the Emir in turn but that with this should go an alternating dynastic system of appointment to the senior titles of Madaki, Uban Gari and Dan Galadima. A similar dissatisfaction with the Emirs had occurred earlier in 1947 when a rumour that Mohamman Agwe was going to abdicate in favour of his son Abubakar, whom he had appointed Dan Galadima, led to a noisy demonstration. In his old age Mohamman Agwe became subject to mental disturbances. Altogether, then, a breakdown in Lafia was not unexpected. In the interregnum Makwangiji Na'ali was appointed the titular Native Authority, but he was so weak that the N.A. Advisory Council took the remarkable step of petitioning Government that the vacant seat of the Emir of Lafia in the House of Chiefs should be given to the Arago Chief of Doma and that he should then take over as Lafia Native Authority. The 1952 solution to the crisis is best told in the Resident's own words:

The work of the Lafia Native Authority and Advisory Council suffered from the growth of faction, intrigue and annoyance arising from the prolonged dispute over the succession to the office of Emir. The deadlock ended in December when I announced to the full Council His Honour's decision to appoint the Madaki Yusufu to be Native Authority and to carry out all the duties of the Chieftaincy of Lafia. The elderly Chamberlain, who had been Native Authority *ad interim* since the late Emir's death, was glad to be quit of an office which he had discharged with credit but found more and more embarrassing and burdensome with the Council divided and himself supporting one of the two rival claimants to the succession. Less than forty-eight hours after the announcement, made on the occasion of the visit of the Walin Bornu to Lafia as Minister of Natural Resources, the Electoral College unanimously appointed Yusufu to be Emir of Lafia. Abubakar, District Head of Assaikio and son of the late Emir, at once assured Yusufu of his co-operation and urged him and the Council to let bygones be bygones and work together for the good of the people and the Emirate. The appointment was endorsed by the Advisory Council and occasioned wide-spread rejoicing.[1]

The demand for a separate Arago state and a separate Keana Native Authority continued, with disturbances necessitating police action breaking out in 1957 and again in 1960. Much was made of the claim that Keana and Doma had been independent at one time and that their chiefs had held some staff of office.

CHIEFS AND EMIRS OF LAFIA*

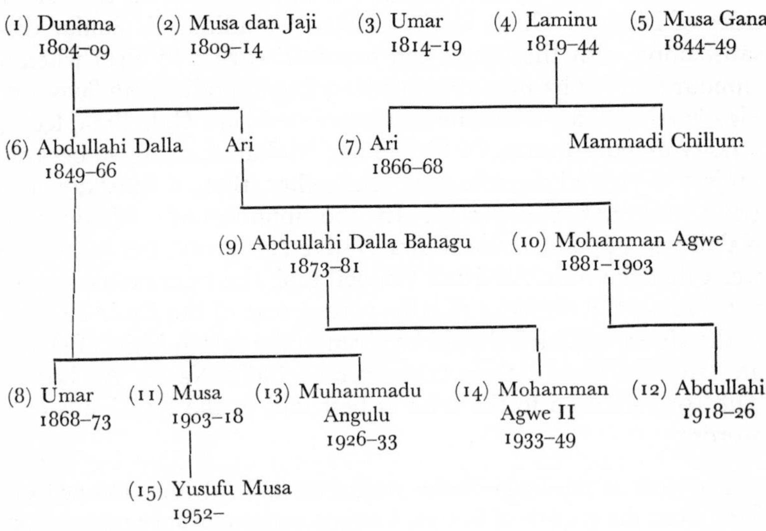

* The title of Emir dates from 1903.

[1] *Annual Report of Benue Province*, 1952, para. 16.

XLVII. JEMA'A

JUST before the outbreak of the jihad, a certain *malam* from Kebbi, by name Usman, went to preach Islam to the Fulani herdsmen who had settled to the east and south of Zaria, mostly on the Kacecare 'plateau' of the Kajuru people. Usman, aided by their *ardo*, 'leader', Abdurrahman (Atona), formed the local Fulani into a cohesive group. Jema'a historians claim that Usman injudiciously warned Sarkin Kajuru that one day his own son would rule them.[1]

Soon after this the Fulani swept the Habe rulers out of Zaria. The Kajuru, anxious about their fate and mindful of Usman's baleful prophecy, decided to eliminate any immediate danger by massacring Usman and his followers. They, however, were warned of the plot by Indema, the favourite Fulani wife of Sarkin Kajuru, and most of them escaped in the night. It is said that when Usman returned home that evening his wife told him of the plot. Usman, thus alerted, picked up his prayer-mat and kettle and slipped away on the pretext of going outside for his ablutions. He headed for Sanga. The Kajuru pursued the Fulani to the edge of the Kagoro plateau, but the main body escaped and settled on the spur of the Darroro hills. Sarkin Sanga welcomed Usman, who hid him from the party of cavalry under Madakin Sarkin Kajuru that searched Sanga. Sarkin Sanga then escorted Usman to join his Fulani brothers at Gumawan-du. Local lore has it that in the deep rift in the ground just outside modern Kafancan lies the body of Indema, buried alive under a pile of stones on the orders of the wrathful Sarkin Kajuru.

The Kajuru made one more attempt to drive out the Fulani, but they were utterly routed and scattered south to Keffi and east as far as Bukuru, being further decimated at the crossing of the

[1] I am indebted to the Jema'a N.A. for supplying a long account of their history, much of which we were able to incorporate in this section, and to many happy history lessons from my students Bulus Gwani, Adam Andow and Yakubu Aboi, with whom I have spent the past four Christmases at Kagoro and to learning from M. Gwamna, Sarkin Kagoro. I have also been allowed to see the unpublished MS. *The History of Kagoro and its Chiefs*, compiled by Mr Yanet Afwai of Kagoro.—A.K-G.

River Kogom. The Fulani at Darroro now sent Usman to Zaria to obtain a flag from the new Emir, Malam Musa, and so to seek his recognition. In granting this, the Emir asked who they were, thus asking for a flag: Usman replied that they were a group, or *jama'a*, of Fulani who had settled round the foothills of Darroro. The Emir then gave his flag and recognition to the settlement of Jema'a-Darroro. This was in about 1810. Abdurrahman (Atona) was persuaded to leave the leadership to Usman, who later accompanied the Emir of Zaria to Sokoto to receive final confirmation of his appointment. It became the tradition for the rulers of Jema'a, like those of Keffi, to be selected by local electoral councils but to be actually turbanned in Zaria. Zaria's first *kofa* or intermediary with Jema'a was the Limamin Juma'a. Usman was now the first Emir of Jema'a. Too late, the Fulani, who had not been particularly keen on having Usman as their chief, woke up to the fact that they had exchanged their *malam* for a master.

One of the former courtesy titles of the Emirs of Jema'a used to be 'Sarkin Kajuru Fellatehu'. This derives from the marriage pact that ended the feud between Jema'a and Kajuru. Jema'a chroniclers write:

> Usman reached Kajuru but found nobody there save a girl, by name Taiba, sitting under a silk-cotton tree. She was the daughter of Sarkin Kajuru. Usman's men seized her and brought her before him. She was wearing *munduwa* on her leg. Usman ordered her to be carried to his house. Then a spy hastened to Sarkin Kajuru and urged him to return to fight the Fulani as they had even captured his daughter. The Kajuru men missed Usman's party with Taiba but they ambushed another group of Fulani and killed Usman's lieutenant Haskiya.

Usman refused all offers of ransom and declared that he would marry her. Sarkin Kajuru complained to the Emir of Zaria, whose judgement had a Solomon-like quality. He ordered Usman to restore Taiba to her father; then he ordered Sarkin Kajuru to give his daughter in marriage to Usman. This was done. Taiba, accompanied by a number of Kajuru families, returned to Jema'a, married Usman, and bore him three sons, each of whom became Emir of Jema'a.

During his reign, Usman conquered the Kaje, Ayu, Mora and Gwandara. The Kagoro were never completely subdued by Jema'a, and they even inflicted a severe attack on the town while

Abdullahi, who had succeeded his father Usman as Emir in 1833, was away on a campaign towards Lafia. The Fulani later retaliated and captured a number of outlying Kagoro villages, which remained as vassals to Jema'a for over a hundred years. One Kagoro legend attributes the fact that they were never completely conquered as a people by the Fulani to the story that Usman had seen in a dream that whoever subjugated the Kagoro would triumph and then immediately die.

Today Jema'a historians suggest that there was never any real war between them and Kagoro except for the conflict brought about by the Tabat Foli affair. They describe it thus:

> The Fulani of Jema'a seized the Kagoro leader Tabat Foli and forced him to take an oath. Hearing this, the men of Kagoro grew angry and burned many houses in Jema'a. The cause of this was that a Kagoro man, by name Mugu Bishut, was very friendly with the people of Jema'a. He and his friend Tabat Foli used to visit them. One day the Kagoro people ambushed a party of Fulani. The Jema'a leaders suspected that Mugu Bishut and Tabat Foli were responsible, so next time they visited Jema'a they were seized. This was the only war between Jema'a and the Kagoro people.

Abdullahi died on a slave-raiding expedition with Zaria against the Doma of Lafia. His brother Musa was such a drunkard that the Emir of Zaria eventually banished him and temporarily gave the throne to the aged Abdurrahman (Atona), whose senility allowed Musa to intrigue successfully enough to regain the emirate. Within a short while, however, Musa was out again, this time deposed by Zaria. Musa is remembered in Jema'a history for his prowess as a warrior. He subdued the Kagoma, and would have annihilated the Kagoro had it not been for their hill-top caves and underground hiding-places. The Kagoro claim they had long used these refuges as a protection against wild beasts.

Musa's brother, Adamu, proved no better as an Emir. He, too, was deposed and then reappointed; he, too, was accused of drunkenness, though Jema'a chroniclers claim that he lost his case because of his inability to produce a large enough bribe to the Zaria court. Adamu was finally deposed in 1885 and yet another son of Usman, Muhammadu Adda, returned as Emir. The family history seemed unstable, for Muhammadu followed in the stormy footsteps of his two brothers, like them being twice deposed by Zaria for maladministration.

In 1888 Abdullahi (Machu) was appointed Emir of Jema'a. During his reign the Sultan of Sokoto had to intervene to stop the civil war between the Fulani of Keffi and of Jema'a. This was after an earlier boundary dispute with the Magajin Keffi which had been settled in favour of Jema'a by the Emir of Zaria. In about 1897 a plot was formed to oust Abdullahi and put in one of his brothers, Usman, then the headman of the Fulani village of Jagindi some fifteen miles south-west of Jema'a. Abdullahi surprised the plotters and had the ringleader, Sarkin Delle, executed. This so incensed the Jagindi Fulani that they rose against Abdullahi, supported by the Kagoma and Kaje.

As a punishment against Zaria for the part played by its vassal Keffi in the murder of Captain Moloney, the emirates of Keffi, Nassarawa and Jema'a were in 1902 removed from the suzerainty of Zaria. Jema'a became a Division of the Nassarawa Province. A detachment of troops was stationed in Jema'a.

The year 1926 brought Jema'a, then described as 'a dream place . . . overcome with a spirit of lethargy', to life again. First, the Emir resigned and was succeeded by Muhammadu. Secondly, the headquarters were removed from the tsetse-ridden town of Jema'an-Darroro (today referred to as Old Jema'a) to the new capital of Jema'an-Sarari (Madakiya). Thirdly, the building of the eastern line from Port Harcourt to Kaduna gave birth to the cosmopolitan if unattractive railway junction town of Jema'a Mallam (later Kafancan), only a few miles away from New Jema'a. So vigorous a town was Kafancan that the Emir, who for some time had been dissatisfied with his backwater, asked permission to move his own headquarters there from Jema'a. This was done in 1933. Meanwhile the Divisional headquarters had been transferred to Kagoro in 1927, but they too were moved again, this time to join the Native Administration in Kafancan. Kafancan has, indeed, stolen the show in Jema'a emirate, though scenically there is nothing to touch the undulating road between Jema'a and Kagoro, with its towering hills on one side and its sudden glimpses of high forest on the other.

Jema'a remained in Plateau Province till 1959, when it was transferred, along with the Federation of the three small Native Authorities of Kagoro, Jaba and Moroa, to form a separate Division of Zaria Province and become the Jema'a Federation. The Emir Muhammadu had for years stoutly resisted the mounting popular wish for a federation of his emirate with these three N.A.s even when he was offered the permanent presidency. The official *Annual Report*, describing Jema'a Emirate as 'an anachronism only held together by the personality of the aged Emir', commented frankly on this:

> Two things prevented agreement: a fear that when the new Division was included in Zaria Province (a proviso politically essential) the Zaria Native Authority would interfere in its affairs; and secondly, the belief that the federal constitution proposed would curtail the rule of the narrow family clique that still controls the Jema'a Emirate. The first fear had no substance, the second was well founded, and in rejecting the federation it is hard to escape the implication that the Emir has preferred his own interests and those of his family to the well-being and progress of his people.

But public opinion against the continuation of the entrenched position of the royal family in such a markedly minority situation was too great. The transfer was effected; the Jema'a Federation was established; and the Emir was appointed president with a council of no less than thirty-one members. Two years later a strained relationship came to a head within the Federation council after 'unfortunate exchanges and major dissensions' between the Emir and his executive councillors.

The eighty-eight-year-old Emir Muhammadu died in 1960. With him passed away a generation; but with his passing the Jema'a crisis—to some extent the dynastic crisis of many an emirate in microcosm, that of a traditional Fulani family ruling over a vast majority of non-Fulani, non-Muslim subjects—came into the open. There was an exceptionally long interregnum, when twelve *malamai* were appointed as the Native Authority; but after an exhaustive examination of the possibility of finding a non-Fulani ruler for the Division, it was found that no chief could yet command an overall support. Accordingly, Muhammadu's son, Isa Muhammadu, then Magajin Gari of Kafancan, was appointed 10th Emir of Jema'a towards the end of 1961.

THE EMIRS OF JEMA'A

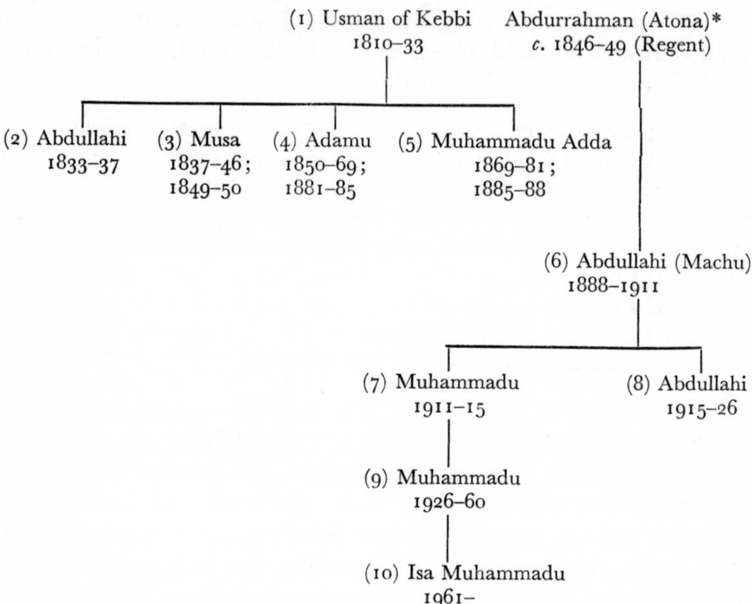

* Some Jema'a sources claim that Abdurrahman (Atona) acted as regent for three months in 1837 and again about 1846 for a period, but he never appears as a ruling emir in any Jema'a king list.

XLVIII. WASE

Of the thirteen Provinces into which Northern Nigeria is now divided, only two—Kabba and Sardauna—have no emirate[1] within their borders; exceptionally, Plateau Province breaks the social pattern of its peoples by including the emirate of Wase within its administrative framework. This is, as we shall see, but a recent accretion.

The original inhabitants of the Wase area were the Basharawa, who had at one time migrated from Konkiok in Bornu and settled on a small hill near the present village of Gaduk. Their first chief was named Tokta. He was followed by one Yamusa, who led his people further south and settled in the vicinity of what is today Wase town. At that time the area came under Jukun control.

The founder of the Fulani dynasty of Wase was one Giwa, who lived at Wuro Mayo in Bauchi. Charmed by a visit to the Wase country, he established firm friendships with the Jukun who lived round the site of modern Wase town. Giwa died in about 1876, leaving three sons, Hassan, Abdu and Umaru. In about 1820 Yakubu, the founder of Bauchi, attacked the Basharawa. One of his generals was Hassan, the son of Giwa, who had become the Madaki of Bauchi. He it was who had told Yakubu about the delights of the country that his father had found so attractive. Yakubu drove them out of their town but allowed them to resettle round the hill of Wase Tofa, lying to the west. He deposed Yamusa, however, and instead appointed Karu as chief of the Basharawa.

Yakubu now gave the land to Hassan, who built the town of Wase as his headquarters. Wase's annual tribute to the Emir of Bauchi is said to have been two men's loads of cloth and three slaves, with a further present of one slave and some salt to the Ajiya. From here Hassan expanded his kingdom by conquering the Ankwe people, who had previously been tributary to the Jukun though recognizing the spiritual leadership of Shendam. Soon after this Yamusa, learning that the Yergam (the Hausa

[1] Mubi is now assuming emirate status.

name for the Tarok of modern Lowland Division) planned to attack the new settlement of Wase Tofa, persuaded Karu to seek a safer site. The Basharawa people now built their town of Ganua.

Hassan was angered by the behaviour of the Basharawa chief, Karu, and had him taken in chains to Bauchi. Yamusa was reinstated; but Karu was later to enjoy the sweetness of revenge. After Hassan's death at Fake in Kano, whither he had been summoned by the Emir of Bauchi to help repel the Bornuese invaders under Shehu Laminu, Karu noised it abroad that Yamusa had in fact sold a number of fugitive Bauchi slaves. Yamusa was disgraced and Karu returned to favour and the chieftaincy of the Basharawa. This was in about 1835. However, fearing the temper of the Emir of Wase, he deemed it wise to evacuate Ganua and withdrew to Gworam, a few miles south-east of Bashar.

Abdu, the 2nd Emir of Wase, first took the title of Sarkin Dutse. He extended his kingdom as far south as Burum Burum beyond Lafia, where on the instructions of the Emir of Zazzau a *kiriya*, an acacia-like tree, was planted to mark the western border of Wase territory. This title, which obtains to this day, derives from the quite remarkable hill (Hausa: *dutse*) which rises abruptly 800 feet above the plain. It has been climbed but rarely in recent history, and in 1959 P. J. Wallace, Divisional Officer, planted the Emir of Wase's flag on the top. Apart from this courageous climb, legend has it that two murderers were offered the chance of saving their lives by one of the Emirs if they could scale Wase Rock. One slipped and plummeted to his death when he was half-way up, but the other, after a valiant struggle, reached the top. By then, however, he was too exhausted or too terrified to try the descent. He gained his freedom but lost his life, for he is said to have died of exposure on the isolated summit of Wase Rock.

On Karu's death in about 1838, the Bashar chieftainship went to Abubakar, whose grandfather had come from Bornu. In 1839 Abubakar moved his people yet again, this time to the new town of Bashar, some twenty miles east of Wase. Meanwhile, the Fulani ruling family had run into trouble and the Emir, Suleimanu, a son of Hassan, found the gates of his own capital shut against him on his return from an unsuccessful expedition against Yelwa. He fled to Dampar and thence to Yergam, eventually being killed in a vain attempt to re-enter Wase.

During the 1880s there was an interregnum in Bashar, when the

Madakin Bashar seized the throne. He was driven out in 1892 by Muhammadu, known as Kobri, the 7th Emir of Wase. Kobri now appointed one of the rightful claimants, Usmanu, the son of Abubakar, but the Emir of Bauchi refused to confirm him and instead turbanned another son of Abubakar, Aliyu, as chief of the Bashar people.

It was Kobri—now called Muhammadu II—who was on the throne when the Royal Niger Company troops under Captain Parker stormed Wase in 1898. Contemporary military records speak of a town wall three miles in circumference and ten feet high, with five gates and a deep moat. The Company's Maxim gun was unable to break such stout defences, so one of the gates had to be rushed. The Emir fled with his people but was killed on the following day by one of his nephews. On the recommendation of the Royal Niger Company, the Ubandoma, Muhammadu, was appointed to the Wase throne by the Emir of Bauchi.[1]

When civil administration was established by the British in 1902, Wase was made independent of Bauchi and placed as a separate district, first in the Shendam Division and then in the Ibi Division of the old Muri Province. The Awe people were separated from Wase in 1905 and the Ankwe of Shendam were freed from the emirate's control in 1909 (Shendam denies that it was ever conquered by Wase), but *en revanche* in 1919 the whole of Yergam district, including the Garkawa, was transferred to Wase. On the general administrative reorganization of 1926, Wase emirate was downgraded (the Emir was deposed) and included in the new Adamawa Province, but in 1946 it was transferred to Plateau Province. Part of the large unpopulated tracts of this new acquisition were gratefully received by the planners of the Shendam Resettlement Scheme.

In 1952 the Emir of Wase regained the rank of 2nd Class Chief, a grade that his father had lost many years earlier. A year later Wase became part of the Federal Council of Lowland Division, which used to meet at Gerkawa. Once the honeymoon was over, however, murmured complaints were heard from the Wase elements. These crystallized into a demand for their own Native Treasury, a plea granted in 1956 when Wase became a

[1] The new Nigerian Army Museum at Zaria houses a remarkable souvenir of the days of the Royal Niger Company's operations at Wase, in the shape of an unexploded shell.

separate Native Administration and opened its Beit-el-Mal with a capital of £6,000. After a shaky start, the emirate has settled down, and in the dubious period of Plateau Province in the 1960s Wase earned praise for being the only N.A. to keep its head above water. This was largely due to the leadership of the Emir, Alhaji Abdullahi Maikano, who was credited with continually placing the welfare of his people, predominantly non-Muslim, above all other considerations.

THE CHIEFS AND EMIRS OF WASE[1]

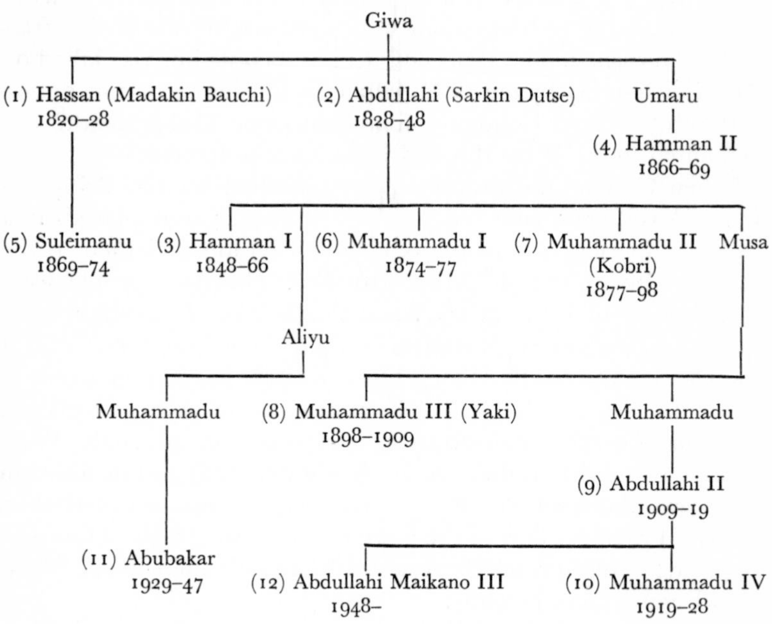

[1] The rank of Emir is said to date from 1902, when Wase was released from its vassal-status to Bauchi.

4. EMIRATES DERIVING INDEPENDENTLY

XLIX. ABUJA

ABUJA, Daura and Argungu represent three small islands which resisted the flood of conquest when a century and a half ago the Fulani overran the rest of what are today the Fulani emirates of Northern Nigeria. Abuja remains the classic model of a genuine and largely unadulterated Hausa emirate, and it is to Abuja that the scholar most happily turns to seek a clear picture of the pre-jihad Habe society.

This is how the chroniclers of Abuja have handed down the story of how in 1804 the Fulani drove Makau, the last Habe ruler of Zaria, out of his city and forced him to seek refuge among his former vassals, the Koro (or Kwararafa) in the south-west:

> A certain *malam* named Musa, who was a teacher of the strict Faith in the land of Zazzau . . . with Yamusa, a Fulani of Bornu, and three hundred and thirty-three men . . . fell upon the King of Zazzau, Muhamman Makau, on Saturday the tenth day of the month of Zulhaji in the year 1804 whilst he was at the prayer-ground of Idi outside the town. Though Makau had many men with him, he was defeated for they could not get back inside the town to arm, and he was forced to flee. That is why, when Abuja was built, the people had their prayer-ground inside the town . . . and that is why the Emir's Bodyguard and the Archers stand behind him, facing west, while he turns in prayer to the east.[1]

The Fulani pursued Makau, first to Kauru, whose chief, Jibrin, shut the gate against the fugitive king, and then to Kajuru. Here the chief, Haruna, gave asylum to Makau and in return suffered a six months' siege. Finally Makau reached the Koro town of Zuba,[2] whose Chief, Muhamman Gwabo, was friendly.

In pre-Fulani Zazzau, Zuba had been administered along with

[1] This section owes a great debt of gratitude to two Abuja scholars, M. Hassan and M. Shu'aibu Na'ibi, on whose work, *A Chronicle of Abuja*, we have gladly drawn heavily and which we commend to all those interested in Habe history.

[2] Some 6 miles south of where Abuja town came to be built.

Izom, Kawu and Jiwa as one of Zaria's four vassal states, each under a Koro chief responsible for exacting *gandu* or tribute. Zuba's chief held the title of Barden Yamma, 'the Warden of the West'. From this war camp the Habe held the Fulani at bay for over a year. When they eventually withdrew to Zaria in 1807, Makau made Zuba his new capital. To this day the Koro call Ali, who succeeded Muhamman Gwabo, 'the Victorious One'. Among the three thousand people who had followed Makau from Zaria were his brothers Abu Ja and Abu Kwaka. Makau and Abu Kwaka were born of the same mother, and when the mother of Abu Ja died it was she who fed him at her breast. So it is that the people of Abuja honour the name of Tasalla who suckled the first three kings of Abuja.

The Gwari and Koro continued to pay tribute to Makau as they had done when he was Sarkin Zazzau. The Gwari of Abuja claim that they came from Bornu where they were subjects of the Koro, and when the Kanuri drove them both out they scattered into Kano and Zaria Provinces. When war broke out in Kano, they were again driven out, the Gwari going wherever the Koro went. It was the chief of Sagwarinpa who led the exodus from their home in Kano to Zaria, then into the area now forming Abuja emirate, first to Lasunta near Guje and then to Jiwa. From Jiwa they went to Gwarinpa. At last they came to Zuba and found the Koro already there. The Koro gave them a place to live on the top of the hill. None can give an exact date when these people left Kano but it seems to have been about 1720.

Makau now raided Jiwa, Toto, Panda and Gulu, and in 1825 considered himself strong enough to attack the powerful Fulani town of Lapai. His soldiers, however, resented the order he had given at Jiwa forbidding them to make slaves of their prisoners. Assuming that any victory at Lapai would again be unprofitable to them, they deserted him in the middle of the battle. Makau, aware of his desperate situation, urged his younger brother Abu Ja to return and unite his people under him as the next Emir. Makau was killed on the battlefield at Lapai. Today his praise is sung in Abuja:

Makau, whose Mother was Tasalla,
The Man of many Spears.
As Peppers make the Eyes run,
So Men run before your Anger.

Abu Ja (meaning 'Abu the Red', on account of his light skin; his real name was Jatau) became the next Habe Sarkin Zazzau and the 1st Emir of Abuja. He remained three years at Izom among the Gwari before deciding to build a new capital further away from the marches of the Fulani of Lapai. Choosing a site at the foot of the Abuchi hills, Abu Ja built his own house in 1828 (on the spot where the old Entrance House of Zazzau still stands to this day) and the following year the walls were started round the town to which he gave his name. Among his symbols of office was a quiver containing two hundred poisoned arrows made specially for him by the people of Burum. They called the poison 'the tribe-slayer', for not only did it kill the person struck by the arrow but also brought death to everyone who set eyes on the corpse. Saddened by the murder of three of his sons captured in battle by the Emir of Nassarawa, Makama Dogo, Abu Ja died in 1851. His praise is sung:

> Light of Skin,
> Lord and Master of the Walled Town,
> And in the open field the first to draw Blood.

Abu Ja was succeeded by his brother Abu Kwaka, nicknamed Dogon Sarki because of his six and half feet stature. He was the first to allow strangers and traders within the gates of Abuja and he reopened the trade routes with Zaria and Bida. In his reign donkeys, camels, ostriches and tame hyaenas were first seen in the market of Abuja, and many cloth-weavers, following the import of strange clothes from the Nupe country, came to settle. Abu Kwaka's religious nature led him to ban the *bori* dancing, an age-old Hausa propitiation of the evil spirits which take possession of the body, usually women's. He was succeeded by Abu Ja's son Ibrahim in 1877, also known as *Iyalai* on account of the number of his followers and *Dodon Gwari* or 'the Terror of the Gwari', whom in his reign he finally subdued. 'Who will stroke the Head of the Wild Buffalo?' ran his *kirari* or praise song, for he not only defeated an incursion by the Emir of Kontagora but also repulsed the Fulani of Zaria with tremendous losses at the Battle of Farin Ruwa, the 'white' or 'clear water', in 1893.

This was the fight in which the most famous of all Abuja warriors, Kauran Caci the Jarmai, distinguished himself in the gorge by the stream called Saiwa. 'Before any man of Zaria shall pass this gate and come to your house,' he swore to the Emir of Abuja as he hurried back to the palace to fetch the Sword of Zazzau, 'we shall be dead with ants crawling into our mouths.' It was at the town's Gate of the White Water, also known as the Bida gate, that the three hundred Fulani prisoners were assembled. Traditionally they should have had their hands cut off and been sent back to Zaria, but the Wambai urged against it: 'No, if we do so, enmity will never cease. Better kill them outright.' Except for one man, the son of the Makaman Zaria who was the half-brother of the Emir Yero and therefore pardoned by the Abuja people as a member of a royal family, all were executed. The chronicle continues:

Then their heads were cut off and put on poles which were stuck along the wall of the town so that everyone who came in or who left by the Gate of the White Water should see them; and this battle increased the enmity between the Fulani and the Abuja . . . But after a little time had passed, the Emir Ibrahim gave the Makama of Zaria's son garments and money for his journey and handed him on to the Sarkin Keffi to be sent back to Zaria.

The first emissary of the British found the gates of Zuba shut in his face when he arrived there from Zaria in 1900. The High Commissioner accepted the chief's subsequent apology but sent back a letter of explanation and a Union Jack, both of which have been preserved to this day. The letter reads:

The Fourth Day of May in the Year 1900.
This letter comes from Governor Lugard:
Greetings and more honour to Mahamman, the Chief of Zuba, together with the expression of my confidence.

After this:—
I let you know that I have seen the messenger whom you sent, and I have heard your message and understood all that you have said.

After this:—
I tell you that you have done wrong; but since you realize this, I will forgive you and pardon your fault.

After this:—
I tell you to watch your actions carefully. I have heard what you have to say and I have also heard all the white man's report.

After this:—

I warn you with the utmost seriousness to take heed of your conduct and to pass on this warning to your people. Also you shall take care of this flag; do not treat it lightly. Every town which possesses a flag such as this becomes thereby a place of importance, for this flag is the flag of our Queen and not to be treated lightly. Should you hold it cheap, it is your own honour and authority which you cheapen.

After this:—

I notify you that I am clearing a road from the bank of the Niger to your town, and from there to the banks of the Kaduna river, so that even a woman travelling alone with her load may pass in safety, or a child. This is my intention. As to the road from Kurmin Giwa to Zaria, all is well; with the road from Lafiya to Wukari, all is well as far as the Birnin Gwari road; every man, woman, and child, the old and the young, may pass in safety.

After this:—

I tell you that we are the rulers of the world. If a man does aught by night, we know of it by morning; if by day, we know of it by night, you may be sure of that. Therefore take heed of your behaviour. I have accepted your explanation and forgiven you for what is past, but for the future take care that nothing shall happen to harm our mutual confidence and respect.

That is all.

After the assassination of Resident Carnegie at Tawari in neighbouring Kabba and the death of a Christian convert, Bako, in a highway robbery along the trade route from Lokoja through Abuja to the Hausa states, it was clear that both the Emir and the Madawaki were involved in the distribution of the loot if not in the actual organization of the brigandry. Accordingly in August 1902, Lieutenant-Colonel Beddoes and the Resident of Nassarawa Province, Captain Moloney, crossed the River Iku and encamped their troops outside Abuja. The Resident sent his messenger, Abdu Tinti, to inform the Emir that he wished to speak to him. After a skirmish the Emir fled to the Abuci Hills but the troops pursued him and Ibrahim was mortally wounded.

Ibrahim was succeeded by Muhamman Gani, the son of Abu Kwaka. It was not till 1904 that a fort was built above the town (on the site of the present D.O.'s house) and Abuja garrisoned to establish administration. At an assembly of all the chiefs of Nassarawa Province at Keffi in 1905, Lugard settled the emirate boundaries, confirmed the chiefs in their titles, and gave each a staff of office. Abuja historians say that Muhamman Gani was afraid to claim certain areas that had traditionally been subject to Abuja. Abuja believes that between 1905 and 1910 it lost the two Zaria vassal states of Jere and Kagarko, which it probably laid claim to after its defeat of the Zaria Fulani under Yero in 1893, and the Gwari-Koro settlements of Kuta, Paiko Gusoro and Abuci.

Lugard chose Keffi in preference to Abuja as the provincial headquarters. Abuja became a separate Division and remained one until the 1926 administrative reorganization, but it lost much of its territory. Koton Karfi was restored to it from Keffi in 1910 but was taken away again three years later, while Jere and Jajjale were handed over to Zaria and the northern boundary drawn back to the River Tafa. During Muhamman Gani's reign the Idi prayer-ground was taken outside the town and the first nomadic Fulani moved in, under their Ardo, Sadiku. When the unpopularity of the transfer of the market to the foot of the Salanke's Hill became evident through its opprobrious name, *kasuwar tilas*, 'the compulsory market', it was moved back to the centre of the town.

On Muhamman Gani's retirement on pension in 1917, Musa Angulu, son of Ibrahim, and Madawaki as well as district head of Izom, became Emir. Among his many claims to fame in Abuja memories are that mining was opened up in his reign and that he was the first Emir to fly in an aeroplane. For the fine work done by the people of Abuja on the railway construction between Lafia and Kafancan the Emir was suitably honoured by a public award in 1926. Waziri Gambo, a Kano man who had been appointed in 1912 to the new title, died in 1929. On the death of his successor nine years later the post was abolished and gradually all the non-Habe titles except Alkali have been done away with. Abuja started its reputation for education in the 1930s when it was one of the first N.A.s to employ ex-schoolboys and teach them typewriting. The district heads were reduced from nine to three, Bwari, Kuje and Zuba, in 1934. The Emir, despite incipient blindness, was described by the Resident in 1935 as 'a delightful personality beloved by his people', stirring up great loyalty among his councillors and affection among his subjects as he toured his districts in a motor car.

The Emir died in March 1944 and was succeeded by his cousin Sulaimanu Barau, next Habe Sarkin Zazzau and 6th Emir of Abuja, of whom it is sung:

> Be patient, and listen not to idle tales.
> Poisoned chaff attracts the silly sheep—and kills them.

Sulaimanu Barau was the first old boy of the famous Katsina Training College to become an Emir, and had been a teacher for several years before his appointment as district head of Diko. 'When he was appointed Emir,' we learn, 'he abolished some of the old customs of the Habe, and in particular he put an end to the practice of people going down on their knees and pouring dust on their heads in obeisance before him or any other person.' In 1958 he became the first Emir of Abuja to perform the pilgrimage. He also visited England, consulting an eye specialist, and has taken a leading part in Red Cross and social works. His was the first emirate to dispense with a permanent District Officer. In the words of the most recent official report on Abuja:

> This compact and economically viable emirate has continued to prosper and to progress under the dominating and energetic leadership of the Chief whose influence pervades at all aspects of local administration to the undoubted benefit of the country at large.

The death of the Madawaki, M. Ahmadu, in 1954 gave rise to a most interesting and significant change, for the Emir chose the Sarkin Yamma, Muhammadu, son of the Koro Chief of Zuba, to succeed to the title and to the position of Chief Councillor. This was the first time that a Koro has been appointed to such a post, though the Emir's grandfather, Abu Kwaka, had wished to appoint Muhammadu's father Bawa, in recognition of his loyalty and services. But Bawa was reluctant, and the Emir gave him one of his daughters in marriage instead. The significance of the appointment lies also in the fact that the Koro of Zuba hold a special place amongst the tribes. They have always been the natural overlords of the Gwari who respect them, and indeed followed them to Abuja from other lands. Moreover they are the guardians of the remarkable Zuma Rock, and as such are regarded as spiritual leaders.

Another interesting appointment was that of Saidu Bubuyi, a Gwari of Ushafa, to the title (once held by the present Emir) of

Iyan Bakin Kasuwai. This was not the first time that a Gwari had held an Abuja title, but previously it had been a military one, such as Jarmai or Hawni, for the Gwari were renowned fighters.

This was in some measure a result of separatist unrest among the Gwari of Diko in 1953. There are three stories about the origin of the name Diko. One is that the Koro who were living there before them called them *diko* meaning strangers. Another story is that when the Gwari of Diko asked the people of Gwazunu to give them yam seed they gave them that kind of yam seed which is called *diko*. Another explanation is that when they came they found Fulani living there whose headman was called Dikko, which is the Fulani title for the head of a group of nomadic Fulani.

Today the Emir's Council is broadly based, consisting of the three permanent members of Madawaki (Koro), Makama Karami (Hausa) and Iyan Bakin Kasuwa (Gwari), together with one of the four elected members, three of whom are Gwari. So wise was the administration of Abuja that it became almost a watchword. In 1957 its District Officer was withdrawn and the Division was legally abolished two years later, Abuja again setting a pattern for other emirates. Abuja's fame has spread far beyond the shores of Nigeria in the last ten years, for exhibitions of its exquisite pottery have been held in London and New York.

The Emir of Abuja is still some times addressed as Ṣarkin Zazzau and it is whispered that until very recently prayers were offered up daily in the mosque for his return to Zaria. The Chief badge of office remains the *Wukar Zazzau*, 'the Knife of Zaria'.

THE EMIRS OF ABUJA

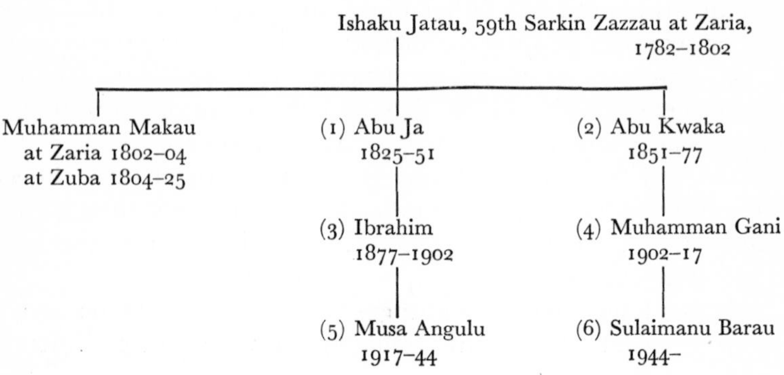

L. BIU

THE area that is today covered by Biu emirate received many of the Chad-sprung migrations in the first millennium. The land between the River Gongola in the west and the Mandara mountains in the east welcomed so many migrant peoples: some stayed and settled, others stayed and then moved on. From about the sixteenth century a number of small kingdoms began to develop here, among them Biu and Shani. Bornu chroniclers such as Ahmed ibn Fartua, the personal *imam* of Mai Idris who wrote his king's biography in about 1583, refers to a chief of Yamta in the south-east.

Now this Yamta-ra-Wala, or Yamta the Great, was the founder of the present royal dynasty of Biu. His real name was Abdullahi. The origin of the name has a number of interpretations. Some connect it with the Bura words *ya*, an honorific prefix, and *mpta*, meaning 'death', and have suggested the sobriquet of 'one who deals out death to his enemies'. A Kanuri *malam* told J. G. Davies, who compiled the standard history of Biu when he was Divisional Officer there,[1] that the name derived from the phrase *yauman-taraku-wallah*, 'he will be leader of the people'. Again, an early *alkali* of Biu affirmed that the chief's real name was Abdullahi but that when he rode out from Birni in anger at his failure to gain the throne of Bornu, he cried out *yauman-tarani-wallahi anasulden insha'allah*, 'one day you shall see that I am a chief, God willing'. Present-day Biu scholars interpret the name as meaning 'you will soon see me or hear of me'. Local tradition asserts that Yamta was the son of a Mandara woman who was already carrying him in her womb at the time she was taken into the Mai of Bornu's household. Yamta was brought up as a Kanuri and because of his proximity to the Mai he stood in line for the kingship. On the death of Mai Idris Katagarmabe in 1526 Yamta was, however, not chosen because, it is said, he did not kill the significant ox in the correct Muslim fashion. Ashamed at this, Yamta left Birni

[1] This chapter acknowledges much to J. G. Davies, *The Biu Book*, 1956. See also the unpublished MSS. of F. Edgar and his *Litafi na Tastuniyoyi na Hausa*, 3 vols.

Ngazargamu for Mandara, accompanied by seventy-two men and their families. There, the historians relate, half the party decided not to stay but to look for fresh lands: 'They entered the country of the Babur and the land of Gombe and settled there in certain places.'[1] The story goes on:

Buba Yero . . . set out for Biu, against those who were descended from the son of the Biu king Yamta or Yamtab the son of Bashar: Yamta's mother Asga was an Arab of Egypt; a caravan of merchants . . . sold her to the son of the Sultan of Auzum; the latter placed her in his harem where the Sultan of Auzum went in to her and she became pregnant by him with a son to whom the name Yamta or Yamtab was given. . . .

(Later she got lost, when) . . . she met three wild men who were hunting elephants and wild sheep and were from the town of Ngasargamo in Bornu. They looked upon her as a great find for she was of a very fair complexion and of such great beauty and handed her over to the king of Bornu Idris ibn Ahmad who placed her in his house where she gave birth to a son . . .; on the day when his hair was clipped they gave him the name of Muhammad but his mother called him Yamta.

She told him . . . how she had come to enter Bornu and said to him, 'Yamta Ula, I have seen a vision that you will leave Bornu and will go to Biu a country of pagans; verily if you do not obtain the rule of that country you will obtain the rule of the rest of the world . . .' Later on, a wager was made regarding the hunting of a black cow and the people said 'he who kills a cow northwards is not the king's son and will not succeed him, but he who kills a cow in the east is the king's son and entitled to the rule of his father'.

Yamta Ula killed a cow in the north whereupon the populace said, 'This is not the king's successor.' His brother however killed cows in the east and all the people cried, 'This is the king's son indeed. . . .' When Yamta saw this he became very angry with his brother and leaving Ngasargamo set out for the mountains of Biu where he found pagans living on the mountain tops . . . he remained with them . . . his descendants are the rulers of Biu today.

Ahmad Al Sanjari says that historians are agreed that the matter is not as related above but that the mother of Yamta Ula was of the royal house of Auzum and that she was stolen away by a thief sent by the Sultan of Egypt. . . .

She remained in (the Sultan's) house until she was five months pregnant at which time she determined to flee and leaving the house by night by stealth she set off . . . but lost her way until she was seized

[1] Quoted in H. R. Palmer, *Sudanese Memoirs*, vol. ii.

by elephant hunters from Bornu who delivered her to the king of Bornu Idris ibn Ahmad; he placed her in his house on account of her beauty and attractions and later on she gave birth to a son; this is the more correct version. They gave him the name of Ahmad but his mother called him Yamta Ula.[1]

These relatives of Yamta spread right across the Biu-Marghi complex, so that today there exist Yamta stock among the Kilba, Higi, Bazza and Marghi peoples of Adamawa and Sardauna Provinces as well as in Biu and Bornu Divisions. Yamta established a sizeable kingdom for himself in the area bounded by the Gongola and the village of Kopchi, with his first capital at a place called Limbur, between Chikorkur and Mandaragarau. The last-named was at one time a kingdom no less important than Babur. Yamta's grave is still identified at Limbur. To do this he was obliged to have recourse to legendary stratagems and oust the Bura from their settlements at Mirnga, Diwar and Buratai. Of his exploits in this connexion, Biu lore has it thus:

Yamta could not take Kiwar so he went there well-dressed and met the slave of a daughter of the Diwar Chief who was drawing water. He got her to take him to the Chief's daughter who, when all were asleep, took Yamta to her father's spear and explained that whatever army came to fight they would be defeated if her father had this spear. Some days later when all the people left to harvest the Chief's corn the daughter remained behind and Yamta came. The daughter offered him drink and he plied her with this drink until she was drunk, whereupon he killed her and took the spear. Three days later Yamta returned with the spear and an army and took the town. He told the people that as he had the spear (symbol of chieftainship) he was now their Chief. Up to 1923 at least the Diwar people are those who pray for rain should it fail in any year. Yamta attacked Old Buratai but was driven back. The Chief of Old Mirnga then helped him and the Chief of Old Buratai went to a baobab tree which opened—he entered and was stopped, every Babur Chief would send a slave and a white horse to Mirnga—the people would try on foot to catch them, those successful being allowed to keep them. Another story is that when Yamta got to Old Mirnga he was several times repulsed by a spear which arose miraculously from the ground and drove him back. He secretly went to Old Mirnga and seduced the Chief's daughter who gave him the spear—he then conquered Mirnga.[2]

Yamta called his followers Babur, and the Babur (or Pabir)

[1] Davies, op. cit., p. 279; Appendices IV and V.
[2] Davies, op. cit., p. 284.

people today derive from intermarriage between Yamta's followers and the indigenous Buram Sha. Yamta's *kirari* or praise-song, freely translated (it is an amalgam of Kanuri and Babur) goes thus:

> He is like a lion, like a lion of the dark forest, yet has no mane; nothing can stand against him except for natural elements like shrubs and the wind.
>
> His importance is such that he is like a pillar holding up the world; although small in size like a sack made from one squirrel's skin yet he controls a large territory as though that sack contained all the meat of one elephant.
>
> Just as a deaf man may appear to be disobedient because of not hearing, so he is brave and fearless, for although he hears he behaves as though he doesn't, nothing dismaying him. He is independent of help from other people, like a baby locust which flies away when born not requiring any milk or assistance from its mother.[1]

By the time of Yamta's death, in *c.* 1580, he had established a viable kingdom. It was, however, never as stable as its neighbour Shani, because of the nomadic element in the Babur people. According to Biu legend, Yamta suddenly disappeared into the ground because he grew annoyed with his son Mari who when tested by his father tried to prove that he could boil and eat a stone. Hence in Biu lore Yamta did not die but 'entered the ground'. Yamta's son was a weaker character. Disintegration appears to have ensued, with the Bura reconquering their motherland to within a few miles of Biu town and later on the Tera reasserting themselves. Not until the reign of Mari Watila Tampta, in about 1670, did the Babur kingdom become really stabilized, though for another century Biu was continuously at war with its neighbouring kingdoms.

These, however, were soon overshadowed by the Fulani wars. The chief of Babur, Garga Moda, is said to have been killed by the Fulani in *c.* 1760, but it was Buba Yero, the founder Emir of Gombe, who really brought war to the upper Gongola valley, with his campaigns in Shani, his attack on Wade (now in Gombe), his foray into Bornu in 1804, and his support of Gwani Mukhtar in the sack of Gujba. The Fulani killed the Babur chief Garga Kopchi, whom they drove from Kogu, the remains of which 200-year-old settlement a mile north of Biu can be seen. He was

[1] Davies, op. cit., p. 286.

killed at Tanga, near Hyema, where he is buried, and for a while the Fulani were able to rule the area as they pleased. It was left to Di Rawa's son, Mari Watirwa, to rid the Biu kingdom of the Fulani. He set up his headquarters at Kogu, summoned every man and woman to his standard, and drove the Fulani from Pubara and Zakam, pursuing them as far as Gurbal, near Gulani. Here Mari Watirwa is said to have received a letter from the Sultan of Sokoto declaring the River Gongola to be his boundary. The Fulani Kitaku of Biu Division originate from this episode.

Mari Watirwa died in 1838 and was succeeded by Ari Paskur, who reigned for thirty-five years. First he lived at Kogu, then he moved to Gura, near Viyukuthla. In about 1870, towards the end of his life, he ordered his people to clear the forest and build the walls of Biu town, but blindness robbed him of ever seeing his new creation. During his reign, Dr Barth passed to the east of Biu, noting in his diary that:

> W.S.W. from the Marghi live the Babur or Babir, scattered in small hamlets over a mountainous basaltic district with the exception of their principal seat Biyu which is called after the name or probably rather the title of their chief. This place . . . is reported to be of large size. The Babur have in certain respects preserved their independence while in others like the Marghi they have begun to yield to the overwhelming influence of their Mohammedan neighbours. But the Marghi claim superiority over their kinsmen in point of courage; for of their relationship there can be no doubt.[1]

Ari Paskur was followed by his son Mari Biya, who moved from Viyukuthla to Biu town in 1878, five years after his accession. He was the first chief to reside in Biu, building his palace of stone on the site of the present Emir's house. As a warrior, Mari Biya delayed just long enough to supervise the laying-out of his courtiers' houses in the new capital before he hurried off to the wars. His reputation as a fighter remains alive in Biu history, and his fierceness is remembered by such epithets as 'porridge of tobacco and soup of pepper'. Legend adds that he was physically so strong that he could break five spears simply by shaking them in his fist. Mari Biya died in 1891.

The next chief of Babur was Garga Kwomting, who even at this late stage in Biu history seems to have been largely nomadic. He had moved to Pelaminta when the British first penetrated

[1] Quoted in Davies, op. cit., p. 39.

Babur country in 1903, from their military post at Gujba. In the following year he was recognized as chief of the Babur and took up his residence in Biu, though it was not till 1918 that the Biu Division was created. Up to then the Biu and Babur Districts came, first, under the jurisdiction of the two Administrative Officers at Gujba, and then in 1907, for a while, under the District Officer of the Marghi Division at Ajimari. Not till 1914 was a Political Officer stationed in Biu itself.

Garga Kwomting died in 1908. He was succeeded by his son Ari (Dogo), then aged thirty-two. Both of his parents were, interestingly enough in the Biu context, Bura. His jurisdiction was now extended over the Bura and he was installed as chief of the Babur and Bura. Meanwhile it was discovered that the Chief of Gulani had over-estimated his original authority over the Tera people when he convinced the Resident of Bornu to appoint him as Chief of the Tera District in 1904. So unsatisfactory was the administration of the Tera chiefs, first Mai Kore of Gulani and then, after his deposition in 1911, Mai Kworianga, that it was decided to abolish the unit. In 1914 the Gulani-Tera area was divided between Gujba and Biu. The Tera in Biu emirate were fortunate in having a man of character, Barde Yamta, as their district head, who ruled them for thirty years.

In 1918 it was agreed, despite the mutual ethnic antipathy, that Mai Biu should extend his control over the Bura. He was upgraded from a District Head (Third Grade Chief) to a Second Class Chief. The Marghi district was shed to Bornu, leaving the districts of Babur, Tera and Bura. From 1920 on we find Mai Ari referred to as the Emir of Biu. The honorific title of Mai was inappropriate because of its Kanuri origin, and locally he is widely known by the Babur-Bura title of Kuthli Viyu—the latter word being the correct pronunciation of 'Biu'. So well did the new emirate seem to function that in 1921 it was enlarged by the transfer of three areas from Yola Province: the trans-Hawal Bura, the Shani enclave (which, thanks to gubernatorial errors, shuttled to and fro again in 1924 and yet once more in 1926), and the Marghi district. This last-named became, in 1937, Askira District, but right from its transfer to Biu Division it was placed in charge of the remarkable Mai Maina. No description of Biu can be complete without a reference to this wonderful old man.[1]

[1] See his autobiography *Mai Maina Sarkin Askira*, written in Hausa in 1957.

The Emir Ari Dogo was seriously ill for the last few years of his reign and he died in 1935. His reign—he had been appointed a chief in 1908—had been an outstanding one and it was thanks to his strong personality and abilities that both the emirate and the Division of Biu were firmly established. At his own request he was buried at Viyukuthla. He was succeeded by his brother, Ari Gurgur, after a split vote by the Birma and his traditional council: the other candidate was Ari I's son, Maidalla Madu, then only twenty-eight.

The Gwani enclave was handed back to Gombe in 1936. A year later both Shani and Askira were made into Native Authorities. When Ari died in 1951, his nephew Maidalla Madu, who had contested the throne in 1935 and was now District Head of Babur, was appointed Emir under the name Muhammad Aliyu. His reign opened inauspiciously, however, for he was soon on strained terms with his council and had to be warned. The Council was then reorganized to give place to representation from the Bura and Tera elements. A disastrous fire in 1956 destroyed much of Biu town and only just missed the Emir's palace.

The Biu Federation was inaugurated in 1957, comprising Biu emirate and the two independent districts of Shani and Askira. But the atmosphere continued uneasy, and after a commission of inquiry the Emir of Biu resigned in 1959. He was succeeded by Maidalla Mustafa, then District Head of Kwaya territory.

One of the celebrated scenic wonders of Biu is Tilla Lake, a few miles south-west of the town, with its hundreds of crocodiles. Many a belief attaches to them, some of them—such as that linked to the Emir of Biu—totemic.[1]

[1] Davies, op. cit., Appendix III.

THE EMIRS OF BIU *

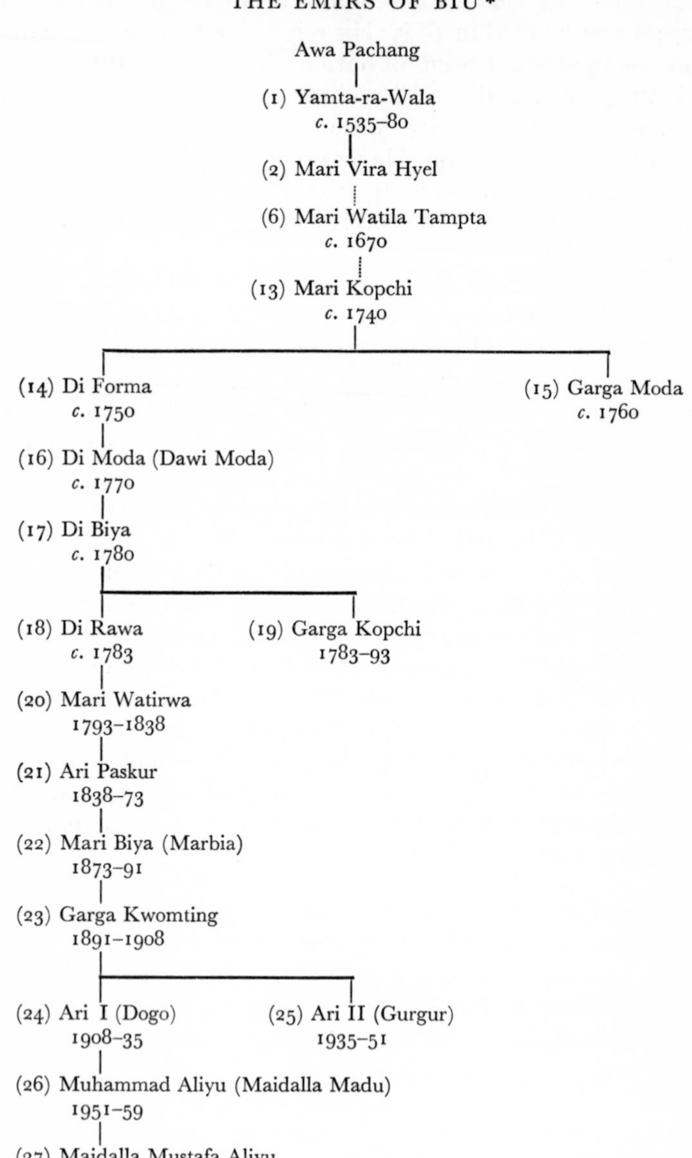

* For a complete list, including all the Babur kings and the Shani dynasty, see Davies, op. cit., pp. 273–6.

LI. BORGU

THERE are many legends about Kisra, the founder of the Borgu people who can, with the Kebbawa, claim to be one of few areas to have successfully repelled the advances of all the empires of the Western Sudan, not excluding the Fulani. Some say that Kisra arose in Mecca preaching a new religion, and was driven thence with his followers by the Muslims. But most accounts give the impression that Kisra was the head of a tiny clan who caused a great stir by refusing to accept the reforms of the Prophet or to be converted to Islam. There was a struggle, in which he was defeated, and with his followers he was forced to cross to Africa and eventually to traverse the continent until they came to the River Niger.

Tradition connects the Yoruba emigration with Kisra's. But here again accounts vary. Some say that Idah's origin is the same as Bussa's, and that when Kisra reached the region of Zaria some of his people broke away and turned south towards the Benue. The Yorubas may have been a part of the group of which Kisra was the head, and it is recounted how they unsuccessfully attempted to persuade Kisra to lead them, and eventually went without him.

However that may be, all legends agree that, though Kisra himself never reached Bussa, his followers, led by his three sons, at last crossed the Niger at Illo, and that the river was immediately afterwards widened to its present size by a miracle. It is not certain who caused the miracle. It may have been Kisra, who, being pursued by Muslims, thus brought pursuit to an end, or it may have been the Muslims, who thus prevented the unbelievers from ever returning to Mecca. Kisra settled at Koko in Gwandu, whence he is said to have mysteriously vanished.

This was the signal for the group, which so long had held together, to break up. Kisra's sons Woru, Sabi and Bio founded the towns of Bussa, Nikki and Illo respectively. They still looked, however, to Kisra as their leader, both spiritual and temporal, and Kisra's semi-priestly status has been handed down to every succeeding king of Bussa and is largely responsible for the spread of their influence.

There are two versions of the descent of the Emir of Bussa. One claims that he springs from Kisra's half-brother by the same mother and a different father, who was the person left in charge at Kisra's death. The other tradition maintains that he is descended from Kisra's second son, brother to the first chief of Nikki, and uncle to the chief of Kaiama. The latter view finds support in the custom whereby the chief of Nikki used to pay homage to the ranks of the chief of Bussa at Karibondi on his appointment to the throne and vice-versa. This tomb of Karibondi, believed to be the chief of Bussa who received Kisra, is, along with the stones marking the doorway of his house, still visible. The Bussawa today disclaim any relationship with the Kaiama people, whom they refer to as Bokoboro and acknowledge as having come from Zamfara. This was substantiated in the 1962 census, when the Kaiama people requested the N.A. that they should be registered as Bokoboro and not as Bussawa.[1] The chief of Bussa claims distant relationship with Bornu,[2] with whom he is said to have exchanged gifts annually up to the end of the eighteenth century. This practice was momentarily revived in 1928. Nikki in time past has had greater territory, following, and wealth than Bussa, but has never denied the latter first place.

Kisra was well received by the inhabitants, who were few and far between. There were a few hunters living in small villages, and a number of Yorubas—the outposts of the Yoruba Empire to the south, already founded, according to Borgu tradition, by Lamurudu. There is a story of an attempt to convert Kisra to Islam, which proved only half successful. It is interesting in so far as it explains a custom maintained to this day. The *malamai*, sent by the Prophet, had succeeded in persuading Kisra to prostrate himself twice, when the latter put an end to the proceedings by entering his house, then mounting a horse and galloping out. He ordered his war-drums to be beaten, and holding his spear in his hand said that twice a year would he consent to prostrate himself, but no more. The *malamai* returned whence they came, and the Prophet had to be satisfied with this partial conversion. A custom

[1] We are grateful to Borgu N.A. for this piece of information. The current Yoruba Research Scheme may have more to add on the Kisra legend.

[2] There is a theory that the early rulers were Zaghawa from Kanem, *vide* p. 68.

symbolic of the king's original disinclination is enacted to this day. When the Salla moon is seen a man with a spear enters the Emir's house and brings him out with a simulation of force to show him the moon. Twice the moon is pointed out to the Emir but he refuses to see it. At the third time, however, he agrees that it is the Salla moon and then the rejoicings begin. A relic said to hail from Kisra days is a large brass drum shaped like a tympanum which is beaten at Salla and on the death of an Emir. It was beaten when news of the late King George's death reached Bussa in 1952. The drum is beaten by strips of hippopotamus hide and is reported to bring death on anyone seeing inside it. If it is necessary to re-skin the drum, it is done by men with their backs to it working with their hands behind them.[1]

From the death of Kisra until the middle of the eighteenth century a gap exists. The names of one or two kings are remembered, such as Kitoro Fulani, but the dates when they reigned are now forgotten. It is said in Bussa that all the records were destroyed when the town was sacked by Gajere, its own king, in 1845. The first king from whom the succession can be traced is Kiseru Brodi, whose son Yerima Bussa defeated the Habe in the Zabayi war of *c.* 1750, so called from the war-camp near Bussa where the Hausawa camped.

It was during the eighteenth century, too, that Kaiama was founded. The word means 'come and rest'. Of the history of Kaiama, the following story was related by an old Bornu *malam*, of Zamfara ancestry, at the end of the last century. The chief of Nikki had two sons, who went hunting. While they were away hunting, their father died. They could not be found by the slaves sent out for them, so a younger brother, born in their absence, was made king. When at last this news reached the two brothers, one said, 'Let us fight for the throne.' But the other replied, 'No, since it is our father's son who has been made chief of Nikki, we must go elsewhere and become kings there.' So one brother went to Buai and the younger to Kaiama, where they were made chiefs.

An event of interest in the history of Bussa is the visit of Mungo Park in 1806, just before he died in the rapids either there or at Tsulu. Kitoro I was King of Bussa at this time. For many years it was believed that the huge silver medallion which has been carefully preserved by succeeding kings of Bussa and mounted as a

[1] *Vide* an article on Borgu in *Nigeria Magazine*, No. 48, 1958.

ring, was a gift to the king from the explorer. Current historical research, however, suggests that this is not so and that the medallion was in fact a present from the Lander brothers.[1] On Jebba island stands a simple obelisk dedicated to the Niger explorers:

> To Mungo Park, 1795, and Richard Lander, 1830,
> who traced the course of the Niger
> from near its source to the sea.
> Both died in Africa for Africa.

During the latter part of Kitoro's reign, soon after 1820, Borgu was involved in war with the Fulani. The country was invaded by the Fulani under the direction, some say, of the Emir of Gwandu, while other Borgu historians accuse an unidentified son of Malam Dendo of Nupe. Twice they were heavily defeated, but finally they attacked and conquered Illo. They never penetrated as far as Bussa, though on one occasion they occupied Luma, only twenty miles away. The practical results of this invasion are not clearly known, but it was probably responsible for the Borgawa sending a large army a few years later to assist the Alafin of Oyo against the Fulani of Ilorin.[2] It was an effort on the part of the combined Borgawa and Yoruba to stem the increasing power of the Fulani in the south.

This war, known as the Eleduwe war in Yorubaland, was the greatest in the history of Borgu, but it had an unhappy outcome, for the Yoruba were not united: discord reigned among the allies and mutual recriminations ensued. During the final assault upon Ilorin the King of Nikki was killed, as were the Alafin and many other chiefs. The war proved an unparalleled disaster to Nikki and Kaiama, from which they did not recover for years. It is said locally that not a single Borgu man returned alive from this war. The friendship with Oyo has, however, been maintained, and for many years it was customary for the Borgawa to visit Oyo at the annual Bere festival.[3] Gwandu historians also record a war with the Borgawa in 1835, when the Borgu army attacked Kaoje and killed the Emir of Gwandu's brother. Curiously enough, there is no memory of this campaign in Bussa, and it may be that the attack was carried out by Nikki and that Bussa was not involved.

[1] See the section on Yauri, p. 256, and the reference to the research of K. Lupton.
[2] See the section on Ilorin, p. 290.
[3] Mr R. Smith has made a study of the exile of Alafin Onigbogi to Borgu after the Nupe invasion of Oyo in the sixteenth century (*c.* 1535–1610).

We have a rare glimpse of Bussa and Wawa in the diary of Sir John Glover, who enterprisingly visited these towns when his ship the *Dayspring* lay wrecked at Jebba in 1857. He noted in his journal:

> Another hour's ride through extensive farms and the walls of new Bussa were in sight, standing on a gentle eminence about 500 yards from the river and embosomed in fine large cotton trees. I dismounted under the shade of a large tree about a ¼ of a mile from the town, while a messenger went on to announce my arrival to the King. He soon returned with permission to enter the town. On reaching the open space in front of the Palace we dismounted. His Majesty came out, and when he had seated himself and his courtiers had made all his arrangements complete, we were led towards him. He motioned me to a seat on his left hand; on his right sat two of his wives who fanned him and brushed away the flies. He received me most graciously, and after eating kola nuts, he told them to conduct me to my quarters. My cavalcade fanning me, we all trooped past him, I (as the custom is on these occasions) making my horse prance and rear, which afterwards produced a compliment from his Majesty and a long conversation on the horses of our own country. . . .
>
> Early in the morning came pap, 3 dishes of fufu for my followers, 6 bowls of fresh milk, a bullock and some yams. Having the bullock immediately killed, I sent (as is the custom) part of it to his Majesty and then distributed the rest among the chief men of the town. I reserved a small piece for my Xmas Dinner the next day. About 10 a.m. I went to visit the King, taking him the presents I had brought him; a sword, a pistol, 2 tobes, a small bournoos of plaid, and some cloth. He invited me into his inner hut, where I delivered to him my message and presents, with both of which he was much pleased, and after a short conversation I left him to examine what I had brought him and returned to my quarters, he promising to pay me a visit in the evening. Visits and presents continued the whole day, so that my larder was well stocked. I had slight fever. About 2 p.m. came the King and one of his wives (all of whom I may here mention keep their heads shaved; such is the custom of the Court of Boussa). He brought with him palm wine sweetened with honey, and said that we must drink together. He stayed about an hour, and I was very glad when he left to lay my aching head upon my pillow.[1]

In the reign of Gajere the hostility between Bussa and Wawa (visited by Clapperton and Lander, with whom the widow

[1] Quoted in A. C. Hastings, *The Voyage of the Dayspring*, 1926, pp. 169–71. This is based on long extracts from Glover's MS. diary.

Zuma[1] fell in love) was finally resolved and Wawa henceforth followed Bussa. Gajere also led a war against Kaoje to revenge an atrocity committed on a Bussa girl who had had both her arms cut off at the elbow in order to remove the ornaments with which they were loaded. This unfortunate woman, Na-iya, was still living at Bussa in 1950. On Gajere's death in 1862, the rightful heir, Kikwassai, was killed by one Dan Toro. His son Kuarra fled to Bida and Dan Toro usurped the throne. In his time Etsu Baba of Nupe was finally defeated by the Fulani at Leaba in Zugurma. Some Nupe were allowed by Bussa to settle and found Leaba in Bussa territory. These events happened about 1882. A few years earlier Bussa had joined forces with Yauri to crush the independent riparian town of Gebi, seventy miles north of Bussa and a noted haunt of canoe pirates. This alliance was followed by an unexpected war between the Bussawa and Yaurawa, which required the peaceful intervention of the Emir of Gwandu to settle.

Borgu had for centuries defied the invading advances of the Moshi, Songhai, Fulani and Dahomey people in turn, for its sparsely inhabited bush was considered impenetrable and perilous. Even today, only three minute hamlets break the monotony of the bush in the forty miles between Kishi and Kaiama. However, in the last decade of the century, European influence began to make itself definitely felt in Borgu, and in 1894 Sir Frederick Lugard visited Kaiama and made treaties with the kings of Kaiama and Nikki. This was the famous 'Nikki steeplechase' of West African history,[2] when Lugard outpaced the Frenchman Decoeur in an heroic march to Borgu and was the first to secure a treaty. Shortly afterwards the French occupied part of the country, and in 1897 occupied Kaiama, but the British and French arrived at an agreement by which the French retired to Nikki and Illo. One of the historical curiosities of the ensuing Anglo-French convention was the grant to the French of a small enclave on the west bank of the River Niger, known as Fort Goldie, at the token annual rent of one franc. As a reward for the valuable services performed by Mora Tsaude, Chief of Kaiama, Lugard granted him the rank of Emir of Kaiama with sway over the western Borgawa and the Bussawa of Kaiama. Up to that time the five districts of Kaiama were

[1] One of the few romantic women in the annals of African exploration, it is claimed.

[2] Miss N. Latham has described the Nikki affair in a number of articles, culminating in her paper read at the annual congress of the Historical Society of Nigeria, 1961.

tributaries of Nikki, the chief of Kaiama enjoying no pre-eminence above his fellow chiefs. The last Emir of Kaiama owned a chair presented to his father by Lugard.[1]

Borgu Province was formed in 1900 by the British, comprising Bussa, Kaiama and Illo, but in 1905 the northern areas were transferred to Sokoto Province. Two years later Borgu was absorbed into Kontagora Province. In 1914 Bussa lost its independence by being joined with Yauri, but the move was a failure and Bussa was separated after only three years.

On the deposition of Kitoro Gani in 1915, a slave named Turaki was appointed to the throne of Bussa. Not without reason, the leading families of Bussa refused to recognize this outsider. They took over the town and put Turaki to flight. After a year's interregnum Kijibrim was installed as the 13th Emir of Bussa, though the chieftainship was now downgraded to second-class. In 1922 Bussa moved to its new site at Ganikassai, some five miles north of Old Bussa visited by Lugard. Kijibrin too, was deposed in 1924, and in his stead Kitoro Gani was recalled from exile in Ilorin town and reinstated. Shortly before this Borgu Division was transferred to Ilorin Province, in 1923. Hopes that the Emir had learned the lessons of adversity were disappointed, and in 1935 he was deposed for the second time and exiled to Mokwa. He was succeeded by his younger brother, Muhammadu Sani (Babaki), District Head of the former independent area of Agwarra, the centre of the picturesque Kambari people originally from Kontagora.

Considerable reorganization in the emirates of Bussa and Kaiama took place in 1954. The latter, as we have seen, was a creation of the British Administration. Haliru Kiyaru had become the second Emir of Kaiama in 1923, but he now resigned because he felt he was too old and no longer enjoyed the confidence of his people. The artificial emirate of Kaiama now reverted to its status of a district under the Emir of Bussa, who took the new title of Emir of Borgu. This crowns the achievements of one of the oldest ruling families in Northern Nigeria. The Divisional headquarters

[1] See Margery Perham, *Lugard: The Years of Adventure*, 1956, p. 507. Lugard's own account of his 1894 journey to Borgu was given in an address to the Royal Geographical Society in 1895, and is reproduced in full in H. B. Hermon-Hodge, *Gazetteer of Ilorin Province*, 1929, pp. 20–35. The most recent, and most enlightening, source is the actual diary of Lugard, now published in *The Diaries of Lord Lugard*, vol. IV, 1962, edited by Margery Perham and Mary Bull.

moved from Kaiama to Borgu and a new subordinate Western Borgu N.A. was established with its centre at Okuta, a town famous already for its dark-coloured *bakin-beri* mats. Borgu today features prominently in the National Development Plan, for the construction of the Niger dam at Kainji by 1968 calls for the complete submersion of Bussa and the building of a new Bussa town on a site some thirty-six miles away. The flooding of the area will affect a large proportion of the emirate's total population, tens of thousands of whom will have to be moved from their homes and resettled for the cause of progress.

THE EMIRS OF BUSSA AND KAIAMA (BORGU)

Bussa

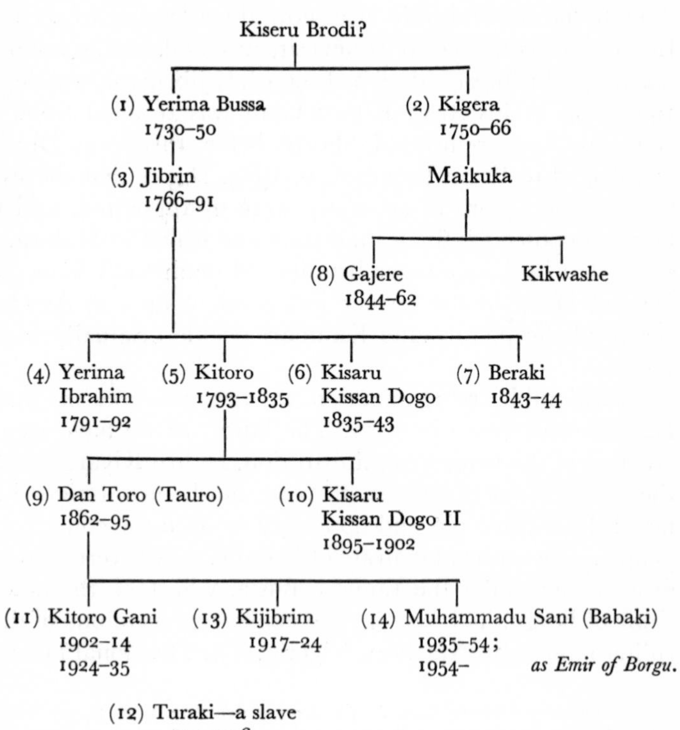

*Kaiama** (1) Mora Tsaude (Murata Sidi)
c. 1901–12

(5) Haliru Kilyaru
1923–54 *Title lapsed.*

* Though the line of Kaiama chiefs is a long one (see *Gazetteer of Kontagora Province*, 1920, pp. 28–29), Mora Tsaude was the first chief on whom the title of Emir was conferred by Lugard, who made him a First-class chief of Southern Borgu.

APPENDIX A

Notes on European Travellers in the Sudan and the Sahara between 1795 and 1880.

1788. Formation in London of The Association for the Promotion of the Discovery of the Interior of Africa. It offered to help any man who would 'cross Africa from east to west, from Egypt to the Atlantic on the latitude of the presumed course of the River Niger'.

1795–97. After three unsuccessful expeditions had been launched, the Association commissioned a young Scottish doctor, Mungo Park, who, starting inland from the Gambia, reached the Niger at Segu. It was then believed that the Niger must flow into some lake or swamp to the east.

1798. A young German student, Frederick Hornemann, told the Association: 'Give me three years. Do not search for me during this time and I will bring back the information you want.' Starting from Cairo, where he received the encouragement of the recently arrived French scientists in Napoleon's expedition, and delayed by the outcome of the defeat of the French fleet by Nelson at the battle of the Nile, he trailed behind a caravan to Siwa and Murzuk. As a Christian his life was always in danger in those intolerant days and he suffered intensely from scurvy. After Murzuk his movements are wrapped in uncertainty but he is believed to have reached the Niger via Aïr. René Lecler in his *World Without Mercy* says that Hornemann's remains were discovered a quarter of a century after his disappearance 'in a small, unmarked wayside grave in the Sudanese town of Nupe on the Niger. He had been murdered.'

1818. Joseph Ritchie and Captain Lyon set out from Tripoli and collected one of Hornemann's notebooks in Murzuk. Ritchie died on his way to the Tassili-n-Ajjer highlands and Lyon gave up.

1805–6. Mungo Park made a second expedition, under the Colonial Office this time, to the Niger, which he had been the first modern European to see. Starting again from the Gambia he got to the Niger at Bamako, but by then he had lost 29 of his European companions from fever. There were only four survivors besides himself to start down the Niger in a canoe. It was subsequently learned from inquiries that they had followed the Niger for more than a thousand miles until they were drowned in the rapids near Bussa early in 1806.

1822-25. Major Dixon Denham, a veteran of Waterloo, Dr Walter Oudney and Lieut. Hugh Clapperton, a naval officer, were sent by the British Government to search for the lower Niger. Following the Tripoli–Murzuk–Aïr route they reached Lake Chad. Oudney died near Katagum about a year later but Clapperton pressed on to Kano and Sokoto, where he was welcomed by Muhammad Bello. Bello was anxious to promote trade with the British, but this was opposed by local Arabs fearing competition. The British attitude to the slave-trade hardened opposition to Clapperton being allowed to go towards Yauri and Nupe and find the course of the lower Niger. Bello produced a map showing the Niger flowing into the Nile, despite the oral assertion that it flowed into the sea at a place called Rakah in Yorubaland, near Fundah. Clapperton rejoined Denham, who had been lucky to escape after being captured in a local affray, and they returned to England by the way they had come, the first to do so after crossing the Sahara.

1825–26. Clapperton returned to Kano and Sokoto in 1825–26, but this time by landing on the Slave Coast at Badagri, west of Lagos, and working his way through the forests. He was the first to show that the Sudan could be approached from the Bight of Benin. He reached the Niger at Bussa but died in Sokoto without having won any concession from Bello in regard to the stoppage of the slave-trade. His young servant, Richard Lander, tried to return by way of the Niger to the sea but he was prevented from doing this and returned to England via Badagri.

1825–26. Major Gordon Laing, a Scottish army officer, set out alone from Tripoli, wearing his uniform and making no disguise of his Christianity. After four months he reached In-Salah, where he was persecuted, but later protected by a prominent merchant, who lent him servants to continue his journey. Within one day's march of Timbuktu he was set upon by marauding Tuareg and nearly killed; but four days later, on 18 August 1826, he was carried into Timbuktu by his servants. After braving the anti-Christian feelings of this Muslim centre for some time he set out to return by way of Arawan, but it was not long before he was waylaid by Berabiches (Moors) and strangled to death.

1827–28. René Caillié, a Frenchman, crossed the western Sahara from Kakondy in Senegal, overland most of the way, to Timbuktu, via Kankan on the upper Niger. The journey took over a year because of sickness. He returned to France via Arawan, Taodeni, and Morocco, after a four months' crossing of the desert under daily torture by heat, thirst and the brutality of his infamous guides. He was the first European in modern times to return alive from Timbuktu, and he had to disguise himself as a Muslim to avoid being killed as a European Christian.

1830. Richard Lander persuaded the Colonial Office to let him return to Africa and try to trace the course of the Niger to the sea. Returning to Bussa he set off in a canoe with his brother John and in due course arrived at the delta after having been captured by some Ibos and having escaped. Eventually they managed to get to Fernando Po and take ship to England, but not without considerable conflict with the tough traders, European as well as African, that they met as they neared the sea.

1850–55. The British Government organized an expedition which was to study the trade routes from Tripoli to the Sudan, and to explore Central Africa; and it was to report on the slave traffic. The appointed leader was James Richardson, who was given two German scientific experts to assist him, Dr Heinrich Barth and Adolf Overweg. Crossing the Red Hammada desert plain from Tripoli to Murzuk they came to Ghat, and climbing the 4,000-foot Tassili-n-Ajjer mountains, they passed the lonely wells of Assiu before stopping a while in the hills of Asben or Aïr. From here the travellers took different routes: Richardson to Bornu, Overweg to Lake Chad via Gobir, Barth to Kano via Katsina. When Barth reached Kukawa in April 1851, he found that Richardson had died of fever; Overweg died near Chad in September 1852 and Barth was ordered from England to go to Timbuktu. Before this he had visited Adamawa and much of the country round Kanem and Bornu. In 1853 he travelled through Katsina and Zamfara to reach Sokoto in April. From there he went on through Gwandu and Kebbi to reach the Niger at Say in June. He then went up river to Timbuktu, arriving in September and staying for many months in fear of his life. In May 1854 he managed to leave Timbuktu and by August he was on his way back to Birnin Kebbi and Gwandu and thence to Sokoto again. In October he reached Kano and in December he met another German explorer, Vogel, who had heard that he was dead. By the end of 1854 he was back in Kukawa. In May 1855 he began the crossing of the desert, and taking the route through Bilma to Murzuk he reached Tripoli at the end of August, having been away for five and a half years and having collected most carefully observed records and information about parts of Africa which at that time were hardly known to exist.

1854–55. Eduard Vogel, a German, with two Englishmen, Church and McGuire, were sent out by the British Government in search of

Barth. They met him in January 1855 on the shores of Lake Chad. Vogel was later murdered in Wadai and McGuire was murdered in Aïr on his way back. Church returned home with Barth.

1858. Cuny, a Frenchman, crossed the eastern Sahara from Egypt to Darfur, where he was murdered.

1860. Duveyrier visited Ghadames and the mountains of Tassili-n-Ajjer, east of Arak, returning by Murzuk and Tripoli.

1864–78. Gerhardt Rohlfs, a German, was the second European to Major Laing to reach the oasis of In-Salah, and he crossed the northern Sahara from west to east. In 1865 he crossed from Tripoli to Kukawa, via Ghadames, Ghat and Zinder; he then traversed Nigeria southwards, emerging at the coast at Lagos in July 1868. In 1869 he crossed the western desert from Cyrenaica to Egypt, and in 1875 he journeyed from the Nile to Darfur and the approaches to Tibesti. Finally, in December 1878, he made the journey to Kufra, the most inaccessible of oases, which had not been visited since antiquity, and returned at Benghazi exhausted but triumphant. He was the first European to become acquainted with the desert from the Atlantic to the Nile, and unequalled as a desert explorer.

1869–74. Dr Gustav Nachtigal, another German, explored the strange mountains of Tibesti and came to Kukawa via Murzuk with long promised presents for the Shehu of Bornu. After three years of travelling as an itinerant doctor in the wilder districts of Wadai and the Bahr-el-Ghazal country, he returned to Alexandria.

1880. Oskar Lenz, an Austrian, crossed the desert from Tangier, Marrakesh, Tinduf (he was the first European here), to Timbuktu. He returned via Senegal.

After 1880. Lenz was not the last of the explorers of the Sahara but he was the last of the pioneers. Thenceforth with a few notable exceptions the great journeys by individuals ended and military expeditions took their place. The above records relate to those who succeeded at least in making the crossing of the desert, but there were many who got murdered in the desert without completing their mission.

APPENDIX B

The Chiefs of the Northern Region of Nigeria

(1). THE PREMIER CHIEFS IN ORDER OF PRECEDENCE (based on the official ranking used in the House of Chiefs in the Regional Legislature, 1964).

		Province
1.	The Sultan of Sokoto (Sarkin Musulmi)	Sokoto
2.	The Shehu of Bornu	Bornu
3.	The Emir of Gwandu	Sokoto
4.	The Emir of Kano	Kano
5.	The Emir of Bauchi	Bauchi
6.	The Lamido of Adamawa	Adamawa
7.	The Emir of Katsina	Katsina
8.	The Emir of Zaria (Sarkin Zazzau)	Zaria
9.	Etsu Nupe of Bida	Niger
10.	The Emir of Ilorin	Ilorin
11.	The Emir of Kontagora (Sarkin Sudan)	Niger
12.	The Emir of Dikwa (Mai Dikwa)	Bornu
13.	The Emir of Argungu (Sarkin Kebbi)	Sokoto
14.	The Emir of Gombe	Bauchi
15.	Tor Tiv	Benue
16.	The Atta of Igala	Kabba
17.	The Emir of Katagum (Sarkin Bornu)	Bauchi
18.	The Emir of Misau (Sarkin Bornu ta Gabas)	Bauchi
19.	The Emir of Hadejia	Kano
20.	The Emir of Daura	Katsina
21.	The Emir of Kazaure (Sarkin Arewa)	Kano
22.	The Emir of Gumel	Kano
23.	The Emir of Agaie	Niger
24.	The Emir of Lapai	Niger
25.	The Emir of Pategi	Ilorin
26.	The Emir of Yauri	Sokoto
27.	The Emir of Borgu	Ilorin
28.	The Emir of Jama'are	Bauchi
29.	The Emir of Muri	Adamawa

30.	The Emir of Fika (Moi Fika)	Bornu
31.	The Emir of Biu	Bornu
32.	The Emir of Bedde (Mai Bedde)	Bornu
33.	Ohinoyi of Igbirra	Kabba
34.	The Emir of Keffi	Benue
35.	The Emir of Nassarawa (Sarkin Kwotto)	Benue
36.	The Emir of Lafia	Benue
37.	The Emir of Jema'a	Zaria
38.	The Emir of Abuja	Niger
39.	The Aku of Wukari	Benue
40.	Ohimege of Koton Karifi	Kabba
41.	The Och' Idoma	Benue
42.	The Emir of Wase (Sarkin Dutse)	Plateau
43.	The Chief of Jos	Plateau
44.	The Chief of Zuru (Sarkin Dabai)	Niger
45.	The Chief of Kagoro	Zaria
46.	The Chief of Mubi	Sardauna
47.	The Chief of Ningi	Bauchi

(2). Other Chiefs by Provinces
(based on the official list of 1st June 1964).

Adamawa

Muri: Chief of Zinna.
Numan Federation: Chiefs of Bacama, Mbula, Batta, Shellen, and Longuda.

Bauchi

Bauchi: Chief of Dass.
Gombe: Chiefs of Kaltungo, Waja, Dadiya, and West Tangale.

Benue

Awe: Sangarin Awe.
Wukari: Chief of Takum.
Gara of Donga.

Bornu

Mai Maina of Askira.
Chief of Shani.

Ilorin

Etsu of Lafiagi.
Etsu of Shonga.
Etsu (Ndakpoto) of Sharagi.

Kabba

Obaro of Kabba.
Olu Jumu of Ijimu.

Agbana of East Yagba.
Olu Okeri of West Yagba.
Maigarin Lokoja.
Aguma of Bassa Komo.
Olu Kiiri of Bunu.
Olu Aworo of Kwara.
Maiyaki of Kwara.
Aganchu of Kwara.
Rogan of Eggan.

Niger

Chief of Kuta, Gwari.
Chief of Wushishi.
Zuru: Marafan Dabai and Chiefs of Danko, Sakaba, Fakai, and Wasagu.
Gwari: Chiefs of Basso, Dangunu, Minna, Fuka, Kurmin Gurmasa, Mainkonkele, Koro, Manta, Gawun, Paiko, Gini, Allawa, Adunu, Ishanu, Guni, G. Kogo, Kushaka.
Kamuku: Chiefs of Tegina, Kusheriki, Gunna, and Kwangoma.

Plateau

Pankshin Federation: Chiefs of Kanam, Angas, Sura Pyem, and Ron Kulere.
Akwanga Federation: Chiefs of Oriye Rindiri, Eggon, and Mada.
Lowland Federation: Long Kemai and Chief of Montol.
Yergam: Ponzhi Tarok.

Sardauna

Chief of Gwoza.

Zaria

Chiefs of Birnin Gwari, Jaba, and Moroa.

BIBLIOGRAPHY

1. Sources Consulted for Part I

AMEER, ALI, *A Short History of the Saracens*. London, 1921.

ARNETT, E. J., *The Rise of the Sokoto Fulani*. Kano, 1922.

Gazetteer of Sokoto Province. London, 1920.

BA, A. H., et DAGET, J., *L'Empire Peul du Macina*, Vol. I, 1818–53; Vol. II, 1853–93. Paris, 1955.

BACKWELL, H. F., *The Occupation of Hausaland* 1900–04*; being a translation of Arabic letters found in the House of the Wazir of Sokoto, Bohari, in* 1903. Lagos, 1927.

BOAHEN, A. ADU, 'Caravan Trade in the 19th Century', *Journal of African History*, III, No. 2, 1962.

Britain, the Sahara, and the Western Sudan 1788–1861. London, 1964.

BARTH, HEINRICH, *Travels and Discoveries in Northern and Central Africa*. London, 1857.

BELLO, SIR AHMADU, *My Life*. London, 1962.

BOVILL, E. W., *The Golden Trade of the Moors*. London, 1958.

Caravans of the Old Sahara. London, 1933.

Missions to the Niger, Vol. I. London, 1964.

BURDON, J. A., *Historical Notes on certain Emirates and tribes in Northern Nigeria*. London, 1909.

CLAPPERTON, HUGH, *Journal of a second expedition into the interior of Africa*. London, 1829.

CROWDER, MICHAEL, *The Story of Nigeria*. London, 1962.

DANIEL, F. DE F., *A History of Katsina, c.* 1937 (private circulation).

Historical Notes, Katsina Emirate, 1928.

'Shedu dan Fodio', *Journal of the African Society*, XXV, 1925–26.

'The Regalia of Katsina', *Journal of the African Society*, January 1932.

DAVIDSON, BASIL, *Old Africa Rediscovered*. London, 1961.

'A New View of the Old Sahara', *West Africa*, 11 January 1964.

DELAFOSSE, M., *Haut-Sénégal-Niger*. 3 vols. Paris, 1912.

DENHAM, D., CLAPPERTON, H., and OUDNEY, W., *Narrative of Travels and Discoveries in Africa*. London, 1826.

DIKE, K. ONWUKA, 100 *years of British Rule in Nigeria*, 1851–1951.

Trade and Politics in the Niger Delta. Lagos, 1956.

DUBOIS, FELIX, *Timbouctou le Mystérieux*. Paris, 1896.

FAGE, J. D., *An Introduction to the History of West Africa*. London, 1955.
An Atlas of African History. London, 1961.

FAGE, J. D., and OLIVER, R., *A Short History of Africa*. London, 1962.

FAGG, BERNARD, 'A Life-sized Terracotta Head from Nok', *Man*, 95, 1956.
'The Nok Culture', *West African Review*, December 1956.
'The Nok Culture in Prehistory', *Journal of the Nigerian Historical Society*, December 1959.

GENTIL, EMILE, *La Chute de l'empire de Rabeh*. Paris, 1901.

GERSTER, GEORG, *Sahara* (translated from the German). London, 1960.

GOUILLY, A., *L'Islam dans l'Afrique Occidentale Française*. Paris, 1952.

HALLETT, R., *The African Association*. London, 1964.

HITTI, PHILIP, *The Arabs: a Short History*. Princeton, 1943.

HODGKIN, THOMAS, *Nigerian Perspectives*. London, 1960.

HOGBEN, S. J., *The Muhammadan Emirates of Nigeria*. London, 1930.

HOPEN, C. EDWARD, *The Pastoral Fulbe Family in Gwandu*. London, 1959.

HUNWICK, J. O., 'Ahmad Baba and the Moroccan Invasion of the Sudan (1591)', *Journal of the Historical Society of Nigeria*, Vol. 2, No. 3, December 1962, pp. 311–28.

JAUNET, H., et BARRY, J., *Histoire de l'Afrique Occidentale Française*. Paris, 1949.

KIRK-GREENE, A. H. M., *Adamawa Past and Present*. London, 1958.
Barth's Travels in Nigeria. London, 1962.

LANDER, RICHARD and JOHN, *Journals of an expedition to explore the course and termination of the Niger, etc.* London, 1832.

LANE-POOLE, S., *The Moors in Spain*. London, 1920.

LHOTE, HENRI, *Les Fresques du Tassili*. Paris, 1958.
'Engravings, paintings and inscriptions of the Kawar, Aïr and Adrar of the Iforas', *Bulletin de l'IFAN*, October 1952, p. 1268.
'Rock paintings in West Takecherouet' (Ahaggar), *Bull. de l'IFAN*, January 1953, p. 283.
'The horse and the camel', *Bull. de l'IFAN*, July 1953, p. 1138.

LUGARD, F. D., *The Dual Mandate in British Tropical Africa*. Edinburgh, 1929.

LUGARD, LADY (Flora Shaw), *A Tropical Dependency*. London, 1905.

MCCALL, D. F., *Africa in Time-Perspective*. Boston and Legon, 1964.

MAUNY, RAYMOND, *Tableau géographique de L'Ouest Africain au Moyen Age d'après les sources écrites, la tradition et l'archéologie*. IFAN, Dakar, 1961.

MEEK, C. K., *Northern Tribes of Nigeria*. London, 1925.
A Sudanese Kingdom. London, 1931.

MONTEIL, CHARLES, 'Les Peuls Rouges', *Journal de la Société des Africanistes*. 1950, pp. 158 *et seq*.

NICHOLSON, R. A., *A Literary History of the Arabs*. Cambridge, 1930.

NIVEN, C. R., *A Short History of Nigeria*. London, 1937.

Our Emirates. Lagos, 1954.

OLIVER, ROLAND, and FAGE, J. D., *A Short History of Africa*. London, 1962.

PALMER, H. R., *Sudanese Memoirs*. 3 vols. Lagos, 1928.

The Bornu Sahara and Sudan. London, 1936.

History of the First Twelve Years of the Reign of Mai Idris Alooma of Bornu (1571–1583) *by his Imam Ahmed ibn Fartua, together with the Diwan of the Sultans of Bornu and Girgam of the Magumi*. Lagos, 1926.

'The central Sahara and Sudan in the XIIth century A.D.', *Journal of the African Society*, 1928–29, p. 368 *et seq*.

'The kingdom of Gaoga of Leo Africanus', *Journal of the African Society*, 1929–30, pp. 280–4; 350–69.

PERHAM, MARGERY, *Lugard: the Years of Authority*, 1899–1945. London, 1960.

PARK, MUNGO, *Travels in the interior districts of Africa, in* 1795, 1796 *and* 1797, *etc*. London, 1799.

Journal of a mission to the interior of Africa in 1805, *etc*. London, 1815.

RATTRAY, R. S., *Tribes of the Ashanti Hinterland*. London, 1932.

RICHARD-MOLARD, JACQUES, *L'Afrique Occidentale Française*. Paris, 1949.

RODD, FRANCIS RENNELL, *The People of the Veil*. London, 1926.

ROUCH, JEAN, *Les Songhay*. Paris, 1954.

SHARWOOD SMITH, B. E., *Kano Survey*. Lagos, 1950.

SKINNER, E. P., *The Mossi of the Upper Volta*.

SMITH, M. G., *Government in Zazzau*. London, 1960.

STENNING, D. J., *Savannah Nomads*. London, 1959.

SURET-CANALE, J., *Afrique Noire occidentale et centrale*. Paris, 1958.

TAUXIER, L., *Moeurs et Histoire des Peuls*. Paris, 1937.

TEMPLE, O. and C. L., *Notes on the Tribes, Provinces, Emirates and States of the Northern Provinces of Nigeria*. Lagos and London, 1922.

URVOY, YVES, *Histoire de l'Empire du Bornou*. Paris, 1949. (Translated by Miss Sheila Richards, 1964, as yet unpublished.)

WARD, W. E. F., *A History of the Gold Coast*. London, 1948.

WHITTING, C. E. J., 'The unprinted indigenous Arabic literature of Northern Nigeria', *Journal of the Royal Asiatic Society*, April 1943.

WILLIAMS, J. J., *Hebrewisms of West Africa: From Nile to Niger with the Jews*. New York, 1930.

BRIEF NOTES ON THE CHIEF ARABIC SOURCES ARRANGED IN CHRONOLOGICAL ORDER

HAUKAL, IBN (tenth century). *Description de l'Afrique.* Translation by De Slane in *Journal Asiatique.* Paris, 1842.

The Oriental Geography, translated by W. Ouseley. London, 1800.

He was a native of Baghdad and visited Ghana. A great traveller. He saw the Niger flowing eastwards, believing it to be the Nile.

BAKRI, Al (1028–94). *Description de l'Afrique Septentrionale*, translated by De Slane. Algiers, 1913, and Paris, 1859. Written in 1068.

He lived in Cordova, where he made a profound study of geography.

IDRISI, AL (*c.* 1100–66). *Description de l'Afrique et de l'Espagne*, translated by R. Dozy. Leyden, 1866.

The well-informed geographer-historian, who compiled the famous *Kitab Rujar.* He also studied in Cordova.

OMARI, AL (1301–49). *Masalik el-Absar fi Mamalik el-Amsar* (translated). Paris, 1927.

An official at the court of the Mamluk Sultan of Egypt. His work was a mine of information for the educated man of his day. Facts are given about Kanem and Mali, the latter based on the experiences of a resident in Mali for thirty-five years. Observations, too, on Mansa Musa's pilgrimage.

BATTUTA, IBN (1304–68). *Travels in Asia and Africa*, translated by H. A. R. Gibb. London, 1929.

A Berber from Tangier, who travelled all over Asia before visiting the court of Mansa Suleiman of Mali and the Niger at Timbuktu.

KHALDUN, IBN (1332–1406). *The Muqaddimah: An Introduction to History*, trans. Franz Rosenthal, 3 vols. New York and London, 1958.

The greatest of the medieval historians, he was born in Tunis and studied in Fez. His later life was spent in Egypt, where he became Qadi in Cairo.

MAQRIZI, AL (1364–1442). *Description Historique et Topographique de l'Egypte*, translated by P. Casanova. Cairo, 1906. There are also translations of extracts in Palmer's *Sudanese Memoirs.*

A celebrated historian of Cairo.

MAGHILI, AL (*c.* 1450–1504). *The Obligations of Princes*, translated by T. H. Baldwin. Beirut, 1932.

He brought a number of Muslim emissaries from Medina to

Kano in the time of Mohamman Rumfa and visited Katsina. This treatise was written for the benefit of Sarkin Kano, to whom he acted as adviser. He later performed similar duties for the first Askia at Gao.

LEO AFRICANUS (1493–1550?). *History and Description of Africa done into English by John Pory*. Hakluyt Society, 3 vols. London, 1896. Also *Jean-Léon l'Africain, Description de l'Afrique*. Paris, 1956.

Born in Granada and originally called Al-Hassan; studied in Fez and made two journeys to Gao and the Sudan in 1509 and 1513. Was captured by pirates in the Mediterranean and presented to the Pope in Rome, who had him freed. He became baptized as Giovanni Leone in 1520.

KATI, MAHMUD (1468–1593 or 1543). *Tarikh al Fattash*, translated and edited by O. Houdas and M. Delafosse. Paris, Leroux, 1913.

Begun in Timbuktu in 1519 and finished by Kati's grandson Ibn el Mukhtar in 1665, this work was not found until 1911. With the *Tarikh al Sudan* it is almost the only local record, and it is the oldest known history by a Sudanese author.

SADI, ABDURRAHMAN AL (1596–1655). *Tarikh al Sudan*, translated by O. Houdas. Paris, 1900. Reprinted 1964.

He was Imam of the Sankore mosque in Timbuktu at the time when the country was dominated by the Moors. Based on the earlier work of Ahmed Baba al Timbukti (1556–1627), this chronicle, like the above, is a priceless record of the period in the Sudan. Its existence was discovered by Barth in Gwandu in 1853.

USMAN DAN FODIO, SHEHU (*c.* 1744 or 1754–1817).

ABDULLAHI DAN FODIO (*c.* 1766–1828 or 1756–1828).

MUHAMMADU BELLO DAN SHEHU (*ob.* 1837).

Works by these great Fulani scholars are deposited in the library of the University archives of Ibadan and elsewhere. See W. E. N. Kensdale, Catalogue of the Arabic MSS. preserved in the University Library, Ibadan, Nigeria, Ibadan 1955–58, and the notes and references in H. F. C. Smith, 'Source Material for the History of the Western Sudan', *Journal of the Historical Society of Nigeria*, 3 December 1958.

Tanbikhu'l-Ikhwan, 'the Admonition to the Brethren', by Shehu has been translated by Palmer under the title 'An early Fulani conception of Islam' in the *Journal of the African Society*, xiii, 1913–14, and xiv, 1914–15.

Muhammadu Bello's famous *Infaq al maisuri* has been translated by H. F. C. Smith in a London edition of 1951 edited by

C. E. J. Whitting, and it is paraphrased in Arnett's *Rise of the Sokoto Fulani*.

Among many works by M. Hiskett and A. D. H. Bivar the following deserve special mention: Hiskett's translation of *Kitab al Farq*, a work on the Habe kingdoms attributed to Uthman dan Fodio (*SOAS Bull.*, xxiii, 3, 1960), and of a work by Abdullahi on the state of learning among the Fulani before their Jihad (*SOAS Bull.*, xix, 3, 1957, pp. 550–78). See also his *Tazyin al Waraqat* by Abdullahi, Ibadan Univ. Press, 1963, which was reviewed in *West Africa*, 23 May 1964. See Bivar's *Arabic Documents of Northern Nigeria* (*SOAS Bull.*, xxii, 2, 1959, pp. 324–49); his *Wathiqat ahl al Sudan*, a manifesto of the Fulani Jihad (*Journal of African Hist.*, 2 February 1961, pp. 235–43); and also his article with Hiskett, 'The Arabic Literature of Nigeria to 1804: a provisional account' (*SOAS Bull.*, xxv, 1, 1962, pp. 104–48). Besides the above there are several articles by both authors in other issues of the Journals mentioned as well as in the *Journal of the Nigerian Historical Society* and in *Nigeria Magazine*.

HAJJI SA'ID. *History of Sokoto*, translated by C. E. J. Whitting, Kano; and extracts published in *African Affairs*, July 1948.

Hajji Sa'id was in the service of Aliyu Babba, Sarkin Musulmi, from 1842 to 1859.

THE KANO CHRONICLE. Translated by H. R. Palmer in the *Journal of the Royal Anthropological Institute*, 38, 1908, and also in vol. III of *Sudanese Memoirs*, 1928.

HISTORY OF KATSINA. Translated by H. R. Palmer in the *Journal of the African Society*, 1927. The Jos Museum has an uncatalogued collection of the Palmer Papers.

Note: A Centre of Arabic Documentation has been set up in the Institute of African Studies of the University of Ibadan to provide a bibliographical service in the field of West African Arabic literature and a central library from which xerograph copies of West African Arabic manuscripts may be obtained. The Hon. Secretary of the Centre is Mr J. O. Hunwick.

2. Some Major Written Sources Consulted For Part II

In the following list of source materials for the individual emirate histories, listed in alphabetical provincial order, no reference is made, although constant recourse had been had, to the principal secondary sources:

1. *Annual Reports of the Provinces of Northern Nigeria*, 1900–1914; 1926–39; and 1950–61. The *Annual Report* for 1961 was not published until mid-1963, and that of 1962 is not yet out.
2. The Provincial Gazetteers, District Notebooks and MS. historical notes held in a number of Native Authority offices, excluding those referring to the non-emirate 'segmentary' societies.
3. The amendments and suggestions offered by all the Native Authorities that have kindly reviewed and given their formal approval of the final draft of the text submitted to them.
4. The published records of the classic travellers to Northern Nigeria in the nineteenth century, such as Denham and Clapperton, Barth, Baikie, etc.
5. The published memoirs of officials who served in the emirates during the first half of the twentieth century, such as Hastings, Kisch, 'Langa Langa', Oakley, etc.
6. Articles in learned journals not easily to hand in Nigeria.

In general, we have preferred to give citation references from works that are now readily available to most Nigerian students rather than to quote from the more *recherché*, out-of-print books. Hence our frequent use of T. L. Hodgkin's *Nigerian Perspectives*, the Kirk-Greene edition of Barth, the anthology *West African Explorers*, etc., and our many references to recent issues of *Nigeria Magazine*, the *Journal of the Nigerian Historical Society*, the *Nigerian Field*, and the interesting historical booklets published in Hausa by Gaskiya Corporation, Zaria.

General

ABDULMALIK MANI, *Zuwan Turawa Nijeriya ta Arewa*. Zaria, 1957.
ALHAJI DOGONDAJI, *Wakakken Labarin Kasa*. Zaria, 1959.
ARNETT, E. J., *The Rise of the Sokoto Fulani*. Kano, 1929.
BACKWELL, H. F., *The Occupation of Hausaland*. Lagos, 1927.

BURDON, J. A., *Historical Notes on Certain Emirates and Tribes in Northern Nigeria*, London, 1909.

HODGKIN, T. L., *Nigerian Perspectives*. London, 1960.

HOWARD, C., ed., *West African Explorers*. London, 1951.

KIRK-GREENE, A. H. M., *Barth's Travels in Nigeria*. London, 1962.

NIVEN, C. R., *Labarin Nijeriya*. London, 1955.

ORR, C. W. J., *The Making of Northern Nigeria*. London, 1911.

TEMPLE, OLIVE, *Notes on the Tribes, Provinces, Emirates and States of the Northern Provinces of Nigeria*. Cape Town, 1919.

Adamawa

AHMADU MARAFA, *Ranar Tabbatad da Lamido*. Zaria, 1955.

EAST, R. M., *Stories of Old Adamawa*. Zaria, 1935.

FROELICH, J. C., 'Le Commandement et l'organisation sociale chez les Foulbé de l'Adamaoua', *Etudes Camerounaises*, No. 45/46. Dakar, 1954.

KIRK-GREENE, A. H. M., *Adamawa Past and Present*. London, 1958.

LEMBEZAT, B., *Les Populations Paiennes du Nord-Cameroun et de l'Adamaoua*. Paris, 1961.

STRUMPELL, F., 'Die Geschichte Adamawas nach mündlichen Überlieferungen . . .', *Mitteilungen der geographischen Gesellschaft*. Hamburg, vol. XXVI, 1912.

Bauchi

ABDULKADIR AKABI, *Yakubu, Bajimin Bauci*. Zaria, 1954.

ABUBAKAR TAFAWA BALEWA, *Shehu Umar*. Zaria, 1955.

FREMANTLE, J. M., 'The Emirate of Katagum', *Journal of the Royal African Society*. 1911.

LOW, V., *et al.*, *Notes for a Preliminary History of Bauchi Province*, unpublished typescript, 1960.

Kafi Garin 'Yan Hausa. Zaria, 1954.

Bornu

AHMED IBN FARTUA, *History of the First Twelve Years of the Reign of Mai Idris Alooma of Bornu*. Lagos, 1926.

BENTON, P. A., *A Bornu Almanack*. London, 1914.

Notes on Some Languages of the Western Sudan. London, 1912.

The Sultanate of Bornu (translation of monograph by Dr. A. Schultze). London, 1913.

COHEN, RONALD, 'The Structure of Kanuri Society', unpublished doctoral thesis. University of Wisconsin, 1960.

'The Bornu King Lists', *Papers in African History*, vol. II. Boston, 1964.

DAVIES, J. G., *The Biu Book*. Zaria, 1956.
ELLISON, R. E., and KAKA MALAM, *Notes for a History of Bornu*, unpublished MS., 1934.
HALLETT, R., 'El Kanemi of Bornu', *Eminent Nigerians*. Cambridge, 1960.
KIRK-GREENE, A. H. M., *Maiduguri and the Capitals of Bornu*. Zaria, 1958.
'The Bornu Stud Farm', *Nigerian Field*, vol. XXVI. 1958.
'The British Consulate at Lake Chad', *African Affairs*, October 1959.
MAI MAINA, *Mai Maina Sarkin Askira*. Zaria, 1957.
PALMER, H. R., *Bornu Sahara and Sudan*. London, 1936.
Sudanese Memoirs. Lagos, 1928.
PATTERSON, J. R., *Kanuri Songs*. Lagos, 1926.
SALIHU BAJOGA, 'The History of Bornu', *Nigerian Citizen*, April 1963.
SCHULTZE, A., *Das Sultanat von Bornu* (see BENTON, above).
STENNING, D. J., *Savannah Nomads*. London, 1959.
URVOY, Y., *Histoire de l'empire de Bornou*. Paris, 1949.
'The Bolewa of Fika', *Nigeria Magazine*, No. 51, 1956.
'Komadugu Yobe', *Nigeria Magazine*, No. 76, 1963.
'From Maiduguri to Lake Chad', *Nigeria Magazine*, No. 79, 1963.

Ilorin

HERMON-HODGE, H. B., *The Gazetteer of Ilorin Province*. London, 1929.
JOHNSON, SAMUEL, *The History of the Yorubas*. London, 1921.
PERHAM, M., and BULL, M., *Diaries of Lord Lugard*, vol. IV. London, 1962.
'Ilorin', *Nigeria Magazine*, No. 49, 1956.
'Sallah at Ilorin', *Nigeria Magazine*, No. 70, 1961.
'The Nupe of Pategi', *Nigeria Magazine*, No. 50, 1956.
'The Pategi Regatta', *Nigeria Magazine*, No. 52, 1956.

Kano

ALHAJI ABUBAKAR DOKAJI, *Kano Ta Dabo Cigari*. Zaria, 1958.
JIRGI HADEJIA, *Sarkin Arewan Hadeja Tatagana*. Zaria, 1954.
KIRK-GREENE, A. H. M., 'The Residencies of Northern Nigeria', *West African Review*, 1962.
PALMER, H. R., *Sudanese Memoirs*, vol. III. Lagos, 1928.
SMITH, MARY, *Baba of Karo*. London, 1954.
Sarkin Kano, Alhaji Abdullahi Bayero. Zaria, 1954.
'The Great Emporium', *Nigeria Magazine*, No. 81, 1964.
Kano Survey, Zaria, 1950.

Katsina

ADEBAYO DUROSINLORUN, 'Daura, The Cradle of the Hausa Race', *Nigerian Citizen*, February 1962.

ALHAJI ABUBAKAR IMAM, *Hausa Bakwai*. Zaria, 1954.

DANIEL, F. DE F., *History of Katsina*, n.d.

'The Regalia of Katsina', *Journal of the Royal African Society*, 1932.

MAIDEN, R. L., 'The Katsina Regalia', *Historical Sketches*. Zaria, 1955.

MANI KANKIYA, *Yaki na karshe tsakanin Katsinawa da Maradawa*. Zaria, 1955.

Dammaliki. Zaria, 1953.

MUHAMMADU BELLO KAGARA, *Sarkin Katsina, Alhaji Muhammadu Dikko*. Zaria, 1951.

PALMER, H. R., *Sudanese Memoirs*, Vol. III. Lagos, 1928.

SMITH, H. F. C., 'A Fragment of 18th Century Katsina' and 'A further adventure in the Chronology of Katsina', *Bull. Nigerian Historical Society*, vol. V, No. 4 and vol. VI, No. 1.

'Daura', *Nigeria Magazine*, No. 50, 1956.

'Katsina', *Nigeria Magazine*, No. 51, 1956.

'Jibiya: A Border Market', *Nigeria Magazine*, No. 60, 1959.

Niger

ALHAJI BELLO, *Gandoki*. Zaria, 1956.

HALLETT, R., 'Umaru and Ibrahim Ngwamatse', *Eminent Nigerians*. Cambridge, 1960.

HASSAN, M., and SHU'AIBU NAI'BI, *A Chronicle of Abuja*. Lagos, 1962.

Makau, Sarkin Abuja. Zaria, 1955.

The Gwari Tribe of Abuja Emirate. Lagos, n.d.

KIRK-GREENE, A. H. M., 'The Battles of Bida', *West African Review*, January 1956.

NADEL, S. F., *A Black Byzantium*. London, 1942.

Nupe Religion. London, 1954.

NDAYAKO, *In Ji Etsu Nupe*. Zaria, 1953.

'The Crafts of Bida', *Nigeria Magazine*, No. 49, 1956.

'Nupe Bronzes', *Nigeria Magazine*, No. 73, 1962.

Sokoto

ARNETT, E. J., *The Rise of the Sokoto Fulani* (a paraphrase of *Infaq al Maisuri*). Kano, 1929.

BELLO, Sir AHMADU, *My Life*. Cambridge, 1962.

BIVAR, A. H. D., 'Arabic Documents of Northern Nigeria', *Bull. School of Oriental & African Languages*, vol. XXII, 1959.

'Wathiqat ahl al Sudan', *Journal of African History*, II, 1961.

HARRIS, P. G., *Sokoto Provincial Gazetteer*, unpublished MS., 1938.

HOPEN, C. E., *The Pastoral Fulbe Family in Gwandu*. London, 1958.

JUNAIDU, WAZIRIN SOKOTO, *Tarihin Fulani*. Zaria, 1957.

Mujaddadi Shehu Usman Dan Hodiyo. Zaria, 1953.

KRIEGER, K., *Geschichte von Zamfara*. Berlin, 1959.

MUFFETT, D. J., *Concerning Brave Captains*. 1964.

SHARWOOD SMITH, B. E., *Sokoto Survey*. Zaria, 1948.

SMITH, H. F. C., 'Usmanu dan Fodio', *Eminent Nigerians*. Cambridge, 1960.

'Muhammadu Bello, Amir Al-Mu'minin', *Ibadan*. June 1960.

ST. CROIX, F., *The Fulani of Northern Nigeria*. Lagos, 1945.

'Desert Blooms', *Nigeria Magazine*, No. 60, 1959.

'Gobir Granaries', *Nigeria Magazine*, No. 67, 1960.

'In the Footsteps of the Shehu', *Nigeria Magazine*, No. 78, 1963.

Zaria

Amina Sarauniyar Zazzau. Zaria, 1954.

MILLER, WALTER, *Autobiography*. Zaria, 1958.

SMITH, H. F. C., 'The Dynastic Chronology of Fulani Zaria', *Journal of Nigerian Historical Society*, December 1961.

SMITH, M. G., *Government in Zazzau*. London, 1960.

The Economy of the Hausa Communities of Zaria. London, 1955.

'The Walls of A City', *Nigeria Magazine*, No. 60, 1959.

'House Decorations of a Northern City', *Nigeria Magazine*, No. 68, 1961.

'Wusasa: an abiding memorial', *Nigeria Magazine*, No. 75, 1962.

INDEX

42